We Stood Shoulder to Shoulder

Jewish Partisans in Byelorussia 1941-1944

Inna Gerasimova, Director, Museum of History and Culture of the Jews of Belarus
Viacheslav Selemenev, Director, National Archive of the Republic of Belarus
Jack Kagan
Foreword by Sir Martin Gilbert
Foreword by Tamara Vershitskaya
Editing and Annotation by Michael Kagan

Published 2010 by arima publishing
www.arimapublishing.com

ISBN 978 1 84549 461 2
© Jack Kagan 2010

All rights reserved

This book is copyright. Subject to statutory exception and to provisions of relevant collective licensing agreements, no part of this publication may be reproduced, stored in a retrieval system, or transmitted in any form or by any means, without the prior written permission of the author.

Printed and bound in the United Kingdom
Typeset in Garamond

This book is sold subject to the conditions that it shall not, by way of trade or otherwise, be lent, re-sold, hired out, or otherwise circulated without the publisher's prior consent in any form of binding or cover other than that which it is published and without a similar condition including this condition being imposed on the subsequent purchaser.

arima publishing
ASK House, Northgate Avenue
Bury St Edmunds, Suffolk IP32 6BB
t: (+44) 01284 700321
www.arimapublishing.com

Contents

Foreword	Sir Martin Gilbert	5
Foreword	Tamara Vershitskaya	6
Introduction	Jack Kagan	7
Jews in the Partisan Movement in Byelorussia: 1941-1944	I. Gerasimova, V. Selemenev	13
Documents and Materials	Complied by I. Gerasimova.	
Part 1: Attitudes towards Jews in Partisan Detachments		31
Part 2: Jewish Partisan Detachments		36
Part 3. Jews in Partisan Detachments		50
Part 4. From the Memoirs of Jewish Partisans		54
Photographs	Compiled by I. Gerasimova, V. Rosakova	69
The Early Days of Occupation	Jack Kagan	95
The Fifty Two Martyrs	Yehuda Slutzki	96
Document: *Order of Conviscation of Jewish Property, 22 Nov. 1941*		98
The First Massacre	Jack Kagan	99
Arrest of the Judenrat	Jack Kagan	99
Documents: *Order for the Transportation of the Jews to Novogrudok Ghetto, 6 March 1942*		100
Partisan attack in Baranowitsche, 16 June 1942		102
Germans attempt to liquidate the partisans, 18 June 1942		103
Photographs	Compiled by Jack Kagan	104
Document: *Order for Combating Partisans in White Russia, 31 July 1942*		105
Preparation for the Second Massacre	Jack Kagan	107
The Remnant	Jack Kagan	108
The Escape Story of Lyuba Rudnicki	L. Rudnicki	109
Anti-Semitism	Jack Kagan	116
The Benye Berkovitz Diary	Trans.: Oscar Delatyski Annotated: Michael Kagan	119
Fourth Massacre	Jack Kagan	130

Operation "HERMAN"	Jack Kagan	131
Escape through the Tunnel	Jack Kagan	134
Document: *Combat Report: Operation at Novogrudok, July 9 1943*		138
Chief Engineer Ribinski	Jack Kagan	140
Map of the Bielski Detachment in Naliboki forest	Chaya Bielski	141
Leaders of the Bielski Detachment	Tuvia Bielski	142
Documents: *Report to the Commander of the Kirov Partisan Brigade, 5 Dec. 1943*		143
Battle Report: March 29 1944		144
Battle Report: May 20 1944		144
Battle Report: June 14 1944		145
Visit by General Platon and its Consequences	Tuvia Bielski	145
The Partisans of Tuvia Belski	Shmuel Amarant	149
Surviving the Holocaust with the Russian Jewish Partisans	Jack Kagan	167
Documents: *Attack on the Yatsuki Railroad Track, Sept. 1942*		177
Battle in the Drachlivo Forest, Novogrudok District, March 12 1943		178
Last Report from Tuvia Bielski to the Chief of Staff		179
Who were these Jewish Partisans?	Yehoshua Yaffe	181
And so finished three years and twelve days of the eclipse of the sun	Jack Kagan	187
Holocaust denial	Jack Kagan	191
List of 92 Jewish commanders in the Byelorussian Partisan movement.	Compiled by I. Gerasimova, S. Moroz, M. Izrailski	193
List of 7742 Jews who were in the Byelorussian Partisan movement, 1941-1944	Compiled by I. Gerasimova, S. Moroz, M. Izrailski	197
List of 1023 fallen Jewish Partisans	Compiled by I. Gerasimova, S. Moroz, M. Izrailski	317
Acknowledgements	I. Gerasimova	335

Foreword
Sir Martin Gilbert

Jack Kagan has done another remarkable service to Holocaust history and Holocaust education. As with his memoirs, Surviving the Holocaust with the Russian Jewish Partisans, and his volume on his hometown Novogrudok, he sets out the narrative and documentation of a savage era, when several hundred Jewish towns in eastern Poland and western Russia – now Belarus - faced the Nazi onslaught on their Jewish citizens, and suffered the terrible fate of ten thousand Jewish localities throughout German-occupied Europe.

Yet for the towns and villages of what is now Belarus, the forests that were a dominant feature of the region's landscape provided a haven – full of risk and danger though it was – for more than eight thousand Jewish partisans, and the women, children and old men whom they sheltered, fed and protected from the repeated German attempts to penetrate the forests and wipe out the partisans and their 'family camps'.

We Stood Shoulder to Shoulder is an essential document for present and future historians. Thanks to the vision and efforts of Jack Kagan, it is now made accessible to a wide English readership. In it are highly researched essays by two scholars from Belarus, Inna Gerasimova, Director of the Museum of the History and Culture of the Jews of Belarus (Minsk), and Viacheslav Selemenev, Director of the National Archive of the Republic of Belarus (Minsk), who tell the story of the Jewish partisans and their contribution to the Soviet war effort behind German lines.

Tamara Vershitskaya, the Curator of the Museum of History and Regional Studies in Novogrudok, supplied the thirty-one documents that are the core of the historical veracity of this book, and translated them from their original Russian to English. Many of these documents are reproduced in facsimile. There are also 143 photographs of individual partisans and groups. Jack Kagan has added important material on his home town, Novogrudok, from which he escaped to the partisans at the age of fourteen.

This book makes clear just how hard the Jewish partisans fought, and how severe were the pressures against them, from the Germans always, and also at times from non-Jewish partisans.

The central feature of We Stood Shoulder to Shoulder is a 143-page list of Jewish partisans in wartime Byelorussia. This list is by far the most detailed ever compiled and published. It gives the names of each partisan, date of birth, the town and region from which each individual reached the partisans, the name of the partisan brigade, and, where known, the individual detachment. There are three lists in all: the ninety-two Jewish partisans who were in the various partisan headquarters; the 7,442 who were active as partisans; and the 1,023 who fell in battle against the Germans. Some of the individuals in these lists were Russian prisoners of war – Jews – who escaped from captivity and made their way to the partisans. The Jews in these three lists were of all ages: Boris Moiseyevich Rozenfeld (who worked in a brigade administration) was seventy-one in 1941; Avram Itskovich Sagalovich was thirteen.

This book serves as a historical guide, as an account of a much-neglected aspect of Jewish history – Jewish resistance – and a memorial to those Jews who fought, and those who fell, in the battle for freedom.

Foreword
Tamara Vershitskaya,
*Director of the Museum of History and Regional Studies in Novogrudok
and Jewish Resistance Museum, Belarus*

The Holocaust is one of the top priorities today in the research of contemporary history, and Jewish resistance during this period is one of the key issues under consideration by many scholars worldwide. Hundreds if not thousands of research papers, collections of documents, and several encyclopedias have been published in Europe, Israel and the USA. Yet very little attention has been given to the events that took place in Belarus and even less attention to the widespread phenomenon of Jewish resistance in that area even though it is in Belarus that more than eight thousand Jews participated in the partisan movement in 1941-1944 fighting against the Nazis. The largest Jewish partisan detachment in the Nazi occupied Europe – the Bielski detachment under Tuvia Bielski – is now known to many thanks to the film 'Defiance' (2009). The Bielski detachment (renamed the Kalinin Detachment in January 1944), together with Detachment #106 under Sholom Zorin, present a unique experience of family partisan units organized by the Jews. Detachments of this kind existed nowhere else but in Belarus. More than 1200 Jews survived the Holocaust thanks to Tuvia Bielski, his brothers and their policy of rescuing Jews and about 550 partisans survived in Detachment #106.

The book 'We stood shoulder to shoulder' is intended to fill in this gap and provide the basis for further investigation of the Jewish resistance in Belarus. Such a wide-scale research would have never been possible without the assistance of the director of the National Archive of the Republic of Belarus - Mr. Viacheslav Selemenev. For the English edition of the book Dr. Inna Gerasimova wrote a special chapter entitled 'How Jews joined the partisans' in order to present all the complexities of the situation in Belarus under the Nazi occupation and to show what it meant for a Jew to be a partisan. This book not only provides accurate information about all the Jews who participated in the partisan movement in Belarus and are registered in the documents kept at the National Archive of the Republic of Belarus (NARB) but also attempts to present the situation in which the Jews joined the partisans and how they operated. A careful reader will find many details about the attitude to the Jews on the part of the partisan command, non-Jewish partisans and local population in the set of documents incorporated into the book which come from the National Archive and the Museum of History and Culture of the Jews of Belarus. Some of the documents concerning the area of Novogrudok where the Bielski partisans operated were collected during Mr. Jack Kagan's long lasting research in the archives of Yad Vashem, Jewish Historical Institute in Warsaw, YIVO, and his cooperation with Scotland Yard on the investigation of war crimes.

Thus the book is a document in itself as it is based on archival materials. It is the first attempt of Belarusian scholars, in cooperation with Mr. Jack Kagan, a former Bielski partisan, to introduce the Jewish resistance in Belarus to researchers and to make it available to the English speaking reader.

Introduction

Dear Reader,

In 2005 Mrs. Inna Gerasimova presented me with her book *We stood Shoulder to Shoulder*[1] . It is a most informative book of Jewish partisans in Byelorussia in the Great Patriotic War 1941-1945. However it was printed in Russian. So I'm grateful to Inna for allowing me to publish it in English allowing people in the West the chance to read, study and learn from it.

In this book Inna lists the names of 8,557 Jewish partisans in Byelorussia during the Second World War. Out of them 92 were leaders of various partisan detachments; 1023 lost their lives. We are of the opinion that many more Jews served in different units without revealing their Jewish identity. We are also certain that many more Jews were killed after escaping the ghettos and camps on the way to reach partisan detachments. Many were killed by partisans themselves, not for any gain, but just for the sake of killing a Jew.

These 8,557 Jews were spread out across many of the Russian brigades but amongst them were two anomalies that almost defy explanation: two outstanding independent Jewish detachments, one led by the Bielski brothers[2] (later renamed after Kalinin[3]) and the other by Zorin[4] (Detachment 106).

At the time of liberation, the Bielski Detachment numbered 1,230 Jews, young and old, men and women, and the Zorin Detachment numbered 740, again of mixed ages. And it was this feature that made them so unique and worthy of our attention and admiration: their motto was *"Save Jews first; harass the Germans second."* Whereas all other partisan groups were defined as fighting groups for fighters only with little or no sympathies for escaping Jews.

Although it has taken an inordinate amount of time to bring the image of the Jew as a partisan fighter - living free and proud in the great forests of Eastern Europe - to the attention of the world, today their exploits are known thanks to a number of excellent publications[5] , documentaries[6], exhibitions[7] and of course the film *Defiance*[8].

It was while preparing Inna's book for publication that I decided to add more documents to the book since it would have been a pity to leave out so many important articles and documents about the Bielski detachment that I have collected over the years[9] . I hope that you will agree that the inclusion of these documents and essays perfectly complements her original material.

In particular, I want to point the reader to an extraordinary eyewitness account of the atrocities and calamities that occurred in the Novogrudok Ghetto – The Binye Berkovich Diary[10] – that is published here for the first time. Although only ten pages long, its tear-filled description of man-made-hell spiced with a sense of irony and the cry of outrage at the injustice of it all, surely makes it one of the most poignant documents of its kind. I would like to thank Prof. Yehuda Bauer for bringing this significant document to my attention; to Oskar Delatycki for the excellent translation; and especially to my son Michael Kagan for his dedicated work in editing and annotating the diary as a Jewish text thereby revealing further layers of the universal tragedy that befell not only the Jewish people but all of humanity.

I wish to thank my important partner in this project, Mrs. Tamara Vershitskaya curator of the museum of History and Regional Studies in Novogrudok, and director of the first and only Jewish Resistance Museum in Belarus. I will always be indebted to her for supplying and translating the documents from Russian to English.

Jack Kagan

Notes:
1   Asobny Dah, Minsk, 2005
2   Tuvia, Zus, and Asael Bielski
3   Mikhail Ivanovich Kalinin (1875 – 1946) nominal head of state of the Soviet Union from 1919 to 1946.
4   Shlomo Zorin, born in Minsk, fought for the Russian communists against the Poles during the First World War, was a carpenter in the interlude. In 1941 he was incarcerated in the Minsk ghetto where he made contact with Russian prisoners of war and helped organize an escape. In the forests he was put in charge of Jewish escapees and was ordered to move to the Naboki Forest area. He was wounded in the last days of the war and lost a leg. He died in Israel in 1974.
5   Nechama Tec: *Defiance*, Oxford University Press (1993); Peter Duffy: *Brothers in Arms*, Century (2003); Jack Kagan: *Surviving the Holocaust with the Russian Jewish Partisans*, Vallentine Mitchell (2nd edition, 2001).
6   *Extreme Survival - Belarus*: Ray Mears, DVD, Discovery Channel/BBC (2002); *The Bielski Brothers*, DVD, History Channel (2009).
7   Permanent Exhibit (opened 1998), Imperial War Museum, London; Permanent Exhibit (opened 1990), Ghetto Fighters Museum, Israel; Bielski Brothers Exhibition (2007-2010), Florida Holocaust Museum, St. Petersburg, Florida.
8   *Defiance*: Dir. Edward Zwick (2008)
9   A number of the documents and essays have already appeared in: *Novogrudok – The History of a Shtetl*: Jack Kagan, Vallentine Mitchell (2006) and are reprinted here with permission.
10 Page 118

Inna Gerasimova, Director, Museum of History and Culture of the Jews of Belarus together with Tamara Vershitskaya curator of the museum of History and Regional Studies in Novogrudok, and director of the first and only Jewish Resistance Museum in Belarus

This book is dedicated to those who saved
and those who were saved.

כל המאבד נפש אחת - מעלה עליו הכתוב כאילו קיים עולם
מלא, וכל המקיים נפש אחת - מעלה עליו הכתוב כאילו איבד
עולם מלא

"Whoever destroys a soul, it is considered as if he destroyed an entire world. And whoever saves a life, it is considered as if he saved an entire world."
Jerusalem Talmud, Sanhedrin 4:1 (22a)

Inna Gerasimova, director of the Museum of History and Culture of the Jews of Belarus,
Dr. of History
Viacheslav Selemenev, director of the National Archive of the Republic of Belarus,
Dr. of History

Jews in the Partisan Movement in Byelorussia: 1941-1944

More than 60 years have passed since the end of WWII but researching and trying to understand the events of that war is still being continued. To a great extent it is connected with the changes of public, social and political situation in modern Belarus. The last decade of the new state – the Republic of Belarus – let scientists and researchers start researching new, unknown before or for political reasons very little known pages of the history of our country thanks to the access to archival materials. In fact there's a process going on today aimed at reexamination and writing the history of our country anew, the history which corresponds to objective scientific methods excluding authors' subjectivism while estimating historic events.

One of the topics which attracts big interest of researchers and public is the topic of heroism and resistance to the occupiers of the Byelorussian people during the war. There were people of different nationalities, including the Jews, among those who took up arms. Participation of the Jews in underground and partisan struggle in Byelorussia during the war has been silenced for decades. It contributed to creating a false conception in public conscience that the Jews hadn't resisted and hadn't participated in the struggle against the occupiers while the fascists were totally destroying the Jewish people.

It's well known that the territory of the BSSR was totally occupied by the German troops. Towns and villages were burnt down, national economy was completely destroyed. The Byelorussian land was the first to receive the attack of Wehrmacht select troops in the horrible days of confusion, chaos and retreat of the Red Army. But most important was destruction of people.

There are more than 500 places known in Belarus where according to different estimates from 600 000 to 810 000 Jews - Byelorussian and deported from different countries of Europe – were killed. Many years have passed since the war but new places of death of innocent people are being revealed even today. Books, articles and films telling about the Holocaust in Byelorussia have appeared in the last decades. I think it is difficult to find a person today who at least in general wouldn't know about the destruction of the Jews by the fascists. Many of those who do know, often ask a question: 'Why did the Jews didn't resist and went to death obediently?'. They don't even suspect that Jewish resistance existed even in the horrible conditions of ghettos and concentration camps.

There were underground organizations in more than 80 ghettos, their members collected arms, ammunition, medicines and prepared themselves for leaving for the forest. In some ghettos underground workers made decisions to use guns during the massacres carried out by the Nazis. Young fighters preferred to die in combat rather than to die obediently. Thus how it happened in the ghettos of Nesvizh, Lakhva, Glubokoye, Kletsk and Kopyl where prisoners organized armed uprisings. As soon as extra German and police detachments arrived and surrounded the ghetto it was clear that the destruction of people would begin. Underground workers set houses to fire, shot fascists and in total mess tried to escape themselves and to take out as many people as possible. Many people were killed but some were rescued. Hundreds of people managed to escape from some ghettos to the forest. For example about 200 prisoners escaped from the ghetto in Slonim in June 1942, about 100 people escaped from the ghetto in Mir at the end of the same year. Underground workers of the ghettos in Baranovichi, Kurenets and other bigger and smaller towns took hundreds of those sentenced to death out to the forest. In Novogrudok prisoners of the ghetto for artisans were digging a tunnel in the course of several months, the tunnel was 170 m long and about 260 people managed to escape.

The underground organization of the Minsk ghetto organized for many prisoners to leave the ghetto for the partisans with the help of city underground organizations. Several partisan detachments and brigades were organized from the escapees. There were cases when partisans attacked enemy garrisons and liberated prisoners from ghettos as, for example, in Novy Sverzhen and Kosovo. Some managed to escape with families, those who escaped massacres, united themselves in groups in the forest. There were people of different ages there, with families and single, united by one fate. They started to live in one family camp which existed thanks to the ability of its members to survive in the forest. It's known today that more than 3 000 people were in such camps.

Little by little young people from family camps acquired arms and organized fighting groups. Thus, a unique phenomenon appeared in the partisan movement in Byelorussia – Jewish family partisan detachments. The most famous among them is the detachment named after Kalinin, commander – Tuvia Bielski, Baranovichi region. There were 1 233 people in this detachment in July 1944 when they met the Red Army troops, including 296 armed fighters. Former prisoners of the Minsk ghetto formed partisan detachment #106 headed by Semion Zorin. It comprised 596 people, 141 of them were in the fighting group. Economical groups of Jewish partisan detachments which consisted of tailors, shoe-makers, bakers, doctors, watchmakers and other artisans formed a base that served many partisan detachments. Women, elderly people and children – all of them tried to make their contribution to the victory.

The Jews who came to the forest in spring – summer 1942 organized fighting Jewish partisan detachments as well. One of the first such detachments under Boris Gindin consisted mainly of Jews who had escaped from captivity or were surrounded by the Germans. Jewish partisan detachment #5 under Lev Gilchik was known in Baranovichi partisan formation. Former prisoners of the Minsk ghetto organized several partisan detachments and brigades: named after Parkhomenko, 25 years of the BSSR, named after Chkalov, named after Chapayev and others. The best known detachment was the one named after Kutuzov under Izrail Lapidus. Separate regiment # 51 which had 151 people was organized from the prisoners of the Slonim ghetto in the detachment headed by Pavel Vasilyevich Pronyagin.

* * *

A contribution to the question of the number of Jews in the partisan movement of Belarus: some statistical data

In the last few years there have appeared both memoirs written by Jewish partisans (including Jack Kagan's *Surviving the Holocaust with the Russian Jewish Partisans*) and research works devoted to the participation of Jews in the partisan movement of Belarus. One of the problems, which both public and researchers have been interested in, is the number of Jews who participated in the partisan movement of Belarus during the war. This question is a central one today in studying the Holocaust on the territory of the Republic of Belarus, as it is important to prove with documents that the Jews resisted and fought the German occupier as well as representatives of other nationalities (Russians, Belarussians, Ukrainians etc) in spite of the fact that they were subjected to attempted annihilation in that period. While the participation and heroism of the Jews on the battle fields of the Second World War are confirmed today by researchers into the military history of 1941-1945, it is much more difficult to do so with regards to the Jewish partisans.

The existing historiography in Belarus has for many years thoroughly excluded, from numerous reference and academic books, and memoirs the topic of a Jewish presence among the Byelorussian partisans. Even in the main reference edition "Partisan Formations of Belarus during the Great Patriotic War (Short information about the organizational structure of partisan formations, brigades, regiments, detachments, battalions and their personnel)", published in Minsk in 1983, the Jews are not mentioned while stating the percentage of partisans of other nationalities in partisan brigades, detachments and separate groups. For example, among 962 partisans of the For Soviet Belarus Brigade, in the Baranovichi region, there were 495 Byelorussians, 237 Russians, 30 Ukrainians and 200 people of other nationalities. In fact, 127 Jews fought in that brigade, of whom thirty perished. The fact that they were Jewish is not mentioned. There are many similar examples in this book.

The problem of studying the number of Jews in the partisan movement of Belarus in 1941-1944 is mainly connected with nature of the sources. Though it may seem strange at first sight, the problem is not in the absence of documents but in their abundance. Researchers who wish to study this problem will have to study a great number of documents: such materials are plentiful in the National Archive of the Republic of Belarus. K. Kazak and E. Savitski[3] wrote about this in 1995: materials about the Jewish partisans are not detached from the whole mass of documents. It is evident that it is a substantial, long-term work to find and pick out information about the Jewish partisans from the general personnel lists of partisan brigades, regiments and detachments that operated in Byelorussia during the war years.

Name lists are basic for each research work connected with studying statistics about the partisans. They were mainly compiled in 1944 after the partisans joined the Red Army units, and have hundreds of thousands of surnames.

There are complete enough lists of 281,007 partisans in the National Archive of the Republic of Belarus, which were checked by the Byelorussian Staff of Partisan Movement (BSPM) in 1946, and which give nationality and social status. A researcher who embarks on this problem must first of all know how many Jews there are in these lists. There is nothing difficult here at first sight, as the number of partisans according to their nationality is stated in the same documents, and in particular in combined data for each brigade. Besides, there is a well known document in the archive, entitled "Information about the number of partisans of the Great Patriotic War who operated on the territory of the Byelorussian SSR, status on January 1, 1946", signed by the chief of the Byelorussian Staff of Partisan Movement personnel department, Colonel V. Romanov. It is in this document that the information about the national composition of the partisans of Byelorussia is presented, and where it is stated that there are 6,014 Jews or 2.14%[4] among the partisans. This information was, and is still used by all the researchers engaged in the studies of the partisan movement of Byelorussia. No research and statistical analysis of the information about the number of the Jews in the partisan movement of Byelorussia has ever been carried out by Belarussian or foreign historians. In some works[5] their authors touched upon this problem in the context of researching the national composition of the partisans in the Republic without detailing their nationality.

In this respect it is necessary to mention the work by V.I.Yermolovich, who analyzed the main archival documents on the personnel of partisan formations that joined the Red Army units, while studying the national composition of the partisans, who had fought in the forests of Byelorussia in 1941-1944. Yermolovich drew an important conclusion: "The results of the analysis carried out have no principal difference with the final information of the BSPM according to the number and national composition of the partisans who joined the Red army units. It lets us consider the statistic materials of the BSPM to a great extent objective and true." 6

Thus, approaching the problem connected with the number of the Jews who participated in the partisan movement in the Byelorussian Soviet Socialist Republic in 1941-1944 we have a starting point – the information of the Byelorussian Staff of Partisan Movement certified by the research based on the archival sources.

The museum of History and Culture of the Jews of Belarus, assisted by the National Archive of the Republic of Belarus, had a task to establish the number of Jewish partisans who had fought on the territory of the Republic and to create a computer database. We understood that we faced an enormous work, as we intended to include not only the first and the second names, and the patronymic of each partisan, into the data base, but also a year of birth, the place he or she came from to join the partisans, the name of the detachment and the brigade, and where that partisan fought. It should have been done to those people who had "Jew" stated in the column "nationality". We were to pick out all these data and put them into the computer database. We applied special methods for this laborious and complicated work and defined some principles from the very beginning:

Picking out information on the partisans, i.e. compiling name lists of Jewish partisans, was made only in accordance with the archival list where in the column "nationality" it was written "Jew". Those partisans who had changed their nationality for well-known reasons while joining a partisan detachment, were not included in the lists even, if their family names or first names were Jewish. It is understandable that the percentage of such people among the partisans was rather high, but that is the topic of a different research. Family names, first names and patronymics in these lists are given according to the archival original.

As has been stated before, the lists of partisan formations compiled in 1944, at the moment of their joining the Red Army, lay at the basis of this research. We defined the number of Jewish partisans not only from the moment when the detachment came out of the forest and joined the Soviet troops, but during the whole period of its existence. Beside the lists from 1944, there are several lists from 1941-1943 in the National Archive of the Republic of Belarus: in Fund 3,500, Inventory 5 - "Personnel list of partisan formations". This information was also included in our list because we defined the presence of Jews in the ranks of Byelorussian partisans during all the war years and not just at the moment of their joining Soviet troops in summer 1944.

Studying the lists of the Byelorussian Staff of Partisan Movement showed that they had not been compiled very grammatically correct and not very accurately, which is understandable taking into account the conditions in which they were made. Some of them were written in pencil and are difficult to read today. As a rule there are several personnel lists of one and the same detachment in different Funds, so we had to compare them in order not to miss a new name. There were lists without the column "nationality". In this case we did not use them, even if there were family names similar to Jewish ones. As it was stated above, the basic criterion for the lists published in this book was the nationality of a partisan certified by the archival documents.

The leaders of the partisan movement were very careful as to how the lists of partisans were compiled, not only after the liberation of the republic in 1944, when they could be compiled under more quiet conditions, but in the years of combat activity as well. Thus, it was required in the order of the chief of the Central Staff of the Partisan Movement on the issues of partisan personnel registration from September 28, 1943: "…a personal list on registration of partisan personnel was filled in for the whole private personnel of partisan brigades and detachments and a detailed reference was compiled."[7]

While compiling general lists of Jewish partisans we ran the risk of repeating the same family names, because the same people could have been in a certain partisan detachment in 1943, and later, when it was disbanded, they could find themselves in a different detachment, and their family names could appear in the lists already in 1944. Putting all the data received into the computer and processing them with the help of a special program excluded repetition of one and the same family name in the final list of Jewish partisans.

There are two basic lists in this book; both are arranged alphabetically. The first one presents the Jewish partisans who were in the partisan formations when they joined the Red Army (June-July 1944); the second one is the list of perished Jewish partisans. A separate list of Jewish leaders of partisan brigades and detachments comes as a supplement. All the information about these people is included into the main list. After processing the information we collected using the methods presented above we received the following results:

According to the lists published there were 8,465 Jews among the partisans in the forests of Byelorussia. 1,023 of them perished or are missing. According to the Byelorussian Staff of Partisan Movement's information dated 1 January 1946, a total of 194,165 people from the personnel of partisan brigades, detachments and regiments joined the Red Army units[8]. According to the lists we present here, there were 7,442 Jews among them or 3,8% and not 5,077 or 2,6% (the Byelorussian Staff of Partisan Movement data).

As stated above, we used the name lists of partisan formations personnel for different years, which were certified by the staff leaders of the partisan movement. Because of the fact that many lists were compiled in different periods of time and some of them even from memory, part of the names were lost in the course of time. Here is what S.S.Shikanov, the commander of the Chernyak partisan detachment of the Stalin Brigade (Brest Formation), writes to the Byelorussian Staff of Partisan Movement in 1946: "I am sending to the department for the registration of perished partisans a list of partisans and contacts who perished during the German occupation in 1941-1942, when we had no connection with Moscow and our contacts and partisans asked us not to put them on the list as they were afraid to cause death to their families and relatives in case they were caught by the Germans or police. I had a list of them but after I had been wounded on 23 August 1943 I was sent to Moscow. The lists were submitted, but those people were not remembered as the commander of the detachment was substituted".[9] 842 Jews are on the list of those perished and missing (the Byelorussian Staff of Partisan Movement information); according to our data, which was obtained from different lists from the archive. They were 1,023.

The analysis of the information about the age (with regards to 1941) of Jewish partisans showed that the most numerous group among them consisted of people at the age from 16 to 37; they were 5,602. Those from 38 to 51 years old were 759. Thus, 6,361 partisans or 85.4% of the total number of Jewish partisans who joined the Red Army units in 1944 were capable of fighting as far as their age was concerned.

The number of the rest of the Jewish partisans included in the lists (from 1 to 15 years old and from 50 to 70 years old) was 982 people. Those people were allowed not to take part in fighting operations. Though 14-15 year old youths (there were 427) fought with arms in their hands. The same can be said about those partisans who were aged 50-55 (110 people). Even if they are not regarded as fighters, they comprise only 13.1% of the total number of Jewish partisans who met the Red Army in the summer of 1944.

This calculation is important to confirm the point that the Jews who are on the list of partisan detachments and brigades took part in fighting operations of partisan formations. There is a widely spread opinion that the Jews were only in family detachments and camps in the forests, as many historians regarded the Byelorussian Staff of Partisan Movement information about the participation of the Jews in the partisan movement of Byelorussia as final and reliable. Thus, "…the Jews in the selection under study were not many – 1.8%. This is explained by the fact that in the surpassing majority the Jews organized Jewish family detachments and camps of their own. Because of the policy carried out by the Germans with regards to the Jews the main aim of such detachments and camps was first of all surviving under the occupation and not armed fighting" is written in one of the recent works on the problems of studying the partisan movement in Byelorussia.[10]

It is necessary to state that family camps were organized not only by the Jews. It is well known that the residents of the villages burnt down by the Germans, especially in partisan zones, often lived in such camps in the forest. As a rule, those who were in the family camps were not included in the personnel lists of partisan detachments. Thus, there is a separate point No.8 in the information of the Byelorussian Staff of Partisan Movement from 1 January 1946 about the number partisans who joined the Red Army units, with 79,484 partisans not included into the general number of partisans as they were "partisans who guarded the villages in partisan zones, family camps and carried out separate assignments of the brigades and detachments' command"[11].

If the partisans who guarded family camps were not included in the total number of partisans, there is no mentioning of family camps members. The exception is two Jewish partisan detachments under T. Bielski and S. Zorin. It is known that these two family detachments were officially recognized as partisan detachments and had names of their own: T. Bielski's detachment was named after Kalinin and S. Zorin's was No.106. It is also well-known, and archival documents prove, that these detachments carried out active fighting. As was stated above, about half of the members of these detachments were part of armed groups and as well as other partisans they fulfilled combat missions of the command.

At the moment when partisan formations joined the Red Army units in 1944, and personnel name lists were compiled, all the Jewish partisan detachments but No.106 and the Kalinin Detachment had been disbanded, and all the Jewish partisans had become fighters in ordinary partisan detachments.

Table No.1
Number of Jewish partisans according to their age

No.	Age (decreasing)	Number from 7,442 (according to list No.1)	Number of the perished and those missing from 1,023 (according to list No.2)	Total Jewish partisans
1	70-50	132	22	154
2	49-41	481	68	549
3	40-38	278	42	320
4	37-26	2,441	313	2,754
5	25-16	3,161	460	3,621
6	15-12	622	43	665
7	11-8	142	4	146
8	7-1	86	4	90

Note: in the personnel name lists the year of birth of partisans is not always mentioned.

There is a column "where from one arrived in the detachment" in the lists. We regard this data important as it gives information (though partial) about the number of Jews who survived the occupation in definite regions of the Republic of Belarus. It is a pity that those who wrote the lists of the detachments were not very attentive to filling in this column, as in some cases geographical names of places are given not precisely and one seldom comes across the word "ghetto". Though, it is known that no less than 80-90% of the Jews came to partisans from ghettos. For example, according to the data from the archival lists only 193 prisoners from the Minsk ghetto and 1,117 all together from Minsk joined the partisans. Yet there is no doubt that it is from the Minsk ghetto that the largest part from this number came to partisans. Those who came to different detachments from different ghettos in Byelorussia are 338 according to the list. Only 85 people came to partisans from Jewish camps (there is such a note). The note that 25 people from Baranovichi "came from home" shows that the authors of the lists did not understand correctly the situation with the Jews who arrived in partisan detachments.

The results obtained on the number of Jewish partisans in the regions of the republic show that most of them were in Baranovichi region: 3,360. Next comes Minsk region, 1,138 and the Vileika region, 648. There is information on ten regions of the Byelorussian Soviet Socialist Republic (according to the administrative division in 1944). The least number of the Jews was in the Gomel region, 127 and the Bialystok region, 63. The residents of the Gomel region are known to have had a chance to be evacuated as the German Army entered the city in August 1941. But in spite of this about 7,000 Jews perished in the city and in the district (according to some data). A small number of Jewish partisans in the Bialystok region, where all the Jews were in the ghettos, shows, that the Jews in this region mainly perished and that very few of them managed to survive.

We determined the presence of the Jews in the brigades and detachments in percentage to the total number of partisans. Those partisan formations where the number of Jewish partisans was no less than 3% were taken into account. This figure was taken as a basic one, as according to the Byelorussian Staff of Partisan Movement, the number of the Jews (in percentage) among the partisans of Byelorussia was 2.14%. We also compared the number of the Jews in each brigade according to the report (archival documents) and according to the actual list. As a rule, the number of the Jews in the report of the brigade was smaller than they were on the list. For example, according to the report of the 18th (Frunze) Brigade, in the Baranovichi region, there were only 735 partisans in the brigade. There were 50 Jews among them.[12] The number of the Jews in the brigade according to the list was 72, and in the list of those perished and missing there were three more partisans of this brigade. Thus, there were 75 Jews in the brigade, which makes 10.7% of the total number of its partisans.

The results of counting the number of Jewish partisans in some brigades are given in table No.2:

Table No.2
The number of Jewish partisans in the partisan brigades of Byelorussia

No.	Name of the brigade, detachment	Total according to the report	Including Jews	Actually Jews according to list No.1	% of Jews to the total number
Baranovichi region					
1	Brigade 'Leninskaya'	1,184	195	260	21.9
2	Brigade Lenin's Comsomol	462	40	86	18.6
3	Brigade 'Forward'	472	61	87	18.4
4	Brigade 'Victory'	901	97	182	20.2
5	Brigade 'Chkalov'	1,063	80	67	6.3
6	Brigade 'Stalin'	1,160	35	92	13.8
Minsk region					
1	2nd Minskaya Brigade	1,234	73	87	7.0
2	Chapayev Brigade	1,513	75	155	10.2
Vitebsk region					
1	named after Chapayev	1,295		45	3.4
2	Nikitin's Brigade	410		51	12.4
Pinsk region					
1	Pinsk Brigade (Shubertidze)	1,071	63	66	6.1

The same principle of establishing the percentage of the number of Jewish partisans to the number of other partisans was used by establishing the number of Jews in separate partisan detachments. It was found out that according to the preliminary data there were from 3% to 30- 35% of Jews in some partisan detachments.

Table No.3
The number of Jews in separate partisan detachments

No.	Name of the detachment	Region	Total according to the report	In fact Jews according to list No.1	% of Jews
1	Chuklai's detachment	Pinsk	123	10	8.1
2	n/a Budenny	Pinsk	1,070	33	3.7
3	n/a Shchors	Brest	340	84	24.7
4	n/a Ponomarenko	Vileika	123	10	8.1
5	n/a Kotovski	Brest	191	19	9.9
6	detachment No.550	Grodno	106	35	33
7	n/a Khmelnitski	Grodno	140	10	7.1

While compiling the second list (of the perished partisans) in accordance with the archival lists the column "date of death" was introduced instead of the column "where from one came to the detachment". It is a pity that the date of death was not in all the archival name lists, that is why it is missing in the lists published.

There is also information about those missing, deserters and captured prisoner in the archival lists in addition to the information about those perished. We put those missing on the list of the perished, then checked the information for everybody in the general lists as the person might have survived and found himself in a different detachment. This was the case with the so-called "deserters" and "captured prisoner". These categories, as they are called, had nothing to do with the Jews, as the Germans did not take the Jews prisoner, the latter preferred to commit suicide. What concerns "Jews-deserters", they could only "desert" to a different detachment as they had nowhere to go to. Proceeding from this, we incorporated "deserters' and "captured prisoner" into list No.1, having checked them in advance. As a rule, a Jew who had been captured prisoner in one detachment, was found later in the lists of a different one.

There is one more category of partisans, whose name lists in the collection of the National Archive are not complete. It concerns different special groups, which arrived at the German-occupied territory of Byelorussia from the rear. The analysis of these lists, which are kept in the National Archive of the Republic of Belarus, showed that there were Jews in such groups; the information about them is included in the lists published. We propose to continue researching this topic in the archives of Minsk and Moscow.

Having made the preliminary analysis of the lists of the Jews who participated in the partisan movement of Byelorussia in 1941-1944, as published in this book, we can conclude that in reality the number of the Jews who fought on the territory of Byelorussia was much larger than it appears in the official documents of the Byelorussian Staff of the Partisan Movement. In addition, we have no opportunity at the moment (because of lack of documents) to find out the number of those Jews who changed their names, family names and nationality when with the partisans. It could be several thousands more, but our research was based only on the archival materials and documents kept in the National Archive of the Republic of Belarus.

The analysis of the name lists database published in this book is on going. We also continue our work on the name list of Jewish partisans, where the information will be organized according to partisan brigades and detachments.

It is necessary to note that we studied about two thousands files in the National Archive of the Republic of Belarus while preparing the lists and documents published here. We also held more than eighty interviews with former partisans and members of their families in Belarus and in Israel. There also documents and materials presented in the book that are published for the first time.

Photos of partisans with some exceptions were provided by the Museum of the History and Culture of the Jews of Belarus (Minsk).

Notes:
1   Such a considerable difference in the number of Byelorussian Jews who died during the war is characteristic of modern Belarus historiography. A well-known Belarusian historiographer, R. Chernoglazova, writes about 400,000 Jews killed (The tragedy of the Jews of Byelorussia in the years of the German occupation (1941-1944). A collection of materials and documents, Minsk, 1995, page 25). It is written in the teaching aids for the eleventh form of secondary schools published on the sixtieth anniversary of the liberation of Belarus from the German invaders: "As a result of the punitive actions carried out during the war more than 600,000 Jews were killed in Belarus" (The Great Patriotic War of the Soviet People (in the context of WWII…Minsk, 2004, page

99). In the last few years there has appeared information about 800,000 killed Jews in a number of newspaper and magazine articles published by Professor E. Ioffe (Minsk). It was stated in the first articles that this number includes Jews from different European countries who had been deported to Belarus (Ioffe E., Akh, voina, chto nadelala, podlaya - *Oh the war, what did you do, you the mean one* - Belaruskaya Dumka, No.8, 2000, pages 147-152; Belaruski Chas, No.526 July 6, 2000). In his new book Professor Ioffe gives a still larger figure – 805,000 perished without any elaboration as to whether they are Belarusian Jews only (Ioffe E., The Byelorussian Jews: tragedy and heroism, 1941-1945 - Minsk, 2003, p. 363.

Some researchers regard these data to be exaggerated and to our mind the following publications may be of interest in this respect:

- Litvin A, "On the question about the number of human losses in Belarus during the Great Patriotic war (1941-1945). Belarus in the 20th century. Part I.," – Minsk, 2002, pages 127-138
- Romanovski D., "How many Jews perished in the industrial cities of Eastern Byelorussia at the beginning of the German occupation (July – December 1941)?", Bulletin of the Jewish University. History, Culture, Civilization. No.4 (22), 2000, Moscow and Jerusalem, pages 151-172.

2   "Partisan formations of Byelorussia in the years of the Great Patriotic War (Short information about the organizational structure of partisan formations, brigades (regiments), detachments (battalions) and their personnel)", – Minsk, 1983, page 40.

3   Kazak K., Savitski E. "Materials of the National Archive of the Republic of Belarus about the participation of the Jews in the partisan and underground movements of Byelorussia (1941 – 1944)", Bulletin of the Jewish University in Moscow, Moscow and Jerusalem, 1995, No.2 (9), p. 124 – 133.

4   National Archive of the Republic of Belarus, f. 4, inv. 33a, file 634, pages 1-3.

5   Kavalenya A.A., Matsko A.N, "Youth Komsomol Underground of Belarus – a factor of national minorities joining the struggle against the enemy (1941-1944), National policy and international relations in Belarus in the 20th century. Collection of scientific articles." Minsk, 1997, pages 125-152; Pavlova Ye. Ya, "Personnel of partisan formations (an attempt to create a data base), Belarus and Germany," History and Present. Materials of the International scientific conference, Minsk, 16 May 2003, Part 2, pages. 140-149 and others.

6   Yermolovich V.I. "On the question about the national composition of partisans and underground activists of Belarus during the war (1941 – 1944)," Natsyyanalnaya palityka, pages 116-117.

7   National Archive of the Republic of Belarus, f. 3500, inv. 17, f. 3, page 58.

8   National Archive of the Republic of Belarus, f. 4, inv. 33-a, f. 634, page 1.

9   National Archive of the Republic of Belarus, f. 3500, f. 6, inv. 6, f. 167, page 14.

10 Pavlova Ye. Ya, "Personnel of partisan formations (an attempt to create a data base), Belarus and Germany," History and Present. Materials of the International scientific conference, Minsk, 16 May 2003, Part 2, page 142.

11 National Archive of the Republic of Belarus, f. 4, inv. 33a, f. 634, page 1.

12 National Archive of the Republic of Belarus, f. 3500, inv. 5, f. 433.

* * *

Situation of Belarusian Jews during the Occupation

That the Belarusian army was totally unprepared for war when Germany carried out its surprise attack on June 22nd 1941, is evidenced by the fact that Wermacht troops entered Minsk, the capital of Belarus, six days after the military actions had begun. Many citizens of the republic including the Jews remained in the occupied territory. The Jewish communities were not ready to accept that their social and economical situation and life in general would radically differ from those of people of other nationalities. Soviet leaders who had signed the German-Soviet non-aggression pact in August 1939 had thoroughly concealed that the annihilation of the Jews had been raised to the level of state policy since the middle of the 1930s. The authorities forbade escaping Polish Jews from divulging information about the real situation the Jews in Poland were facing.

One factor that mitigated the situation was that not so many years had passed since World War I when the Kaiser's troops had occupied Belorussia and many Jews remembered perfectly well the lenient attitude of the Germans towards them. The Soviet authorities kept silent the fact that the Germans in 1914 were not the same as the Germans in 1941 and that now they were actively looking to solve 'the Jewish question' something that was unheard of just 27 years earlier.

No announcements were made even during the first days of the war when it would have still been possible to warn the Jewish population about the immediate threat of mortal danger if the German onslaught succeeded. In fact, on the first day of the war the government of the BSSR announced over the radio the need for the citizens of Minsk to stay in their places and to continue work assuring them that the heroic Red Army was adequately rebuffing the enemy. These messages calmed the population down a bit but by June 24, as German bomber planes started turning Minsk into ruins, it began to be appreciated how strong the enemy was.

It was only on the morning of June 25 when the citizens of Minsk learned that their leaders had fled the capital that many of them tried to escape the burning city on foot. Very few of them succeeded because German troops had already surrounded it. The situation was similar in other towns of the republic with the exception of the Gomel region where evacuation was organized; Gomel was occupied by the enemy only on August 19, 1941. Thus most of the Jews who living in the BSSR suddenly found themselves in territories occupied by the Nazis.

Jews in both big cities and small towns were driven into ad-hoc ghettos which as a rule were fenced-in with wire and guarded. Often Jews from surrounding shtetls and villages were brought there as well. In small villages that were far from major towns, the Germans registered them and let them stay in their houses. Then, without warning, they were taken by lorries or marched out of their villages to prepared pits in the forests or on the fields and killed. There were no exceptions: babies, teenagers, elderly people, the young, women and men – everybody was exterminated.

In the big cities 'the final solution of the Jewish question' by the Nazis was implemented in several stages. While the ghettos were being established certain limiting measures were introduced with regards to the Jews. The authorities set up Judenrats. The main task of these administrative bodies, comprised of the communities' most respected members, was to regulate the life of the Jews and to be responsible for fulfilling all the orders and instructions of the occupational authorities. The next stage was the creation of the ghetto itself where the whole Jewish population of the city and small surrounding towns was concentrated. The Judenrat was thus turned into an inner self-government and Jewish police was set up to keep order in the ghetto. A German commandant was the chief of the ghetto and the Judenrat were to fulfill his orders. External guarding was exercised by SS troops and the police.

Conditions in which prisoners of the ghettos were forced to live (extraordinary crowding, hunger, continual harassment, intolerable labour and, more importantly the state of lawlessness, permanent humiliation and defenselessness) were calculatedly designed by the Nazis to induce the moral and spiritual destruction of the personality thus leading the population to feelings of despair, obedience and reluctance to resist authority. All these conditions made it easier for the occupiers to carry out the last and main stage of their plan – the actual physical destruction of the Jews.

Psychologically, the Jews in the ghettos were not ready to accept that the Germans would destroy them without any reason. There was no example in history where one people annialated another and many Jews were convinced that civilized states and world powers would not let it happen. Some of them hoped that the Germans, being an educated, cultural nation, would exhibit humaneness and mercy. Others explained the impossibility of killing all the ghetto prisoners for a more pragmatic reason: the Germans needed a free working force. These illusions inspired hope at least until the mass killings began. As the mass killings spread, those who remained alive began to think about survival. It was clear for many that the only way to live was to escape from the ghetto and subordination under the fascists. But they faced unavoidable questions – 'How to escape?', 'Where to escape to?', 'Where was it possible for Jews to survive?' Underground organizations usually set up by the youth in many ghettos in cities and small towns were a response to these difficult questions.

Some Jews, because of their "non-Jewish" appearance, were able to change their surnames and acquire false documents, stayed outside the ghettos living in 'the Russian districts'. They were under constant threat of being informed to the police by their former colleagues, neighbors and acquaintances. In the long term, going to the forests to join the partisans was the only way for them to survive as well.

Fascists set up many concentration camps for captured soldiers and officers of the Red Army on the territory of the republic. Though Jews, like commissars and commanders, were shot by the occupiers immediately some of them managed to hide their nationality. It is natural that they tried to escape as soon as they had a chance. In case they were lucky, they looked for the partisans or found shelter with peasants in villages and helped them about the household.

Thus the Jews under the German occupation in Byelorussia were left with one option if they wanted the possibility to survive and fight the Nazis and that was in the forests with the partisan detachments.

* * *

How the Jews joined the Partisans: Problems and Obstacles

During the German occupation that began in June 1941 there were more than a hundred ghettos in Belarus. By the beginning of 1942 most of their inhabitants, especially in the eastern regions of the country, had been murdered, with the exception of the Jews in the Minsk ghetto, where there were about 100,000 people. In the western part of Belarus, ghettos continued to exist; about eighty of them had underground organizations[1]. As a rule they were organized by members of the numerous Jewish youth organizations that had operated in Western Belarus during the Polish Republic (1919-1939).

Underground Jewish workers tried to acquire guns, establish contacts with partisans and leave for the forest. But they faced a very complicated obstacle – confrontation with members of the Judenrat (Jewish Council), parents, and other ghetto inmates who were older and did not appreciate underground activities. The very idea of using guns even to save lives seemed impossible to many of those in the ghettos, because Jews who had lived in Diaspora for so many centuries had no tradition of armed resistance to the authorities. The injunction, 'You will live according to the rule of the sword' was unacceptable for a Jew who lived according to tradition. Even more decisive, the German-imposed order of collective responsibility for the slightest alleged fault of a Jewish family member led to execution of dozens of ghetto inmates for the escape of several, or even a single Jew.

Family has always been the basis of the very existence of the Jewish people. Family ties became even stronger during those terrible days. There were unbearably difficult situations in those circumstances. Sometimes parents asked their children to escape from the ghetto in order to save their lives while they themselves remained hostages. Young people faced a tragic dilemma – on one hand they could display individual courage and use the possibilities to save themselves by escaping and fighting the enemy; on the other hand, by escaping, they condemned their elderly parents or wives with small children to death by leaving them in the ghetto. That is why in many cases the decision was: 'I won't leave without them. If they go, I'll go too'.

There were many cases when young prisoners escaped to the partisans and then returned because they did not want to be the reason for the death of their relatives and other prisoners. Those who escaped to the partisans gave way to despair when their families were killed in the ghetto, and felt guilty till the end of their days. Those who were against escape justified their position by citing both the punitive measures and also the impossibility – as they saw it – of those Jews who could not fight – elderly people, women and children - surviving in the forests.

During the first year and a half of the German occupation, the partisan movement in the Belarus was not as strong or as widely spread as it was to become by the beginning of 1943. In the early period, some leaders of partisan detachments refused to accept weak people without guns, in particular elderly people, women and children who impeded the mobility of the partisans. But this was not the only reason for the refusal to accept the Jews in partisan detachments; Jews who had miraculously escaped from the ghettos and were wandering in the forests were suspected of espionage.

Rachil Rapoport, a former prisoner of the Minsk ghetto, who managed to join the partisans in 1943, wrote: «...*A horsecart with armed people is coming towards us. They stop me, look suspiciously, they obviously don't trust me. I must say that the Fascists have recently spread rumors that the Jews who had escaped from the ghettos were sent by the Gestapo to partisan detachments for espionage. Unlikely though this is, some partisans believed it. People from the Gestapo spread the news that they had set up a school for spies for the Jews. Their intention was more than evident – those who had escaped from death in the ghetto were to be destroyed by local people. It happened indeed that some Jews were shot because of having been suspected of espionage*[2].

Leaders of the Central Staff of Partisan Movement, and of the Belorussian Army Staff, who were worried about the protection of partisan units from saboteurs and agent provocateurs sent by the German occupiers, regarded escapees wandering in the forests as potential spies. The reports of special reconnaissance groups that worked behind German lines confirm that special schools for preparing such agents were set up in Minsk, Borisov and Bobruisk, where Jews had comprised about half the population. Here is a report sent on 9 September 1942, by one of these reconnaissance groups:

"*About the German espionage school in Minsk and Borisov. The capacity is 700-800 people. It is divided into 3 departments: fighting partisans, military and strategic issues and the industrial department. The military department is busy with reconnaissance, and the industrial department is finding out where military enterprises had been evacuated to and where they are now*". [3]

The following secret order, signed by P.A. Zhuchkevich, a leader of the Borisov inter-district party center, who was later a member of the Vitebsk underground regional committee - CP(b)B - was sent to commanders and commissars of partisan detachments 'for continued execution':

"*According to the information available at the Gestapo, a great number of Jews and Jewesses were released from Minsk with the aim to be sent to detachments to poison the command staff. Strong, effective substances were found with the latter in the sleeves of their clothes, and in their hair; agents also poison wells.*

Check newcomers thoroughly, as well as those who have been with you and are working in the kitchen." [4]

It is natural that such a warning was a reason for the leaders of partisan detachments to refuse to take Jews into partisan ranks. Partisans felt distrust towards the Jews only because the latter remained alive, and were rescued from the ghetto in an incomprehensible way. Partisans were especially suspicious of Jewish teenagers who had escaped from the ghetto. Such a partisan attitude is explained by the radiogram signed by P. Kalinin, the chief of the Belorussian Staff of Partisan Movement (BSPM) on 22 April 1943. It read: *"The enemy sends local children at the ages of 8 to 15, armed with pistols, knives and poison, to partisan detachments. Take measures to protect detachments from such facts of espionage."* [5]

These orders blocked the way to saving the lives of Jews who had risked escaping from the ghetto. If the leaders of the partisan moment had analysed the situation in light of the German 'the solution of the Jewish question' in Byelorussia in 1941-1942, they could have understood the whole absurdity of accusing the Jews of espionage on behalf of the Germans. The partisan command undoubtedly knew the real situation with the Jewish population. This is proven by numerous reports by Soviet scouts that are kept in the National Archive of the Republic of Belarus. The personal attitude towards the Jews of the Central Committee of the Communist Party of Bolsheviks of Belorussia, First secretary P.K. Ponomarenko, when he occupied the position of the Chief of Staff of the Partisan Movement, was seen in his note to Stalin on 12 July 1941, entitled: 'Development of the partisan movement".

Together with the description of the heroic activity of partisan detachments, Ponomarenko writes: *"… in conclusion I must stress the exceptional fearlessness, firmness and irreconcilability to the enemy of collective farmers as opposed to some party officials from towns and cities who don't think about anything else but how to save their hides. To a great extent this can be explained by a vast Jewish stratum in towns. They are filled with animal fear of Hitler and instead of fighting they run away."*[6]

Anti-Semitism propagated by the Germans also influenced the leaders of many partisan detachments - as well as the local population frightened by the German orders about the death penalty for sheltering Jews - who did not want to accept Jews. [7] With rare exceptions they did not strive to risk their lives in order to rescue Jews. In many cases real danger came from peasants, who, for the material reward, handed over Jews whom they caught to the police or gendarmerie. Thus there was a question how prisoners could survive in the forest, even after a successful escape. Besides, it was clear that not all ghetto inmates could escape, which meant that those who remained would be destroyed by the Germans immediately.

The arguments made by Jewish underground workers, who insisted that sooner or later all the ghettos would be destroyed, and that as many as possible had to run away in order to keep at least some Jews alive, were not supported by the Judenrat or by the older ghetto inmates. Many of them thought that it was the underground in the ghetto, the collecting and keeping of guns, and the preparations to leave for the partisans, that made life in the ghetto still more dangerous, and drew massacres nearer. To explain the choice between death in the ghetto and life in the forest they said: *"It is better to die together in the ghetto than to live in the forest when you don't know what expects you."*

There were also arguments in the Jewish underground organizations, between those who thought it was necessary to resist inside the ghetto and those who insisted on fighting in the forest, where there were more possibilities for armed resistance to the German occupation forces. These arguments were settled by reality. The actual situation led Jewish underground workers in some of the ghettos to decide to use arms during the mass annihilation carried out by the SS and Gestapo. Young fighters preferred death in combat to being resigned to death. This was so in the ghettos of Nesvizh, Lakhva, Glubokoye, Kletsk and Kopyl, where ghetto inmates organized armed uprisings.

As soon as additional German SS and police detachments surrounded the ghetto, it was clear that the killings would begin. Jewish underground workers set houses on fire, shot the German murderers, and under the cover of the total confusion and noise, tried to escape and take out as many people as possible with them. For example, about 200 escaped from the Slonim ghetto in June 1942, and about 100 from the ghetto in Mir that September.

Jewish underground workers in the ghettos in Baranovichi, Kurenets and other towns and villages took out hundreds of people, who were effectively sentenced to death, into the forests. In Novogrudok, where slave labourers dug a tunnel about 250 metres long in the course of four months, about 260 Jews managed to escape. The Jewish underground organization in the Minsk ghetto organized an escape of an even larger number of Jews with the help of Jewish workers in the city.

Several partisan detachments and brigades were organized from the escapees: among them the Kutuzov detachment, the Parkhomenko detachment, the Chapayev detachment and the Kalinin detachment. Some families also managed to escape. There were even cases when partisans attacked German garrisons and liberated Jews, as, for example, in Novy Sverzhen and Kosovo. But even when they escaped to the forest at the cost of enormous effort, the Jews understood that it was not a guarantee for their complete rescue. As we have seen, it was not easy to become a fighter in a partisan detachment.

There were not many routes leading to partisan detachments, and to take them one needed to risk one's life. An escape from the ghetto or a concentration camp needed courage. In many cases it was accomplished without anyone else's help.

Jews in the Partisans

As to the possibility of Jews being accepted in a partisan unit, it was Jewish prisoners of war – Red Army soldiers who had been captured by the Germans and escaped from captivity - who would most likely be accepted, because, as a rule, having changed their surnames and thus not obviously Jews, they had professional military experience, which was in demand in the partisans.

Jews who took part in the anti-German underground movement usually changed their Jewish surnames and were sent to partisan units by the underground Communist Party organizations or Young Communist League. Even if the leaders knew that the member of the underground was a Jew, he was first of all considered to be a comrade in arms. Such Jews were sent to partisan units by the Communist Party underground. But such former Red Army soldiers were few under the German occupation; the majority of the Jews who were eager to join partisan units were in the ghettos.

Jews in the ghetto had to think how to save their own lives, and to find an opportunity to reach a partisan unit. It is necessary to admit that, despite the strong anti-Semitic attitude among the Soviet partisans, especially during the first years of the war, some of them tried to help Jews escape from the ghetto and supported their desire to fight against the Germans. While some of the partisan commanders thought that the Jews were joining the partisans only to save their lives, and with no desire to fight, and that they would be a burden, other commanders helped create units from ghetto escapees and from Jewish prisoners of war.

In spring of 1942, Philipp Phillipovich Kapusta, who later became a commander of a partisan formation, helped organize a unit under Lev Gilchik. It was a purely Jewish unit. The legendary partisan commander, and Hero of the Soviet Union, Kirill Prokopovich Orlovski wrote later: "*I organized a detachment entirely from the Jews who had escaped from the shooting.*

Partisan detachments around us rejected those people. There were cases when they killed those people. During two and a half months, former venders, craftsmen and others conducted fifteen combat operations, willing to revenge the German savages for the spilled blood. They killed Hitlerites, blew up bridges and derailed trains.'[8]

The Commander of the People's Avengers Brigade, Vasili Timofeyevich Voronyansky, accepted Jews without any limitations. The story of organizing the Victory Detachment under Nikolai Yakovlevich Kiselev, in People's Avengers Brigade, is of interest. 58% of the detachment were Jews from family camps situated in the neighborhood. Kiselev's name is connected to a unique case in the partisan movement: at the end of 1942 this fearless and honorable man led the unprecedented march of more than two hundred Jews who had escaped from the ghettos of the Vileika region - women, children and elderly people - across areas occupied by the Germans for more than three months, saving them by taking them across the front line to Soviet controlled territory.[9]

There were not many commanders such as Kiselev. A Jew who had escaped from a ghetto and met partisans could be denied acceptance even if he was young and strong. He had to find his own weapons and prove that he could fight. There were many such Jews wandering in the forests. When they met, they organized groups consisting of people of different age, married and single, united by one fate. They started to live in a family camp that existed thanks to their ability to survive in the forest. The main problems the Jews faced were: to provide security, procure food and obtain living quarters, however harsh.

Some partisan commanders understood the circumstances of the Jews who had escaped from the ghettos, and allowed them to settle nearby. Partisan units with such camps took responsibility for the safety of these Jews and helped them with food. For example, in the People's Avengers Brigade, Gennadi Ivanovich Safonov, assistant of the commander of one of the detachments, organized a tannery in the forest and employed about two hundred Jews from the nearby family camps. Witnesses say that Safonov created this tannery with the aim of saving the Jews giving them a chance to be with the large partisan unit.

Most of family camps were situated near those partisan units where there were Jewish partisans striving to defend their families, relatives and fellow Jewish townsmen and women from constant danger and hunger. It is known today that more than three thousand people lived in such camps.

Step by step, young people from family camps began to get arms and form combat groups, creating a unique phenomenon of Jewish family partisan units in the partisan movement of Belarus. The best-known was the Kalinin Detachment under Tuvia Bielski, in the Baranovichi region. At the time of joining the Red Army in July 1944 the detachment numbered 1,233 people, 296 of whom were armed. Partisan detachment No.106, under Semion Zorin, consisted mainly of the Jews from the Minsk ghetto. It numbered 596 people, 141 of whom were members of the combat group. "Economical" groups in Jewish family camps consisted of tailors, shoemakers, bakers, doctors, watchmakers, repairers and other specialists: these became a base that served many partisan detachments. Women, children and elderly people - everybody tried to make their contribution to the Victory.

The Jews who came to the forest in spring and summer of 1942 organized Jewish partisan detachments with battle-ready fighters. One of the first detachments under Boris Gindin consisted mainly of Jewish escapees or those who had been surrounded and had escaped. Former inmates of the Minsk ghetto organized several partisan detachments. The best known one was the Kutuzov Detachment under Israel Lapidus. A separate 51st regiment with more than 150 Jews from the Slonim ghetto was created in a detachment under Pavel Vasilyevich Pronyagin.

In 1943, on orders from the partisan movement headquarters, Jewish partisan detachments were disbanded and the partisans were assigned to different brigades. The newly arrived Jewish partisans were sent to Zorin's or Bielski's detachments. One of the reasons for taking this decision by the leaders of the partisan movement headquarters was the fight against anti-Semitism. They thought that if the number of the Jews in a detachment was small, they would not be so evident among the partisans of other nationalities – Belorussians, Ukrainians, Russians etc. - and that the attitude towards the Jews would change for the better. In reality, the situation in many detachments became even worse, while it became more difficult for small numbers of Jews to fight against the anti-Semitic partisans.

Judging by the documents of the Belarus National Archive, however, despite all that, Jewish partisans fought with dignity in the ranks of the People's Avengers. Many of them were honored with high military awards.

Considering the situation of the Jews in the partisan units, it is necessary to stress the difference in their situation to that of non-Jewish partisans. The first factor is the moral state of the Jewish partisans. The all-too-recent memory of the massacre of their fellow-Jews, which they had witnessed and which they by their own efforts had managed to escape, the memory of their murdered families, relatives and friends never left them. Revenge and loneliness were their companions. Jewish partisans had also constantly to prove their courage and ability to fight, overcoming the mistrust of others towards them as warriors. It is not by chance that among many memoirs of Belarusian partisans of different nationalities published after the war, and until almost the middle of 1990s, there are only few memoirs written by Jews, who could not write the truth at that time. This is proved by the words of Anna Davydovna Krasnopiorko, a former Jewish ghetto inmate, partisan and author of a courageous book about the Minsk ghetto 'Letters of My Memory'.

The journalist M. Knizhnik recalls: "…*Anna Davydovna told how many horrible things there were after the escape from ghetto. How they were rejected by the partisans. "I don't need the Jews", the commander of one detachment told them. Another commander was afraid of the information leaking out and sent a man to shoot them. I asked: 'Why don't you write about it? What are you talking about! Is it possible to write about it?!'- said she, sincerely astonished.*"[10]

Notes:

[1] Not much is known about Jewish resistance in Belarus as researchers in Belarus have began to research this topic only recently. There is a chapter "Resistance and uprisings of the prisoners of ghettos" in the book 'The Belarusian Jews. Tragedy and heroism' by E. Ioffe (pages 158-178). Historiography on the topic is presented in the article 'Jewish resistance in Belarus during the Shoa. Historical aspect: The Holocaust and the Anti-Fascist Committee. Materials of the IV International Conference (Moscow, October 1-2, 2002), M. 2003, pages 108-112' by I. Gerasimova. There is an exhibition 'Jewish resistance in Belarus, 1941-1944' at the Museum of History and Culture of the Jews of Belarus.
Research papers on Jewish resistance in Belarus by Sh. Kholyavski, I. Arad, and M. Altshuler (Israel) have been published in Israel, the United States and Poland in the 1960s and 1970s. Research by D. Meltser (Uunited States) and L. Smilovitski (Israel) were published at the end of the 1990s. There are many memoirs of the former ghetto underground members in different languages. The first book about the underground in the ghetto was H. Smolyar 'In the Minsk ghetto' published in Yiddish in 1946 in Moscow. Important information about the Minsk ghetto underground is presented the reference book 'The Minsk Anti-Fascist Underground' by Ya. Baranovski, G. Knatsko, T. Antanovich and others, Minsk, 1995.

[2] Rapoport R.S., Memoirs about the Ghetto, Minsk, 1962, p. 107, Museum of History of the Jews of Belarus, Minsk, Archive, f.2, inv.1, f.12.

[3] NARB, f.1405, inv.1, f.789. pp.2-3.

4   R. Rapoport, Memoirs about the Ghetto, Minsk, 1962, Manuscript, Archive of the Museum of History and Culture of the Jews of Belarus, f. 2, op. 1, d. 12.
5   National Archive of the Republic of Belarus (NARB), f. 1405, op. 1, d. 789, pages. 2-3.
6   NARB, f. 1405, op. 1, d. 958, page 87.
7   NARB, f. 1405, op. 1, d. 802, page 20.
8   Izvestiya of the Central Committee of the Communist Party of the Soviet Union, No.7., 1990.
9   In spite of great danger, there were noble and courageous people who rescued Jews at the risk of their lives. In the early 1960s the Government and the people of Israel established the honorary title of the Righteous Among Nations as a sign of gratitude for rescuing Jews. There are more than 500 such 'Righteous' in Belarus today. The book 'The Righteous Among Nations in Belarus', compiled by I. Gerasimova and A. Shulman, was published in Minsk in 2004.
10 L. Zubarev, Belarusian Jews, Minsk, 2004, page 69.
11 Yad Vashem Commission (Jerusalem) awarded the title of Righteous Among Nations to N. Kiselev for having rescued 210 Jews. The award was based on a report presented by the Museum of History and Culture of the Jews of Belarus.
12 M. Knizhnik, from notebooks, Znamya, No.9, 1993.

Documents and Materials

(All the documents presented preserve the transcription of personal and geographical names and the style of the original)

Part 1: Attitudes towards Jews in Partisan Detachments

No.1

From the report of Chekunov Vasili Dmitrievich, born in 1912, Ushakov G.M., born in 1908, Amochayev A.N., born in 1921 - the contacts of the partisan brigade Spartak - to the secretary of the Vileika regional committee of the Communist Party (of Bolsheviks) of Belarus from 23.12.42

German bands deal especially brutally with the Jewish population. Fascists shoot thousands of Jews and Gypsies in all the small towns of the Vileika region. During the executions of the Jews from the towns of Braslav, Yezdy, Vindza, Opsa, Gadutishki and others, babies were thrown into the graves by the Germans. Their backs were broken, legs and arms torn off. Earrings were torn off together with ears, golden rings – together with fingers.

Belarusian and Polish population feel exceptional sympathy to the sufferings of the Jews, provide every possible assistance with food, hide them in their houses in spite of the fact that they are severely punished according to fascists' laws, right up to shooting.

There was a case in the town of Braslav, when the Jews asked a catholic priest to rescue them from death. The priest treated the Jews with sympathy and helped some of them. When the Germans learned about it, they shot the priest. The priests in Postavy and Lyntupy were shot by the Germans.

Source: NARB (National Archive of the Republic of Belarus) f. 4, inv. 33, f. 264, p. 50 (original)

No.2

From the report to Commissioner of the Central Committee of the All-Union Communist Party (of Bolsheviks) of Belarus and the commissioner of the Workers and Peasants' Red Army General Headquarters comr. Platon from 10.11.42

There are many Jews in partisan detachments. A considerable amount of them are excellent fighters who try to wreak revenge on the fascists for the brutal murders of Jews. The attitude of some brigades' staff to this question is not correct: it is not allowed to set up separate Jewish detachments. The population here doesn't like Jews; they don't call them otherwise than Zhidy (Yids – interpr.) When a Jew comes into a house and asks for food, the peasant says that the Jews have robbed him. When a Russian comes together with the Jew, everything goes well. The Orlyanski detachment Bor'ba (Struggle – interpr.), Lenin brigade has 80% of Jews. There were cases when a Jewish group went for food to the other side of the Niemen. It was disarmed, the weapons were given to peasants and the group was beaten with shouts: "Beat the Yids (Jews), save Russia". Many Jewish families are hiding in the woods, few of them are armed. These Jews burst into villages and seize anything. There are detachments that don't take in Jews.

Source: NARB, f. 3500, inv. 4, f. 241/1, p. 98. (original)

No.3

From the report of V.B. Karpov, deputy commander of the reconnaissance and communication service group of the Minsk regional committee of Communist Party (of Bolsheviks) of Belarus to the secretary of the Vileika regional committee comr. Klimov from 27.11.42

Jewish population, terrorized and disarmed, takes shelter in the forests, gets food and clothes from local peasants, begging and sometimes using violent measures. There is a group of Jews about 300 people near Nivka, 250 - near Krasnoye, 63 - in the area of Panyshevo, 87 – near Zacherna and others. Sometimes fighters who escaped from captivity join them. And then they go on the so-called economical missions collecting particular supplies from population. Partisan detachments don't help them; they reluctantly take Jewish youth in. There were reports when partisans from N.N. Bogatyrev's detachment, having deprived the newcomers from their weapons, sent them back because anti-Semitism is developed rather strongly among partisans. A positive initiative in providing help to Jewish population was made by Timchuk, a commissar of the detachment "Mstitel" (Revenger – interp.) who set up a tannery in the Malinin forest where the Jews who have escaped from the ghetto are working. Jewish youth and men display their wish to join partisan detachments but going behind the frontline should be regarded as their main wish.

The decision on the fate of Jews in Vileika region must be taken as quickly as possible in order not only to relieve them from their sufferings but also in order to release peasants from supporting the mass of people that doesn't produce anything.

Source: NARB, f. 4, inv. 33-a, f. 264, p. 64 (original)

No.4

Some partisan detachments take in the Jews; some shoot or drive them away. Thus Grozny has got a considerable amount of Jews, Zotov has enough of them as well. But on the other hand neither Markov, nor Strelkov take in Jews.

Source: NARB, f. 1399, inv. 1, f. 13, p. 99 (original)

No.5

From the conversation of N.A. Kossoi, the assistant to the chief of the information department, with the partisans of the brigade "Dyadya Vasya" (Uncle Vasya – interp.) Meizeles Yelena Peisakhovna and Gurvich Frida Shlemovna on 29.10.1942 in the village of Khvorost'yevo

…On May 3 our group joined the detachment "Dyadya Vasya" as a platoon of the third company. In the period when we were left alone, the commander of the group Comr. Binun decided to send comrades Pruslin, Vaskin and Feldman to Minsk to be treated there as the latter had got frost-bitten and we had no means to treat them. We arranged a horse cart, allocated a person and sent them away in the evening.

Having reached the place of our previous location they stopped for the night and in the morning on having left the camp they were caught by a German punitive detachment in the very first village and hung at the place.

With regards to the situation, difficult for our group, which had arisen at the place of our previous location, Binun announced to all the partisans that those who wanted to leave the detachment could go away. As a result communists Khanin, Mirski, a Comsomol member Knyazev and a guide-communist Semka, who had brought us to the detachment, left the detachment.

Source: NARB, f. 3500, inv. 4, f. 136, p. 20-21 (original)

No.6

To the deputy chief of a Special Detachment in Baranovichi Region comr. Zukhba

Report

There is an unbearably difficult atmosphere of Anti-Semitism among the staff of Chapayev brigade, which has recently been severely aggravated.

Squeamishly mocking talks about the Jews are held; Jewish pronunciation is exaggerated; names are mispronounced; the word 'Zhid' is used in the insulting sense – all this acquires a mass character because the brigade command not only doesn't put an end to it but even encourages it.

Let's point to some most characteristic factors:

1. Brigade commissar's aide-de-camp Shilov constantly claims all the Jews to be cowards, traitors; that they all have joined the partisans in order to save their lives; "that if the Germans didn't persecute you, all of you would be spies and provocateurs"; that the Jews leave their comrades when in trouble and they cannot be relied on as a nation on the whole. Answering the question, whether he would have talked like that in the Soviet Union, Shilov said: "No, I would have received a ten year sentence". The same Shilov approached a ten year-old Igor Sadovski and said: "You are a Zhidyuga and a Jewish mug".

The chief of staff's aide-de-camp Burlakov claims that all the Jews must always remember that they are not equal, they stand lower than other nations and to all what is said about them they must keep silence and bend their heads.

Such talks, with rare exception, are characteristic of nearly all aide-de-camps as well as of partisans from the brigade staff. When the brigade commander's aide-de-camp Yakovlev doesn't take part in these talks, they claim he "has sold himself to Jews".

All these talks took place in the presence of district Comsomol Committee secretary Cezar Pavlyuts who not only doesn't explain the harm of such talks, not only doesn't he put an end to them but even supports them. To comrade Liebovich's pointing out to comrade Pavlyuts he answered: "It's none of your business".

The Jews meet especially squeamish attitude on the part of Mariya Borisovna – you can hear now and then: "Abrams", "parkhuls", "Yids" and so on.

All these facts were presented to the Chief of the Special Department comrade Vetelkin orally while talking to him. The atmosphere became especially aggravated after the case of Tsukkerman's desertion from the detachment "26 years of the October". Paying no attention to the Jews being present, talks of the following kind started in nearly all the dug-outs: it's a pity the Germans haven't destroyed all the Jews; all the Jews are beasts and traitors.

Especially ferocious in such talks were Kh. Burlakov, scout Piotr Minin supported by the chief of staff deputy on reconnaissance A. Myagkih.

It is characteristic that if some partisan, a Jew according to the nationality, does something wrong or commits a crime, all the Jews are made guilty of it.

There are many such facts. It is enough that the attitude has become hostile.

We think that such behavior and ideology of partisans are only to the benefit of the enemy and bring discord among partisans. It is by no means the result of the fascist propaganda, on which all enemy policy is based. It is necessary to take measures to eliminate the facts pointed out and to immediately explain the essence of the real national policy of our party and government to the partisans.

Our Motherland is no less dear to us than to the others, and we are ready like other partisans to give our lives for it.

March 20, 1944

Leibovich
Sadovskaya
Kostelyanets

Source: NARB, f. 1329, inv. 1, f. 109, p. 226-226 (back side) (original)

No.7

From the testimony of Faiva Solomyanski, the former partisan of the detachment "Mstitel" (Revenger – interp.) given by him to the department "The righteous of the World" at the Museum of Yad Vashem on 27.08.1992 (Jerusalem)

In summer 1942, when the Germans destroyed the ghetto in the village of Ilya, where I had been born and lived, I was miraculously saved. I was hiding in the forest and later I managed to join the partisan detachment "Mstitel". On the second day I met there Safonov Gennadi Nikolayevich who at that time was a commander of the economical platoon in the partisan brigade and was the rank of a senior lieutenant. Gennadi Nikolayevich did a lot to save Jews – elderly people, women and children who managed to escape from the ghettos of different towns and villages to the forest. But they were not accepted by partisan detachments and had to set up family camps themselves, but they lived there without food, in hunger and cold. I saw how Safonov used to bring food to the camp, and warm clothes which gave them a chance to survive.

Work on struggling against Anti-Semitism was carried out in the partisan detachment and Safonov watched that the Jews didn't suffer from those partisans who were filled with Anti-Semitism.

During the German round-up of the partisans, Gennadi Nikolayevich took the Jews out of the family camp to the places where they could hide or showed them on the map where they could find rescue. Many Jews were saved from inevitable death.

Source: Archive of the department "The Righteous of the World" of the institute of Yad Vashem (Jerusalem). Translation from Hebrew by M. Abeleva).

No.8

From the report about the work done by the political leader Kiselev Nikolai Yakovlevich since the beginning of the war till his coming out of the encirclement according to the task of the brigade "Dyadya Vasya", in accordance with the instructions of the secretary of the Central Committee of the Communist Party (of Bolsheviks) of Belarus comr. Ponomarenko

During the brutal pogroms organized by German executioners peaceful citizens of the cities of Minsk, Logoisk, the towns of Dolginovo, Krivichi, Knyaginino and others escaped to the forest. Poorly dressed and half hungry, they took shelter near the acting detachments "Mstitel', "Bor'ba" and others and were prevented them working.

On June 16, 1942 the command of the mentioned detachments instructed me as the head of five partisans to gather all the families in the forest as well as prisoners of war who had escaped from the enemy captivity, to allot a combat group and set up a detachment.

This task was fulfilled by me. Then my detachment was assigned to feed the collected group of about 270 people in order not to bind the hands of the acting detachments, and then to arm the young detachment.

Autumn was approaching: the people were barefoot and poorly dressed, besides there were 35 children from 2 to 12 years old, elderly people and women among those gathered. Economical missions have changed to combat ones. We had to take minimal quantity of food from the Germans and the police by fighting.

What concerns weapons the young detachment had 1 PPD submachine gun, 15 rifles, the same amount of grenades and up to 5,000 cartridges before going to the Big Land. But it was necessary to carry out economical missions every day and on a large scale in order to feed the people gathered.

On your instruction the command of the detachments mentioned above entrusted me to take the people gathered to the Big Land. The way was difficult and dangerous. Several times we were subjected to danger but always managed to get out unharmed.

The group of 218 people, whom I took out of the deep enemy rear, owe rescue of their lives to you, comr. Ponomarenko.

These people entrusted me to express sincere gratitude to you in their names and wish you long years of life and fruitful work to the benefit of our Motherland and our people. They also asked me to tell you that in their turn they will do their best to stand up to your care about them.

I ask you to take this sincere gratitude and wishes of 218 people, whose lives were saved by you.

Commander of the detachment, political leader Kiselev
19.01.43

Source: NARB, f. 4, inv. 33a, f. 155, p. 167 (back side) – 168 (original)

No.9

ORDER OF THE BELARUSSIAN STAFF OF PARTISAN MOVEMENT

January 14, 1943   City of Moscow
No. 90/15

For active combat actions against the German occupiers and accomplishing the task of the command on taking out from the German rear 210 Jewish families to award the partisans of the detachment "Mstitel":
1. Kiselev Nikolai Yakovlevich – 800 roubles
2. Rogov Nikolai Ivanovich – 800 roubles
3. Bannikov Vasili Pavlovich – 600 roubles
4. Gorodishchev Viktor Ivanovich – 600 roubles
5. Il'yin Afanasi Petrovich – 400 roubles
6. Asyutin Ivan Andreyevich – 400 roubles
7. Blokhin Ivan Fimich – 400 roubles
8. Koksharev Semion Stepanovich – 400 roubles

Chief of Staff of Belorussian partisan movement
– brigade commissar   (P. Kalinin)

Source: NARB, f. 3500, inv. 17, f. in cust. 7, p. 3 (original)

Part 2: Jewish Partisan Detachments

No.10

About the partisan detachment under L. Gilchik

Gilchik managed to penetrate into the ghettos of the towns Niesvizh and Kletsk and after a thorough preparation took out thirty people from these places.

At the beginning I was supposed to distribute the people who came from the ghettos among the detachments but having changed this intention I instructed Gilchik whose character had been clear to me already to form from them a new independent detachment. We allocated several rifles for the initial armament of this detachment and the rest was the task of the newcomers. I appointed senior lieutenant from the aviation Razuvayev a commissar of the detachment. And in a short period of time this new partisan unit grew up to one hundred and forty people – all of them being Jews. The people of this detachment showed how to arm themselves and how to fight.

F.F.Kapusta, major-general, former partisan formation commander.

Source: "Partisan friendship" – M., 1948, pp. 92-93

No.11

About the partisan detachment named after Kutuzov under I. Lapidus

In April 1942 a group of 13 people headed by Lapidus Izrail Abramovich left Minsk by lorry with the agreement of the driver, which had been reached through the underground committee. Having taken several rifles, pistols and grenades they got off on the 43-45th km on the road Minsk-Slutsk and went to the Kolodinski forest where they stopped and where others who could get out of the ghetto would gather… By April 10, 1942 a group up to 25-30 people gathered at this place, which had been previously fixed – all came out of the Minsk ghetto… By April 25, 1942 the detachment reached 40-45 people. The growth was exceptional thanks to the Jews from ghettos… The detachment was formed in the absolute majority on the basis of good knowledge of each other from the period of living together in town and in the ghetto, which guaranteed from penetrating spies into the detachment, and also other countermeasures with regards to the formation of the detachment.

After this the detachment was replenished in the same way and by May 15, 1942 there were up to 90 people in its ranks.

The best partisans-fighters in the detachment, who really won respect, are: Khalyavski Abram Borisovich: he has been in the detachment since May 1942, has got 26 combat operations on his account, 10 blows of enemy echelons among them. Aginski Yefim Samuilovich: being brave and capable of carrying combat, was appointed a platoon commander; he has been with partisans since April 1942, has 34 combat operations on his account, 12 blows and firing at enemy vehicles among them. Shultz Vilhelm Aleksandrovich: partisan since November 1942, has 22 combat operations on his account, 13 blows of enemy echelons among them… Shneider Yefim Semionovich: he has been with partisans since April 1942, has 22 combat operations on his account, 11 blows of enemy echelons and two sabotages on blowing enemy vehicles among them…

Commander of the detachment named after Kutuzov	Kolitvintsev
Commissar of the detachment	Abramov
Chief of Staff	Orlov

Source: NARB, f. 3500, inv. 4, f. 149, pp. 111-112 (original)

No.12

From the memoirs of a former commissioner of the Minsk underground city communist party committee N. Dement'yev

In 1942 I was sent to the partisan zone in the Rudensk district on the assignment of the underground committee to make stronger the connection with the partisans. When I came to Comr. Tishchenko's detachment in the partisan zone, I also visited Lapidus' Jewish detachment.

There was a printing house in Lapidus' detachment. There were types and a printing press; there was compositor Oppenheim from the printing house named after Stalin. He was assigned a mission to organize printing in the shortest time possible.

Everything was made ready during one night and at ten o'clock in the morning one could start printing. There was no need to train people as there were qualified printers and composers in Lapidus' detachment. Commissar Murav'yev wrote the first leaflet, edited it and an appeal to the population was printed right next to the headquarters tent in the equipped and adjusted to forest conditions printing house.

Source: NARB, f. 4683, inv. 3, f. 830, pp. 79-82 (original)

No.13

From the report of the secretary of the Ivieniets CP(b)B district committee Sidorok to the Chief of Belarussian Staff of partisan movement Kalinin from 31.01.1944

In the course of the summer 556 Jews – children, women, and the elderly – were taken out of the Minsk ghetto and organized into a Jewish family detachment. The commander of the detachment is Zorin Semion Natanovich, commissar – Feigelman Khaim Izrailevich, chief of staff – Vertheim Anatoli I.

Source: NARB, f. 1329, inv. 1, f. 7, p. 3. (original)

No.14

From the report about combat activity of detachment No.106

On July 9, 1944 partisan detachment No.106 of the Ivieniets district center, Baranovichi region under Zorin Semion Natanovich, commander of the detachment, commissar Feigelman Khaim Srolevich and chief of staff Vertheim Anatoli Isaakovich operating on the territory of the Ivieniets district, Baranovichi region came out of the enemy rear and joined the advancing units of the Red army in the area of Budy, Naliboki dense forest.

Beginning from July 5, 1944 the detachment was in permanent engagement with German dispersed groups which were trying to break through the Naliboki dense forest in the direction of Novogrudok. On 06.07.1944 the detachment lost 6 people killed, 3 people were heavily wounded including the commander of the detachment Zorin, platoon commander Marashek and one private in the fight with 150 German submachine gunners near the farmstead of Boryaki.

9 Germans were killed, 2 –wounded, 5 captured alive in this action.

On July 7-8 the fighting company repulsed the attacks of different German groups which tried to attack our family camp to capture food.

On 09.07.1944 a battle was unleashed 2 km from our camp between German groups and the 1st Baranovichi brigade, Bielski's detachment and the detachment named after Kutuzov. The command of the detachment decided to take the family group of 421 people to Kromen and the fighting company laid an ambush to cover the retreat of the family group in case the Germans would break through. When the family group accompanied by an armed platoon headed to Kromen, our reconnaissance reported that advanced units of the Red Army were moving from Kromen.

Before going out the detachment had 137 people armed and 421 in the unarmed family group who in fact all came out.

Source: NARB, f. 3500, inv. 5, f. 402, pp. 46-47. (original)

No.15

CONFIDENTIAL

To the deputy chief of the Special Detachment in Baranovichi region
Colonel from Justice comr. Zukhba
On your request from March 20, 1944 I inform you:
I considered the submitted compromising material on the partisan of our detachment Khurgina Emiliya immediately after it arrived and in February the case was closed.

The facts of Khurgina Emiliya's espionage activity were not proved by the investigation materials.

In view of the lack of proves I closed Khurgina Emiliya's case.

Commissioner of the SD of detachment No.106   /Meltser/

31.03.44

Source: NARB, f. 1329, inv. 1, f. 109, p. 232

PARTISAN DETACHMENT named after KALININ

No.16

The history of the partisan detachment named after M.I. Kalinin,
Lida zone, Baranovichi region

Since the arrival of the German invaders into the western Byelorussia the situation in the Novogrudok district of the Baranovichi region had been extremely tense from the moment the detachment was established. All the centers with large populations were filled with German and police outposts. In view of these circumstances, life in those centers was nearly totally impossible as German authorities hunted former Soviet employees and officials everywhere, and subjected them to dreadful punishment. The economical situation in the region was getting worse with each new day because of the predatory rule of German authorities.

The Baranovichi – Lida railroad, the Novogrudok – Lida and Novogrudok – Vsielub highways ran through the district, and German and police outposts were in Novogrudok, as the district centre, in the village of Berezovka, Novogrudok district, protecting the glassware factory situated there and a wooden bridge across the Nieman River on the Novogrudok – Lida highway, in the village of Ruda, Berezovka village soviet, the outpost on the railroad and on the bridge across the Nieman River, on the Baranovichi – Lida line, and in the small town of Vsielub. The garrisons there were big.

Our partisan detachment started to organize itself in the Bochkovichi forests of the Novogrudok district on the initiative of the Bielski brothers – Anatoli, Alexander and Sigizmund, who with a group of twenty people went to the forest, being afraid of the German invaders' persecution.

During the initial period when the group was being organized, there were no weapons. There was only one pistol with insufficient ammunition. Thus, with such an amount of weapons it was impossible to undertake any combat operations. The group was involved only in procuring means of surviving, and propaganda among the local population to join the partisan movement. At first the population reacted unfavourably to the partisans because of the fact that part of them were Poles. They traced the movement of the group and single partisans, tried to capture them, and reported them to the German authorities. Having learned about the organizers of the detachment, the authorities visited their homes in the village of Stankevichi, Petrevichi village soviet in the Novogrudok district several times. However, they were unable to find them because the latter were in contact with part of the local population who informed them about it in advance.

The group named itself after Zhukov, and from the first days of July 1941, elected Anatoly (Tuvia) Davidovich Bielski a commander by their common decision. Thus, having taken upon itself the task of fighting German occupiers in their rear, and preserving lives of Soviet citizens, women, children and the elderly, the group of twenty people, grew to eighty members by August 1942. The new recruits came mainly from the Lida and Novogrudok ghettos. Alongside with the growth in number, there was also an increase in weaponry possessed by the detachment, thanks to local population.

The detachment did not have a permanent base, and moved around in the forests in order not to be discovered and was difficult to catch. The system of managing the detachment came from its commander through the platoons' commanders. Because of the small number of people there was no commissar and no chief of staff in the detachment as such. In order to protect the members of the detachment when at rest, a special outpost was allocated, which provided security of the detachment. At times when the detachment changed its location and was on the move, a reinforced reconnaissance on foot provided security of its movement, both ahead and in the rear, and from the sides.

Information about the situation in the surrounding villages was obtained through the contacts of the detachment, who were permanent residents of these villages, whom the command had known since the pre-war times. At that time the detachment had no means of transportation, and since we were afraid of the treachery of some peasants, we did not use their horses and wagons.

Thus, from July 1941 to August 1942, the detachment was involved in disseminating propaganda among local population, increasing and arming its membership, as well as in researching the area for forthcoming operations.

In August 1942, having established contacts with the Novogrudok ghetto, we began to take out of it young element capable of fighting, who escaped the hands of the Germans and were often armed with their own weapons and in a short time the detachment grew up to 250 members.

Since that time, groups of partisans began to appear in various places in the forest and in populated areas, about which peaceful population knew as they were seen. At that time, informers started reporting about the presence of partisan groups to German outposts and police stations. As a result, and due to their small number, some of the partisans were caught alive by the Germans, and either punished or killed on the spot. The reason for these mishaps were the informers, and because these informers were many enough, we set our main aim to put an end to their activities by warning them, and even eliminating them. The detachment actually killed single policemen who sometimes came to the area where it was located.

In September 1942, the command of the detachment established contact with lieutenant comr. Panchenkov, who operated with his detachment in the region nearby, and joined him in the fighting operation on 16/10/42 on the Novogrudok – Novoyelnya highway, which took the form of an ambush against German gendarmes and resulted in the destruction of an automobile, and the capture of two hand machineguns, three rifles, and a few thousands of cartridges. During that ambush we lost neither men, nor equipment. On September 20, together with comr. Panchenkov's detachment as well, we attacked the Yatsuki railway juncture on the Baranovichi – Lida railroad, where four Germans were killed and seven more were wounded (description and Scheme No. 1).

After these operations, the Germans expanded their garrisons, especially in the village of Berezovka where they guarded the glassware factory and the bridge across the Nieman, which was the only means of communication along the highway between Novogrudok and Lida, and in the village of Ruda where they guarded the railroad bridge across the river Nieman, on the Baranovichi – Lida line.

The attitude of the local population towards the partisans improved after such operations, besides partisan movement had grown in the meantime. Neither local population, nor German authorities were able to determine the number of partisans because their location changed frequently. German authorities were already afraid of them.

The telegraph and telephone connection on the Novogrudok – Lida highway was repeatedly destroyed by the detachment. On 8/12/42, an ambush was organized on the railroad detour on the Yatsuki – Novoyelnya section, where two Germans were killed and two rifles with cartridges were captured.

In the autumn of 1942 a saw and drying mill was burned down together with a large supply of raw material at the Novoyelnya station, and eight German state estates with all their supplies of grain and agricultural inventory were burnt down in the district.

In December 1942, being afraid of a blockade in the region after the Germans had blocked the Lipichanski dense forest, the detachment moved to the Khrepieniovo forests in the Lubcha district, where on 1/5/43 the Germans made an expedition against the detachment, which resulted in our loosing nine men, two machine guns and five rifles. The reason for these losses was that there were few partisans at the location left as the rest had gone on their assignments. The Germans were about 400 and they were led by a local traitor who knew the area and the conditions well. The camp was surrounded on three sides simultaneously and the partisans fought to the last cartridge until the Germans burned the buildings that served cover to them. When they were escaping the fire, all the nine men were killed outside in various places.

After that, the detachment made for the Novogrudok district, where it had a permanent location, i.e. bases where they stayed till 15/2/43, the day of the second attack on part of our detachment. These bases were earth houses that could not be seen from above, which housed 20-25 people who had already experience they had received in Khrepienievo. There were several bases scattered on the 15 square kilometres of territory. There were approximately 150 people at the central base, a hospital where 5 people with frostbitten feet were treated at that time. Medical services was already set up and staffed by two doctors and two nurses. The base was surrounded by guards at a distance of 600-800 meters from the earth houses; reconnaissance missions travelled around the area, but the weapons in the detachment were very few to engage in combat with a large number of police, besides there were many women and children. As a result of the attack, in which almost 200 well-armed policemen participated under the leadership of a policeman, a local resident, who knew the area perfectly well, one partisan was wounded on our side; he was standing guard, noticed the police and gave a warning shot, after which the whole personnel that was at the base escaped without any casualties. On that same night all the bases of the detachment were abandoned. Three days later the Germans and the Lithuanians – approximately 600 men, 50 on horseback with dogs and very well armed, under the leadership of that same policeman undertook the second expedition on that same base, but the detachment had already gone. From February 15, 1943 to April 15, 1943 the detachment was divided into groups, and dispersed throughout the vast territory of the Novogrudok district.

On February 1943, a joint command for partisan detachments was established and our detachment which had 250 members was incorporated into the Octyabr detachment of the Lenin Brigade, the headquarters of which were located in the Lipichanski dense forest, under the previous command, as the second company, in which that command from November 1942 was included because of the growth of the detachment; the chief of staff was comr. L.A. Malbin.

On March 12, 1943, part of the detachment together with the detachment of Lieut. comr. Panchenkov, participated in the fight against the police in the village of Drachilovo, Novogrudok district, where fifteen policemen were killed and wounded. (Description and Scheme No. 2).

In March, telephone and telegraph connections on the Novogrudok – Lida highway on the section of five kilometres long was repeatedly destroyed to such a degree that the Germans ceased rebuilding it, three bridges were also burned down on this highway, and two bridges on the Novogrudok –Vsielub highway.

On April 15, 1943 the entire detachment was gathered at the base in Staraya Guta, in the Berezovka village soviet, where it was divided into companies and platoons because of the large number of armed people, and reconnaissance groups on foot and mounted ones were allocated, secret outposts and patrols were established. The reconnaissance forces constantly travelled around their districts; monitoring car movements on the highway was established, so that the command of the detachment always knew about the situation and the movements of the garrisons and other units in their part of the district. From that place broken contacts with the Lida ghetto were renewed, and people from there were extricated and brought into the detachment, and in the course of six weeks the detachment grew from 250 people to 750 members. With such numbers, and with more than 70% unarmed people, the detachment was moved to a different base in the Yasenovo Forest of the same Novogrudok district. It made the move with the reinforced reconnaissance, protected from ahead, from the rear and at the flanks. Besides this, there were mounted contacts from the command in all the detachments and while crossing the Novogrudok – Lida highway there were ambushes laid on both sides with reinforced armament. At the base there were again posts and patrols set up; reconnaissance operated day and night, both on foot and on horseback. On June 9, 1943 at 4 a.m. the Germans once again sent out an expedition against the detachment, but thanks to timely and precise reports of the mounted reconnaissance and patrols that detained the vanguard of the police, we managed to take away almost all unarmed men, women and children from the camp as part of the armed men engaged in fighting with the Germans and the police who arrived in sixty cars, two armoured vehicles and with a good amount of ammunition. They were led by a local resident whom we subsequently shot. After almost an hour-long battle we retreated, having lost five men killed and two rifles. The Germans lost eight of their men and policemen.

Because of the large number of people and the small number of weapons, the entire detachment with its women, children and the elderly moved to the Naliboki dense forest after this expedition, where according to Major-General Chernyshev's order No. M026 from June 19, 1943 the detachment was separated from the Oktyabr detachment and became an independent detachment named after Ordzhonikidze, Kirov Brigade. At the same time the detachment was to have a backup base in the Naliboki – Ivieniets dense forest where the women, the children and the elderly were to be based under armed protection. The fighting part of the unit, composed of 140 men, was to remain on their own in the Novogrudok district to carry out operations, moreover the fighting group was responsible for supplying and assuring food provisions to those remained at the family base. The detachment began to build a permanent base, but was unable to finish it because of the Great Blockade of the Naliboki dense forest by a great number of German regular forces. This lasted from July to August 14, 1943 during which the entire unit of 750 people had been taken away before the blockade without any human losses thanks to the knowledge of the area and the guides from the detachment. They had to return to the Novogrudok district again because of the difficult situation with food supplies in the dense forest as all the villages situated on the territory of the dense forest had been burned down or destroyed and most of the population had been driven away to German slavery.

In September 1943, the detachment participated in the 'rail war' and destroyed up to 800 meters of the railway bed on the Baranovichi – Lida line. All partisan detachments and brigades participated in the 'rail war' and specially went out on this mission to certain districts. The results of the battle were very good: after the 'Great Concert' the Baranovichi – Lida railway line was put out of service for one month and a half, and the Germans had to spend a great deal of effort, energy and equipment to get it back in service.

Since it was impossible with so few people and weapons to remain in the region any longer, about 500 people were gathered and sent back to the Naliboki dense forest on the order of the Kirov Brigade command, where they started to build a new base for the entire detachment and that base was built. On January 3, 1944 according to Order No. 001, Major-General Chernyshev separated the armed part of the detachment which had about 100 men into an independent detachment named after Ordzhonikidze under a different command as part of the Kirov Brigade. Our detachment, that was left, was called the Bielski detachment and subsequently named after M. I. Kalinin under the previous command and directly subordinated to the Lida Zone Centre, and the assignments were set to preserve the members of the detachment until the arrival of the Red army, to arm those capable of fighting and to organize them into subversive sabotage groups, and to start sabotage activity in the Novogrudok district, which was done. Since February till the liberation by the Red Army, the combat account of the detachment listed 6 derailed German troop trains and 6 locomotives, 34 carriages with personnel and technical equipment damaged, 14 automobiles with personnel blown up, 3 blown up bridges on the highway, 1 kilometre of a telegraph and telephone line cut on the railroad, 113 policemen and Nazis killed, 12 wounded and 31 man captured prisoner.

Since March 1944 comr. Ivan Vasilevich Shemyatovets was appointed commissar of the detachment on the order of the commissioner of the Central Staff of partisan movement Major-General comr. Chernyshev and occupied this position till the liberation.

Additional workshops were set up at the base, in which more than 200 non-armed specialists worked as shoemakers, tailors, saddlers, carpenters, locksmiths, weapon makers, tanners, sausage makers, hat makers; a mill, a bakery, a blacksmith shop, and other workshops provided everything possible not only to the members of the detachment, but other detachments and brigades located near our detachment in the Naliboki dense forest. In the period from January to June the detachment grew from 750 people to 1000.

Beginning from July 5 to 11 the detachment was involved in tracking down groups of destroyed German units. On July 6 a group of partisans returning from the operation became engaged in a battle with the Germans. As a result 4 Germans were killed and 3 captured prisoner, on our side one partisan was killed. On July 9, the detachment had a fight with a large German group composed of more than 200 men as a result of which eight people were killed, one wounded; on the German side there were 45 dead. (description and scheme No. 3). Two hours later Soviet armoured troops entered the camp, which were provided with assistance in reconnaissance as there were big dispersed German groups in the area and the scouts of the detachment led the armoured troops through the swamps to Kletishche.

The detachment had no direct connection to the Big Land (the territory east of the front line). The only link was through direct local command centres, i.e through the district centre or the Regional Communist party committee.

During the entire period of its existence the detachment received from the Big Land two machine guns, 2500 cartridges, 32 grenades and 45 kilograms of explosives. Some medicines were received as well. Uniforms were not received at all. The infirmed and the wounded were not taken to the rear.

Regular contact with the Soviet rear was of very great significance to the partisan movement: 1. Provision to the detachments of improved automatic weaponry, ammunition, explosives and medicine. 2. A fighter, going to battle, went much more courageously, knowing that in case of injury he would be picked up by his comrades and some time later evacuated to the rear. 3. Local populations saw that the Soviet government was helping the partisan movement by sending weapons, ammunition, medicine, uniforms and literature. The literature received was immediately distributed among the local population.

The detachment always accommodated itself in the forest trying to choose the largest, thickest areas, or a dry island, so that the enemy had no chance to approach it from any side. We tried to choose a place farther from villages so that the local population would not know the number of members and the location of the detachment and each person who came to the location of the detachment by chance or on purpose was interrogated and checked by the commissioner of the Special Detachment as there were cases when the Germans sent in spies under the pretext that they were partisans.

In order to obtain provisions a domestic or household platoon was set up, which was charged with the mission of supplying the whole detachment. As long as the detachment was small, the domestic platoon managed to fulfill its mission, but with the number of the members in the detachment about 750 and growing, a greater part of the partisans in the detachment had to do it. When the detachment was operating in the region, permanent food supply bases were not created because of the possible daily changes in our location. However, when in the Naliboki dense forest, where part of the detachment returned to after the Great Blockade in the autumn of 1943, the permission was received to harvest grain from the fields and to dig potatoes for our own needs. Special working groups and brigades were organized from the non-armed part of the detachment, which were occupied exclusively with this task and with the storing of the potatoes that had been picked up by our people. The detachment was provided through till February 1944 taking into account that 1 ton per day was used. Special pits were dug out, to which potatoes were brought, special transport was organized.

Since February on the permission of the regional party committee the detachment took potatoes from those people in the area who had picked their potatoes but moved from the dense forest to the area where German garrisons were stationed. They were mostly Poles who went to White Poles legions that fought together with the Germans against the Soviet power. Meat and other products such as grain, fat and others were procured from the families of policemen or in the villages that were near German garrisons. It occurred very often that some amount of food provisions had to be taken by force as very frequently armed self-defence was organized by the Germans in the villages, which also fought against the partisans. Due to the fact that most mills were controlled by the Germans, our detachment built a mill and grain seeder of its own in the Naliboki dense forest, that worked using horse power. We also built our own bakery. A grain-base was made, and every member of the unit received about two kilos of bread-crumbs and one kilo of sausage, also made by ourselves. We also had an NZ (*untouchable reserve – interpr.*).

The average daily ration for each partisan not involved in fighting operations was 500 grams of bread, 300 grams of meat and 1.5 kilos of potatoes. While in the region and during combat operations the rations were not fixed and depended on the circumstances. Sometimes it happened that one go without food for a couple of days.

We set up our own hospital in the detachment where we treated the injured and the infirm not only of our own detachment but of other detachments and brigades as well. A medical service chief was appointed, and he had 27 doctors to assist him and a whole staff of nurses. We had a dentist's office for the dentist, an epidemiological hospital, which was totally isolated from the camp. Food for the wounded and the infirm was prepared in a separate kitchen under the supervision of a doctor and a shift nurse. The population of our region willingly assisted with provisions, taking into account and knowing the situation of the partisans. The attitude of the population to the partisans radically changed for the better since the Stalingrad campaign. Uniforms and shoes were also received from the local population. In 1944 a leather factory was organized, which was able to provide our detachment with shoes but we didn't make leather yet. To repair and to sew uniforms and shoes big workshops were set up in the detachment, more than 200 people altogether worked there, serving all the detachments and brigades located near our detachment. Special women's brigades were organized to handle the laundry, and they did the washing for everybody who needed it. Soap was given out in the detachment as we had our own soap production that supplied the detachment with soap in sufficient amounts we didn't have to apply for help to the population in this respect. Underwear was mostly made from parachutes, and laces were made from parachute cables.

Pursuant to the instructions of the government, the detachment sowed approximately 8 hectares of cultivated grain of wheat and barley on its own, and provided assistance to the local population with horses.

General moral state of the detachment was good. The detachment had a burning wish to carry out revenge attacks on the enemy for the losses suffered by our motherland; the military tasks of destroying German communications assigned by the commanders were carried out by the fighting staff with great enthusiasm. There were no especially negative aspects observed while fulfilling the orders of the commanding staff, except for some cases of looting the local population by the partisans of our detachment, which was rooted out by the commanding staff of the detachment using measures of extreme punishment – shooting of two partisans.

A Party and Communist youth organization (Comsomol) was organized in the detachment, which alongside with political and educational activities among the membership and the population of our region also issued wall newspapers. Besides a Pioneer Communist children's group was organized, with some fifty-five members, and at the same time a school for sixty children from the first to the third grade was set up. In order to carry out these activities, teaching staff from among former Soviet school teachers was enlisted. The Pioneer group regularly issued its own 'Pioneer Newspaper' three times a month. This was organized by comr. Cheslava Solomonovna Genish under the supervision of the commanding staff of the detachment and the underground regional Comsomol committee.

In the leisure time partisans' amateur performances were arranged: their own songs, dances and music.

Some 23% of the members of the detachment were women of various ages; few of them were armed and participated in military operations of the detachment and the rest worked in the workshops according to their trade, in the kitchen and in the other workshops in the detachment. Women enjoyed authority among the members of the detachment, served guard duty alongside with men, carried out various tasks of the commanding staff, were members of the All-Union Leninist Communist Youth Union and the All-Union Communist Party of Belarus, and took an active part both in political and economical life of the detachment.

The detachment also had its own heroes, who courageously and bravely carried out military assignments of the commanding staff of the detachment, for example, Alexander Davidovich Bielski stopped a German automobile by accurate shooting on the Novogrudok – Novoyelnya highway during the ambush on the German gendarmerie on 16.10.43, and was engaged in a battle with superior forces of the enemy in the Yasenovo forests for more than an hour during the German operation against the detachment; together with the detachment he burned down several bridges on the Novogrudok – Lida highway, derailed 1 (one) enemy troop train, destroyed 3 (three) automobiles, took part in a number of other fights. Comrades Makhins Mihel Movshovich and Shimanovich Kiva Yevelevich, who knew the Naliboki dense forest perfectly well, served as guides during the Big Blockade in 1943 and actively assisted the commanding staff to withdraw the detachment from the blockade without any losses of the personnel. Comrade Ferdman Lev Zelmanovich, a landmine specialist, who had 4 (four) derailed enemy troop trains on his combat list, 10 (ten) automobiles and 2 (two) blown up bridges, had a burning wish to inflict still more losses on the enemy despite of his poor health. He taught landmining to 27 other partisans. Comr. Pressman Khonya Gertsovich, a deputy commissar on the Comsomol, called on Comsomol members and non-Union youth to energetic activity. He personally had 1 (one) derailed enemy troop train and 9 destroyed automobiles on his combat activities list.

General Summary

During the period of the detachment's existence a considerable amount of work was done: about 1,000 Soviet citizens were rescued from death or German slavery; 6 enemy troop trains were derailed, thus 6 locomotives were put out of service and 34 enemy carriages with personnel and equipment were destroyed, 1 railway bridge was blown up, 11 bridges on highways, 16 automobiles with personnel and about 9 kilometres of telegraph and telephone communication lines were destroyed; 8 German state estates with all surplus of grain and farming inventory and 1 sawmill and a wood drying factory with a big surplus of raw materials were burned down;

12 open battles and ambushes were carried out. 261 German soldiers and officers, police and vlasovtsies were killed, 800 meters of rail line beds were destroyed.

The detachment could have carried out much greater work, had it had sufficient reserves of weapon-trained members. However, it did not have the opportunity to arm everyone because of the absence of weapons and ammunition. Besides, the detachment did not have a sufficient amounts of explosives. All the materials mentioned above had to be obtained in various ways, and were found in small amounts. The detachment also did not have the opportunity to move around quickly because of the fact that 50 per cent of those under its protection were non-combatants – elderly men, women and children of school age and pre-school age.

The tactics of the adversary didn't make much damage to the partisan movement because the enemy didn't have a reliable rear. The overwhelming majority of the peaceful population supported the partisan movement in all possible ways, such as food provisions, weapons, ammunition and uniforms. Therefore, in order to strike certain blows on the partisans, it was necessary for the adversary to concentrate a big amount of well-armed regular troops; as a result, the effectiveness of its activity was minimal. Thus, the partisans distracted big formations of troops from the front and in this way made the activity of the invaders at the front weaker. Partisans' activity in small groups and sometimes in large ones, in the districts and in garrisons, inflicted great damage on the enemy in personnel, equipment, communications; it disrupted various deliveries, total mobilization and the transportation of peaceful populations into German slavery.

Commander of the Detachment: Bielski (signature)
Chief of Staff: Malbin (signature)
Commissar of the detachment: Shemyatovets (signature)

16/9/44

Source: NARB, f.3500, inv.4, f.272, pp.33-48. (original)

No.17

Confidential
Copy No.2

Order

Assistant to the Commissioner of the partisan movement Staff and the Central Committee of the Communist Party of Bolsheviks of Belarus on the Baranovichi Region

On the Lida Zone

May 1944 "N – ki dense forest"

No.011

§1

In connection with the application of the Bielski detachment command about the renaming of the detachment I satisfy the request and the detachment should be ffom here on named after Kalinin.

§2

I appoint Shemyatovets Ivan Vasil'yevich commissar of the detachment named after Kalinin considering him to occupy this position from March 25, 1944 on.

Assistant to the Commissioner
of the partisan movement Staff
and the Central Committee of the
Communist Party of Bolsheviks of Belarus
on Baranovichi Region

(signature) /Sokolov/

Source: NARB, f. 1399, inv. 1, f. 377, p. 17. (original)

No.18

ABSOLUTELY CONFIDENTIAL
Copy No.3

ORDER
of the Central Staff of partisan movement and
Central Committee of the Communist Party of Bolsheviks of Belarus
on the Baranovichi Region Commissioner

January 3, 1944   "Naliboki dense forest"

No.001

§ 1

To separate reserve Bielski's detachment from the brigade named after Kirov and make it a separate detachment directly subordinated to my assistant comr. Sokolov.

§ 2

I appoint comr. Bielski Anatoli Davidovich a commander of the detachment.
Comr. Molbin Lazar Abramovich – a Chief of Staff of the detachment, comr. Gordon Tyankhel Yefimovich - an acting deputy commander on political part.

§ 3

The reserve detachment must have its base in the Naliboki dense forest. Economical operations must be carried out in the Novogrudok district.
The exact villages included into the detachment's zone of operations will be defined by comr. Sokolov.

§ 4

I put forward the task for the detachment's command: to provide the family population of the detachment with food and armed protection.
To take measures to find weapons and to arm those capable of fighting.
To widely involve those not armed in the destruction of communication, bridges, roads and carrying out reconnaissance.
To organize no less than 2-3 sabotage groups from 150 armed people and blow up vehicles and other machinery.
To set ambushes in order to destroy enemy personnel and machinery.

Commissioner of the Central Staff of partisan movement and the Central Committee of the Communist Party of Bolsheviks of Belarus in Baranovichi Region
Major-General Platonov   (signature)

Source: NARB, f. 1399, inv.377, p. 17 (original)

No.19

Partisan district self-service industrial complex

The detachment named after Kalinin was a big partisan camp. It consisted of an armed detachment of more than 100 people, an economical group of more than 800 people and about 200 of the elderly and children. The detachment and the camp were subordinated to the Lida interdistrict party center.

Hundreds of people, different kinds of specialists, who miraculously escaped from ghettos, joined the detachments to save themselves from death and the detachment became a base that served the needs of many brigades of the Baranovichi partisan formation.

Imagine a path in the forest on both sides of which there are dug-outs camouflaged with moss and green plants. There were two hospitals with doctors, hospital attendants and qualified nurses, an out-patients' department for permanent reception of the sick there. They equipped a chamber for disinfection and a bath house at the out-patients' department, where not only those who lived in the camp took a bath but also those partisans who came to the detachment on some mission.

There were some kitchens a little bit aside. Nearby was a bakery, a mill, a soap factory. Different workshops were situated separately and the main one was where guns were repaired and even self-made mortars were made.

Blacksmiths shoed horses, made nails, knives, axes, hammers, rifled sows. Cups, buckets, iron ovens were made from tin. Carpenters' workshop produced rifle butts, wooden parts for saddles, bunks, stools, doors for dug-outs and other necessary things. Specialists tanned skins, from which shoe-makers made shoes, and saddle-makers made horse-collars, saddles, cut belts and other harness.

There was also a tailoring workshop, where jackets, trousers, military shirts were sewed from the materials captured while German garrisons and bases were destroyed. Hat-makers made hats and caps.

Watch workshops worked. Women knitted sweaters and scarves, barbers cut hair and shaved.

Each order was authorized by a written permission of the command, and only then, when there was a real need to produce the thing.

Work began at dawn and lasted till dark.

There were people from different bigger and smaller towns, but mostly from the Baranovichi Region. Everybody had lost somebody from the family, many had lost all. There were wives, whose husbands had been tortured to deaths by the Germans, mothers mourning for the children killed in front of their eyes, men, who had seen their wives and children being shot. I was struck by the special tense silence in all the workshops. People sometimes exchanged remarks but mainly kept silence – they worked at their best trying to suppress memories with work, so horrible, leaving no rest by day and at night memories. To speak was to disturb an unhealed wound. Better to keep silent…

Source: Schensnovich N.I., "Notes of an actor and a partisan", Minsk, 1976, pp. 88-89

Part 3. Jews in partisan detachments

No.20

To the commander of the "Mstitel" (Revenger) partisan detachment

At night from 31.12.42 to 01.01.43 communication near Myadel was broken along the length of 2 km. Khodos Grigori Davydovich, Alperovich Zalman Shlemovich and others were distinguished in this operation. 9 people all together.

Source: NARB, f. 1405, inv. 1, f. 843, p. 19. (original)

No.21

Order No.124 from 22.12.42. Partisan detachment "Mstitel"
To set free from his direct duties Rotblat, a partisan of the second company. To set free from the duties of a section commander Levin, a commander of the 1st company. To send Levin and Rotblat to do special work on a special mission.

Source: NARB, f. 1405, inv. 1, f. 844, p. 27. (original)

No.22

From order No.19 from 9.11.42 on the brigade "Dyadi Vasi" (Uncle Vasya's) about awarding partisans "For excellent fulfillment of fighting assignments in the enemy rear, active reconnaissance of the area and the enemy and organizing a tannery in the forest conditions I produce the following partisans of the detachment "Mstitel" to governmental awards... partisan Mindel Leiba Abramovich – to the order of The Great Patriotic war of the 2nd degree.

Source: F. 1405, inv. 1, f. 775, p. 9-9 (back side). (original)

No.23

From order No.48 from 17.03.43
I produce comr. Kotlyar Leonid Abramovich, a doctor, to a governmental award – the order of "The Red Star" - for treating seriously wounded partisans in conditions of a forest partisan hospital and displaying care and insistence.

Source: F. 1405, inv. 1, f. 775, p. 80. (original)

No.24

From the history of the detachment named after Parkhomenko, brigade named after Stalin, Baranovichi region
While destroying the police station in the small town of Rubezhevichi on July 16, 1942 partisan Figa Leib Yankelevich was the first to burst into the building, where from the police were firing machine guns, and overran all the firing points. Thus he made it possible for the detachment to destroy the whole police station.

Source: NARB, f. 3500, inv. 4, f. 248-a, p. 338. (original)

No.25

Order No.020

On the partisan detachment named after Parkhomenko, brigade named after Stalin

From August 22, 1943

§ 1

According to the verification of the perished and missing partisans – men and women – in the detachment named after Parkhomenko, carried out by the commission including commissar of the detachment Geiman, chief of staff Varvashenya, party organizer Gazman, commander of the 1st platoon Feigin and partisan Golub it was established that:

1. 24 people from the personnel of the detachment according to the list attached, hiding in a pit on the farm-stead near the camp-site, were brutally murdered after the dense forest had been blocked.
2. Those missing – 10 people
3. Partisan Khazanovich Tanya committed suicide in order not to be captured alive by the fascists.

§ 2

It is stated that partisans Nyusinson F. and Gurvich A. perished in the village of Zabor'ye while carrying out an economical mission on August 17 this year.

Among the latter was Shimshelevich who had not been on the personnel list and was killed together with them.

§ 3

The chief of staff of the detachment must exclude the mentioned above partisans – men and women - from the personnel list.

§ 4

Beginning from today partisans Klionski D. and Fiterson S. should be regarded on a business trip to Minsk accomplishing a special task of the partisans. The date of their return is September 7 of this year. Partisan Krontsenblyum should be regarded on a business trip carrying out reconnaissance in the district of Rubiezhevichi, the date of her return is September 7 of this year.

§ 5

Partisans Shimanovich I., Shimanovich B. and Shimanovich Kh., who didn't come back at the time established, should be regarded as deserters. On their return they must be sent to the special detachment of the brigade to be called to account.

§ 6

For the perfectly fulfilled economical mission on supplying the detachment with food stuff to express gratitude in the name of the command to a group of partisans headed by the commander of the group Antonenko Dmitri, fighters: Golub I., Shparber I., Dezhin V., Dovedenko Ya. And Merlis L.

To reprimand the commander of the 2nd platoon Tsukerman, fighter Katsnelbogin for being carelessness while fulfilling his duties during the economical mission.

§ 7

Partisan Shparger G. is appointed a secretary-typist of the detachment beginning from this date.

Commissar of the detachment named after Parkhomenko		
Quartermaster of the 2nd rank	(signature)	/Geiman/
Chief of staff of the detachment		
Military technician	(signature)	/Varvashenya/

Source: NARB, f. 3500, inv. 4, f. 248-a, p. 563. (original)

No. 26

List of partisans – men and women – from the detachment named after Parkhomenko, who tragically perished during the blockade of the dense forest while hiding in a pit at the farmstead near the camp.

The group was brutally tortured, arms and legs were twisted, pots were put on their heads, faces were not recognizable; some people, who tried to escape from the pit, were killed near it; the people were recognized by their clothes and build; after the brutal massacre the group was burnt.

1. Bass S.
2. Levin S.
3. Bronitski L.
4. Sheinberg O.
5. Sheinberg R.
6. Sheiberg T.
7. Kleorin
8. Krigel
9. Frumkin
10. Levina F.
11. Levina D.
12. Kagan A.
13. Khabai N.
14. Alperovich N.
15. Shuster
16. Gammer
17. Ptushkina
18. Shgarber R.
19. Baskina Z.
20. Zeldovich
21. Kotina S.
22. Vashkevich F.
23. Pashkevich F.
24. Khazanovich T. committed suicide in order not to be caught alive
25. Rubinchik D.
26. Vashkevich A. /a child/

The partisans who went missing during the blockade of the dense forest:

1. Kukhtin I.
2. Tishkov
3. Kulik I
4. Cidarovski P.
5. Maleikin
6. Leikind D.
7. Khanin L.
8. Turov V.
9. Rogovina G.
10. Frantsuz G.

The partisans who were sent to Zorin's detachment:

1. Rybakova I.
2. Golland S.
3. Gurvich M.
4. Siterman S.
5. Charno Kh.
6. Kargilovich L.
7. Sorokin B.
8. Bril T.

Children:
9. Golland Lena
10. Golland Nina
11. Gurvich Nahama

The partisans of the detachment killed during the economical mission in the village of Zabor'ye:

1. Nyusinson Fedya
2. Gurvich Alexander

Comrades who arrived from Minsk on the 22nd of July 1943, who were not on the list of the detachment and who were transferred to Zorin's detachment:

1. Shimshelevich Asya
2. Murokh Sima
3. Marshak Rema
4. Tsirlin Lilya
5. Tsirlin Rakhil
6. Livshits Dora
7. Lapidus Renya
8. Peisakhovich M.
9. Shuster N.
10. Levin L.
11. Kravets L.

List of people who arrived from Minsk on August 19, 1943 and were sent to Zorin's detachment

1. Grudinski Victor
2. Openheim Fanya
3. Lyandres Fanya
4. Openheim Doba
5. Plavchik Movsha
6. Eizrakh Samuil
7. Eizrakh Simon

Comissar of the detachment named after Parkhomenko Quatermaster of the 2nd rank
    (signature)   /Geiman/

Chief of staff of the detachment Military technician
    (signature)   /Varvashenya/

Source: NARB, f. 3500, inv. 4, f. 248-a, p. 556 (back side). (original)

Part 4. From the memoirs of Jewish partisans

No.27

M. Kravets. From the memoirs of a Jewish partisan. My town of Lenin. Meeting with partisans.

We are walking, our feet feel comfortable and there is plenty of room for them, but the head is bursting from different thoughts, how it all will end. But the thoughts give nothing, we must go further. We came to some ditch and stopped – it is not clear whether we should cross it or go along… Suddenly we noticed some people approaching us. We wanted to run away but it was too late. They saw us and somebody shouted: "Wait!"- for us not to move. They took the rifles off their shoulders and came nearer.

I see that they are neither police, nor the Germans. I was right. While they were holding their submachine guns ready, my heart was beating well. There were six of them. "Who are you? – they ask. "We are Jews, ran away from Gantsevichi, from the ghetto". "And where are you going?" "We are looking for partisans". "But you have no rifles". I can't answer anything. "You know it is not allowed to walk in the forests. We can shoot you". I dared to say: "The Germans shoot us, we have escaped to you and you want to kill us?" I noticed there was a Jew among them but he kept silence. The Jew was worried but he couldn't do anything. "So what shall we do now? Perhaps throw ourselves in this ditch? There is no place for us anywhere". They explained to us that without the permission of the commander of their detachment they couldn't take us in. They ordered us to sit here till the next day. They would inform the commander and come back to pick us up the next day. They went away through the big dry swamp.

An idea came to my mind to follow them when they were far away so that they wouldn't need to come back to pick us up. One peasant said that partisans were in the area of Starobin, it meant that they couldn't come back the next day. One needed some days to go there and back on foot – they simply wanted to get rid of us.

Thus we followed them at a distance of one kilometer and they were looking back all the time. When they stopped, we did the same. We see that one of them is returning to us. I see he is a Jew. OK. He came nearer and began to speak Yiddish to us. He asked us to return, because, if we followed them they would shoot us. "What should we do? Go back to the occupiers again? Better you shoot us, the less we suffer". I see the Jewish partisan take out his handkerchief to wipe out his tears. The boys and I started to cry too. Here he says to me: "Listen to me. There's a stack of hay there, sleep one night there. I'm not your enemy. And tomorrow you will go the same way through the swamp. You'll come to Rekhovets and there you should ask further". We went back to the stack of hay, made a fire (the day was cold) and fell asleep.

I woke up at night and started to listen. There was silence all around; the forest was rustling in the distance. I felt shivering. I was not alone, there were children with me but there was nobody to speak to. It was getting colder and colder. I came up to the stack, took an armful of hay and covered the children. I tried to fall asleep myself but sleep didn't come because I was scared. When the day was breaking, I woke up the children. They were cold. We made a fire, warmed ourselves and got ready to start on the way. We went the same way that we had taken the day before…

Source: Archive of the Museum of History and Culture of the Jews of Belarus, f. 2, inv. 1, f. 5

Translation from Yiddish by A. Zhenikhovski, manuscript

No.28

From Turetski Meer's memoirs, a former prisoner of the Minsk ghetto and partisan of detachment No.106.

Joining a partisan detachment was connected with great difficulties. First of all it was difficult to establish a contact with a partisan detachment. While looking for such contacts, people often got caught in the intelligence net of agent provocateurs. Besides, everybody was put on a card by the Judenrat. If an escape took place from the ghetto all the inhabitants of the house were to be shot. That's why it was necessary to make anyone who left the ghetto be regarded as having died.

Going out of the town was risky. That's how it was in those days. My two comrades and I decided to leave the town.

It was April 22, 1943. As in each morning we had to stand in the column, which was led to work. When we reached the place of work, we tore away our yellow round patches and white numbers, which were sewed on the jacket breast and on the back. It was the first serious violation, which was punishable by death, because Jews could walk only along the roadway in columns accompanied by the guide of the column. On the way we noticed that the places where the patches had been sewed on were clearly different. These places hadn't lost color and now could be evidently seen. This had not been foreseen but at the moment nothing could be done. I went ahead and my comrades – about ten meters behind so that they would be able to run away, if I were detained. There was one thought in the head, which pressed on us – to get out of town as quickly as possible. The street seemed endless, but when we came to the end of the street, we saw that it was blocked and the exit from town was guarded by the Germans. With our hearts full of pain we had to turn back, go back along the same long street and try to take the parallel road to leave town. Two policemen approached in our direction on the other side of the street, but we were lucky and they didn't pay us any attention. At last the houses were behind us; the fields ahead of us; and no guards in between. It became easier to breathe.

Soon we met up with partisans.

Source: Archive of the Museum of History and Culture of the Jews of Belarus, f. 2, inv. 1, f. 4. Manuscript

No.29

F. Solomyanski. From the memoirs (translation from Yiddish by M. Akkerman)

We proved that we were devoted to the goals of our detachment "Mstitel" and ready to accomplish any task set before us. And really nobody dared to say openly and to address us with accusations.

However it was very difficult to clear the clouds of suspicion and hostility. Danger always awaited a Jewish partisan. A Jewish partisan had to be more careful not only with the Germans but with comrades in arms in his own detachment. Dozens and hundreds of Jews met their death at the hands of their comrades in arms. The air was poisoned with anti-Semitism. German propaganda also helped a lot. It stated that the war had been unleashed because of the Jews and it was their fault.

Such was the atmosphere in which Jewish partisans had to live and fight. But we knew that we had to suffer and fight until the victory came, because understanding that we were revenging the Germans was stronger than anything else and it made us stronger. We believed that in the future it would be better. And we continued to fight – went to the railroad, attacked the Germans – caused losses to German troops.

The Red army continued its assault – took Minsk, liberated Vilno. Soon an order came: all partisan brigades must gather in Minsk – since at that time we were considered soldiers of the Red army and not partisans. Several days later all the former partisans paraded on the main square of Minsk and listened to a special order of the chief staff. It was about the activity of the partisans. Waves of joy were warming up our hearts but we, the Jews, were crying without stop. Everybody was mentioned in the order: the Russians, the Belarussians, the Lithuanians, the Poles, the Latvians, the Tatars, but only we, the Jews, remained unmentioned. Thus we stood and later marched with the whole parade that wanted us to forget the blood of our relatives, our wives, our parents, our children that lay in the death pits…

Source: Archive of the Museum of History and Culture of the Jews of Belarus, f. 2, inv. 1, f. 3. Translation from Yiddish by Akkerman. Manuscript

No.30

From the list of a Raisa Kh., a former prisoner of the Minsk ghetto, partisan of the detachment named after Kotovski, to her friends from the partisan detachment.

March 18, 1983

Dear Sasha and Anya!
First of all I want to beg your pardon that I'm so over-familiar while addressing you. But I can't address you by the name and patronymic the people who were fighting with me together in one partisan detachment in the most difficult years.

May this letter appeal to your memories. The matter is that on January 14 it was 40 years since the first fighting operation of the detachment named after Kotovski while destroying the garrison in Iliya.

I know that Sasha was with the detachment from the very beginning and directly took part in the fight in Iliya. That's why I ask you to describe the fight in Iliya in more detail.

I can tell you, that I arrived in the detachment on December 27, 1942 after it had been organized. My section commander was Melnikov Georgi. I don't remember what company I belonged to. I participated in the fight together with Zhitukhin and G. Melnikov and remember only the events in my zone. I remember well, that the submachine gunner Sasha Kuznetsov was severely wounded in his head in this fight. He died in my hands…

Source: Archive of the Museum of History and Culture of the Jews of Belarus, f. 3, inv. 1, f. 2, p.1. (original, manuscript)

No.31

December 20, 1985

Dear Anechka!
You were a witness of the events, when in July 1943 my daughter and I arrived at the detachment that was crushed by the siege.

Frost bitten, exhausted, hungry partisans from many brigades (Zheleznyak, "Dyadi Koli", named after Kirov and others) decided to breakout that night. Ella and I remained alone by ourselves in complete darkness lying in the endless poisonous swamp. My strength was expiring. Ella, her teeth chattering, asked:

Mum, lift me up, I'm cold...

Feeling that we would not get out of the swamp, I took out my revolver, groped for the girl's temple and wanted to pull the trigger. I decided to shoot her and myself. But then I heard children crying and cows bellowing. I thought it all seemed to me that it was a hallucination before death.

I listened carefully: The cow was bellowing very close and the children were crying. Then I raised my voice:

Good people, help! I've lagged behind with a child, we are lost!

But the crying and bellowing kept going on. It meant they didn't hear me. It meant my voice was too weak. I strained my efforts and repeated the request louder. The crying of the children stopped. During those times, when in danger ,mothers know how to make hungry children be quiet.

It meant they had heard me. I heard the sound of sloshing steps in the swamp coming towards us. Then they stopped still at a distance from us and the voice of a man started to reproach us without any shame:

How could it be! How could you have got her! Speak up, woman!

I raised my voice. An elderly man with a beard approached, lifted the girl carefully out of the swamp, shook her, as if shaking wet clothes, opened his fur coat, pressed the girl to his chest to warm her up and covered her with the flaps of his fur coat. I didn't understand anything. The old man helped me to get up and said:

I'll go slowly and you, woman, hold me. We are close by here.

How we got there I don't remember. I only heard somebody exclaimed:

Larisa, is that you?!

At that moment I lost consciousness. Later, when I came to, I learned that it was one of several small islands in the Domzhershin swamps, on which the population of some village had found safety.

Having come out of the dangerous entrapment of the swamps we continued a long way along forest paths. We found ourselves in the territory of the brigade named after Kirov. We saw a fire, around which a woman was cooking some food. Ella ran up to the woman and began singing:

A cook is making cutlets and cooking Russian salads. Mum, I love the cook.

When the woman saw us and heard such a song from the little girl, she began to cry. Everybody thought we had been lost.

Where could Ella have heard this song? Partisans had no cutlets and moreover no Russian salad. And the girl was only 4 years old.

Have patience, daughter - said the woman – *The soup will be ready soon. And I'll give you to eat.*

They asked me to stay in that brigade but I stubbornly wanted to return to my detachment, to the partisans with whom we were brothers, with whom we bonded during the first fight when on January 14 we attacked and destroyed the village Iliya.

Our way led us across the river Beresina. It was raining and Ella and I had to cross along two logs bound to stakes. When we reached the middle of the river, my head began to spin, I slipped and we fell into the river. Ella began to drown and a stake, to which the logs were bound, pierced through my foot when I fell on it. I couldn't swim. In those minutes I thought that I had miraculously survived the horrible siege and now my daughter would die because of me. I began to call for help:

-*We're drowning, help!*

Nobody was close at hand. Suddenly I noticed some partisans on the opposite bank who seemed to be busy burying one of their comrades. And again one more time someone took pity on us. We were saved.

Because of my previous foot injury received during the siege and now being pierced by the stake I couldn't walk further. We were brought to the village of Uborki where I met a wonderful person, Mariya Fedorovna (her surname seems to be Osipova). She was a member of the underground district Comsomol committee. She found a towel made from rough canvas and bandaged my bleeding and swollen foot. She asked women from the village to sow my torn, ragged skirt using their rough threads.

Thus Ella and I managed to drag ourselves in these rags to the detachment. My skin was also hanging in rags and we were covered with boils. You, Anechka, saw us, began to cry, and took us to the hospital…

Many years passed. At one of the annual gatherings of our partisan group, which I attended for the first time, I don't remember in what year, a beautiful woman with long, lose hair approached me and crying fell onto my chest. Through her sobbing I heard her say:

-*Larisa, how tattered you were then!*

"Then" meant after the siege on July 16, 1943. It was you, Anya. You told me this. The memory of your heart hadn't forgotten me. Thank you for the memory, for your tears!

The memory of those hard times during the last war will not fail us till the end of our lives. It is our weapon in the battle for peace. Our children and grandchildren must know how we fought for Victory.

And we, those who lived through so much, who fought with weapons in our hands, we deserve the right to joy…

Source: Archive of the Museum of History and Culture of the Jews of Belarus, f. 3, inv. 1, f. 2, p.2-3 (original manuscript)

List of documents

Part I. Attitude towards the Jews in partisan detachments

No.1 From the report of Ushakov G.M., born in 1908; Amochaev A.N., born in 1921, the contacts of partisan brigade "Spartak" under Chekunov Vasili Dmitrievich, born in 1912; from 23.12.42 to the secretary of Vileika regional committee of the CP(b)B comr. Klimov.

No.2 From the report to the commissioner of the TsK VKP(b)B (Central Committee of the All-Union Communist Party (of bolsheviks) of Byelorussia) and the representative of the RKKA (Workers and peasants' Red army) General Staff comr. Platon from 10.11.42.

No.3 From the report of Karpov V.B., deputy commander of the reconnaissance and communication group of Minsk regional committee of the CPB(b) to the secretary of Vileika regional committee comr. Klimov from 27.11.42.

No.4 From the report of partisan contacts in1942.

No.5 From the conversation of the assistant to the chief of information department N.A. Kossoi with partisans of the brigade "Dyadya Vasya's" Meizeles Yenta Peisakhovna and Gurvich Frida Shlemovna from 29.10.1942, v. of Khvorostyevo.

No.6 Report of the partisans Leibovich, Sadovskaya and Kostelyants, brigade named after Chapayev, to the deputy commander of the Special Detachment comr. Zukhaba.

No.7 From the evidence of the former partisan Faiva Solomyanski, detachment "Mstitel", given by him at the department "The Righteous of the World" in the Yad Vashem Museum from 27.08,1992 (Jersalem). Translation from Hebrew.

No.8 From the report about the work done by political leader Kiselev Nickolai Yakovlevich from the beginning of the war till they came out of the encirclement on the assignment of the brigade "Dyadya Vasya's" according to the instructions of the CC of the CP(b)B secretary comr. Ponomarenko.

No.9 Order about the Byelorussian staff of partisan movement from January 14, 1943 about rewarding partisans of the detachment "Mstitel" for taking out of the German rear 210 Jewish families.

Part 2. Jewish partisan detachments

No.10 Memoirs of F.F. Kapusta about L. Gilchik's partisan detachment.

No.11 About the partisan detachment named after Kutuzov under I. Lapidus.

No.12 From the memoirs of the underground Minsk city committee former commissioner N. Dement'yev.

No.13 From the report of Ivieniets district committee of the CP(b)B secretary Sidorok to the Chief of the Byelorussian staff of partisan movement Kalinin from 31.01.1944 about organizing Jewish family detachment No.106.

No.14 The report about fighting activity of detachment No.106.

No.15 The report of Meltser, a special detachment commissioner of detachment No.106 to Zukhba, a deputy chief of the Special Detachment on Baranovichi region from 31.03.44.

No.16 The history of origin of the partisan detachment named after Kalinin, Lida zone, Baranovichi region.

No.17 The order of the Staff of partisan movement and CC of the CP(b)B on Baranovichi region Commissioner Sokolov about renaming Bielski's detachment into the detachment named after Kalinin.

No.18 The order of the Central Staff of partisan movement and CC of the CP(b)B on Baranovichi region Platon about the Jewish partisan detachment named after Kalinin from January 3, 1944.

No.19 From the book of memoirs by the partisan of the detachment named after Kalinin Schensnovich N.I. "Notes of an actor and a partisan", - Minsk, 1976.

Part 3. Jews in partisan detachments

No.20 From the message to the commander of partisan detachment "Mstitel".

No.21 From order No.124 from 22.12.42, detachment "Mstitel".

No.22 From order No.19 from 9.11.42 about the brigade "Dyadya Vasya's" about rewarding partisans of the detachment "Mstitel".

No.23 From the order No.48 from 17.3.43 about producing doctor KOtlyar Leonid Abramovich to an award.

No.24 From the history of the detachment named after Parkhomenko, brigade named after Stalin, Baranovichi region.

No.25 Order No.020 about the detachment named after Parkhomenko, brigade named after Stalin from August 22, 1943 about the perished partisans of the detachment.

No.26 The list of tragically killed partisans – men and women – of the detachment named after Parkhomenko.

Part 4. From the memoirs of Jewish partisans

No.27 Kraviets M. From the memoirs of a Jewish partisan. My town of Lenin.

No.28 From the memoirs of Meyer Turetski, a former prisoner of the Minsk ghetto, a partisan of detachment No.106.

No.29 Solomyanski F. From the memoirs of a former prisoner of Ilya ghetto, a partisan of the detachment. Translation from Yiddish.

No.30 From the letter of a prisoner of Minsk ghetto, partisan of the detachment named after Kotovski, Raisa Kh. to the friends in the partisan detachment (from March 18, 1983).

No.31 A letter of Raisa Kh. from December 20, 1985.

Part 5. List of photocopies of documents

1. Information about the personnel of the 2nd company of the partisan detachment "Oktyabrski" under Tuv'ye Bielski by the end of 1943 (MI and KEB, f. 2, inv. 1, f. 4, p. 3).
2. Plan of the family Jewish partisan detachment named after Kalinin.
3. Certificate of Esfir Lvovna Pashkova, an underground activist from the village of Ilya, Vileika region, issued by the command staff of the partisan brigade named after Frunze.
(NARB, f. 3500, inv. 2, f. 182, p. 31)
4. Information about the composition of the partisan detachment named after Kalinin (commander T. Bielski) on March 1, 1944 (NARB, f. 3500, inv. 4. f. 2460, p. 104).
5. List of the command of the Jewish family partisan detachment No.106 to the deputy director of the Institute of History at the CC of the CP(b)B about the personnel lists of the detachment from April 13, 1970 (NARB, f. 3500, inv. 5, f. 4, p. 234).
6. Extract from the personal card on registration of partisans of Kuziniets Iosif, a fighter of the partisan detachment "Pobieda", brigade "Narodnyye mstiteli" (NARB, f. 3500. inv. 5. f. 99, p. 51).
7. Extract from the personal card on registration of partisans of the partisan detachment No.620 named after Chapayev, fighter Altshuler Moisei (NARB, f. 3500, inv. 7, f. 301, p.6).
8. Extract from the personal card on registration of partisans of the partisan detachment "Mstitel" Solomyanski Faivl (NARB, f. 3500, inv. 2, f. 152, p. 12).

Location of the Jewish family partisan forest camp of the Kalinin (Bielski) Detachment

Left side from the top

Mill
Tannery
Workshops: shoe-makers'
           tailors'
           watchmakers'
           carpenters'
           barbers'
           hat-makers'
           leather goods
Kitchen

Distribution of bread
Prison
Food storage

Hospital for contagious diseases

Right side from the top

Bathhouse
Bakery
Metal workshop
Soap factory
Sausage shop
Slaughter house
Cattle shed
Blacksmith
Stable
Health center
Headquarters
School
Assembly place
Kessler's camp 1,5 km away from the main camp

Copy

2nd company
list of partisan detachment personnel

1. 1941		7
2. the first half of 1942		7
3. the second half of 1942		63
4. 1943		16
according to education		
1. primary		21
2. secondary		20
3. Higher		7
according to age		
1. up to 20		32
2. from 20 to 30		71
3. from 30 to 40		45
4. older than 40		5

    company commander Bielski
    company political leader
    chief of staff

Information about the personnel of the 2nd company of the partisan detachment "Oktyabrski" under Tuvye Bielski by the end of 1943

Source: MHiKEB, f. 2, inv. 1, f. 4, p. 3

Certificate

Issued to Pashkova Esfir Lvovna, the village of Vyazynka, Ilya district to certify that she is a contact of the partisan brigade named after Frunze and actively works on behalf of the partisans.

This certificate is issued to show partisans when passing through the posts on the assignment of partisans and also none of the partisans is allowed to take anything from the household of Pashkova E.L.

The term of this certificate is till the arrival of the Red army

Chief of Staff of the brigade
Captain   /Ko..../
January 15, 1944

    certified true copy
    chief of general department
    secr. of district Soviet

Certificate of the underground activist from the v. of Ilya, Vileika district Pashkova Esfir Lvovna issued by the leaders of the partisan brigade named after Frunze

Source: NARB, f. 3500, inv. 2, f. 182, p. 31

Personal card
for registration of partisans

1. Name, first name, patronymic _____*Kuzieniets Iosif Foliyevich*_____
2. Date and place of birth _____*1920*_____ *t. of Dolginovo, Molodechno*_____
3. Nationality _*Jew*_ 4. Social position _____*employee*_____
5. Time of joining the VKP(b) or VLKSM, the number of party or Comsomol card
   _____*non-party*_____
6. Education, general and military (where from and when graduated)
   _____*7 grades*_____
7. By what RMC and when conscripted to the Red arm _____*no*_____
8. Participation at the fronts (what and where) _____*no*_____
9. Where from, when and from what position came to partisans
   _____*from the Dolginovo ghetto, t. of Dolginovo, Molodechno region, May 1942*_____
10. Whether was in prison (where and when) _____
11. Part of what partisan detachments (or groups) was, position in the area of operation of the detachment _____*"Mstitel"*_____

   1. From _*May*_ 194*2* till _*August*_ 194*2*
   _____*private*_____ (private, platoon commander, etc.)
   detachment _____*Mstitel*_____
   operated in _*Logoisk   Pleshchenitsy*_ district _____*Minsk*_____ region

   2. From _*August*_ 194*2* till _*October*_ 194*2*
   _____*private*_____ (private, platoon commander, etc.)
   detachment _____*Pobieda*_____
   operated in _____*Pleshchenitsy*_____ district _____*Minsk*_____ region
   _____*crossed the front line to join the RKKA*_____

   3. From _____ 194_ till _____ 194_
   _____ (private, platoon commander, etc.)
   detachment _____
   operated in _____ district _____ region

12. Wounds and contusions (when and where) _____

Fragment of the personal card on registration of partisans of the fighter from the detachment "Pobieda", brigade "Narodnyye mstiteli" under Kuziniets Iosif.

Source: NARB, f.3500, inv. 5, f. 99, p. 51

Personal card
for registration of partisans

1. Name, first name, patronymic _____Altshuler Moisei Khaimovich_____
2. Date and place of birth _1948 Mogilev region, Bobruisk district, v. of Nazarovka_
3. Nationality _Jew_   4. Social position _____peasant_____
5. Time of joining the VKP(b) or VLKSM, the number of party or Comsomol card
_____non-party_____
6. Education, general and military (where from and when graduated)
_____2 grades, no military_____
7. By what RMC and when conscripted to the Red arm _____Bobruisk_____
8. Participation at the fronts (what and where) _____wasn't_____
9. Where from, when and from what position came to partisans
_____from Gomel region, Rogachev district, v. of Pobolovo_____
10. Whether was in prison (where and when) _____wasn't_____
11. Part of what partisan detachments (or groups) was, position in the area of operation of the detachment _____"Mstitel"_____

1. From _May 5_ 194_2_ till _December 10_ 194_3_
_____private_____ (private, platoon commander, etc.)
detachment _____Chapayev No.620_____
operated in _Klichev, Bykhov, Propoisk_ district _____Mogilev_____ region

2. From _December 10_ 194_3_ till _July 1_ 194_4_
_____private_____ (private, platoon commander, etc.)
detachment _____Chapayev No.620_____
operated in _____Kletsk_____ district _____Baranovichi_____ region

3. From _____ 194_ till _____ 194_
_____ (private, platoon commander, etc.)
detachment _____
operated in _____ district _____ region

12. Wounds and contusions (when and where) _____wasn't_____

Fragment of the personal card on partisans' registration of a fighter from partisan detachment No.620 named after Chapayev Altshuler Moisei.

Source: NARB, f. 3500, inv. 7, f. 301, p. 6

Personal card
for registration of partisans

1. Name, first name, patronymic _____Solomyanski Faivel Eilevich_____
2. Date and place of birth _____1908   t. of Ilya_____
3. Nationality __Jew__   4. Social position _____employee_____
5. Time of joining the VKP(b) or VLKSM, the number of party or Comsomol card
_____no_____
6. Education, general and military (where from and when graduated)
_____7 grades_____
7. By what RMC and when conscripted to the Red arm _____no_____
8. Participation at the fronts (what and where) _____no_____
9. Where from, when and from what position came to partisans
_____to the underground organization_____
10. Whether was in prison (where and when) _____no_____
11. Part of what partisan detachments (or groups) was, position in the area of operation of the detachment _____member of an underground organization which_____
 1. From _September 1_ 194_1_ till _September 1_ 194_2_
  was in contact with the partisan detachment (private, platoon commander, etc.)
 detachment _____Kotovski's_____
 operated in _____Ilya_____ district _____Molodechn_____ region

 2. From _October 10_ 194_2_ till _arrival of Red Army_ 194_4_
  _____scout_____ (private, platoon commander, etc.)
 detachment _____Mstitel_____
 operated in _____Luban-Pleshchenitsy_____ district _____Minsk_____ region

 3. From _____ 194__ till _____ 194__
  _____ (private, platoon commander, etc.)
 detachment _____
 operated in _____ district _____ region

12. Wounds and contusions (when and where) _____no_____

Fragment of the personal card on partisans' registration of a fighter from the partisan detachment N...e Mstitel Solomyanski Faivl.

Source: NARB, f. 3500, inv. 2, f. 152, p. 12

> Deputy director of the Institute on the Party History
> at the CC of the CPB on the party archive
> Comr. Pochanin S.V.
> Zorin S.N. (former commander of the p/d No.106)
> Feigelman Kh.S. (commissar of the p/dNo.106)
> Meltser A.R. (former chief of the fighting department of the p/d No.106)

On the instruction of the Ivenets District Center personnel lists of the detachment were compiled several times.

On the last occasion personnel lists were compiled according to the state on July 15, 1944, i.e. when the detachment was disbanded. These lists were given to the Belorussian Staff of Partisan Movement together with the lists that had been compiled previously and with other documents. But the lists from July 15, 1944 haven't been preserved for a part of the partisans and the latter lost the possibility to receive certificates of the same kind. Because of the fact that no one could have left the detachment from October 1943 with the exception of those killed, when former partisans of the detachment No.106 apply for documents we think it possible to regard the list preserved reliable and to define the time of their stay with the detachment up until its disbandment on July 15, 1944.

We also inform about the names of the partisans killed:
Openheim, Fishkin, Raskin, Ozerski, Segelchik, Plavchik, Sholkov, Cherno, Zager, Mindel, Pekker, Tunik, Ezrakh, Parkhutski, Parkhutskaya, Kushner, Perchenok (father), Perchenok (son),.......

Zorin S.N.	The signature of comr. Zorin is certified
Feigelman Kh.S.	The signature of comr. Feigelman is certified
Meltser A.R.	The signature of comr. Meltser is certified

A letter of Jewish partisan detachment No.106 leaders to the deputy director of the Institute of party history at the CC of the CP(b)B about the personnel lists from April 13, 1970.

Source: NARB, f. 3500, inv. 5, f. 4, p. 234

Information about the composition of the Kalinin partisan detachment under the command of Tuvia Bielski on March 1, 1944

Bielski detachment	Name of the detachment
780	Number of partisans
5	Members and candidates of the VKP(b)
19	Comsomol members
2	Russians
no	Byelorussians
no	Ukrainians
778	Jews
no	Poles
no	Other nationalities
no	Party workers
168	Soviet workers
200	School children
16	Engineers and technicians
2	Doctors
no	Chairmen of collective farms
343	Workers
20	Collective farmers and peasants
6	NKVD and militia workers
2	Junior commanders
1	Middle commanders
no	Higher command
9	Local
no	From the encirclement
no	From prison
no	Sent
no	From the forest
no	From the landlord
771	From the ghetto
no	From the Ukrainian battalion
461	Men
313	Women
8	Since 1941
3	Since 1942 till June 1942
200	Since 6. 1942 till 1943
569	Since 1943
686	Lower than secondary
80	Secondary
8	Higher
177	Up to 20 years old
289	From 20 to 30
181	From 30 to 40
133	From 40 and older
There are 23 children in the detachment up till the age of 7 years old. 80 people up till the age of 16 years old.	Remarks

Information about the composition of the partisan detachment named after Kalinin (commander T. Bielski) on March 1, 1944

Source: NARB, f. 3500, inv. 4, f. 2460, p. 104

JEWISH PARTISANS IN BYELORUSSIA 1941-1944   71

74 WE STOOD SHOULDER TO SHOULDER

JEWISH PARTISANS IN BYELORUSSIA 1941-1944

JEWISH PARTISANS IN BYELORUSSIA 1941-1944 77

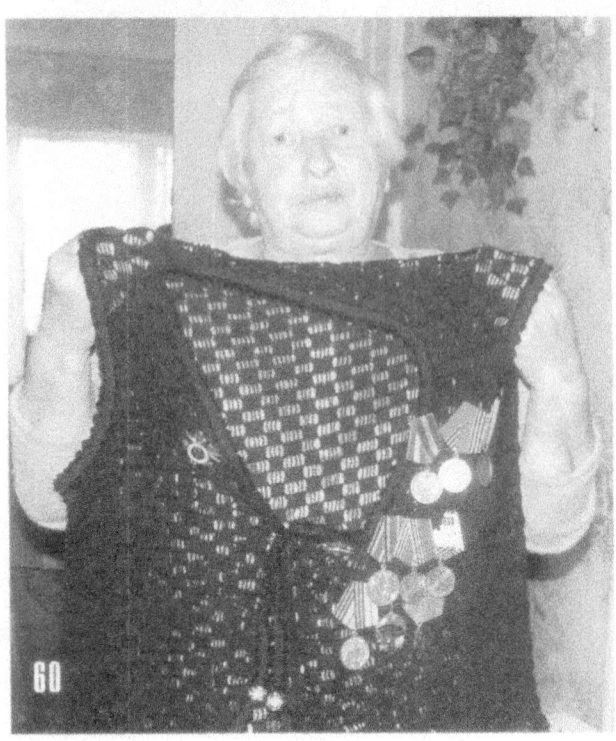

JEWISH PARTISANS IN BYELORUSSIA 1941-1944

JEWISH PARTISANS IN BYELORUSSIA 1941-1944   81

JEWISH PARTISANS IN BYELORUSSIA 1941-1944 83

84 WE STOOD SHOULDER TO SHOULDER

JEWISH PARTISANS IN BYELORUSSIA 1941-1944   85

86 WE STOOD SHOULDER TO SHOULDER

88 WE STOOD SHOULDER TO SHOULDER

JEWISH PARTISANS IN BYELORUSSIA 1941-1944   89

Photos

1. A group of former ghetto prisoners in a family camp. Pinsk region. 1943
2. Sophia Kustanovich. A partisan of the detachment named after Chukhlai in the partisan bakery.
3. An escapee from the ghetto on the occupied territory. Photo from the MH and CJB archive.
4. In the partisan camp. Drawing by Boiko L. (Rozenshtekher Abram), a partisan of the brigade "Razgrom", Minsk region, 1944
5. David Keimakh. Commander of the partisan detachment "Dima" (later the detachment named after V.V. Shcherbina).
6. Lev Gilchik. Commander of partisan detachment No.5, later renamed after Zhukov.
7. Samuil Sverdlov. Secretary of Rogachev underground district party committee, a commissar and later a commander of the First Rogachev partisan detachment.
8. Izrail Lapidus. Commander of the partisan detachment named after Kutuzov.
9. Gerasim Kruglikov. Chief of staff of the partisan detachment named after Budenny, brigade named after Suvorov.
10. Samuil Sverdlov. 1943. Drawing by S. Romanov.
11. Leonid Okun. Commander of detachment No.208 of the partisan regiment, Mogilev region.
12. Eugeni Mironovich (Tevye Finkelshtein), commander of the detachment named after Voroshilov, brigade named after Frunze, with his wife ithe partisan detachment. 1944.
13. Faina Lazebnik in the partisan detachment named after Shish, brigade named after Molotov.
14. The Jews – partisan commanders. Sitting from left to right: Boris Khaimovich, commissar of the 1st battalion, 208th partisan regiment named after Stalin; Sholom Zorin, commander of partisan detachment No.106; Girsh Smolyar, commissar of the partisan detachment named after Lazo. Standing from left to right: Khaim Feigelman, commissar of detachment No106, Vladimir Kravchinski, commander of the sabotage group, detachment named after Budenny, brigade named after Stalin; Naum Feldman, commissar of the detachment "25 years of the BSSR", brigade named after Ponomarenko.
15. Nickolai Nikitin (Beines Shteingardt). Commander of the brigade named after Nikitin. In October 1942 the brigade named after Nikitin made a raid through the enemy rear and crossed the front line.
16. Boris Gindin. Platoon commander, later chief of staff of the "Batya" sabotage group.
17. Detachments commanders of the brigade named after Molotov.
18. Leaders of the brigade "Narodnyye mstiteli": from left to right – commissar V.V. Semenov, commander V.T. Voronyanski, chief of staff D.I. Kopanev.
19. Philip Philippovich Kapusta. Commander of the brigade named after Voroshilov, later – of the formation of partisans of Slutsk Zone.
20. Ivan Matveyevich Timchuk. Commissar of the partisan detachment "Mstitel". In 1943-44 – commander of the 1st anti-fascist brigade of Minsk region.
21. Ivan Leonovich Satsunkevich. Commissar of the partisan brigade "Razgrom".
22. Gennadi Ivanovich Safonov. Deputy commander of the detachment "Mstitel". In 1992 Safonov was distinguished with the title of "The Righteous of the World".
23. Nickolai Yakovlevich Kiselev. Commander of the detachment "Pobieda". In September 2005 Kiselev was distinguished with the title of "The Righteous of the World".

24. Headquarters of the partisan brigade named after the newspaper "Pravda". Grigori Gertsovich (4th on the left) – chief of staff, his wife Valentina Gertsovich (the first on the left) – staff typist.
25. Natan Liker (on the right), partisan of the detachment named after Shchors, with PavelVasilyevich Pronyagin, commander of the partisan detachment named after Shchors.
26. Nickolai Shchensnovich. Partisan of the detachment named after Kalinin.
27. Partisans of the 208th regiment named after Stalin with a four-year-old Lenya Satsunkevich rescued by them. Photo from 1943.
28. Naum Tseitlin. Partisan of detachment No.258, the 8th Rogachev brigade.
29. Yelena Gringauz. Partisan of detachment No.106.
30. Newly-weds. Partisans of the detachment "Za Sovetskuyu Rodinu", brigade named after Chkalov.
31. Lev Gurevich. Partisan of Fedotov's detachment, Pinsk partisan formation.
32. Abram Aleksandrovich. Commander of the 1st squad, detachment named after Voroshilov, brigade named after Zhukov.
33. Partisans of the detachment named after Katovski. The first row at the top (from left to right) – Nickolai Shevchenko, Izya Galin, Feiga Geller; 2nd row – Yakov Klin, Zlata Rubina, Motl Shifron; 3rd row – Ivan Panov, Abram Tsukerman. Volkovysk. July, 1944.
34. Musya Rozental. Partisan of the 5th Vorginskaya brigade.
35. Rakhil Rapoport. Partisan of detachment No.106.
36. Maria Mints. Partisan of the detachment named after Gastello, brigade named after Bragin. Drawing by A. Rabkin.
37. Grigori Erenburg. Partisan of the detachment named after Akhromenko, Lelchitsy brigade.
38. Revekka Gringauz. Partisan of detachment No.106.
39. Gisya Bukhovtsova. Partisan of Podgoyetski's detachment, Gomel region.
40. In the partisan printing house.
41. Anshel Delyatitski. Partisan of the detachment named after Shchors, 51st Jewish group.
42. Yitsek Gershengorn. Partisan of the detachment named after Suvorov, brigade named after Zaslonov.
43. Khaim Aleksandrovich. Partisan of the detachment "Borba", brigade "Narodnyye Mstiteli".
44. Galina Relkina-Kulchayeva. Partisan of the detachment "Burevestnik", brigade "Burevestnik".
45. Michail Lev. Partisan of brigade No.537, Mogilev region.
46. Uri Kaplan. Partisan of the detachment named after Zhukov.
47. Bronislava Zavalo. Partisan of the detachment named after Dzerzhinski, brigade named after Frunze.
48. Maria Kerzon. Doctor of the detachment named after Chapayev, brigade named after Chapayev with her friends-partisans Fima and Semen.
49. Berta Bruk. Doctor of the detachment named after Suvorov, 2nd Minsk brigade.
50. Yakov Mogilnitski. Partisan of the 20th Kalinin brigade.
51. Faivl Solomyanski. Partisan of the detachment "Mstitel", brigade "Narodnyye mstiteli".
52. Yankel Liberman. Partisan of I.G. Shubertidze's brigade.
53. The Dorski brothers: Grigori (on the left) and Michail. Partisans of the detachment named after Bydenny, F. Kapusta's formation.

54. Yakov Glazshneider (second on the right). Partisan of Makagonov's detachment, brigade "Vpered".
55. Michail Kantarovich. Partisan of the detachment named after Zhukov.
56. Dina Beninson. Partisan of the detachment named after Sergeyev, Mogilev region.
57. Rakhmail Kheifets. Partisan of the detachment named after Dovator, brigade named after Chkalov.
58. Lazar Losik (on the left) and Khaim Oginski. Partisas-scouts of the detachment named after Kutuzov.
59. Partisan family – Sofia and Alter Kustanovich. Sofia – partisan of the detachment named after Chuklai, Pinsk formation; Alter – detachment named after Gastello, brigade No121.
60. Raisa Lifshits. Partisan of detachment No.30, Ilyin's brigade.
61. Partisans of the brigade named after Chkalov, from left to right: Shepsl Shpringer, Yekhiel Okun and Lelya Shukhman. Photo from 1942.
62. Anna Taits.   Partisan of the detachment named after Chkalov, brigade "Vpered".
63. Yuri Taits. Chief of Baranovichi formation medical service.
64. Khaim Feigelman and his wife Faina, partsans of the detachment No.106.
65. GalinaKostelyanets. Partisan of the detachment "Za Sovetskuyu Byelorussiyu", brigade named after Chkalov.
66. Leonid Boiko (Abram Rozenshtekher). Partisan of the brigade "Razgrom". Selfportrait. Drawing.
67. Taking an oath by the partisans of the detachment "Razgrom". On the left – commissar of the brigade Satsunkevich I.L. Drawing by L.Boiko.
68. Anna Gorelik. Partisan of Bukhov's special group, Minsk region.
69. Khasya Pruslina. Partisan of the brigade named after Suvorov.
70. Vladimir Shatsman. Partisan of the brigade named after kalinin, brigade named after Molotov.
71. March at night. Drawing by L.Boiko.
72. Abram Zhitelzeyev. Partisan of the brigade named after Ponomarenko.
73. Portrait of a partisan. Drawing by L.Boiko.
74. Partisan family: Vulf Losik (left), partisan of the detachment named after Kutuzov, his brother moisei Losik (fought at the front), Lazar Losik (Vulf's son), partisan of the detachment named after Kutuzov.
75. Rakhil Krasnoperko. Doctor of the brigade named after Stalin.
76. Anna Sirotkova. Scout of the detachment "Pobieda", brigade "Narodnyye mstiteli".
77. Yekaterina Klimovich. Partisan of the detachment named after Chkalov, brigade named after Suvorov.
78. Yelena Drabkina. Partisan of the detachment "Spartak", brigade "Bolshevik".
79. Raya Epshtein. Partisan of the detachment "Sokol", brigade named after Ponomarenko.
80. Riva Sosland. Partisan of the detachment "Belarus", brigade "Belarus".
81. Faina Lazebnik (on the right) with her partisan friends.
82. Anna Krasnoperko. Partisan of the brigade named after Stalin.
83. Ilya Vilenski. Partisan of the detachment "Iskra", brigade named after Kirov.
84. Yakov Grinshtein. Partisan of detachment No.106.
85. Abram Rubenchik. Partisan of the Jewish detachment No.106.
86. Anna Machiz. Partisan of the brigade named after Zhukov.

87. Abram Tsukerman. Partisan of the detachment named after Kotovski, brigade named after A. Nevski.
88. Bronislav Rotblat. Partisan of the detachment "Mstitel", brigade "Narodnyye mstiteli".
89. Group of Jewish partisans of the detachment named after Voroshilov, brigade named after Frunze after the war. From left to right: Abram Aleksandrovich, Lazar Vizenfeld, last on the right – commander of the detachment E. Mironovich (T.Finkelshtein).
90. Roza Yulevich. Partisan of the detachment named after Shish, brigade named after Molotov.
91. Shaya Berkovich. Partisan of Pinsk formation, died on 31.12.1942.
92. Anna Minkova (left) with her sister Lyuba and Aleksander Zakharov. Partisan s of the detachment named after Kotovski, brigade "Narodnyye mstiteli".
93. Grigori Shepetinski (down on the right) with his partisan friends. 1944. Pinsk.
94. Sholom Kholavski (in the middle). Partisan of the detachment named after Zhukov with his partisan friends. Photo from 1944.
95. Leva Kravets and Misha Stolyar. Partisans of the detachment No.106.
96. Partisans of the 51st Jewish group of the detachment named after Shchors. In front – Grigori Shepetinski.
97. Sholom Kaplan. Partisan of detachment No.106.
98. Michail Treister. Partisan of detachment No.106.
99. Izrail Mazel. Partisan of detachment No.106.
100. Leonid Melamed. Partisan of detachment No.106.
101. Semen Berkovich. Partisan of detachment No.106.
102. Yefim Goldin (left) and Leonid Okun. Partisan of detachment No.106.
103. Maks Konyuk and abram Teif. Partisans of detachment No.106.
104. Yakov Puchinski. Partisan of detachment No.106.
105. Genya Pasternak. Partisan of detachment No.106.
106. Boris Mlynski. Partisan of detachment No.106.
107. Darya and Yefim Vapne. Partisans of detachment No.106.
108. Sholom Zorin. Commander of partisan detachment No.106.
109. Partisans of the detachment named after Shish, brigade named after Molotov.
110. Group of partisans from detachment No.106 at the monument to the fallen friends. Photo from the 60-ies.
111. Tuvye Bielski. Commander of the partisan detachment named after Kalinin.
112. Zus Bielski. Partisan of the detachment named after Kalinin.
113. Asael Bielski. Partisan of the detachment named after Kalinin.
114. Raya and Yakov Shepetinskis. Partisans of the brigade named after Lenin.
115. Meyer Turetski. Partisan of the detachment No.106.
116. Michail Pertsev. Partisan of the detachment named after Kutuzov, brigade named after Lenin.
117. Group of partisans from the detachment named after Kalinin. Photo from 1944.
118. Pesakh Friedberg. Partisan of the detachment named after Kalinin.
119. Mirra Levina. Partisan of the detachment named after Kalinin.
120. Partisans of the detachment named after Kalinin: Pinya Boldo, Pesakh Abramovich and Ishe Openheim.
121. In the partisan hospital. Chief of the hospital – Yuri Taits.
122. Faina Lazebnik with her partisan friends from the brigade named after Molotov, Pinsk region.

123. Faina Lazebnik. Partisan of the brigade named after Molotov.
124. Guarding the aerodrome in the Naliboki dense forest. Detachment named after Kalinin.
125. Vilik Rubezhin. Partisan of the detachment named after Dzerzhinski, 18th brigade named after Frunze.
126. Iosif Shelyubski. Partisan of the detachment named after Furmanov, brigade named after Chapayev.
127. Sonya Petrashkevich. Partisan of the detachment "Za Sovetskuyu Byelorussiyu", brigade named after Kirov.
128. Alik Lapidus. Partisan of the detachment named after Kutuzov.
129. Yekha Rubenchik. Partisan of the detachment No.106.
130. Yidel Kagan (left). Partisan of the detachment named after Kalinin.
131. Igor Sadovski. Partisan of the brigade named after Chkalov.
132. Vyacheslav Tamarkin. Partisan of I. Kovpak's formation.
133. Lazar Vizenfeld. Partisan of the detachment named after Voroshilov, brigade named after Zhukov.
134. Iosif Berman. Partisan of the brigade named after CC of the CP(b)B. Fell in May 1944.
135. Lyalya Bruk. Partisan of the detachment named after Suvorov, 2nd Minsk brigade.
136. Miron Margolin. Partisan of the detachment named after KIM. Fell on 09.03.1943.
137. Iosif Margolin. Partisan of the detachment "Zvezda". Fell on 31.05.1944.
138. Matvei Pruslin. Partisan of the detachment "Mstitel". Fell in 1942.
139. Olga Kostelyanets (Gringauz). Partisan of the detachment "Za Sovetskuyu Rodinu". Fell on 02.08.1943.
140. Abram Kostelyanets. Partisan of the detachment "Za Sovetskuyu Rodinu". Fell on 02.08.1943.
141. Shlema Markus. Doctor of the partisan detachment "Borba", Lenin brigade. Fell in September 1942.
142. Maks Khanin. Partisan of the brigade named after Parkhomenko. Fell in 1944.
143. Isaak Kagan. Partisan of I.Shubertidze's brigade. Fell in 1944.

Novogrudok: part of the market place - December 1941

The Early Days of Occupation
Jack Kagan

Novogrudok was bombed on Tuesday 24 June 1941 and again on Saturday 28, June. More than half the town burned down including the whole Jewish centre. There were many casualties.

On 4 July the German army entered the town and immediately began enforcing anti-Jewish laws. On the third day of the occupation, an order was issued stating that Jews were to wear Yellow Stars on the front and back of their clothing. Additionally, a curfew was imposed from 6 p.m.; Jews were not allowed to walk on the pavement; every Jew between the ages of twelve and sixty had to do forced labour; Jews were not allowed to travel on public transport, go to any market place or have any contact with non-Jews. Finally Jews lost their right of citizenship. A Judenrat (Jewish Council) was formed. Its members being the lawyer Zeldovitz (Chairman), the chemist Moshe Leizerovski, Yehoshua Ivenecki, Moishe and Leizer Israelit, Shalom Lubcianski, Momik Dobrin and Landau.

Within a few days Jews were arrested for work. In fact they were taken outside the town and shot. On 26 July the SS arrived and demanded that the Judenrat provide 100 Jews for special work. The Jews were assembled in the centre of the Market Square, then fifty-two of them were taken out and shot, while a German army band played Strauss. The bodies lay in the Market Square for nearly three hours. After that the Germans ordered five horses and carts to remove the bodies to the Jewish cemetery for burial. Then they ordered the Judenrat to provide Jewish women to wash the blood from the stones.

Among the fifty-two victims were two Judenrat members, Yehoshua Iveniecki and Moshe Leizerovski.

The Fifty Two Martyrs
Yehuda Slutzki

It was Saturday 26 July 1941, and during the morning there were frightening rumours circulating in the town. We thought that it would be an opportune time to clean the streets. Jewish policemen went from house to house and urged us to assemble in the Market Square; they told us that by doing so we would avoid a general slaughter. My father, David Slutzki, prayed the Morning Prayer at the Breslin house of our neighbour. I hid in the garden of my friend Halperin, and my brother Mulik was at home. After we heard that we had to assemble in the Market Square we returned home, then all three of us went there. The square was full of people and encircled by armed Germans. We understood immediately that we were facing great danger.

We were ordered to stand in lines, then the Germans started the selection, sending people to either the right or to the left. There was no pattern to the selection process; it simply depended on the whim of the selector as to who would be sent to death and who would remain alive. So, we were then in two groups. There was a rumour that we were to be taken to work somewhere but we realized soon enough that this was not the case. The Germans ran around us like predatory animals, screaming out orders. They separated out fifty people, among them my father and brother.

One of the Germans, apparently the commander, gave a speech. Although I did not understand him, I was stunned – his voice was that of a menacing animal. At the end of the speech the Germans took out ten people from the group of fifty and positioned them opposite ten Germans and, on the order Feuer (Fire!) they shot them. Then they took another ten. In that way they murdered all fifty.

There were a few who tried to escape from the Market Square, among them the teacher Solomon. The Germans, who stood in a chain around us, shot him and another. The rest of us, who watched the atrocities – that terrible disaster – believed that our end was near and that we would go the same way as the others. However the Germans ordered us to go to the Judenrat where we were given spades. Carts were brought in, we loaded our dead onto them, drove them to the Jewish cemetery, and buried them in a Brothers' grave. Then an incident occurred that haunts me. One of the fifty was still alive. He asked us to put him on top of the grave – he thought that he would be saved that way – but a Pole overheard him and attracted the attention of a German, who shot him again. We were terrified that the Germans would shoot us too following the burial. They only beat us brutally; they did not kill us.

That black day came to a close at twilight. In the cemetery near the Brothers' grave I said good bye for ever to my father and my brother, without even saying Kaddish for fear of the Germans around us. Beaten and traumatized we returned from the cemetery. The martyrs' blood that had been spilled on the ground had now been washed away by our grieving Jewish women. Amongst the victims were 2 Judenrat members Yehoshua Ivenecki and the chemist Moishe Leizerovski.

About a month later the SS arrived and asked the Judenrat for fifty workers. It took time, but eventually the Jews assembled in the Market Square. They were then taken away, as if they were being taken to work. In fact the SS took them to Skridlewo forest and shot them there.

Robbery by German soldiers and by the local Byelorussian and Polish police was a daily occurrence. The Gebeits commissar SS-Hauptsturmfuehrer Wilhelm Traub arrived and took over the civil administration and gave an order to shoot three members of the Judenrat. Zeldovitz, Lubchanski and Landau were arrested and shot in Scridlevo. Then, on 22 November 1941, he ordered that the Jews must give up all valuables, such as gold, silver, copper and fur coats. As always, the end of the order went the words: 'If you disobey YOU WILL BE SHOT.'

Yudl Slutzki served as a fighter in the Bielski detachment. Mobilized in the Red army in July 1944, he fought bravely against the enemy. In 1946 he reached Palestine where he fought for the establishment of the State of Israel. He died in Tel Aviv in 1999.

EVERLASTING PEACE

In this cemetery, the deceased from Novogrudok Jewish community were laid to rest for 500 years. During the Holocaust their graves were desecrated and their tombstones were removed. On July 26, 1941, before the four huge massacres in which the Nazis and their henchmen murdered 11,100 Jews from the town and its surroundings, the Germans shot 52 Jewish citizens dead in the market place and they were buried in a mass grave in that cemetery.

*In memory of the martyrs of our community who perished in the Holocaust,
the partisans and those who fell at the front during the war.
Whose last place is not known.*

May they rest in everlasting peace.

Fencing of the cemetery and setting the tombstone was performed by the Novogrudok Jewish Association in Israel and in the Diaspora during the month of Av, July 1997.

**Regional Commissar
in Novogrudok
in the General Commissariat of White Russia**

Circular Letter
To all District Mayors, Commune Mayors and Village Elders

I am enclosing a series of wall posters concerning the confiscation of Jewish property. These are to be posted in sufficient numbers on sites which are clearly visible. The collection of Jewish property will take place on 28.11.1941. On that day every Mayor's office will prepare one room, which will serve as a collection point, and will be occupied by two officials of the District of the Commissariat. For the preparation of those rooms, which must be neat and orderly the District Mayor is responsible.

To enable the Jews, who are ordered to hand over their possessions, to pass along the street to the district offices, I am also enclosing pass forms. These pass forms are to be handed to the Commune Mayor or Village Elder according to the numbers of Jews in their area. Jews, whose duty it is to hand over their possessions, will report to the Commune Mayor or Village Elder in order to obtain a pass form.

They will enter in the relevant spaces the name of the Jew and the place where he lives. The pass form must be returned to the Village Elder and must be handed on to the District Commissar via the Commune Mayor.

The Jews, who are with their possessions to be handed over, will assemble in the communes and villages and will march in close formation to the district town, under the supervision of the Jewish Council. After handing over their possessions and valuables they will be led back, again marching in close formation.

Every misuse of the pass forms or travel permits will be punished. The Jewish Councils are responsible for this.

The District and Commune Mayors, as well as the Village Elders, are responsible that all orders regarding the handing over of the property of the Jews are carried out.

In the district towns, the civilian police will line up the Jews in front of the District Mayors' offices. They will then be dealt with in alphabetical order.

Two civilian policemen will be on duty at the collection point in case of special need.

Unpleasantness during the preparations for the handover, and refusal to hand over or hiding of valuable items, is to be reported immediately to the German officials.

Novogrudok, 22 November 1941.

Signed: Traub
Regional Commissar

Source: (NARB), Central National Archives (Partisan section) Minsk.

The First Massacre
Jack Kagan

On 6 December 1941 all the Jews of Novogrudok were ordered to assemble at the courthouse. The elderly, the sick and the children from the orphanage had to go to the convent on First of May Street. From the convent they were taken straight to Skridlewo forest to be killed. More than 6,000 of us assembled at the courthouse in the bitter cold. In the evening we were let into the five buildings. On 8th December 5,100 men, women and children were selected to be killed. They were beaten on the way to the waiting lorries, then loaded on, fifty people to each vehicle. They were taken to Skridlevo, three kilometres (about two miles) from Novogrudok. There they were forced to lie face down in the cold snow. Then fifty at a time, they were made to undress, and fifty at a time they were made to run to the pit that had been dug where they were shot. Additionally, the Germans brought some Jews from the surrounding villages to Skridlevo and also killed them there.

The mass grave and memorial for the 5,100 victims massacred on the 8th December 1941.

Arrest of the Judenrat

A ghetto was formed in Novogrudok on 10 December 1941, in the suburb of Pieresika; the living conditions were terrible. Workshops were created for the tradesmen in the courthouse. They were then forced to work for the Germans as well as for the local population.

The Germans also ordered the formation of a Jewish police force. Mr. Kalinski a refugee from Lodz became the Jewish police commandant. He had about twenty young men in his force, including Yudl Ostashinski, Yichok Bercovitz, Hercl Nachimovski, and also Herman Kritz who was not from Novogrudok. At this time the Judenrat chairman was Lawyer Ciechanowski, Moshe and Leizer Israelit, Motl Yankovski, Shlomo Kabak, Momik Dobrin, Shlomo Gershenovski and Munie Dzienciolski.

About 300 Jews were working in the German barracks; the rest were working for the municipality. Food was allocated: we were given about 200 grams (7 ounces) of bread a day, but the situation worsened daily. In May/June 42 the Gebiets Commissar accused the Judenrat of not doing their job properly. They were arrested and shot in Skridlevo.

**Regional Commissar
in Novogrudok
in the General Commissariat of White Russia**

Announcement
To all Regional Mayors and Village Elders
ORDER regarding the JEWS

1. When the transfer of the Jews from the surrounding areas to the ghettos in district centers has been completed, no Jew may stay in the villages and small towns of those districts
2. I therefore order all community Mayors and village elders that, if any Jew appears, to have him arrested by the police and brought to Novogrudok.
3. The only exception are the Jews who are in possession of an identity document issued by the Regional Commissar of Novogrudok. Nevertheless, I request that each document is to be thoroughly scrutinized to check whether it is genuine.
4. Persons without stars (the recognition badge of the Jews) but who by their appearance are recognizable as Jews, in other words it can be suspected that they have removed their Jewish recognition badge, are also to be arrested and to be delivered to the prison in Novogrudok.

Novogrudok, 6 March 1942

Signed: Traub Regional Commissar

Judenverordnung

1. Mit dem Abschluss der Überführung der Juden des flachen Landes in die Ghettos der Rayonstädte darf sich in den Gemeinden und Ortschaften sämtlicher Rayons des Gebiets Nowogrodek kein Jude mehr aufhalten.

2. Ich weise deshalb sämtliche Gemeindebürgermeister und Dorfälteste an, jeden auftauchenden Juden sofort durch die Schutzmannschaften festnehmen und nach Nowogrodek bringen zu lassen.

3. Allein ausgenommen sind Juden, die sich im Besitz eines Ausweises des Gebietskommissars Nowogrodek befinden. Jedoch bitte ich jeden Ausweis genauestens auf seine Gültigkeit zu prüfen.

4. Personen ohne Stern (Kennzeichen der Juden), die aber an ihrem Aussehen, als Juden erkenntlich sind, bzw. in dem Verdacht stehen ihre Kennzeichen entfernt zu haben, sind ebenfalls festzunehmen und in das Gefängnis Nowogrodek einzuliefern.

NOWOGRODEK, DEN 6. MÄRZ 1942

gez.

TRAUB

Gebietskommissar

Загад адносна жыдоў.

1. З заканьчэньнем пераводу жыдоў з усяго абшару у гэтта раённых гарадоў, ані адзін жыд не можа знаходзіцца у вёсках і гмінах паасобных раёнаў Наваградзкай Акругі.

2. Дзеля гэтага загадываю усім гмінным Бурмістрам і Соцкім кожнага натрапленага жыда заразжа затрымаць паліцыяй і загадаць адправіць да Наваградка.

3. Свабодна адпушчанымі могуць быць жыды, якія маюць пасьведчаньне Акружнага Камісара Наваградка. Аднак прашу кожнае пасьведчаньне дакладна праанялізаваць адносна яго важнасьці.

4. Асобы бяз зоран (разпазнальныя азнакі жыдоў), якія аднак па свайму воннкаваму выгляду могуць быць прызнаныя жыдамі, або падазроныя, што скінулі азнакі, павінны таксама быць затрыманымі і даста́ўленымі у Наваградзкую цямніцу.

НАВАГРАДАК, ДНЯ 6 САКАВІКА 1942 г.

падпісана

ТРАУБ

Акружны Камісар

Source: State Archive of Brest Region, f. 684. op. 1, d. 4, p.6

Translation from German 450/93
Copy

The commander of the Security Police and the Security Service Riga, 16.6.1942
- Ostland -
Dept. 1 P Diary No. 1919/42

To the Reich Commissioner for Ostland Riga

Subject: Partisan attack in Baranowitsche

The Baranowitsche Unit of the Commander of the Security Police and the Security Service, White Ruthenia, with a strength of 8 German SS-Unterfuhrer and Unterfuhrer, 2 members of the District Commissioner's Office, Novogrodek, 1 Lieutenant and 1 Sergeant in the Gendarmerie and 15 Lithuanians and Russians, had gone out on an operation against Jews and at about 5.00pm on 9.6.1942 reached Naliboki north of Stolpce. The village is in a fairly large wooded area; in front of the village however there is a fairly large, completely open and flat area.

When the Unit's cars and lorries had left the wood and wanted to drive into the village, they were fired on from two sides by heavy machine-guns. The Unit left the vehicles and tried to storm the village. In the open ground it was, however, exposed to strong fire. Besides the fact that the terrain was unfavourable, in that it offered no possibility of cover, the Unit was also at a disadvantage because the weapons they had brought with them had too limited a range compared with those of the partisans. In the unequal battle all the members of the Unit fell one by one, only an SS-Oberscharfuhrer and an SS man along with 4 interpreters and drivers could withdraw and fight their way out alive. In the course of this one interpreter was wounded.

On 10.6.1942 the Commander of the Security Police and the Security Service, White Ruthenia, set out for Baranowitsche with almost all the forces at his command. He received reinforcements from the motorised gendarmerie and the local police. He found 15 dead bodies in Naliboki, just as they had fallen in battle. All those who had fallen had had their boots taken off, the SS men had also been undressed down to their underpants and all their identity documents and identifying marks had been stolen. One SS-Obersturmfuhrer had had a swastika and a Soviet star burnt into his chest. From an interrogation of villages it was established that 4 Germans, probably the two SS-Unterfuhrer and the two gendarmerie officers, had been captured and taken through Naliboki on a lorry stolen by the partisans. They had placed red flags in their bound hands. In addition the partisans had scornfully shouted: "Look, these are your masters!" The bands of partisans consisted of 90-100 Russians, including parachutists wearing Russian uniform. They were armed with heavy weapons and had radio equipment.

From further questioning of the villagers it has been established that the four captured officers were shot on 9.6.1942 in a wood near Naliboki. A search operation for the bodies has been set in motion.

Measures necessary to combat the partisan group have been taken without delay, but because of the weakness of our forces these have not so far been successful.

On instructions
Sgd. Stuber
ss-Sturmbannfuhrer

Source: Scotland Yard War Crime Section.
Original: Bundearchiv Koblenz: BA Koblenz R58/697, p. 168, 175-8

The Germans had tried to liquidate the partisans, but were unable to do so. Below is a German document to this effect.

Report of 18 June 1942, 0076 Wilejka,

From SS Unterscharfuhrer Lipps, Wilejka Group
to SS Untersturmfuhrer Burgdorf
My last report covered the period to 24 May 1942.

The time between 24 May 1942 and 18 June 1942 has been filled with more or less unsuccessful operations against partisans who have been disagreeably active in this area in recent weeks.

On 30 May we brought in two parachutists who surrendered to us voluntarily. Between 1 June and 3 June we concentrated our operations in the region of Dolhinow where, according to reports, a large band (of partisans), which had a fortified encampment in the forest, was carrying out acts of terror. We located the camp on the third day, but the partisans had left it the previous day.

On 4 June the entire Waffen SS group was ordered to Minsk, where a major operation was to be launched against the partisans in the area. On 5 June we drove to Stolpce, 75 Km SW of Minsk. On 6 June we came back to Minsk, only to return to Stolpce again on 7 June. The operation began on 8 June. Substantial forces were committed. The preparations had taken several days. After all that, the operation was a total failure! We found one camp, but it was deserted. All our efforts against the partisans, in conjunction with the Wehrmacht, came to nothing because the machinery operates too slowly. On the evening of 9 June we returned to Minsk and on 10 June continued on to Wilejka. On the evening of 10 June we received orders to return to Minsk. We set out early on the morning of 11 June. Our route took us through Wilna-Lida-Nowogrodek to Mir, where we met up the next day with the Minsk group. We had been summoned because a detachment from the Baranowitschi group had been ambushed by partisans the previous day. It was an unfortunate encounter in which fifteen of our men, mostly Lithuanians, were killed. Six others, including four Germans, were taken prisoner by the partisans. The dead were buried in Baranowitschi on 13 June. We then returned to Minsk. On 14 June we came back to Wilejka and on the same evening received orders to return once again to Minsk. SS Obersturmfuhrer Burkhardt had unfortunately been killed in action against the partisans. The group set out for Minsk once more on 15 June, took part in the funeral ceremony for the dead Obersturmfuhrer and returned to Wilejka on 17 June.

This concludes my report of the major events between 24 May and 18 June.

There have been no incidents within the group which would give any cause for complaint.

(signature)
Lipps
SS Unterscharfuhrer

Source: Military History Archive Prague. Group Wilejka to Burgdorf 18.6.1942

Konstantin Kozlovky, the Righteous Gentile

Mrs. Maria Bobrovskaya receiving a Righteous Gentile certificate on behalf of her late father, for saving Jews, Novogrudok 1994

The Belski brothers partisans guarding the airport in the Naliboki dence forest together with other partisans.

Raya Kalmanovitz (Kaplinska) The Secretary to the Chief of Staff of the Bielski detachment

Yudel Levin, the Commander of the Mounted Platoon of the Bielski group, and Yankiel Abramovich, another of the Bielski Commanders

Bella Einess (née Dzienciolska) in 1993, visiting the house where she was being hidden for two years in the cellar under the floor

Report by Wilhelm Kube[1]   Minsk July 31, 1942
General Commissar for Byelorussia
Gauleiter ?G507/42 g

To the Reichskommissar for the Ostland, Gauleiter Hinrich Lohse
Riga

Secret!

Re: Combating Partisans and Judenaktion (mass killing of Jews) in the White Russia General District

It has become apparent during the course of all the clashes with partisans in White Russia, in both the former Polish and the former Soviet parts of the Generalbezirk (General District), that the Jews, together with the Polish resistance movement and the Moscow Red Army in the east, are the principal supporters of the partisan movement. Consequently, the question of how the Jews in White Russia should be handled is a political matter taking priority over all considerations about risks to the economy as a whole. Accordingly, it has to be solved not from an economic but from a political point of view. During the course of extensive discussions with SS-Brigadefuhrer (brigade commander) Zenner and the very competent leader of the SD, SS-Obersturmbannfuhrer Dr jur. Strauch, it was established that we have liquidated about 55,000 Jews in the past ten weeks. In the Minsk area ('Gebiet Minsk-Land') the Jews have been completely eradicated, without any negative effect on the workforce. In the mainly Polish area of Lida 16,000 Jews have been liquidated, in Slonim 8,000 Jews. Our preparations for the liquidation of the Jews in the Globokie area were disrupted when the rear army area pre-empted us, liquidating 10,000 Jews whom we had been due to eradicate systematically, without any prior liaison with us. (A report on this incursion has already been submitted.) On 28 and 29 July about 10,000 Jews were liquidated in the city of Minsk, 6,500 of them Russian Jews – for the most part old people, women and children –and the rest Jews unfit for work, who had mostly been sent from Vienna, Brunn, Bremen and Berlin in November of last year to Minsk on the Fuhrer's orders.

In addition, the Slutsk area has been alleviated of several thousand Jews. The same applies for Nowogrodek (Novogrudok) and Wilejka (Vileyka). Radical measures have yet to be taken in Baranovichi and Gantsevichi. There are still some 10,000 living in the city of Baranovichi alone, of who 9,000 will be liquidated next month.

There are 2,600 Jews from Germany left in the city of Minsk. In addition to these, there are a total of 6,000 Russian Jews and Jewesses still alive, left over from the labour units in which they were employed during the action. Minsk will continue to retain the largest Jewish workforce. This is currently necessary because of the high concentration of armaments factories and work related to the railway. In all the other areas the SD and I have limited the number of Jews coming for work to a maximum of 800 and, where possible, 500. Thus, at the conclusion of the actions we have reported, we retain in the city of Minsk 8,600 Jews and in the other ten areas, including the Minsk Region, which is free of Jews, some 7,000 Jews. This means the risk that partisans will continue to gain vital support from the Jews has been removed. Naturally the SD and I would prefer to eliminate the Jews in the General District of White Russia once and for all as soon as the Jews are no longer needed by the Wehrmacht for economic reasons. For the time being, the Wehrmacht's requirements, as the principal employer of Jewish labour, are being taken into account.

Coming into conflict with this clear brief regarding the Jews is the difficult task the SD in White Russia is faced with of having to ensure that the continuous flow of Jewish transports reaches its destination. This takes a terrible toll on the physical and mental strength of the men of the SD as well as distracting them from their duties, which lie within the area of White Russia itself.

I should therefore be grateful if Herr Reichskommissar could arrange for further Jewish transports to Minsk to be suspended, at least until the danger from the partisans has been overcome conclusively. I require the SD for 100 per cent deployment against the partisans and the Polish resistance movement, both of which demand all the strength of the not exceptionally strong SD units.

Tonight, after the Minsk Judenaktion was over, SS-Obersturmbannfuhrer Dr. Strauch reported to me with justified anger that a transport of 1,000 had suddenly arrived from Warsaw for the district air command here without any instructions from the Reichsfuhrer-SS or prior notification from the General Commissar.

I would ask Herr Reichskommissar, as the most senior authority in the Ostland (my request is already prepared by teleprinter) to call halt to such transports. The Polish Jew is as much an enemy of the German people as the Russian Jew. He poses a political danger far more significant than his worth as a skilled worker. Under no circumstances in an area under civil administration can army or air force personnel bring Jews from the General-Gouvernement or elsewhere without authorization from you, Herr Reichskommissar, as they jeopardize all the political work and the security of the General District. I am fully in agreement with the commander of the SD in White Russia that we should liquidate every Jewish transport which has not been ordered by our superiors or for which we have not received notification from our superiors, in order to prevent further unrest in White Russia.

General Commissar for White Russia

Signed Kube

Source: Documents on the Holocaust, ed. Y. Arad, Y. Gutman, A. Margaliot, Yad Vashem Jerusalem 1981

Notes:
[1] General Commissar Wilhelm Kube was assassinated 21 September 1943 by Russian partisans

Preparation for the Second Massacre
Jack Kagan

In May and June 1942, Jews were brought into the Novogrudok ghetto from the neighbouring towns of Lubcha, Ivieniec, Naliboki, Koreliche, Rubiezheviche and Vsielub. The conditions in the ghetto at that time were indescribable. The Regional commissar Traub accused the Judenrat of allowing Jews to escape to the forests. The Judenrat was arrested and shot. A two-person Judenrat was formed with Chaim Ajzikovitch as its chairman and Daniel Ostashinski responsible for labour.

We just waited for a massacre, and there was nothing we could do about it. Some young people escaped, but bad news came back quickly: either they had been killed by the Germans, or by the local population, or by the Russian/Polish partisans.

On 7 August 1942, Estonian 36th Police battalion and German soldiers surrounded the courthouse, the ghetto and the barracks, and on the same day 5,500 Jewish men women and children were killed in Litovka, about a kilometre (just over half a mile) from the ghetto.

In the late afternoon, Regional Commissar Traub together with Wilhelm Reuter who was in charge of the Jewish affairs, came with Estonian soldiers and searched the courthouse buildings for hidden children. About thirty children were found. They were thrown brutally into a lorry and taken to Litovka, where they were shot.

Monument for the victims of the second
massacre on the 7th of August 1942,
and the third massacre on the 4th of
February 1943

The Remnant
Jack Kagan

After the second massacre there were just over 1,000 Jews left, around 500 in a much smaller ghetto in Pieresika (Chaim Ajzikovitz was the one-man Judenrat) and about another 500 in a labour camp for tradesmen in the courthouse in Novogrudok.

The courthouse was surrounded by double sets of barbed wire with a fence on the outside. It was overlooked by five towers manned with machine guns and on the tall building a searchlight, probed into every dark recess. Our living conditions were very cramped and we were watched by Byelorussian guards at all times. The new Jewish police commandant was Salek Yakubovitz, and a one-man Judenrat, Moshe Burstein.

Jewish joiners were sent to us from the nearby town of Dziatlovo, (Zdzienciol); and within days most of them managed to escape to the partisans. We then made contact with partisan groups. We heard about the Bielski brothers, and then escapes took place both from the ghetto and from the labour camp with the help of the farmer Konstantin Kozlowski, and the dog catcher Bobrovski. Both have been awarded the Righteous among the Nations medal by Yad Vashem in Jerusalem.

The Bielski detachment took in every Jew who came to it, including the old, the very young and the crippled; it became a haven for escapees. The Bielski group fought a double battle against the Germans and against collaborators.

The Escape Story of Lyuba Rudnicki
Lyuba Rudnicki
To the memory of my brother-in-law Meir Rudnicki

May 1942, life in the Novogrudok ghetto is 'as usual'. Every morning the Jews go to work outside the ghetto under heavy guard. Those who stay behind the ghetto walls wait for their loved ones safe return, consumed by fear. Rumours start to circulate that there are partisans near Novogrudok and that their chief is someone called Gromov. People are curious, but there is no concrete information. Someone says that Gromov left a note in the barbershop which read: 'Gromov was here'. Everyone wants to see or contact him.

People would do anything to leave the ghetto. Those of us who are still alive begin to comprehend that gradually all of us will be killed. Yet the Germans promised that the ones who were allowed to live were needed and nothing untoward would happen to them. Despite that, the aspiration of most of us is to get out of the ghetto. But where can we hide? We continually look for contacts among the villagers.

One bright morning we discovered that a few people had left the ghetto overnight including the tar-maker (I have forgotten his name), Ben-Zion (Benche), Movshovich, David Golvicki and Ada Ziskind-Shapiro. They went to an acquaintance of the tar-maker, near the village of Shchorsy but after two days the tar-maker and David Golvicki returned saying that the guard near the Shchorsy Bridge had spotted them and opened fire. The two managed to escape, but Movshovich and Ada Ziskind-Shapiro were killed on the spot.

That incident shook us all. If anyone had held out any hope of escape, it now disappeared. We realized that there was no safe refuge. New rumours were circulating that a second slaughter was about to take place. No doubt the murderers were preparing themselves with all the thoroughness (planmaessig) that only the Germans could achieve.

The rumours materialized, the terrible 'day of judgment' arrived. It was 7 August 1942. In the morning, as usual, people left under heavy guard for work. My husband and I both worked in the infirmary in the house of Mordechai Movshovich on Third of May Street. Every one was restless, sensing what was to come; we were looking for a hiding place until the killings ended.

From the experience of the first massacre we knew that those who had managed to hide for the duration had returned unharmed to the ghetto. But now the Judenrat prepared a list of all the tradesmen who would have to move to the building of the district court - up until now the ghetto had been only in Pieresika. Many people begged to be among the lucky ones who were to be transferred to the second ghetto. We wanted to move too, but were met with the stubborn reluctance of the Judenrat and the police, although the medical personnel, to which we belonged (my husband was a dentist and I was a nurse) had been previously promised that they would be left alive. Now our trust evaporated and we found a hiding place in the cellar of the house owned by the dentist Shimon Kaminiecki.

The Kaminiecki house was next to the German police station. We entered in the hope that they would not look for us there. 'Who would think that someone would dare hide there?' Fifteen people were concealed in the cellar. We moved a kitchen cupboard in front of the entrance door to the cellar, we took with us water and bread, and then waited for the 'terrible storm' to pass. During the night we heard sirens above our heads. From the police station next door, we heard desperate cries cursing, sobbing, moaning the sound of beatings and, from time to time shots being fired. We set huddled close together, we did not move and just waited, hoping to survive, to let all the troubles pass. We had no idea of the time; light did not penetrate the cellar. But by listening to the traffic we estimated that it was dawn. We were desperate, to find out if the slaughter had ended. Who would tell us when to come out? No one knew where we were.

While we were thinking and whispering to each other, we heard the sound of steps from the other side of the cellar. The cellar under the house of the Kaminiecki family extended under the vacant apartment of Kushi Plazenski (who lives today in Israel). The entrance to that apartment was from the main thoroughfare, the Market Square, and only a thin wall separated our cellar from the abandoned and dilapidated apartment. We did not know about this at the time. Before our eyes the wall was pulled down and, as the light penetrated, policemen appeared, their guns at the ready. The order was given for us to come out. They pulled us out one by one; but it was still dark inside and I managed to hide under a sink in the cellar. I curled up under it and lay there dead still. Suddenly I heard screams from the police station. Had they have killed everyone? I wanted to go out. Was there any value to my life alone? When facing death one does not know what to hold on to; one moment one has a strong will to overcome all and the next one is enveloped in such despair that one wants to die without resistance.

Suddenly the sink was lifted, a policeman lit a match and recognized me. I knew him too, he was a Byelorussian policeman. I took off my gold watch, gave it to him, and told him to go and save my husband. I promised him that if we were spared we would give him money. He agreed, covered me with the sink again and went out. From time to time policemen entered the cellar and moved the sink, but I moved with it. It is hard to say how long it took, although a very long time passed, but suddenly I heard a familiar voice calling out: 'Lyubinka, come out!' I thought I was dreaming. It was my husband's voice. Was this possible?

The call was repeated again and again, and eventually I came out and saw my husband without his yellow star with the police officer. They asked me to follow them and gathering my courage, I walked into the police station. An interrogation started. Why did I hide? Did I know what was going to happen to me? I do not remember my answers, but to this day I can hear my cry: 'I want to live. This is the right of every human being.' My cry was not normal it was a cry for life.

Later, in the police station, I saw many acquaintances among the hundreds of people there. One was sobbing, another tearing at his clothes in desperation. All of them wanted to know what I had been asked. After a few hours nine people were taken out, among them, my husband and me. They led us under guard to the court house. We stayed alive thanks to the head of the Polish police for whom my husband had treated his teeth and had made a bridge for him. Later we found out that the Byelorussian policeman was in contact with the partisans, but we do not know what happened to him.

In the ghetto we met some members of our family: my brother-in-law Meir, who had been saved by a miracle, and my uncle Rafael Kaplinski and his wife. Alas, their daughter Lea had been killed in the slaughter.

Some 800 to 900 Jews, broken and traumatized, remained alive. We entered empty rooms which smelled of mould. Still shaken, the survivors were brought in, numbering approximately 250. Every one had horrific stories to tell about the slaughter. One man had witnessed his babies being torn out of their mother's arms by the brutal oppressors then their heads smashed against a wall. Others told us how many had been saved by staying in the lavatories in the yard.

Soon the order came to divide the ghetto. The courthouses were to accommodate the tradesmen, and the professionals, and those with no trade were to be moved to Pieresieka. Everyone tried to stay in the place they thought safe, and people started to invent trades. Like everywhere else, friendship and family relations were useful, and talk with the 'Judenrat' could help too. I however thought about one thing only – escape! Where could we escape to, and how? After the first massacre, when I lost all my dear family, I was desperate and nothing interested me but later, after facing death myself, a strong will to live overtook me.

At this stage we had heard nothing about the partisans. I contacted a devout Christian woman, by the name of Pargowicka, who lived two kilometres (just over a mile) from the courthouse in the village of Selco (Selec). She was an honest woman and I trusted her. I told her everything and asked her for help. She had relatives in the village of Khrapienevo near Ivje, and she told me that she had heard that there were Russian soldiers in the area, who had not managed to escape and were hiding in the forests. Her readiness to help us was great. She believed that if she saved us, God would bring back her husband, who had been taken prisoner by the Germans. She had been left with four small children.

My husband, brother-in-law and I decided to break out of the ghetto. One day Dr Sasha Ziskind a 'good friend' approached us and asked if we would allow himself his wife, Tamara Viner from Volkovisk and Dr Mark Berkman, a surgeon from Warsaw, to join us. They did not know Mrs. Pargowicka; they had learned about our plan from a friend of hers.

We agreed of course, to let them join us, without doubt or hesitation. Leaving the ghetto was a very risky undertaking; getting out was, in itself, a very dangerous operation, and then there was the problem of surviving 'on the outside'. However the idea of leaving the ghetto was stronger then any doubts we had. We decided to do it; we would escape on 19 August 1942.

In the end our group consisted of five people: Dr Berkman, Dr Tamara Viner, Meir Rudnicki, my dear brother-in-law and a school-master, my husband Yakov and me. Sasha Ziskind and his wife stayed in the ghetto because of ill health and were to join us in the winter. We were to meet at the water well in Karelicher Street, where people from the ghetto, under heavy police guard, were allowed to draw water every evening.

On the appointed day we returned from our work in the town in time to fetch water from the well. We hid in the barn of Benzlavski, a postman, until it was dark. We had to pass by the ghetto, there was no alternative, except walking through the fields, which was far too conspicuous and dangerous. We took off our yellow patches and walked on the road, singing so as not to arouse suspicion. Our hearts thumping, we passed by the barbed wire fence of the ghetto. It is an unusual courage that grows from desperation and the strong will to live. We arrived safely at Mrs. Pargowicka's house where a guide was waiting to take us to Khrapienevo.

We set off again at midnight, taking a meandering route, circumventing the police station in Gorodilovka. While crossing the River Volovka at a shallow place next to Selec, we realized that the searchlights of the ghetto lit the surroundings. Crawling, we crossed a wide field and entered the forest. We felt safer there but, as our bad luck would have it, it was harvest time and Russian planes appeared and bombed the granaries. The bombing started fires, which lit a large area all about us. Slowly we advanced towards the town of Vsielub. We did not know exactly where we were; we thought we were in the depths of the forest then to our surprise, we saw villagers going to the church in Vsielub. Our guide also went, telling us to hide until it was dark.

We entered the forest again, hid among the bushes, and waited for darkness to come, we discussed what to do. Tamara wanted to return to the ghetto but my husband, brother-in-law and I stood by our decision to go forward even if we were to meet the most horrible fate we did not wish to return to the ghetto. The waiting was frightful. We were crowded behind a bush with no food or water. Now and then we heard voices of Germans going to and from Novogrudok. Hour after hour passed, then finally it was dark but our guide did not return and doubts started forming in our minds. We began to wonder whether we should go on alone, but we had no knowledge of the area. At last at ten o'clock our guide returned. We walked all night along narrow tracks among the bushes. Eventually, at dawn, we reached our destination Khrapienevo, which lay some twenty-five kilometres north (fifteen miles) of Novogrudok and about four kilometres (two and half miles) south of the River Niemen. It was desolate country, full of swamps and isolated villages. The nearest town of any size, Ivje, was fifteen kilometres (nine miles) away on the other side of the Niemen.

Our new life started here. We were in a swamp, and we had to sit there all day. Only at night were we allowed to move to the granary, which was at a distance of 200 metres (218 yards). The main thing that was demanded of us was to sit in absolute silence, lest the shepherds near the swamp detect us. The guide's sister and kind mother supplied us with food. We did not hear anything about partisans at this time. We were told that some Russian soldiers had been in the district but that they had left. It was a quiet area with just an isolated house far from the road. A month passed, and winter was approaching. We decided to dig a hiding place - a 'bunker' in the forest. The men went out at night; they tied a stick or a hoe to their shoulder, which in the dark looked like a rifle, to deter villagers, if they were to meet them. The women stayed put. The aim was to dig a hiding place two metres deep, because my brother-in-law was very tall. They dug even deeper, until they reached water, which was a necessity if we were to live there.

Once, early in the morning, we were fortunate to meet two Jews one from Vsielub and the other from Swencany, but both living in Vsielub at present. They put us in contact with partisans who operated in the area, a very small unit of seven. Their leader was an escaped Russian prisoner of war called Anton. Our life changed again. Our men went out for reprisal operations. They returned to their bunker, but did not tell their friends about the women in the bunker. Later, only in one operation, the women were involved.

At the beginning the operations were small. There was a shortage of weapons and not everyone had a rifle. The first big and important operation was to destroy the bridge across the Niemen that led to Zboisk. All of us went out one night to fetch barrels of tar, which we took from a tar factory, located about six kilometres (just under four miles) from our shelter. We also appropriated some kerosene from a nearby village. We successfully set fire to the bridge and it burned for a few days. No one dared to come over for fear of partisans. It was an audacious operation.

Thus one of our big enemies - the bridge - was destroyed and it was not repaired all the time we were there. We felt safer and moved around more freely. First and foremost we were looking for weapons. The men ambushed a group of Germans, killed them and took their rifles. With the passing of time the men started to worry about the safety of the women that is, myself and my friend Tamara Viner-Ziskind. We did not take part in night operations but waited, fearful, for the return of the men. It was also necessary to obtain food. The men crossed the Niemen, went into the villages which were hostile to partisans and stole food where they were able.

We passed the days by telling each other stories about our lives. That is how I learned about the life of Dr. Mark Berkman. His home town was Warsaw, and he worked there before the war as a surgeon at the hospital on Czyste Street. He was clever and intelligent, but had a steely character; he said himself that he would walk over dead bodies to achieve his aims. Nevertheless we liked him, he had a good sense of humour and was a great storyteller. He had reached Novogrudok from Lvov, whence he had escaped after the Germans conquered Warsaw in September 1939. Dr Limon, who was then the manager of the district hospital in Novogrudok, accepted him as a surgeon. Dr Berkman had left his wife and daughter behind in Warsaw; he was indeed a brave man.

My dear brother-in-law, Meir Rudnicki, was born in Novogrudok. He finished high school there and then enrolled at the faculty of history at the University of Vilna. When the Soviets came in October 1939 he was the headmaster of a school near Slonim. He was an honest, quiet and modest fellow, good hearted and unpretentious. He never liked people to talk about him or praise him. Always with a smile on his face, he used to say: 'If we get through all this, I will show you that I am not that shy!' When he took a rifle for the first time, his hands trembled. People had always said that he would never hurt a fly, and yet he had to become a fighter. The first operation was hard on him; he could not shoot from an ambush. But when he reminded himself who the people he was shooting at were, he found the courage and used his bullets well. Poor man, he did not survive.

We lived together like a family, and we became close to each other despite our differences. Dr. Berkman and my husband Yaakov (who had completed his dentistry training in France at the University of Bordeaux) helped the villagers many times. The partisans did not have a permanent location; everyone was hiding separately, waiting for the spring when the aim was to unite and create a united fighting body.

At that time we did not know about any other Jewish partisans; we thought we were the only ones. The Russian partisans also did their rounds in the villages, and if someone was sick they came straight to us, and asked Dr. Berkman to help. My husband always accompanied him. Once, when one of the partisans was wounded and Dr. Berkman attended him, my husband pulled out a rotten tooth and made a primitive prosthesis from a piece of wire. Contacts between us the locals, and the Christian partisans were firm, but that friendship and trust brought a disaster upon us in the end. We believed that we were all in the same situation and we had all the same aims: we forgot about the ever present anti-Semitism.

From time to time we sent messengers from the village to find out about the situation in the ghetto. We received news that the conditions in the ghetto had worsened: guarding was stricter and food was in short supply.

Dr. Sasha Ziskind managed to send us a message that he intended to join us. Born in 1915, Sasha was a handsome man very talented, quiet and modest, always ready to help anyone in trouble. He finished his high school studies in Novogrudok and later finished medicine at the University of Vilna. During the Soviet rule he worked as a general practitioner at the hospital in Novogrudok. He and I had gone to school together from early childhood. He was a good and a loyal friend.

On 5 January 1943 Sasha, disguised as a villager, set off to our hiding place, but a policeman from Vsielub, who had once been his patient, recognized him and turned him over to the Germans. They imprisoned him in Novogrudok, put him through horrific tortures and pressurized him to reveal our hiding place. He died a martyr without uttering a word; I honour his memory. (We heard the details of his imprisonment much later from the prison wardens.)

On the same fatal day that the Bielski detachment was attacked by the Germans and some escaped to the district of Khrapienevo, we were waiting at a house in Khrapienevo for the arrival of Sasha. Searching the area for him, we came face to face with the Bielskis. We had never heard of Tuvia Bielski before, but we willingly accepted his offer to join his unit in the spring. We had just said good bye to each other and left the house when it was attacked. The five partisans in it were killed, including Tuvia Bielski's wife and her brother, Grisha. The house was just half a kilometre (a quarter of a mile) from our bunker. We found out about the killings the next morning, when we went to Khrapienevo and found the burning embers of the house.

It was clear that we had to change our location; too many of the partisans in the area were a threat to us. We just wanted the winter to pass so we could join a large and strong unit that would be able to stand up against the enemy that surrounded us in the spring.

The fatal day arrived, Red Army Day, 23 February. Early in the morning we heard knocking, and two Russian partisans asked my husband and Dr. Berkman to come to their dwelling, because a third partisan, Vania, had been injured during a night operation the previous night. Without any suspicion, they went with the partisans in their sledge. My brother-in-law Meir stayed with us. A few minutes later we heard machine-gun shots and we knew it was bad news. Had the Germans attacked them? Meir took his rifle and went to stand guard. Tamara and I followed him, although previously we, the women, did not show ourselves to the villagers in daytime. My brother-in-law went ahead. Suddenly we heard blood-curdling cry. They have killed my brother, I thought.

Tamara and I started to run away, but where to? There was forest all around, the snow was knee deep, and our legs could not move. We had walked a few paces from our bunker when we heard the call of the two partisans, who only a short time ago had taken my husband and Dr. Berkman to their injured colleague. I approached them first. With a pistol directed at my heart they ordered me to climb on their sledge, which stood beside our bunker. I started to ask questions: '*What were the shots? Where were my husband and his friend?*' Dr. Tamara, who was usually brave and cool, lost her head, could not utter a word, and pulled me on to the sledge.

An unusual strength came over me, the strength of desperation. I continued to ask about the fate of my husband, Dr. Berkman and my brother-in-law. One of them blurted out: '*We killed everyone and we will kill you too. Today is Red Army Day; we have received an order to kill all Jews.*' I had a flicker of hope that one of our three missing men was still alive; it gave me the will to go on questioning and talking. One thing was clear to me: if one of them was still alive, he would return early; so, we must get rid of these murderers, both of whom were drunk.

Even now I cannot believe the coolness with which I manipulated them. Calm and relaxed, I promised them that we would come to them, but only in the evening. I advised them to go home and sleep, rest for a while, and we would wait for them to come and pick us up. I explained to them that women cannot survive in the forest alone, that we did not know the surroundings, and that we would not move without them. They accepted this, and told us to wait until the evening. I advised them that it was not good to see women among the partisans.

After they left the bunker, we set out in the snow, desperate, with no hope, and not knowing what to do. We saw in the deep snow the prints of a man's boots. We ran towards them. It was my husband, who was rushing back to help us. He was stunned, tired and broken.

"*They killed Dr. Berkman. Where is my brother Meir? A miracle saved me, I managed to knock Sasha's hand (that was the partisan's name) and his revolver dropped to the ground, the second man was the driver of the sledge and had no weapon. Sasha took the machine gun, but I managed to jump into the forest, and hung my coat on one of the trees. They shot at it, thinking that it was me. In the meantime I returned to you. Where is my brother?*"

Those were short, broken, terrible sentences. We told him the atrocious news that his brother had been murdered. Hearing that left him deaf and dumb for a few days.

Our rifles had stayed on the sledge with the murderers. Only one rifle with a broken barrel was left in the bunker. I picked it up and we started to walk away from the bunker. Where should we go? Broken, shattered and fatigued we walked, leaving behind brothers and friends, sacred corpses. We could not even bury them; we could not even go close to them, lest we were also killed. After a short time we heard deafening shots from the direction of the bunker. It seemed that the murderers had regretted leaving us and had come back to pick us up. Thanks to the dense forest we managed to escape, but we remained in the vicinity of the bunker. We were afraid to walk during the day, for fear of being informed on; there were enemies all around us. Where could we go and what was going to happen? My husband was deaf and unable talk. The persistent question hounded us: where should we go? With nightfall my husband recovered a little; he was our only hope. He decided to go in the direction of Konstantin Kozlowski, who was a friendly villager and a contact man of the Bielski's. Kozlowski lived far from us. We walked for a few days, with great fear, along winding tracks. We did not know the area and feared every stranger. We made a great effort not to be seen. Those were torturous and troubled days.

It was our bad luck to reach Kozlowski only a few hours after the Germans had left his yard. Swiftly he led us away and hid us in a small wood. The Germans were again attacking the Bielski's, who were back in their old base. We could see from a distance the Germans retreating towards Novogrudok. After a few days we finally met the Bielskis. There, a new chapter opened in our lives.

During all our time with the Bielski's our first aim was to take revenge on the family of the policeman who caught Sasha Ziskind. My husband could not rest; the thought depressed him. He found out from the villagers where the policeman lived and took a few men with him to the policeman's house. It was a very dangerous operation; first, his house was close to the police station; second, in order to reach the house one had to pass an area where Germans and policemen hung around. But that did not deter my husband. Finding that the policeman was not home, my husband killed with his own hands the man's mother, sister and everyone else who was in the house. They left a note to explain the murder, and burnt the house down.

Dr. Rosenbloom was a good friend of Dr. Berkman. Hearing about the horrific murder of Dr. Berkman and my brother-in-law, he sought and found the two partisans, as well as the family they stayed with, who had assisted them. He killed them all.

Meir Rudnicki. Killed by Russian Partisans in the forest of Khrapienevo, 23 February 1943

Anti-Semitism
Jack Kagan

The local population gave the Jews away to the Germans or killed them themselves. There was no safety, even if one managed to escape. The only salvation was to find large Jewish groups of partisans.

Mir is a small town about thirty-seven kilometres (twenty-three miles) from Novogrudok. I found an interesting document about the Mir Police. The document, signed by the officer in charge of the Mir police, and witnessed, was addressed to the Regional Office in Baranowicze:

Re: The arrest and shooting of five Jews as well as the destruction of a Jewish band near the forest of Miranda in the region of Mir.

On 14.11.42 around 6 o'clock I was informed by the man in charge of the forest estate in Miranda, in the region of Mir, that about 6 km to the north of the town of Mir, he discovered in the woods a hole in the ground where a band of Jews were hiding. Immediately, I sent there 3 gendarmes and 60 policemen together with the forester. They confirmed the information given by the forester by discovering the hole in the ground which was covered with a wooden cover and well camouflaged. After removing the cover they found the people who were hiding there. They were ordered to come out without weapons otherwise a hand grenade would be thrown into the hole. They obeyed this command and as a result 3 Jews, among them the ringleader of Mir and 2 Jewish women came out from the hole. After a short interrogation, in accordance with legal practice, they were killed and as per order, buried. They had on them a few rags but no articles of any value. Afterwards the hole was searched, approximately 100 kg of potatoes, some bread and cooking utensils were found. Arms and ammunition were not found. The hole was destroyed by the policemen. The foodstuff as well as the rags was given to the police force.

```
Gend.-Außenposten „Mir"
Gend.-Kreis Baranowitsch(i)              Mir, den 15. 11. 1942.
Generalbezirk Weißruthenien

An den
Gend.-Gebietsführer
in Baranowitsche .


Betr.:  Festnahme und standrechtliche Erschiessung von 5 Juden, sowie
        Vernichtung eines Judenlagers in der Nähe der Försterei Miranka
        Rayon Mir.
Bezug:  ohne.


         Am 14.11.42, gegen 6 Uhr, teilte mir der Waldwärter der Försterei
Miranka, Rayon Mir mit, dass er etwa 6 km nördlich der Stadt M i r
und zwar in einem Walde eine Erdhöhle entdeckt habe, in der sich eine
Judenbande aufhalte. Sofort wurden von mir 3 Gendarmen und 60 Schutz=
männer unter Mitnahme des Waldwärters nach dorthin entsandt. Sie stell
ten fest, dass die von dem Waldwärter gemachten Angaben zutrafen. Es
wurde eine Erdhöhle entdeckt, die mit einem Holzdeckel zugedeckt und
gut getarnt war. Nach Entfernung des Deckels wurden die Insassen der
Höhle aufgefordert, ohne Waffen herauszukommen andernfalls eine Hand=
Granate in die Höhle geworfen würde. Dieser Aufforderung leisteten
sie Folge und es kamen 3 Juden, darunter der Judenrat von Mir und 2
Jüdinnen aus der Höhle heraus. Nach kurzem Verhör wurden sie stand -
rechtlich erschossen und ordnungsmässig vergraben. Sie führten ausser
ein paar zerlumpte Bekleidungsstücke keinerlei Wertgegenstände mit sic
Sodann wurde die Höhle durchsucht. Es wurden etwa 100 klg. Kartoffeln,
einige Brote und ein paar alte Kochtöpfe gefunden. Waffen sowie Mu-
nition wurden nicht gefunden. Die Höhle wurde hierauf von den Schutz=
männern zerstört. Die Lebensmitteln, sowie die zerlumpten Bekleidungs=
stücke wurden der Schutzmannschaft Mir übergeben.

Gesehen:
                                                      Hauptwachtmeister d.Sch. 4101
Z. d. A.
```

Source: Scotland Yard War Crime Section. Original From the 28.6.42 BA Koblenz R6/348 p. 47-48

The main escapes from the ghetto and labour camps started in the autumn of 1942, when the Germans began the second round of massacres in the area of Novogrudok.

To survive one needed winter clothing. There was only one way to get it; take it by force from the local population. Hunger was another serious problem. Some escapees reached the Russian partisans but they only accepted people with rifles or the young ones who had served in the army. So the Jews had to form their own detachments, even though this was against Russian policy.

We had a radio in our camp and on 4 February 1943 we heard the best news yet. The Germans had suffered a disastrous defeat in Stalingrad, and had lost a whole army. The order was issued that the German flag should fly at half-mast in all official buildings. But our joy was short lived, for we found out that on the same day the Germans had killed all 500 remaining Jews in the ghetto. Now only 500 Jews remained in the courthouse.

Before the killings in the ghetto the Germans arrested a couple from Korelicze and promised the husband that they would be kept alive if he agreed to spy on the Jews in the courthouse. On the following day we found that there was an additional man in the camp. After a long investigation, we decided to kill him.

The next day the Gestapo came and arrested Moshe Burstein the Judenrat representative. He was then tortured and killed. Daniel Ostashinski was appointed in his stead.

Conditions deteriorated in the courthouse. The daily food ration was cut to 125 grams {barely four and a half ounces} of bread mixed with straw, and soup. It was a starvation diet. We were told to work hard, as the Reich needed our production of fur coats, fur gloves, felt boots, saddles and overcoats for the German army. Everybody worked hard to ensure a steady supply of goods for the army in the hope that they would continue to need us and keep us alive.

Source: document: Scotland Yard War Crime Section

The Diary of Binye Berkovich[1]

This diary written in Hebrew by Binye Berkovich, a captive in the Novogrudok Ghetto, was given to the historical commission in Warsaw by Romuald Pielachowski a Pole and also a citizen of Novogrudok sometime after the conclusion of the war. Pielachowski was sent to work in the Novogrudok ghetto by the German authorities. According to his own words he won the confidence and trust of the Jewish inhabitants of the ghetto by *making their difficult lives easier including escapes from the ghetto*. At the end of 1942 or perhaps at the beginning of 1943, Pielachowski received the diary from Binye Berkovich with the request to keep and protect his eyewitness testimony. The manuscript was written on eight separate cards in which the massacres of the Jews of Novogrudok and the surrounding villages are described. Binye Berkovich asked that the manuscript be put into a glass jar, for it to be sealed, and hidden in the ground so that after the war the contents could reach *Jewish organizations in the USA*. Fulfilling the will of Binye Berkovich, Pielachowski protected the manuscript and after the war gave it to the Historical Commission[2] in Warsaw. The manuscript was eventually found by Dr. Havi Dreyfus-Ben Sasson[3] in 2005 in the archives of the Jewish Historical Institute in Warsaw entitled: Binye Berkovich's Diary. She passed in on to Prof. Yehuda Bauer[4] who brought it to the attention of Jack Kagan in 2005 and it is published here for the first time in English[5]. The translation was made by Oskar Delatycki and the English text edited and annotated by Michael Kagan.

Although the fate of the author is unknown it is clear from the date of the last entry (26th February, 1943) that he survived the third massacre which took place on 4th February, 1943. In the list of partisan fighters complied by I. Gerasimova, S. Moroz, and M. Izrailski, and presented in this volume, the name Binye Berkovich appears. His birth year is given as 1922, which would make him 19-22 years old at the time of the horrific events that he experienced. There is no record that this Berkovich died in the forests, so it can only be assumed that he lived until the liberation by the Red Army on July 4th 1944. Was this Berkovich the same as the author of the diary? We can never know for sure although a man of such tender years might be considered too young to write with such maturity as exhibited in this document. For what is obvious is that the author of this chilling record was a widely read intellectual who had proficiency in secular as well as Jewish sources. He seems equally at home with the Bible as he does with Dostoyevsky and Ahad Ha'Am, whom I am sure he identified with. He was a person of high culture brought to his knees by the extreme sadism of the people who developed that very same culture that he adored. His sense of the ironic is masterful as he twists and turns his penetrating eye to record the horrors taking place around him. It is also clear that he struggled daily not only to keep himself alive but also to stay human in the face of such inhumanity. And in the end, as hope slips out of his grasp, he leaves us with his final gasp – a wish: *do not compile lamentations about our destruction, only a book of curses, and more to the point, one huge and firm curse to all humanity and culture.*

Page 1*:

Kaf' Tet' in the month of Nisan[6], Taf' Shin' Bet' (16th April 1942):

This is twentieth week since the big slaughter[7] and the second since the killing of the Judenrat. The pain did not ease, not a bit. On the contrary, the beautiful days of the early spring increase the darkness and deep sorrow of the wounded heart. Mixed emotions overwhelm my brain: what if it was this or that perhaps we could be saved.

The most difficult and oppressive moments start at dawn. All the efforts to change my thoughts are of no avail. On the one hand starting work late is good for me simply because the day is too long. The people are on the move from the dawn. The "world" prepares itself for the day of work. It is impossible to think of anything other than of the big slaughter. The days are getting longer, but nobody notices.

Zayin' of Tamuz Taf' Shin' Alef' until Yud' Het' of Kislev Taf' Shin' Bet'
(22nd June 1941 until 8th December 1941):

Very long weeks and an eventful period. No period passes without some news e.g. an edict the Jews are forbidden to walk outside the town or leave their homes without their "badge of shame" – the yellow star. Each edict ended with the threat of death for not abiding the rules.

On top of that we had to work beyond our strength supplying the "Komendantura" with furniture, utensils etc. from Jewish assets. One could feel the poison in the air, something unknown was approaching, the … of naked bodies… On Wednesday, Friday and Sunday in the month of July[8] people were picked out under the pretext of being taken to work but they were murdered. Fifty Jews lost their lives by the order of the "good" Komendant.

This was only a short interval, but it was rich in events. This continued until the horrific days of 6-8th December (1941). One was under the impression that all the previous threats and tortures were a prolog to a big and horrifying drama.

The period after the slaughter, 20 weeks to date, could be considered as usual, if one neglects to think of the constant pressure on the heart. The little slaughters are usual occurrences, small things, there is no time to stop and think about them.

Page 2:

Even the dates of the deaths are forgotten by all except the living relatives of the victims. For example, the shooting of three women after the slaughter, on Friday the 14th December. If you wish, it was not an unusual or different slaughter; it was just an epilogue of the former. On the other hand it could be considered to be their own fault: could you have imagined that three women decided to walk to their own houses to bring back to the Ghetto some food that was left there, such as some flour? They have forgotten that the houses were not theirs. Jews don't own any property anymore. And also another slaughter, 40 people arrested on the way to a village, without the "badges of shame"[9] and not hiding in dugouts and caves.

On another occasion four Jews were caught: three were from ------ and were on guard duty, one was from the Karelich Judenrat. Three were shot and burned in the middle of the night; the fourth was miraculously left alive. All these slaughters did not cause great excitement.

However, the next incident of "Harugei Malchut" (Martyred by the Rulers[10]) when 12 members of the Judenrat were killed, shattered everyone in the Ghetto. It was an attack on the right to life of the members of the administration.

Ideas dart through my head: it is absurd to continue my life. Indeed what hope could I have? There is not a ray of light penetrating the dark clouds that cover our sky.
All my family: my wife and two dear sons, my sister and her husband, my father – all of them were brutally killed by the murderers who are building a "new Europe".
But on the other hand, I am gripped by another idea: I must live to be able to take part in the Day of Judgment which must come, a day of revenge and retribution.
I must live in spite of my will so that when I will taste the blood of the killers of innocent children on the lap of their mothers and in front of their parents, it may be possible to sooth my wounded heart.

Those thoughts don't leave me.

Ideas and feelings pile up in my head and disperse; the brain weakens and the heart breaks and there as no escape, no relief.

The 22nd week (since the first slaughter):

The spring is at its zenith. The hills are green around the Ghetto as if to highlight the separation between us and the free world. The sun is shining as it did last year, as if to show that nothing happened to it, as if it says: "I am not to be blamed". Unlike the poet who called it "the deceiving sun".

Page 3:

But on the other hand there are the words of the Russian author Dostoyevsky "the world will be destroyed (in order) to save a child from tears"[11].

And a thought troubles my heart: thousands of children are slaughtered in horrific cruelty under the same sun, their screams pierce the sky, but the sun continues to shine as before in a perfect regularity…

However, if you think about it, there is no base for such complaints, even those people who by some luck stayed alive after the murderers' sword was laying on their throats, even those have forgotten everything already. Life goes on, the same laugh and wit. This is for me so shocking and infuriating.

The justification of the well-known adage: "Eat and drink for tomorrow we will die"[12] can not sooth my irritated nerves.

The 25th week:

Till now there was no obvious change in the life of the Ghetto. The monotonous life crawls slowly on.

The news about the slaughters in Lida, ?, Ivia, ? and the burning alive of the Jews of ? doesn't freeze the blood of the Ghetto Jews. Their hair doesn't stand on end, as it would have happened before the slaughter in Novogrudok.

I try to explain that reaction to myself and I think that the reason is the egotism of the human being; before the slaughter each feared that it would be his fate too. But when the slaughter was over and by miracle or by bribing a gendarme one was saved from death, one knows that in the meantime, as long as there is no other slaughter, his hope to live strengthens again and he rejects any frightening thoughts.

I think that it is worthwhile to write down the approximate numbers of those slaughtered. In Lida – 5500, ? – 1200, Ivia – 2400, Volozin – 1300. The brutality is unlimited, even Stalin could not invent such methods, such as making the victims to undress near the trenches, throwing in toddlers and babies alive in front of their parents. It is certain that to hear things like that breaks everyone's heart, sorrow overwhelms you, yet after a day or two those feelings disperse.

Sometimes ? some moaning or a belated tear from the eye of an old woman as she is peeling potatoes…

Page 4:

The 30th week:

The head cools down; the ideas are fewer and concentrated. There is the feeling that it is possible already to create a complete picture of all that happened till today. It does not mean that it is the final account of the slaughters of the multitude or of a few, because every week something happens. A fortnight ago a young man, Binyamin Kushchinski, was killed. He finished his day's work and wanted to get some milk and a piece of bread from his gentile acquaintance when he was shot. Another two fellows who went with him managed to escape. A week ago a 17-year-old girl was killed; a woman who walked beside her was wounded; they were shot "without intention" only because a militiaman wanted to practice his "sacred" profession of shooting. This happened on their way back from work. This is the situation in the Ghetto now, lives go on as normal, as before.

When the month July, the period of the Three Weeks[13], comes "one reduces one's festive activities[14]."

The horrifying rumors from Slonim have been confirmed, a real slaughter of Jews in all its details. Of the approximate 10,000 people who were alive after the first slaughter in the winter, approximately 7000 people were killed in this second slaughter (a small slaughter of about a dozen Jews is not included in this account). Approximately 2500 Jews were left.

There is a rumor passed on in whispers of a slaughter in Molchad. According to that rumor everyone was slaughtered, no one was left. The aim in Molchad had been achieved: it is clean of Jews, no one will disrupt its future development.

The impression is that these rumors did not impact heavily on the life of the Ghetto. One starts to get used to the idea of death. And really, why should we expect different things from those who are already asleep eternally underground.

Tisha B'Av - The 9th day of Av (23rd July, 1942):[15]

The religious Jews study on this day the book of Job. I, though I am not religious, would like very much to study that book. Though Job's grievance is directed towards the Divine leadership, meaning world order in general, this is the old problem of the tragic fate on earth of the humans. But there is nothing in his grievance regarding social injustice and human relationships. This could be because in Job's generation there wasn't yet a developed culture and the wonderful invention of the "cultured" German people; people of visionaries, thinkers, philosophers and poets; the racial theory. Then, in the ancient days, people understood that German blood is no better than Jewish blood.

Page 5:

Saturday, Parshat Ekev:[16]

There is restlessness in the Ghetto. Today all tradesmen were called to the courthouse, the … are there. The Judenrat was ordered to select 150 people to act as the service people in the Ghetto: the Judenrat, police, bakers, hospital attendance and the kitchen. The others are to go to work outside the Ghetto. A fear of the unknown prevails. Hearts hammer in fear with the events in Slonim fresh in mind… no one wants to put in words what is felt inside.

Tuesday, Parshat Ra'eh:[17]

Yesterday late at night, Hauptmann (captain) ? visited the hospital, the residence of the Jewish doctors and a few other houses. A watchtower was built opposite the Ghetto and machine guns were mounted there. An electric light was installed on the watchtower and in the night the Ghetto was illuminated.

All that means something. These are preparations for the second slaughter.

Friday, the 15th day in the month of Elul, Taf' Shin' Bet' (28th August 1942):

Today is the third week since the second mass slaughter. Three weeks ago at this hour I was lying hidden in the septic waste tanks of the Ghetto hospital.

No, I don't want to think again of the events. The voices of the babies, toddlers and children, who should be going to a school, they are going to the slaughter, their screams and cries: "mummy, … me". No, no. I have to stop writing, I am choked by tears. Why didn't I come out of my hiding place, approach a gendarme and ask him to shoot me in my heart, but before that ask him a simple questioning in a resigned voice: *"My dear Mr. German, You are a son of the nation of writers and thinkers, why do you kill small children? You to must have small children in*

Germany and they must be basking now in the beauty of nature". And then getting or expecting an answer I would go to my grave, having crossed over from life to the void.

The mood is depressed. The issue is clear. Europe will be cleansed of Jews. We will all die; our fate is death.

The execution of the rest was postponed only for a short time.

Victor Hugo wrote a whole book "The Last Day of a Condemned Man"[18] about the thoughts of a man who was condemned to death and was waiting to be executed within an hour or two. There is no need to write a book about our secrets and thoughts, resignation.

Page 6:

There are rumours about a third slaughter in Slonim.

Perhaps I should not write anymore. The Byelorussians and the Poles know all the details of the tortures and slaughters. I have no strength left to write anymore. I noted only a few psychological moments and mentioned a few events.

My name is Binye (B"R) Yehuda Berkovich. My father was ------- (a cook?). I still hope to stay alive. My only sister lives in Bialystok with her family (she is still alive). I ask the person who will find these notes to try to establish if my sister, brother-in-law or any of the children are still alive and if he will find them to give them these last pages of mine.

This is my last testimony: "Jews! A people who live alone among nations (*am la'vadad ishkon*)[19] remain like that, don't act for other people, and don't work other people's fields! In one hand hold the hoe and in the other the sword of revenge. Revenge our blood and the spilt blood of our children!

The name of my sister, who lives in Bialystok, is Bluma (Alter?), her husband's name is Meir Itzchak. Pre-war they lived in ? St. 48, flat No. 8.

I forgot to add a small note: a week after the slaughter I met two young women, whose husbands were taken with the "third party" last year. I asked them what they did with their babies (did the women survive by bribing??). Their answer was short: *They cried so we strangled them.* The mothers did not cry. Now they are waiting. Their turn will come. There is no salvation.

Saturday...

The proof. When we went to the well to fetch water we saw a cart loaded with torn Torah parchment. They were taking it probably to the tannery. The parchment will make good ? for people. I was told about the evil Roman Emperor Titus[20] who burned the books of the Torah in the Temple. This happened 2000 years ago. The Titus' of the 20th Century know how to make use of the Torah parchment.

Last year in Karelich they forced the Rabbi to put fire to the Torah in the yard of the Beit Hamidrash[21] and to carry water to extinguish the fire. In another incident the Jews of the town were burnt alive. The method is to kill using rifles, machine guns, by burning alive or by suffocation. But death by burning is unusual. The Ghetto is filled with graves. About 20 people were found strangled in their hiding places.

Page 7:

The living are still lying with the dead 4-5 days later. The living said that they did not feel that their friends have died, but when they try to "wake them up from their sleep" their fingers dug into the rotting flesh and there was a stench.

I forgot to note an incident. A Miss Lipkin was found in her hiding place and she was taken to prison. Two days later she was taken to be killed with a group of about 100 other Jews. But she was saved and is now in the Ghetto. She said that they were put alive face down into a trench, which had been prepared beforehand. In that position they were shot. She felt that she was slightly wounded. What should she do? People above her and under her that were wounded moaned, struggled and died. The murderers went off. Slowly she pushed aside the corpses above her and sneaked out into the forest. Now she lives in the Ghetto. She eats and drinks…till the next action.

The news from Slonim had been confirmed. After the third mass slaughter, 300 Jews were left alive. The Jewish population of Slonim before the war was app. 23,000.

Tet' Vav' in the month of Tevet, Taf' Shin' Gimel' (23rd Dec. 1942):

I stopped writing my notes approximately three weeks after the second slaughter. I thought that our days were numbered. I was mistaken. The murderers are not satisfied to proceed with a usual murder. They are thirsty for blood and torment of the soul.

About 20 people were murdered in the last few months through their own fault. One jumped the Ghetto fence to gather some marrows which were sown by the Jews before the second slaughter. One Jew from Karelich was killed while carrying water from the well. A gendarme searched him and found a kilogram of potatoes in his bag. Others were killed whilst trying to escape into the forest.

The hope to escape from the Ghetto and the creation of an organization to aid the escape take a special place in the events of the Jews in Byelorussia. There is some hope that, despite it all, some Jews will survive in Byelorussia to tell the historians the true facts about the life and fights in the forest.

It is of use to write about the horrific cruelty that is increasing from day to day. Beating with sticks. Forcing the women to take off their upper garments and whipping them 25 times.

The accountant Yosif –alianski was buried yesterday close to the Ghetto in a field. His corps was left in the open for three weeks and was eaten by pigs, dogs and ravens.

Page 8:

There are rumours about a third slaughter in Baranovichi. It is not possible to obtain details. It is not possible now to escape from the Ghetto. The mood is of complete resignation.

Thursday Caf' Bet' in the month of Tebeth (30th Dec. 1942):

The town Dworec (?) with a Jewish population of app. 2000 had become "clean of Jews" (Judenrein) a few days ago. Most were shot. Those who escaped, but returned after the slaughter, including people who were hiding underground, were killed by burning.

One bitter thought kept returning to my mind: Our ancestors died as martyrs (Kiddush Hashem[22]) with "Shma Isroel"[23] on their lips. They were killed because they were Jews, they desired not to break the chain[24] and their hope that the chain will not be broken gave them courage in their last moments.

We are the generation of emancipation yet we are being erased off the face of the earth and nothing will be left of our culture that was nourished for 3000 years. We will not die with the cry "Shma Israel - Hear O Israel!" Our last words will be a fierce, big curse of all humanity and its culture.

The beast in the man broke out of his hiding place, naked and wild, and is showing his cruelty and brutality.

A new group of victims: 15 people tried to escape from the Ghetto No 1, the courthouse building. A young woman Lea Schumerchik was killed together with her sister-in-law and her child. Lea was taken to Ghetto No 1 and the others to Ghetto No 2. The husband and father of the victims didn't cry at the open grave, he was just moving his lips, because the best hiding place is the grave. Here the murderers can do nothing.

Saturday mevarchim[25] in the month of Tebeth (2nd Jan. 1943):

New and infuriating news. The pharmacist Leizerowski and his two assistants, the women Botnik and Berlinerblau, were found dead near the town in a ditch besides the road. They were naked without their cloths and shoes. It was assumed that their acquaintances who pretended to help them in their escape, deceived them, robbed them of their money and killed them. They were lying there like corpses of dogs or cats and nobody took them away.

On the same day two 12-year-old children, who escaped from Dworec, after a week of wandering in the forest came to Novogrudok. They wanted to sneak into the Ghetto, but did not meet any Jews. As the fate would have it, they met a German girl who led them straight to the gendarmes.

Suicide by hanging. It supposed to be an easier way to die.

Let the murderers mutilate my corpse after my death, but not before.

Page 9:

It is worthwhile to leave a few remarks about the life of the few surviving Jews in the Ghetto. They are in a state of complete demoralization. People are moving around hungry, looking for bread with no one to give it to them.

All one is interested in is a slice of bread and a potato. Some gather to pray. I don't want to join them. The books of mine and others, which I kept during the first and second slaughter, were scattered in the wind. There is no reason to keep them. For whom?

The torn pages of our literature, some of them thousands of years old, are scattered in the gutter, so what? The brains which created them are there too…

Jewish brothers! We are martyrs and this is our wish to you: we are a generation of dwarfs, small people but big egoists. For twenty-two years[26] we could have done something for ourselves and we have done nothing. We have no justification for the spilt blood of our children, for their lives which were cut short.

The eyes of our children demand from us and from you, our American brothers, revenge for their spilt blood. I repeat my words from the previous page: when the hoped for day will arrive you have two tasks: revenge with no mercy and construction.

Construction of the two: the country and the people.

Achad Ha'am[27] said: "*If a nation is destroyed, who is going to build it? I don't mean in size, in numbers but only in quality.*" If you are to find some Jewish songs, collect them anew and start to construct Judaism again. Do not cease. I am not a religious man and I don't believe in the providence of God, but I believe in the maxim: "*The Eternal One of Israel will not deceive.*"[28]

Berkovich Binye

Page 10:

Let the people stand up! Everything is disproved! Everything is an utter lie! What a bitter irony and ridicule is heard from all the promises quoting Isaiah's vision of the end of the days. Every New Year we cited all the prophets about the vision of a better world – what are all those phraseologies? ------ or childish innocence? So we become disbelievers in the providence of God and the Messianic ideal.

If, in front of the civilized world, under the shining sun such deeds are done. If we will take all the brutal deeds the people did to each other during the human history and put them on one end of the scale and then take "the beautiful things" that the nation of the great philosophers and poets did from 1942, the latter would tip the scales. But the most important issue is that those were done in the name of the "superior" ideal – the "saving of Europe".

In my notes I wrote only about one thousandth of these horrific events. The historian will find a lot of material given to him by the nations of the world who will remain alive. But who will tell him about this fact? In the courthouse on the day of the second slaughter, the murderers grabbed babies and young children out of their parents' hands, dragged them like dogs to the trucks, "the slaughter trucks", and while the children were screaming *mummy, mummy* they were thrown to the ground and murdered with rifle butts. And when a 12 year old girl, Shulamit Taritski (Tavaritski?), tried to resist the man who was dragging her, Herr Haltsher, 'a son of the most cultured nation in the world' grabbed her by the neck and choked her till her tongue came out of her mouth, and then threw her into the truck. All this was done in front of her mother, who could do nothing but tear out her hair.

A small baby who was hidden in the ceiling of the third floor was found and thrown down to the ground, whilst those who were still alive could see it. The parents who hid him saw everything... they could not cry, their hearts turned to stone. And you American and English Jews, you certainly still dream about all that humanity created, is creating and will create. Transcending and transcending.... What a lie! What cynicism!

If you could only see for five minutes one picture, one scene of our life in the Ghetto it would be enough to shock your hearts and cause you to spit in the face of humanity and its culture.

I am approaching the last moment of my life. I cannot write details. I think that you will see everything in the cinema. I want to tell you only my thread of thoughts, the ideas of one of the last European Jews who is waiting for his slaughter.

Dreams are meaningless, I never believed in dreams and never told anyone, not even my family, about my dream. But I want to tell you about an amazing dream.

It was back in 1938: I dreamt that my brother (David Berkovich who lived in Karelich) was murdered, and that my sister Bluma Alter was also murdered! Now my brother was killed with his family in the second slaughter I know nothing about my sister, who lives (lived) in Bialystok.

We were rooted out. Everything was erased; no remains of us are left. We have no interest in what will happen after the blood shed. But for whom are you going to build a new land and a new life? All the hope and pride of the Jewish people was the Eastern Jewry and it is no more.

My request to you, American brothers: do not compile lamentations about our destruction, only a book of curses, and more to the point, one huge and firm curse to all humanity and culture, as I already wrote in my previous pages.

Berkovich Binye
Tet' Vav' in the month of Shvat, Taf' Shin' Gimel'
(26th February 1943)

Source: The Archives of the Institute of Jewish History in Warsaw, File 5394

Notes:

* The numbered pages refer to the pages of the manuscript found at the Jewish Historical Institute in Warsaw which is a typed copy of the original handwritten cards.

1 The original document (5394) is located at the Jewish Historical Institute in Warsaw.

2 The Central Jewish Committee in Poland (CKZ) was founded in the summer 1944 with the liberation of Poland by the Soviet and Polish armies. The CKZ established a Jewish Historical Commission in August 1944.

3 Havi Dreyfus Ben-Sasson is a historian specializing in Holocaust studies and 20th Century Polish history at Tel Aviv University

4 Yehuda Bauer – eminent historian and scholar of the Holocaust - is a Professor of Holocaust Institute of Contemporary Jewry at the Hebrew University of Jerusalem.

5 It is being simultaneously published in Russian by Literary Historical Society 'Vozvrashchenie', Moscow.

6 Many of the dates given in the diary are the Hebrew dates. The day of the (lunar) month and the year (from Creation) are given in the Hebrew numerological form where numbers are replaced by letters. The Gregorian dates are given in parenthesis.

7 The first massacre of 5,100 Jews took place on 8th December 1941.

8 The murder of the 52 took place on Saturday 26th July 1941.

9 See: Order for the Transportation of the Jews to Novogrudok Ghetto, March 6 1942 page 100 in this volume.

10 Reference to the hideous murder of the 10 great sages by the Romans, recited during the Yom Kippur liturgy: *The Angels cried out bitterly, "Is this the Torah and its reward? ... The enemy insults Your great and awesome Name and reviles and balsphemes against the words of the Torah!" A Heavenly voice replied: "If I hear hear another sound, I will return the universe to fluids and the earth to utter emptiness. This is My degree – accept it...!*

11 The Brothers Karamazov is Dostoyevsky's passionate philosophical novel that explores deep into the ethical debates of God, free will, and morality. *The highest harmony is not worth a single tear even of a single killed child* - Ivan Karamazov.

12 Isaiah 22:13

13 From the 17th Tammuz to 9th Av – the Three Weeks – is a time when traditionally Jews reduce celebrating as there begins the commemorations of the destruction of the Temples and other catastrophes that occurred during this time frame throughout history.

14 In accordance with the Talmudic dictum (Ta'anit 26).

15 This is the saddest and darkest day of the Jewish year. It was on this day both the First and Second Temples were destroyed and the expulsion of Jews from Spain in 1492 took place.

16 The Torah (Bible) is divided into weekly portions (parshat) that are read on each Sabbath in synagogues. Parshat Ekev refers to Deut. 7:12 - 11:25, which occurred on 1st August 1942. The opening verse reads: *This shall be the reward when you hearken to these commands...*

17 Parshat Re'eh refers to Deut. 11:26 – 16:17, which opens with the verse: *See, I present before you this day a blessing and a curse.* The Tuesday of that week was 11th August 1942.

18 *Le Dernier Jour d'un Condamné* - a short novel by Victor Hugo first published in 1829

19 Numbers 23:9, said by Balaam as he tried to curse the Israelites but failed, praising them instead.

20 Titus Flavius Vespasianus (39 – 81): In the year 70 he laid siege to Jerusalem and destroyed the Temple. He was Roman Emperor from 79 to 81.

21 House of Torah Study

22 lit.: Sanctification of the Holy Name

23 *Hear Israel – the Eternal is our God, the Eternal is One!* (Deut. 6:4). This declaration is recited twice every day in prayer and again before sleep and, if possible, before death.

24 Presumably the author is referring to the 'chain of tradition'.

25 Lit.: The blessing Shabbat. The Sabbath immediately preceding the appearance of the new moon and hence the new lunar month when special prayers are said for a good life.

26 From the rise of Hitler and the Nazi Party until that day.

27 Nom de plume of Asher Zvi Hirsch Ginsberg (1856 – 1927) meaning *one of the people* (Genesis 26:10). He is known as the founder of Cultural Zionism with which the author would have probably identified.

28 *Netzach Israel Lo Ishaker* is said by the Prophet Samuel (Samuel 1 15:29) after he tells King Saul that God has abandoned him and will not accept his repentance for not killing the King of Amalek as instructed. The verse has been used (out of context) as a rallying call: The Eternal will never abandon Israel. In the First World War a Jewish spy ring against the Turks was called NILI, an acronym based on this phrase.

Fourth Massacre
Jack Kagan

On May 7, 1943 the Germans separated two hundred and fifty out of the five hundred skilled workers and shot them in Hardzilovka, less than a kilometre away from the Labour Camp. The war against the Jews was more important than the war against Russia.

The monument to the fourth massacre - in Hardzilovka – when 250 skilled workers from the Labour Camp were killed on 7 May 1943

Operation "Herman"
Jack Kagan

We knew that the Germans were planning to liquidate the last Jews in the Novogrudok labour camp. The digging of the tunnel was going according to plan. By the end of July we had reached the centre of the wheat field that would give us the protection we needed. The wheat was over a meter high. It would have been easy to crawl the 150 meters behind the mound, far away from the eyes of the guards. An escape list was made; each man made his plan or route where he would run to. The Germans had their own plan. The first days of August they brought a tractor to the field to harvest the wheat. The people in the camp were in panic would the tunnel collapse under the weight of the tractor? And what about the escape? The exit point would be too exposed. The escape committee decided to dig the tunnel a further 150 meters, behind a little hill. The digging would take another two months, if they will not kill us before then.

It turned out that had we escaped in early August as planned, none of us would have survived. The Germans made a plan to liquidate the partisans in the Novogrudok/ Ivenietz area. They named the operation "**Herman**"; they assembled in Novogrudok and the surrounding villages 52,000 soldiers and police. *These consisted of: the 1st Infantry SS brigade under Nazi major-general Curt von Gottberg, 2nd infantry SS regiment, 30th police regiment, 4 separate SS-Sondercommando unit led by SS lieutenant-colonel Oscar Dirlewanger. A group of three separate SS battalions under Kerner, the 15th, 57th, 116th and 118th Ukrainian battalions, a Latvian battalion, Gendarmie group under Kraikenborn, police from towns and villages in the area of the operation, special commandos of General Kube.**

The operation started on the 13th July 1943. Their intention was to surround the vast forest, to push the partisans to the centre and destroy them. They did not taken into consideration the difficult terrain and the swamps. On the 24th July the partisan leader General Platon reported that the Ivieniets-Naliboki dense forest was blockaded.

In the Naliboki dense forest were 4500 partisans in July/August 1943.

1. Brigade named after Kirov. Commander Fiodor Sinichkin. (The Bielski detachment belonged to this brigade).
2. Brigade named after Zhukov Commander Severin Klyuchko March 1943 to August 1943.
3. Brigade Pervomayskaya Commander Naum Kovalev.
4. Brigade named after Stalin. Commander Pavel Gulevich. (The Zorin detachment belonged to this brigade).
5. Brigade named after Chkalov. Commander Mikhail Gribanov.
6. Separate detachments named after Kutuzov. Commander Grigori Zhurenko.
7. Separate detachment named after Nevski. Commander Aleksei Boikov.
8. Separate detachment named after Chkalov #621 Frol Zaitsev.
9. Separate detachment Bolshevik. Commander Yakov Pridannikov.
10. Separate detachment named after Kotovski. Commander Mikhail Chaikovski.
11. Separate cavalry detachment Dmitri Denisenko.

At the beginning of the offensive, the partisan headquarters requested that each detachment should send 200 fighters to fight the Germans at the edge of the river Niemen. General Platon soon realised the strength of the German army, and ordered each detachment to retreat separately.

For the Russian or Polish partisans the decision to run to avoid the onslaught was easier than for Bielski or Zorin; both leaders had family groups, old people and a number of small children. Zorin had about 500/600 people from the Minsk area only a few of which were fighters; Bielski had 750 people with about 200 fighters. Zorin decided to run with the Russian partisans. Tuvia could not decide what to do. He knew for certain that running after the Russian armed partisans would spell disaster and that he would not be able to keep up with so many people.

Friendly Polish partisans passed by and told Bielski that the Germans were near and they would reach Bielski's camp in the morning. Gun-fire could already be heard. The people were panicking. Russian partisans passed and told Tuvia that he must retreat right now, but where could he retreat to? All that Tuvia could say to his Jews was "*Don't panic - we will find a way out*". Tuvia had predicted that the Germans would not attack during the night.

Two people approached – Michol Mechlis and Akiva Shemonovich; Mechlis had been a forest surveyor before the war and Shemonovich had been a merchant in Naliboki. They told Bielski about a small unknown island in the swamps, Krasnaya Gorka (Red Island) about 12 Kilometres away: "*We cannot guarantee that the Germans won't follow but we can see no other way out*".

Bielski immediately spoke to the people and explained the position telling them they must maintain absolute silence and must obey orders. He told them about the terrain they would be facing, and he ordered the food stores to be opened so that everybody chould take as much food as they could carry. He ordered the release of the cows and horses.

They started the night march into the marshes. Mechlis and a few armed young men went first. Tuvia wanted to see that everybody followed. Children were carried on the shoulders; the armed men made sure that their rifles did not get wet.

They made slow progress in the deep mud. Everybody was quiet and hoped that the Germans would not follow this route. They stayed there during the day and heard continued shooting and "*Catch the Jews*" being shouted in German. They went deeper in the swamps. It seemed that the German went in but as the swamps got deeper they turned back. The shooting continued. With great difficulty they reached the island. The island was too small to accommodate everyone, which meant that some people had to stay in the mud.

After arriving on the island the people were counted and it seemed that 6 were missing. Volunteers were found to go and search for them, and luckily they were found. A few days later the guards found a Byelorussian woman not far from the island. They decided that she was a spy and executed her on the spot.

The hunger started to bite. Ten days had passed since they went into the swamps. The people started suffering from blisters and swellings. The doctors said these were symptoms of starvation. Akiva took a party to a nearby village for food: they came back empty handed - the Germans were still in the villages.

They could not stay there any longer. Zus took eighty fighters out of the swamps to try and break through the German lines. When he got out of the swamps he separated the group into small units. They scouted around and soon realised that the Germans had gone. Tuvia waited another two days and they left Krasnaya Gorka.

The Germans had burned down 150 villages round the dense forest. Everything went up in smoke. 4,934 people from the villages and small towns in the area of operation were killed. 20,944 people including 4,173 children were taken to forced labour in Germany.

Guerrilla battles took place between various partisan detachments and the withdrawing German forces. The German losses were high: 3000 killed, 29 captured prisoners, 2 tanks,

2 armoured vehicles, 55 lorries and 5 cars destroyed. 130 partisans were killed and about 50 wounded.

The Bielskis decided to go back to the district in the forests round Novogrudok. However they left a party of about 70 people to stay in the Naliboki forest and to collect the harvest which had been left in the ground. They collected 200 tons of potatoes, 3 tons of cabbages, 5 tons of sugar beet, 5 tons of grain and different vegetables all of which was put in special warehouses.

On the way to the district the group had to cross the Niemen River. The water in the river was treacherous and during the crossing one man drowned. That was the sole loss to the Bielskis in the biggest German raid on the partisans in Belarus. Zorin was not so lucky; he lost quite a lot of people in his escape.

Notes:
* Encyclopedia "Гісторыя Беларусі" (History of Belarus), vol. 2, Minsk, 1994, p. 518

Escape Through the Tunnel
Jack Kagan

An escape committee, led by Berl Yoselevitz, was established in the labour camp. The committee decided to attempt a mass break out from the labour camp. Between them they had only six rifles, and a few pistols and hand grenades.

The original plan was to attack the guards and run. However as ninety-five per cent of the would-be escapees would probably have been killed this idea was rejected. It was then decided to dig a tunnel 100 metres (328 feet) long to the other side of the barbed wire, into a field of growing wheat. To succeed would not only be a major engineering feat, which would have to be carried out without discovery.

The work started[1] but then had to be stopped for a while because there was not enough oxygen for the lamps to burn inside the tunnel. We had no electricity in our living quarters, but Mr. Rukovski, one of the inmates, was an electrician. He found the camp's main power cable leading to the workshops, and made a hidden switchboard, so that the camp searchlights could be turned on and off, and the tunnel could be lit up.

The joiners among the prisoners prepared railway lines and a trolley. The tailors prepared bags and reins to pull the trolley. The loft was reinforced, and the dug-out earth hidden there. Work went on secretly twenty four hours a day, seven days a week. The tunnel was 1.5 metres {just under 5 feet}below ground, about 60 centimetres (24 inches) wide and 75 centimetres high (30 inches) just enough for a person to crawl through.

In August 1943 the tunnel was nearly ready. Suddenly there was a serious setback the Germans brought in a tractor and cut the corn. The fear was that the tunnel might collapse from the weight of the tractor, but it did not. However, if we had escaped then, probably none of us would have survived, as the German army had brought in 52,000 soldiers to launch a month-long raid on the Soviet partisans Operation Herman. The main German base was at Novogrudok. Once the cover of the cornfield had been removed, we were forced to extend the tunnel by another 150 metres {nearly 500 feet}.

As the day of the escape grew nearer, a list was drawn up of the order in which we were to go through the tunnel. I was one of the last. In front of me was my friend Pesach Abramovitz.

The escape was on the night of 26 September 1943. It was a dark, moonless, stormy, night, as if made to order. We assembled in the loft, very quietly, and waited in a very orderly manner. At 9 p.m. the line started moving forward. Fresh air could be felt coming in from the tunnel as we broke through to the outside world. We made a big mistake, however, by leaving the lights on in the tunnel. Coming out into terrible darkness, some people became disorientated and ran towards the camp. The guards, not knowing what had happened, started shooting in all directions. But most of us ran towards the forest and freedom. Of those who escaped, about 170 made it to the partisans, mostly to the Bielskis' group, and about eighty were caught and killed.

Ten elderly people had hidden themselves in a specially built hiding place in the loft, reasoning that they were too weak to escape through the tunnel. Five days later, after the labour camp had been abandoned by the Germans, they simply walked out of the main gates and were able to join the partisans.

The Nazis had wanted to declare the area Juderein (free of Jews). The only Jews left in Western Belarus at the beginning of 1944 were ninety-eight, in Koldychevo concentration camp. They escaped in February 1944.

The Labour Camp and the escape route
Photograph taken from a model in the Imperial War Museum, London

Key to the model

1. Living quarters
2. Workshops
3. Police station
4. Police station, watch tower and searchlight
5. Machine-gun towers
6. Two rows of barbed wire
7. Wooden fence to prevent prisoners seeing the outside world
8. Toilets
9. Graveyard
10. Gates
11. Tunnel
12. Main road to Minsk
13. Tunnel exit

136 WE STOOD SHOULDER TO SHOULDER

In the camp, Yitzhak Rosenhouse kept a list of the inmates. His list was used as the escape list. Part of it is shown here.

Yitzhak Rosenhouse, creator of the escape list Bielski Brigade. Died in Israel.

Photographs of some of the escapees from the Labour Camp

Notke Sucharski
Bielski Detachment.
Died after liberation.

Issac Yarmovski
Bielski Detachment.
He later lived in Israel.

Yakov Shepsman
Soviet partisan Detachment.
Died in Britain.

Lionke Portnoy
Bielski Detachment.
Died in Israel.

Chaim Ostashinski
Bielski Detachment.
Died in Israel.

Elia Berkovitz
Bielski Detachment.
Died in Israel.

Avram Chertok
Soviet partisan Detachment.
Died in France.

Zeidl Kushner
Bielski Detachment.
Died in the US.

Chonia Kushner
Killed during the escape.

Shaul Gorodinski
Bielski Detachment.
Died in Israel.

Rita Volozhinska
Killed during the escape.

Moshe Niegnievicki
Bielski Detachment.
Lives in Israel.

Chaim Liebovitz
Bielski Detachment.
Died in the US.

Yacov Oshman
Bielski Detachment.
Died in Israel.

Sonia Oshman
Bielski Detachment.
Lives in the US.

Raya Kushner
Bielski Detachment.
Died in the US.

Jack Kagan
Bielski Detachment.
Lives in Britain.

Yakov Shepsman
Soviet partisan Detachment.
Lives in the US.

Had we not escaped on 26 September 1943, the Germans would have killed us within a week. They wanted to liquidate the Lida ghetto before us, as the German document below indicates. The ghetto of Lida was destroyed between 17 and 19 September 1943.

Tamara Vershitskaya was responsible for uncovering the tunnel in July 2007 and for creating the first Jewish resistance museum in Belarus on that section of the labour camp.

The uncovered entrance to the tunnel in the Novogrudok Resistance Museum

Combat Report: Operation at Novogrudok, 9 July 1943
SS Haupsturmführer Wilke
Baranovichi, 11 July 1943

On 9 July I went to Novogrudok to carry out a special mission at the order of the security police and SD commander. The combat order said that I must arrive in Baranovichi to receive a mission in Novogrudok. In his office in Minsk Obersturmführer Muller told me that the talk was about several hundreds of arrests which were to take place in Novogrudok. I was not given a definite and specific mission by Obersturmführer Muller. In connection with the forthcoming numerous arrests and taking into account especially the dangerous area around Novogrudok I decided to take a Latvian platoon with me, so the total number of the party was 37 people.

When I arrived in Baranovichi on the evening of July 9 Untersturmfuhrer Anders and Untersturmfuehrer Dadishek told me that Untersturmfuehrer Amelung had not informed them about any mission for me in Novogrudok, which was why they could not tell me what mission I had to carry out there. They were only given a hint that some kind of investigation was taking place regarding Jews who had connection with the Polish resistance movement. It was now my turn to be surprised. I could learn nothing about my mission in Baranovichi even through a radiogram with the request to send a strengthened SD party had been sent from Baranovichi to Minsk.

I went by the most direct route to Novogrudok in order not to lose any more time, and hoped I would learn about the mission from SS Sturmbannfuehrer Traub. Traub received me in Novogrudok with much surprise and asked me what operation I was going to carry out in his region.

I told him about my mission and asked him in turn to inform me about his large mission. It was then that SS Sturmbannfuehrer Traub showed surprise and said that it appeared that Untersturmfuehrer Amelung must have misunderstood him. Apparently some time ago he had spoken to Untersturmfuehrer Amelung and an SD interpreter in Baranovichi Gurnevichius about an SD party of four to five men which was to come to Novogrudok to study general questions regarding the security police, which had been totally neglected up to that time. They were to carry out a thorough investigation of the Ivenets case to try to discover to what extent Polish police corporals had inspired the Polish resistance movement. There was a rising suspicion that this had been the case in Novogrudok. He further told me of Untersturmfuehrer Amelung's wish to liquidate a Jewish labour camp in Novogrudok.

I discussed with Sturmbannfuehrer Traub what I thought I should do on this matter, and stated my decision. I would not undertake any investigation regarding the question of the Polish resistance movement, as the matter required more time than I had been given by the order for me to carry out executions. Once again I reminded Untersturmfuehrer Amelung about my mission and he agreed to send two or three agents in civilian clothes to Novogrudok to accomplish this. I said I would not carry out the desired resettlement of the Jewish labour camp either, as Sturmbannfuehrer Traub had wished, because to my mind it could not be done without carrying out a simultaneous action involving 2,000 Jews in Lida. It would be impossible to resettle 250 Jews in Novogrudok without it becoming known in Lida very soon. The risk was too great that many Jews would escape to the forest and become bandits.

Sturmbannfuehrer Traub especially insisted on the liquidation of the Jewish labour camp because of the great fear that Jews would escape from the camp disposed in Novogrudok. He pointed out that bandits had recently taken the guards of the camp prisoner and, relying on the intelligence he had about the situation in the camp, he was convinced that the bandits would undertake a big operation to liberate the camp in the very near future. As things stood, Sturmbannfuehrer Traub asked me to transfer 250 Jews to a labour camp in Baranovichi. I had to refuse him on this matter too, because to my mind such a transfer of Novogrudok Jews would be regarded by Lida Jews as an execution, and also the camp in Baranovichi would not be able to accommodate such an influx of Jews. I promised Sturmbannfuehrer Traub to report the state of affairs and my decision to the security police and SD commander.

Original: Special Moscow Archive, 500-1-769, p. 218

According to the German historian Christian Gerlach, in his book, Calculated Murder[2], Traub himself took part in the shooting in the fourth massacre in Hardzielovka, and also participated in killing the Jews who were caught escaping from the tunnel.

Traub was born on 2 April 1919. Only on 21 November 2002, did I find out that Wilhelm Traub the murderer died on 18 February 1946, as a prisoner of war in a camp in Yugoslavia.

Notes:
[1] Two or three weeks after May 7th 1943
[2] Christian Gerlach Kalkulierte Morde: Die deutsche Wirtschafts- und Vernichtungspolitik in Weißrußland 1941 bis 1944 [Calculated Murder: The German economic and annihilation policy in Belorussia 1941 to 1944] in German. Hamburger Edition, Hamburg (1999)

Chief Engineer Ribinski
Jack Kagan

Very few people have ever written about engineer Ribinski; he was the most enthusiastic, dedicated and efficient man I have ever met.

When the order arrived[1] that we should leave the Novogrudok District and move to the old base in the Naliboki Forests, Ribinski was put in charge of building the new base. On the day the order arrived he chose about a dozen horsemen to ride out and borrow tools from friendly farmers. He needed many spades, saws and axes. He arrived ahead of the column and for 2 days he searched for a perfect site for the permanent camp.

The site had to be well camouflaged from aircraft; a minimum of a metre above the water table; hidden from strangers yet with access to a nearby road. At last he found it. The group arrived and there was no time to loose. It was now past the middle of October, which left about eight weeks in which to build a minimum 20 huts for the 1000 people, separate huts for the commanders, plus a Central Headquarters. Once winter hit it would be impossible to build as the ground would be too frozen and fires would not be permissible to soften it.

He divided the workers into three groups: the first group to dig holes twenty metres by six metres; the second group to cut trees than clean the branches; the third group to construct the hut (ziemlanka)

Because he was worried that German aeroplanes would find the place his plan was to build just behind the trees, but that created a tremendous amount of extra work because of the tree roots. He had a special force of young people axing away the exposed roots that were in the way.

The first hut was dug one metre deep but at that depth we hit the water table and water began to seep in and cover the floor. So the next 3 were only 90 cm deep. The other huts were built on slightly hilly terrain so he went back to the metre.

The huts was built without nails, since they were such a scarce commodity, so precision was required; as the hole was finished 20 metre long logs were dropped in followed immediately by about six one metre long logs to support it. Mr Ribinski made sure that trees were cut accurately. He swore like a trooper, and threatened to shoot some people as saboteurs if the measurements were not precise enough.

Sleeping bunks for 25 people along either side were erected.

The roof had to be logged in accurately as well. And finally, the roofs were camouflaged with grass. It was a tremendous job; he managed not only to build the living quarters but also a food warehouse, a mill, a bakery, kitchens, a small hut for bread distribution, workshops for shoemakers, tailors, watchmakers, carpenters, hat makers, leatherworks and even a barber's shop, a separate hut for making sausages, Pupko's hut for making soap, and a metal workshop where Oppenheim repaired all sorts of armaments. Later he added a hospital, school, and a bathhouse[2].

While all this was going on two parties of workers went to the villages and the town of Naliboki that the Germans had destroyed and salvaged anything of use. They came back with such things as metal ovens, burned sewing machines, window frames and doors. Joiners put in the window frames and doors into the huts, and the burned sewing machines were put in kerosene to await it repairs.

In my opinion Ribinski was a genius that everyone took for granted. He had the good fortune that Tuvia gave him a free hand. He was the construction boss and it was thanks to him that when the very cold winter weather came in the second week of December we were prepared. **In eight weeks he had built a small town.** Finally a prison was built. After it was finished the workers deserved a well-earned rest.

Map of the Bielski Otriad in Nalibocka Forest
During the Last Phase of Existence
(Autumn 1943 - Summer 1944)

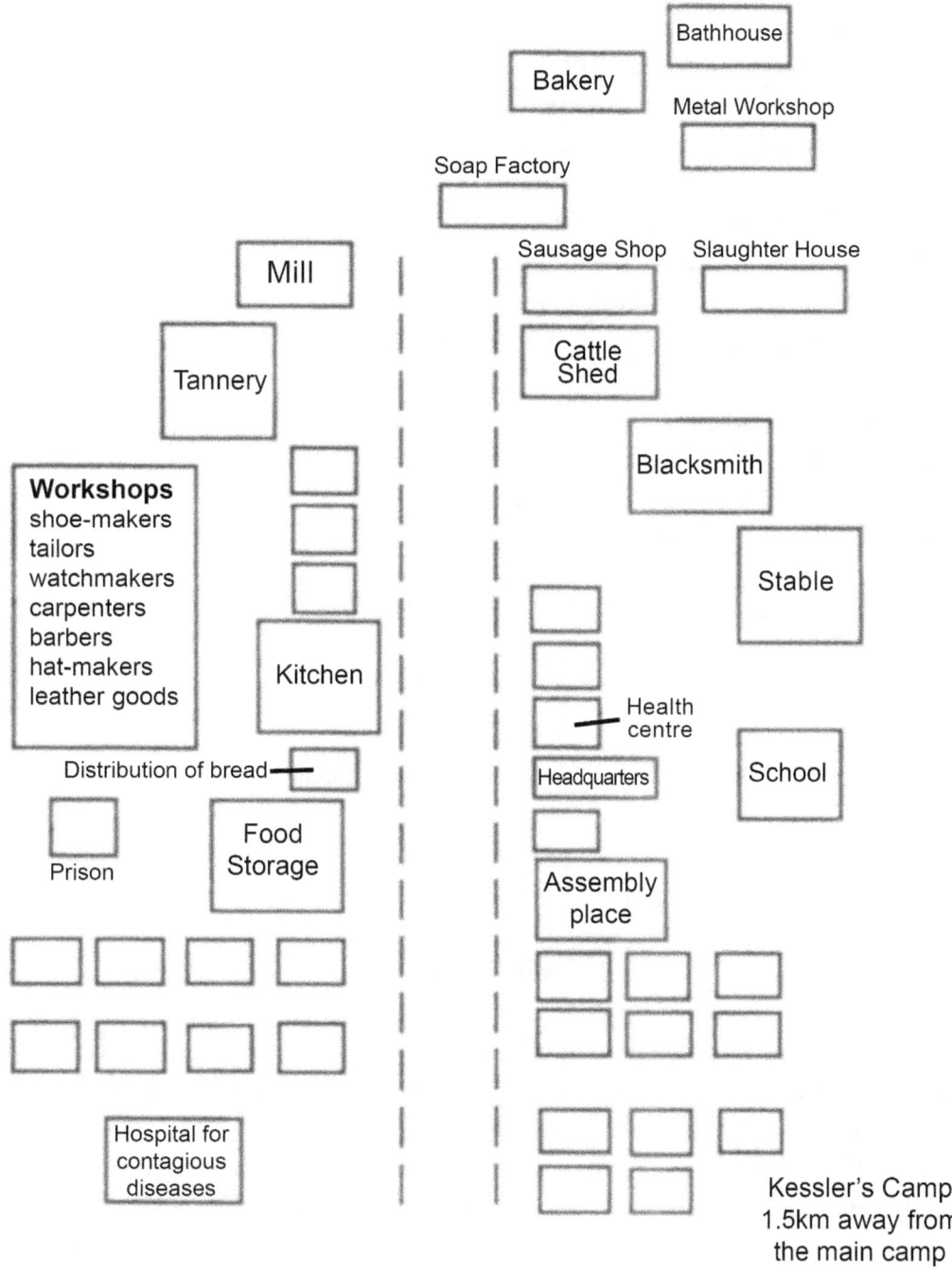

This map is based on information provided by Chaya Bielski

Notes:
[1] First day of Succot (Oct. 1943) they left and seven days later they arrived at the new site.
[2] In February 44, 96 escapees arrived from Koldichevo concentration camp most of them were tanners. So in March he added a tannery.

Leaders of the Bielski Detachment by Tuvia Bielski

1. Commander: Tuvia Bielski
2. Head of the fighting group and Second in Command: Asoel Bielski
3. Chief of Staff: Lazar Malbin
4. Political Commissar: Shmatoviec, Ivan Vasilievich (Byelorussian)
5. Secretary to the Headquarters: Raya Kaplinski
6. Second Secretary: Yisrael Bedzovski
7. Third Secretary: Avrohom Viner
8. Quartermaster: Pesach Friedberg
9. Chief of special Operations: Solomon Volkovisky
10. Chief of Sabotage: Leibush Feldman
11. Training Instructor: Yehuda Bielski
12. Reconnaissance Leader: Yehuda Levin
13. Reconnaissance: Yankl Abramovitz.
14. Platoon Heads: Chaim Abramovitz, Navitzki
15. Medical Officer; Dr Henrik Isler
16. Medical Assistant: Dr. Hirsh
17. Commander of the Camp: Maks Potashnik
18. Workshops Manager: Maciek Kabak
19. Responsible for food supply: Mordechay Gershovitz
20. Kitchen Manager: Yichak Rosenhaus
21. Building Engineer: Rubinski
22. Historian: Dr Shmuel Amarant

Source: Jews of the Forest, Tuvia Bielski, published in Hebrew, Jerusalem 1946.

The Bielski Detachment

The Soviet partisan movement named the Bielski detachment after the Soviet Prime Minister, M. I. Kalinin. Its members took part in fighting the enemy and in committing various acts of sabotage, which included blowing up bridges and cutting down telegraph poles. During the German offence against the partisans in August 1943, the Germans had arrested and killed many of the farmers, burned their houses, and left the potatoes and cabbage harvest in the ground. The Bielski group took the opportunity and dug up more then 200 tons of potatoes. They put them away in a secret hideaway, to be eaten during the winter.
During a period of six month in 1944, the Bielski fighters stopped German trains for a total of fifty-one hours.

The following four documents relating to the Bielski partisans were found in the Minsk National Archives (NARB).

Kirov Partisan Brigade
Detachment named after
S. Ordzhonikidze
Family Group
Naliboki dense forest
5 December 1943
N 0020

Report to the Commander of the Kirov
Partisan brigade Capt. Comr Vasiljev

Concerning work done:

On 17 September 1943 on having gathered the family group of 250 people and having left a fighting unit with the whole Staff in our operation's area, according to the order of the brigades staff, and taking into account the impossibility of coexistence of the detachment and families in the area of hostilities, I returned with them to the old base in the dense Naliboki Forest. Having arrived at the place, I found out that the group of 36 people whom I had left had grown to 63 people and was engaged in digging up potatoes for their own needs and building a summer camp.

Having come to the representative of the CCCP/6/B in Ivenec Inter District Centre, in whose district the camp was situated, I started to build a base for 700 to 800 people. Besides this group, I had also received an order to bring in all the families who were in the dense forest and in the Stolpcy and Mir districts, about another 100 people. We at once began a planned stocking up of potatoes and building a winter camp. Taking into account our situation, we immediately began a bakery and a mill of our own, in a part of the dense forest that had been burnt during the round up. We also started to arrange different workshops: shoemaker's, tailors, gunsmiths, joiners, saddlers, sausage makers and others, where more than a hundred people are working now serving other brigades located near us beside our own detachment. The bakery and the sausage making department served the other detachments. The group began to build a winter camp, the plan of which is enclosed.

The camp is built already and the group began to build a secret reserve for winter. On 30 October the last family group was brought in and now the group has about 800 people. It is still in 4 camps as different kinds of work are carried out everywhere. Now the group has the following stockpiles: about 200 tons of potatoes, 3 tons of cabbages, 5 tons of sugar beet, 5 tons of grain, and different vegetables, about 3 tons of meat and 1 ton of sausages. Part of it is kept in a secret place. There is also flour for bread for everyday use. There is one common kitchen, which provides hot meals for the whole group three times a day. Three groups including sixty people are on economic operations in different districts. Sixty-six rifle men plus a reconnaissance party of six people and four messengers are on daily service. There are no epidemically or infectiously ill people on the base. There are 16 people in hospital, 1 doctor and 2 nurses work in hospital.

Commander of the family group Assistant to the Chief of Staff.
Bielski Malbin

Source: NARB, f. 3623, op. 1, d. 2,

Statement

Drawn up on 29 March 1944, on the fact that a group of partisans from the Bielski detachment, consisting of eight people, cut a telephone telegraph communication line at night from 26 to 27 March 1944 on the line Baranovichi-Lida line on the Novoyelna Dvorec sector over the length of 1 km (21 poles).

During the retreat the group was fired on by a police ambush, moreover one policeman was killed and spoils of war were taken: one bag with 100 cartridges for a Russian rifle. There were no victims from the side of our group.

The following took part in the destruction of the communication line:

1   Bielski, Alexander Davidovich Commander of the fighting group
2   Gulkovich, Boris Shlemovich
3   Leibovich, Archer Notkovich
4   Leibovich, Zahnan Notkovich
5   Pshenica, Alexander Semionovich
6   Berkovich, Benjamin Berkovich
7   Kotler, Izrael Moiseevich
8   Venburg, Morduch Isaakovich

Three copies of the statement were drawn up. To:
Tuvia Bielski, Commander
Asoel Bielski , Commander of fighting group
Lazar Malbin, Chief of Staff

Source: NARB, f. 3617, op. 1, d. 9, pp. 61-61 P.T.O.

Transmitted by radio:

Statement

Drawn up on 20 May 1944, on the fact that a group of partisans from the detachment named after Kalinin blew up one German car on the Lida - Novogrudok road at the distance of 17 km from Novogrudok and 4 km from Novaya Guta on 12 May, 1944. Four Germans were killed. The above said is confirmed by the messenger Iosif Zodzkim, a resident of Novaya Guta.

There were neither victims from the partisan group, nor spoils of war. The following took part in the blowing up:

1   Ostashinski, Ilja Gilkovich, Commander of the platoon, Chief of group
2   Shenvald, Pavel Ludvikovich Sapper
3   Dvorecki, Abram Peisachovich
4   Leib Genach, Samuilovich
5   Litavorski, Litman Alterovich

Three copies of the statement were drawn up.
To: Shemyatovec, Commissar of the Detachment
        Ostashinski, Commander of the Platoon
        Lazar Malbin, Chief of Staff

Source: NARB, f. 3617, op. 1, d. 9, p.77

To the Central Staff of Partisan Movement.
Fighting Dispatch

I report, that a group of partisans from the detachment named after M. I. Kalinin, Lida Zone, including seven people, the man in charge of the group is Kukelko Anton, there is sapper Baran Benjamin, and there are participants: Berman Yaacov, Slutski Yudel, Sinder Efraim, Golman Nina, Borecki Yosel, mined the railway on the Lida -Molodechno line near the station of Gavja at night from 14 to 15 June. On 15 June, 3 o'clock an enemy transportation going from Molodechno to Lida was derailed, the locomotive and four medical carriages were derailed. The number of killed and wounded is not established. The movement of trains was stopped for six hours. The same group on the same night and in the same place mined the railway and on June 15 at 7 o'clock derailed an enemy transportation going from Lida to Molodechno. A locomotive and five carriages with military equipment were damaged. The movement of trains was stopped for eight hours.

The above said is confirmed by the messenger Zmitrovich Vladislav, a resident of the farmstead Zastenok near the village of Rusaki, Ivje district.

Commander of the detachment Bielski   Commissar of the detachment Shemyatovec

Chief of Staff Malbin   Chief of the group Kukelko

Sources: NARB, f. 3618, inv. 1, f. 30, p. 158-158a

Visit by General Platon to our Camp and its Consequences
Tuvia Bielski

When we heard that the regional Soviet partisan commander, General Platon[1], was coming for a visit, the people set to work to clean and beautify the camp. Platon arrived at our camp on 31 December 1943, with an entourage of forty people, mostly from the Kutuzov group, who acted as his personal guards. They were from Russia and their modern equipment was the envy of the entire camp. While Platon came to our command hut, the rest of his entourage toured the camp. We treated the guest to a meal with the best of our products: sausages, pickled meats, stuffed cabbages and of course schnapps (vodka).

We first entered the large light industries building. Matitiyahu Kabak, a lawyer, called the group to attention. Platon made a few remarks and then told the people to get back to work. We moved from group to group, and the General was astonished at the industriousness and dedication of the workers. Esther Goroditzskaya, from Stolovichi, was responsible for the twelve women and two sewing machines that continually hummed. Platon shook her hand and asked about the conditions, the way of life and the food. He did this with every workshop leader.

They all praised me, their commander. The hat makers sat close by, and Platon spoke with Leibovitch, the foreman. He spent some time with the saddle makers and told the foreman that every saddle made in the camp was like ambushing the enemy. The shoemaker's workshop employed twenty-two people, and he saw a number of rifles hanging on the walls. Kolchak, the foreman of the shoemakers, described how the shoemakers kept their weapons close at hand, twenty-four hours a day. There were four hairdressers working, and Platon invited the chief hairdresser to make a working visit to his headquarters. With this he finished meeting with the first group of workshops.

Platon started the second round of visits with the tailors. Shmuel Kagan from Novogrudok headed a group of eighteen tailors. Platon was surprised at the quality of the goods. He was even more surprised when he met the watchmakers. They were working on many watches. Pinchuk, the foreman, explained that they did work for many people in the region. This concluded our visit to the workshops.

Then we went over to meet with the three people in the metal workshop. Oppenheim the foreman was also a watchmaker, who had been seriously wounded during the German attack on the Zabielovo forest. He had been on guard duty at the time. There were many weapons under repair, from rifles to machine guns and sub-machine guns, and they were assembling new weapons from spare parts too.

After that we went to the carpentry workshop where Netta Huberman from Mir, was in charge. Here we manufactured the stocks for the rifles and sub-machine guns, plus windows and doorframes and other articles. Mordecai Berkowitz was in charge of our four blacksmiths, and we prepared the charcoal ourselves. We simply burnt trees in the forest. Even the bakery supplied us with large quantities of charcoal. At the time of our visit, Bashitz the blacksmith was busy manufacturing the upper parts of rifle breeches, very delicate work indeed. This made an impression on Platon and he asked for more information about the work.

Then Platon interjected: *'Many breeches Comrade, to attack the German fascists!'*

I took him next to see the tannery, where Orkovitz from Baranovitchi was in charge. His assistant was Muksay, and they worked with a dozen people. There were six wooden tanks full of hides outside the workshops. With the final product we produced soles and other leather goods. Platon was amazed at the ingenuity and all within the confines of the forest.

Then we moved to the bakery where the ovens were full of bread. Mordecai Gershovitz, from Lida and a noted baker, was in charge. But Platon was even more surprised when he saw our sausage factory. So I said to him: *'Visit us often and we will be glad to share our bounty with you.'* From there I took our guest to show him our food stores, where we had a three-day supply of bread, meat and two kilograms (about four and a half pounds) of dry bread per person. Small bags of dried produce were hanging on the walls. Our guest sampled several of the products.

Following that we moved on to the soap-making workshop, and he requested that we send soap to his headquarters. From there we visited the slaughterhouse. There were two ritual slaughterers, Rabbi David Brook from Novogrudok and an old man from Varnuva. They had prepared the knives and they deemed them completely kosher. We moved to the flour mill and met with the miller, Reznick. Finally, in our last stop we witnessed the production of resins from the barks of the fir trees for use in the tannery. Shmuel Mikolitzky from Novogrudok was the expert in charge of this process.

'Is it possible that you also make vodka here?' joked Platon.

Then we moved on to the hospital, where we met with Dr. Hirsch, who complained to Platon about the difficult conditions and the lack of medical supplies. Platon promised that with the next supply aircraft he would send them parachute silk and more medical supplies. There were two other doctors with us at the time, Dr. Lepkovitz and a woman, but I cannot remember her name; there were also twenty nurses.

We then returned to our staff hut where Platon spoke for half an hour, promising help, and praising us. He then requested that I ride with him to visit Sokolov. He also insisted on seconding me to his staff, to stop all further interference and improve relations amongst the groups.

Four of us accompanied Platon. Besides me, there was Lazar Malbin, Gordon, who had known Platon before the war, and Eliyahu Bleicher, my second-in-command. We visited the

Dzerzhinsky brigade, and all night we partied in honour of the New Year. The following morning we drank some more, and then rode over to visit Sokolov. We reached his headquarters on the afternoon of 1 January 1944, and the partying started again. Later that night we finally sat down to a serious meeting that continued into the morning of 2 January. We did not hold back on our drinking, but we never forgot where we came from or who we were.

Besides Platon and Sokolov, Major Valery from the central 'Special Section', Sashkin, the commander of the Dzerzhinsky brigade, Malbin, Gordon and I participated in the meeting. Genia, who was in charge of the radio, and had parachuted in from Russia, acted as secretary.

When my turn came I suggested that we change the name of our group to Platon, but Platon insisted that the group would now be known simply as the Bielski Group. He appointed Gordon to be Deputy Commissar. (It seems that Gordon and Platon were friends from Radun. When the Russians occupied eastern Poland in the early summer of 1944, Platon had an important position in the Soviet Regional government. Gordon was a cripple; he walked with great difficulty and it seems to me that he had connections with the Communist party).

Before we left for home, Sokolov had told me that in another week to ten days I would accompany him on a tour to visit the various units in his brigade.

The most important thing that was achieved at this meeting was the cancellation of the orders concerning Asael. He was now appointed Commander of the Partisan Fighting Forces of our group. I pressed for this, and used the fact that Platon was so impressed with our camp as an additional lever. I noted Asael's military prowess and all that he had done up until that time, and what he still was capable of doing in the military arena. Without him, I said, I could not maintain a cohesive fighting force, and without this force I could not maintain the integrity of our group; and we all know how important it was for our group to continue to exist. Our 1,000 and productive loyal citizens were certainly worth preserving.

So I rode with Sokolov on his tour. We also visited the Kirov brigade, who's Commander was Vasil'yev. We had come to inspect conditions and review his partisans. Sokolov spoke with several members of the brigade and called a meeting of the brigade commanders among them, Zusia who was commander of the Ordzonikidze brigade. Victor Panchenko presented a report on his group, 'October'. Sasha Kanonov reported on the 'Iskara' group, and the 'Gypsy' gave a report on the Baltiets Group. This gypsy had served in the Russian Baltic Fleet, hence the name of his group. I gave a report on the activities of our group. The last one to speak was Vasil'yev.

I spoke about what had occurred after Vasil'yev had robbed my partisan fighters. I reminded everyone of Sokolov's promise during the bad days in the dense forest that all the partisans would help us. I reminded them of Vasil'yev's promise that our partisans of the Ordzonikidze brigade, with Zusia at its head, would help us, the families. Yet, despite these promises they were delaying our food convoys. First time, this was done by some of Panchenko's men, and the second time, Vasil'yev's men. I didn't complain about Victor, because I knew that his people had done it without his authorization, while Vasilayev, as commander, had given the order personally. Vasil'yev interrupted me and said he had only expropriated salt. I answered: *'Why did you search our wagons if there were no other things than food aboard? You know that there are women and children and elderly people with us and we have a hospital. We need honey. We need clothes for the women and children. How can you interfere? If you had wanted salt, I would have given you the salt. But what you did was simply an act of plunder.'*

'Let's not get excited here,' said Sokolov, trying to calm me down.

I told him that according to Soviet law, the guilty should be punished. Vasil'yev apologized and reiterated that he was not against us. On the contrary he respected my talents. Later, Vasil'yev's conduct was noted officially in his military file.

In January, Asael and his partisans destroyed many trains and several German army vehicles and in every case we retrieved much military booty. During that time, Major Shastakov came from the east to the dense forest with 600 soldiers. His targeted area was Novogrudok and amongst his group there were some Jews unrecognizable as Jews. The Major did not pay particular attention to anyone's background.

Shastakov lunched with us and made a very good impression. We could see that he was a good man. He viewed the camp and realized that many people did not have weapons. He promised me a few rifles in exchange for sausages, and to this end he sent us fifteen head of cattle. We completed the work in a few days, and then I rode over to visit him with the sausages. Shastakov ordered his supply officer to give me any extra rifles and a 25 kilogram (55 pounds) box of explosives, together with parachute silk for the hospital. The supply officer loaded the wagons with seventeen good rifles, the explosives and the silk. Later I heard that the supply officer was Jewish.

General Vasily Chernyshev[1]

Notes:
[1] General Vasily Chernyshev was known by his codename as "General Platon".

The Partisans of Tuvia Bielski*
Dr. Shmuel Amarant,
An Historian with the Bielski Group

The Bielski partisans who were based in the forests of western Byelorussia provided a refuge to people who escaped from the ghettos and working camps, and to small family groups, which escaped from the ghettos to the countryside and wandered without cover and protection from constant danger. They also gave refuge to the Jewish partisans who suffered from anti-Semitism in the Russian partisan movement, or were expelled by the Russians because of anti-Semitism, which was usually disguised under all sorts of pretexts. Often they were made to leave without weapons or an alternative hiding place.

The unit's core developed in stages within the Bielski family; it grew slowly with every new arrival of escapees from the camps and ghettos. Every wave of people fleeing to the forests brought with them their own way of life and influenced the life of the growing group of partisans. The history of that family camp, the largest in the Jewish partisan movement, reflects the evolvement of family camps with the process of unification on the one hand and the trend towards division and disintegration on the other. The importance of the dependence of those camps on the conditions of the general partisan movement, their aspirations and achievements was underlined.

The Bielski family escaped from their village of Stankievichi, near Novogrudok, at the beginning of 1942. They wandered in the forests of Bochkovichi. Little groups of relatives and friends from the ghetto of Novogrudok began to join them during the spring and summer of 1942. The people armed themselves and started to take revenge on the murderous peasants and German collaborators. They contacted a group of Russian partisans under the command of Victor Panchenko, and together they carried out daring raids in the Novogrudok district.

From the beginning there were different opinions as to how the group should operate. Many of its members tended to favour isolation. They wanted to take advantage of their good relations with the farmers around them and hide in the depth of the forests until the day of liberation. The fact that the family group turned into a huge unit was due to the personal influence of Tuvia Bielski who was chosen as the leader of the partisans.

Tuvia Bielski was, from the beginning, bent on absorbing all Jewish escapees. The struggle over the decision as to decide how the partisans should act lasted a long time, especially in times of danger. When the shortage of supplies was severe, there was a desire by some, particularly those who carried arms, to divide the camp and separate it into closed units, thus taking advantage of having weapons and having connections with the local population, and to leave the rest of the people, who had no weapons or fighting skills, to fend for themselves. They did not see why they had to take care of the malbushim 'Jacketted-ones' as they called the unarmed people. They wanted to get rid of them and only take care of themselves.

Tuvia Bielski held a different opinion; he exhibited a statesman-like responsibility and an understanding of the hour's needs. He accepted any Jew who came to join him with or without a weapon, with or without fighting skills. He said again and again: 'I wish that thousands of Jews would join us, we will absorb them all'. Disintegration of partisan units was very common in 1942 at the beginning of the partisan war. At this time there was no central authority and every group of partisans was an independent unit. If it had not been for Tuvia Bielski, his partisans would also have been divided into tiny groups, each looking for hiding places in the depths of the forests. But Bielski maintained his line of action, and his personal intervention saved the unity of the partisans and the lives of hundreds of its members. In the primitive conditions of the forest, at the beginning of the partisan war, when selfish tendencies were common, Tuvia Bielski's stand deserves high commendation and praise.

In the winter of 1942/43, because of the increased danger and difficulty in supplying the camp, the unit was forced to divide into five groups, which settled in different locations in the district of Novogrudok. Some then tried, together with their families and relatives, to separate themselves and abandon the unarmed people. Bielski assembled his partisans and ordered that no Jew should be left alone in the forest.

The Jews of Novogrudok and the surrounding area were the first to join the unit. Bielski's messengers started to smuggle groups of Jews from the ghetto of Novogrudok, using prepared lists of names. Later the Jews of Ivje abandoned their ghetto and joined the partisans - after they learned that they were going to be removed from the town. The remnants of the Dworec population, the bulk of whom was slaughtered in December 1942, also joined the Bielski's partisans. Their camp was a refuge to small groups of Jews from Novogrudok and Dworec. They tried initially to survive independently but, having encountered the murderous behaviour of the Russian partisans, they were forced to look for protection from the Bielski partisans. The commanders of the Russian partisans also started to press little family groups and forced them to join Bielski's unit.

In the spring of 1943 the Jews of Lida started to arrive. Initially they had tried to join the Russian partisan group 'Iskra' on the banks of the Niemen, but met with an anti-Semitic attitude, were disarmed and sent off to the Bielski partisans. These Jews formed the connecting link between the forest and the Lida ghetto, and hundreds of people from Lida began to arrive at the bases of the Bielski partisans, in the forests of the Novogrudok district, Stara Huta and other locations.

Groups of Jewish partisans from the Russian units also joined the Bielski camp. They came, for example, from the 'Arlianski' partisans, from the Lipichanska wilderness, the 'First of May' partisan unit, and others. They resented the anti-semitic atmosphere that prevailed in the Russian units and left them of their own free will, carrying their arms with them. They wanted to fight together with the Bielski partisans, among their fellow Jews.

Bielski's unit thrived. On the eve of the 'Big Hunt' in July 1943 it had reached more than 700 souls. However, during the 'Big Hunt', through July and August 1943, the divisive opinions were heard again. The units, which had moved to the forests of Naliboki, were forced to split into many small groups. They than wandered in the area, trying to survive in those troubled days. Often the armed groups drove off the unarmed partisans, and even threatened them with their weapons. There was no lack of display of extreme selfishness, which sometimes bordered on cruelty.

After the 'Big Hunt', in September 1943, in the forests of Volsov, the commander of the 'Kirov' brigade, captain Snichkin - Bielski's partisans were under his overall command - decided to separate the fighting men from the non-fighting family members. From then on the armed people formed the fighting Ordzonikidze Brigade named after the early Bolshevik leader under Soviet command of Captain Lyashenko.

Tuvia Bielski was appointed commander of the family unit. They camped in the old forests of Naliboki. All the groups that wandered in that area were ordered by the district partisan staff under the command of 'Platon' General Chernyshev who had been parachuted in from the Soviet Union to concentrate on the family camp. Those who were reluctant were threatened with severe penalties.

At the end of the summer of 1943 a process of concentration started, and the small groups were united into large family groups. Small groups of the former Bielski units and escapees from the ghetto also joined the new unit.

The Lida ghetto was eliminated on 18 September 1943. Soon after that, a group of fighting partisans from Lida joined the Bielski partisans in the forests of Volsov. At the same time, a base for a large family unit was organized in the forests of Naliboki. Its core was a group of forty people under the command of Israel Kesler. The base was established in the heart of the wilderness, about seven kilometres (just over four miles) from Naliboki, within a dense forest of birches and pine trees. Many small groups started to join them: those who were with the fighting partisans and those who were just wandering and looking for a refuge in a large Jewish partisan group.

Kesler organized the base and took care of the supplies for the future camp. He collected potatoes, which had remained in the abandoned villages that had been burned and destroyed by the Germans at the time of the 'Hunt'. He prepared storage to preserve the foodstuffs over the coming winter.

The Commander of the district under General Platon-Chernyshev ordered that, from then on, the camp would be an independent unit under the Commander of the Lida district. Bielski was appointed the commander of the unit. One branch of the unit was an armed platoon under the command of Tuvia Bielski's brother, Asael. Its task was to protect and supply the camp. Asael was often seen throughout the camp, riding on his horse and inspecting every corner. He was daring and devoted to his duties. His simplicity and honesty were reflected in his handsome, smiling and open face. He was friendly, loved by his companions and by the people under his command. After the return of the Soviets, Asael was conscripted into the Red Army and died soon afterwards on the Prussian front.

The elimination of the ghettos, labour camps and concentration camps in Byelorussia was completed. The last of the escapees from the ghettos and camps found shelter in Bielski's unit. Small groups of Jews from the forests of Krinicy near Stolpce, and of Jews from Mir who were hiding in the forests of Zlushin, near their town, joined the Bielski unit.

100 Jews from the labour camp of Koldychevo arrived. On the way they had met partisans from a Soviet Circassian unit who cruelly taunted and robbed them. In October 1943, 150 people arrived from the labour camp of Novogrudok, which was located in the buildings of the district court. These were the Jews who had managed to escape through an underground tunnel they had dug.

Jews from Novogrudok were the initial group of the Bielski unit. The camp grew month by month, and in the winter of 1944 there were 1,230 people in the unit. The Naliboki base of the camp had developed in the months from September 1943 until the liberation in July 1944 into an excellently organized camp. The stability of its existence in the last ten months made it look like a settlement, the atmosphere of a Jewish town was evident; a community whose population was the last remains of dozens of towns and villages which had been razed to the ground.

The camp was located in the heart of the Naliboki wilderness. Around it were hundreds of square kilometres of forests and marshes. The whole area was 'Partisan Country', a territory under Soviet rule surrounded by the Nazi enemy. All that large area was under the control of the partisan commands, which were growing, and who ruled and directed all that was happening in that area. On the edge of the forests, on the banks of the River Niemen, there were strong partisan groups, including 'Iskra' and 'Mit'kovtsy', who supervised the movements and carefully examined all comings and goings in the vicinity. Platoons of partisans from different units periodically left the wilderness to raid the villages and fringes of towns where German soldiers were encamped and to confiscate food and clothing for the people in the forest, right under the nose of the enemy.

Only in times of the 'Great Hunt', when the Germans deployed full military divisions, and dared to penetrate the wilderness with artillery, tanks and planes, only then did the partisan units retreat into the dense forests, looking for hiding places until the end of the 'Hunt'. Afterwards the 'Partisan Country' returned to normality.

In the autumn of 1943, after the 'Hunt', Soviet control of the Naliboki wilderness grew stronger. Hundreds joined the partisan groups: Byelorussian and Ukrainian policemen who realized that they had backed the wrong side, and were in a hurry to join the 'partisanka' to atone for their collaboration with the bitter enemy; residents of villages and towns who did not want to be sent as forced labourers to Germany; Jews, escapees from the ghettos and labour camps - all these people looked for a haven in the ancient forests.

The Germans destroyed all the Byelorussian villages, even the smallest hamlets, at the time of the 'Hunt'. Part of the population was sent to Germany as forced labour and the rest was ruthlessly eliminated on the spot. Often a person approaching Bielski's camp trudging along endless, winding, rough roads and crossing swamps on precarious plank tracks stumbled upon the ruins of these towns and settlements. Ruined peasants' huts would appear, charred chimneys, partly burnt fences, corpses of decomposed farm animals strewn around, stench in the air, and frightened cats meowing amidst the destruction.

For many months, the people from the Bielski camp went into those settlements, and to the ruins of Naliboki and Derevnoye, which were close by – between seven and ten kilometres (four and six miles) away, to collect anything that could be of use. From Naliboki and Derevnoye they brought whole parts of buildings, which could be useful, and also complete windows, heaters, boilers, barrels and kitchen utensils. They found all these strewn among the ruins. In September 1943 the camp people still went out every day in carts, dug the fields, collected potatoes in sacks, loaded them, and brought them to the camouflaged stores, to be kept for the winter months.

When the camps were first set up people lived in huts built out of pine branches. Small groups or individuals made provisional shelters ('succah', plural 'succot'). They spread soft branches on the ground and covered them with blankets and peasants' fur coats. From a distance the 'succot' looked like kennels. On wet autumn nights, the people who lived in them were soaked to the skin and were forced to get up, shivering in their wet clothes, to dry themselves in front of their bonfires.

The snows came and often, when we emerged from the 'succah' in the morning, the whiteness and sparkle of it surprised us. The commanders started the project of building larger huts, following the design of Ribinski, the building manager, who was appointed to supervise the project. Every person had a duty to take part in the work. To begin with, the foundations were dug, rectangles to the depth of 80-100 centimetres {31-39 inches}. Next, tree trunks from the forest were placed in the foundations. The trunks were held tightly together with barbed wire, and the spaces between the logs were filled with moss. The roofs of the huts were made of rough timber planks, topped with soil and camouflaged with tree branches. German planes often flew over, on reconnaissance missions, looking for partisans but the huts were well hidden in the dense forest.

At the entrance to the hut there was a door, followed just inside it by a couple of steps. It was dark in the hut and it took a while to get used to the thin light filtering through the open door, and through a tiny window in the opposite wall. These were wooden benches covered with straw along both sides of the wall. Forty people slept in each hut, side by side. In the middle of the hut stood a small iron stove, looted from one of the abandoned villages.

The huts were erected in two long rows, both sides of the 'main street'. Every hut had a number and even a nickname, depending on the origin of its occupiers or their trade. For example, hut number 11 was called 'intelligentsia': because the camp doctor Dr H., a woman dentist from Pinsk, the lawyer Volkovyski from Baranovichi, and a few other professional people lived there. The 'main street' was the major traffic route; it was always alive with people and all sorts of goings on. Men and women strolled in the street in their typical 'uniforms', partly peasants' garb, partly military, and a strange combination of peasants' furs. Their boots were made of light yellow leather, which was a product of the camp, and they wore army caps, Russian and German, or peasants' fur hats, and carried weapons gathered from different sources. Friends met here, as did groups of guests who frequented the camp.

The onlooker who watched the traffic at twilight could distinguish easily the rank and social importance of each person[1]. That ranking was established in the camp, and was understood by everyone. Even there, in the heart of the forest, the order was the same; social status played its part - and it drew people closer or kept them apart, bred arrogance and envy, gossip and bitterness. The commanders and their relatives, along with the scouts; were the elite. They galloped on their horses wearing leather coats and breeches high-status clothing with pistols in their belts. Their wives did the same, riding around in breeches, also armed with pistols. They behaved like salon ladies, their image reflecting an arrogant self-assurance and personal success. The elite had a kitchen to themselves, and good food, which made them feel even more special.

Of lower status were members of the two fighting platoons. They were the defence force, took part in battles, and were responsible for obtaining supplies. Their status symbol was the rifle, ever present on their shoulder. Their clothing was of lesser quality, gathered from wherever they could find it. They also felt important and behaved accordingly. They looked with disdain upon the 'Malbushim' the unarmed people. The members of the fighting platoons were tall, strong fellows, most of them sons of the lower class families from the towns and villages - small timber merchants, peddlers, coachmen and tradesmen. Their education was minimal, but they were close to the forest and adapted quickly to the conditions that existed in the camp.

Among the 'Malbushim' too, there were different class strata. Tradesmen involved in the food industry, especially the essential ones such as baking and sausage-making, enjoyed a better position than those whose trades were not as useful in the camp. At the bottom were the real 'Malbushim', who were employed in a range of service tasks within the camp-kitchen work, tree cutting and transporting, guarding the horses and cows and so on. They were the lowest class, the 'amcha' of the camp. They were instantly recognizable on the 'main street' by their untidy appearance, torn and patched clothing, thin and pale faces, and slow and heavy walk.

At night during the rainy season, the floor of the huts became a sticky swamp, and the cold dampness caused many inhabitants to suffer rheumatic pain in their leg and arm joints. Frequently, problems arose when people had to relieve themselves in the cold night; they walked like drunks and stumbled against the benches where other partisans slept. It was a nightmare to many, but eventually we became immune to it.

It was forbidden to light stoves or a bonfire during the day for fear of the German planes discovering the camp. Those without alternative jobs prepared wood for the fire. In the winter they went out in groups to the forest close to their huts to select dry birch trees. They cut them down, sawed them into short pieces, and brought them to the huts, where they split the logs. In the evenings they lit the iron stoves, which stood in the centre of each hut. They became red hot, and the hut dwellers huddled around enjoying the warmth. Sometimes water was boiled on the stove for laundering an only shirt, or for a wash. Some of the people, who sat close to the stove, held pine bark soaked with resin to rekindle the dying fire. Some held splits of pine tree which were used as candles in the long evenings, their dim light leaping on to the faces of the men and women who sat around drawn, thin, pale, weather beaten faces. They sat and entertained themselves by singing lively songs or by telling adventurous partisan or pre-war stories, in a special partisan style. Nightmarish memories of the Holocaust were never mentioned on those occasions. An intimate family atmosphere enveloped the group sitting around the stove. Sometimes the commander visited the huts, going from hut to hut, and taking part in their conversations.

In the winter[2] months, small groups started to build huts that would be more comfortable for themselves, in higher and drier places. The first builders were my wife and I and two other young, intelligent couples. After receiving permission from the commander, we started to build our hut a little further from the 'main street', on a higher spot. We went to the destroyed town of Naliboki and found a large window with its windowpanes intact, a door and an iron stove. We made three separate benches, a table, and chairs out of tree stumps. The window let through a pleasant bright light, and a crowded clump of birches, like a green wall, could be seen through it. Our new hut felt like 'home'; it looked to us like a splendid villa and we were proud of it. People from the camp came to feast their eyes on the miracle of 'architecture', and praised its relative comfort. In Naliboki we also found a large tin tub, in which we could bathe. In the forest it was a valued treasure. We dug a well near the hut and had water–it was dirty, but it still enabled us to wash every day. What a good life! In that same tin tub we laundered our clothes and boiled potatoes it was a wonder-utensil for universal use.

Others followed our example, and a little neighbourhood of small family huts appeared on the slopes of the hill above the main street – the 'villas' of the camp.

In our neighbourhood lived the camp Komissar, Shemyatoviec, with his young Jewish wife and father-in-law. He belonged to one of the Russian fighting partisan groups in the area, but when the chief of staff demanded that he should be separated from his family and they should be transferred to the family camp, he preferred to come with them and join our partisans. He was a true Russian, a middle aged man, fifty years or more, with a large Cossack moustache, an angry expression on his face, broad shouldered, and he moved in a heavy, bear-like fashion.

Shemyatoviec had met his wife near his partisan camp; she was with a group of Jews who wandered in the forest. He gave her and her father shelter and protection in his partisan hut. It was not a union made in heaven: she was eighteen years old, dark, tall, pale-faced with a Jewish prettiness, and there was never a smile on her face. Her father was the same age as his son-in-law, bearded and religious. We often saw him through the window of his hut, wrapped in 'talit' and 'tefilin' praying.[3]

In the evenings the father went to the tannery, which was used as a place in which to pray. Was that religious Jew happy with his Russian son-in-law, with whom he was made to live day and night? Was he suffering because his daughter was forced to be a wife to that man? No one could tell. There were many couples like that in the forest. The times and the hard forest life resulted in strange unions that would have been inconceivable in normal times. One of the couples who lived in our hut was like that. He was middle-aged, a crude man and a butcher; she was a widow who had lost her husband and sons, and went with the butcher because of his physical strength and his work in the sausage factory. All that made her life comfortable. Joining together as couples was premeditated. It is not, perhaps, surprising, that after suffering such traumatic family experiences, people were keen to start new family relationships and make themselves forget the past.

I have made a 'detour' to the 'villa' neighbourhood. Now I shall come back to the 'main street'. In the central street was the hut of Tuvia Bielski, the camp commander. Family huts of his relatives and friends were close by: his brother Asael Bielski, the Boldo family, Dzienciolski and others. The elite of the camp often met there, and spent time together there. Next to the commander's hut was the surgery, where every day Dr. Hirsh received the waiting sick. The dentist, a Jewish woman from Pinsk who turned up in our partisan camp, also worked there, used ordinary pincers to pull rotten teeth; there was a severe lack of equipment. However, both the doctor and dentist had nurses to assist them.

Further on, at the end of the street, was the camp's communal kitchen. Potato soup was cooked daily in a huge blackened boiler. A deep ditch was dug under the boiler, flames burst out of the smoking fire under it. A few boys, who worked in the kitchen, split tree stumps and threw them into the fire when necessary. The soup was usually thin and poor; it was a miracle if you managed to find some bones in it, which were sent from the sausage factory. Sometimes, in times of 'plenty', one could get some potatoes boiled in their skins. The commanders and their relatives and friends had food prepared in a separate kitchen, which was across the street. There was a great difference between the quality and the nutritional value of the food made in the two kitchens. This fact stirred up a lot of jealousy and anger, especially among the armed people, who demanded better food. In front of the common kitchen, long queues of people with eating utensils in their hands formed. The people standing in the queue regularly pushed each other in order to get the first servings, which were thicker, which caused many quarrels. The daily portions of bread were distributed at the same time.

The social differences influenced the way people ate. The partisans who went on 'farm' operations, took for themselves - whether it was permitted or not - products that they cooked in their huts. The communal kitchen was confined gradually to serving only the lower 'classes' of the camp, the 'malbushim', who had to make do with the thin, meagre portions given to them. A short distance from the huge kitchen, a bakery was built with a large oven, typical of that area. It was equipped with all the tools that could be found in the surrounding villages. Near the bakery was a primitive flour mill, where two horses circled around pulling heavy millstones which milled the flour. During the winter the bakery was a nice, place to keep warm. On the holiday of November 7, the anniversary of the Bolshevik Revolution, after the parade in the open air, in the square decorated with flags, the commanders met at the bakery, and enjoyed drinking brandy out of a barrel, which was brought from somewhere for the holiday.

Further on there was the bathhouse. The partisans were proud of this establishment; guests visiting the camp were taken to it and admired its excellent arrangements. The inhabitants of each hut bathed in a certain order from the early hours of the morning. There was also a room for disinfecting clothes within the bathhouse. This was vital, because the third Egyptian curse - lice - was very troubling to us all. And in spite of the ongoing struggle with them, the lice came again with greater force to trouble the partisans in their crowded huts.

An honourable place among the projects was held by the sausage-making factory, which was in a hut nearby. On one of the forays to the villages, a meat-mincer was found, which was a huge bonus. A separate structure for smoking the sausages was also built. Partisans from the neighbouring units brought cattle in exchange for sausages.

In the same area there was also a soap factory. Soap was made from a mixture of discarded cow's milk and ashes, and resembled a dark brown dough. There was not much of it, but it enabled the people to have a good wash and, now and then, launder their clothes.

Outside the 'main street' there was a fenced in area for the herd of cows owned by the camp. They grazed there, and their number reached at times up to sixty head. From the cow paddock, the horses of the camp could be seen in the distance grazing in the forest, fenced in by empty peasants' carts, with a few boys tending to their needs.

In the winter, during the long, freezing nights, packs of wolves roamed around, filling the air with their incessant howling, like crowds of women yelling desperately. Often, when the wolves drew closer, and their shining eyes could be seen in the dark, the guard on duty was forced to shoot in the air to frighten them off. Further out there was a muddy swamp with dense bushes and reeds. The incessant croaking of frogs always filled the air.

Further along the 'main street', was the nerve centre of the camp. The large square was flanked on one side by the centre of command and on the other by workshops. In the command room one could find the commander, Tuvia Bielski, and his brother Asael, the commander of the fighting platoons. Also there were Malbin, who was the chief of staff, Gordon, second in command, Pesach Fridberg from Novogrudok, the store man, and Volkovyski, a lawyer from Baranovichi who was the head of the 'special unit'. The operations were planned in the commander's room. Fighting units departed from there as well as units on missions to gather food from the farms. Everyday management was also concentrated in that room. There was the court, which dealt with cases of discipline in the unit and sentences were handed down with the help of Volkovyski, the lawyer. The camp prison was in a special hut.

The workshops were located in a wide and roomy hut. The sound of work could be heard from afar: the pounding of the sledgehammers and the digging machines, the hammering, the sawing of wood, the wild laughter and animated conversation, spiced with the partisan slang. The workshops were an organized project, which deserved praise. Dozens of craftsmen, divided according to their craft, worked away hut. Its tall ceiling and large windows that more than enough light into every corner of the building gave it the appearance of a factory. It looked as if you had found yourself in workshop of ages ago.

The individual workshops were separated by timber partitions. Several craftsmen worked in each of them. But not all crafts were concentrated in the central building; other production facilities were scattered all over the camp. Because of security or hygiene requirements, some had to be located at some distance from the centre.

All production lines were interconnected with each other. All the materials supplied by nature were utilized to the maximum. In the heart of the dense forest, much creative imagination was invested and lots of fruitful inventiveness was used to keep the supplies going. The carpenters made huge barrels for the tanners to soak the skins of the slaughtered animals; they made shelves for the storeroom, lasts for the cobblers and wooden soles for sandals. The tanners - among them were survivors of the Koldychevo camp - erected a tannery in a remote place. They supplied leather to the shoemakers, and a few weeks after the production started one could see the camp partisans wearing boots that had been made locally - they were instantly recognizable because of their raw light-yellow colour.

The saddlers made harnesses and saddles for the horses and belts for the partisans. The shoemakers were always loaded with work, because the people who arrived at the camp came with their shoes barely holding together after their long ordeals. There were always long queues of people wanting shoes. Some clients from other partisan groups came too, and paid the shoemakers with other essential products. Often that was reason enough to favour one client over another. Gifts and products were brought from the 'farm operations'. Some girls received their boots quickly, because their friends who came back from an expedition bestowed a suitable gift on the shoemaker. There were about a dozen craftsmen in the shoemakers' workshop, stooping and sewing new shoes and patching old ones, making sandals with wooden or rubber soles cut from tyres.

Opposite the shoemakers worked the tailors. They were also kept very busy by the demands of hundreds of partisans whose clothing was worn out and often needed patching. The tailors also received orders from other partisan units; often they received arms and cattle for their tailoring services.

Nightshirts made from coarse peasant cloth were also made in the tailors' workshop. The partisans brought the material from the surrounding villages. Most of them had to wear their nightshirt for a long time without changing. No wonder that the shirt, in spite of the disinfecting room in the bathhouse, hurt and tortured the body. However in the spring months of 1944 Soviet planes started to drop weapons into the dense forest. The parachutes they used were made of an excellent fine silk, which was used to make shirts and nightshirts. The partisan's pleasure, when he was awarded a shirt made out of fine light beige silk, was great.

You could get a haircut and a shave from one of the three barbers who worked near the workshops. Their instruments were blunt and scratched the skin ruthlessly, but there was no other choice. When not fighting on missions partisans took the opportunity to come to the barbershop to have a chat, to gossip about what was going on in the camp, to listen to news from the front, and to have a joke. The conversations, in typical partisan style were in Yiddish spiced with Russian expressions, mostly crude jokes. The girls tried to compete and outdo the men with their outrageous use of language.

At a little distance from the workshops was the smithy, where the blacksmiths shoed not only the camp's horses but the horses of a number of other partisan units in the area. One could hear the beating of the blacksmiths' hammers from far away. In a separate building mechanics worked cleaning and repairing arms. They put together new weapons, using old parts, as well. As the stock of the fighting units increased, more rifles and machine guns became available. The mechanics also served other partisans in the area and were rewarded with more arms, which the clients left in the camp.

In the spring the economic situation of the camp improved. New lines of production were initiated, the allocating of chores and tasks became more efficient, and almost everyone in the camp was employed and productive. Hundreds of people were involved in camp activities. They made an effort to forget their loneliness, the loss of their loved ones, and all the traumatic experiences that they had been through only a short time before. Being productive helped the partisans to adapt to the forest's conditions, and was a blessing to many of them. Sometimes the camp sent its own experts to fulfil important tasks in other units, such as the printers who published papers for the partisans in Russian and Byelorussian. These workshops helped to save hundreds of people from the jaws of the enemy, and generally raised the morale in the 'land of the partisans'. They contributed to fortifying the battle against the Nazi conqueror. The non-military workshops also fulfilled partisan missions that cannot be ignored. Their efforts were also part of the struggle of the whole partisan movement.

Bielski's camp contained hundreds of people who, in the pre-war days, would have required continuous medical treatment. Some would have been hospitalised; yet others would have been buried in the cemetery. But in the partisan forest, apparently, this did not follow. One would think that the harsh life and physical abuse in the ghettos, the wandering without a roof over their heads, with no place to lie down and no protection from the elements, the unhygienic food and lack of nutritious meals, would have destroyed the strongest of men. But amazingly, in Bielski's camp almost no one died. As far as I can remember the typhus plague killed only one person, a young partisan whom we buried in the camp.

Had it not been for the Germans and their allies, there would have been almost no need for a cemetery in the forest. The angel of death took a holiday; the few escapees from the ghettos the concentration camps and the 'hunts' bore the lot of the partisan and hope for the end of the war. Old people, women and children wandered for weeks in the swampy forests. The sun assaulted them during the day and dampness tormented them at night, when they permitted themselves a short nap on the soggy ground while their stomachs shrank because of hunger. Yet, in spite of all that, no one among them lagged behind because of fatigue. The sick and feverish were forced out of their sick beds to flee. They dragged themselves along as best they could, usually their sickness was forgotten and, somehow, they survived.

When we escaped from the Lida ghetto, a deep wound developed on my wife's left leg, exuding pus. Her leg was swollen, it looked like blood poisoning, and she was in excruciating pain which prevented her from walking. But how could we stop, when the ground was burning under our feet? There was nowhere we could go for medical help, and the enemy was all around us. My wife continued walking, or rather hopping on one foot, and she did so for days and days, while every muscle in her body was crying out in pain. As we made our way at night through slush and muddy clay, she was forced to walk with both legs deep in mud and in filthy, cold water. But as it happened, this was her saving; the mud cured the infection - the swelling diminished and the wound started to heal.

Pregnant women, or those who had just given birth, left their hospital beds to find refuge in the depths of the forest. They all walked day and night without showing signs of fatigue that anyone would notice, while fleeing the horrific enemy.

I remember one woman, a young, lonely widow whose husband had perished in Lida. Grieving and looking for consolation she had a short love affair with a partisan. As a result, she, like many other women partisans, turned to Dr. Hirsh the camp doctor for an abortion. We were still living then in our temporary 'succot', while the work groups were digging the foundations for our new huts. Dr. Hirsh took the woman out of her group of diggers, went with her to one of the uncompleted huts, and asked for my wife's help. My wife held the patient and the operation was done quickly. The woman lay on the bench, and did not make a sound. After a short while she came out, pale and shaky on her legs, and rejoined the group of diggers as if nothing had happened.

The bespectacled Dr. Hirsh always smiling, very thin, his clothes in tatters, holding his surgical case, which contained his instruments and medicines, he fulfilled his role faithfully. He was widely known as an expert in abortions, and women partisans arrived from the most distant units for his help, usually leaving after a few hours, relieved of their burden. His wife, a qualified nurse, usually helped him with these operations. For his services the doctor received different payments such as pork fat and flour, which were unimaginable treasures in the forest. From the partisans who went out on 'farm operations', the doctor asked for food products; from people with means he asked for gold coins. Gossip circulated in the camp that the bag, around the doctor's neck, was gradually filling with gold coins. But those Bielski's camp partisans who could not pay had the operation for free. Dr. Hirsh was polite and ever ready for his task. One could meet him in the morning hours, in his surgery, a hut on the 'main street' near commander

Bielski's hut. There he received his patients, who waited in a queue. Helping him were a few qualified nurses including his wife, and Chana Rivak from Novogrudok. In the afternoon the doctor made 'home visits', hurrying from hut to hut to treat bedridden patients. Then every day he went to the isolated 'hospital', one and a half kilometres {a mile} from the camp. He travelled in a wagon pulled by a 'skeleton' of a horse.

The groups of partisans who went out hunting in the area for supplies were ordered to look for medicines. Farmers who acted as contact men obtained medicines, which they ordered in the towns and delivered them to the partisans. But there was always a shortage, even of the basic of medicines, in the forest.

The doctor resided in hut number 11 – the hut that was called Intelligentsia and which housed forty people in all. I was his nearest neighbour, and I saw that he did not sustain his personal hygiene nor the hygiene of his children. He did not take advantage of the washing facilities which were available and he was shabbily dressed, when we brought our meagre, often revolting, meals to our hut from the communal kitchen, the doctor, with all the seriousness of an expert, convinced us that there might be some vital nutritious ingredients in our bowls. *'There is no need to get overanxious!'* he would say. He spiced his talk with a few scientific terms, and eventually we made ourselves swallow the food.

The typhus plague recurred every year in the partisans' units. It spread into the Bielski camp after the partisans of the Zhukov brigade decided to leave the forest of Naliboki to move to a distant place. The Zhukov commanders permitted the Bielski partisans to collect whatever was left after the brigade's departure. In exchange we had to take care of their wounded, their sick and a number of women whom they could do without. We collected kitchen utensils and food products; parts of weaponry, horses, cows and clothing such as peasants furs, trousers and boots.

A short time after, the typhus plague erupted in our camp and we connected it to the gifts we had received from the Zhukov brigade. There had been a few cases of typhus in that brigade, and with the clothing came lice that carried the contagious disease. It played havoc in our camp. Every day, many times a day, the wagon was busy taking feverish people to the 'hospital'. Rivak Shlomo, who had been a teacher in Novogrudok, was responsible for transferring the sick to Dr. Hirsh's hut. The pace was hectic, the hospital huts were crammed, and the overcrowding started to worry the commanders. A qualified nurse from Minsk, devoted to her profession, worked in the hospital. She was the wife of the director and theatre actor from Minsk, Shchesnovich, who was one of the partisans.

There was a shortage of the simplest of drugs in the hospital. We cured the sick with a relatively healthy diet and boiled water as their only drink. (As usual we drank filthy water from the shallow wells we dug near the huts). The multitude of the dangerously sick people did not have any other medicine but, in spite of the extent of the disease, most of the sick recovered. Rivak's wagon started to take the convalescing people back to the camp. They were weak, skeletal, a dreadful sight. They were given a cup of milk a day, and satisfying meals for lunch and supper which came from the commander's special kitchen.

The quarrels, the personal frictions and the tension were more acute than usual in the crowded huts, but this was to be expected under the circumstances. There was only one mentally ill person in the camp, a seventeen-year-old boy, Yankl. In the ghetto, German soldiers had severely beaten him around his head with their rifle butts. Yankel was a lonely, neglected boy, in torn clothes. He wandered aimlessly about the camp, his madness reflected in his eyes. During the heavy bombardments, when everything was collapsing all around us, Yankel would stroll around; no one could convince him to hide. However much they tried; he just went on wandering.

Daily life in our hut was stressful, verging on the manic, but there was no room to escape to real madness. People in the camp preferred to escape to health, to strengthen their minds and bodies, to use their vitality, whatever they had, to continue the struggle. With hyperactivity and sometimes aimless activity, we tried to distract our minds from the terrors of our lives.

Sleep in the camp was mostly restless. We got out of bed a lot to urinate, especially during the rainy season, when the earth in the hut was wet; and people often tripped over each other in the dark. The atmosphere in the hut at night was always restive; people did not have nightmares, at least that seemed the case with most of my relatives. We dreamed a lot about food. One of our neighbours, Sonya, a lively girl who lived in our hut with her mother, used to relate in the morning her culinary dreams. *'I dreamed about a plate full of gefilte fish and you, Mum, grabbed it from under my nose. Why did you do it Mum?'* asked the girl. The listeners implored the girl to continue her description of that gefilte fish plate and the rest of the delicacies she had enjoyed in her sleep.

There were a few dozen children in the camp. They used to gather together and watch that was going on. They were near the commander's room when units departed for operations and when the partisans returned from their missions; they followed guests from other partisan units, who visited our camp; they were at every corner, wandering between the huts, and they never took their eye off the ball. In their tattered clothing, these waifs looked like lost creatures from a different world. They had come to the heart of the wilderness – the great forest - on their parents' shoulders. They had been carried for days, fleeing from the Germans, from the ghetto, or during the 'hunt'.

I remember a small girl in our group of Lida Jews, which slowly meandered toward the Naliboki camp in the forest. October's cold rains and the misty nights, which we spent on the damp ground, weakened the girl. She was feverish, and her parents could hardly carry her; she was slowly deteriorating in front of our eyes. Then one evening, at twilight, her father managed to catch a wild pigeon with his hat. He killed it and cooked it for his daughter. She felt better and in time returned to good health.

With time all the children grew stronger; they got used to the forest and learned to withstand the hardship of life there. I cannot recall a child dying in Bielski camp. During typhus plagues, the children suffered too, but recovered quickly in spite of the dreadful conditions. There was one boy, about fifteen years of age, Y. Epstein tall, skinny and fragile. He came to the forest with his older sister, their parents were gone. He visited me often, craving knowledge, alert and asking many questions; he was a terrific listener. He caught typhus and we were fearful that his sickly body would not withstand the disease. But after a few weeks the boy returned from the 'hospital', a walking skeleton. But soon he started to grow again and the symptoms of the disease disappeared. He grew taller and became a handsome, broad-shouldered fellow, only to be killed by the retreating German soldiers in June 1944. We buried him with eight other victims before we left the camp in the wilderness.

A young couple from Mir settled in one of the huts. They had a baby just a few weeks old who gave them a lot of trouble at night. It is a wonder how those parents had managed to reach the depths of the forest. One autumn morning the mother screamed that the baby was not breathing. The camp doctor decided that he had been suffocated by his mother's body while sleeping as a result of over-crowdedness. The parents cried for many days and for a long time they were inconsolable.

Other children grew without any supervision. They peeped into every corner of the camp it seemed as if they were studying the residents; they knew all their comings and goings. They adopted the coarse partisans' language, and loved to spice their talk with loud curses, like the best of the partisans, who kept the Russian cursing heritage going. These youngsters knew all that happened in the huts and gossiped like the adults.

Older boys were recruited for farm work. Some guarded the herd of cows and horses and helped the people responsible for the cowshed and stables. They took the cows to graze, and also helped in the kitchen. Some of them found occupation in the workshops and became apprentices. A few children learned carpentry and others became apprentice shoemakers. Coming out of the forest, they could boast that they would be able to make a living because they had learned a trade in the 'partisanka'. A few boys aged thirteen and fourteen, kept the communication lines open between the Lida ghetto and the forest. On a few occasions they managed to smuggle Jews out from the ghetto; they never feared the most dangerous of operations.

The children assembled in the morning, after the first milking, with tins in their hands, in order to get their daily portion of milk. The leftovers were given to women, old people and the frail. The children tried to compensate for the severe deficit of nourishment in their diet by collecting the red berries that grew on tiny bushes during the winter. Groups of children looked for the red berries that peeped through the snow on a sunny day. Their happy voices rang in the forest.

In the summer the children filled their tins with blackberries or raspberries, and brought them back to their parents. Sometimes, when hunger troubled them, the adults joined the children and collected mushrooms and sorrel. They also cut the birch tree bark with knives and collected the oozing sap. Then they cooked swamp berries in the juice. The result was a thin, sweet-and-sour compote with a sharp medical smell that felt so reviving. Those juices, Dr. Hirsh told us, immunized our bodies, and the nutrients in them added something to the two daily portions of thin potato soup that most people survived on.

Confronting the neglect among the camp's children, the leadership decided to create a learning environment, like a school. Dozens of children congregated every day and spent time together in a special hut, under the supervision of the woman partisan, Tsesya. They went on excursions with her, they did gymnastics and they played team games. They also were taught traditional songs.

Preparations for festivities[4] were one of the important operations of this education group. For Purim, the children made masks for their parents and other adults. In the afternoon, every one in the group assembled to watch the performance on a specially prepared stage in the hut. It was a winter day, with wind and whirlpools of snow. We watched the children sing, and recite in Yiddish or in Russian. They were dressed up for the holiday in white shirts and red ties. They did gymnastics and they danced, with the beauty of innocence on their faces and in their bodies. With tears in our eyes the audience followed the performance. Old, hidden memories came back, memories that had been blunted by the harsh reality of the partisans' existence. The wounds of the bereaved parents started to bleed again. By being hectically active they had tried to forget their sorrow, but with the performances all their lost loved ones reappeared.

Suddenly, after a dance of a pretty group of children, the Political Commissar, A Shlachtovic, stood up and shouted in Yiddish: '*Where are my children? Revenge! Revenge!*' His freckled red face became even redder under his mop of red hair. He drew out his pistol and shot into the air. And again he cried: '*Revenge, revenge!*' At last he left the hut, but the audience sat glued to their seats, their heads lowered and the sounds of stifled weeping could be heard.

It was as if cruel reality had burst through the dark wooden walls of the workshops. Those innocent children reminded us what should have been. Their childish gaiety congealed inside us turning into a terrible cry and lamentation. Finally we lifted ourselves us from our seats, drying our eyes, and departed.

Time passed, the snow thawed, the birch trees started to put out green leaves, the air was perfumed with aromas of the forest, and above the top of the trees a soft spring sun was shining. The expectation of change grew daily. Every evening people congregated in the square near the commander's hut, eager for encouraging news. Scouts, or guests from the partisan units who had a wireless, brought us news from the front and messages from the chief of staff of the Red Army. Connection by air with Moscow across the German lines was improving all the time. More frequently, Soviet planes landed on the airstrip in the wilderness near Poldoruzshka. The partisans of our unit, under the command of Assoel Bielski, guarded it for a number of weeks.

The scope of the partisan attacks on the German lines of communication grew considerably. During the nights, thousands of partisans would raid the railways over a huge area and sabotage them, blowing up trains and cutting the enemy's movement for long periods. Echoes of explosions could be heard at night from all directions. The partisans called those operations 'concerts'.

The towns and villages were filled with Ukrainian collaborators – including Kuban Cossacks who had been brought with the retreating German army from inside Russia. They were stationed in the Byelorussian villages. There were many clashes with them, and as a result supply of provisions for the camp became harder to obtain.

Sometimes we received Soviet newspapers, which were parachuted from planes with other supplies. We read them eagerly, trying to draw our own conclusions. Occasionally some German papers fell into the hands of the partisans out on operations; we read them too, compared them, trying to read between the lines. The partisans' chief of staff issued broadsheets in Russian and Byelorussian. These were distributed in the area among the local population and the partisans. They were printed in the forest on tiny dark yellow pages, crammed with printed letters. So we did have some good information, and every now and then we assembled the partisans together for political lectures and debate.

The German front collapsed and the Red Army advanced. Names of liberated places became more and more familiar. The Red Army penetrated Pole'je and Volyn, and liberated Pinsk and Rovno. Ferocious battles went on during April near Tarnopol. The First of May festivities in 1944 were accompanied by encouraging messages from the front, which was advancing towards us, bringing liberation.

The celebration of the First of May[5] that year was a very festive occasion. In the afternoon everyone in the camp congregated in the square in front of the commander's hut, red flags were flying and the huts were decorated. It was a brilliant day, the spring sky was high and peaceful, and about 1,200 people stood in the wide square. On three sides were the fighting units, the scouts and the mounted units, their horses beautifully turned out and the armed platoons headed by their commanders. On the fourth side stood unarmed people in military uniform.

In the centre of the square stood the commanders, headed by Tuvia Bielski. He read to us the message of the Red Army chief of staff. It said that the war effort had succeeded and that after fierce battles over many weeks Tarnopol had been conquered and the enemy had retreated in panic. Applause and shouting interrupted his words. After that the commander gave a short speech: '*Shortly we will take the war to the Nazi beast's den in Germany, and there we will exterminate him. We partisans have taken our part in the struggle against the cruel enemy.*

The front is coming close fast, we can expect hard days ahead of us and we must be ready for them. Victory is looking us in the face'.

What a joy it was, to hear those words! Everyone was excited. The rule of evil was collapsing, the day we had hoped for, the day of payback and revenge, was approaching. That hope strengthened most of the people; it gave meaning to their sufferings, meaning to their worst moments. We danced and sang late into the night. But there was a hidden anxiety that everyone had, but no one talked about: 'What would happen to us when we return home? We, the last of our people, the remnants; how would we continue?'

In June 1944 the Soviets broke the front near Vitbesk and advanced rapidly towards Minsk. The German army retreated in panic from wide areas of eastern Byelorussia, and many German divisions were surrounded near Minsk. At night, one could hear from a distance the sounds from the front - a constant hum and noises like muffled thunder. At night we sat long at night, on the grass in front of our huts, waiting for the signs of the storm which would bring our redemption. Excitement and tension in the camp grew stronger every day as the echoes from the front grew louder.

Scattered groups of German soldiers, trying to escape the Soviet encirclement, started to appear in the area and instructions came to be on our guard. The armed platoons of Bielski's partisans operated against the German soldiers who wandered in the forest. The partisans lay in ambush on roads and tracks that crossed the wilderness, and eliminated many German units. Our armed units also clashed a few times with German groups. No prisoners were taken; they were all killed on the spot. Two of our members were wounded in battle, and one of them had to be taken to hospital.

Our roles changed. The partisans hunted down Germans, and their mood was elated. Our armed units enjoyed the activity; every evening they returned, flushed and excited with new stories about their encounters in the forest. They savoured the sweet taste of revenge. Four German prisoners were brought before the camp commanders. Three were young. The fourth, who was older, was crying. Two of them said that they were Communists and blamed the others for being Nazis. Only one kept his 'identity' and continued to curse the Jews. They were executed in the camp in front of all of us.

The partisan chief of staff called repeatedly on the camp to be at the ready. It was not known how events would develop. The front could shift to our part of the wilderness and it was possible that the Germans would penetrate the forests and employ all their power in battle. We had to be on guard. We were prepared for evacuation at any moment, night or day. There were trial evacuations to train the people for a fast departure - taking a matter of minutes. Detailed instructions were given; new locations in the forest for each unit were decided upon; tasks were allotted. We lived in an atmosphere of constant tension. Rumours chased rumours, one contradicting the last. We swung between desperation and anticipation. Alternately, we saw in our imagination the Red Army saving us and the Germans attacking us. Since the big 'hunt' in July 1943, we had gained experience, and we were ready to use it when necessary, and to find cover in the great swamps of the forest.

Once, in the early hours of the morning, we were woken by shots coming from the camp's central square. We could clearly hear German voices, loud orders, screams and curses. Bullets whistled over our heads. We ran out of the hut and hid in the undergrowth. The bullets continued to come. We ran down to the swamp and lay down between the dense reeds, gripped with terror. After a while there was silence. And then we found out that a group of a 100 German soldiers was marching through the forest and had surprised our people. Our armed partisans were away, and guarding the camp had been forgotten. The Germans had got into a few huts surprising people in their sleep. They seriously wounded Gordon, the deputy commander, who was sleeping on his bench. They threw a hand grenade into one of the communal huts and shot a few people on their way. But they had to retreat quickly. The partisans in the area heard the shots and came back. The Germans left the camp, but they were brought to battle by the partisans, who chased and eliminated them.

That sudden raid by the Germans on our camp cost us nine lives. Among the dead was Gordon[6], who was wounded in the stomach and died after a few hours of terrible suffering, Epstein the sixteen year old boy who had survived typhus, Patzovski and Ostashinski.

After an hour, a scout unit of the Red Army passed by near the camp. We all went towards them. We encircled the dusty, sweaty figures, hugged them, shook their hands and kissed them. '*Welcome, comrades, redeemers*', we cried.

The soldiers continued on their mission and we returned to the camp - liberated!

Nothing was left for us to do in that camp but to bury our dead. On the hill behind the 'main street' we dug a common grave, the commander delivered a short eulogy, and a salvo of gunshots ended the sad ceremony.

With heavy steps, our heads bowed, we went to spend our last night in the huts. It was a restless night. I sat outside the door, unable to sleep. In the darkness I recognized the tall figure of a man, who was walking slowly. It was the theatre director and actor of the state theatre, Shchesnovich, a Russian, who had been transferred to us after his partisan unit had dispensed with its entire group of non-fighting men. '*Going home comrade?*' he asked me, '*Very soon we will be back at our places and will start anew*'. '*You, comrade, are going home,*' I answered him, '*It might be a destroyed home, but a home that you will be able to rebuild. We have got nowhere to return to. Nothing remains of our homes. We will go to our home towns, but only to say goodbye.*'

In the early hours of the next morning we vacated the camp. An order was given to destroy the huts, so that 'White' anti-Soviet partisans would not be able to use them. We smashed the windows, destroyed the doors and benches, filled in the wells, and buried our tools. Afterwards an order was given to take only the things we could carry on our backs. Only two wagons for the wounded followed the marching people. There was a long way ahead of us, fraught with unexpected dangers, and we had to be alert. The commander, riding on his horse, scanned the marching people. One of the members of our partisan unit, 'P' did not follow the instruction and was pushing a cart loaded with personal items. He was shot on the spot, in front of his wife and his small child who sat in the cart. The woman screamed a desperate scream, which shattered all of us. It was a tragic end. The camp that had been established to save Jewish life from the hands of the Nazis, ended its existence with the murder of a Jew and the destruction of a Jewish family. The suffering woman cried for days, and her screams accompanied us all the way. We marched traumatized through the forest. The corpses of German soldiers in their uniforms and the corpses of animals were scattered among the tall trees. We passed the Kroman Lake, its blue water seen between the tree trunks, and continued to walk into the dense forest. The summer heat was oppressive. We walked tired and sweating. Bluish mist started to envelope the forest undergrowth, which became denser. A smell of smoke reached us. The forests were burning. The battles that were being fought there caused fires that spread quickly. Huge areas went up in flames, clouds of bluish-grey smoke filled the air, choking us and making our eyes water. We could see the silhouettes of burning trees; the fire licked the bushes, climbed up the trees and spread towards the horizon. We marched in a landscape of flames, in the depth of the forest, a small distance from the sea of fire.

At last we reached the Niemen and the fire stopped. We camped under the sky. We marched like that for a few days. Leaving the wilderness, we came to a busy road and marched through the village of Shchorsy. The residents came out of their huts, looking with surprise in their eyes: 'So many Jews! So many Jews!'

At the beginning we marched in a military fashion with the armed units in front of us and behind us. Later, people dispersed, walking in groups, slowly, in the heat of the day. We advanced with heavy hearts. As we came closer to areas that were once Jewish, the extent of our catastrophe became clearer. It looked as if flames had devoured everything that was Jewish, had burnt to cinders our past, our homes and our loved ones. And now we prepared to re-entered that scorched earth.

Then on the horizon we could see the houses of Novogrudok. We slept outside the town in a farmhouse with a big yard and threshing floors. We stretched ourselves on the chaff, exhausted from the long march. The next day we explored the town. The people from Novogrudok, who were members of Bielski's unit, took us to the places where the ghetto had been. We stood at the extermination sites, near graves of thousands of ghetto victims. The people of Novogrudok brought up memories. They walked, mourning in their own town, and so did we.

That was how all of us would return to our destroyed homes. That was the welcome that every Jew could expect on his return to the ruins of his community. We walked around the houses in what was once a ghetto. Christians were living there. Strange apathetic eyes stared at us through the windows. Those were our inheritors. The Jewish community was completely erased.

Hundreds of German prisoners were concentrated in a fenced-off yard. Through the fence we stared at those figures. A short time ago they had brought with them murder and extermination; now their eyes were dull. They were lying on the ground weak and impotent.

So the day passed. In the evening, after our walk around the town, the partisans assembled on the slope of the ancient castle for a liberation celebration. Thousands of partisans from all over the forest crowded into the wide square, and the ruins of the castle were lit with a searchlight. The speakers - partisan commanders and officers of the Red Army - stood on a stage below the castle wall. They raised the flag of the liberator, the Red Army. The army delegates praised the partisan struggle that had struck the Nazi conqueror in the rear helping in its defeat.

The partisans' last assembly was on the following day, at the farmyard where we were staying. We stood in a rectangle, the commander gave a short speech, and every one received a partisan certificate. We parted with warm handshakes and went to the centre of the town. We had to go back to our pre-war towns; the saga of the forest was at an end.

The story of the partisan newspaper in the forests deserves a mention. Eliyahu Dameshek from Lida, who reached the partisans in 1943, had the idea of building a printing press in the wilderness, to inform the partisans and the general population of the district. Dameshek returned to the Lida ghetto and with the help of the partisans from the Russian unit 'Iskra', which was then camped on the banks of the Niemen, he brought the entire printing house of Shapira (who was also a member of the Bielski's partisans) to the camp. The printing presses were brought in cases in a farmer's wagon by a man trusted by the partisans, to the 'Iskra' camp, in an operation that lasted eighteen days. Dameshek moved to the dense forest of Lipichanski following the orders of General Platon. There, near the area controlled by the 'Lenin brigade', they built the printing house. The first partisan paper in the area was published there, its name was 'Krasnoye Znamia' (Red Flag), and it was issued three times a week. Later, the printing house was moved to the forests near Slonim, where the team of printers was augmented by parachutists who came from the Soviet lines.

The newspaper deeply influenced the local population and encouraged it -especially on the eve of the repeated recruitment to German labour forced camps - to abandon their villages and join the partisans in the forests.

Dr. Shmuel Amarant,
historian with the
Bielski group

Notes:
* This essay first appeared in the Pinkas Navaredok, Tel Aviv 1963. Translated from Hebrew by Aviva Kamil; edited and annotated by Michael Kagan (MK).
1 The social stratification of the camp, while unpopular and the cause of considerable complaint, was absolutely necessary since the detachment had to act as an authentic, fully Soviet structure. Thus the party members and the commanders enjoyed priviliges that others could only dream about. A true reminder of Orwell's quip: All are equal except some are more equal than others.
2 This is probably a mistake since it was impossible to build in the winter because of the frozen earth. These houses were actually built in early spring (March) as the ground thawed out.
3 Any expression of religious activity was forbidden in the camp due to the need to preserve the strict Soviet façade. It was this façade that gave the Bielskis the stamp of true comrades of the Soviet Union and won them the respect of General Platon and the other Soviet commanders without which they would not have been able to survive.
4 Such activities were extremely dangerous. Communist informers were everywhere and any hint that the Bielski detachment was not fully Soviet e.g. that they were practicing Judaism, would have put them in extreme danger.
5 The Bielski Detachment was forced to act in all ways like true Soviet patriots. Tuvia often would talk about 'defending the Soviet Union' as their primary goal while downplaying the Jewish aspect and significance of what he was doing.
6 This tragedy on the last day before liberation robbed the Bielskis of one of their finest heros. Tanchel (Tankhel) Yefimovich Gordon, born in Radun, was a barber in Vasilishki (a small town in Grodno region). When the Soviets came in 1939 he was a secretary at the executive committee. Gordon joined the Bielskis in April 1943 together with other Jews from the Lida ghetto. He was appointed a deputy commander on political matters some time in 1944, at the very end. He had been a friend of General Platon before the war and it was this friendship that won the trust between the Jewish warrior and the Soviet warrior.

Surviving the Holocaust with the Russian Jewish Partisans
Jack (Idel) Kagan

I was born in 1929 in Novogrodek to a unique family. Two brothers married two sisters - and harmony reigned in the house! Although we had two houses, we lived in one. Everything was togetherness; the most important thing in life was family. My father Yankel was a businessman. My mother, Dvore, was a businesswoman who looked after our two shops, where we sold the saddles and sandals produced in our workshops. I had a sister, Nachama, two years older than myself.

We were a middle-class family; we were not short of anything. Novogrudok had a Jewish population of between 6,000 and 6,500, which made up half the town's inhabitants. There were really no problems between the Jews and the local population - until 1935, when the situation began to change. Poles from western Poland started to settle in our town, bringing strong feelings of anti-Semitism with them. The Jews lived in the centre of the town, and most of the shops belonged to them; they formed the majority of the professional people. Jewish community life was organized through the synagogues and guilds. There were all sorts of Jewish institutions-hospitals, Hebrew schools, orphanages-and there was a Jewish theatre, a library, a Jewish bank and Yiddish newspapers.

All this changed on 17 September 1939. War had broken out on the first day of September and we were very worried about a probable German occupation. But on the afternoon of 17 September we heard the roar of Soviet tanks coming down the street. Some Jews cried with joy, because the alternative to the Red army was occupation by the Germans. But our life changed. We had to close down our shop, as private enterprise was not allowed. We had to close all the shops and workshops, and stop going to the synagogue, because the use of the Hebrew language was not allowed. Everything Jewish connected with religion or Palestine had to stop. Every institution that was Jewish had to change. Our lives became totally different. The wealthier business people were arrested during the night and sent to Siberia, together with the leaders of the community. Thinking back on it now, I realize that the Russians wanted to destroy our rich Jewish culture.

Then on 22 June 1941 the war between Germany and the Soviet Union broke out. By the following day the whole Russian army was in retreat. We knew that we would suffer under the Germans; we expected labour camps and imprisonment, but never imagined that they would try to liquidate us all. I remember the discussion between my father and my uncle. *'There is no point in running. We are used to work. They won't kill us!'* And so we stayed.

On 24 June 1941 the town was bombed. Four days later, planes flew overhead and dropped incendiary bombs. Most of the town was burnt down. Large numbers of people lost their lives. We, the Kagan family, lost everything. I was left with a pair of short trousers and a shirt. We found an empty house and moved in with about eight other families.

The Germans entered Novogrudok on 4 July 1941 and immediately started enforcing anti-Jewish laws. Yellow stars had to be worn on the front and back of our clothes, Jews were not allowed to walk on the pavement, and everyone from the age of twelve to sixty had to report for work. My father and uncle worked as saddle-makers. My mother, aunt and others, including myself, worked on clearing up the bombed streets. For that we were issued food cards for 300 grams {10.5 ounces} of bread and potatoes. Jews lost their rights of citizenship, which meant that if someone wanted to rob you (and many did) there was no point in complaining to the authorities, because you had no protection.

On Saturday 26 July 1941, some Jewish men were rounded up by the local police and taken to the Market Square, where a group of SS men were waiting. I was near the Market Square at the time, and hid behind the ruins of a burned-out house. I heard shots being fired and an orchestra playing music. I waited there for quite a while and when I reached home, I heard the awful news that the SS had selected fifty-two men and shot them. Jewish women were ordered to wash the blood off the cobblestones. From time to time after that, groups of Jews were rounded-up in the street and told that they were being sent to work. But later we would find out that they had been shot a short distance from town.

On Friday, 5 December 1941, posters appeared stating that as from six o'clock that evening no Jews could leave town and that the next morning all Jews must assemble at the courthouse. They could only take with them whatever they could carry. Saturday was a bitterly cold day, -20 degrees centigrade. All 6,500 Jews assembled in the yard of the courthouse. We waited all day in the cold. Late in the afternoon, they opened the doors and there was just about room for us all to stand inside. We did not sleep that night.

We were locked up there all Saturday and Sunday. On Sunday, the Wehrmacht (the German army) arrived and took a party of about 100 men to build a fence around twenty-eight houses in the suburb of Peresika. They were creating a ghetto. Early on Monday morning, 8 December 1941, lorries arrived with the SS and local police. We had to form a line, families together. The head of the family had to approach the SS man, and two questions were asked: 'Profession?' and 'How many children?' The SS man, just signalled with his gloved hand-right or left: life or death. My uncle went first with his family. *'Profession?' 'Saddle-maker.' 'How many children?' 'Two children'.* The signal from the SS man was to the left. My father followed: Saddle-maker; two children, signal to the right. In all 5,100 people were selected to the left and taken to the village of Skridlevo. They were beaten-up on entering the forest, and ordered in groups of fifty to lie face down on the ground. From there, again in groups of fifty, they had to hand over all their valuables, undress in the bitterly cold weather, and were driven into freshly dug pits where they were shot. That day we lost my uncle Moshe and aunt Shoshke their younger son Leizerke, and Berele from Karelitz. Berl, by some miracle, survived. It was an appalling blow to us all. The remaining 1,500 of us were taken to Peresika, where the ghetto had been formed. It was very small. We built bunks, about 60 centimetres (approximately two feet) of space per person. If you turned over in the night, you would wake up the nine other people who slept in your row.

It was an 'open' ghetto, which meant we had to go out to work. My father worked as a saddler, and my mother stitched fur gloves for the German army. I worked in the Russian barracks, along with about 250 men. The work was hard, and I had a four kilometre walk to work {two and a half mile}. I was barely thirteen years old - I believe I was the youngest worker in the barracks. After a while I was transferred to a better job - transporting stones in a wheelbarrow. This work was also hard, and I received plenty of beatings too.

Various regulations were being issued daily against the Jewish population. From beginning of May 1942, Jews from the surrounding towns and villages were brought to Novogrudok. Altogether the ghetto came to hold about 6,500 people, making it incredibly overcrowded. It is difficult to describe the misery of that time. People walked around aimlessly, knowing that they were sentenced to death but not knowing when the execution would take place. Yet there was nowhere to run.

One day at the beginning of July, we arrived for work as usual. At lunchtime, I drifted away from the workplace, as I had done every day, to search for cigarette ends or pieces of bread, which the German soldiers might have thrown out. Suddenly, from nowhere, a German soldier jumped out at me shouting '*Raus, raus du verfluchter Jude!* (Out, out, you cursed Jew!)' I felt a crack from his rifle butt and he pushed me into the middle of the barracks square together with about fifty other people.

The SS troops surrounding our group shouted insults at us and made us line up in a single row. Within a few minutes a machine gun was assembled. I thought they were going to shoot us, and my legs turned to jelly. They kept us there for a long time but, eventually, a high-ranking SS officer arrived. He did not say anything but just released us and we went back to work. After that, I went to work with my father to learn the craft of saddle-making. Father was friendly with the foreman, who had given permission for me to join.

On 7 August 1942 we arrived at work as usual, and immediately we were surrounded by the police and the SS. There were about 500 of us, men and women. At the same time the SS also surrounded the ghetto and the barracks. They then took everybody from the ghetto to Litovka, one kilometre {about a third of a mile} from the ghetto, to mass graves, which had been specially prepared. They killed everybody from the ghetto; including my relatives from Karelitz, my old grandmother among them. On that day, 5,500 men, women and children were killed in Litovka.

That same evening everybody in the workshops had to line up for inspection. I stood next to my father, dressed in his jacket and long trousers in an attempt to look older. The Nazi chief passed and did not say anything, but all the children hidden in the lofts and basements were found and thrown out of the windows. Then they were taken by lorry to Litovka where they were killed. From that day the ghetto in Peresika contained 500 Jews and the Courthouse 500 skilled tradesmen. I was one of the youngest among them. From our family, my mother, father, sister, cousin Berl and myself had survived so far.

We were kept locked up for a number of days without food or water. Then a van was driven into the Courthouse yard, where we were assembled, and loaves of bread were thrown at us. The Germans took pleasure in seeing us struggle to get hold of a piece. Then the camp commandant told us we were the lucky ones; we would remain alive because the Reich needed us, but we would have to work hard. We were issued numbers which we had to stitch on to the back of our clothes. Mine was 334.

Now we no longer lived in a ghetto, but a work camp. We were enclosed by two circles of barbed wire with a wooden fence on the outside. Towers with searchlights and machine guns were installed. The camp had no water facilities, so every day a number of workers had to fetch drinking water. This was our only contact with the outside world.

After the second massacre, the young people began to escape. There would be a lot of whispering then they would disappear at night. Contact with the Bielski partisans in the woods had been established, and the Bielski brothers gave me hope - they provided a place to run to. I knew the youngest brother, Archik Bielski, very well as we had gone to the same school and had been in the same class. The four Bielski brothers had refused to submit to the German terror and had gone into hiding in the forest. They were joined by other families and people from the ghetto in Novogrudok, and the Bielski brigade was formed. Once it became known in the ghetto that there was a place to run to, people began to take the chance.

By the end of October 1942 the Bielski group consisted of more than 300 people. I started to prepare myself for escape. Getting out of the camp was still quite easy; the danger was that in winter you could freeze to death. Then there was the problem of food, and the fact that the outside world was unfriendly. People were ready to sell you to the Germans or give you away just for the sake of it.

I became friendly with the Jewish warehouseman in charge of the store of felt boots. He had lost a son of my age and therefore wanted me to succeed in my escape. He risked his life and gave me a pair of the most beautiful, hard felt boots. I told my parents that I planned to escape and they gave me their blessing.

On 22 December 1942, the gates were opened to let in lorries to unload raw material for the workshops. It was very cold. I put on my special felt boots, loosened the yellow star and number, and then tore them off when I got nearer to the gates. There were no guards to be seen and I walked through the gates without looking back. I crossed the highway and went on to the small forest where a few people were already waiting. By the afternoon there were fourteen of us.

We waited until dark, then started to skirt around the town because a rendezvous had been arranged with the partisans at midnight. The going was very difficult, with waist-deep soft snow, and we had to cover approximately eight kilometres {five miles}. We reached the little River Britanka, which we had to cross. Step by step we felt the ice under the snow, but suddenly it gave way and most of us fell in. I was the worst off; my felt boots immediately absorbed the water, and snow started sticking to them. Each step became more and more difficult.

We all reached the rendezvous place but we were too late. The partisans had not waited, but we knew they were due to come back three nights later. We were advised to stay in the small forest for the next three days. After a while, I just wanted to sleep. I started to dream and realized immediately that if I fell asleep now, it would be forever. I fought hard with myself and made a decision: I must return to the camp otherwise I would freeze to death. I crawled to the road and put my life in the hands of fate. I was fortunate. A peasant passed by in his sleigh and did not notice me when I climbed on to the back. When we got near the camp, I just jumped off and started walking towards the well. I knew that in a few hours time the first party would come to fetch water. I waited in the bitter cold, and eventually they came. The guards were so wrapped up that they could not see anything.

I moved forwards and was noticed by one of the carriers. He must have immediately told the others, as I suddenly found myself in the middle of the group. Before I knew what was happening I was back in my room. My father tried to take off my boots but it was impossible - a file and sharp knife had to be used. My toes were black with frostbite on both feet. There was no doctor to help and no medicine; there was nothing we could do. After a few days the flesh started to rot, and my toes had to be amputated. Now I felt sure that I had signed my own death certificate by being in a camp, unable to walk. The strain on my parents and sister was unbearable: if I could not work, I could not bring in any food, which meant a decrease in rations for all of them.

We had a hidden radio in the camp. On the fourth of February the person that listened to the radio shouted out. We will most probably survive. The Germans had had a great disaster in Stalingrad. They lost a whole army, half of them through frostbite.

That means that we are stitching fur coats, fur boots for no money. They must keep us alive. Later the same day we heard that the ghetto in Pieresika was liquidated.

Gradually I started to feel better, but a new enemy had arrived - bugs, millions of them. They made my life a misery. Because of the dirty conditions, lice and bugs reigned. They got under the so-called bandages and into my wounds. I had to scratch, and with the slightest scratch the wounds would bleed again.

In April 1943 there was a new announcement that specialist workers, including my father, would receive extra food rations. On 7 May 1943, my window was open and I watched the workers going to get their extra rations of food as usual. Suddenly I saw local and foreign police running about, hitting out with their rifles. My mother came to the window to reassure me. I was sure she had come to say goodbye. (I had a feeling about things like that then, and when my mother came to me, it was as if she were saying goodbye.) I could no longer stand hearing the shouting and seeing the beatings. I turned towards the wall, covered myself, put my fingers in my ears and lay quietly, crying my heart out.

Suddenly I heard guards coming into the room. They had killed everybody and were now coming to rob us, but we did not have anything that they could steal. They grabbed some items of clothing took some belongings and threw them on the top bunk, and so covered me even more. How long I lay there I do not know, but soon I heard crying and realized the workers had been sent back, my father among them. All the others, including my mother, sister and aunt, had been taken just outside the camp and killed.

After this massacre, food was cut down to 125 grams {just over four ounces} of bread, mixed with straw, and a bowl of soup a day - a slow starvation diet. It was impossible for me to get used to the hunger. I was not occupied, and the days passed very slowly, laying there just waiting twenty-four hours for the next slice of bread.

An escape committee was formed, because we were now certain that nobody would be left alive, the war against the Jews was more important to them than the war against the Russians. The first plan was to wait for a dark night, throw hand grenades into the guardroom, and escape. Some would definitely reach the forest, but what about me? I could not run and could not let myself be taken alive. In desperation my father prepared two nooses. As soon as we would hear the first explosion, we would hang ourselves. However after about a week, this plan was dropped and a new one devised: To dig a tunnel 100 metres {328 feet} long to the other side of the barbed wire, into a field of growing wheat. The plan was laid down by Berl Yoselevitz. The work would need to start immediately at a rate of two meters per day. It actually started 2nd week in May.

A work's committee was formed and met in the room where I still lay on the top bunk unable to walk. They used to meet three or four times a week to discuss the progress. Two permanent members lived in my room Notke Sucharski and Ruvke Shabakovski. It is difficult to know how many members served on the committee - people were called in as needed. The word tunnel changed the whole atmosphere of the camp. It was no secret, everybody but

Mr. Mendelson knew about it. For me it was a god send. I felt well, maybe I will recover and participate in the escape. For people that believed in escape that was it. For people that did not want to escape that gave them the delay action. It was decided to start digging in the stable. It was the furthest building from the guards and less occupied, I can't remember but I believe that in the stable was an earth floor. Notke Sucharski and Lionke Portnoi promised within a week to deliver the necessary tools, and to keep them in perfect condition. The lower bunk was hinged to the wall, for quick lift up. A shaft was dug 2 mtr deep. Sosnovski the tailor was called in and told to collect blankets and to make 60 bags. 40 cm X 50 cm, A joiner was called in and asked to cut a trap door from the stable to the loft of the next building. Salek Jacubovitz the policeman to be responsible to appoint diggers and for people to find extra food for them. It was established that the tunnel should be 65 cm X 70cm. The earth to be put on either side of the loft. There was a house builder in the camp, I can't remember his name. He was later sent to Koldichevo. He was responsible for location of the dug out earth. To make sure that the loft will not cave in under the weight of the earth. After two weeks it was realized that it would be impossible to keep to the two meters per day. The lamp did not burn properly. Difficult for people to sit inside the tunnel and to pass on the bags.

We had no lights in the living quarters, Rukovski the best electrician in the area was called in and told to look for live electric cable and provide electric light in the tunnel. After a few days he reported that he found the main cable and he can do it.

Skolnik the carpenter from Karelitz was called in and told that a platform on wheels was required as quickly as possible, the size to be 50x 50 cm. They asked my father to stitch up two reigns 50 mtr each. It must be strong and have a ring in the end. It was like magic, everything materialized under such difficult situation. Skolnik built the platform in pieces to be able to smuggle out from the joiners workshop.

I think that within three week it was electricity inside the tunnel, the platform was functioning, but not good enough. Earth was spilling over and the platform was hitting the walls.

Skolnik was called in again, this time to produce a box 50 cm X 50 cm x 50 cm on 2 sides of the panels should be hinged, for quick loading an unloading the earth. To make wider wheels and guiding rails at the side so that the box should not hit the walls. The request was enormous, it meant making and stealing four, one meter rails a day. If caught stealing German property was hanging. Skolnik himself was caught carrying a piece of wood about six month before; he was hung by the arms. He survived.

The aim was to pull out 9 to 10 trolleys of earth a day. Get reid of it in the evening and night. In the shaft was built in a place for two people to sit and pass on the earth that was put in bags. From there a line of about sixty to seventy people were sitting passing on the small bags and emptying at both sides of the loft. Nobody complained. From the tunnel shaft to the barbed wire was 40 mtr. On a Sunday morning at end of June Loinke Portnoy was installing a breathing pipe to let in air in the tunnel. At the same time a test was made to see the deeps of the tunnel. This was not a simple exercise, he needed to push through a two meter rod, in a 65 cm cavity. Lionke brought with him 4 sticks they had to be assembled into one. The top one was painted white so it should be easily seen. At the same time Joselevitz went up on the loft, took out some tiles to be able to see the direction. Everything was perfect.

At the beginning of July 1943, my father came to me during the working day, took some belongings, and said goodbye. He told me that they were sending him and another ten specialists for a short while to a different camp. It was a very sad day for me, the parting was so quick. To this day I can see him with his small packet in his hands, putting on a brave face, saying he would see me soon, knowing very well that this was goodbye for ever. He was killed in the Koldichevo escape in February 1944.

His job to look after the reigns was given over to Efroim Sielubski. he made a good job of it.

When I began to feel better, I started to test my strength. After six months of lying still, I felt pins and needles and pain when I lowered my legs. I was very weak but I was also tremendously determined. I was still only fourteen years old and life was hard for me. I could more or less get around on crutches, but I was just like a skeleton. I had to live completely on charity, for someone to give me a slice of bread and some 'soup water'. I started to participate in building the tunnel. Every evening I was seating on the loft in line and passing on the small bags.

The digging of the tunnel progressed well. The escape plan was put in motion the electrician Rukovski managed to make a switch board so that he can control the two large searchlights. To the end, the Germans could not find out the reason the searchlight was not functioning properly. The escape was planed for the second week in August. The wheat outside the camp was the best camouflage.

Then one day in August the Germans brought a tractor into the field and cut the wheat. We were afraid that the tunnel would collapse under the tractor's weight but luckily it held. However, we were left with a problem. Escape is impossible into an open field.

Had we escaped early August as planned, none of us would have survived. The Germans made a plan to liquidate the partisans in Novogrudok Ivenietz area. They named the operation "**Herman**"; they assembled in Novogrudok and the surrounding villages 52,000 soldiers and police.[1]

Their intention was to surround the vast forest, to push the partisans to the centre and liquidate them.

The committee met and decided to dig further to the end of the ridge, more than 150 metres more. Nobody can imagine how much earth accumulates from such a project. First the loft was filled, then double walls were built and filled. All incriminating evidence had to be hidden. Sunday was the sanitary day in the camp. We had to make sure that outside the buildings were all clean. We were told that new toilets had to be dug and that gave us an ideal opportunity to dispose of the earth from the tunnel.

At the end of August there were further problems: rain started seeping through and earth was falling from the roof of the tunnel. Wood had to be found/stolen and some bunks destroyed to make supports to prevent the tunnel from collapsing.

In the middle of September a meeting was called and a vote taken. There were still some people who said it was better to die in the camp than to run, but the majority preferred escape. So the escape was on. Mr Yitzhak Rosenhouse put together the list of the inmates and gave it to the committee to decide the order of escape. The only name that was left off was that of Mr. Mendelson. Mr. Mendelson was a convert from Vienna and was not trusted. He lived separately, knew nothing about the tunnel and consequently was left behind. On the 27th he was arrested and later shot in prison.

The first to go through would be the tunnel diggers, followed by five armed men, then the strong ones. I would be among the last, along with my friend Pesach, who had also lost some toes. I had to make a trial run to see whether I was capable of making the distance. It went perfectly well (I was already walking without sticks).

On 19 September 1943 another meeting was called, and we were notified that the tunnel would be completed the following week. So started the longest week in my life, but I was not afraid. People were saying goodbye to each other, and exchanging tips about the route and the best way to go. It was thought that if we all went our separate ways, we would stand a better chance of survival.

The day arrived, 26 September 1943, our chosen day of escape. We assembled at in the front building, which consisted of about 10 rooms. Orders were given for some people to go up to the loft. The committee was afraid if all 250 people would go up on the loft at the same time the ceiling might collapse.

The night was dark and stormy. Made to order. The searchlights had been cut off and some of the nails removed from the zinc roof in the stable, so it would rattle a lot in the wind. The leaders did not let anybody into the tunnel until the exit was broken through. This was to ensure that there would be enough air for the first 120 people that would fill the tunnel. The moment we felt the rush of fresh air the 120 people crawled in side. The rest went up on the loft and formed a line that stretched back towards the stable. The first lot that went into the tunnel lay there for about ten to fifteen minutes until the exit hole was sufficiently enlarged. Then the line started to move forwards. But we had not reckoned on the effect of the lighting in the tunnel. When people came out at the other end, the sudden darkness after the brightness in the tunnel disorientated them and some began to run back towards the camp. The guards opened fire. Although the searchlights were cut off, they could still see movements in the dark, and probably thought that partisans were attacking to liberate the camp.[2]

When I came out of the tunnel I could see the whole field alive with flying bullets. I saw figures in the dark running towards the forest, and was certain that in the morning the Germans would search that area. So Pesach and I stuck to our original plan to skirt around the town and wait on the other side. The fields had recently been ploughed, so walking was difficult. We took the same route I had taken on my first escape and crossed the same river, which was now flowing gently.

Dawn started to break. We lay behind a bush and stayed there all day, about two kilometres {just over a mile} from the town. As soon as darkness fell, we got up and went to the nearest house and asked for food. A man gave us a loaf of the most beautiful bread and some milk. We walked for five nights in the same direction. It rained for some of this time, and I was afraid to take off my tattered shoes. Around the hole that had developed in one of them, I could see dried blood. On the morning of 1 October 1943, we settling down for rest after a night's walking when we saw a group of people with a cart and horses. We hid ourselves but then we heard them speaking Yiddish we realized that they were Jewish partisans – I even recognized one of them!

They were fighters returning from a mission. We were very lucky to have met them: it is impossible to calculate the odds of going into that forest, without really knowing the way, and reaching the group we were searching for.

The partisans took us to their base, where I was reunited with my cousin Berl. We laughed and cried at the same time. I had reached the Ordzhonikidze Detachment of the Kirov Brigade. This was the name of the former Bielski fighting group of 180 men and women. Not long afterwards, Berl decided that we should join the family group of the Kalinin Detachment, better known as the Bielski Detachment, so that we could stay together. He got permission for us to transfer, and we left the fighting group.

We only had a short journey on foot to reach the Kalinin group, whose commander was Tuvia Bielski. It was strange to see so many Jews in this place, quite unafraid, although it was so close to German police stations.

A reconnaissance group arrived and told Bielski that the Germans and local police were on the move. That meant immediate evacuation of the camp. It could not have happened at a worse time for me as my wounds were just beginning to heal. We moved out slowly in the middle of the day, a large convoy. The danger was great because we had to cross several major roads. Berl decided that he and I should leave the convoy because if shooting took place, I would not be able to run. He found out the route the convoy was taking and we left on our own.

Berl knew the way and we walked slowly. We met the group on the following day and heard that shots had been exchanged with the local police. We had something to eat and moved on again to the next meeting place. I got used to sleeping in the forest without fear. We carried on moving for the next few days until we reached the main base in the huge Naliboki forest[3]. We arrived late and I was very tired. I took the outer rags off my feet with difficulty, then I took off my sweater and wrapped it around my feet. I covered myself with an overcoat and fell into an exhausted sleep. I woke up early in the morning; the pain in my feet was almost unbearable.

The Bielski base in the forest developed into a little town with a bakery, a sausage-maker, shoe workshops, tailoring and engineering workshops and, later, a tannery. Partisans from all over the region used to come to get their guns, shoes and uniforms repaired there, and would exchange flour for bread and cows for sausages. I did all sorts of work in the camp.

In the forest the Jewish partisans had another enemy - the 'White' Poles. Their slogan was, *'Poland without Jews and Communists'* and many Jews who managed to escape from the ghettos were killed by them. The Bielski group took an active part in fighting the enemy and in committing various acts of sabotage, which included blowing up bridges and cutting down telegraph poles. Over a period of six months in 1944, the Bielski fighters stopped the German trains for a total of fifty-one hours, which was a great achievement.

At four o'clock in the morning of 22 June 1944, almost exactly three years after the Nazis started the terrible war against Russia, the Red Army began its great offensive on the Byelorussian front. On 3 July Minsk was liberated. As the fighting got closer we could hear the sound of artillery by lying down and placing our ears on the ground. We prepared for a fight with the German Army as we knew their retreat would be through the forest. Sure enough, one morning a large retreating group of Germans broke through our reinforcements. Unfortunately, nine of our members were killed.

On the following day we heard that the Russian army was in Novogrudok. We were pleased that the nightmare was over, but each one of us felt terribly sad. We all knew what we would find in Novogrudok - a destroyed town without Jews, without the people we had known before the war. It was decided that we would return to Novogrodek. Bielski requested that everybody march out of the forest in an organized body and so it was. I walked without difficulty the 100 kilometres {62 miles} and more to the town. Thanks to the Bielski brothers, 1,230 Jews arrived in the suburbs on 16 July 1944. Although we were free, nobody talked or laughed or sang. We were all sad.

Long columns of German prisoners of war were being led through the streets of Novogrodek. They were a scruffy lot, no longer the victorious army. I saw a high-ranking officer marching with the men, in a fine pair of boots. I called the Russian guard and asked his permission to remove the boots. The soldier smiled with full approval and said, *'Please help yourself!'* I caught up with the officer and spoke to him in Yiddish, which is similar to German. I wanted him to know that I was a Jew. I told him to stop and remove his boots, saying they were too good for him. Then the Russian soldier approached and gave him a push with his rifle, whereupon he sat down and pulled off his boots. I wore them for a long time after that; in fact I was still wearing them when I eventually arrived in England in 1947.

When I first came to England, I found a job as a cutter in a handbag factory. Then after fifteen months, I started my own company, Princelet Handbags, followed by another one,

Hi-Speed Plastics. After that, I started up a number of other successful companies. I also met Barbara Steinfeld, fell in love with her, and we were married in 1955. We have two sons, Michael Leon and Jeffrey David, and one daughter, Deborah Judith. Between them all, we now have ten grandchildren and three great grandchildren. I eventually settled down to a normal life, but I can never forget the past. I regret missing out on my youth and educational opportunities. But I continue my study of resistance in the Holocaust, and enjoy speaking to groups about the role of the remarkable Bielski brothers. To me they are among the greatest of Jewish heroes.

Over the last fifty years I have given many talks to children, to university students, and to the general public both Jewish and Gentile and always the same question is raised? How could it be that you dug for more than 4 months without being discovered?
There are two answers:

1) The workers always fulfilled the quotas demanded of them by the Belarusian/Polish foremen. If they could not fulfil it in 12 hours they worked for 14 hours. The aim was not to give anybody a reason to be suspicious and look. As far as they were concerned the job was always done.

2) As I explained, we did not have any water inside the camp. We were dirty. I did not wash properly from March to September, did not change my clothes. We were full of lice and the premises were full of bugs. It was so bad that the SS man Reuter used to put on white gloves when he had to beat a Jew.

Nevertheless we were always on guard and we built all kinds of signals and buzzers to warn if anyone suspicious was approaching. The moving of the earth was done during the evenings and at night.

The most important thing though – and this may sound strange after everything I have described - WE WERE LUCKY!

Notes:
[1] See Operation Herman above, page 131.
[2] Traub had apparently left Novogrudok on September 20 and there was nobody in charge of the Gebietskommissariat.
[3] See Shmuel Amarant's account above describing the building and layout of the base.

Plan No. 1

Attack on the Yatsuki Railroad Track

In September 1942, the detachment under the command of Anatoly Davidovich Bielski, had already almost 150 armed members, two German trophy machine guns captured when an automobile was destroyed on the Novogrudok – Novoyelna highway and about 40 rifles and was manoeuvring in the Novogrudok district of the Baranovichi region among the German garrisons located in Ruda, Yatsuki station, and the police stations situated in the village of Berezovka and in the town of Novogrudok. Due to the fact that there still was no connection between the detachments, decisions about the tasks were made by our own commanders. The adversary stood well-armed in the garrison, having built pillboxes everywhere, but it did not expect to be attacked by partisans in villages.

The commander of the detachment, having reached an agreement with the commander of the neighbouring detachment, Lieut. Panchenkov, decided to destroy the German garrison stationed at the Yatsuki station on the Lida – Baranovichi railway line because it had few people there, good approach from every direction as it was surrounded by a forest and the precise information received from one scout, a local resident who worked on the railroad, despite the fact that the small numbers and the quality of arms were still superior to those of the partisans.

The garrison consisted of forty Germans who accommodated themselves in a wooden building of the station and were armed with two mortars and four machine guns standing in 3 pillboxes. The plan of the attack was to approach the siding at night, surround it, and to open such fire at the station where they were situated, that they could not enter the pillboxes at the station and destroy them. Having destroyed the adversary and if possible captured their weapons, we would then set fire to the walls of the railway station and withdraw.

After two reconnaissance raids, the commanders of both detachments decided to carry out this plan. About sixty men were chosen from both detachments; they were armed with four machine guns, and the task was explained to everybody who took part in the attack; everybody was shown his place; all were divided into platoons, and commanders were appointed. Instructions were given regarding the exact positions, time and signal for opening fire. The positions were to be occupied by the platoons while it was still dark so that on September 20 at 6 am it would be possible to open fire at the sleeping Germans. The station was watched by one guard who was to be killed by a single shot.

On the night of September 20, the detachment occupied its positions according to the plan and at 6 sharp the commander of the Bielski Detachment, who was in charge of the first platoon in this operation, gave the signal by firing, and all the three platoons opened fire at the station.

The Germans, being only half-awake, got confused, and their response was chaotic at the beginning, then, under the command of their chief, they coordinated their activity and, protected by the machine gun fire, they began to crawl over into the pillboxes. As soon as the first Germans got into the pillboxes, they opened heavy mortar and machine gun fire at the detachment. Besides, a train had been sent from Lida to Baranovichi in the morning and during the engagement flank guards reported that 'the train was approaching'; trains usually were escorted by a heavy protection, and we had to leave the place of combat, thus, the assignment put forward by the commanders was not completely carried out.

178   WE STOOD SHOULDER TO SHOULDER

Subsequent intelligence information revealed that at the time of the operation four Germans were killed and seven were wounded, but we were unable to capture any weapons. We had no human or material losses from our side.

Following the engagement, reinforcements, 60 men strong, arrived from Lida with heavy weapons and, with such a strength the garrison was encircled by a trench and surrounded by barbed wire. Guards were put forward; the surrounding forest was cut down in order to prevent anyone from approaching the station.

* * *

Plan No. 2

Battle in the Drachlivo Forest, Novogrudok District

On March 12, 1943 part of the detachment 35 people strong, headed by the detachment commander Anatoli Davidovich Bielski and the chief of staff Lazar Anatolyevich Malbin, were at the meeting with the October detachment headed by Lieutenant Panchenkov in the village of Negrimovo, that belonged to the Drachilovo village soviet in the Novogrudok district. Both detachments operated in the Novogrudok district, and had about 150 rifles and six machine guns all together.

About 70 men attended the meeting with submachine guns. Meetings of the commanders took place in order to exchange information, news and to coordinate their activities. The detachments were searched for three or four times a month in different places; therefore, the place and the time of these meetings were known only to the commanders of the detachments.

During the meeting, outposts were put forward around the village of Negrimovo because at that time the police were patrolling the collection of supplies. The distance from the village of Negrimovo to the village of Drachilovo was a two kilometre forest road. The situation in the region was as follows:

The village of Drachilovo is situated at a distance of twelve kilometres from Novogrudok, and was linked to it by a good road. In Novogrudok, however, because of frequent ambushes and attacks of partisans on the police, there was a Lithuanian battalion constantly standing battle-ready with 20 automobiles and two armoured cars with full armament to a battle place at first signal.

p. end-------illegible

p. beginning --- illegible

At midnight, the scouts of our detachment who had been sent out to the village of Drachilovo to get some horses, informed us about the imminent arrival of the police in Drachilovo. A decision was taken immediately to prevent the police from entering the village, to occupy positions in front of the village and to prepare an ambush.

All the 70 people present at the meeting were gathered together immediately, divided into four platoons, machine guns distributed among the platoons and the detachment marched to the village of Drachilovo protected from the front and from the rear, with strong reconnaissance sent ahead.

The plan was as follows: because of the fact that it was not known exactly from which direction the police would arrive and how many they were, it was decided to prepare two ambushes on both ends of the village. In case the police were encountered at one end, the other end would take a detour and get the police from behind.

Approaching the village the detachment stopped and sent a reconnaissance team ahead. As soon as the scouts appeared on the mountain towering over the village, a hailstorm of fire was opened up at them. Apparently the village had been occupied by the police before the partisans arrived. It was then decided to drive out the police from the village immediately.

The detachment was immediately ordered in a defence line, and began rushing in the direction of the village. We had to run across the open field under heavy enemy fire. In spite of the hail of fire, the partisans courageously headed for the village. The platoons occupied one end of the village; the fourth platoon lay in wait at the cemetery in order to cut off ---- in the direction of the road to Novogrudok. Then a fierce battle began, we had to drive the policemen one by one out of each house trying not to kill or hurt local residents, or damage the houses. The job was difficult but thanks to the courage of the partisans it was successfully accomplished. After a two-hour battle, the police were driven out of the village, having left fifteen men dead and injured, and abandoning arms, ammunition, uniforms and wagons, having received no supplies from the village.

We suffered four injured, but captured a few Holland rifles of the old model with cartridges. There were no casualties or losses on the part of the local population, except for a few broken windows.

After the police were driven out of the village, having picked up and sent off its wounded, the detachment set off back to the place of the meeting because of the small amount of ammunition and knowing that the Lithuanian battalion would be approaching. Actually, after we had travelled one kilometre, the rear security section reported that a chain of armed forces was approaching the village, which we had just cleared up. They were Lithuanians. Having entered the village, they interrogated the peasants about the number of partisans, their armaments, where the partisans came from, and where they went to. Having received no distinct answer from the local population and the defeated police, the Lithuanians started firing mortars at the forest and ----- (the document ends)

Source: National Archives Republic of Belarus (NARB) f.3618, inv.1, f.26

* * *

This is the last report from Tuvia Bielski to the chief of staff. On liberation, over 1000 Jews survived in the Bielski family group and 230 in the fighting group Ordzhonikidze.

To the chief of Byelorussian Staff of the Partisan Movement comrade Kalinin

In July 1941 a group of 20 people organised a partisan detachment. The organisers of the detachment were the Bielski brothers, Anatoli (Tuvia), Alexander (Asael) and Sigismund Davidovichi (Zusha). The Detachment was given the name Zhukov, with Anatoli Davidovich in charge. There was no commissar/ enlistment officer/ and no chief of staff in the detachment in view of the small number of people.

From May 1942 onwards the detachment began to grow and by August 1942 the detachment put itself in touch with the Novogrudok ghetto and began to take people out of it. By January

1943 it grew to 300 people under the command of Anatoli Davidovich as Commander and Malbin Lazar Abramovitch as Chief of Staff. In February 1943 the detachment was renamed into second company of 'Octyabr' detachment by order of the Lenin brigade. From April to June 1943 on having put itself in touch with the ghettos in Lida, Ivje and other towns, the detachment grew to 750 people and on 1 June 1943 by the order of Major-General Chernyshev it became an independent detachment renamed Ordzhonikidze, Kirov brigade, Lida Inter-district centre under the same command. In September 1943 the Ordzhonikidze detachment was separated and given another command, and on Major-General Chernyshev's order, our detachment was named the Bielski detachment under the same command and by order of the Lida Zone Centre of April 1944 it became the Kalinin under direct subordination to the Lida Zone Centre with 1,000 people. The commander of the detachment from its inception into the Red Army units was Bielski Anatoli Davidovich, and from November 1942 to the Liberation the Chief of Staff was Malbin Lazar Abramovich and Commissar of the detachment from 18 March 1944 to the Liberation was Shemyatovec Ivan Vasil'yevich attached by Major-General Chernyshev's order from the Kalinin detachment, brigade of Komsomolec Stolpcy Inter-district centre.

The first German expedition against the detachment took place on 5 January 1943 in the village of Chrepienovo and Vsielub village, Soviet Novogrudok district, Baranovichi region where 9 people were killed.

The second expedition was on 15 February 1943 in the forest village of Berezovka, Soviet Novogrudok where 5 people were lost.

The fourth expedition was 'The Big Blockade' in the Naliboki dense forest in August 1943, from which the detachment was withdrawn with no losses.

Commander of the detachment   Commissar of the detachment
/Bielski/   /Shemyatovec/

Source: National Archives Republic of Belarus (NARB) f.3618, inv.1, f.26

Who were those Jewish Partisans?
Y. Yaffe

Asael Bielski

Asael Bielski knew all the roads and trails that connected the villages. All peasants in the area knew him, because they used to come to mill their grain in Bielski flour-mill in Stankiewicze. He had to leave school and work in the flourmill from an early age, because of his father's ill-health. He was a quiet modest man, who loved work and was ready to help anyone. His good character stood him in good stead in troubled times.

At first, Asael hid on his own, close to the village of Stankievichi. His brothers joined him later. Before the first slaughter in Novogrudok, he assembled all his family, some fifteen people, and hid them in the homes of friendly peasants.

The Bielski's then joined a group of Russian partisans lead by Victor Panchenkov, to fight the Germans. In the meantime Tuvia, the oldest brother, arrived from the Lida ghetto; he was tall and broad shouldered, full of initiative, courage and a warm Jewish heart. He accepted the task of the leader of the partisans. Tuvia was the commander and Asael his loyal helper.

Asael carried out every undertaking with devotion and precision. He took part in scouting, fighting and negotiating with the Russian partisans. He was the commander of the group's internal punishment unit, and, in dangerous conditions, he successfully completed his assignments.

Everyone loved Asael and put their trust in him. They were glad to participate in battles under his command. It was a pleasure to scout with him, or just to be with him. He was a loyal and pleasant friend.

By the end of the summer of 1942 the first groups from the Novogrudok ghetto joined the Bielski's. Everyone feared the Germans. Many Jews, who were roaming in the countryside, were captured by Christians and delivered to the Germans. The art of being a partisan was not, as yet, familiar.

Asael and his group fought bravely. They also took revenge on the Christians who betrayed Jews to the Germans. As this became known, the peasants did not dare to assault Jews any more, and even helped them to find their way to the forest.

In November 1942 the Bielski's, with Victor Panchenkov's Russian partisans, ambushed German military convoys on the Novoyelna-Novogrudok road. Asael was the commander of the Jewish unit. Scores of Germans were killed, and many weapons were captured on that occasion. The weapons were used to equip the fighters from the Novogrudok ghetto.

There was a second battle that November under Asael's command, at the railway station of Yatsuki, on the Niemen-Lida line. It was a fierce battle with the Germans, who were dug-in in a bunker that guarded the station. It ended successfully[1].

The third action involved setting fire to granaries, where grain destined for Germany was stored. All of these operations created a favourable reputation of the Jewish partisans, and helped other Jews to be accepted in Russian partisan units.

The fighters and non-fighters all loved Asael; he befriended the fighters and was one of them. But he was also a friend of the non-fighters. He noticed the good qualities in every person. "We would not always be like Gypsies in the forest", he said. "After liberation every one will return to his profession or trade and will be successful, even if he was not a fighting partisan".

Asael was the first in a battle, and the first to aid the injured. "There is no need to fear death, we will die anyway, sooner or later", he would say. "Our aim is to fight the Germans and their collaborators, who hate us. We have to avenge our brethren's blood. I am not interested in tomorrow".

Asael was glad on one occasion, to go on an operation to punish a Belorussian family for betraying to the Germans some Jewish partisans who were visiting their house. He killed them with his own hands. "Jewish blood is not cheap", he shouted, as he set fire to the family and their house. Later he used to remind himself of that punishment operation to calm his aching heart.

Asael was a brave much-loved man, who always went out and returned from actions with his partisans safe and sound. He survived the forest, joined the Russian Army, and fell in the war against the Germans in a foreign land. Blessed be his memory.

Arie Volkin
Arie Volkin came to the forest at the age of eighteen. He was a child when his father died long before the war. The obligation of providing for the family had fallen on his mother, who was too busy to take good care of him. She was a milliner. He received his education at the Polish State School and studied Jewish subjects with private teachers. The prophets and their visions did not attract him. I was his teacher for half a year. I taught him Isaiah and Ezekiel. We were reading the phrase about the end of days - when the lamb and the wolf will live in peace together. He erupted, 'It will never happen, the goyim hate us to death.'

Every day he had to wrestle with non-Jewish children at school. Among them he learned that you have to fight back. He got beaten, but he could give a good beating too, and the Christian children knew not to mock him with their call of "zhid" as they called other Jewish children.

When the Germans came, Arie worked in their camp. The German soldiers liked him; he was a good worker, cleaned the horses and the stables. They also let him clean their weapons, take them apart and put them together again; this knowledge helped him in the forest.

While working with the Germans he saw death every day. Every day people were shot. He got used to that. It was a familiar occurrence for him to see how scores of people were buried in ditches.

After the second slaughter in Novogrudok, he escaped from the ghetto. He was searched until he found the Bielski camp. He was a good partisan and had no fear. On occasions he went back to town and entered the ghetto, right under the noses of the Germans. He was successful in accomplishing all sorts of missions.

In the ambush that the Bielski's and Victor's partisans set on the Germans in the forest of Koshelevo, he fought like a lion, killed a German, and took his sub-machine gun, which he used as his own weapon.

Arie was a scout, and the first in every action, until the bitter morning in December 1942 when a few hundred policemen surrounded the house that was called Khrapienevo, and opened fire with machine guns on a dozen Jewish partisans, who were sleeping there: Efroimski, Leibovich and Volkin, as well as Bielski's wife and her brother Grisha. Bielski, in his recollections, considered the event a major setback and mentioned more victims. The fight was fierce, with no hope of survival. Arie Volkin, shooting through the window, used his sub machine gun to the last bullet and was wounded.

Arie was the only one to be taken alive by the Germans. They brought him to Novogrudok prison, and tortured him, but he did not utter a word. He knew a lot but said nothing. He endured the torture for several weeks, and when the Germans realised that they would not be able to extract anything from him, they hanged him in Novogrudok jail. God will avenge his blood.

Eliyahu Yavnovich
Eliyahu Yavnovich was born in 1908 in the Nasvich farm, ten kilometres from Novogrudok. He completed primary school and later learned to repair sewing machines in Novogrudok and worked at the Singer Company in Lida. In the summer of 1942, he was brought by the Germans from Lubcz to the ghetto in Pieresieka. He survived the slaughter of August 1942, and immediately after that he escaped to join Bielski's unit.

Eliyahu was an educated man with an inherent intelligence. He was self-taught, read a great deal, and studied at night after a day of hard and strenuous work. He was well-mannered and a pleasure to talk to. He had a vast general knowledge, and was among the few who brought some culture and knowledge to the forest.

As a mechanic, Eliyahu was among those who repaired and cleaned the weapons of the unit. He was a capable partisan with military knowledge and became a group leader after the division of the Bielski camp into two, when the unit "Ordzonikidze" was established.

As a leader of his group he was meticulous in supervising their duties, such as guarding, scouting and fighting. He was serious and devoted, and was liked by his men. He insisted on order and discipline, and fought for equality in the group. He was always ready to help. He was a good fighter and a good friend. With his help, many left the Lida ghetto. He instructed them and cheered them up in times of danger or crisis.

On the fatal day, Eliyahu went with another partisan for a special operation in the village of Zeshirialnik. When they were there, a group of policemen appeared in the village. When they heard about the partisans they surrounded the house they were in and sprayed it with bullets from automatic guns. There was no hope of surviving. Eliyahu was wounded in his leg and could not escape. He came out of the house and hurled a hand grenade. As he did so, he was killed, but during the explosion the second partisan managed to escape to the nearby forest. After his death Eliyahu was awarded a posthumous medal for bravery by the unit commanders, and was promoted to a higher rank. God will avenge his blood.

Eliyahu Ostashinski
Eliyahu Ostashinski was born near Selib. He married Rachel Berman, the daughter of the blacksmith. The blacksmith was known for his strength. Eliyahu was a blacksmith too. Before the war he served in the Polish Army and was promoted to sergeant. He was among the few in Bielski's unit who had proper military training and a rank. He had many acquaintances among the peasants, which made his escape from the ghetto easier. He joined Bielski's unit together with his wife. He became an instructor of the partisans and was a unit leader. He put a great deal of work into the training of partisans, from the use of a rifle to battle exercises. He took part with his men in fighting the enemy and in scouting operations.

Eliyahu's unit brought food supplies to the camp. During all his time in the forest he was busy, planning and organising operations, carrying them out with success. Quiet and polite, he was loved by all of the people in the camp and by those in the fighting units.

Two days before we left the forest, a few hundred retreating Germans, who were fleeing from the Russians, came near the camp. They overcame the guard and entered the camp. Eliyahu Ostashinski organised the defence and with a small group of fighters fought the Germans. It was a short face-to-face battle and he was killed. God will avenge his blood

The Zuchovitski brothers

Moshe Zuchovitski was born in 1922 and his brother Nisan in 1924. Their father Aharon had a small grocery store. Their mother was a dressmaker. The children received a traditional religious and national education. The influence of their education on them was noticeable in the forest.

The Zuchovitski brothers were quiet, decent, helpful fellows and were liked by all.

Moshe Zuchovitski was a brave partisan and an excellent fighter. He felt bitterness and hatred towards the Goyim who helped to kill and rob their Jewish neighbours, and was full of hate for the Germans. Only one thing motivated him – revenge. He did not fear for his own young life, took part in the hardest of the battles, and went to the most dangerous places. He took part in many operations in the Bielski unit and later in the Ordzonikidze group. After liberation he joined the Russian Army with his brother Nisan. Both fell on German soil. God will avenge their blood.

Chayemke Bloch

Chayemke Bloch was born in 1930 in Novogrudok. His father was a shoemaker. He studied at the Tarbut School. The Germans separated him from his family and sent his parents to death. Aged eleven, he was left solitary and lost, but with a strong will to live. He also survived the second slaughter. He heard talk about people who were escaping the ghetto; about something happening outside; he followed the actions of the underground in the ghetto. Watching someone escaping the ghetto he followed by running after him. He hid for three days. When he returned to the ghetto he found out that all his relatives had been killed. He was starving, and pleaded with friends and strangers for food. He wanted to live. There were people who helped him, gave him a piece of bread, and comforted him, as he was one of them.

There was no safety in the ghetto. Many knew that their days were numbered. In a week, in a month, they will also be killed. People escaped to the forest, they hoped to survive there. Chayemke was among them. He was twelve years old, the only child among the partisans. In the forest they took pity on him, befriended him, washed his clothes and gave him food. He obeyed everyone. He used to say that at home he had been a good boy too, and had helped his mother and father. The partisans loved him. We moved from forest to forest, we walked at night, sometimes fifty kilometres and more, and Chayemke was with us. He was alert and never tired, carried water, cut wood, lit the fire, and helped anyone who asked him for help. He was the partisans' helper, their apprentice, cleaning their rifles. He wanted to stand on guard and hold a rifle, hoping that he would grow up to be a good partisan and even take revenge on the Germans. He went through a difficult winter in the forest, but later in the summer it was easier. He was given a job as one of the horses keepers.

One morning, at dawn, when we were in the forest of Yasinovo near the Niemen, when the Germans attacked the camp from several directions, with hundreds of Byelorussian policemen. We escaped from the forest, and when we met again on the other bank of the Niemen for a head count, Chayemke was not with us. He was left dead in the forest of Yasinovo, and his desire for revenge was not fulfilled. God will avenge his blood.

Shlomo Stoler

Shlomo Stoler was born in 1926 in the town Korelichi near Novogrudok. His father was a hawker, who went from village to village selling haberdashery and kitchen utensils to the peasants. Though Shlomo was a very talented boy, he had studied very little. He finished only a few classes of the Polish Primary School. At a young age he left school to help his father provide for their large family. During the week they went from village to village and before Sabbath they returned to their poor family in the small town with their profits.

In July 1942 the Germans brought the Jews of Korelichi to the Novogrudok ghetto. Most of them were killed there in August 1942. Only a few escaped, among them was Shlomo Stoler and his brothers. For months they were roaming the villages around their town. He knew the area, and the peasants knew him and took pity on him. They let him sleep in their granaries, and in the morning they gave him a loaf of bread and a bottle of milk and sent him on his way. So he roamed until winter. Almost no Jews were left in the area, and the peasants were afraid of the Germans and did not want to hide a Jew. Then he found out about the Bielski units. But unfortunately the Bielski camp was divided into many groups, and these groups were hiding in different places. It was difficult to find them. When an acquaintance brought him, together with his cousin, to the Yankelevich group, Yankelevitch rejected him. I stood guard then, and heard their conversation. "*Why are you so stubborn?*" Shlomo asked. "*You have got a house underground. My father had a nicer house than you, and they still drove him out of his house and killed him. Who knows if soon someone will drive you out of your hut.*" The boy did not know that it was a prophesying. A month later the Germans raided our huts in the middle of the day, but we all escaped.

Shlomo Stoler was accepted by the Abramovich group, where he had an uncle. From the first day you could see that he was a devoted and energetic fellow, used to hardship, to cold, and to complicated situations. He matured and became a courageous and disciplined partisan. He revealed all his skills when we were in the Naliboki forest, and the whole area was full of Russian partisans.

There were 1,100 Jews in Bielski's camp. It was hard to provide for all of them. Shlomo was the leader of a group of twenty people. They roamed the Korelichi area and took from under the German noses grain and meat to the camp.

I went with Shlomo a few times and saw how well he operated. He was a very modest and practical person; he knew that everything should be endured until the time when the Jews would be able to come out of the forest. After the liberation he reached Italy and was in the Displaced Persons camps for a couple of years. With the outbreak of the Israeli War of Independence, he heard the "old man's" - Ben-Gurion's – call. He came on a boat to Israel, and immediately joined the army. He fell at Latrun, as our State was established. Blessed be his memory.

Yaakov Slutski

Yaakov Slutski was born in 1914 in Korelichi. His father was a farmer, with cattle, but his main occupation was growing cucumbers. Yaakov studied in a Polish school. A private teacher taught him Yiddish and Hebrew. When he grew up he learned mechanics and became a mechanic in the flourmill in town. He loved reading and solitude, talked little and thought deeply.

With the elimination of the ghetto in Korelichi, Yaakov was brought to the Peresike ghetto. At the beginning of 1943 he escaped to the forest and joined the Bielski camp. He was a good partisan, tall, broad-shouldered, healthy and loved to work. He never avoided an action; the hardest of missions were given to him. Though he had no weapon he always came along, never afraid, possibly apathetic towards life - as he himself said. His aim was to get his own weapon. Once at a peasant's farm he found a dismantled rifle with no butt, he borrowed some tools from another peasant and made a butt, he had never worked in carpentry before. He said: "My rifle is not beautiful – but it shoots". It was his until he moved to a Russian partisan unit. There he received a sub-machine gun and a pistol. He helped a lot with the building of the bunkers in the forest and the organising of the camps when we moved from place to place.

Yaakov was a bachelor, forlorn and lonely. He had no one from his family. He befriended other lonely people like himself, and helped the weak who could not go to the villages to fend for themselves, and whose situation was therefore worse. Eventually he became disillusioned with the inequality in Bielski's camp. It started when the Lida people arrived in the forest, after which silver and gold were to be found in the hands of forest people and the commanders. He befriended Nachman Kirzner, the son of the milliner Shmerl Kirzner from Novogrudok. He was a student at the Warsaw Conservatorium, who also disliked the arrangements in the camp. When people came from the Alexander Nevski partisan group to ask who wanted to move to their camp, Yaakov and Nachman were the first to volunteer.

Yaakov Slutski became a professional saboteur. He made the bombs, mined the roads and railways, and was known as the best in the battalion. On the fatal night he went with three other partisans to mine the railway. Due to human error they detonated the bomb too early and all of them were killed. He was known among the partisans as a brave Jewish fighter, partisan, and a courageous and efficient saboteur. God will avenge his blood.

Just over one hundred Jews from Novogrudok were killed in the partisan movement: Sixty-three in the Bielski/Ordzonikidze detachments, and forty in other detachments.

Notes:
1 This contradicts the report above.

And So Finished Three Years and Twelve Days of the Eclipse of the Sun
Jack Kagan

The German army entered Novogrudok on 4 July 1941, and on 16 July 1944 1,230 Bielski partisans entered the town.

There were about 400 hundred survivors from Novogrudok. The other 300 survived by escaping to the Red Army, serving in the Red army, in Siberia, in General Anders' Polish army, or being hidden by Righteous Gentiles.

Approximately 6,000 Jews lived in Novogrudok and around it when the Germans arrived. Only 700 survived, and that was in large part thanks to the brave and noble efforts of the Bielski brothers.

We returned to Novogrudok, but many partisans were mobilized into the Red Army and never returned. It seemed impossible to live again in the town where so many tragedies had taken place, and some survivors moved away to Lida.

Soon a movement formed, and many of us left the Soviet Union and travelled to Poland. In Poland we heard about the Displaced Persons camps in Germany, Austria and Italy. These camps were run by UNRRA (the United Nations Relief and Rehabilitation Administration established in 1943). In the Displaced Persons camps groups were formed with one intention only: to go to Palestine.

Nearly all the Novogrudok Jews who returned from the depths of Russia and went straight to the Displaced Persons camps, with a strong will to go, illegally if necessary, to Palestine. Some managed to get through the British blockade, some were interned in a British-run camp at Atlit, on the coast of Palestine, others behind British barbed wire in Cyprus. Some of the Novogrudok survivors were on the ship Exodus, and were sent by the British back to the DP camps in Germany. Many went to the United States and settled there.

The incident around the ship EXODUS 1947 helped in the creation the State of Israel. On 29 November 1947 the United Nations General Assembly voted in favour of the establishment of the State of Israel. I was proud of those Jews from Novogrudok who were on the ship. They included my cousin, Berl Dov Kagan, and Shloimele Zhuk.

We shall never forget or forgive the generation of murderers that killed our people just for being Jewish.

Jack Kagan's cousin, a pre-war photograph (1935): Front row: Shiendl Sucharski, Leizer Kagan, Nachama Kagan, Berl Kagan. Second row: Srolik Sucharski, Leizer Senderovski, Idel Kagan

188 WE STOOD SHOULDER TO SHOULDER

Displaced Persons camp, Fohrenwald, Germany. A second reunion of survivors, 1946

The Fohrenwald reunion, 1946

In 1999 Jack Kagan's book Surviving the Holocaust with Russian Jewish
Partisans was translated into Byelorussian and published in Minsk.
In 2002 it was translated into French and published in Paris

Jack Kagan being introduced to the Queen, at the opening of the Holocaust Museum at the Imperial War Museum

Tuvia Bielski receiving a plaque in recognition of his services as partisan commander, given in New York by the Federation of Jewish Underground Fighters and Holocaust Survivors on November 14, 1976. From left to right: Lilka Bielski, Tuvia Bielski, Sam Gruber, Isaac Mendelson, Aaron Oshman, Sam Halpern

Lilke's and Tuvia's Bielski's grave in Jerusalem

Dr. Alyaksei Mazhukhou, Ambassador of the Republic of Belarus (with some of his staff) at the Novogrudok exhibition at the Imperial War Museum, 9th May 2004

Invitation from the President of Belarus Mr. Lukashenko to Jack Kagan to celebrate the 60th anniversary of the liberation of Belarus

Holocaust denial
Jack Kagan

Dr. Boris Ragula was a Byelorussian born near Novogrudok. During the German occupation he became an interpreter to the German regiment commissar, Traub. He wore a German SS uniform and knew everything that went on in district of Novogrudok.

At the end of the war Dr. Ragula managed to leave Europe. He settled in Canada in the town of London in the province of Ontario. There he wrote a book about his life, in Byelorussian. Below is what he wrote about the Jews of Novogrudok.

> 'Germans, assisted by the SS, drew the Jewish population from villages and towns together to the ghetto, which was situated on the territory of the former district Courthouse in Korelitskaya Street. They were kept behind the fence and had to work for the Germans sewing military uniforms, and making shoes. They were literally stealing material for these from the local Byelorussian population. The fact that Jews had to sew for the German army was children's play in comparison to what Stalin had done. But both these dictators - Stalin and Hitler - brought equal sorrow to people by their cruelty and destruction directed against man.'

In his English manuscript, Dr. Ragula writes:
> 'As far as I am concerned no harm came to the Jews until August 1942, when a group of Jews, perhaps two or three hundred, were selected from the camp. They were formed into a column and brought to the centre of Novogrudok to Slonimskaya Street. They were marched towards Novoyelnya by perhaps a couple of dozen people: SS men, German citizens, and some local police. It was rumoured that the Jews were going to be loaded on to a train in Novoyelnya and taken to a bigger camp to work.
> The Jews were marched through the streets of Novogrudok to Novoyelnya and were never seen again. About five or six kilometres from Novogrudok, there apparently were mass graves prepared and this group of Jews was executed there. No one witnessed it and there was no real proof of it.'

In fact, Ragula knew everything that went on. Fifty-two Jews were killed on July 26, 1941, and 5,100 on December 7, 1941. On August 7, 1942 the Germans took 5,500 Jews out of the ghetto and killed them about a kilometre {just over half a mile} from town. On February 4, 1943 they liquidated the 500 people from the ghetto and on May 7, 1943 the last 250 skilled workers from the Labour Camp.

Ragula's version of our escape through the tunnel is this:
> 'One day, to our great surprise, the news broke all over Novogrudok – the great escape of the Jews from camp! This news was passed quietly from person to person, but no one dared to say it aloud. We found out that the Jews had been digging a tunnel under the fence and had got in touch with the local population, who met them in the tunnel, took them out into the village of Sielec, and then put them in touch with the Red guerrillas. This was a great, daring attempt. Not all the Jews escaped, however. The older people and more skilled craftsman stayed, but nothing happened to them afterwards. The Germans did not touch them or continue further persecution.'

In fact, many of the eighty who were killed during the daring escape were killed by the local population. And further: according to Ragula seventy-five per cent of the Jews in Byelorussia survived the Holocaust. In fact, it was less than ten percent.

Finally: Ragula had organized a Byelorussian army to fight the partisans. His army was called Ragulevtsy – 'Ragula's Men'.

Two photographs of Boris Ragula with the President of Byelorussia (far left) inspecting the troops. They are dressed in German uniforms. Ragula is talking to the President of Byelorussia

Document issued by the Byelorussian headquarters of partisan movement to Yudel Kagan certifying that he was a soldier in the Kalinin detachment from September 1943 to June 1944

List of 92 Jewish commanders in the Byelorussian Partisan movement

Avrutin Iakov Mironovich	Chief of Detachment Stuff	Nepobedimy	3rd Minsk
Aizenberg Boris Lvovich	Chief of Detachment Stuff	Petrakov	Rokossovski
Angelchik Iosif Mikhaylovich	Detachment Commissar	Budenny	Stalin
Babishchev Samuil Ilyich	Brigade Commissar		? 125
Belov Mikhail Rufimovich	Detachment Commander	Za Sovetskuyu Belorussiyu	Frunze
Belskii Anatolii Davidovich	Detachment Commander	Kalinin	
Berkovich Isaak Zelikovich	Chief of Detachment Stuff	? 5	Chapaev
Bodnev Aizik Elevich	Chief of Detachment Stuff	Shturmovik	TsK KP(b)B
Boiko Zakhar Antonovich	Commissar, Chief of Brigade Stuff		Ponomarenko
Bolotin Boris Abramovich	Detachment Commissar	Shchors	Bogushevskaya
Bolotin Efim Evseevich	Chief of Detachment Stuff	Shchors	? 37 Parkhomenko
Borodulin Mordukh Movshevich	Chief of Detachment Stuff	? 212	Osipovichskaya VOG
Breido Isak Markovich	Chief of Detachment Stuff	Stalin	1st Baranovichi
Burmak Moisei Isaakovich	Chief of Detachment Stuff	? 1	2nd Belorusskaya
Bukhman Abram Solomonovich	Detachment Commissar	Zaluzhye	Grizodubova
Byvalyi Boris Grigorevich	Brigade Commissar		Starik
Vertgeim Anatolii Isaakovich	Chief of Detachment Stuff	detachment ? 106	
Vertkin Boris Moiseevich	Detachment Commissar	Kotovski	Narodnye mstiteli
Gertsovich Grigorii Efimovich	Chief of Detachment Stuff		Pravda
Gershovich Isaak Moiseevich	Regiment Commissar		Partizanski polk ? 277
Gilchik Leva Moiseevich	Detachment Commander	? 5	Chapaev
Golant Ruvim Khaimovich	Detachment Commissar	? 210	Osipovichskaya VOG
Goldberg Ruvim Lvovich	Detachment Commissar	Gastello	Diadi Koli
Gonikman Isaak Khaimovich	Detachment Commander	? 3	Zhelezniak
Gonikman Mikhail Izrailevich	Detachment Commissar	Bolshevik	37th Elskaya
Gorelik Aleksandr Aleksandrovich	Detachment Commander	Oktiabr	Pervomaiskaya
Grenader Petr Izrailevich	Detachment Commander	? 4	Kirov
Gripoded Petr Izrailevich	Detachment Commander	? 4	Zhelezniak
Gubler Efim Efimovich	Detachment Commissar	KIM	VLKSM
Danovich Fedor Afanasevich	Detachment Commander	I.Kolas	Pervomaiskaya
Egudkin Samson Solomonovich	Brigade Commissar		Mstitel
Elkanovich Samuil Isaakovich	Detachment Commissar	? 5	Chekist
Zager Mikhail Sakhnovich	Chief of Detachment Stuff		2-ia Zaslonov
Ziniakov Leonid Sergeevich	Detachment Commissar	? 60	Chekist
Zorin Semen Natanovich	Detachment Commander	detachment ? 106	
Kantser Ilya Abramovich	Detachment Commissar	Smert Fashizmu	? 123 25th Anniversary of BSSR
Keimakh David Ilyich	Detachment Commander	Shcherbin	
Kleinburg Leonid Leonovich	Chief of Detachment Stuff	Malenkov	Chapaev
Koron David Elevich	Detachment Commissar	Gvardeets	Donukalov
Korotkov Evsei Naumovich	Chief of Detachment Stuff	Molotov	Za Rodinu
Kruglikov Gerasim Litmanovich	Chief of Stuff, Detachment Commissar	Dzerzhinski	Frunze
Kumbarg Konstantin Solomonovich	Battalion Commissar	battalion ? 1	Smolenski partizanski polk
Lando Natan Borisovich	Detachment Commissar	Kalinkovichski	
Lapidus Izrail Abramovich	Detachment Commander	Kutuzov	2nd Minsk
Lapin Matvei Leontevich	Detachment Commissar	Ponomarenko	Rokossovski
Lev Mikhail Andreevich	Chief of Regiment Stuff		? 537
Levitan Mikhail Semenovich	Detachment Commissar	Shchors	? 37 Parkhomenko
Likhter Efim Iakovlevich	Brigade Commissar		Starik
Lvov Aleksandr Vasilevich	Detachment Commissar	? 721	
Lianger Iosif Veniaminovich	Detachment Commander	? 3	Lenin
Malbin Lazar Abramovich	Chief of Detachment Stuff	Kalinin	
Merson Afanasii Moiseevich	Detachment Commissar	Ponomarenko	
Milshtein Isaak Efimovich	Detachment Commissar	? 4	Nikitin
Mindlin Abram Iakovlevich	Detachment Commander	Kalinkovichski	
Mindlin David Iakovlevich	Detachment Commander	Parichski	
Motienko Mikhail Anatolevich	Chief of Detachment Stuff	? 55	? 125
Mugerman Miron Naumovich	Detachment Commissar	? 135	
Mukatser Zakhar Moiseevich	Detachment Commander	Razzhalovichski	Grizodubova
Nikitin Nikolai Mikhailovich	Brigade Commander		Nikitin
Okun Leonid Mikhailovich	Detachment Commander	? 4	208th partizanski polk
Pavlovich Engels Vulfovich	Detachment Commissar	Zaslonov	? 121 Bragina
Perlov Efim Davydovich	Detachment Commissar	Smert Fashizmu	37th Elskaya

Podolnyi Mikhail Pavlovich	Detachment Commander	Istrebitel	Voroshilov
Prokopets David Iakovlevich	Chief of Detachment Stuff	? 5	Chekist
Prusak Moisei Peisakhovich	Brigade Commissar		Shchors
Reznik Semen Borisovich	Detachment Commissar	Zhelezniak	Chkalov
Reznitski Lev Isaakovich	Chief of Detachment Stuff	reserve	Za Sovetskuyu Belarus
Reider Pinia Meerovich	Battalion Commissar	battalion ? 2	Partizanski polk ? 255
Rudnitski Semen Mikhailovich	Battalion Commissar	battalion ? 3	? 425
Rutman Ilyia Borisovich	Chief of Regiment Stuff		152nd partizanski polk
Sverdlov Samuil Monusovich	Regiment Commander		Partizanski polk ? 255
Solomon Eduard Borisovich	Chief of Detachment Stuff	Shirokov	Neulovimye
Stoler Semen Iakovlevich	Detachment Commissar	Chkalov	? 225 A.Suvorov
Tkach Mikhail Aizikovich	Detachment Commissar	? 4	Lepel Brigade Stalin
Fedorov David Ilich	Chief of Regiment Stuff		polk ? 113
Feigelman Khaim Afroimovich	Detachment Commissar	detachment ? 106	
Feldman Naum Lvovich	Detachment Commissar	25th Anniversary of BSSR	Ponomarenko
Fogel Iosif Lazarevich	Brigade Commander		Shturmovaya
Khazan Semen Mendelevich	Detachment Commissar	Ryzhak	Stalin
Khaimovich Boris Faivelevich	Battalion Commissar	battalion ? 1	208th partizanski polk
Khinich Aron Izrailevich	Detachment Commissar	Bondarovets	? 101 A.Nevski
Tsivin Gilel Aronovich	Chief of Detachment Stuff	? 61	? 61
Tsimkovski Ziama Mendelevich	Detachment Commissar	Za Sovetskuyu Rodinu	Glusskaya Brigade ? 100
Chernoglaz Zus Iakovlevich	Brigade Commissar		37th Elskaya Brigade
Chernyi Izrail Iakovlevich	Chief of Detachment Stuff	Za Sovetskuyu Belorussiyu	Za Sovetskuyu Belorussiyu
Cherniak Iakov Lvovich	Detachment Commander	? 6	Kutuzov
Cherniakov Iakov Moiseevich	Detachment Commander	Dzerzhinski	? 200 Rokossovski
Chirlin Edit Iankelevich	Detachment Commander	Leninski Komsomol	Iazykovich
Shvartsman Samuil Iakovlevich	Detachment Commissar	Zvezda	Kalinovski
Shulgin Monia Abramovich	Chief of Detachment Stuff		Vpered
Erkin Girsha Nasonovich	Detachment Commissar	Bolshevik	Bolshevik
Erlakh Iankel Shevelevich	Detachment Commissar	detached Lelchitski	

List of 7742 Jews that were in the
Byelorussian Partisan Movement 1941-44

198 WE STOOD SHOULDER TO SHOULDER

NAME	YEAR	CAME FROM	REGION	BRIGADE	DETACHMENT
Abelevich Natan Meyerovich	1904	Zelva	Belostok	A.Nevski	
Abilevich Liza Yakovlevna	1921	Dyatlovo	Baranovichi	Pobieda	Molotov
Abramzon Abram Zalmanovich	1926	from captivity	Vitebsk	Rokossovski	Kotovski
Abramzon Grigori Borisovich	1914	Disna	Vileyka	4th Belorussian	? 1
Abramov Genadi Mikhailovich	1900	Ulla	Vitebsk	Chapayev	detachments
Abramovitski Yakov Zalmanovich	1907	getto, Pruzhany	Brest	Ponomarenko	Kirov
Abramovich Abram Leibovich	1911	Novogrudok getto	Baranovichi	Kirov	Ordzhonikidze
Abramovich Abram Ovseyevich	1894	Korelichi	Baranovichi	Kalinin	
Abramovich Aleksandr Meyerovich	1918	Gorodishchensk district	Baranovichi	2? 5 annversary of BSSR	Kotovski
Abramovich Berta Khatskovna	1909	Minsk getto	Baranovichi	18th Frunze	brigade headquarters
Abramovich Boris Vulfovich	1924	Minsk	Mogilev	208th regiment, which grew to a regiment	
Abramovich David Aronovich	1900	Byten	Brest	Ponomarenko	Sovetskaya Belarus
Abramovich Yevel Gershevich	1900	s/kh Bolshevik	Vileyka	Frunze	Voroshilov
Abramovich Yefim Yakovlevich	1919	from captivity	Minsk	Dyadi Koli	Dzerzhinski
Abramovich Zelda Moiseyevna	1936	Lida	Baranovichi	Kalinin	
Abramovich Izrail Yevseyevich	1920	from captivity	Minsk	Razgrom (Crushing defeat)	
Abramovich Yosif Abramovich	1920	Korelichi	Baranovichi	Kalinin	
Abramovich Isaak Girshevich	1922		Baranovichi	Oktyabr	
Abramovich Leya Ovseyevna	1923	Korelichi	Baranovichi	Kalinin	
Abramovich Lyuba Leibovna	1925	Minsk	Baranovichi	Kalinin	
Abramovich Lyubov Izrailevna	1920	Slonim	Baranovichi	Voroshilov	Voroshilov
Abramovich Mikhail Gershevich	1917	Pruzhany	Brest	Ponomarenko	Kirov
Abramovich Movsha Khaimovich	1922	Dyatlovo	Baranovichi	Leninskaya	family detachment group
Abramovich Mordukh Zelikovich	1901	Lida	Baranovichi	Kalinin	
Abramovich Peisakh Faivelevich	1924	Novogrudok	Baranovichi	Kalinin	
Abramovich Rakhelya Girshevna	1925	Lida	Baranovichi	Kalinin	
Abramovich Sulamita Leibovna	1943	Naliboki dense forest	Baranovichi	Kalinin	
Abramovich Felya Zalmanovna	1923	Novogrudok	Baranovichi	Kalinin	
Abramovich Khaim Abramovich	1910	Korelichi	Baranovichi	Kalinin	
Abramovich Khaya Greimenovna	1923	Novogrudok getto	Baranovichi	Kirov	Ordzhonikidze
Abramovich Tsypa Meyerovna	1914	Novogrudok	Baranovichi	Kalinin	
Abramovich Shimon Abramovich	1925	Mir	Baranovichi	Kalinin	
Abramovich Yankel Leizerovich	1913	Korelichi	Baranovichi	Kalinin	
Abramovich Yankel Mordukhovich	1911	Lakhva	Pinsk	Kirov	Za Rodinu (For Motherland)
Abramovskaya Anna Shayevna	1919	Byten, Baranovichi region	Brest	Za Sovetskuyu Belarus	Suvorov
Abramovski Leonid Yevelevich	1923	Mir	Baranovichi	Chkalov	
Abramovski Elya Sholomovich	1910	Slonim	Brest	Sikorski's headquarters	
Abramovski Yakov Zelmanovich	1907	Slonim	Brest	Za Sovetskuyu Belarus	brigade headquarters
Abramovshchik Izrail Movshevich	1915	Minsk	Baranovichi	Stalin	Budenny
Abramson Aleksei Moisevich	1932	Slonim	Brest		Kotovski
Abramson Lenya Leonidovich	1931	Slonim	Brest	Sikorski's headquarters	
Abramchik Krusya Ovseyevna	1921	Slonim	Brest	Sikorski's headquarters	
Abramchik Liza Moiseyevna	1925	Slonim	Brest	Sikorski's headquarters	
Abramchik Lyubov ShiyYevna	1922	Slonim	Brest	Ponomarenko	
Avdenshtat Mariya Pavlovna	1911		Palesye	? 123	Pavlovski's
Avinovitski Lipa Mikhailovich	1915	K. Kashirski	Pinsk	Molotov	Potalakh
Avrukin Semen Naumovich	1910	Minsk	Mogilev	208th partisan regiment	? 3
Avrukina Mariya Naumovna	1920	Minsk	Mogilev	partisan regiment ? 277	? 277
Avrutin Yakov Mironovich	1919	Cherven district, v. Dubovruchi	Minsk	3rd Minskaya	Lazo
Avrukh Avrum Borukhovich	1909	Volynskaya region, Ukraine	Brest	Sikorski's headquarters	
Avsishcher Galina Abramovna	1923	Sennenski district, Vileika region	Mogilev	Chekist	Mon. group
Avtsin Yosif Ilyich	1915	from captivity	Belostok		Boyevoi (Fighting)
Aginskaya Aleksandra Aronovna	1919	from the detachment polkovnika Ldova	Brest	Dzerzhinski	Chertkov
Aginski Grigori Samoilovich	1926	Stolbtsovskoe getto	Minsk	Chapayev	Ponomarenko
Aginski Zalman Girshevich	1896	Stolbtsy	Baranovichi	Kalinin	
Agulnik Volf Shmerovich	1914	Baranovichi, from home	Baranovichi	Grizodubova	Matrosov
Adamovich Arkadi Ivanovich	1914	Minsk	Minsk	Grishin's 13th regiment	
Adzhaev Grigori Konstantinovich	1916	from captivity	Vitebsk	Prudnikov's	Sirotin's
Adinailo Edya Ionovna	1924	GrizoDubov's's brigade	Grodno		B.Khmelnitski
Adinailo Edya Shayevna	1926	Stolbtsy	Grodno		B.Khmelnitski
Adoneilo Yuzik Shayevich	1923	Ostrov Mazovetski	Baranovichi	Kirov	
Adoneiyum Moisei Shayevich	1914	N. Sverzhen	Baranovichi	Zhdanov	
Azeiman Yakov Khaimovich	1904		Minsk	Grishin's 13th regiment	

JEWISH PARTISANS IN BYELORUSSIA 1941-1944 199

Azenberg Samuil Abramovich	1896	Lida	Baranovichi	Vpered (Forward)	Chkalov
Azentat Aizik Meyerovich	1915	Martikantsy	Baranovichi	Lenin's komsomol	Kotovski
Azenshtat Borukh Abramovich	1921	Martikantsy	Baranovichi	Lenin's komsomol	Kotovski
Azimberg Sofiya Abramovna	1915	Minsk	Vitebsk	1st Zaslonov	Kutuzov
Aizenbut Ita Elevna	1914	Rubezhevichi	Baranovichi	Kalinin	
Aizenshtadt Daba Borisovna	1921	Novogrudok	Baranovichi	Kalinin	
Aizenshtadt Shenshel Leibovich	1912	Novogrudok	Baranovichi	Kalinin	
Aizel Lev Yankelevich	1909	Nevir, Volyn region	Pinsk	Shubetidze	Ordzhonikidze
Aizel MIlya Shlemovna	1915	Nevir, Volyn region	Pinsk	Shubetidze	Ordzhonikidze
Aizen Foma Samuilovich	1919	Poland	Pinsk	Molotov	Shish
Aizenberg Aizik Shayevich	1910	Lyubashovski district, Volyn region	Pinsk	Sovetskaya Belarus	Kutuzov
Aizenberg Boris Lvovich	1902	from captivity	Vitebsk	Rokossovski	brigade headquarters
Aizenberg Gershko Yoselevich	1900	Domachevo	Pinsk	Molotov	Lazo
Aizenberg Yelizaveta Yefimovna	1916	Lyubashovski district, Volyn region	Pinsk	Sovetskaya Belarus	Kutuzov
Aizenberg Izrail Mikhailovich	1923	Belarusian Staff of Partisan Movement	BSPM		
Aizenberg Ilya Mikhailovich	1923	VShON, Moskva	Vileyka	Voroshilov	Vileika center
Aizenberg Mendel Nevakhovich	1912	Stolbtsy	Baranovichi	detachment ? 106	
Aizenberg Yankel Nevakhovich	1924	Peshkovo, Ivanovo district	Pinsk	Shubetidze	Nemytov
Aizenshtadt Semen Martynovich	1903	Ivatsevichi	Brest	Dzerzhinski	Chertkov
Aizenshtat Mariya Naumovna	1926	Glussk	Palesye	? 123	Krasny Oktyabr
Aizenshtat Naum Leibovich	1904	Rudobelka	Palesye	? 123	administration platoon
Aizenshtein Leiba Moiseyevich	1912	Derechin	Baranovichi	Pobieda	Molotov
Aizenshtein Nokhim Zavelevich	1908	Odrizhin	Pinsk	Molotov	brigade headquarters
Aizina Yelizaveta Borisovna	1920	Naliboki	Vitebsk	Nikitin's	? 1
Aitel Aron Gerisovich	1920	Byten	Pinsk	Lenin	Dzerzhinski
Aishtein Khaya Aronovna	1924	Derechin	Baranovichi	Pobieda	
Akerman Manya Shlemovna	1917	Slonim	Brest	Sikorski's headquarters	
Akim Aleksei Yakovlevich	1922	Semiatichi	Brest		Kutuzov
Akselrod Abram Vasilevich		getto, Vilno	Vileyka	Voroshilov	Kalinin
Akselrod Benyamin Berkovich	1924	Molodechno, getto	Baranovichi	Za Sovetskuyu Belarus	Shturm
Akselrod Brazd Osherovich	1914	StoLyutsy, getto	Baranovichi	Stalin	
Akselrod Lev Zalmanovich	1926	Krasnoye	Vileyka	Frunze	Voroshilov
Akselrod Lyuba Ovseyevna	1915	Stolbtsy	Baranovichi	Kalinin	
Akselrod Manya Abramovna	1923	Minsk	Baranovichi	detachment ? 106	
Akselrod Khana Ovseyevna	1918	Stolbtsy	Baranovichi	Kalinin	
Akselrod Yakov Zalmanovich	1922	Krasnoye	Vileyka	Frunze	Voroshilov
Aleev Izya Abasovich	1927		Baranovichi	detachment ? 106	
Aleksandrov Mikhail Pavlovich	1912	iz partizanskoi gruppy, Slutsk	Grodno		Kalinin
Aleksandrovich Abram Izrailevich	1904	Jewish camp, Minsk	Vileyka	Frunze	Voroshilov
Aleksandrovich Yakim Moiseyevich	1903	Minsk, underground, regional committee of the CP(b)B	Minsk	Narodnye Mstitel (Revenger)i Voronyanski	Voronyanski
Aleksandrovich-Barsar Regina Semenovna	1923	Minsk	Baranovichi	Komsomolets	brigade headquarters
Aleksandrovski Aron Gershkovich	1915	Sverzhen	Minsk	Chapayev	Shchors
Alekhnovich Boris Zundelevich	1923	Minsk	Baranovichi	detachment ? 106	
Alekhnovich Grigori Venyaminovich	1927	Minsk	Baranovichi	detachment ? 106	
Albert Isaak Falkovich	1916	Dyatlovo	Baranovichi	Kirov	Ordzhonikidze
Albershtein Yelizaveta KushElevna	1919	Lida	Baranovichi	Kirov	Iskra
Alperin Khonya Movshovich	1881	Novogrudok	Baranovichi	Kalinin	
Alperovich Abram Naftalevich	1913	Kurenets, Vileika region	Vitebsk	Voroshilov	Mstitel (Revenger)
Alperovich Vulf Yevelevich	1924	Jewish camp	Vileyka	Voroshilov	headquarters' production group
Alperovich Gaves Aogdukhovich	1926	getto	Vileyka	Voroshilov	Chapayev
Alperovich Dora Borisovna	1910	Minsk	Minsk	Shturmovaya	Za Otechestvo (For Fatherland)
Alperovich Yelizaveta Aronovna	1921	Vileika, getto	Baranovichi	Kutuzov	
Alperovich Zalman Abelevich	1908	Logoiski district, Kremenets	Minsk	Dima	
Alperovich Zalman Moiseyevich	1926	Kurenets, Vileika region	Vitebsk	Ponomarenko	Dovator
Alperovich Izrail Izrailevich	1923	iz ukrainskogo batalona	Vileyka	Voroshilov	Istrebitel (Destroyer)
Alperovich Moisei Zalmanovich	1922	getto	Vileyka	Suvorov	
Alperovich Noson Rubinovich	1924	Kurenets	Vileyka	Dovator	brigade headquarters
Alperovich Perets Abramovich	1926		Minsk	Narodnye Mstitel (Revenger)i Voronyanski	brigade hospital
Alperovich Polya Yakovlevna	1925	Minsk	Baranovichi	detachment ? 106	
Alperovich Raisa Ivanovna	1926	Krivichi, Vileika region	Vitebsk	Ponomarenko	Kirov
Alperovich Revekka Khaimovna	1925	Minsk	Baranovichi	detachment ? 106	
Alperovich Rubin Nosonovich	1905	Kurenets	Vileyka	Dovator	

Alperovich Rubin Yankelevich	1903	getto, Vileika	Vileyka	Gastello	Za Sovetskuyu Rodinu
Alperovich Semen Zakharovich	1915	Kurenets, Vileika region	Vitebsk	Ponomarenko	Kirov
Alperovich Fanya Mendeleyevna	1901		Vitebsk	Chapayev	detachments
Alperovich Fanya YudolYevna	1919	Roichino	Vileyka	Kutuzov	
Alperovich Khaya Yakovlevna	1913		Vitebsk	Chapayev	brigade headquarters
Alperovich Eser Markovich	1928	Minsk	Baranovichi	detachment ? 106	
Alperovich Yakov Aronovich	1923	Kurenets	Minsk	Voronyanski	Kotovski
Alpert Abram Isaakovich	1914	Dyatlovo	Baranovichi	Leninskaya	family detachment group
Alpert Abram Mordukhovich	1909	Lida	Baranovichi	Pobieda	brigade headquarters
Alpert Anna Peisakhovna	1925	Slonim	Brest	Sikorski's headquarters	
Alpert Borukh Isaakovich	1925	Dyatlovo	Baranovichi	Leninskaya	Leninski
Alpert David Leibovich	1884	Dyatlovo	Baranovichi	Leninskaya	Krasnogvardeiski
Alpert Isaak Falkovich	1916	Dyatlovo getto	Baranovichi	Kirov	Ordzhonikidze
Alpert Lazar Abramovich	1924	Sverzhen	Baranovichi	Kirov	
Alpert Mulya Abramovich	1934		Baranovichi	Leninskaya	Borba
Alpert Peisakh Zakharovich	1898	Slonim	Pinsk	Lenin	Kutuzov
Alpert Raisa Peisakhovna	1924	Slonim	Pinsk	Lenin	Kutuzov
Alpert Raya Khonovna	1912		Baranovichi	Leninskaya	Borba
Alpert Riva Aizikovna	1901	Slonim	Pinsk	Lenin	Kutuzov
Alpert Khana Peisakhovna	1925	Slonim	Pinsk	Lenin	Kutuzov
Alpershtein Meyer Leibovich	1910	Dyatlovo getto	Baranovichi	Kirov	Ordzhonikidze
Alpershtein Moisei Kushelevich	1920	Ivye	Baranovichi	Kirov	Iskra
Altman Aleksandra KushElevna	1909	Stolbtsovskoe getto	Minsk	Chapayev	Ponomarenko
Altman David Nikolayevich	1909	br. Rodionova	Minsk	1st Antifashistskaya	
Altman Izrail Yakovlevich	1927	Vitebsk obl., Lioznenski district	Minsk	Za Sovetskuyu Belorussiyu	Pobeditel
Altman Markek	1912	Kalinkovichi, iz madiarsk. rab. garniz.	Palesye	99th Kalinkovichskaya	Kotovski
Altman Pushel Khachkovich	1895	Stolbtsy, getto	Baranovichi	Stalin	Parkhomenko
Altmark Mikhail Borisovich	1929	Orsha	Mogilev	Chekist	Kalyushnikov's
Altshuler Anna Naumovna	1924	Dikov	Gomel		Kotovski
Altshuler Venyamin Abramovich	1905	Mogilev, concentration camp	Pinsk		? 200
Altshuler Tatyana Naumovna	1918	Shklov	Mogilev	Ilyin's	? 24
Alshits Galina IdElevna	1909	Bobr	Mogilev	Ilyin's	? 5
Alshuler Moisei Khaimovich	1898	Rogachevski district	Baranovichi	? 620	
Amarant Samuil Adolfovich	1904	Vilno	Baranovichi	Kalinin	
Amarant Tamara Ilyichna	1913	Vilno	Baranovichi	Kalinin	
Amburg Raisa Khaimovna	1929	Ukhvala, Krupki district	Mogilev	Ilyin's	? 30
Amburg Khaim Shmuilovich	1904	Ukhvala, Krupki district	Mogilev	Ilyin's	? 30
Amelchenko Fira Mikhailovna	1908	Novoselki, Borisov district	Minsk	Shchors	Shchors
Amstibovski Leva Yudelevich	1921	Kosovo	Brest	Ponomarenko	Sovetskaya Belarus
Angelchik Yakov Sholomovich	1909	Novogrudok, getto	Baranovichi	1st Baranovichskaya	Frunze
Angelchik Yosif Mikhailovich	1888	from captivity	Gomel	Stalin	Budenny
Andreichik Yevgeni Yosifovich	1938	Minsk	Baranovichi	Kalinin	
Andreichik Lyubov Yosifovna	1933	Minsk	Baranovichi	Kalinin	
Andreichik Mariya Salomonovna	1905	Minsk	Baranovichi	Kalinin	
Antipenko Klavdiya FadeYevna	1919	Rechen, Lyuban district	Minsk	Ponomarenko	Selnitski
Apel Shlema Yesilevich	1923	Lida	Baranovichi	Kalinin	
Aranovich Yefim Zalmanovich	1924	Minsk			
Aranovich Yosif Shlemovich	1915	Baranovichi, from home	Baranovichi	Grizodubova	Matrosov
Aranovich Elya Shlemovich	1908	from the civil camp	Vileyka	4th Belorusskaya	? 6
Aranovski Alter Yeselevich	1902	Litva, g. Velt	Baranovichi	Leninskaya	Niepobedimy (Undefeated)
Arbitman Semen Borisovich	1922	Uzdenski district, v. TElyakovo	Minsk	Rokossovski	Furmanov
Arinovich Zus Peisakhovich	1924	Domanovichi, Starobin district	Pinsk	Komarov-Korzh's	Komarov's 3rd group
Arinovich Roza Peisakhovna	1921	Domanovichi, Starobin district	Pinsk	Komarov-Korzh's	Komarov's 3rd group
Arlyuk Zakhar Ilyich	1914	Lida	Baranovichi	Kirov	Iskra
Arlyuk Sonya Berkovna	1921	Lida	Baranovichi	Kalinin	
Arman Khaim Moiseyevich	1904	v. Khotovo	Baranovichi	Kalinin	
Arnatskaya Elena Borisovna	1920	Borisov	Minsk	Shchors	Bolshevik
Arnover Filipp Leontevich	1913	Poland	Brest	Stalin	Chernyak
Aron Avsei Mendelevich	1895	Germanovichi	Vileyka	Zhdanov	
Aron Genya Moiseyevna	1920	Mery	Vileyka	4th Belorusskaya	? 1
Aron Itsik Moiseyevich	1915	Mery	Vileyka	4th Belorusskaya	? 6
Aronzon Naum Zelmanovich	1914	from the encirclement	Mogilev		? 19
Aronik Mikhail Lvovich	1914	from captivity	Vitebsk	Prudnikov's	Grinenko's's
Aronov Berzon Mendelevich	1915	Disna	Vileyka	4th Belorusskaya	? 6
Aronov Isaak Matveyevich	1915	Mery	Vileyka	4th Belorusskaya	? 6

Aronov Yudel Sholomovich	1904	N. Sverzhen	Minsk	Chapayev	Shchors
Aronovich Aron Malkonovich	1913		Baranovichi	Oktyabr	
Arotsker Polina Vulfovna	1925	Minsk	Baranovichi	Stalin	Bolshevik
Asner Abram Itskovich	1916	Nachi	Baranovichi	Lenin's komsomol	Lenin's komsomol
Asner Aron Itskovich	1918	Nachi	Baranovichi	Lenin's komsomol	Lenin's komsomol
Asner Rakhil Abramovna	1925	Eishishki	Baranovichi	Lenin's komsomol	Lenin's komsomol
Asner Khaim Itskovich	1915	Eishishki	Baranovichi	Lenin's komsomol	Lenin's komsomol
Asner Tsilya Abramovna	1927	Eishishki	Baranovichi	Lenin's komsomol	Lenin's komsomol
Asner Yankel Itskovich	1913	Nachi	Baranovichi	Lenin's komsomol	Lenin's komsomol
Asnis Isaak Yefimovich	1923	Minsk	Baranovichi	Vpered (Forward)	Chkalov
Asovski Izya Aronovich	1929	Glussk	Palesye	? 100	Budenny
Ass Bellya Itskovna	1897	Novogrudok	Baranovichi	Kalinin	
Ass Berta Yefimovna	1908	Slutsk	Baranovichi	Zhdanov	
Ass Ida Mendeleyevna	1924	Novogrudok	Baranovichi	Kalinin	
Ass Ilya Khatskelevich	1906	Pesochnoe, Kopyl district	Grodno	Kapusta's brigade hospital	
Ass Yosif Mendelevich	1927	Novogrudok	Baranovichi	Baranovichskaya	Kalinin
Ass Leva Khatskelevich	1895	Slutsk	Baranovichi	Zhdanov	
Ass Mendel Yosifovich	1894	Novogrudok	Baranovichi	Kalinin	
Ass Mikhail Solomonovich	1918	Bobruisk	Pinsk	Molotov	Kalinin
Ass Polina Semenovna	1926	Minsk getto	Minsk		Mstitel (Revenger)
Ass Solomon Khatskelevich	1887	Bobruisk	Minsk	Bragin	Panfilov
Ass Eduard Leonovich	1928	Slutsk	Minsk	Chapayev	Shchors
Ass Etya Mendeleyevna	1927	Novogrudok	Baranovichi	Kalinin	
Astashinskaya Manya Yakovlevna	1919	Minsk	Baranovichi	detachment ? 106	
Astrin Semen Zalmanovich	1918	Zazvorinets	Vileyka	Spartak	? 6
Astrinski Maks Moiseyevich	1903	Baranovichi, from home	Baranovichi	Grizodubova	Matrosov
Atlas Khatskel Sipayevich	1913	Velikaia VOlya	Baranovichi	Pobieda	Pobieda
Ausker Etya Eserovna	1925	Stolbtsy	Baranovichi	detachment ? 106	
Afanasyev Petr Leonidovich	1908		Vitebsk	Donukalov	brigade headquarters
Aframovich Lyuba Leibovna	1925	Minsk	Baranovichi		
Ash Tsiva Yakovlevna	1920	Belarusian Staff of Partisan Movement	Gomel	Stalin	headquarters
Ashkenadzi Aleksei Grigorevich	1911	from captivity	Minsk	Voronyanski	Mstitel (Revenger)
Ashkenadi Samuil Aleksandrovich	1908	Vileika district, Kurenets	Minsk	Kirov	Frunze
Ashman Boris Lazarevich	1922	from the camp	Palesye	? 225	Suvorov
Babaev Rustan Pashayevich	1919	from captivity	Mogilev	208th partisan regiment	headquarters
Babendur Raisa Mikhailovna	1921	Minsk	Minsk	Shturmovaya	Za Otechestvo (For Fatherland)
Babich Lev Isaakovich	1908	Minsk	Mogilev	208th partisan regiment	headquarters
Babishchev Samuil Ilyich			Palesye	? 125	
Babchik Naum Khaimovich	1898	Minsk	Baranovichi	detachment ? 106	
Babchik Rakhil Itskovna	1906	Minsk	Baranovichi	detachment ? 106	
Babchik Ruva Naumovich	1927	Minsk	Baranovichi	detachment ? 106	
Badovski N.K.	1914	Kopyl district	Minsk	Voroshilov	? 1
Baer Lyuba Khaimovna	1926	Yody	Vileyka	Za Rodinu (For Motherland)	Zhdanov
Bainer Meyer Isaakovich	1907	Gomel	Grodno	Izyumski's	
Bairan Pesya Yankelevna	1921	Lida	Baranovichi	Kalinin	
Baitman Boris Zusevich	1926	Kalinovka	Palesye	? 100	Budenny
Baitman Zus Zelikovich	1891	Kalinovka, Lyuban district	Minsk	Ponomarenko	Kalinovski
Baitman Pinya Zelikovich	1888	Lelchitsy	Palesye	Lelchitskaya	administration platoon
Bakalchuk Mikhail Abramovich	1926	Jewish camp, Rovno region.	Pinsk	Shubetidze	Ordzhonikidze
BakaLyar David Rubinovich	1921	Selets, Kartuz-Berezski district	Brest	Za Sovetskuyu Belarus	Suvorov
BakaLyash Vera Samuilovna	1911	Radostovo	Brest	Dzerzhinski	Molotov
Bakenshtein Galina Semenovna	1922	Gorodishche district	Baranovichi	25 years of the BSSR	Grozny
Bakman Boris Yosifovich	1915	Kobrin, from captivity	Pinsk	Molotov	Suvorov
Baksht Basya Borisovna	1926	Lida	Baranovichi	Kirov	Iskra
Baksht Boris Leibovich	1893	Lida	Baranovichi	Kirov	Iskra
Baksht David Borisovich	1922	Lida	Baranovichi	Kirov	Iskra
Baksht Yosif Movshevich	1918	Belarusian Staff of Partisan Movement	Vileyka	Dovator	Sverdlov
Baksht Leiba Shlemovich	1926	Ivye	Baranovichi	Kalinin	
Baksht Menukha Davidovna	1914	Ivye	Baranovichi	Kalinin	
Baksht Ovsei Shlemovich	1922	Ivye	Baranovichi	Kalinin	
Baksht Samuil Yakovlevich	1923	Dyatlovo getto	Baranovichi	Kirov	Ordzhonikidze
Bakshtein Grisha Mikhailovich	1924	Timkovichi	Minsk	Chapayev	Ponomarenko
Bal Karl	1934	Minsk	Baranovichi	detachment ? 106	

Baltsin Shavel Izrailevich	1901	Boyanichi, Lyuban district	Minsk	Ponomarenko	Selnitski
Band Abram Khatskelevich	1921	Shilovichi	Brest		Budenny
Band Arsik Khatskelevich	1914	Slonim district	Brest	Sikorski's headquarters	Shchors
Bandelsman Sroel Isaakovich	1897		Baranovichi	detachment ? 106	
Bank Aron Ilyich	1905	Vidzy	Vitebsk	Prudnikov's	colonel Nikitin's
Banshchik Isaak Davidovich	1896	Baranovichi, from home	Baranovichi	Grizodubova	Matrosov
Baran Aleksandr Rubinovich	1921	Lida	Baranovichi	Voroshilov	Voroshilov
Baran Barik Lazarevich	1924	Ivye	Baranovichi	Vpered (Forward)	A.Nevski
Baran Boris Yosifovich	1925	Minsk	Baranovichi	detachment ? 106	
Baran Bronya Borisovna	1923	Minsk	Baranovichi	Chkalov	reserve group
Baran Zalman Mordukhovich	1908	from the civil camp	Vileyka	4th Belorusskaya	? 6
Baran Itsko Faivelevich	1924		Baranovichi	Oktyabr	
Baran Moisei Yosifovich	1920	Krasnoye, Minsk region	Minsk	Shturmovaya	brigade headquarters
Baranov Boris Davidovich	1910	Druya	Vileyka	4th Belorusskaya	? 1
Baranov Dmitri Grigorevich	1913	from the detachment Nikitin's	Minsk	Chapayev	Shchors
Baranova Rita Abramovna	1917	Baranovichi	Minsk		Chapayev
Baranovich Abram Rubinovich	1913	Ivienets	Baranovichi	Kalinin	
Baranovskaya Sonya Moiseyevna	1925	Derechin	Baranovichi	Pobieda	Pobieda
Baranovski Isaak Shlemovich	1912	Derechin	Baranovichi	Pobieda	Pobieda
Baranskaya Sonya Naumovna	1913	Minsk	Baranovichi	detachment ? 106	
Baranchik David Yeselevich	1928	Zheludok	Baranovichi	Leninskaya	Krasnogvardeiski
Baranchik Leib Semenovich	1911	Lida	Baranovichi	Kalinin	
Baranchik Sonya IsElevna	1923	Zheludok	Baranovichi	Leninskaya	Borba
Baranchuk Yosif Aizikovich	1898	Zheludok	Baranovichi	Leninskaya	Borba
Baranchuk Khasya Khaimovna	1920	Belitsa	Baranovichi	Leninskaya	Borba
Baranchuk Yankel Mordukhovich	1902		Baranovichi	Oktyabr	
Barg Viktor Movshevich	1927	Alitus	Baranovichi	Lenin's komsomol	Ivanov's
Barg Movsha Girshevich	1903	Alitus	Baranovichi	Lenin's komsomol	Ivanov's
Bard Mendel Yanilovich	1913	Slutsk	Brest	Sikorski's headquarters	
Bardakh Chernya					
Baretski Isaak Srolevich	1925	Slonim	Pinsk	Lenin	Kutuzov
Barkan Boris Samuilovich	1905	detachment ismall town of Budennogo	Vileyka	Voroshilov	headquarters' production group
Barkan Izrail Gerukhmovich	1904	Minsk	Baranovichi	18th Frunze	Frunze
Barlas Sender Yankelevich	1909	Domachevo	Pinsk	Molotov	Lazo
Barlas Sonya Yosifovna	1923	Rudobelka	Palesye	? 123	Vezhnovets'
Barman Mera Berkovna	1923	concentration camp	Pinsk	Kuibyshev	Shchors
Barnamov Leiba Aftaleyevich	1923	Yody	Vileyka	Spartak	? 3
Barovski Volf Yosifovich	1916	Novogrudok	Baranovichi	Kalinin	
Barok David Buinimovich	1913	Germanovichi	Vileyka	Spartak	? 6
Barsov Pavel Vasilevich	1918	Vitebsk	Vitebsk	Kirillov	Kirillov's
Baru Aleksandr Markovich	1910	Zaslavl	Vitebsk	Nikitin's	? 2
Barshai Bella Yosifovna	1924	s/factory Oktyabr	Mogilev		? 115 Dolgov-Rudov's
Barshai Sara Borukhovna	1895	Batsevichi, Klichev district	Mogilev		? 278
Barshai Khaim Yosifovich	1926	s/factory Oktyabr	Mogilev	Osipovichskaya VOG	? 210
Baryshanskaya Bela Abramovna	1921	Dyatlovo	Baranovichi	Za Sovetskuyu Belarus	family detachment
Baryshnikova Olga Mikhailovna	1900	Shklov	Mogilev	Chekist	? 1
Basist Zlata Mordukhovna	1920	Lida	Baranovichi	Kalinin	
Basist Mordukh Benyaminovich	1912	Lida	Baranovichi	Kalinin	
Basket Kalman Moiseyevich	1897	Lida	Baranovichi	Kalinin	
Basket Sima Moiseyevna	1899	Lida	Baranovichi	Kalinin	
Basket Faina Kalmanovna	1923	Lida	Baranovichi	Kalinin	
Basket Khaim Kalmanovich	1927	Lida	Baranovichi	Kalinin	
Baskin Yosif Lazarevich	1923	Minsk getto	Baranovichi	Shchors	Shchors
Baskin Samuil Matveyevich	1896	Checkersk	Gomel	1st Gomelskaya	Kalinin
Baskina Ira Lazarevna	1924	Minsk	Baranovichi	Chkalov	? 4 "Za Sovetskuyu Belarus"
Bastomski Sadek Isaakovich	1917		Baranovichi	Leninskaya	Niepobedimy (Undefeated)
Baumovich Boris Yakovlevich	1912	Drogichin	Pinsk	Shubetidze	Stalin
Bakhrakh Abram	1925	Dobrush	Gomel	Stalin	headquarters
Bashanski Abram Khaimovich	1912		Baranovichi	Oktyabr	
Bashikhis Grigori Fadeyevich	1921	Minsk	Grodno	Chapayev	
Begelman Lev Zalmanovich	1909	? 1 vost. b-n nemetskoi armii	Vitebsk	Stalin	Suvorov
Begelman Yankel Aronovich	1913	Lenin	Pinsk	Molotov	Kalinin
Begun Kastrel Khaimovich	1906	from the civil camp	Vileyka	4th Belorusskaya	? 6
Begun Tsalya Abramovich	1912	Baranovichi	Baranovichi	Chkalov	? 4 "Za Sovetskuyu Belarus"

Begun Shlema Aizikovich	1926	Boyanichi, Lyuban district	Minsk	Ponomarenko	Korneyev's
Beder Yosif Itskovich	1905	Khomsk, Pinsk region	Brest	Sverdlov	Makarevich
Bedzovskaya Lilya Mikhailovna	1922	Lida	Baranovichi	Kalinin	
Bedzovskaya Khasya Moiseyevna	1902	Lida	Baranovichi	Kalinin	
Bedzovski Benyamin Mikhailovich	1933	Lida	Baranovichi	Kalinin	
Bedzovski Izrail Borukhovich	1920	Lida	Baranovichi	Kalinin	
Bedzovski Khonon Mikhailovich	1924	Lida	Baranovichi	Kalinin	
Bedynerman Raisa Meyerovna	1915	Minsk getto	Baranovichi	Chapayev	Parkhomenko
Beyerzon Girsha Mendelevich	1897	from the camp v/plen-nykh, Orsha	Minsk	Kirov	? 4
Bezdetski Mokha Srulevich	1913	Ivanovo	Pinsk	Molotov	Lazo
Bezrodny Mikhail Grigorevich	1918	from captivity	Mogilev	? 13	? 719
Bezruchki Izrail Movshevich	1924	Shchuchin	Baranovichi	Leninskaya	family detachment group
Beikelman Yankel Aronovich	1913	Lenin	Pinsk	Molotov	Shish
Beilin Benyamin Leizerovich	1907	Mir	Baranovichi	Kalinin	
Beilin Lev Grigorevich	1924	Minsk	Baranovichi	Ponomarenko	25 years of the BSSR
Bellyin's Tseita Borisovna	1912	from the civil camp	Vileyka	4th Belorusskaya	? 6
Beiman Abram Bayumovich	1924	Kozyany	Vileyka	Spartak	? 3
Beinenson Girsha Zalmanovich	1897	Zapole, Krupki district	Minsk	Shchors	Bolshevik
Beinenson Yelizaveta Yefimovna	1926	Zapole, Krupki district	Minsk	Shchors	Bolshevik
Beinesovich Beines Khaimovich	1900	Lagoisk	Baranovichi	Kalinin	
Beirakh Movsha Yekhilevich	1918	Lida	Baranovichi	Kalinin	
Bekenshtein Galina Semenovna	1922	Derechin	Baranovichi	Pervomaiskaya	Zhdanov
Bekenshtein Zalman Semenovich	1922	Derechin	Baranovichi	Pervomaiskaya	Pervomaiski
Beker Belya S.	1920	Derechin	Baranovichi	Pobieda	Pobieda
Beker Braiko Shimonovna	1908	Kaidanavo	Baranovichi	Kalinin	
Beker Liza Leibovna	1904	Derechin	Baranovichi	Pobieda	1st May
Beker Khaim Kivovich	1918	Belostok	Grodno	Chapayev	
Beker Shura Isaakovna	1930	Derechin	Baranovichi	Pobieda	1st May
Bekerman Berko Gershkovich	1915	Poland	Pinsk	Molotov	
Bekerman Mukha Abramovich	1924	concentration camp, Vlodava	Pinsk	Molotov	Kalinin
Bekker Alter Girshevich	1909	Derechin	Baranovichi	Leninskaya	hospital
Bekker Boris Samuilovich	1922	Derechin	Baranovichi	Pobieda	Pobieda
Bekker Lyubov Itskovna	1927	Derechin	Baranovichi	Pobieda	Suvorov
Bekker Solomon Samuilovich	1914	Belarusian Staff of Partisan Movement	Minsk	Special groups	gr. Filimonenko
Bekman Dora Elevna	1921	Baranovichi	Baranovichi	18th Frunze	Lenin
Bekrman Berko Gershkovich	1924	Poland	Pinsk	Molotov	Shish
Belanovskaya Renata Grigorevna	1914	Minsk	Baranovichi	18th Frunze	Kutuzov
Belevich TsElya	1923	Sharkovshchina	Vitebsk	Rokossovski	Shchors
Belitskaya Basya Girshevna	1907	Lida	Baranovichi	Kalinin	
Belitski Abram Yakovlevich	1906	Lida	Baranovichi	Kalinin	
Belitski Girsh Abramovich	1934	Lida	Baranovichi	Kalinin	
Belk Leiba Solomonovich	1927	Krulevshchizna	Minsk	1st Antifashistskaya	? 5
Belkin Grigori Yevelevich	1930		Mogilev	? 113	
Belkin Maksim Leizerovich	1923	Rubezhevichi	Baranovichi	Chkalov	? 4 "Za Sovetskuyu Belarus"
Belkin Samuil Abramovich	1927	Rubezhevichi	Baranovichi	Kalinin	
Belkina Yevgeniya Nor.	1912		Brest		Kirov
Belkina Riva Judenovna	1925	Minsk	Grodno	Chapayev	
Belkina Sara Moiseyevna	1893	Batsevichi, Klichev district	Mogilev	? 113	
Belkovski Leon Yefimovich	1915	Baranovichi	Brest	Ponomarenko	Sovetskaya Belarus
Beloboroda Feliks Izrailevich	1922	Lida	Baranovichi	Kirov	Iskra
Belov Mikhail Rufimovich		Vileyka	Frunze	Za Sovetskuyu Belorus-siyu	
Belokurski Mikhail Davidovich	1922	Klichev district	Baranovichi	? 620	
Belorusskaya Yelizaveta Lvovna	1906		Palesye	? 123	Vezhnovets'
Belostotskaya Katya Lyubovovna	1920	Derechin	Baranovichi	Pobieda	Pobieda
Belostotski David Lazarevich	1928	Minsk getto	Minsk	3rd Minskaya	brigade headquarters
Belostotski Lazar Isaakovich	1902	Minsk getto	Minsk	3rd Minskaya	brigade headquarters
Beloshkurnik Yesil Izrailevich	1920	from the camp	Baranovichi	Grizodubova	
Beloshkurnik Izrail Yeselevich	1894	from the camp	Baranovichi	Grizodubova	
Beloshkurnik Nadezhda Arkadevna	1913	Baranovichi	Baranovichi	Grizodubova	
BYelskaya Dora Moiseyevna	1923	Novogrudok	Baranovichi	Chapayev	Parkhomenko
BYelskaya Zelda Zelikovna	1920	Novogrudok	Baranovichi	Kalinin	
BYelski Aleksandr Davidovich	1908	v. Stankevichi	Baranovichi	Kalinin	
BYelski Anatoli Davidovich	1906	v. Stankevichi	Baranovichi	Kalinin	
BYelski Aron Davidovich	1927	v. Stankevichi	Baranovichi	Kalinin	
BYelski Zigizmund Davidovich	1912	Novogrudok district	Baranovichi	Kirov	Ordzhonikidze
BYelski Moisei Davidovich	1920	Gorodishche district	Baranovichi	Pobieda	Pobieda

BYelski Yudel Zelikovich	1909	Novogrudok	Baranovichi	Kalinin	
BYelskind Irina YulyYevna	1925	Minsk getto	Baranovichi	Stalin	Bolshevik
Belyavski Leonid Sergeyevich	1922	from captivity	Mogilev	Chekist	? 10
Belyak Abram Notkovich	1923	Jewish camp	Vileyka	Spartak	? 2
Belyak Leiba Peisakhovich	1911	Dunilovichi, Vileika region	Minsk	Voroshilov	? 5
Belyak Osip Leibovich	1927	Dunilovichi, Vileika region	Minsk	Voroshilov	? 5
Belyak Rakhmil Leibovich	1906	Braslav	Vileyka	Za Rodinu (For Motherland)	Kirov
Belyak Tevel Lazarevich	1920	Ivye	Baranovichi	Vpered (Forward)	A.Nevski
Belyakov Anatoli Yefimovich	1911	from captivity Borisov	Minsk	Death to Fascism	Kutuzov
Benderovskaya Roza Germovna	1915	from the camp	Baranovichi	Grizodubova	
Bener Benyamin Yudelevich	1917	Slonim	Brest	Ponomarenko	Sovetskaya Belarus
Beneshkevich Roza Girshevna	1914	Novogrudok	Baranovichi	Leninskaya	Borba
Benilsdorf Elya Khaimovna	1929	Dvorets	Baranovichi	Kalinin	
Beninson Grigori Zakharovich	1928	Orekhovo, Ushachi district	Vitebsk	Dubov's	commandant platoon
Beninson Dina Grigorevna	1909	Minsk	Mogilev	208th regiment	
Beninson Yevgeniya Pavlovna	1923	Minsk	Vileyka	Frunze	Krasnoye znamya (Red Banner)
Benya Minson Nikolayevich	1916	Glubokoye	Minsk	1st Antifashistskaya	? 6
Benyaminovich Isaak Berkovich	1880	Dyatlovo	Baranovichi	Leninskaya	family detachment group
Benyamenson Shlema Borukhovich	1916	Glubokoye	Minsk	1st Antifashistskaya	? 5
Ber Abram Yakovlevich	1911	K. Kashirski	Pinsk	Shubetidze	Kostyushko
Bergaut Moisei Ivanovich	1909	Vlodava (Poland)	Pinsk	Molotov	Shish
Berger Yefim Grigorevich	1906	Minsk	Baranovichi	detachment ? 106	
Berger Meilakh Abovich	1912	Novogrudok getto	Baranovichi	Kirov	Ordzhonikidze
Berger Roza Yevseyevna	1911	Minsk	Vileyka	Frunze	Voroshilov
Berger Sima Leizerovna	1895	Mir	Baranovichi	Kalinin	
Berdovski Grigori Aizikovich	1897	Ivye	Baranovichi	Kirov	Za Sovetskuyu Belarus
Berezovskaya Anna Matveyevna	1912	Minsk	Pinsk	Lenin	Dzerzhinski
Berezovski Noi Borisovich	1925	Grodno, getto	Belostok	A.Nevski	
Berenzon Ruvim Berkovich	1899	Central Committee of the CP (b) B	Palesye	formation headquarters	detachment at the headquarters
Berenshtein Isaak Movshevich	1924		Baranovichi	Oktyabr	
Berenshtein Leiba Girshevich	1904	concentration camp, Pogost-Zagorodski	Pinsk	Kuibyshev	Shchors
Berestetski Izrail Yankelevich	1925		Brest	Ponomarenko	Kirov
Berzhan Peisakh Khaimovich	1923	Kozyany	Vileyka	Spartak	? 3
Berzak Petr Yosifovich	1919	Baranovichi	Baranovichi	Chkalov	? 4 "Za Sovetskuyu Belarus"
Berzak Tsesya Yosifovna	1924	Baranovichi	Baranovichi	Chkalov	? 4 "Za Sovetskuyu Belarus"
Berzon Anna Gershevna	1918	from the civil camp	Vileyka	4th Belorusskaya	? 6
Berzon Leiba Mendelevich	1914	from the civil camp	Vileyka	4th Belorusskaya	? 6
Berzon Riva Grigorevna	1925	Sharkovshchina	Vitebsk	4th Belorusskaya	
Berzon Khana Pertsovna	1908	Jewish camp	Vileyka	4th Belorusskaya	? 6
Berinshtein Shaya Abramovich	1918	Volozhin	Baranovichi	Chkalov	
Berkner Kalman Yudelevich	1925	Byten	Pinsk	Lenin	Kutuzov
Berkner Shmerl Semdilovich	1923	Belostok	Grodno		Kirshner's group
Berkner Yudel Kalmanovich	1900	Byten	Pinsk	Lenin	Frunze
Berkovich Aizik Berkovich	1893	Stolbtsy, getto	Baranovichi	Za Sovetskuyu Belarus	Kirov
Berkovich Aizik Berkovich	1924	Stolbtsy	Baranovichi	Chkalov	? 4 "Za Sovetskuyu Belarus"
Berkovich Benyamin Berkovich	1922	v. Nikolasy	Baranovichi	Kalinin	
Berkovich Berko Aizikovich	1892	Mir	Baranovichi	Chkalov	
Berkovich Boris Gdalevich	1925	Novogrudok	Baranovichi	Kalinin	
Berkovich Viktor Gdalevich	1914		Baranovichi	Oktyabr	
Berkovich Galina Yosifovna	1923	Gomel	Gomel	Bolshevik	Bolshevik
Berkovich Genya Berovna	1928	Iuratishkinski district	Baranovichi	Stalin	Stalin
Berkovich Genya Moiseyevna	1922	Korelichi	Baranovichi	Kalinin	
Berkovich David Aronovich	1885	Radun	Baranovichi	Lenin's komsomol	Lenin's komsomol
Berkovich David Meyerevich	1913	Lida	Baranovichi	Kirov	Iskra
Berkovich Dasha Gdalevna	1913	Novogrudok	Baranovichi	Kalinin	
Berkovich Yeakhim Gdalevich	1921		Baranovichi	Oktyabr	
Berkovich Zalman Aronovich	1924		Baranovichi	Oktyabr	
Berkovich Izrail Yefimovich	1906	Baranovichi, from home	Baranovichi	Grizodubova	Matrosov
Berkovich Yosif Moiseyevich	1922	Korelichi	Baranovichi	Kalinin	
Berkovich Isaak Gdalevich	1915	Novogrudok	Baranovichi	Kalinin	
Berkovich Isaak Zelikovich	1913	Kopyl	Minsk	Chapayev	Ponomarenko
Berkovich Itsko Leizerovich	1926	Rubezhevichi	Baranovichi	Kalinin	
Berkovich Kunya Mordukhovna	1913	Lida	Baranovichi	Kalinin	

Berkovich Lazar Volfovich	1924	Korelichi	Baranovichi	Kalinin	
Berkovich Lazar Moiseyevich	1928	Voronovo	Baranovichi	Kalinin	
Berkovich Leizer Mikhailovich	1883	Rubezhevichi	Baranovichi	Kalinin	
Berkovich Meyer Borukhovich	1912	Novogrudok	Baranovichi	Kalinin	
Berkovich Mikhail Leibovich	1909	Baranovichi	Baranovichi	Leninskaya	Borba
Berkovich Movsha Mordukhovich	1923		Baranovichi	Oktyabr	
Berkovich Moisei Aronovich	1898	Voronovo	Baranovichi	Kalinin	
Berkovich Mordukh Girshevich	1900	Novogrudok	Baranovichi	Kalinin	
Berkovich MotLya Davidovna	1935	Lida	Baranovichi	Kalinin	
Berkovich Nokhim Yakovlevich	1927	Novogrudok getto	Baranovichi	Kirov	Ordzhonikidze
Berkovich Rakhil Yevseyevna	1910	Baranovichi, from home	Baranovichi	Grizodubova	Matrosov
Berkovich Rakhil Lazarevna	1900	Voronovo	Baranovichi		
Berkovich Samuil Meyerovich	1920	Slonim	Brest	Sikorski's headquarters	
Berkovich Seva Borukhovich	1921	Kopyl	Minsk	Chapayev	Ponomarenko
Berkovich Sema Mikhailovich	1927	Minsk	Baranovichi	detachment ? 106	
Berkovich Taiba Moiseyevna	1902	Novogrudok	Baranovichi	Kalinin	
Berkovich Todis Berkovich	1911	Iuratishkinski district	Baranovichi	Stalin	Stalin
Berkovich Khaim Davidovich	1922	Radun	Baranovichi	Lenin's komsomol	Lenin's komsomol
Berkovich Khaim Sholomovich	1926	Radun	Baranovichi	Lenin's komsomol	Kotovski
Berkovich Khona Berkovich	1917	Iuratishki, getto	Baranovichi	Stalin	Suvorov
Berkovich Tsira Moiseyevna	1919	Korelichi	Baranovichi	Kalinin	
Berkovich Shlema Izrailevich	1925	Baranovichi, from home	Baranovichi	Grizodubova	Matrosov
Berkovich Shmaier		Slonim	Brest	Za Sovetskuyu Belarus	Suvorov
Berkovich Sholom Borukhovich	1921	Kopyl	Minsk	Chapayev	Ponomarenko
Berkovich Elya Berkovich	1907	Novogrudok	Baranovichi	Kalinin	
Berkovich Yakov Leibovich	1914	Novogrudok getto	Baranovichi	Kirov	Ordzhonikidze
Berkovskaya Gita Kivovna	1881	Vselyub	Baranovichi	Kalinin	
Berkovskaya Leya Gutelevna	1923	Novogrudok	Baranovichi	Kalinin	
Berkovskaya Sonya Gershovna	1916	Vselyub	Baranovichi	Kalinin	
Berkovskaya Frida Nokhimovna	1910	Novogrudok	Baranovichi	Kalinin	
Berkovskaya Cherno Yeselevna	1902	Novogrudok	Baranovichi	Kalinin	
Berkovskaya Yusla Moiseyevna	1918	Korelichi	Baranovichi	Kalinin	
Berkovski Gutel Borukhovich	1895	Novogrudok	Baranovichi	Kalinin	
Berkovski Rubin Aronovich	1904	Dyatlovo	Baranovichi	Leninskaya	Borba
Berkovski Samuil Isaakovich	1918	Minsk	Baranovichi	detachment ? 106	
Berkovski Khaim Moiseyevich	1911	Korelichi	Baranovichi	Kalinin	
Berkovski Shimon Isaakovich	1905	Baranovichi	Baranovichi	Kalinin	
Berkon Boris Vulfovich	1921	Sharkovshchina	Vileyka	Spartak	? 6
Berkshtein Abram Simkovich	1905	getto, Vileika	Vileyka	Gastello	brigade headquarters
Berlina Yelizaveta Sholomovna	1917	Skidel	Baranovichi	Lenin's komsomol	Kotovski
Berlina Roza Borisovna	1921	Belarusian Staff of Partisan Movement	Grodno		Bezlyudov's
Berliner Zina Benyaminovna	1923	Slonim	Brest	Ponomarenko	Sovetskaya Belarus
Berman Abram Borisovich	1922	Granichi	Baranovichi	detachment ? 106	
Berman Abrasha Davidovich	1916	Baranovichi	Baranovichi	detachment ? 106	
Berman Bentsion Shimonovich	1906	Stolbtsy	Minsk	Chapayev	Ponomarenko
Berman Boris Khaimovich	1920	Mir	Baranovichi	Za Sovetskuyu Belarus	Shturm
Berman Girsh Dymelevich	1916	small town of Vishnevo	Baranovichi	Chapayev	Chapayev
Berman Girsh Yankelevich	1907	Gorodok	Baranovichi	Chkalov	
Berman Grigori Gomelevich	1916	Vishnevo	Baranovichi	Stalin	Chapayev
Berman Yosif Samuilovich	1930	Minsk	Baranovichi	Chkalov	reserve group
Berman Isaak Yankelevich	1908	Gorodok	Baranovichi	Chkalov	? 4 "Za Sovetskuyu Belarus"
Berman Mikhail Gendelevich	1910	getto	Vitebsk	Nikitin's	? 1
Berman Naum Gilerovich	1922	Baranovichi	Baranovichi	detachment ? 106	
Berman Nokhim Isokhorovich	1926		Baranovichi	Oktyabr	
Berman Sokhor Nakhimovich	1905	Dyatlovo	Baranovichi	Leninskaya	Borba
Berman Tatyana Grigorevna	1916	Minsk	Mogilev	regiment ? 208	
Berman Yakov Ziselevich	1926	Novogrudok	Baranovichi	Kalinin	
Bernadski Leonid Mikhailovich	1917	Belostok	Minsk	Chkalov	Gromov
Bernamov Ilya Gdalevich	1921	Yody	Vileyka	Spartak	? 4
Bernshtein Eina Moiseyevich	1921	Stomshche	Baranovichi	Kalinin	
Bernshtein Yefim Yosifovich	1904	iz Baranovichskoi tiurmy	Baranovichi	Grizodubova	Chkalov
Bernshtein Zalman Movshevich	1911	Fedorenki, Ushachi district	Vitebsk	Chapayev	detachments
Bernshtein Izrail Abramovich	1923	Byten	Brest	Ponomarenko	Sovetskaya Belarus
Bernshtein Isaak Koletovich	1914	from captivity	Gomel	Ponomarenko	Zhukov
Bernshtein Isaak Movshevich	1924	Ivienets, getto	Baranovichi	Kirov	Ordzhonikidze
Bernshtein Mikhail Vlasovich	1914	Baranovichi, from home	Baranovichi	Grizodubova	Matrosov
Bernshtein Raisa Borisovna	1922	Berezino district, Belichany	Minsk	3rd Minskaya	Niepobedimy (Undefeated)
Bernshtein Semen Isaakovich	1918	getto, Pruzhany	Brest	Za Sovetskuyu Belarus	Chkalov

Name	Year	Origin	Region	Detachment	Brigade
Bernshtein Khaim Vulfovich	1914	Minsk getto	Baranovichi	Chapayev	brigade headquarters
Bernshtein Khaya Movshevna	1922	Ivienets, getto	Baranovichi	Kirov	Ordzhonikidze
Bernshtein Shner Abramovich	1918	Stolbtsy, getto	Baranovichi	Stalin	Parkhomenko
Bernshtein Sholom Movshevich	1895	Orany	Baranovichi	Lenin's komsomol	Lenin's komsomol
Berson Ilya Abramovich	1907	Vilno, getto	Vileyka		Za Sovetskuyu Belorussiyu
Berson Mera Yevelevna	1902	Dzerzhinsk	Baranovichi	detachment ? 106	
Berson Yankel Leizerovich	1896	Minsk getto	Minsk	Ponomarenko	Za Rodinu (For Motherland)
Berkhan Zalman Mendelevich	1912	Sharkovshchina	Vitebsk	4th Belorusskaya	
Berkhman Zuska Khatskelevich	1928	Leompol	Vileyka	4th Belorusskaya	? 1
Berkhman Khatskel Izrailevich	1898	Leompol	Vileyka	4th Belorusskaya	? 1
Berkhovskaya Leya Gutelevna	1923	Novogrudok	Baranovichi	Kalinin	
Berkhovskaya Cherna Yeselevna	1902	Novogrudok	Baranovichi	Kalinin	
Berkhon Boris Vulfovich	1921	getto, Sharkovshchina	Vileyka	1st Suvorov	Bolshevik
Berkhon Riva Grigorevna	1925	from the civil camp	Vileyka	4th Belorusskaya	? 6
Berkhun Matvei Mendelevich	1908	from the civil camp	Vileyka	4th Belorusskaya	? 6
Bertsiyavski Sadiya Leiyzerovna	1895	Novogrudok	Baranovichi	Kalinin	
Bershchanski Aron Shmuilovich	1916	Lida	Baranovichi	Leninskaya	Niepobedimy (Undefeated)
Betser Movsha Yankelevich	1922	Glussk	Brest	? 99 Gulyaev	Grabko
Betser Khaim Yankelevich	1925	Glussk	Brest	? 99 Gulyaev	Grabko
Betser Yankel Froimovich	1893	Glussk	Minsk	A.Nevski	Lomatko
Beshkina Resha Abramovna	1925	Derechin	Baranovichi	Pobieda	Pobieda
Biber Izak Davidovich	1925	K. Kashirski	Pinsk	Molotov	Suvorov
Biber Sarra Davidovna	1919	Kamen-Kashirski	Pinsk	Molotov	
Bibinov Mikhail Leibovich	1915	Lyuban district, Zhivun	Minsk	Bragin	Zaslonov
Bibman Sergei Rubinovich	1895	Pruzhany	Brest	Ponomarenko	
Bilnik Itsko Moiseyevich	1912	Slonim district	Brest	Ponomarenko	Sovetskaya Belarus
Bim Lyubov Mikhailovna	1915	Polikarpovka, Gressk district	Minsk	Suvorov	
Bimbat Mariyan Girshevich	1925	Vilno	Vileyka	CC of the CP(b)B	Parkhomenko
Bindel Bruno Moiseyevich	1895	Gorodishche district	Baranovichi	25 years of the BSSR	Kotovski
Binder Mariya Mordukhovna	1922	Gorodok	Baranovichi	Za Sovetskuyu Belarus	family detachment
Binder Roza Peisakhovna	1940	Smorgon	Baranovichi	Za Sovetskuyu Belarus	family detachment
Binder Sonya Iserovna	1914	Smorgon	Baranovichi	Za Sovetskuyu Belarus	family detachment
Bindler Asya Yuryevna	1909	Minsk	Vitebsk	Nikitin's	brigade administration
Bindum VIlya Pavlovich	1934	Stavsk	Baranovichi	detachment ? 106	
BinenBoym Abram Khaimovich	1922	Osovo	Pinsk	Shubetidze	Chapayev
Binkevich Ilya Maksimovich	1928	Braslav district	Vileyka	Zhdanov	
Binshtok Gdalya Isaakovich	1922	Minsk	Mogilev	Chekist	Kalyushnikov's
Binshtok Mikhail Davidovich	1922	Domachevo	Pinsk	Molotov	Kalinin
Birger Izak	1910	Lyakhovichi	Brest	Sikorski's headquarters	
Bireyer Aizik Davidovich	1912	Slonim	Brest	Sikorski's headquarters	
Birenbaum Vladislav	1923	Minsk	Minsk	Dyadi Koli	Dzerzhinski
Birzh Aron Genikhovich	1923	Glubokoye	Vileyka	CC of the CP(b)B	brigade sanitary service
Birkovich Shaya Yosifovich	1918	RK VLKSM	Pinsk	Komarov-Korzh's	
Bitkovski Movsha A.	1904	Byten	Brest	Ponomarenko	Sovetskaya Belarus
Bichunskaya Riva Notkovna	1923	Glubokoye	Vileyka		Ponomarenko
Bichunski Yosif Avseyevich	1914	Sventiany	Vileyka		Ponomarenko
Bishanski Abram Khaimovich	1912	Lida, getto	Baranovichi	Kirov	Ordzhonikidze
Bishinkevich Roza GeorgiYevna	1914	Baranovichi	Baranovichi	Leninskaya	Leninski
Blekharovich Sholom Yosifovich	1905	Lida	Belostok		Boyevoi (Fighting)
Bliznianski Yosif Faivelevich	1923	Derechin	Baranovichi	Pobieda	Suvorov
Bliznianski Samuil Solomonovich	1912	camp, Volkovyssk	Brest	Ponomarenko	brigade headquarters
Blimshtein David Zemelevich	1911	Gorodok	Baranovichi	Chkalov	? 4 "Za Sovetskuyu Belarus"
Blishch Eti Zakharovna	1923	Zaspa	Gomel	Mstitel (Revenger)	Mstitel (Revenger)
Blonshtein Abram Semenovich	1927	Minsk	Baranovichi	detachment ? 106	
Blokh Vera Yosifovna	1918	getto	Vitebsk	Nikitin's	? 1
Blokh Yosif Yakovlevich	1924	Ivye, getto	Baranovichi	Kirov	Ordzhonikidze
Blokh Isaak Moiseyevich	1926	Zaslavski district	Minsk	Shturmovaya	Zhukov
Blokh Leizer Sholimovich	1886	Minsk	Baranovichi	detachment ? 106	
Blokh Maksim Mordukhovich	1924	Bakshty	Baranovichi	Dzerzhinski	Dzerzhinski
Blokh Mikhail Rubinovich	1918	Novogrudok	Baranovichi	Komsomolets	Kalinin
Blokh Moisei Ovseyevich	1936	Ivye	Baranovichi	Kalinin	
Blokh Moisei Khonovich	1920	Ivye, getto	Baranovichi	Kirov	Ordzhonikidze
Blokh Moisei Yakovlevich	1923	Novogrudok	Baranovichi	Kirov	Ordzhonikidze
Blokh Sonya Moiseyevna	1902	Ivye	Baranovichi	Kalinin	
Blokh Fira Leizerovna	1927	Minsk	Baranovichi	detachment ? 106	
Blokh Shmaya Ovseyevna	1924	Ivye	Baranovichi	Kalinin	
Bloshtein Isaak Samuilovich	1902	Zheludok	Baranovichi	Leninskaya	Borba
Blyukshtein Ignat Mikhailovich	1924	Warsaw	Brest	Lenin	Zhukov

Name	Year	Place	Region	Detachment	Brigade
Blyum Boris Yudelevich	1915	Poland	Brest	Stalin	Chernyak
Blyum Mordukh Yakovlevich	1912	Baranovichi	Pinsk		Chukhlai
Blyumenfeld Ilya Izrailevich	1918	Slonim	Brest	Sikorski's headquarters	Shchors
Blyumenfeld Lilya Izrailevna	1918	Slonim	Brest	Ponomarenko	Sovetskaya Belarus
Blyumenshtok Vova Isaakovich	1926	Warsaw	Baranovichi	detachment ? 106	
Blyumin Aron Moiseyevich	1924	Staroselye	Mogilev	Chekist	? 1
Blyumin Yevgeni Moiseyevich	1926	Staroselye	Mogilev	Chekist	? 1
Blyumin Leonid Alterovich	1910	from captivity	Minsk	Zheleznyak	? 3
Blyumina Masha Aronovna	1898	Staroselye	Mogilev	Chekist	? 1
Blyumkin Yosif Semenovich	1924	from captivity	Vitebsk	2nd Zaslonov	Chapayev
Blyumovich Abram Isaak Yakovlevich	1909	Slonim	Brest	Sikorski's headquarters	
Blyushtein Bentsion Motolevich	1924	Domachevo	Brest	Stalin	Frunze
Blyankleider Fima Abramovich	1907	Domachevo	Brest	Stalin	Chernyak
Blyakhar Bellya Khaimovna	1913	Voronovo	Baranovichi	Kalinin	
Blyakhar Khaim Elevich	1940	Voronovo	Baranovichi	Kalinin	
Blyakharovich Sholom Yeselevich	1905	Zabolote	Baranovichi	Lenin's komsomol	Lenin's komsomol
Blyakher Ida Samuilovna	1890	Minsk	Baranovichi	detachment ? 106	
Blyakher Ida Solomonovna	1929	Minsk	Baranovichi	detachment ? 106	
Blyakher Mikhail Romanovich	1916	Rudenski district	Mogilev	208th regiment	
Blyakher Moisei Vulfovich	1906	Parichi	Palesye		Volkov's
B'lyakher Samuil Konstantinovich	1920	Minsk	Baranovichi	detachment ? 106	
Blyakher Folya Konstantinovich	1925	Minsk getto	Baranovichi	Chapayev	Parkhomenko
Blyakher Sholom Pinkhusovich	1913	Krivichi, Vileika region	Vitebsk	Ponomarenko	Kirov
Blyakher Elya Movshevich	1916	Lida	Baranovichi	Oktyabr	
Blyakhman Aleksei Yuryevich	1909	Chashniki	Vitebsk	Dubov's	? 7
Blyakhman Boynes Danilovich	1916	Budslav, Krivichi district	Vileyka	Kutuzov	
Blyakhman Genya Yefimovna	1927	Litove, Sirotinski district	Vitebsk	Korotkin	Levkovich's
Blyakhman Ilyas Moiseyevich	1919		Minsk	Voronyanski	Mstitel (Revenger)
Blyakhman Yosif Markovich	1904	Osveia	Vitebsk	Frunze	Kotovski
Blyakhman Meyer Benyaminovich	1924	Glubokoye	Vileyka	Budenny	Lesnoi, special group
Blyakhman Ramuel Abramovich	1921	Dyatlovo	Baranovichi	Leninskaya	family detachment group
Blyakhman Rona Zalmanovna	1921	from the civil camp	Vileyka	4th Belorusskaya	? 6
Blyakhman Sima Mendeleyevna	1920	from the civil camp	Vileyka	4th Belorusskaya	? 6
Blyakhman Yudel Gershkovich	1914	Domachevo	Pinsk	Molotov	Lazo
Blyashko Betya Khaimovna	1923	detachment Matrosova GrizoDubov's's brigade	Grodno	B. Khmelnitski	
Blyashko Natan Yankelevich	1921	detachment Kotovskogo brigade Molotova	Grodno	B. Khmelnitski	
Bobman Izrail Rubinovich	1902	getto, Pruzhany	Brest	Ponomarenko	Kirov
Bobman Sergei Rubinovich	1895	Pruzhany	Brest	Ponomarenko	Kirov
Bobrov Lev Samuilovich	1913	concentration camp, Pogost-Zagorodski	Pinsk	Kuibyshev	Shchors
Bobrov Mikhail Yankelevich	1922	Serniki, Rovno region.	Pinsk	Shubetidze	brigade headquarters
Bobrov Nokhim Moiseyevich	1911	Minsk	Baranovichi	detachment ? 106	
Bobrova Zhenya Verkhovna	1911	detachment Kaganovicha	Pinsk	Kuibyshev	Ordzhonikidze
Bobrova Maya Samuilovna	1930	Minsk	Baranovichi	Kalinin	
Bogat Isaak Aronovich	1912	Jewish camp	Vileyka	Voroshilov	headquarters' production group
Bogatin Vasili Khatskelevich	1904	concentration camp	Pinsk	Kuibyshev	Shchors
Bogdush Yosif Lipovich	1920	Slonim	Baranovichi	Pobieda	Budenny
Bogovich Sofiya Borisovna	1923	Beldiuchi, Sharkovshchina district	Vileyka	CC of the CP(b)B	brigade headquarters
Bograd Anna Isaakovna	1921	Sennenski district, Vileika region	Mogilev	Chekist	? 1
Boguslavyak Boris Ilyich	1927	Vitebsk, d/dom ?9	Vitebsk	VLKSM	Raitsev's
Bodnev Aizik Elevich	1904	Bobrovshchina	Vileyka	CC of the CP(b)B	Parkhomenko
Bodneva Sofiya Elevna	1919	Glubokoye	Minsk	Ponomarenko	Voroshilov
Bozhein Mikhail Borisovich	1928	Gressk district Minsk region, Vetereevichi	Minsk	Burevestnik	Gromov
Boyko Zakhar Antonovich	1918	from captivity	Baranovichi	Ponomarenko	Voronov's
Boyko Leonid Semenovich	1912	Dymanovichskaya Rudnya	Minsk	Razgrom (Crushing defeat)	
Boyman Shlema Kerinovich	1914	Lenin	Pinsk	Molotov	Kalinin
Bokov Noyakh Berkovich	1904	N. Sverzhen	Minsk	Chapayev	Shchors
Boksenbaum Gersh Moikovich	1907	Domachevo	Brest	Lenin	Zhukov
Bokshtein Simkha Osherovich	1902	Bereza	Brest	Sverdlov	Chkalov
Boldo Yosif Khonovich	1922	Lyubcha	Baranovichi	Kalinin	
Boldo Lyuba Khonovna	1927	Lyubcha	Baranovichi	Kalinin	
Boldo Mozes Samuilovich	1883	Novogrudok	Baranovichi	Kalinin	
Boldo Pesya Girshevna	1890	Novogrudok	Baranovichi	Kalinin	
Boldo Petr Kholovich	1924	Novogrudok getto	Baranovichi	Kirov	Ordzhonikidze

Boldo Rakhelya Aronovna	1898	Lyubcha	Baranovichi	Kalinin	
Boldo Sonya Moiseyevna	1922	Novogrudok getto	Baranovichi	Kirov	Ordzhonikidze
Boldo Khonon Shmuilovich	1893	Lyubcha	Baranovichi	Kalinin	
Bolotin Boris Abramovich	1911	Svistuny, Vitebsk region	Vitebsk	Bogushevskaya	Shchors
Bolotin Yefim Yevseyevich	1919	Glussk	Minsk	Parkhomenko	Shchors
Bolotnitskaya Lyuba Meyerovna	1914	Rubezhevichi	Baranovichi	Kalinin	
Bolotnitski Izrail Zalmanovich	1913	Naliboki	Baranovichi	Kalinin	
Bolotnitski Tevel Zalmanovich	1909	Naliboki	Baranovichi	Kalinin	
Boltariskaya Sara Girshevna	1897	Lida	Baranovichi	Kalinin	
Bomshtein Leva Sholomovich	1927	Radoshkovichi	Minsk	Voronyanski	Kotovski
Bomshtein Polya Sholomovna	1918	Radoshkovichi district	Minsk	Voronyanski	Kotovski
Bondarenko Dina Isaakovna	1918	Demekhi	Gomel	Voroshilov	Voroshilov
Bondarenko Sima Samuilovna	1918	Tolochin district	Mogilev	Chekist	? 5
Bonk Volf Genokhovich	1906	Belarusian Staff of Partisan Movement			
Bonk Yakov Girshevich	1908	Belarusian Staff of Partisan Movement	Grodno		Samutin's group
Boravskaya Khana Khaimovna	1923	Vselyub	Baranovichi	Kalinin	
Boravski Volf Yoselevich	1915	Novogrudok	Baranovichi	Kalinin	
Bord Mendel Yankelevich	1913	Slutsk	Brest	Dzerzhinski	Chertkov
Bordovich Yevsei Simkhovich	1920	Osveia	Vitebsk	Frunze	Frunze ? 2
Bordovski Grigori Aizikovich	1897	Novogrudok	Baranovichi	Kirov	Za Sovetskuyu Belarus
Bordovski Yegor Leibovich	1925	getto, Pruzhany	Brest	Ponomarenko	Kirov
Borenshtein Belya Markovna	1926	Derechin	Baranovichi	Leninskaya	Leninski
Borenshtein Samuil Abramovich	1916	Derechin	Baranovichi	Pobieda	Suvorov
Boretski Yosif Itskovich	1898	Novogrudok	Baranovichi	Kalinin	
Boretski Isaak Izrailevich	1925	Slonim	Brest	Sikorski's headquarters	Shchors
Boretski Isaak Yoselevich	1928	Novogrudok	Baranovichi	Kalinin	
Boretski Osher Yoselevich	1930	Novogrudok	Baranovichi	Kalinin	
Bornshtain Samuil Abramovich	1916	Derechin	Baranovichi	Leninskaya	hospital
Borovski Aron Yoselevich	1904	Novogrudok	Baranovichi	Kalinin	
Borodina Basya Yakovlevna	1916	Logoisk	Minsk	Kirov	? 4
Borodulin Mordukh Movshevich (Mikhail Matveyevich)	1918	iz 210 detachmenta	Mogilev	Osipovichskaya VOG	? 212
Borok David Bunimovich	1922	Germanovichi	Vileyka	4th Belorusskaya	? 1
Boron Zalman Mordukhovich	1908		Vitebsk	4th Belorusskaya	
Bortkovski G.Kh.	1912		Minsk	Voroshilov	? 1
Bortnik Boris Isaakovich	1926	Kosovo	Brest	Ponomarenko	Sovetskaya Belarus
Borushanskaya Rima Venyaminovna	1915	Minsk getto	Minsk	2nd Minskaya	Kutuzov
Borushanski Miron Venyaminovich	1918	Minsk getto	Minsk	2nd Minskaya	Molotov
Borkhan Zalman Mendelevich	1912	from the civil camp	Vileyka	4th Belorusskaya	? 6
Borshtein Falvyel Abramovich	1909	K. Kashirski	Pinsk	Sovetskaya Belarus	Kutuzov
Borys Abram Moiseyevich		from the civil camp	Vileyka	4th Belorusskaya	? 6
Bosak Gidel Faitelevich	1913	Derechin	Baranovichi	Pobieda	Suvorov
Bostomski Isaak Aizikovich	1902	getto	Vileyka	Voroshilov	Chapayev
Bosyak Mordukh Faitelevich	1909	Derechin	Baranovichi	Pobieda	Budenny
Botvinnik Abram Yakubovich	1925	Minsk	Baranovichi	detachment ? 106	
Botvinnik Anna Markovna	1920	Minsk	Minsk	2nd Minskaya	Kutuzov
Botvinnik Genya Mordukhovna	1926	Minsk	Baranovichi	18th Frunze	Kutuzov
Botvinnik Yelizaveta Borisovna	1916	from the brigade "Starik (Old man)"	Minsk	Kirov	? 4
Botvinnik Isaak Yakubovich	1924	Eishishki	Baranovichi	Lenin's komsomol	Lenin's komsomol
Botvinnik Maks Moiseyevich	1934	Minsk	Baranovichi	detachment ? 106	
Botvinnik Mordukh Sholomovich	1895	Minsk	Baranovichi	18th Frunze	Kutuzov
Botvinnik Semen Vulfovich	1913	Minsk	Minsk	Za Sovetskuyu Belorussiyu	Lazo
Botvinnik Sofiya Borisovna	1923	Smolevichi district, v. Topilka	Minsk	Ponomarenko	Voroshilov
Botvinnik Tsilya Yakovlevna	1917	Minsk	Baranovichi	Kalinin	
Boyanev Aizik Elevich	1904	Plissa, Vileika region	Minsk	Voroshilov	? 3
Boyarskaya	1906	Baranovichi	Baranovichi	Grizodubova	Chkalov
Boyarski David	1904	Baranovichi	Baranovichi	Grizodubova	Chkalov
Boyarski David Solomonovich	1925		Baranovichi	Oktyabr	
Boyarski Kushel Girshevich	1924	Voronovo, camp	Belostok	A.Nevski	
Boyarski Samuil Yudolevich	1914	Zheludok	Baranovichi	Pervomaiskaya	Oktyabr
Boyarski Tankhum Falkovich	1922	Lida	Baranovichi	Kalinin	
Boyarski Shlema Aronovich	1914	Vasilishki	Baranovichi	Leninskaya	Borba
Bravda Abram Semenovich	1909	Chashniki	Vitebsk	Kirillov	Kirillov's
Braverman Yelizaveta Grigorevna		from the encirclement	Baranovichi	25 years of the BSSR	Budenny
Braide Isaak Lazarevich	1926	Bryansk getto, Belostok region	Grodno	Vo imya Rodiny (In the name of Motherland)	Zhukov

Name	Year	Place	Region	Unit	Sub-unit
Braide Osip Lazarevich	1922	Bryansk getto, Belostok region	Grodno	Vo imya Rodiny (In the name of Motherland)	Zhukov
Braido Movsha Abramovich	1924	Minsk	Baranovichi	detachment ? 106	
Brainin Benyamin Yosifovich	1924	Belarusian Staff of Partisan Movement	Mogilev	partisan regiment ? 277	
BraisbLyat Khashka Shmuilovna	1925	Vlodava (Poland)	Pinsk	Molotov	Shish
Braitman Zus Zelikovich	1891	from captivity	Minsk	Suvorov	
Branchuk Yosif Aizikovich	1898	Zheludok	Baranovichi	Leninskaya	Borba
Bratkovskaya Tamara Yefimovna	1922	Timkovichi	Grodno	Kapusta's brigade	hospital
Bratkovski Grigori Kharitonovich	1912	Timkovichi, Kopyl district	Minsk	Voroshilov	Kotovski
Bratkovski Mendel Yosifovich	1901	Kopyl	Minsk	Chapayev	Ponomarenko
Bratkovski Naum Kharitonovich	1915	Timkovichi, Kopyl district	Minsk	Voroshilov	Kotovski
Bratkovski Samuil Zavelevich	1898	Koldychevo	Baranovichi	Kalinin	
Braun German Shamelevich	1911	from the Hungarian army	Brest	Stalin	Chernyak
Brashkovski Samuil Zavelevich	1898	Baranovichi	Baranovichi	Kalinin	
Brevda Zelik Itskovich	1924	concentration camp, Pogost-Zagorodski	Pinsk	Kuibyshev	Shchors
Brevda Nikolai Itskovich	1913	concentration camp, Pogost-Zagorodski	Pinsk	Kuibyshev	Shchors
Brevdo Aron Abramovich	1915	Kopyl getto	Minsk	Frunze	Budenny
Bregman Sofiya Izrailevna	1918	iz otr. ismall town of Dzerzhinskogo	Palesye	? 27 Kirov	Kirov
Breidbort Khaya Simkhovna	1922	getto, Pruzhany	Brest	Ponomarenko	Kirov
Breitman Isaak Pinkhusovich	1925	Minsk getto	Minsk	2nd Minskaya	Kutuzov
Breiebarde Kusel Aronovich	1912	Baranovichi	Brest	Za Sovetskuyu Belarus	Suvorov
Brem Peisakh Benyaminovich	1914	getto	Baranovichi	Kirov	Orel
Bremer Srul Meyerovich	1922	Bryansk getto, Belostok region	Grodno	Vo imya Rodiny (In the name of Motherland)	Zhukov
Breslav Girsh Markovich	1907	Baranovichi	Baranovichi	Kalinin	
Bresler Aleksandr Mendelevich	1917	Minsk getto	Baranovichi	Ivienets DC CP(b)B company	
Bresler Yankel Shlemovich	1915	from the forest, grazh-danski camp	Vileyka	Za Rodinu (For Motherland)	Molotov
Breslin Lazar Moiseyevich	1907	Mir	Baranovichi	Chkalov	
Breslin Mariyan Moiseyevich	1924	small town of Mir	Baranovichi	Stolbtsy zone	
Brest Solomon Vulfovich	1921	getto, Brest	Vileyka	Voroshilov	Chapayev
Brestovitski Ikhno Gdalevich	1921	Dyatlovo	Baranovichi	Leninskaya	Borba
Brigadir Khonya Abramovich	1924	Minsk getto	Baranovichi	18th Frunze	Frunze
Brik Yasha Borisovich	1930	Dolginovo	Minsk	Starik (Old man)	
Brllyant Mariyam Markovna	1920	Bragin	Gomel	Za Rodinu (For Motherland)	Stalin
Bril Tevel Meyerovich	1926	Minsk	Baranovichi	detachment ? 106	
Bril Frida Meyerovna	1928	Minsk	Baranovichi	detachment ? 106	
Brio Abram Moiseyevich	1919	Leompol	Vileyka	4th Belorusskaya	? 2
Brio Sterna Moiseyevna	1920	Leompol	Vileyka	4th Belorusskaya	? 2
Brover Khonon Abramovich	1922	Grodno	Brest	Za Sovetskuyu Belarus	Chkalov
Broderzon Bunim Naftanovich	1902	Byten	Brest	Ponomarenko	Sovetskaya Belarus
Broderzon Mikhail Itskovich	1924	Derechin	Baranovichi	Pobieda	Pobieda
Broide Abram Zaselevich	1894	Derevno	Baranovichi	detachment ? 106	
Brok Yosif Moiritovich	1915	Kosovo	Brest	Sikorski's headquarters	Shchors
Brolnik Mordukh Rakhmilevich	1925	Ivienets	Baranovichi	Kalinin	
Bromtein Bens Martianovich	1924	Domachevo	Brest	Lenin	Zelenin
Bronak Danich	1918	Belostok	Grodno	Samutin's group	Kirshner's group
Bronitskaya Goda Faivelevna	1881	Dvorets	Baranovichi	Kalinin	
Bronitski Meyer Faivelevich	1922	Dvorets	Baranovichi	Kalinin	
Bronitski Rakhmil Gershavich	1928	Molchad	Baranovichi	Kalinin	
Bronitski Khaikel Faivelevich	1926	Dvorets	Baranovichi	Kalinin	
Bronshtein Anna Grigorevna	1918	Minsk	Minsk	Krasnoye znamya (Red Banner)	brigade headquarters
Bronshtein Meyer Sheyevich	1922	Domachevo	Pinsk	Molotov	Shish
Bronshtein Yuri Georgievich	1922	Belarusian Staff of Partisan Movement	Minsk		Mstitel (Revenger)
BrubergTevel Moiseyevich	1924	Ignalina	Vileyka	Spartak	? 1
Brudner Moisei Yoselevich	1910	Minsk	Baranovichi		
Bruk Berta Moiseyevna	1896	Piatevshchina	Minsk	2nd Minskaya	Suvorov
Bruk David Shteyevich	1921	Novogrudok	Baranovichi	Voroshilov	Kalinin
Bruk Klara YevgenyYevna	1926	Minsk	Minsk	2nd Minskaya	Suvorov
Bruk Lidiya Mikhailovna	1925	Minsk getto	Baranovichi	Vpered (Forward)	Chkalov
Bruk Movsha Shlemovich	1919	Novogrudok	Baranovichi	Kalinin	
Bruk Riva Khaimovna	1924	Dyatlovo	Baranovichi	Leninskaya	hospital
Brukhanskaya Fanya Yosifovna	1900	Stolbtsy	Baranovichi	Zhdanov	

Brukhanski Isaak Abramovich	1893	Stolbtsy	Baranovichi	Zhdanov	
Brukhanski Elya Semenovich	1912	Stolbtsy	Baranovichi	detachment ? 106	
Bryukhanskaya Khela Isaakovna	1925	getto N. Sverzhen	Minsk	Chapayev	Ponomarenko
Bryanski Moisei Yankelevich	1912	getto N. Sverzhen	Minsk	Chapayev	Ponomarenko
Bryanski Tsalka Yankelevich	1925	N. Sverzhen	Minsk	Chapayev	Shchors
Buber Dmitri Borisovich	1917	Borisov	Mogilev	208th partisan regiment	? 3
Bubnyatski Abram Berestovich	1921	Slonim	Brest	Sikorski's headquarters	Shchors
Budova Bellya Samuilovna	1913	Sharkovshchina	Vileyka	4th Belorusskaya	? 1
Budovich Rubin Yosifovich	1921	Jewish camp	Vileyka	Spartak	? 2
Buiman Shlema Gershkovich	1914	concentration camp	Pinsk	Molotov	Shish
Bukengolts Moisei Izrailevich	1909	Glussk	Pinsk	Komarov-Korzh's	Komarov's 3rd group
Bukshman Sofiya Gershovna	1921	from the forest	Pinsk	Molotov	Kalinin
Bumar Yefim Meyerovich	1917	Minsk getto	Baranovichi	18th Frunze	Dzerzhinski
Bumar Fanya Yakovlevna	1922	Minsk getto	Baranovichi	18th Frunze	Dzerzhinski
Bunilovich Berko Itskovich	1895	getto	Baranovichi	Za Sovetskuyu Belarus	Kirov
Bunimovich Aizik Leibovich	1909	Naliboki	Baranovichi	Kalinin	
Bunimovich Aleksei Ovseyevich	1921	from Melnikov's brigade	Vileyka	Kalinin	? 2
Bunimovich Movsha Leibovich	1921	N. Sverzhen	Minsk	Chapayev	Shchors
Bunimovich Sofiya AvseYevna	1925		Vitebsk	Chapayev	detachments
Bur Khaim Leibovich	1923	from the civil camp	Vileyka	4th Belorusskaya	? 6
Burgin Yekhil Nakhitovich	1914	getto	Vileyka	Voroshilov	Propaganda detachment
Burdo Izrail Shlemovich	1915	Dyatlovo	Baranovichi	Leninskaya	Borba
Burdo Yosif Moiseyevich	1915	Zalese, Oktyabr district	Palesye	? 123	komandant platoon
Burmak Moisei Isaakovich		Vitebsk	2nd Be-lorusskaya	? 1	
Burmanshtein Groinom Aronovich	1912	Slonim district	Brest	Ponomarenko	Sovetskaya Belarus
Burshtein Motel Aronovich	1922	Volna	Belostok	A.Nevski	Kotovski
Busel Yosel Mordukhovich	1912	Baranovichi	Grodno		B.Khmelnitski
Busel Leon Yakubovich	1917	Poland	Brest	Stalin	Chernyak
Busel Perets Isaakovich	1925	Dyatlovo	Baranovichi	Leninskaya	Borba
Buslen Yosif Zelikovich	1922	Dyatlovo	Baranovichi	Kirov	Ordzhonikidze
Buslovich Genrikh Yosifovich	1911	Minsk	Baranovichi	Vpered (Forward)	Chkalov
Buslovich Yevgeniya Solomonovna	1924	Minsk	Baranovichi	Za Sovetskuyu Belarus	Kirov
Bussel Zavel Izrailevich	1909	Baranovichi	Baranovichi	Chkalov	? 4 "Za Sovetskuyu Belarus"
Bussel Mordukh Shlemovich	1910	Lyakhovichi	Brest	Sikorski's headquarters	Shchors
Bukh Moisei Zelikovich	1915	Jewish camp, Belostok	Grodno		Kalinin
Bukhman Abram Solomonovich	1916	Minsk	Minsk	Parkhomenko	Kirov
Bukhovtseva Gisya Yudovna	1917	Belarusian Staff of Partisan Movement	Gomel	Kozhar's	Podgaetski's group
Bukhheadquarterser Yosif Yakovlevich	1917	from the encirclement	Minsk	Parkhomenko	Shchors
Buchin Rafail Mikhailovich	1920	from captivity	Mogilev	1st Bobruiskaya	? 753
Bushkanets Semen Shmulevich	1908	getto	Vileyka	Voroshilov	Chapayev
Bushkov Zalman Shlemovich	1897	s/kh Zhaly, Lyubanskogo districta	Minsk	Ponomarenko	brigade headquarters
Bushkova Mariya Lazarevna	1924	Starosek, Lyuban district	Minsk	Ponomarenko	Kalinovski
Bushmen Mordukh Zelikovich	1920	Dyatlovo	Baranovichi	Leninskaya	family detachment group
Buianovski Isaak Leonovich	1890		Gomel	1st Gomelskaya	Kalinin
Byvaly Boris Grigorevich	1906	Minsk, posle okruzheniia	Minsk	Starik (Old man)	
Bykov Abram Lazarevich	1924	from the forest, grazhdanski camp	Vileyka	Za Rodinu (For Motherland)	Molotov
Bykov Aleksandr Shlemovich	1928	Germanovichi, Vileika region	Vitebsk	Donukalov	brigade headquarters
BytYelski Shlema Yoselevich	1905	st. Lesnaia, Baranovichi region	Brest	Ponomarenko	Sovetskaya Belarus
Bytenski Zalman Abramovich	1905	Slonim	Brest	Za Sovetskuyu Belarus	Suvorov
Bykhovskaya Klara Semenovna	1922	Belarusian Staff of Partisan Movement	Gomel	Kozhar's	Drozdov's group
Byala Riva Yankelevna	1923	Tomashevka	Pinsk	Molotov	Shish
Byalkin Petr Or.	1909	farm-stead Lediopol	Brest		Kirov
Vagengeim Olga Robertovna	1925	Rechitsa	Vitebsk	Lenin	Kutuzov
Vagengeim Robert Moiseyevich	1890	Rechitsa	Vitebsk	Lenin	Kutuzov
Vainrit Tsalik Kasilovich	1908	Novogrudok	Baranovichi	A.Nevski	brigade headquarters
Vaibus Shmul Khaskelevich	1924	concentration camp, Poland	Pinsk	Molotov	Kalinin
Vaizer Adolf Arturovich	1919	cheshski evrei iz nemetskoi chasti	Gomel		Kotovski
Vaiman Mariya Davidovna	1924	Braslav district	Vileyka	Zhdanov	
Vain Bentsion Volfovich	1928	Eishishki	Baranovichi	Lenin's komsomol	Lenin's komsomol
Vainberg Abram Moiseyevich	1919	getto N. Sverzhen	Minsk	Chapayev	Ponomarenko

Name	Year	Origin	Region	Detachment	Brigade
Vainberg Anastasiya Lvovna	1898	Zarechenski vrachebnyi uch-k	Vitebsk	Chapayev	hospital
Vainberg Bronya Nekhovna	1924	from the camp	Baranovichi	Grizodubova	
Vainberg Khaim Abramovich	1920	Martikantsy	Baranovichi	Lenin's komsomol	Kotovski
Vaingarten Abram Meizashevich	1915	madiarski work camp	Palesye	99th Kalinkovichskaya	Kuksa's
Vainer Abram Berkovich	1909	Mir	Baranovichi	Kalinin	
Vainer Lipa Davidovich	1912	Belostok	Minsk	Chapayev	Ponomarenko
Vainer Lyuba Moiseyevna	1920	from the civil camp	Vileyka	4th Belorusskaya	? 6
Vainer Masha Sholomovna	1920	Mir	Baranovichi	Kalinin	
Vainer Meir Itskovich	1907	Kopyl getto	Minsk	Frunze	Budenny
Vainer Mera Girshevna	1920	Viazan	Vileyka	Voroshilov	Kalinin
Vainer Movsha Leibovich	1901	Ivanovo	Pinsk	Shubetidze	Nemytov
Vainer Mordukh Berkovich	1904	Mir	Baranovichi	Kalinin	
Vainer Motol Movshovich	1925	Ivanovo	Pinsk	Shubetidze	Nemytov
Vainer Raya Davidovna	1926	Minsk	Baranovichi	detachment ? 106	
Vainer Roza Mordukhovna	1925	Mir	Baranovichi	Kalinin	
Vainer Semen Khaimovich	1910	from the encirclement	Minsk	Chkalov	Gromov
Vainer Fedya Moiseyevich	1912	Kremenets	Baranovichi	detachment ? 106	
Vainerit Tsalik Kasilovich	1908	Ivye	Baranovichi	Vpered (Forward)	A.Nevski
Vainreb Boris Yakubovich	1920	Vilno	Vileyka	Voroshilov	Propaganda detachment
Vainrid Yankel Kushelevich	1910	Novogrudok, getto	Baranovichi	1st Baranovichskaya	Frunze
Vaintroib Itsko Movshovich	1912	Korelichi	Baranovichi	Kalinin	
Vaintshuk Fanya Borisovna	1927	Batsevichi, Klichev district	Mogilev		? 115 Dolgov-Rudov's
Vainfeld Leiba Girshevich	1925	from the work camp	Palesye	? 123	Papruga's
Vainshtein Abram Moiseyevich	1923	Kena	Vitebsk	Lepelskaya Stalin	
Vainshtein Isaak Shmoilovich	1923	Zheludok, Baranovichi region	Baranovichi	Vpered (Forward)	Sibiryak
Vainshtein Itska Leibovich	1924	Zheludok, Baranovichi region	Baranovichi	Vpered (Forward)	Roshcha
Vainshtein Moisei Isaakovich	1918	Stolbtsy, getto	Baranovichi	Stalin	Parkhomenko
Vainshtein Yakov Samuilovich	1926	Minsk	Baranovichi	Vpered (Forward)	Chkalov
Vais Andrei Izrailevich	1912	iz madiarskoi armii	Pinsk	Sovetskaya Belarus	Chkalov
Vais Bernard Samuilovich	1915	madiarski work camp	Palesye	99th Kalinkovichskaya	Kuksa's
Vais Ivan Ludvigovich	1915	from the Hungarian army	Brest	Stalin	Chernyak
Vaisbrot Riva Zelikovna	1925	Tomashevka	Pinsk	Molotov	Shish
Vaisbrot Sara Zelikovna	1920	Poland	Pinsk	Molotov	Shish
Vaisenblyum Meyer Gertovich	1914	Minsk	Minsk	Shturmovaya	Grozny
Vaisman Masha Lazarevna	1923	Mozyr	Baranovichi	detachment ? 106	
Vaispapir Arkadi Moiseyevich	1891	st. Sabibor (concentration camp), Poland	Brest	Stalin	Frunze
Vaitsen Aleksei Anglovich	1922	st. Sabibor (concentration camp), Poland	Brest	Stalin	Frunze
Vaitsen Yosif Morovich	1916	from the Hungarian army	Brest	Stalin	Chernyak
Vaksman Alter Elyashevich	1917	Slonim	Grodno		B.Khmelnitski
Valitskaya R.I.	1920	Derechin	Baranovichi	Pobieda	Pobieda
Valkaver Gdali Khaimovich	1919	from Melnikov's brigade	Vileyka	Kalinin	? 2
Valovich Zelik Izrailevich	1913	Priluki, Ukraine	Palesye		Ponomarenko
Valkovich Mikhail	1927	detdom	Baranovichi	Zhukov	
Valter Meyer Yoselevich	1919	Mir	Baranovichi	Kalinin	
Valshtein Avsei Isaakovich	1925	from the civil camp	Vileyka	4th Belorusskaya	? 6
Vand Goda Matveyevna	1918	Postavy	Minsk	Kirov	? 4
Vand Ruvim Zelikovich	1913	Postavy	Minsk	Kirov	
Vanne Yefim Yulyanovich	1919	Minsk	Baranovichi	detachment ? 106	
Vanne Revekka Yosifovna	1890	Minsk	Baranovichi	detachment ? 106	
Vannik Sonya Saulovna	1912	Minsk	Baranovichi	detachment ? 106	
Vansover Zlata Borisovna	1912	Derechin	Baranovichi	Leninskaya	hospital
Vantrub Ruvin Itskovich	1913	Lyakhovichi	Pinsk	Lenin	Dzerzhinski
Vanshtein Abram Moiseyevich	1923	Kivilishki	Vitebsk	Donukalov	brigade headquarters
Vanshtein Mariya Lvovna	1924	Starosek, Lyuban district	Minsk	Ponomarenko	Kalinovski
Vargavtik Yefim Izrailevich	1902				
Vargaftik Solomon Shimonovich	1912		Pinsk	Molotov	Kalinin
Varemba Viktor Viktorovich	1917	Mogilev region	Gomel	1st Gomelskaya	? 1 Chapayev
Vartman Mota Simonovich	1921	Dokshitsy	Vitebsk	Donukalov	brigade headquarters
Varfman Moisha Moishevich	1917	Myadel	Minsk	Voronyanski	Kotovski
Varfman Shlema Noselevich	1917	Dokshitsy	Minsk	Voronyanski	Suvorov
Vaserman Shlema Yankelevich	1911	Tolmachevka	Pinsk	Molotov	Lazo
Vasilyevich Yesil Yankelevich	1920	from captivity	Baranovichi	Grizodubova	
Vasilishkin Aizik Abramovich	1903	Radun	Baranovichi	Chkalov	reserve group
Vasilishski Ruban Khatskelevich	1922	Radun	Baranovichi	Lenin's komsomol	Lenin's komsomol

Vaskovich Lyubov Naumovna	1920	Minsk	Baranovichi	Ponomarenko	25 years of the BSSR
Vasser Riva Isaakovna	1914	Stolbtsy	Baranovichi	Zhukov	
Vasserman Naftal Leibovich	1909	Milevichi, Pinsk region	Pinsk		Chukhlai
Vasserman Shulim	1913	Zalyadyne	Pinsk	Molotov	brigade headquarters
Vaskovich Manya Lvovna	1930	Minsk	Baranovichi	detachment ? 106	
Vaskovich Fanya Elevna	1914	Smilovichi	Baranovichi	detachment ? 106	
Vakhenberg Maksim Abramovich	1927	local	Baranovichi	Lenin's komsomol	Kotovski
Vatskal Yosif Makarovich	1905	Central Committee of the CP (b) B	Minsk	Suvorov	
Vezhba Khil Borukhovich	1903	Mir	Baranovichi	Kalinin	
Vezinfeld Lazar Izrailevich	1927	Jewish camp, Kremenets	Vileyka	Frunze	Voroshilov
Veinerovich Yosif Naumovich	1909	Belarusian Staff of Partisan Movement	Vitebsk	Belyaev's filmgroups	Belyaev's group
Veif Leiba Yosifovich	1928	from the civil camp	Vileyka	4th Belorusskaya	? 6
Veif Moisei Rubinovich	1915	escapee	Vileyka	Suvorov	
Veif Fanya Isaakovna	1920	Luzhki	Vileyka	Suvorov	
Veitsshan Mikhail Ovseyevich	1924	Vilno	Vitebsk	Lenin	? 1
Vekman Samuil Isaakovich	1913	from the encirclement	Palesye	? 123	Death to Fascism
Veksler Yevel Mendelevich	1905	detachment ismall town of Budennogo	Vileyka	Voroshilov	headquarters' production group
Veksler Nekhama Ovseyevna	1915	detachment "Mest"	Vileyka	Voroshilov	headquarters' production group
Velitovskaya Riva Yefremovna	1919	N. Sverzhen	Baranovichi	Zhdanov	
Velkin Dvosya Samuilovna	1920	Novogrudok	Baranovichi	Kalinin	
Velkin Khaim Shmuilovich	1903	Novogrudok	Baranovichi	Kalinin	
Velkitskaya Lyubov Moiseyevna	1926	Yody	Vileyka	Gastello	Zaslonov
Veltman Moisei Vulfovich	1917	Minsk	Minsk	3rd Minskaya	Niepobedimy (Undefeated)
Vemburg Mordukh Benyaminovich	1921	Rubezhevichi	Baranovichi	Kalinin	
Vemburg Sonya Girshevna	1924	Baranovichi	Baranovichi	Kalinin	
Venger Abram Khaimovich	1895	Mir	Baranovichi	Kalinin	
Venger David Abramovich	1922	Mir	Baranovichi	Kalinin	
Vendrov Litor Naumovich	1898	Shatsk	Mogilev	208th regiment	
Vendrov Mikhail Borisovich	1927	Gantsevichi	Pinsk	Lenin	Dzerzhinski
Venitskiy Boris Isaakovich	1919	from captivity	Vitebsk	Prudnikov's	Luchenok's
Verabeichik Shenkel Izrailevich	1899	Minsk, Uzlyany	Minsk	2nd Minskaya	Kutuzov
Vernik Khava Izrailevna	1922	Korelichi getto	Baranovichi	Kirov	Ordzhonikidze
Vernikovskaya Belya Moiseyevna	1922	Baranovichi	Baranovichi	Leninskaya	family detachment group
Vernikovskaya Genya Gvidonovna	Minsk	Kirov	Budenny		
Vertgeim Anatoli Isaakovich	1912	Stolbtsy	Baranovichi	detachment ? 106	
Vertgeim Moisei Isaakovich	1919	Stolbtsy	Baranovichi	detachment ? 106	
Vertkin Boris Moiseyevich	1902	Minsk	Minsk	Voronyanski	Kotovski
Vertlib Abram Yudovich	1888	Zabolote	Mogilev		Chapai
Vertlib Anna Abramovna	1925	Zabolote	Mogilev		Chapai
Vertlib Emma Abramovna	1922	Zabolote	Mogilev		Chapai
Vertkhan Sholko Itskevich	1923	Vlodava (Poland)	Pinsk	Molotov	Kalinin
Verkh Anani Lazarevich	1895	Rovno region	Pinsk	Kirov	Kalinin
Vetler Leonid Abramovich	1909	Dolginovo	Minsk	Voronyanski	Borba
Vecherebina Bronya Itskovna	1924	Starobin	Pinsk	Komarov-Korzh's	1 group
Vibinov David Shulimovich	1917	concentration camp, Lafa	Minsk	Chkalov	Zheleznyak
Vibinov Rafail Sulimovich	1926	Lyuban district, Sosny	Minsk	Chkalov	Kotovski
Vigdorchik Isaak Yefimovich	1910	Urechye, Slutsk district	Mogilev		? 760 Berezovski
Vigdorchik Tatyana Markovna	1918	detachment Plamya	Mogilev		Yakimov's
Vikos Leiba Abramovich	1892	from the encirclement	Palesye	? 123	komandant platoon
Vilenskiy Aron Yudelevich	1920	Novogrudok	Baranovichi	Kalinin	
Vilenskiy Ilya Leibovich	1917	Lida	Baranovichi	Kirov	Iskra
Vilenskiy Mordukh Mordukhovich	1926	Lida	Baranovichi	Kalinin	
Vilenskiy Simkha Yudelevich	1913	Novogrudok	Baranovichi	Kalinin	
Vilinskaya Eddya Matveyevna	1920	from captivity	Baranovichi	Grizodubova	
Viltsin Shevel Izrailevich	1901	Boyanichi, Lyuban district	Minsk	Ponomarenko	Korneyev's
Vllyanovski Zus Itskovich	1924	Lida	Baranovichi	Kalinin	
Viner Simon Abramovich	1891	Glussk	Palesye	? 123	Pavlovski's
Vinik Liza Arkadevna	1921	Minsk	Baranovichi	detachment ? 106	
Vinik Riva Aronovna	1927	Minsk	Baranovichi	detachment ? 106	
Vinnik Itsko Davydovich	1907	Lakhva	Pinsk	Kirov	
Vinnik Mikhail Khononovich	1927	Minsk	Baranovichi	detachment ? 106	
Vinnik Riva Mikhailovna	1910	Varichinets	Minsk	258th Kuibyshev	Chapayev
Vinnik Susanna Arkadevna	1925	Minsk	Baranovichi	Chkalov	
Vinograd Vigdor Bentsionovich	1907	Byten	Brest	Ponomarenko	Sovetskaya Belarus
Vinograd Osher Peisakhovich	1925	concentration camp	Pinsk	Kuibyshev	Shchors

Vinogradova Olga Semenovna	1906	Kopyl	Grodno	Kapusta's brigade	hospital
Vinokurov Volka Naumovich	1917	from captivity	Gomel	Bolshevik	Chapayev
Vint Shondor Adolfovich	1909	from the Hungarian army	Brest	Stalin	Chernyak
Vismonskiy Boris Isaakovich	1913	Belitsa	Baranovichi	Leninskaya	Leninski
Vitenberg Ruta Davidovna	1911	Belostok	Baranovichi	Kalinin	
Vitenberg Sonya KhatskElevna	1920	Mir	Baranovichi	detachment ? 106	
Vitenberg Khatskel Vulfovich	1913	Mir	Baranovichi	detachment ? 106	
Vitman Aron Yakubovich	1910	getto, Vilno	Vileyka	Voroshilov	Kalinin
Vitnevich Meyer Yankelevich	1922	Bryansk, getto	Belostok	Vo imya Rodiny (In the name of Motherland)	Zhukov
Vikhman Ida Aronovna	1924	Minsk	Baranovichi	detachment ? 106	
Vikhman Roza KhatskElevna	1907	Bobruisk	Gomel	8th Rogachevskaya	? 255
Vikhnevich Yosif Mordukhovich	1912	St. Dorogi	Pinsk	Komarov-Korzh's	2 group
Vishko Yosif Zalmanovich	1910	Slonim	Baranovichi	Kalinin	
Vishko Khana Davidovna	1921	Lomzha	Baranovichi	Kalinin	
Vishnevskaya Braina Faivelevna	1903	Glussk	Minsk	A.Nevski	? 1
Vishnevskaya Nikhama Moiseyevna	1923	Novogrudok getto	Baranovichi	Kirov	Ordzhonikidze
Vishnevskaya Fanya Isaakovna	1920	Novogrudok getto	Baranovichi	Kirov	Ordzhonikidze
Vishnevskaya Khaya Markovna	1925		Minsk	Parkhomenko	Kirov
Vishnevski Aba Isaakovich	1922	Korelichi getto	Baranovichi	Kirov	Ordzhonikidze
Vishnevski Moisei Isaakovich	1912	Korelichi getto	Baranovichi	Kirov	Ordzhonikidze
Vishnevski Mordukh Gershovich	1899	Glussk	Brest	? 99 Gulyaev	Grabko
Vishnevski Fima Motolevich	1923	Glussk	Minsk	A.Nevski	? 1
Vishnya Bronya Borisovna	1924	Baranovichi, from home	Baranovichi	Grizodubova	Matrosov
Vishnya Yevgeniya Yudelevna	1922	from the camp	Baranovichi	Grizodubova	
Vishnya Mordukh Izrailevich	1923	Baranovichi, from home	Baranovichi	Grizodubova	Matrosov
Vladavski Roman Mikhailovich	1917	Ivanovo	Pinsk	Molotov	Lazo
Vladykina Nina Mikhailovna	1918	Minsk	Minsk	Rokossovski	Chkalov
Vober Khana Moiseyevna	1920	Molodechno	Baranovichi	Kalinin	
Vovshovich Mikhail Gavrilovich	1898	Baranovichi, getto	Baranovichi	special Cossack brigade	
Vodnitski Peisakh Nokhimovich	1910		Pinsk	Komarov-Korzh's	4 group
Vodovoz Itsko Shepshelevich	1913	Volna, camp	Belostok	A.Nevski	
Vodopyanov Izseslav Yevseyevich	1924	Omsk	Vitebsk	VLKSM	? 3
Voyencher Zelman Shmerkhovich	1897	Botki	Belostok	Vo imya Rodiny (In the name of Motherland)	
Voitekhovich Dora Markovna	1908	Kopyl district, v. Savichi	Minsk	Suvorov	
Voitik Mikhail Pavlovich	1932	Minsk	Minsk	Shturmovaya	Shturm
Voichik Lazar Yudolevich	1906	Minsk	Baranovichi	detachment ? 106	
Volik Leiba Peisakhovich	1901		Vileyka	Kutuzov	
Volk Vulf Simonovich	1905	Kremenets	Minsk	Voronyanski	Kotovski
Volk Elena Girshevna	1925	Kosovo	Brest	Ponomarenko	Sovetskaya Belarus
Volk Zyama Falevich	1933	Minsk	Baranovichi	detachment ? 106	
Volk Isaak Girshevich	1922	Kosovo	Brest	Ponomarenko	Sovetskaya Belarus
Volk Lazar Mordukhovich	1924	Kremenets	Minsk	Voronyanski	Kotovski
Volk Mulya Falevich	1931	Minsk	Baranovichi	detachment ? 106	
Volk Raisa	1921	Kosovo	Brest	Ponomarenko	Sovetskaya Belarus
Volk Sonya Yosifovna	1911	Minsk getto	Minsk		Mstitel (Revenger)
Volk Khelya Gertsovna	1925	Kosovo	Brest	Sikorski's headquarters	Shchors
Volkin Yakov Grigorevich	1908	Baranovichi	Baranovichi	Chkalov	reserve group
Volkov Yakov Borisovich	1929	Kostenevichi	Vileyka	Dovator	Furmanov
Volkovitskaya Mina	1920	Slonim	Brest	Ponomarenko	Sovetskaya Belarus
Volkovitski Khasel Alterovich	1922	Kozyany	Vileyka	Spartak	? 6
Volkovyiski Solomon Yefimovich	1909	Slonim	Brest	Za Sovetskuyu Belarus	brigade headquarters
Volkovyskaya Genya Moiseyevna	1918	Baranovichi	Baranovichi	Kalinin	
Volkovyskaya Sonya Abramovna	1922	Lida district	Baranovichi	Oktyabr	
Volkovyski Aleksei Leibovich	1924		Baranovichi	Pobieda	Pobieda
Volkovyski Mordukh Shimonovich	1925	Lida	Baranovichi	Kalinin	
Volkovyski Perets Shimonovich	1921	Lida	Baranovichi	Kalinin	
Volkovyski Solomon Moiseyevich	1906	Baranovichi	Baranovichi	Kalinin	
Volkovysskaya Mina Isaakovna	1920	Slonim	Brest	Za Sovetskuyu Belarus	brigade headquarters
Volkovysski Leonid Abramovich	1929	Zheludok	Baranovichi	Voroshilov	Voroshilov
Volkomirski Aizik Yevnokhovich	1908		Baranovichi	Pobieda	Pobieda
Volmen Asya Yefimovna	1911		Vitebsk	2nd Belorusskaya	
Volnets-Gurevich Sofiya Zalmanovna	1911	Minsk	Minsk	Shturmovaya	Za Otechestvo (For Fatherland)
VolovYelskaya NataLya Benekovna	1922	getto, Pruzhany	Brest	Za Sovetskuyu Belarus	Chkalov
Volovik Zelik Izrailevich	1913	Belarusian Staff of Partisan Movement	Pinsk	groups in the region	Bobrov's group
Volozhinski Mariyan Bendikovich	1924	Molodechno	Baranovichi	Chkalov	? 4 "Za Sovetskuyu Belarus"
Volokhnyanski Aron Mordukhovich	1908	Lakhva	Pinsk	Kirov	

Voloshin Boris Abramovich	1911	from the encirclement	Vitebsk	Kirillov	Suvorov
Volukh Arnold Yakubovich	1900	from the detachment Kovpaka	Baranovichi	Kirov	Baltiets
Volkhovianski Movsha Abramovich	1919	from home	Baranovichi	Grizodubova	
Volchek Asya Meyerovna	1908	from behind the front line	Baranovichi	Pervomaiskaya	Oktyabr
Volfovich Borukh Moiseyevich	1904	Dyatlovo	Baranovichi	Voroshilov	Kalinin
Volfovich David Notovich	1900	Novogrudok	Baranovichi	Kalinin	
Volfovich Lazar Mironovich	1929	Novogrudok	Baranovichi	Kalinin	
Volfovich Leizer Movshovich	1912	Novogrudok	Baranovichi	Kalinin	
Volfovich Roza Ilinichna	1914	Dyatlovo	Baranovichi	Leninskaya	Borba
Volfovskaya Mira Ilinichna	1923	Dyatlovo	Baranovichi	Leninskaya	Borba
Volfson Kalman Afroimovich	1922	Belarusian Staff of Partisan Movement	Brest	groups of party leaders	Mech (Sword)
Volfson Shneer Movshevich	1912	Glussk	Minsk	Ponomarenko	A.Nevski
Volfianski Rakhim Abramovich	1921	Baranovichi, from home	Baranovichi	Grizodubova	Matrosov
Volshtein Avsei Isaakovich	1925	Pogost	Vileyka	Spartak	? 6
VOlyak Yosif Leibovich	1927		Vileyka	Voroshilov	brigade headquarters
VOlyanskaya Raya Moiseyevna	1926	Derechin	Baranovichi	Pobieda	Pobieda
VOlyanski Meyer Leibovich	1914	getto Baranovichi	Minsk	Chapayev	Ponomarenko
Vonchak Nokhman Moshenovich	1907	Gorodishche district	Baranovichi	25 years of the BSSR	Grozny
Vorobeichik Aron Abramovich	1908	Zabolote	Baranovichi	Lenin's komsomol	Lenin's komsomol
Vorobeichik Afroim Gershenovich	1916	Minsk getto	Minsk		Mstitel (Revenger)
Vorobeichik Berko Abramovich	1924	Zabolote	Baranovichi	Lenin's komsomol	Lenin's komsomol
Vorobeichik Leiba Borisovich	1904		Vitebsk	Chapayev	detachments
Vorobev Grigori Abramovich	1913	Berchuki, Rudnya district	Minsk	2nd Minskaya	Kutuzov
Voronovich Lyuba Rubinovna	1913	Pukhovichi district, Gorelets	Minsk		Stalin
Vorot Ilya Davidovich	1917	Jewish camp, Belostok	Grodno		Kalinin
Vorotilov Abram Meyerovich	1923	Minsk	Minsk	3rd Minskaya	25years of the A-ULCYL
Vrubel Lyubov Yankelevna	1924	Bryansk getto, Belostok region	Grodno	Vo imya Rodiny (In the name of Motherland)	Zhukov
Vuzek Adel Leibovna	1909	Nesvizh	Minsk	Chapayev	Ponomarenko
Vulfina Zinaida Moiseyevna	1918		Gomel	1st Gomelskaya	Suvorov
Vulfovich Borukh Mordukhovich	1904	Dyatlovo	Baranovichi	Shchuchin IDC	
Vurtselman Lyudvig Yakovlevich	1925	Poland, a small partisan group	Pinsk	Molotov	Lazo
Vusiker Semen Arkadevichi	1923	Bronnoe,prison	Gomel	Bolshevik	Chapayev
Vygotski David Volfovich	1920	Baranovichi	Baranovichi	Kalinin	
Vymenets Mikhail Yakovlevich	1923	p/o Bolshevik, Khotenchitsy	Vileyka	Frunze	Fighter
Vysotskaya Dina Mironovna	1915	Zaskorki	Vitebsk	Chapayev	brigade headquarters
Vyshkin Motka Davidovich	1923	Kozianski les	Vileyka	Voroshilov	A.Nevski
Gabel Solomon Markovich	1907	getto, Vilno	Vileyka	Voroshilov	Kalinin
Gabrielov Lev Moiseyevich	1927	Minsk	Baranovichi	detachment ? 106	
Gabrielov Sema Moiseyevich	1930	Minsk	Baranovichi	detachment ? 106	
Gabrielova Sofiya Moiseyevna	1921	Minsk	Baranovichi	detachment ? 106	
Gavi Lev Naumovich	1941	Minsk	Baranovichi	detachment ? 106	
Gavi Yosif Naumovich	1931	Minsk	Baranovichi	18th Frunze	Kutuzov
Gavurin Gidin Yudelevich	1928	Dvorets	Baranovichi	Kalinin	
Gazhanski Semen Itskovich	1905	Lokhva	Palesye	? 225	Chapayev
Gazevich Yelizaveta Yefimovna	1911	Lakhva	Pinsk	Kirov	
Gazeevich Kalman Movshevich	1918	Lakhva	Pinsk	Kirov	
Gazenpud Khasya Lazarevna	1913	Minsk	Baranovichi	Vpered (Forward)	Chkalov
Gazman Vulf Lvovich	1908	Minsk getto	Baranovichi	Chapayev	Parkhomenko
Gaidenson Rubin Solomonovich	1911	getto, Kurenetski district	Vileyka	Suvorov	
Gaidokovski Mordukh Yakovlevich	1912	Dyatlovo	Baranovichi	Leninskaya	Borba
Gaidukovskaya Ida Gershevna	1924	Lida	Baranovichi	Kalinin	
Gaidukovski Aron Girshevich	1924	Dyatlovo	Baranovichi	Leninskaya	Borba
Gaidukovski Yevsei Yankelevich	1904	Dyatlovo	Baranovichi	Leninskaya	Borba
Gaidukovski Zelik Girshevich	1921	Dyatlovo	Baranovichi	Leninskaya	Borba
Gaister Venyamin Leibovich	1921	Belarusian Staff of Partisan Movement	Vitebsk	Lepelskaya Stalin	sabotage detachment
Gaitler Yeremei Yosifovich	1925	Krasnoye, Vileika region	Minsk	Shturmovaya	Frunze
Gaikhman Leon Lazarevich	1910	Yelsk	Palesye	? 27 Kirov	Kirov
Gaishman Berta Lvovna	1921	Minsk	Baranovichi	Ponomarenko	Budenny
Galershtein Berta Samuilovna	1905	Minsk	Baranovichi	detachment ? 106	
Galershtein Leva Naumovich	1930	Minsk	Baranovichi	detachment ? 106	
Galershtein Tatyana Moiseyevna	1924	Byten	Brest	Ponomarenko	Sovetskaya Belarus
Galimbovskaya Bella Volfovna	1920	Lida	Baranovichi	Pobieda	Pobieda
Galimbovski Volf Abramovich	1890	Lida	Baranovichi	Pobieda	Pobieda

JEWISH PARTISANS IN BYELORUSSIA 1941-1944 215

Galin Igor Semenovich	1923	Volkovyssk, camp	Belostok	A.Nevski	
Galinson Semen Borisovich	1924	Lakhva	Baranovichi	Kirov	
Galburt Aleksandr Yefimovich	1925	Minsk	Baranovichi	detachment ? 106	
Galperin Boris Milevich	1927	Ryzhkovichi, Shklov district	Mogilev		? 345
Galperin Volf Moiseyevich	1920	Bryansk getto, Belostok region	Grodno	Vo imya Rodiny (In the name of Motherland)	Zhukov
Galperin I.N.	1923	Minsk	Minsk	Rokossovski	25 years of Oktyabr
Galperin Maksim	1904	Dyatlovo	Baranovichi	Pobieda	
Galperin Samuil Aronovich	1922	Druya	Vileyka	4th Belorusskaya	? 1
Galperin Khaim Izrailevich	1922	Dzhanka, Baranovich-skoi obl.	Baranovichi	Pervomaiskaya	Oktyabr
Galperin Shlema Aronovich	1910	Druya	Vileyka	4th Belorusskaya	? 1
Galperina Liza I.	1917	Belitsa	Baranovichi	Pobieda	
Galperina Nina Naumovna	1923	Minsk getto	Baranovichi	18th Frunze	Kotovski
Galperina Rakhil Naumovna	1923	Minsk	Baranovichi	18th Frunze	Kutuzov
Galperina Esfir Zelikovna	1908	Ryzhkovichi, Shklov district	Mogilev		? 345
Gamburg Mariya Semenovna	1912	Brest	Brest	Chapayev	25 years of Oktyabr
Gamburg Moisei Yefimovich	1909	Pinsk	Pinsk	Molotov	brigade headquarters
Gamburg Sofiya Samuilovna	1923	concentration camp Oboltsy	Vitebsk	Groza	
Gamer Abrasha Yakovlevich	1938	Minsk	Baranovichi	detachment ? 106	
Gamer Lyuba Yakovlevna	1932	Minsk	Baranovichi	detachment ? 106	
Gamer Nekhama Izrailevna	1905	Minsk	Baranovichi	detachment ? 106	
Gamulinskaya Mariya Ivanovna	1913	Warsaw	Baranovichi	Pobieda	Pobieda
Gamulinski Aleksandr Ignatovich	1911	Warsaw	Baranovichi	Pobieda	Pobieda
Gamush Lyubov Lazarevna	1919	from the forest, grazhdanski camp	Vileyka	Za Rodinu (For Motherland)	Molotov
Gandelsman Aron Nisovich	1901		Pinsk	Kuibyshev	Shchors
Ganzenko Faina Fedorovna	1922	Minsk	Baranovichi	Ponomarenko	Voronov's
Ganik Shlema Peisakhovich	1915		Pinsk	Shubetidze	Stalin
Gankin Shimon Abramovich	1891	getto, Postavy	Vileyka	1st Suvorov	Voroshilov
Gans Viktor Samsonovich	1917	from the Hungarian army	Brest	Stalin	Chernyak
Gantverger Semen Shmulevich	1907	Central Committee of the CP (b) B	Brest	Chapayev	
Gantman Abram Samuilovich	1915	Minsk	Minsk	2nd Minskaya	Kutuzov
Gantman Boris Borisovich	1916	Pruzhany	Brest	Za Sovetskuyu Belarus	Chkalov
Gantman Genya Solomonovna	1927	Pisiuta,Borisovski district	Minsk	Shchors	Shchors
Gantman Isaak Abramovich	1925	Minsk	Baranovichi	Ponomarenko	Voronov's
Gantman Petr Movshevich	1924	Pisiuta,Borisovski district	Minsk	Shchors	Bolshevik
Gantman Raya Yosifovna	1921	Minsk	Baranovichi	detachment ? 106	
Gants Samuil Meilakhovich	1914	Poland	Pinsk	Molotov	Shish
Gapartsin Grigori Yakovlevich	1913	from captivity	Mogilev	208th partisan regiment	? 2
Garbalevski Grisha Rafailovich	1926	Minsk	Baranovichi	detachment ? 106	
Garbar Grigori Yakovlevich	1918	from the encirclement	Pinsk	Shubetidze	Chapayev
Garbar Eva Yakovlevna	1918	getto, Pruzhany	Brest	Za Sovetskuyu Belarus	Chkalov
Garbarovich Mira Abramovna	1922	getto, Vilno	Vileyka	Voroshilov	Kalinin
Garbarovich Semen Davidovich	1912	getto, Glubokoye	Vileyka	Voroshilov	Kalinin
Garber Abram Samuilovich	1925	Grodno	Baranovichi	Leninskaya	Borba
Garbuz Leiba Aronovich	1897	concentration camp	Pinsk	Kuibyshev	Shchors
Garbuz Tevel Yankelevich	1924	Molodechno, getto	Baranovichi	Za Sovetskuyu Belarus	Shturm
Garbulski Lev Levelich	1914	Konstantinovo, Ruzhanski district	Brest	Ponomarenko	Kirov
Garbulski Shepsel Khaimovich	1914	Grodno	Baranovichi	Lenin's komsomol	Ivanov's
Garde Rubin Beinashevich	1921	Mir	Baranovichi	Chkalov	
Gardon Lyuba Zalmanovna	1919	Ivienets	Baranovichi	Kalinin	
Garkavy Yosif Aronovich	1921	Sverzhen	Minsk	Chapayev	Shchors
Garmoza Grigori Mikhailovich	1925	Minsk	Minsk	2nd Minskaya	Suvorov
Garnek Yevgeniya Itskovna	1919		Baranovichi	Leninskaya	hospital
Garonovski Tsalya Yosifovich	1924	Baranovichi	Baranovichi		
Gartbei Fisher Motelevich	1901		Palesye	? 130	? 132
Gartman Falvyel Davidovich	1917	Koldychevo, getto	Baranovichi	Pervomaiskaya	Ya.Kolas
Gartsovski Gutel Shlemovich	1903	Dyatlovo	Baranovichi	Leninskaya	Leninski
Gartsovski Leiba Gutelevich	1924	Dyatlovo	Baranovichi	Leninskaya	family detachment group
Garkavy Yosif Solomonovich	1912	Stolbtsy	Baranovichi	Stalin	Parkhomenko
Gaskel Yosif Aleksandrovich	1907	Shilena	Vitebsk	Dubov's	? 14
Gaudman Lyusya Isaakovna	1930	Lida	Baranovichi	Kalinin	
Gaudman Maks Isaakovich	1930	Lida	Baranovichi	Kalinin	
GauzerAnatoli Yanya Samuilovich	1912	Lida	Baranovichi	Vpered (Forward)	A.Nevski
Gaufman Adam Rakhimulevich	1914	Lakhva	Pinsk	Lenin	Kutuzov

Gaft Yosif Zalmanovich	1924	Minsk	Vitebsk	Nikitin's	? 2
Gvardian Regina AndreYevna	1924	from captivity	Vitebsk	Nikitin's	? 5
Gebeleva Slava (Glory) Solomonovna	1914	Minsk	Baranovichi	detachment ? 106	
Geyerov Khenik Yoselevich	1917	getto Vlodava	Pinsk	Molotov	Kalinin
Gezhes Kushel Mikhailovich	1914	Poland, camp, prisoner of war	Pinsk	Molotov	Kalinin
Geizenblozen Rakhmel Isaakovich	1923	Kopyl	Minsk	Chapayev	Ponomarenko
Geiman Mikhail Yankelevich	1918	Kobrin	Pinsk	Molotov	Suvorov
Geiman Nikolai Abramovich	1914	Minsk	Baranovichi	Ponomarenko	Budenny
Geinish CheSlava (Glory) Solomonovna	1916	Lida	Baranovichi	Kalinin	
Geirush Benyamin Samuilovich	1919	Novogrudok	Baranovichi	Leninskaya	Borba
Geiserman Naum Yosifovich	1910	Krivoi Rog	Baranovichi	detachment ? 106	
Geisman Semen Isaakovich	1910	from captivity	Palesye	? 123	Death to Fascism
Geister Venyamin Leibovich	1921	Belarusian Staff of Partisan Movement	Brest	groups of party leaders	Terekhovich's group
Geitler Aron Girtlevich	1924	Krasnoye, Vileika region	Minsk	Shturmovaya	Grozny
Geitler Moisei Yoselevich	1924	Krasnoye, Vileika region	Minsk	Shturmovaya	Grozny
Geikhman Bronya Meyerovna	1913	Central Committee of the CP (b) B	Gomel	Buda-Koshelevskaya	Chkalov
Geikhman Leon Lazarevich	1910	Yelsk	Palesye	? 27 Kirov	
Geikhman Oleg Lazarevich	1920	from behind the front line	Minsk	Ponomarenko	Gvardeyets (Guardsman)
Geler Samuil Khaimovich	1910	Ivye	Baranovichi	Kalinin	
Geler Yankel Movshevich	1905	Kletsk	Minsk	Chapayev	Ponomarenko
Gelimson Berta Isaakovna	1927	Minsk	Baranovichi	detachment ? 106	
Geller Grigori Natanovich	1913		Minsk	Voronyanski	Pobieda
Geller Solomon Borisovich	1904	from captivity	Vitebsk	Sennenskaya brigade (Leonov's)	A.Nevski
Geller Fedor Ruvimovich	1921	Zapole, Cherven district	Mogilev	Osipovichskaya VOG	? 210
Geller Edya Lvovna	1920	Baranovichi	Minsk	Chapayev	Shchors
Geller Yankel Movshevich	1905	Kletsk	Minsk	Chapayev	Shchors
Gellerman Boris Borisovich	1911	Stolbtsy	Baranovichi	Grizodubova	Chkalov
Gelberger Sheps Borisovich	1918	Rogachev	Mogilev	? 425	? 425
Gelvan Boris Ilyich	1893	from the civil camp	Vileyka	4th Belorusskaya	? 6
Gelvan David Ilyich	1893	Mirony	Vitebsk	Stalin (Okhotin's)	Lapenko
Gelvan Zorukh Berkovich	1925	from the civil camp	Vileyka	4th Belorusskaya	? 6
Gelman Abo Samuilovich	1919	from the civil camp	Vileyka	4th Belorusskaya	? 6
Gelman Eva Meyerovna	1914	Minsk	Baranovichi	detachment ? 106	
Gelman Rakhil Ruvinovna	1915	Minsk	Baranovichi	detachment ? 106	
Gelman Rubin Lazarevich	1902	Volozhin	Baranovichi	Chkalov	
Gelman Fanya Solomonovna	1937	Minsk	Baranovichi	detachment ? 106	
Gelmanovskaya Mariya Ilinichna	1922	Baranovichi	Baranovichi	Chkalov	
GYelski Arkadi Davidovich	1924	Staiki, Vitebsk region	Vitebsk	Kirillov	Suvorov
GYelski Vladimir Davidovich	1929	Staiki, Vitebsk region	Vitebsk	Kirillov	Suvorov
GYelski David Artilovich	1895	Staiki, Vitebsk region	Vitebsk	Kirillov	Govedo
Gelfan Motal Khaimovich	1923	Baranovichi, from home	Baranovichi	Grizodubova	Matrosov
Gelfand Abram Vulfovich	1910	Starye Dorogi	Minsk	Ponomarenko	Gorbachev
Gelfand Aizik Shevelevich	1904	Starye Dorogi district	Minsk	Kirov ? 100	Kutuzov ? 2
Gelfand Boris Arkadevichi	1926	Starye Dorogi district	Minsk	Kirov ? 100	Kutuzov ? 2
Gelfand Boris Zakharovich	1909	Klichev	Mogilev		? 278
Gelfand Girsha Isaakovich	1902	Stoianovo	Mogilev	partisan regiment ? 277	? 277
Gelfand Yosif	1930	Starye Dorogi	Minsk	Kirov ? 100	brigade economical service
Gelfand Liza Vladimirovna	1903	Starye Dorogi	Minsk	Kirov ? 100	brigade economical service
Gelfand Masha Matveyevna	1913	Klichev	Mogilev		? 278
Gelfand Fanya Markovna	1920	getto	Vitebsk	Nikitin's	? 5
Gelfand Tsilya Yakovlevna	1926	Smilovichi	Baranovichi	detachment ? 106	
Gelfand Etl Elevna	1904	Smilovichi	Baranovichi	detachment ? 106	
Gelfand Yakov Faivelevich	1899	Smilovichi	Baranovichi	detachment ? 106	
Gelfer Saul Yoselevich	1907	Vilno	Baranovichi	Kalinin	
Gelfman Anna Solomonovna	1915	Minsk	Baranovichi	detachment ? 106	
Gelfman Rakhil Moiseyevna	1908	Minsk	Baranovichi	detachment ? 106	
Geltsman Samuil Gershonovich	1910	Lakhva	Pinsk	Kirov	
Gendel Benyamin Mendelevich	1918	Sharkovshchina	Vileyka	Spartak	brigade headquarters
Gendelzon Khana Solomonovna	1910	Jewish camp	Vileyka	Voroshilov	headquarters' production group
Gendelman Kalman Mirovich	1903	Rovno region	Pinsk	Kirov	Za Rodinu (For Motherland)
Gendlin Yosif Borisovich	1905	Starobin	Pinsk	Komarov-Korzh's	Komarov's 3rd group

Name	Year	Origin	Region	Detachment	Brigade
Genz Borukh Davidovich	1903	Evev	Baranovichi	Kalinin	
Genzelbul Mordukh Shayevich	1899	Stolbtsy	Minsk	Chapayev	Ponomarenko
Genikovich Abram Elevich	1925	Plissa	Vileyka	CC of the CP(b)B	brigade headquarters
Genkin David Borisovich	1911	Stolbtsy	Baranovichi	Zhukov	
Genkin Naum Sholomovich	1923	Postavy	Minsk	Voroshilov	? 1
Genkina Khana Yakovlevna	1913	Stolbtsy	Baranovichi	Zhukov	
Genov Isaak Leibovich	1911	concentration camp, Slutsk	Pinsk	Komarov-Korzh's	Komarov's 3rd group
Gens Zinaida Kaumanovna	1919	Slobodka, Braslav district	Vileyka	Za Rodinu (For Motherland)	Zhdanov
Gens Semen Abramovich	1912	Slobodka, Braslav district	Vileyka	Za Rodinu (For Motherland)	Zhdanov
Gens Etka Kaumanovna	1914	Slobodka, Braslav district	Vileyka	Za Rodinu (For Motherland)	Zhdanov
Genshtein Matvei Aronovich	1925	getto	Vileyka	Voroshilov	Grozny
Genkin Abram Leizerovich	1905	Central Committee of the CP (b) B	Gomel	Shemyakin's "Vpered (Forward)"	Makagonov's
Gepner Sanya Oskarovich	1909	Byten	Brest	Ponomarenko	Sovetskaya Belarus
Gerasun Mikhail Lvovich	1914	from captivity	Pinsk	Sovetskaya Belarus	Chkalov
Gering Ida Khilovna	1924	Poland	Pinsk	Shubetidze	Chapayev
Gerling Aleksandr	1915	Dyatlovo	Baranovichi	Leninskaya	Krasnogvardeiski
Gerling Leon Yakovlevich	1903	Baranovichi	Brest	Dzerzhinski	brigade headquarters
Gerling Khristina Lipovna	1916	Dyatlovo	Baranovichi	Leninskaya	Borba
Gerling Sholom Shimelevich	1915	Lida	Baranovichi	Leninskaya	Borba
Germanov	1913	from the encirclement	Vitebsk	Kirillov	Kirillov's
Gertner Raya ElyashYevna	1922	detachment ismall town of Chapaeva	Vileyka	Voroshilov	headquarters' production group
Gertseva Sheina Yosifovna	1907	Mir	Baranovichi	Kalinin	
Gertsevski Khonon Berkovich	1921	Novogrudok	Baranovichi	Kalinin	
Gertsek Masha Abramovna	1930	Mir	Baranovichi	Kalinin	
Gertsek Mordukh Abramovich	1906	Mir	Baranovichi	Kalinin	
Gertsekov Yankel Movshovich	1909	Baranovichi	Baranovichi	Kalinin	
Gertsekh Semen Adolfovich	1918	from the Hungarian army	Brest	Stalin	Chernyak
Gertsovich Grigori Yefimovich	1913	iz RKKA	Minsk	Pravda (Truth)	Pravda (Truth)
Gertsovskaya Golda Zomonovna	1919	Slonim	Brest	Sikorski's headquarters	Shchors
Gertsovskaya Yevgeniya Yosifovna	1914	Novogrudok	Baranovichi	Shchuchin IDC headquarters' company	
Gertsovskaya Perla Syadova	1927	Korelichi	Baranovichi	Kalinin	
Gertsovskaya Khana Nevakhovna	1891	Novogrudok	Baranovichi	Kalinin	
Gertsovskaya Khaya Abramovna	1922	Novogrudok getto	Baranovichi	Kirov	Ordzhonikidze
Gertsovskaya Khaya Isaakovna	1919	Dyatlovo	Baranovichi	Leninskaya	Borba
Gertsovski Aron Zalmanovich	1915	Dyatlovo getto	Baranovichi	Kirov	Ordzhonikidze
Gertsovski Gutel Shlemovich	1906		Baranovichi	Leninskaya	hospital
Gertsovski David Girshevich	1914	Mir, Baranovichi region	Minsk	Chapayev	Ponomarenko
Gertsovski Mikhail Abramovich	1911	Gorodishche	Baranovichi	Kalinin	
Gertsovski Samuil Yeselevich	1920	Dyatlovo	Baranovichi	Leninskaya	Krasnogvardeiski
Gertsovski Yankel Movshevich	1909	Baranovichi	Baranovichi	Kalinin	
Gerchikova Zinaida Abramovna	1913	Bobr	Mogilev	Ilyin's	? 28
Gershanovich Mairim Yudelevich	1895	Novogrudok, getto	Baranovichi	1st Baranovichskaya	Frunze
Gershanovich Shevakh Mairimovich	1923	Novogrudok, getto	Baranovichi	1st Baranovichskaya	Frunze
Gershanok Boris Grigorevich	1914	Checherski district	Gomel	Buda-Koshelevskaya	Kutuzov
Gershanski Aron Shmuilovich	1916	Lida	Baranovichi	Lenin's komsomol	Lenin's komsomol
Gershberg Zelman Shepselevich	1903	Malorita	Brest		Kotovski
Gershberg Pavel Abramovich	1921	Gorodishche district	Baranovichi	25 years of the BSSR	Kotovski
Gershgorn Belya Markovna	1926	Derechin	Baranovichi	Pobieda	Pobieda
Gershekovskaya Roza Samuilovna	1923	Novogrudok	Baranovichi	Kalinin	
Gershengorn Itsek-Borukh Mordukhovich	1913	from the encirclement	Vitebsk	Donukalov	brigade headquarters
Gershenovich Bentsian Yudelevich	1899	Minsk	Baranovichi	detachment ? 106	
Gershenovich Girsh Germanovich	1893	Uzda	Mogilev	208th regiment	
Gershkovich Zoltan Ede	1917	from the Hungarian army	Brest	Stalin	Chernyak
Gershman Venyamin Movshevich	1900	Glussk	Palesye	Lelchitskaya	Shantar's
Gershovich David Meyerovich	1919	Voronovo	Baranovichi	Kalinin	
Gershovich Isaak Moiseyevich	1911	Okolitsa	Mogilev	partisan regiment ? 277	headquarters
Gershovich Fanya Rubinovna	1923	Ivye	Baranovichi	Dzerzhinski	Kotovski
Gershovich Shevakh Meyerovich	1923	Novogrudok	Baranovichi	Kalinin	
Gershon Yakov Samoilovich	1916	Glussk	Minsk	Chkalov	Gromov
Gershper Moisei Shlomovich	1911	detachment Kaganovicha	Pinsk	Kuibyshev	Ordzhonikidze
Gershtein Yosif Yakovlevich	1917		Minsk	Grishin's 13th regiment	
Gershtovski Solomon Volfovich	1913	Baranovichi	Baranovichi	Kalinin	
Gershun Mikhail Mendelevich	1926	Minsk	Minsk	Voroshilov	B.Khmelnitski

Gershun Nikolai Maksimovich	1916	from captivity	Minsk	Voroshilov	Patriots of Motherland
Gesman Anofrii Kondratevich	1901	Minsk	Baranovichi	18th Frunze	Kutuzov
Getin Nikolai Yakovlevich	1919		Gomel	1st Gomelskaya	Kalinin
Getrein Isaak Samuilovich	1916	Baranovichi	Baranovichi	Kalinin	
Geshelevich Tsalya Shlemovich	1913	Slonim	Baranovichi	Pobieda	Pobieda
Gibal Yaik Lezerovich	1923	Derechin	Baranovichi	Pobieda	Pobieda
Gibal Aleksandra Lazarevna	1925	Derechin	Baranovichi	Pobieda	Pobieda
Gibs Nikolai Adamovich	1904	Minsk	Minsk		Kalinin
Gibs Sofiya Stanislavovna	1918	Minsk	Minsk		Kalinin
Gilemovich Abram Zelikovich	1918	Turets	Baranovichi	Kalinin	
Gilemovich Kushel Zelikovich	1908	Turets	Baranovichi	Kalinin	
Gilerovich Zelda Izrailevna	1920	Molchad	Baranovichi	Kalinin	
Gilinski Moisei Davidovich	1906	getto	Vileyka	Voroshilov	headquarters' production group
Gilkin Mikhail Abramovich	1928	Snegiri	Mogilev	? 117	? 124
Giller Foma Khatskelevich	1922	Volkovyssk, camp	Belostok	A.Nevski	
Gilodi Leonid Yosifovich	1924	Orsha	Vitebsk	Kirillov	Voroshilov
Gild Blyum Khaskel	1916	Baranovichi	Grodno		B.Khmelnitski
Gilderman Leon Ovseyevich	1911	work camp, Gantsevichi	Pinsk	Molotov	Kalinin
Gildizgeim Arty Khaimovich	1915	Stolbtsy	Baranovichi	Stalin	Bolshevik
Gildin Lazar Aizikovich	1914	Minsk	Baranovichi	detachment ? 106	
Gildiner Lidiya Borisovna	1919	Minsk getto	Baranovichi	18th Frunze	Frunze
Gilkin Abram Isaevich	1906	Snegiri	Mogilev	? 117	? 124
Gilman Nikolai Leontevich	1925	Ushachi district, Kublichi	Minsk	Zheleznyak	? 5
Gilman Foma Leibovich	1922	getto	Vileyka	Voroshilov	Istrebitel (Destroyer)
Gilmovskaya Mariya Ilinichna	1922	Mir	Baranovichi	Za Sovetskuyu Belarus	Za Sovetskuyu Belarus
Gilmovskaya Mariya Mikhailovna	1903	Mir	Baranovichi	Chkalov	? 4 "Za Sovetskuyu Belarus"
Gilchik Leva Moiseyevich	1906	Kopyl	Minsk	Chapayev	Ponomarenko
Gilchik Mikhail Mikhailovich	1922	Kopyl	Minsk	Voroshilov	Kotovski
Gilchik Raya Mikhailovna	1925	Stolbtsy	Minsk	Chapayev	Ponomarenko
Gimelshtein Asya Ilinichna	1910	Minsk	Baranovichi	detachment ? 106	
Gimelshtein Boris Yakovlevich	1922	Minsk	Grodno	Kapusta's brigade	hospital
Gimelshtein Grigori Yosifovich	1930	Minsk	Baranovichi	detachment ? 106	
Gimelshtein Yosif Abramovich	1902	Minsk	Baranovichi	detachment ? 106	
Gimelshtein Monya Isaakovich	1922	Slutsk	Pinsk	Komarov-Korzh's	2 group
Gimelshtein Naum Shayevich	1905	Minsk getto	Minsk	Rokossovski	25 years of Oktyabr
Gimelshtein Revekka Yakovlevna	1912	Uzda	Baranovichi	detachment ? 106	
Gimelshtein Ruvel Pinkovich	1886	Glussk	Palesye	? 100	Budenny
Gimelshtein Yakov Samuilovich	1914	Minsk getto	Baranovichi	Chkalov	
Gimpeleva Sonya Izrailevna	1909	Minsk	Baranovichi	detachment ? 106	
Gimpeleva Fanya Izrailevna	1930	Minsk	Baranovichi	detachment ? 106	
Gimpelevich Girsh Davidovich	1912	Novogrudok	Baranovichi	Kalinin	
Gimpelevich Mariya Semenovna	1896	Tolochin district	Vitebsk	Kirillov	Govedo
Gimpilevich Yosif Samuilovich	1893	Tolochin district	Vitebsk	Kirillov	Govedo
Gindelsman Abram Meyerovich	1910	from captivity	Baranovichi	Grizodubova	
Gindin Rakhil Mendeleyevna	1910	Jewish camp	Vileyka	4th Belorusskaya	? 6
Gindin Sholom Samuilovich	1923	Novogrudok	Baranovichi	detachment ? 106	
Ginenskaya Bellya Aronovna	1901	Novogrudok	Baranovichi	Kalinin	
Ginenskaya Grunya ShepshElevna	1925	Novogrudok	Baranovichi	Kalinin	
Ginenskaya Dana ShepsElevna	1922	Novogrudok	Baranovichi	Leninskaya	family detachment group
Ginenskaya Riva ShepshElevna	1928	Novogrudok	Baranovichi	Kalinin	
Ginenski Isaak Girshevich	1925	Novogrudok	Baranovichi	Leninskaya	Borba
Ginenski Malkiel Movshovich	1914	Novogrudok	Baranovichi	Kalinin	
Ginenski Meyer Shmuilovich	1925	Novogrudok	Baranovichi	Kalinin	
Ginenski Yakub Girmovich	1921	Novogrudok	Baranovichi	Pobieda	Pobieda
Ginzburg Abram Borukhovich	1915	Minsk getto	Minsk	Ponomarenko	Za Rodinu (For Motherland)
Ginzburg Abram Davidovich	1920	Minsk	Baranovichi	detachment ? 106	
Ginzburg Boris Yosifovich	1923	work camp, Gantsevichi	Pinsk	Molotov	Kalinin
Ginzburg Yelizaveta Shlemovna	1920	Ivye, getto	Baranovichi	Kirov	brigade headquarters
Ginzburg Zinaida Yuryevna	1921	Moskva, Belarusian Staff of Partisan Movement	Minsk	Rokossovski	brigade headquarters
Ginzburg Isaak Lazarevich	1906	from the encirclement	Mogilev		? 41
Ginzburg Lev Izrailevich	1911	Central Committee of the CP (b) B	Gomel	Bolshevik	Chapayev
Ginzburg Lev Mironovich	1913	Minsk	Minsk	Rokossovski	Chkalov
Ginzburg Matvei Shlemovich	1914	Ivye	Baranovichi	Kirov	Iskra
Ginzburg Movsha Iserovich	1925	Vulka	Pinsk	Kirov	

Ginzburg Moisei Aleksandrovich	1917	from captivity	Minsk		Chapayev
Ginzburg Nina Shlemovna	1921	Lida	Baranovichi	Kirov	Iskra
Ginzburg Peisakh Izrailevich	1912	Timkovichi	Minsk	Chapayev	Ponomarenko
Ginzburg Riva Solomonovna	1905	Minsk	Baranovichi	18th Frunze	Kutuzov
Ginzburg Roman Isaakovich	1913	Rudnya, Belynichski district	Mogilev		? 345
Ginzburg Khonon Davidovich	1915	Svintyany	Vitebsk	Stalin (Okhotin's)	hospital
Ginzburg Tsali Shlemovich	1922	Ivye	Baranovichi	Kirov	Iskra
Ginzburg Shlema Matveyevich	1890	Lida	Baranovichi	Kirov	Iskra
Ginzburg Yankel Elevich	1917	Lenin	Pinsk	Komarov-Korzh's	2 group
Ginsburg Faina Yefimovna	1922	Minsk	Minsk	Shturmovaya	Shturm
Ginsburg Shevel Meyerovich	1901	StoLyutsy	Baranovichi	Kalinin	
Ginfin Petr Yefimovich	1925	Martynovka	Mogilev		Za Sovetskuyu Belorussiyu
Ginfina Fanya Natovna	1902	Martynovka	Mogilev		Za Sovetskuyu Belorussiyu
Girkus Yosif Alterovich	1928	Gorodok	Baranovichi	Za Sovetskuyu Belarus	Za Sovetskuyu Belarus
Girkus Yosif Alterovich	1909	Volma	Baranovichi	Chkalov	? 4 "Za Sovetskuyu Belarus"
Girtsovski Mikhel Abramovich	1911	Gorodishche	Baranovichi	Kalinin	
Girsh Benyamin Maksovich	1940	Ivienets	Baranovichi		
Girsh Lyudvik Maksovich	1936	Ivienets	Baranovichi	Kalinin	
Girsh Maks Samuilovich	1907	Ivienets	Baranovichi	Kalinin	
Girsh Rozaliya Benyaminovna	1910	Ivienets	Baranovichi	Kalinin	
Girshevich Benyamin Yakovlevich	1928	Mir	Baranovichi	Kalinin	
Girshevich Mordukh Davidovich	1904	Lida	Baranovichi	Kalinin	
Girshevich Ovsei Yakovlevich	1926	Mir	Baranovichi	Kalinin	
Girshik Yankel Shlemovich	1912	Parichi	Mogilev	1st Bobruiskaya	? 252
Girshovski Yosif Khonovich	1921	Dyatlovo	Baranovichi	Leninskaya	Borba
Girshtavski Salomon Volfovich	1913	Baranovichi	Baranovichi	Kalinin	
Gitelzon Benyamin Isaakovich	1894	from the civil camp	Vileyka	4th Belorusskaya	? 6
Gitelzon Sonya Alterovna	1924	from the civil camp	Vileyka	4th Belorusskaya	? 6
Gitelzon Sonya Leibovna	1903	from the civil camp	Vileyka	4th Belorusskaya	? 6
Gitelzon Khaya Benyaminovna	1928	Jewish camp	Vileyka	4th Belorusskaya	? 6
Gitelman Boris Mordukhovich	1903	from the camp	Minsk	Chkalov	Gromov
Gitelman David Leizerovich	1897	Pinsk	Pinsk	Shubetidze	Stalin
Gitelman Itsko Shlemovich	1908	David Gorodok	Pinsk	Sovetskaya Belarus	Chkalov
Giterman Asya VasilYevna	1920	Glussk district, Gorodok	Minsk	Parkhomenko	Shchors
Gitin Shlema Tsalevich	1907	concentration camp	Pinsk	Kuibyshev	Shchors
Gitlets Samuil Borukhovich	1891	Vileika district, Ilets	Minsk	Kirov	Frunze
Gitlin Yevgeniya Mordukhovna	1922		Vitebsk	Chapayev	detachments
Gitlin Meyer Motovich	1913	Jewish camp Dolginovo	Minsk	Voronyanski	Pobieda
Gitlits Genya Isaakovna	1922	Myadel district	Vileyka	Dovator	Sverdlov
Gitlits Rafail Mendelevich	1923	Opsa	Vileyka	1st Suvorov	Chkalov
Gitlits Khaim Urovich	1925	Krivichi district, Vileika region	Vitebsk	2nd Belorusskaya	
Gishler Daniil Isaakovich	1906	Kopisitsy	Vitebsk	Za Sovetskuyu Belarus	Sibiryak
Glazar Mikhail Yosifovich	1910	Petrikov	Baranovichi	Grizodubova	Chkalov
Glazunova Sofiya Grigorevna	1916	Sloboda	Gomel	Shemyakin's "Vpered (Forward)"	Makagonov's
Glazshneider Yakov Mikhailovich	1898	Mogilev	Gomel	Shemyakin's "Vpered (Forward)"	Makagonov's
Glaikhengauz Aron Lazarevich	1923	Minsk	Minsk	Belarus	Belarus
Glanzet Samuil Shakhovich	1927	Novo-Pogost	Vileyka	Budenny	Orel
Glauberman Aba Yefimovich	1917	lag. v/pl. Osintorf	Vitebsk	2nd Zaslonov	brigade headquarters
Glezer Leiba Rubinovich	1920	Vilno	Vitebsk	Lenin	2-oi
Glezer Liliya Samuilovna	1922	Minsk	Belostok	Chapayev	Zhukov
Glezer Elya Yankelevich	1911	Kletsk	Minsk	Chapayev	Ponomarenko
Gleizer Liza FaiflYevna	1913	Minsk getto	Minsk		Mstitel (Revenger)
Gleizer Semen Failovich	1922	getto	Vileyka	Suvorov	
Gliznianski Yosif Favelevich	1924	Derechin	Baranovichi	Pobieda	Pobieda
Gliker Semen Matveyevich	1904	N. Belitsa	Gomel	Bolshevik	headquarters
Glikman Galina Sholomovna	1919	Dyatlovo	Baranovichi	Leninskaya	Krasnogvardeiski
Glikman Lipa Yosifovna	1915	Dyatlovo	Baranovichi	Leninskaya	Borba
Glikfeld Anna Yakovlevna	1926	Derechin	Baranovichi	Pobieda	Pobieda
Glinik Yakov Abramovich	1906	from captivity Minsk	Minsk	Death to Fascism	Kutuzov
Glintsman Yakov Leibovich	1928	Vlodava (Poland)	Pinsk	Molotov	Potalakh
Glitsman Lipa Davidovich	1913	Vlodava (Poland)	Pinsk	Molotov	Potalakh
Glomberg Aleksandr Moiseyevich	1915	from captivity	Vitebsk	Za Sovetskuyu Belarus	Sibiryak
Glukh Isaak Aizikovich	1907	getto, Vilno	Vileyka	Voroshilov	Bagration
GLyazburg Zoya Naumovna	1924	Minsk	Baranovichi	Kalinin	
GLyazburg Mariya Mikhailovna	1906	Minsk	Baranovichi	Kalinin	

GLyazburg SaLya Naumovna	1931	Minsk	Baranovichi	Kalinin	
GLyaikhengauz Yosif Davidovich	1910	Mogilev	Minsk	Belarus	Belarus
GLyaikhengauz Rakhil Aronovna	1923	Minsk	Baranovichi	detachment ? 106	
GLyauberman Lev Aronovich	1914	Lida	Baranovichi	Kalinin	
Gnesin Fedor Yakovlevich	1923	Minsk	Minsk	Burevestnik	Gromov
Goberman Abram Rubinovich	1914	getto, Glubokoye	Vitebsk	Korotkin	Voroshilov
Goberman Zalman Mendelevich	1905	Druya	Vileyka	4th Belorusskaya	? 6
Goberman Ida Yefimovna	1910	Borisov	Baranovichi	detachment ? 106	
Goberman Kopel Girshovich	1912	getto, Glubokoye	Vileyka	1st Suvorov	Bolshevik
Goberman Moisei Notkovich	1927	Novogrudok	Baranovichi	Kalinin	
Goberman Nina Yakovlevna	1926	Rudnenski district, Minsk region	Baranovichi	Voroshilov	Voroshilov
Goberman Nota Movshovich	1888	Novogrudok	Baranovichi	Kalinin	
Goberman Pelageya YulyYevna	1907	from the Jewish camp, Kozianski les	Vileyka	Zhdanov	
Goberman Estera Solomonovna	1918	getto, Glubokoye	Vitebsk	Korotkin	Voroshilov
GovLyach Peisakh Yudelevich	1922	Molchad	Baranovichi	Kalinin	
GovLyach Yudel Monessovich	1890	Molchad	Baranovichi	Kalinin	
Godina Sonya Lvovna	1923	Klinok, Cherven district	Minsk	Pravda (Truth)	Pravda (Truth)
Godina Tsilya Semenovna	1898	from the detachment ? 208	Minsk	Pravda (Truth)	Pravda (Truth)
Godkina Fanya Yakovlevna	1921	Begomlski district, Pasperezhe	Minsk	Kirov	? 4
Gozhanski Samuil Bentsionovich	1923	Shklyary	Belostok		separate detachment Zhukov
Gozenpud Sofiya Tevelevna	1900	Minsk getto	Minsk		Mstitel (Revenger)
Goida Shepsa Mordukhovich	1921	Lida	Belostok	A.Nevski	
Goland Boris Yudolovich	1923	Bobruisk	Minsk	Parkhomenko	Shchors
Goland Lena Izrailevna	1932	Minsk	Baranovichi	detachment ? 106	
Goland Matvei Yudolovich	1924	Bobruisk	Minsk	Parkhomenko	Shchors
Goland Masha Matveyevna	1912	Klichev	Mogilev		? 278
Goland Nina Izrailevna	1936	Minsk	Baranovichi	detachment ? 106	
Golant Leiba Elikovich	1910	Jewish camp	Vileyka	Voroshilov	headquarters' production group
Golant Ruvim Khaimovich	1909	Central Committee of the CP (b) B	Mogilev	Osipovichskaya VOG	? 210
Goldin Meyer Mendelevich	1901	from the civil camp	Vileyka	4th Belorusskaya	? 6
Goldin Semen Mendelevich	1905	from the civil camp	Vileyka	4th Belorusskaya	? 6
Goldin Semen Yakovlevich	1914	Pukhovichi district, Kobylitsy	Minsk		Stalin
Goldina Blyuma Mendeleyevna	1918	from the civil camp	Vileyka	4th Belorusskaya	? 6
Golevitski David Shmuilovich	1913	Novogrudok getto	Baranovichi	Kirov	Ordzhonikidze
Golevski Semen Yoselevich	1911	detachment "Mest"	Vileyka	Voroshilov	headquarters' production group
Golenbiker Aleksandr Mech (Sword) eslavovich	1936	Volozhin	Baranovichi	Kalinin	
Golik Srol Yeselevich	1903	Filipovichi, Kopatkevi-chski district	Palesye	? 125	Mikhailovski's
Golimbovskaya Bella Volfovna	1920	Lida	Baranovichi	Leninskaya	Pobieda
Golinder Galina Zakharovna	1919	Mogilevski district	Mogilev	? 425	? 425
Golod Anna Yakovlevna	1903	Lyuban	Palesye	? 225	Chapayev
Golod Khaim Itskovich	1925	Ozarichi	Palesye	? 123	Artyushka's
Golod Yankel Samoilovich	1901	Ozarichi	Palesye	Ponomarenko	
Golomb Klara Yosifovna	1909	Vilno	Vitebsk	Rokossovski	Kotovski
Golombevski Vulf Abramovich	1890	Lida	Baranovichi	Leninskaya	Pobieda
Goltshtein Natan	1921	Belostok	Grodno	Samutin's group	Kirshner's group
Golub Aleksei Mikhailovich	1921	Minsk	Grodno	Chapayev	
Golub Zori Georgievich	1920	Lida	Baranovichi	Kirov	brigade headquarters
Golub Yosif Nosinovich	1914	Minsk getto	Baranovichi	Chapayev	Parkhomenko
Golub Lev Lvovich	1913	Minsk getto	Baranovichi	Chapayev	Parkhomenko
Golub Nikolai Semenovich	1925	Glussk	Minsk	Chkalov	Dovator
Golub Semen Mikhailovich	1925	Minsk	Grodno	Chapayev	
Golub Shlema Aronovich	1905				
Golubok Shalem Mendelevich	1912	Lida	Baranovichi	Kirov	Iskra
Golubtsov Girsh Mendelevich	1898	from the civil camp	Vileyka	4th Belorusskaya	? 6
Golubchik Fefel Khaimovich	1908	Grodno	Baranovichi	Lenin's komsomol	Kotovski
Golub Abram Ovseyevich	1922		Vitebsk	Nikitin's	? 3
Golub Leizer Shlemovich	1909		Pinsk	Molotov	Kalinin
Golub Lyubov Leibovna	1921	Krasnoye	Minsk	Voronyanski	Kotovski
Golub Khaim Yevnovich	1905		Pinsk	Molotov	Kalinin
Golfond Motya Khaimovich	1922	Kletsk	Minsk	Chapayev	Ponomarenko
Golshmid Gita Yakovlevna	1922	Lida	Baranovichi	Kalinin	
Golynbekker Mech (Sword)eslav Isaakovich	1905	Volozhin	Baranovichi	Kalinin	

Golynbekker Tatyana Pavlovna	1907	Volozhin	Baranovichi	Kalinin	
Golynker Yakov Borisovich	1899	Krugloye	Mogilev	Ilyin's	? 30
Golynskaya Lidiya Semenovna	1916	Bobruisk	Gomel	formation headquarters of Gomel partisans	
Golynskaya Sofiya Semenovna	1918	Bobruisk	Gomel	formation headquarters of Gomel partisans	
Golberg Genya Borisovna	1910	Minsk	Minsk	2nd Minskaya	Kutuzov
Golberg Yevgenii Lipovich	1925	Minsk getto	Baranovichi	Chkalov	
Golberg Yosif Movshevich	1917	Neman	Baranovichi	Leninskaya	Borba
Golberg Lipa Meyerovich	1901	Minsk	Baranovichi	Chkalov	
Golberg Khaim Leibovich	1922	Pruzhany	Brest	Ponomarenko	Kirov
Golberg Tsilya Lvovna	1924	Urechye, Slutsk district	Minsk	Ponomarenko	Komsomolets
Golberg Shai Borisovich	1918	Rogachev	Baranovichi	? 620	
Golberg Shevel Khononovich	1909	Starye Dorogi	Minsk	Kirov ? 100	Kutuzov ? 2
Golbershtein Benyamin Leibovich	1918	Vilno	Baranovichi	Leninskaya	Niepobedimy (Undefeated)
Golburd Aleksandr Yefimovich	1925	Minsk	Baranovichi	detachment ? 106	
Gold Lev Antonovich	1918	getto	Brest		Kutuzov
Goldberg Abram Moiseyevich	1913	from captivity	Mogilev	Chekist	? 60
Goldberg Adam Moritsevich	1939	Nesvizh	Baranovichi	detachment ? 106	
Goldberg Arkadi Pavlovich	1907	Baranovichi	Baranovichi	Vpered (Forward)	Bolshevik
Goldberg Vladimir Yosifovich	1929	Pogost, Starobin district	Pinsk	Komarov-Korzh's	1 group
Goldberg Zhenya Borisovna	1920		Mogilev	? 425	? 425
Goldberg Igor	1931	Slutsk	Minsk	Frunze	Budenny
Goldberg Lekim Leibovich	1903	Minsk	Baranovichi	Vpered (Forward)	Chkalov
Goldberg Liza Grigorevna	1917	Baranovichi	Baranovichi	detachment ? 106	
Goldberg Mai Borisovich	1918	Rogachev			
Goldberg Moisei Lazarevich	1911	Lyubcha	Baranovichi	detachment ? 106	
Goldberg Morits Abramovich	1892	Nesvizh	Baranovichi	detachment ? 106	
Goldberg Nakha Shmulevich	1897	Derechin	Baranovichi	Pobieda	Pobieda
Goldberg Ruvim Lvovich	1917	Central Committee of the CP (b) B	Minsk	Dyadi Koli	Burya (Storm)
Goldberg Ruvim Lvovich	1917	from behind the front line	Minsk	Zheleznyak	? 5
Goldberg Salim Gershovich	1921	Belostok	Grodno	Samutin's group	Kirshner's group
Goldberg Sofiya Yefimovna	1910	Minsk getto	Baranovichi	18th Frunze	Frunze
Goldberg TOlya Yudelevna	1907	Nesvizh	Baranovichi	detachment ? 106	
Goldberg Fanya Leibovna	1915	Minsk	Baranovichi	detachment ? 106	
Goldberg Khana Peisakhovna	1926	detachment "Mest"	Vileyka	Voroshilov	headquarters' production group
Goldburg Simkha Iserovich	1912	Vilenskaya obl.	Baranovichi	Leninskaya	Niepobedimy (Undefeated)
Goldburd Anna Moiseyevna	1920	Bobruisk	Baranovichi	detachment ? 106	
Goldburd Venyamin Neukhovich	1893	Bobruisk	Palesye	? 123	
Goldvaser Samuil Isaakovich	1919	Baranovichi region ?	Baranovichi	Kirov	Ordzhonikidze
Goldgamer Gershko Movshevich	1910	Poland	Pinsk	Molotov	Lazo
Golde Volf Mordkovich	1916	Bryansk getto, Belostok region	Grodno	Vo imya Rodiny (In the name of Motherland)	Zhukov
Golde Eva Mordkovna	1918	Bryansk getto, Belostok region	Grodno	Vo imya Rodiny (In the name of Motherland)	Zhukov
Golder Irina Venyaminovna	1924	Odrizhin	Pinsk	Molotov	Lazo
Goldzeger Yakub Abramovich	1922	getto, Vilno	Vileyka	Voroshilov	brigade headquarters
Goldin Yefim Kalmanovich	1928	Minsk	Baranovichi	Chkalov	? 4 "Za Sovetskuyu Belarus"
Goldin Meyer Abramovich	1895	Glussk	Minsk	Ponomarenko	A.Nevski
Goldin Fima Kalmanovich	1926	Minsk	Baranovichi	detachment ? 106	
Goldin Elya Khononovich	1905	Belarusian Staff of Partisan Movement			
Goldina Blyuma Mikhailovna	1917	Minsk	Baranovichi	Stalin	Budenny
Goldina Golda Meyerovna	1927	Glussk	Minsk	Ponomarenko	A.Nevski
Goldina Sarra Kalmanovna	1920	Minsk	Baranovichi	detachment ? 106	
Goldiner Yevgeniya Matveyevna	1917	Poreche, Pukhovichi district	Minsk	2nd Minskaya	Molotov
Goldman Aron Abasovich	1900	Lunin, Pinsk region	Pinsk	Kuibyshev	Shchors
Goldman Movsha Srulevich	1925	concentration camp	Pinsk	Kuibyshev	Shchors
Goldman Nuta Iorukhovich	1920	Malorita	Brest	Stalin	Voroshilov
Goldman Omar Itskovich	1923	detachment Kaganovicha	Pinsk	Kuibyshev	Ordzhonikidze
Goldman Riva SrulYevna	1915	concentration camp, Pogost-Zagorodski	Pinsk	Kuibyshev	Shchors
Goldman Samuil Girshenovich	1910	David-Gorodok	Pinsk	Kirov	Petrovich's
Goldman Sender Itskovich	1925	detachment Kaganovicha	Pinsk	Kuibyshev	Ordzhonikidze
Goldman Solomon Moiseyevich	1908	Novogrudok	Baranovichi	Leninskaya	family detachment group

Goldman Urcha Tsukovich	1904	Lakhva	Brest	Sikorski's headquarters	Shchors
Goldshmid Abram Yosifovich	1904	Novogrudok getto	Baranovichi	Kirov	Ordzhonikidze
Goldshmit Shlema Berkovich	1917	Novogrudok getto	Baranovichi	Kirov	Ordzhonikidze
Goldshtein Abram Girshevich	1904	Dyatlovo	Baranovichi	Kalinin	
Goldshtein David Leibovich	1898	from Poslavy forest	Pinsk	Molotov	Lazo
Goldshtein Yosif Isaakovich	1921		Baranovichi	Leninskaya	hospital
Golzak Naum Yankelevich	1912	Minsk	Baranovichi	18th Frunze	Kutuzov
Golzberg Roman Nokhovich	1932	Kletsk	Minsk	Voroshilov	Kotovski
Golman Anatoli Markovich	1913	Belarusian Staff of Partisan Movement	Brest	groups of party leaders	gr. Golovneva
Golman Meyer Mendelevich	1911	Vilno	Vileyka	4th Belorusskaya	? 6
Golman NIlyin's NikolaYevna	1924	Minsk	Baranovichi	18th Frunze	Kutuzov
Golman Reveka Isaakovna	1922	Minsk	Baranovichi	Kalinin	
Golman Yudel Yefimovich	1911	Byten	Brest	Ponomarenko	Sovetskaya Belarus
Golnshtein Isaak Shlemovich	1896	Dyatlovo	Baranovichi	Leninskaya	Borba
Golnshtein Leizer Itskovich	1926	Dyatlovo	Baranovichi	Leninskaya	Borba
Golpern Liza I.	1917	Belitsa	Baranovichi	Pobieda	Pobieda
Golpern Maksim I.	1904	Dyatlovo	Baranovichi	Pobieda	Pobieda
Goltburt Venyamin Neukhovich	1893	Bobruisk	Palesye	? 123	Pavlovski's
Golshenid Abram Yoselevich	1904	Voronovo	Baranovichi	Kalinin	
Golshmid Berko Girshevich	1936	Ivienets	Baranovichi	Kalinin	
Golshmid Girsh Khaimovich	1901	Ivienets	Baranovichi	Kalinin	
Golshmid Gita Pinkhusovna	1922	Lida	Baranovichi	Kalinin	
Golshmid Khaim Leizerovich	1916	Lida	Baranovichi	Kalinin	
Golyanskaya Masha Yudelevna	1918	Dyatlovo	Baranovichi	Leninskaya	Borba
Golyanski Mairam Aronovich	1912	Dyatlovo	Baranovichi	Leninskaya	Borba
Golyanski Shlema Aronovich	1921	v. Zabelt	Baranovichi	Kalinin	
Gomberg Zhenya Itskovna	1921	Vilno	Baranovichi	A.Nevski	brigade headquarters
Gomberg Khena Itskovna	1925	Vilno	Baranovichi	Kalinin	
Gomolinskaya Mariya Gdalevna	1913	Bolotnia	Baranovichi	Pobieda	Pobieda
Gomolinski Aleksandr Isaakovich	1911	Zelva	Baranovichi	Pobieda	Pobieda
Gompelevich Nokhim Isaakovich	1919	Lida	Baranovichi	Kalinin	
Gonikman Isaak Khaimovich		Belarusian Staff of Partisan Movement	Minsk	Special groups	Abramov's group
Gonikman Mikhail Romanovich	1914	from the encirclement	Palesye	? 125	Bolotnikov's
Gonikman Moisei Izrailevich	1906	Yelsk	Palesye	37th Yelskaya	Bolshevik
Gonikman Ester Meyerovna		zhena Gonikmana small town of I.	Palesye	37th Yelskaya	Death to Fascism
Goninski Isaak Girshevich	1925	getto	Belostok	A.Nevski	
Gonski Yakov Khaimovich	1915	Grodno	Baranovichi	Kalinin	
Gontovich German Matusovich	1919	Kletsk	Minsk	Chapayev	Ponomarenko
Gonts Viktor Samsonovich	1917	from the Hungarian army	Brest	Stalin	Chernyak
Gonchar Meyer Leizerovich	1922	N. Sverzhen	Minsk	Chapayev	Shchors
Goncharovski Meyer Shlemovich	1915	Iavorskaya Ruda	Baranovichi	Leninskaya	Borba
Goncharovski Mordukh Moiseyevich	1909	Dyatlovo	Baranovichi	Leninskaya	Borba
Gopershtein Leizer Ilyich	1927	Lida	Baranovichi	Kalinin	
Gopershtein Elya Kushelevich	1900	Lida	Baranovichi	Kalinin	
Gopershtein Ester Iliyanovna	1929	Lida	Baranovichi	Kalinin	
Gopershtein Yankel Rubinovich	1922	Lida	Baranovichi	Lenin's komsomol	Lenin's komsomol
Gopshtein Ivan ElYekhimovich	1925	Vilno	Vileyka	Dovator	Sverdlov
Gorban Fili	1901		Palesye	? 130	? 136
Gorbatovski Semen Davidovich	1915	Gorbatovichi	Baranovichi	Pervomaiskaya	Ya.Kolas
Gorbachevskaya Berta Aronovna	1925	Minsk	Baranovichi	detachment ? 106	
Gorgel Ser Yakovlevich	1924	Braslav district	Vileyka	Zhdanov	
Gordes Movrits Samoilovich	1914	iz Baranovichskoi tiurmy	Baranovichi	Grizodubova	Chkalov
Gordin Kalman Raifovich	1909	Lida	Baranovichi	Kirov	Iskra
Gordina Esfir Moiseyevna	1916	Lida	Baranovichi	Kirov	Iskra
Gordinskaya Estera Faivelevna	1906	Mir	Baranovichi	Kalinin	
Gordon Abram Einovich	1921		Minsk	Voronyanski	Mstitel (Revenger)
Gordon Aron Abramovich	1916	Martikantsy	Baranovichi	Lenin's komsomol	Kotovski
Gordon Braina Osherovna	1927	Krivichi district, Vileika region	Vitebsk	2nd Belorusskaya	
Gordon Venyamin Neukhovich	1926		Vileyka	Budenny	Orel
Gordon Grigori Ovseyevich	1923	getto, Kobylniki	Vileyka	Budenny	Budenny
Gordon Grigori Samuilovich	1920	Minsk	Mogilev	208th partisan regiment	? 1
Gordon Zoya KushElevna	1927		Minsk	Voronyanski	Mstitel (Revenger)
Gordon Yosif Pavlovich	1887	Dnepropetrovsk	Gomel	Shemyakin's "Vpered (Forward)"	Makagonov's
Gordon Isaak Abramovich	1910	Vasilishki	Baranovichi	Lenin's komsomol	Lenin's komsomol
Gordon Isaak Lazarevich	1922	Iuratishkinski district	Baranovichi	Vpered (Forward)	A.Nevski
Gordon Lyuba Zalmanovna	1919	Ivienets	Baranovichi		

Gordon Miron Iozelevich	1909	getto, Vilno	Vileyka	Voroshilov	Kalinin
Gordon Moisei Karlovich	1905	getto	Vileyka	Voroshilov	Istrebitel (Destroyer)
Gordon Monya Gershenovich	1929	Ushachi district	Minsk	1st Antifashistskaya	
Gordon Mordukh Khaimovich	1902	Minsk getto	Baranovichi	Chapayev	Parkhomenko
Gordon Noemi Borisovna	1912	getto, Vilno	Vileyka	Voroshilov	Kalinin
Gordon Rakhelya Davidovna	1925	Lida	Baranovichi	Kalinin	
Gordon Tank (Anton) Ivanovich	1918	Gaidutishki, camp	Vileyka	Budenny	Budenny
Gordon Khaim Moiseyevich	1924	Olkhovka	Vileyka	Za Rodinu (For Motherland)	Zhdanov
Gordon KhIlya AvElevna	1927	Minsk	Baranovichi	detachment ? 106	
Gordon Emma KushElevna	1923	Postavy	Minsk	Zheleznyak	? 5
Gorevoi Meyer Natanovich	1908	from the encirclement	Gomel	formation headquarters of Gomel partisans	
Gorelik Aleksandr Aleksandrovich	1902	Vilno	Baranovichi	Pervomaiskaya	Oktyabr
Gorelik Aron Isaakovich	1908	Bobruisk	Pinsk	Molotov	Kalinin
Gorelik Boris Leizerovich	1925	Shchedrin	Palesye	? 123	Pavlovski's
Gorelik Yevgeni Pavlovich	1905	Khabaly, BYelski district	Grodno	Vo imya Rodiny (In the name of Motherland)	Parkhomenko
Gorelik Yevsei Gershenovich	1909	Central Committee of the CP (b) B	Mogilev	? 17	? 2
Gorelik Lazar Gertsovich	1883	Shchedrin	Palesye	? 123	Artyushka's
Gorelik Mikhail Lvovich	1923	Minsk	Baranovichi	Chkalov	
Gorelik Moisei Khaimovich	1924	Smilovichi	Baranovichi	detachment ? 106	
Gorelik Mordukh Aronovich	1924	Baranovichi	Baranovichi	Kalinin	
Gorelik Mota Rafailovich	1902	Osipovichi	Mogilev	Osipovichskaya VOG	? 210
Gorelik Khaim Abramovich	1897	Smilovichi	Baranovichi	detachment ? 106	
Gorelik Shneer Abramovich	1906	Central Committee of the CP (b) B	Baranovichi	Komsomolets	Kalinin
Gorenkrig Genya Solomonovna	1898	Minsk	Baranovichi	detachment ? 106	
Gorenkrig Danil Isaakovich	1899	Stolbtsy	Baranovichi	detachment ? 106	
Gorenkrig Klara Danilovna	1926	Stolbtsy	Baranovichi	detachment ? 106	
Gorenkrig Musya Danilovna	1924	Stolbtsy	Baranovichi	Za Sovetskuyu Belarus	family detachment
Gormoza Izrail Khaimovich	1900	from behind the front line	Minsk	Ponomarenko	Gvardeyets (Guardsman)
Gorodetski Zakhar Srolevich	1927		Pinsk	Budenny	Ponomarenko
Gorodetski Sergei Makarovich	1920	from captivity	Mogilev	Chekist	Kovalev's
Gorodinskaya Ester Faivelevna	1906	Mir	Baranovichi		
Gorodnitski Yankel Shmoilovich	1893	Pogost, Starobin district	Pinsk	Komarov-Korzh's	1 group
Gorodynskaya Sonya Abramovna	1921	Novogrudok	Baranovichi	Kalinin	
Gorodynski Shevel Abramovich	1925	Novogrudok	Baranovichi	Kalinin	
Gorodynski Shlema Movshovich	1916	Korelichi	Baranovichi	Kalinin	
Goronovski Tsalya Yosifovich	1924	Baranovichi	Baranovichi	Kalinin	
Gorokhova Dora Faivelevna	1920	Trelosino, Shklov district	Mogilev	Ilyin's	? 30
Gorfinkel Mikhel Venyaminovich	1910	Kurenets	Vitebsk	Lepelskaya Stalin	? 2
Gorfinkel Shaya Mikhailovich	1929	Poland	Brest	Lenin	Zelenin
Gorfung Mordukh Borisovich	1941	Lida	Baranovichi	Kalinin	
Gorfunk Boris Lvovotich	1920	Lida	Baranovichi		
Gorfunk Lyuba Yakovlevna	1921	Lida	Baranovichi		
Gorshkov Boris Solomonovich	1913	N. Sverzhen	Vileyka	Zhdanov	
Gorshtein Sonya Yudelevna	1915	Novogrudok	Baranovichi	Kalinin	
Goskind Isaak Irsifovich	1898		Baranovichi	Shchuchin IDC	
Gotkin Mendel	1910	from the civil camp	Vileyka	4th Belorusskaya	? 6
Gotkin Motka Itskovich	1899	Machulishche, Sharkovshchina district	Vileyka	Za Rodinu (For Motherland)	Zhdanov
Gotlib Vera Mikhailovna	1926	Minsk	Baranovichi	Za Sovetskuyu Belarus	family detachment
Gotlib Semen Mikhailovich	1924	Minsk	Baranovichi	Vpered (Forward)	Chkalov
Gotlibovich Boris Ilyich	1910	Minsk	Minsk	2nd Minskaya	Kutuzov
Gofman Bronya Borisovna	1918	Minsk	Baranovichi	Stalin	brigade headquarters
Gofman Izrail Kopelevich	1911	Turets	Baranovichi	Shchors	Chapayev
Gofman Martin Simonovich	1919	from the working Magyar batallion	Pinsk	Sovetskaya Belarus	Chkalov
Gofman Mikhail Matveyevich	1913	Pukhovichi	Minsk	Chapayev	Ponomarenko
Gofman Moisei Samoilovich	1920	Jewish camp	Vileyka	Spartak	? 2
Gofman Naum Semenovich					
Gofman Tevel Leizerovich	1907	concentration camp, Vilno	Vileyka	Spartak	? 6
Gofman Yakov Isaakovich	1926	Lida	Belostok	A.Nevski	
Gofshtein David Khaimovich	1902	Dubrovno	Mogilev	Osipovichskaya VOG	? 210
Gokhman Ivan Nasonovich	1929	getto, Glubokoye	Vitebsk	Korotkin	Voroshilov
Gokhman Isaak Abramovich	1908	N. Belitsa	Gomel	Bolshevik	Bolshevik
Grabe Simkha Abramovich	1920	Baranovichi	Baranovichi	Kalinin	
Graver Leon Benyaminovich	1920	st. Lesnaia, Baranovichi region	Brest	Ponomarenko	Sovetskaya Belarus

Gradenabel Yakov Gershkovich	1920	Lida	Baranovichi	Kirov	Iskra
Grazhevski Volf Volfovich	1920		Baranovichi	Leninskaya	Pobieda
Grazhevski Shmul Volfovich	1920	Derechin	Baranovichi	Pobieda	Suvorov
Grazovskaya Zinaida Elevna	1909	Uzda	Minsk	Rokossovski	Chkalov
Grazovskaya Fanya Khaimovna	1930	Uzda	Minsk	Rokossovski	Chkalov
Grazovski Khaim Aizikovich	1905	Uzda	Minsk	Rokossovski	Chkalov
Gralvyer Girsh Rubinovich	1902	Minsk	Minsk	Chapayev	Ponomarenko
Graizhevski Girsh Lazarevich	1912	Zheludok	Baranovichi	Lenin's komsomol	Lenin's komsomol
Graizhevski Grigori Movshevich	1911	Kozlovshchina	Baranovichi	Lenin's komsomol	Lenin's komsomol
Graizel Boris Khlavtsovich	1929		Brest	? 99 Gulyaev	Grabko
Grakus Khatskel Borisovich	1922	Novogrudok	Baranovichi	Kalinin	
Granatshtein Filipp Solomonovich	1914	Slonim	Baranovichi	Slonim IDC	
Grande Khatskel Borisovich	1922	Novogrudok	Baranovichi		
GrankovskiAnatoli Yanya Lazarevich	1924	Derechin	Baranovichi	Pobieda	Pobieda
Granovski Abram Yakovlevich	1909	l/vpl Smolevichi	Minsk	Za Sovetskuyu Belorussiyu	Lazo
Graf Sender Aronovich	1913	Malorita	Brest	Lenin	Voroshilov
Grachuk David Movshevich	1909	Slonim	Baranovichi	Pervomaiskaya	Ya.Kolas
Grachuk Ilya Moiseyevich	1918	Slonim	Pinsk	Lenin	Dzerzhinski
Grachuk Mariya Movshevna	1916	Slonim	Pinsk	Lenin	Dzerzhinski
Grelvyer Mariya Aronovna	1913	Minsk	Minsk	Chapayev	Ponomarenko
Greider Nokhim Danilovich	1922	detachment "Mest"	Vileyka	Voroshilov	headquarters' production group
Greizdorf Leiba Lazarevich	1909	Kozyany	Vileyka	Spartak	? 6
Greizdorf Mina Leizerovna	1910	Kozyany	Vileyka	Spartak	? 4
Greizdorf Pavel Lazarevich	1908	getto, KozLyany	Vileyka	1st Suvorov	Voroshilov
Greizel Aizik Khlaunovich	1926	Glussk	Palesye	? 100	Budenny
Greiman Boris Yosifovich	1913	from the encirclement	Vileyka	Voroshilov	Vileika center
Greiman Fima Lekhelevich	1910	Dunilovichi	Vileyka	Voroshilov	Suvorov
Greis Ilya Izrailevich	1917	from captivity	Baranovichi	Lenin's komsomol	Lenin's komsomol
Greisukh Khaya Shmoimovna	1915	Grozovo, Minsk region	Minsk	Chapayev	Ponomarenko
Greifer Leiba Mordukhovich	1895	Shchedrin, Parichi district	Minsk	Parkhomenko	Kirov
Grenader Petr Izrailevich	1909	Belarusian Staff of Partisan Movement	Minsk	Special groups	Tekhanovich's group
Grenadir Osher Meyerovich	1926	Jewish camp, David Gorodok	Pinsk	Shubetidze	Ordzhonikidze
Grengauz Grigori Shepselevich	1921	Slonim	Pinsk	Lenin	Kutuzov
Grengauz Shepsel Yakovlevich	1893	Slonim	Pinsk	Lenin	Kutuzov
Gres Boris Mikhailovich	1915	Minsk	Minsk	Rokossovski	Chkalov
Grechanik small town ofl.	1911	Kopyl	Minsk	Rokossovski	25 years of Oktyabr
Grechanik Sofiya	1923	Minsk	Minsk	Rokossovski	25 years of Oktyabr
Gribovski Grigori Konstantinovich	1904	Minsk	Minsk	Rokossovski	Chkalov
Grivner Abram Antonovich	1888	Orsha	Vitebsk	1st Belorusskaya	
Gridman Estera Mendeleyevna	1915	detachment "Mest"	Vileyka	Voroshilov	headquarters' production group
Grimberg Abram Borisovich	1922	Parichi district, Shchedrin	Minsk	Parkhomenko	Shchors
Grimberg Bela Yankelevna	1881	Glussk	Minsk	Ponomarenko	A.Nevski
Grinberg Genrikh Aronovich	1916	iz cheshskogo rabochego batalona	Brest	Ponomarenko	Kirov
Grinberg Daniil Genukhovich	1905	Borisov	Minsk	Shchors	Shchors
Grinberg Yosif Rafailovich	1905	Mir	Baranovichi	Kalinin	
Grinberg Isaak Grigorevich	1925	Minsk	Baranovichi	detachment ? 106	
Grinberg Minya Rafailovna	1913	Mir	Baranovichi	Kalinin	
Grinberg Mikhail I.	1927		Palesye	? 123	Krasny Oktyabr
Grinberg Rakhil Davidovna	1925	Minsk	Baranovichi	detachment ? 106	
Grinberg Estera Yakovlevna	1923	Novogrudok	Baranovichi	Kalinin	
Grinvald Mariya Samuilovna	1922	Mir, getto	Baranovichi	Za Sovetskuyu Belarus	Kirov
Grinvald Nikolai Eduardovich	1920	from the working Magyar batallion	Pinsk	Sovetskaya Belarus	Chkalov
Gringauz Leva Aronovich	1939	Minsk	Baranovichi	detachment ? 106	
Gringauz Lena Aronovna	1925	Minsk	Baranovichi	detachment ? 106	
Gringauz Khaim Abelevich	1906	Minsk	Baranovichi	detachment ? 106	
Gringauz Shura Aronovich	1928	Minsk	Baranovichi	detachment ? 106	
Gringaus Girsh Shepselevich	1921	Slonim	Brest	Sikorski's headquarters	Shchors
Gringaus Zusya Abramovich	1911	Radoshkovichi	Minsk	Voronyanski	Kotovski
Gringaus Ida Ilinichna	1909	Minsk	Baranovichi	detachment ? 106	
Gringaus Khaim Khatskelevich	1890	Radoshkovichi	Minsk	Voronyanski	Kotovski
Gringaus Shepsel Yankelevich	1893	Slonim	Brest	Sikorski's headquarters	Shchors
Gringolts Naum Moiseyevich	1924	Rakov	Vileyka	Dovator	Sverdlov
Gringruk Ida Ilinichna	1909	Minsk	Baranovichi		

Name	Year	Origin	Region	Detachment	Group
Grinkovski Abram Shlemovich	1916		Baranovichi	Oktyabr	
Grinkovski Isaak Borisovich	1920		Baranovichi	Oktyabr	
Grinoder Shigel Yankelevich	1925	Belarusian Staff of Partisan Movement	Vitebsk	Special groups	Melnikov's group
Grinshian Miriam Barukhovna	1918	Warsaw	Baranovichi	Kalinin	
Grinshpan Zyama Mikhailovich	1915	Uzda	Minsk	Voroshilov	Patriots of Motherland
Grinshpan Meilakh Solomonovich	1939	Lida	Baranovichi	Kalinin	
Grinshpan Pesya Shmuilovna	1925	Vlodava (Poland)	Pinsk	Molotov	Shish
Grinshpan Riva Falkovna	1914	Lida	Baranovichi	Kalinin	
Grinshtein Bella PertsYevna	1920	Minsk getto	Baranovichi	Ponomarenko	Voronov's
Grinshtein Yakov Abramovich	1919	Uzda	Baranovichi	Stalin	Budenny
Grinkovskaya YAnya ManYevna	1923	Golynka	Baranovichi	Leninskaya	Leninski
Grinkovski Abram small town of	1920	local	Baranovichi	Pobieda	Pobieda
Grinkovski Anatoli Yakovlevich	1923	Dyatlovo getto	Baranovichi	Kirov	Ordzhonikidze
Grinkovski Lazar Izrailevich	1888	Dyatlovo getto	Baranovichi	Kirov	Ordzhonikidze
Gripoded Petr Izrailevich	1909	from behind the front line	Minsk	Zheleznyak	? 5
Grifeld Yakov Vladimirovich		Minsk	Dyadi Koli	Gastello	
Grodens Yosif Navtulovich	1900	Minsk	Minsk	Rokossovski	Chkalov
Grodens Sofiya Isaakovna	1917	Minsk	Minsk	Rokossovski	Chkalov
Grodenchik Blyuma Abramovna	1924	Lida	Baranovichi	Kalinin	
Grodenchik Khaim Yankelevich	1926	Voronovo	Baranovichi	Kalinin	
Grodner Rakhil Izrailevna	1905	Minsk getto	Baranovichi	18th Frunze	Frunze
Groner Maksim Samuilovich	1907	otr. "Za Rodinu (For Motherland)"	Brest	Dzerzhinski	Selnitski
Gros Vaitetekh Germanovich	1912	from the Hungarian army	Brest	Stalin	Chernyak
Grosberg Vasili Germanovich	1917	from the Hungarian army	Brest	Stalin	Chernyak
Grunberger Adolf Leopoldovich	1906	cheshski evrei iz nemetskoi chasti	Gomel		Kotovski
Grundshtein Boris Shulmovich	1922	Domachevo	Brest	Lenin	Zhukov
Gryshkan Vladimir Mikhailovich	1928	Domachevo	Vitebsk	Kirillov	Suvorov
Guberman Boleslav Abovich	1924	concentration camp, Vlodava	Pinsk	Molotov	Kalinin
Guberman Dmitri Simkhovich	1922	Derechin	Baranovichi	Pobieda	Suvorov
Guberman Ekheskel Abovich	1922	Vlodava (Poland)	Pinsk	Molotov	Kalinin
Gubler Yefim Yefimovich	1914	Central Committee of the CP (b) B	Vitebsk	VLKSM	? 3
Gudeeva Tasya Pavlovna	1919	Rudinka	Mogilev	partisan regiment ? 277	? 277
Gudis Yosif Khaimovich	1900	Koniushevshchina	Baranovichi	Za Sovetskuyu Belarus	Kirov
Gudse Leya Grigorevna	1920	Lodz	Baranovichi	Kalinin	
Guz Osher Yankelevich	1922	Jewish camp	Pinsk	Shubetidze	Ordzhonikidze
Gulkovich Bentsian Shlemovich	1909	Korelichi	Baranovichi	Kalinin	
Gulkovich Fruma Samuilovna	1917	Korelichi	Baranovichi	Kalinin	
Gulkovich Yudes Abramovna	1917		Baranovichi	Oktyabr	
Gulman Riva Izrailevna	1898		Pinsk	Kuibyshev	Shchors
Gulnik Moisei Movshovich	1922	Lida	Baranovichi	Kalinin	
Gumanits Matvei Rubinovich	1921		Baranovichi	Kirov	Iskra
Gumanova Mira Gutelevna	1919	Minsk	Baranovichi	detachment ? 106	
Gumnits Vigdor Khaimovich	1874	Ivye	Baranovichi	Kalinin	
Gumnits Matvei Rubinovich	1921	Lida	Baranovichi	Kirov	Iskra
Gumnits Mnukha Vigdorovna	1926	Lida	Baranovichi	Kalinin	
Gumnits Rokha Aronovna	1880	Ivye	Baranovichi	Kalinin	
Gumnits Shoma Vigdorovna	1929	Lida	Baranovichi	Kalinin	
Guppershmidt Naum Semenovich	1926	skryvaiushchaiAsya evreiskaya group	Pinsk	Molotov	Kalinin
Gurvach Riva Lebetsovna	1918	detachment "Mest"	Vileyka	Voroshilov	headquarters' production group
Gurvich Alter Girshevich	1907	Lyubcha	Baranovichi	detachment ? 106	
Gurvich Benyamin Aleksandrovich	1922	Minsk getto	Baranovichi	Chapayev	Parkhomenko
Gurvich Venyamin Yankelevich	1921	concentration camp	Brest	? 99 Gulyaev	Grabko
Gurvich Girsh Khaimovich	1911	Novogrudok, getto	Baranovichi	1st Baranovichskaya	Frunze
Gurvich Grigori Tubyanovich	1922	Vilno	Baranovichi	Lenin's komsomol	Lenin's komsomol
Gurvich Masha Isaakovna	1903	Rakov	Baranovichi	detachment ? 106	
Gurvich Nekhama Aleksandrovna	1933	Rakov	Baranovichi	detachment ? 106	
Gurvich Ovsei Davidovich	1915	Krevo	Baranovichi	Chkalov	? 4 "Za Sovetskuyu Belarus"
Gurvich Ovsei Yankelevich	1926	Mir	Baranovichi	Kalinin	
Gurvich Freida Shlemovna	1902	Minsk, underground, regional committee of the CP(b)B	Minsk	Voronyanski	Mstitel (Revenger)
Gurvich Yakov Gedalovich	1919	Warsaw	Baranovichi	Pobieda	Pobieda

Gurevich		Belarusian Staff of Partisan Movement	Gomel	Kozhar's	Shemyakin's group
Gurevich Anna Moiseyevna	1910	Glussk	Palesye	? 123	Krasny Oktyabr
Gurevich Basya Yefimovna	1912		Palesye	? 123	Vezhnovets'
Gurevich Boris Vulfovich	1910	Belarusian Staff of Partisan Movement	Minsk	Special groups	Khonyak's group
Gurevich Boris Leibovich	1911	getto, Vilno	Vileyka	Voroshilov	brigade headquarters
Gurevich Yevgeniya Semenovna	1923	Lepel	Vitebsk	Lepelskaya Stalin	cavalry squadron
Gurevich Zusya Genukhovich	1894	Slizhin, Shklov district	Mogilev	? 115	? 2
Gurevich Ivan Romanovich	1926	from captivity	Vileyka	Suvorov	
Gurevich Igor Lazarevich	1920	Borisov	Mogilev	208th partisan regiment	? 3
Gurevich Lazar Kalmanovich	1906	Minsk	Minsk	Voronyanski	Kotovski
Gurevich Lev Grigorevich	1917	from captivity	Vileyka	Voroshilov	Istrebitel (Destroyer)
Gurevich Lev Semenovich	1918	from captivity	Pinsk	Lenin	Chapayev
Gurevich Lena Izrailevna	1922	small town of Vishnevo	Baranovichi	Chapayev	Parkhomenko
Gurevich Leonid Grigorevich	1919	Minsk	Minsk	2nd Minskaya	Kutuzov
Gurevich Liza Grigorevna	1920	Minsk	Baranovichi	Za Sovetskuyu Belarus	family detachment
Gurevich Mariya Yakovlevna	1913	Lyuban	Minsk	Chkalov	Gromov
Gurevich Mikhail Osirovich	1925	Novogrudok	Baranovichi	Ivienets DC CP(b)B company	
Gurevich Movsha Davidovich	1915	Krevo, getto	Baranovichi	Za Sovetskuyu Belarus	Kirov
Gurevich Moisei Yakovlevich	1905	Belarusian Staff of Partisan Movement	Minsk	Chapayev	Shchors
Gurevich Mordukh Leibovich	1906	Glussk	Minsk	Ponomarenko	Gorbachev
Gurevich Nikolai Vladimirovich	1920	Ganskoe	Mogilev	? 117	? 124
Gurevich Pesya Khaimovna	1923	Bobruisk	Palesye	Lelchitskaya	Shantar's
Gurevich Raya Yakovlevna	1923	Glussk	Brest	? 99 Gulyaev	Grabko
Gurevich Rita Samoilovna	1914	getto, Vilno	Vileyka	Voroshilov	brigade headquarters
Gurevich Sarra Izrailevna	1920	Minsk	Baranovichi	detachment ? 106	
Gurevich Solomon Natanovich	1924		Vileyka	Suvorov	
Gurevich Sonya Sholomovna	1914	Minsk	Baranovichi	detachment ? 106	
Gurevich Faina Solomonovna	1920	Baranovichi	Baranovichi	Chkalov	
Gurevich Fanya Girshevna	1912	Minsk	Baranovichi	detachment ? 106	
Gurevich Khaya Yevelevna	1921	Lenin	Pinsk	Kirov	
Gurevich Shaya Abramovich	1893	Rubezhevichi, getto	Baranovichi	Zhukov	
Gurevich Yakov Yakovlevich	1925	Glussk	Minsk	A.Nevski	Lomatko
GurkofYelskaya Anna Borisovna	1918	Lida	Baranovichi	Kalinin	
Gurman Isaak Faivelevich	1915	Stolbtsy	Baranovichi	Kalinin	
GurnofYelski Isaak Borisovich	1920		Baranovichi	Oktyabr	
Gurskaya Sara Osherovna	1922	Skidel	Baranovichi	Kalinin	
Gurski Izrail Girshevich	1917	Chekhovo	Baranovichi	Kalinin	
Gurfinkel Yevgeni	1921	Nasalsk	Baranovichi	Pobieda	Pobieda
Gurian Basya Movshovna	1924	Rubezhevichi	Baranovichi	Kalinin	
Gurian Yosif Faivelevich	1912	Rubezhevichi	Baranovichi	Kalinin	
Gurian Leizer Leibovich	1905	Rubezhevichi	Baranovichi	Kalinin	
Gurian Movsha Leibovich	1887	Rubezhevichi	Baranovichi	Kalinin	
Gurian Samuil Lazarovich	1931	Rubezhevichi	Baranovichi	Kalinin	
Gurian Sonya Benyaminovna	1905	Rubezhevichi	Baranovichi	Kalinin	
Gurian Fanya Movshovna	1927	Rubezhevichi	Baranovichi	Kalinin	
Gurian Khaya Movshovna	1897	Rubezhevichi	Baranovichi	Kalinin	
Gurian Shmeir Movshevich	1903	Minsk getto	Minsk	3rd Minskaya	Lazo
Gurian Iavzer Itskovich	1893	Minsk getto	Minsk	3rd Minskaya	Lazo
Gusev Mikhail Semenovich	1916	Minsk camp, prisoner of war	Minsk	3rd Minskaya	Lazo
Guseva Galina Petrovna	1922	Uvarovichi	Gomel	Bolshevik	Bolshevik
Gusman Lev Zakharovich	1912	from captivity	Baranovichi	Kutuzov	
Gus Fedor Maksimovich	1919		Minsk	2nd Minskaya	Chapayev
Guskova Zinaida Ivanovna	1910	Minsk	Baranovichi	Stalinskaya	Suvorov
Gut Yefim Mikhailovich	1906	Selektra	Vitebsk	1st Zaslonov	Kutuzov
Guterman Lev Maksimovich	1900	Mikhanovichi	Grodno	Ponomarenko	squadron
Guterman Samuil Azrelovich	1923	Belarusian Staff of Partisan Movement	Gomel	Kozhar's	Arbuzov's group
Guterman Srul Moiseyevich	1915	Poland	Brest	Lenin	Zelenin
Guterman Shmul Volfovich	1916	Slonim	Brest	Sikorski's headquarters	Shchors
Gutermas Zigmund Mikhailovich	1915	Kaunas	Vileyka	Gastello	Za Sovetskuyu Rodinu
Gutermas Raisa Abramovna	1923	Kaunas	Vileyka	Gastello	Za Sovetskuyu Rodinu
Gutin Izrail Zyamovich	1928	Samotevichi	Gomel	Shemyakin's "Vpered (Forward)"	Makagonov's
Gutin Yankel Abramovich	1911	Chashniki district, Vitebsk obl., v. Charia	Minsk	Ponomarenko	Gvardeyets (Guardsman)
Gutina Nina Zamanovna	1926	Samotevichi	Gomel	Shemyakin's "Vpered (Forward)"	Makagonov's
Gutkevich Leya Zalmanovna	1917	Minsk getto	Minsk	Belarus	Stalin

Gutkin Grigori Abramovich	1894	Slaveni	Mogilev	Ilyin's	? 24
Gutkin Yosif Zelikovich	1923	Glubokoye	Vileyka	Spartak	? 1
Gutkin Lazar Samoilovich	1919	Minsk	Baranovichi	Chkalov	
Gutkin Moisei Abramovich	1870	Slaveni	Mogilev	Ilyin's	? 24
Gutlits Benyamin Davidovich	1894	Jewish camp	Vileyka	Voroshilov	headquarters' production group
Gutlits Rakhil Venyaminovna	1925	Jewish camp	Vileyka	Voroshilov	headquarters' production group
Gutman (Sergienko) Raya Yefimovna	1920	Borisov	Minsk	Shchors	Bolshevik
Gutman Aleksandr Moiseyevich	1907	Minsk, camp, prisoner of war	Vileyka	Frunze	Voroshilov
Gutman Aleksei Yakovlevich	1923	Belarusian Staff of Partisan Movement	Vitebsk	Belyaev's filmgroups	gr. Posnichenko
Gutman Golda Shayevna		zhena Gutmana small town of L.	Palesye	37th Yelskaya	Death to Fascism
Gutman Menash Leibovich	1891	Skorodnoe	Palesye	37th Yelskaya	Death to Fascism
Gutman Movsha Yosifovich	1920	Dyatlovo	Baranovichi	Leninskaya	Borba
Gutman Movsha Mordukhovich	1902	Molchad	Baranovichi	Kalinin	
Gutman Tamara Girshevna	1920	Pavlovka, Yelski district	Palesye	37th Yelskaya	Bolshevik
Gutman Fegel Khononovich	1920	Kozyany	Vileyka	Spartak	? 6
Gutman Sholom Zalmanovich	1904	Moskalevshchina, Vitebsk region	Vitebsk	Voroshilov	KIM
Gutman Yakov Aleksandrovich		Gomel	Buda-Koshelevskaya	Kutuzov	
Gutnik Yefim Ilyich	1898	K. Kashirski	Pinsk	Molotov	Suvorov
Gutfeld Mendel Aronovich	1908	Baranovichi	Baranovichi	Kalinin	
Gutfraint Ester Mikhailovna	1929	Minsk	Baranovichi	detachment ? 106	
Guttsait Aron Itskovich	1911	Belarusian Staff of Partisan Movement	Brest	groups of party leaders	Kokhov's group
Guttsait Venyamin Aronovich	1910	Slutsk	Minsk	2nd Minskaya	Kutuzov
Davidan Nison Girshevich	1913	from the encirclement	Pinsk	Komarov-Korzh's	Komarov's 3rd group
Davidovich Lazar Khaimovich	1914	Minsk	Baranovichi	18th Frunze	brigade headquarters
Davidovich Leya Moiseyevna	1900	Novogrudok	Baranovichi	Kalinin	
Davidovich Mikhail (Meilakh) Khaimovich	1928	Minsk getto	Baranovichi	18th Frunze	brigade headquarters
Davidovich Riva Aronovna	1930	Ivye	Baranovichi	Kalinin	
Davidovich Sofiya Lazarevna	1907	Minsk getto	Baranovichi	18th Frunze	brigade headquarters
Davidovich Frida Gershovna	1923	Novogrudok	Baranovichi	Kalinin	
Davidovich Yudel Natanovich	1914	Minsk	Baranovichi	detachment ? 106	
Davidovski Lev Berkovich	1925	Novogrudok getto	Baranovichi	Kirov	Ordzhonikidze
Davidovski Shlema Movshovich	1909	Nesvizh	Baranovichi	Kalinin	
Davidson Vladimir Izrailevich	1939	Minsk	Baranovichi	detachment ? 106	
Davidson Izrail Abramovich	1906	Minsk	Baranovichi	detachment ? 106	
Davidson Mira Izrailevna	1935	Minsk	Baranovichi	detachment ? 106	
Davidson Rakhil Izrailevna	1932	Minsk	Baranovichi	detachment ? 106	
Davidson Rakhmel Abramovich	1915	camp, prisoner of war	Minsk	2nd Minskaya	Suvorov
Davidson Fruma Meyerovna	1912	Minsk	Baranovichi	detachment ? 106	
Davidson Esfir Abramovna	1910	Smorgon	Baranovichi	detachment ? 106	
Davydovich Isaak Georgievich	1924		Baranovichi	Slonim IDC	
Dagovich Meyer Abramovich	1922	from the detachment Konopelki	Vileyka	Zhdanov	
Dagutskaya Bella Lvovna	1925	getto	Baranovichi	Kirov	Orel
Daineko Fedor Afanasyevich	1918	Svisloch, Osipovichi district	Mogilev		? 760 Berezovski
Daichik Sofiya Isaakovna	1927	Berezino	Minsk	Razgrom (Crushing defeat)	
Damesik Ilya Isaakovich	1912	Lida	Baranovichi	Slonim IDC	
Dameshek Sonya Borisovna	1922	Nesvizh	Baranovichi	Za Sovetskuyu Belarus	family detachment
DanIlyin's Anna Abramovna	1910	Kulazhin, Komarin district	Palesye		Kotovski
Danishevski Lazar Girshevich	1913	Krevo	Baranovichi	Chkalov	reserve group
Danishevski Mariya FaibElevna	1916	Krevo	Baranovichi	Chkalov	reserve group
Danovich Faiva Aizikovich	1910	Belarusian Staff of Partisan Movement	Minsk	Special groups	Kovalev's group
Dantsig Khanka Froimovna	1925		Pinsk	Molotov	Kalinin
Dantsiger Liza Yefimovna	1919	Lida	Baranovichi	Kalinin	
Dantsiger Yakov Rubinovich	1910	Lida	Baranovichi	Kalinin	
Dantsik Sheya Mordukhovich	1923	Ivanovo	Pinsk	Molotov	Shish
Daroshka Movsha Isaakovich	1893	Ostrozhanka, Lelchitski district	Palesye	Lelchitskaya	brigade headquarters and administration platoon
Datner Shimon Markovich	1902	Belostok	Grodno	Samutin's group	Kirshner's group
Dauer Eva Yosifovna	1918	Byten	Pinsk	Lenin	Chapayev
Dachkovskaya Golda Pertsovna	1915	Rubezhevichi	Baranovichi		

Dveerman Mikhail Yosifovich	1903	Borisov	Minsk	Kirov	? 4
Dvigun Gavrel Mikhailovich	1904	Disna	Vitebsk	Chapayev	detachments
DvIlyanskaya Elya Yankelevna	1922	Lida	Baranovichi	Kalinin	
DvIlyanski Itsko Volfovich	1920	Lida	Baranovichi	Kalinin	
DvIlyanski Yakov Abramovich	1915	Lida	Baranovichi	Kalinin	
Dvint Reveka Zelikovna	1919	Jewish camp	Vileyka	Voroshilov	headquarters' production group
Dvovrina Lyubov Solomonovna	1924	Belarusian Staff of Partisan Movement	Minsk		Putilova
Dvozhinskaya Tamara	1914	Lida	Baranovichi	Kalinin	
Dvozhinski Nekhemya Abramovich	1938	Lida	Baranovichi	Kalinin	
Dvoinina Vasilisa I.	1910	Sergeiki, Sennenski district	Vitebsk	Sennenskaya brigade (Leonov's)	Karaketov's
Dvoretskaya Lyuba Khaimovna	1928	Ivye	Baranovichi	Kalinin	
Dvoretskaya Rakhelya Abramovna	1927	Dvorets	Baranovichi	Kalinin	
Dvoretskaya Sofiya	1906	Volkovyssk	Belostok	A.Nevski	Kotovski
Dvoretskaya Taiba Shmuilovna	1905	Ivye	Baranovichi	Kalinin	
Dvoretskaya Tsylya Khaimovna	1930	Ivye	Baranovichi	Kalinin	
Dvoretski Abram Peisakhovich	1896	Dvorets	Baranovichi	Kalinin	
Dvoretski Khaim Mirovich	1897	Ivye	Baranovichi	Kalinin	
Dvoretski Khaim Shmulovich	1927	Ivye	Baranovichi	Kalinin	
Dvoretski Yuli Yosifovich	1926	Minsk	Baranovichi	detachment ? 106	
Dvorzhetskaya Vita Yakovlevna	1919	Volkovyssk	Baranovichi	Pobieda	Pobieda
Dvorzhinski Daniil Moiseyevich	1910	Poland	Brest	Lenin	Zelenin
Dvorin Boris Arkadevich	1910	Kniazevka, Borisov district	Minsk	Shchors	Bolshevik
Dvorina Genya Zolina	1925	Minsk	Baranovichi	detachment ? 106	
Dvorkind Klara Zalmanovna	1921	Borisovski district, v. Zhitkovo	Minsk	Kirov	Kirov
Dvoskin Fima Borisovich	1927	Minsk getto	Baranovichi	Chapayev	Parkhomenko
Degenorish Blyuma Izrailevna	1906	Lida	Baranovichi	Leninskaya	Borba
Degenorish Yosif Mendelevich	1905	Lida	Baranovichi	Leninskaya	Borba
Deich Semen Moiseyevich	1924	Minsk	Vileyka	Frunze	Voroshilov
DElyatitski Andrei Izv.	1905	Slonim	Brest	Sikorski's headquarters	Shchors
DElyatskaya Khanna Movshevna	1926	getto	Vitebsk	Nikitin's	? 6
DElyatski Yevsei Movshevich	1913	getto	Vitebsk	Nikitin's	? 6
DElyatski Movsha Khaimovich	1890	getto	Vitebsk	Nikitin's	? 6
Dembovski Leonid Mikhailovich	1923	Minsk	Minsk	Shturmovaya	Za Otechestvo (For Fatherland)
Demburg Sara Benyaminovna	1925	Kopyl getto	Minsk	Frunze	Budenny
Dement Genya Naumovna	1918	Minsk	Minsk	Rokossovski	Chkalov
Dement Naum Fisolevich	1894	Minsk	Minsk	Rokossovski	Chkalov
Demenshtein Zelik Leontevich	1922	Dolginovo	Minsk	Zheleznyak	? 3
Demonshtein Abram Yeselevich	1900	Knyaginino	Minsk	Voronyanski	Mstitel (Revenger)
Demyakhovskaya Esfir Solomonovna	1907	Kostenevichi	Minsk	Voronyanski	Borba
Denburg Yakov Benyaminovich	1922	Kopyl getto	Minsk	Frunze	Budenny
Denenberg Itsko Zelikovich	1914	concentration camp, Pogost-Zagorodski	Pinsk	Kuibyshev	Shchors
Denenberg Itsko Senderovich	1921	concentration camp	Pinsk	Kuibyshev	Shchors
Denenburg Peiser Naumovich	1911	Gantsevichi	Mogilev	208th partisan regiment	headquarters
Denershtein Semen Markovich	1924	Minsk	Minsk	Ponomarenko	Gvardeyets (Guardsman)
Dentalski Abram Aronovich	1909	v. Izva	Baranovichi	Kalinin	
DentYelskaya Rakhil Movshevna	1926	Kletsk	Minsk	Chapayev	Shchors
DentYelskaya Khaya Abramovna	1918		Baranovichi	Oktyabr	
DentYelski Isaak Shlemovich	1922	Belitsa	Baranovichi	Pobieda	Pobieda
DentYelski Semen Aronovich	1898		Baranovichi	Oktyabr	
Derachinski Aron Yefimovich	1921	getto, Vilno	Vileyka	Voroshilov	Kalinin
Derevenski Adam Leibovich	1903	Baranovichi	Brest	Za Sovetskuyu Belarus	Suvorov
Derevenski Ovsei Leibovich	1909	Stolin	Brest	Za Sovetskuyu Belarus	Pozharski
Derevo Roza Yefimovna	1922	Nesvizh	Baranovichi	Za Sovetskuyu Belarus	Kirov
Derevo Yulya Khaimovna	1922	Nesvizh	Baranovichi	Chkalov	
Derevianko Ilya Isaakovich	1915	Gorodishche	Baranovichi	Pobieda	Pobieda
Derevianski Benyamin Zavelevich	1923	Zheludok, Baranovichi region	Baranovichi	Vpered (Forward)	Roshcha
Derevianski Girsh Zavelevich	1922	Voronovo	Baranovichi	Kalinin	
Derevianski Moisei Zelikovich	1924	Lida, getto	Baranovichi	Kirov	Ordzhonikidze
Deresevich Khengel Romanovich	1914	K. Kashirski	Pinsk	Shubetidze	Kostyushko
Derechinski Tsodik Shlemovich	1924	Slonim	Pinsk	Lenin	Dzerzhinski
Derchenskaya Elena Rubinovna	1911	Korelichski district	Baranovichi	Stalin	Bolshevik
Deul David Iserovich	1912	Oshmiany, getto	Baranovichi	Chapayev	Furmanov
DzengYelski Mikhail Elevich	1906	Baranovichi	Brest	Ponomarenko	Sovetskaya Belarus
DzentYelski Yankel Yovtelevich	1900	Derechin	Baranovichi	Leninskaya	hospital

DzentsYelskaya Bellya Shlemovna	1939	Izvi	Baranovichi	Kalinin	
DzentsYelskaya Ita Pinkhusovna	1878	Izvi	Baranovichi	Kalinin	
DzentsYelskaya MikhLya Gershevna	1909	Izvi	Baranovichi	Kalinin	
DzentsYelskaya Sonya Shlemovna	1936	Izvi	Baranovichi	Kalinin	
DzentsYelskaya Taiba Davidovna	1907	Stankevichi	Baranovichi	Kalinin	
DzentsYelskaya Khaya Aronovna	1918	v. Izva	Baranovichi	Kalinin	
DzentsYelski Aron Shayevich	1872	Izvi	Baranovichi	Kalinin	
DzentsYelski Shlema Dronovich	1895	Izvi	Baranovichi	Kalinin	
Dizengauz Isaak Moiseyevich	1913	Lida	Baranovichi	Kalinin	
Dizengauz Eva Girshevna	1913	Lida	Baranovichi	Kalinin	
Dik Lazar Zelmanovich	1923	Jewish camp	Pinsk	Shubetidze	Ordzhonikidze
Dik Yakov Zelikovich	1909	Jewish camp	Pinsk	Shubetidze	Ordzhonikidze
Dikshtein Manya Abramovna	1926	Minsk	Baranovichi	detachment ? 106	
Dimenshtein Girsh Lazarevich	1904	getto	Vileyka	Voroshilov	Suvorov
Dimenshtein Zinaida Yefimovna	1918	Glubokoye	Vileyka	CC of the CP(b)B	Parkhomenko
Dimenshtein Khaya Yakovlevna	1925	Krivichi district, Vileika region	Vitebsk	2nd Belorusskaya	
Diminshtein Abram Isaakovich	1905	getto Dolginovo	Minsk	Voronyanski	Pobieda
Diminshtein Movsha Aronovich	1911	Dolginovo	Minsk	Zheleznyak	? 5
Dinerman Gersh Fishelevich	1915	Belostok	Brest	Ponomarenko	Kirov
Dinershtein Aron Gotlibovich	1894		Vitebsk	Chapayev	detachments
Dinershtein Neukh Lvovich	1915	Vileika	Minsk	Voronyanski	Kotovski
Dinershtein Rakhil Lvovna	1922	getto, Ushachi	Vitebsk	Ponomarenko	hospital
Dinershtein Faiba Moiseyevich	1909	getto, Glubokoye	Vitebsk	Rokossovski	Dzerzhinski
Ditkovski Aron Grigorevich	1925	Minsk	Baranovichi	detachment ? 106	
Ditkovski Rubin Isaakovich	1904	Byten	Brest	Ponomarenko	Sovetskaya Belarus
Dlot Goda Aizikovna	1909	Pudenichi	Minsk	Voronyanski	Pobieda
Dobin Grigori Izrailevich	1905	Minsk, underground, regional committee of the CP(b)B	Minsk	Voronyanski	Borba
Dobrai Mark Petrovich	1920	from the encirclement	Gomel	8th Rogachevskaya	headquarters
Dobrin Izrail Lazarevich	1923	Mir	Baranovichi	Chkalov	
Dobrin Moisei Samonovich	1928	Mir	Baranovichi	Kalinin	
Dobrinski Yevsei Saulovich	1896	Minsk	Mogilev		
Dobrotkina Ida MotseyYevna	1908	Minsk	Vitebsk	Nikitin's	brigade administration
Dogim Isaak Abramovich	1916	Ponarov	Vileyka	Voroshilov	A.Nevski
Dogutskaya Bela Lvovna	1923	Lida	Baranovichi	1st Baranovichskaya	sabotage detachment "Orel"
Dogutski Yudol Abramovich	1915	Lida	Baranovichi	1st Baranovichskaya	sabotage detachment "Orel"
Dozortsev Viktor Markovich	1907		Minsk	Grishin's 13th regiment	
Doich Ivan Shlemovich	1922	Kobrin	Pinsk	Molotov	Kalinin
Doich Shlema Ovseyevich	1888	Ushkovichi	Brest		Kotovski
Doktorovich Sofiya Grigorevna	1906	Minsk	Minsk		Kalinin
Doktorchik Abram Mendelevich	1916	Slonim	Brest	Sikorski's headquarters	Shchors
Dokshitskaya Anna Adamovna	1920	Borisov	Baranovichi	Za Sovetskuyu Belarus	family detachment
Dokshitskaya Raya Yankelevna	1910		Minsk	Voronyanski	Pobieda
Dokshitskaya Emma Sholomovna	1925	Dolginovo	Vileyka	Kutuzov	
Dokshitski Zelik Semenovich	1913		Minsk	Voronyanski	Pobieda
Dokshitski Leonid Lvovich	1923	Minsk getto	Baranovichi	Chapayev	Parkhomenko
Dolgin Vladimir Semenovich	1924	Minsk	Minsk	Ponomarenko	Voroshilov
Dolgin Mikhail Filippovich	1921	Starobin	Pinsk	Komarov-Korzh's	1 group
Dolgina Genya Faivelevna	1924	Starobin	Pinsk	Komarov-Korzh's	1 group
Dolgopolski Mikhail Aleksandrovich		Chashniki	Vitebsk	Chapayev	detachments
Dolgopiatov Boris Zelikovich	1927	Lyuban district, Zhivun	Minsk	Bragin	Zaslonov
Dolgopiatyi Shlema Zelikovich	1911	Lakhva	Pinsk	Lenin	Kutuzov
Dolenko Anna Solomonovna	1893	Minsk	Baranovichi	Ponomarenko	25 years of the BSSR
Dolenko Moisei Khonovich	1893	Minsk	Baranovichi	Ponomarenko	25 years of the BSSR
Dolzhanski Mikhail Kalmanovich	1922	Belarusian Staff of Partisan Movement	Gomel	Kozhar's	Drozdov's group
Dolinko Khaim Davidovich	1897	Lyubashev, Volyn region	Pinsk	Shubetidze	Kostyushko
Dolino Ekha Solomonovna	1893	Minsk	Baranovichi	detachment ? 106	
Dolinskaya Ida Yosifovna	1913	small town of Golshany, getto	Baranovichi	Chapayev	Lazo
Dolinski Aron Samuilovich	1909	small town of Golshany, getto	Baranovichi	Chapayev	Lazo
Domashek Moisei Khaimovich	1916	Nesvizh	Baranovichi	Chkalov	
Domashek Sonya Borisovna	1922	Radoshkovichi district	Baranovichi	Chkalov	reserve group
Domashek Yuzef Yefimovich	1927	Nesvizh	Baranovichi	Chkalov	
Dombrovski Benyamin Shlemovich	1916	Brest	Baranovichi	Kalinin	
Domeshek Yevgeniya Khaimovna	1924	Mir	Baranovichi	Za Sovetskuyu Belarus	Shturm

Domeshek Yosif Yefimovich	1927	Mir	Baranovichi	Za Sovetskuyu Belarus	Shturm
Dominshtein Zakhar Abovich	1913	Krasnoye, getto	Baranovichi	Chkalov	
Domnich Bronya	1924	Slutsk	Pinsk	Budenny	Kotovski
Domnich Grigori Izrailevich	1918	Pogost, Starobin district	Minsk	Dyadi Koli	Stalin
Domnich David Izrailevich	1923	Pogost, Starobin district	Pinsk	Komarov-Korzh's	Komarov's 3rd group
Domnich Yefim Zakharovich	1922	Slutsk	Pinsk	Budenny	Kotovski
Domnich Yosif Khaimovich	1902	Pogost, Starobin district	Pinsk	Komarov-Korzh's	1 group
Domnich Sonya Abramovna	1902	Pogost, Starobin district	Pinsk	Komarov-Korzh's	1 group
Domnich Khaim Zelikovich	1922	Slutsk	Pinsk	Komarov-Korzh's	2 group
Dondo Rakhil Ionovna	1898		Vitebsk	Sadchikov's	batalon ? 2
Donishevski Khaim Abramovich	1927	Ivienets	Baranovichi	Kalinin	
Doniushevskaya Sofiya Yuryevna	1893	Smorgon	Minsk	Voronyanski	Kotovski
Dordik Matvei Lvovich	1908	from captivity Minsk	Minsk	Burevestnik	Burevestnik
Dorozhinski Danil Moiseyevich	1910	Poland	Brest	Lenin	
Dorosinski Aleksandr Lvovich	1913	ShLyakhetki	Vitebsk	1st Belorusskaya	
Dorski Grigori Anatolevich	1922	Slutsk district, Lenino	Minsk	Frunze	Budenny
Dorski Mikhail Anatolevich	1925	Slutsk district, Lenino	Minsk	Frunze	Budenny
Dorfman Gita Yakovlevna	1918	Minsk	Baranovichi	detachment ? 106	
Drapkina Khaya Davidovna	1903	Minsk	Baranovichi	detachment ? 106	
Drapski Izrail Isaakovich	1922	Minsk	Baranovichi	detachment ? 106	
Drapshi (Tropish) Khenik Ilyanovich	1913	Slonim district	Baranovichi	Rokossovski	Stalin
Drapshi Guta Samoilovna	1919	Slonim district	Baranovichi	Rokossovski	Stalin
Drebskaya Genya Yosifovna	1926	Lyuban district, Zagale	Minsk	Chkalov	Gromov
Drevin David Lazarevich	1917	Glussk	Minsk	Parkhomenko	Shchors
Drevina Anna Benyaminovna	1921	Glussk	Minsk	Parkhomenko	Shchors
Dreer Abram Greinovich	1891	Glussk	Palesye	? 123	brigade headquarters and administration platoon
Dreizen Leiba Mikhailovich	1905	Druya	Vileyka	4th Belorusskaya	? 3
Dreizenshtok Rubin Lvovich	1924	Glubokoye	Vileyka	4th Belorusskaya	? 1
Drendel Isaak Naumovich					
Drizhun Yosif Faivelevich	1915	Jewish camp, Stolin district	Pinsk	Shubetidze	Ordzhonikidze
Drizin Shepsel Gavrilovich	1909	Lida	Baranovichi	Kalinin	
Drovenko Ilya Meyerovich	1911	Gorodishche	Belostok	A.Nevski	
Drogachinski Leonid Girshevich	1920	from captivity	Brest	Za Sovetskuyu Belarus	Pozharski
Droznik Mikhail Ilyich	1909	Moskva, spetsshkola TsK VLKSM	Vitebsk	Donukalov	brigade headquarters
Droznik Moisei Ilyich	1904	Belarusian Staff of Partisan Movement	Brest	groups of party leaders	Krotov's group
Dronova Lidiya Mironovna	1917	iz tiurmy, Orsha	Vitebsk	Sadchikov's	battallion ? 3
Drug Boris Moiseyevich	1917	K. Kashirski	Pinsk	Molotov	Lazo
Druk Yosif Yakovlevich	1938	Lida	Baranovichi	Kalinin	
Druk Feiga Natanovna	1914	Lida	Baranovichi	Kalinin	
Druk Yakov Moiseyevich	1908	Lida	Baranovichi	Kalinin	
Druyak Meyer Lipmanovich	1919	Vilno	Baranovichi	Leninskaya	Niepobedimy (Undefeated)
Dubershtein Zina Matveyevna	1925		Minsk	Voronyanski	Mstitel (Revenger)
Dubershtein Elya Vulfovich	1923	Jewish camp Pleshchenitsy	Minsk	Voronyanski	Pobieda
Dubin Zelik Abramovich	1924	Starobin	Pinsk	Komarov-Korzh's	Komarov's 3rd group
Dubin Yakov Yeselevich	1929	getto	Vileyka	Voroshilov	Kutuzov
Dubinski Aron Genrikhovich	1922	Cherven	Pinsk	Lenin	Kutuzov
Dubinski Mikhail Izrailevich	1922	Radun	Baranovichi	Lenin's komsomol	Lenin's komsomol
Dubitski Berka Leizerovich	1925	Yelsk	Palesye	37th Yelskaya	Bolshevik
Dubkovski	1925	Baranovichi	Pinsk	Budenny	Kotovski
Dubovski Semen Naumovich	1924	Lyubanskaya nemetskaya tiurma	Palesye	? 225	Chapayev
Dubrovkina Sima Nokhimovna	1919	Novogrudok	Baranovichi	Leninskaya	hospital
Dubrovski Yosif Borisovich	1925	Shchedrin, Parichi district	Minsk	Ponomarenko	Selnitski
Dubchak Vladimir Yevseyevich	1917	iz tiurmy, Ovruch	Minsk	Ponomarenko	Selnitski
Dubchanski Meyer Isaakovich	1925	Lida	Baranovichi	Kirov	Iskra
Dudman Gedalp Mordukhovich	1908	Vishnevo	Baranovichi	Kalinin	
Dudnik Raisa Lvovna	1919	B. Dubrova	Mogilev		Za Sovetskuyu Belorussiyu
Dudritsa Naum Lvovich	1904		Mogilev	208th regiment	
Dukorskaya Bronya Aleksandrovna	1927	Minsk	Baranovichi	detachment ? 106	
Dukorski Grigori Leonidovich	1911	Minsk	Minsk	2nd Minskaya	brigade headquarters
Dukorski Solomon Shimonovich	1903	Uzlyany	Mogilev	208th regiment	
Duksin Genya Moiseyevna	1910	Byten	Brest	Ponomarenko	Sovetskaya Belarus
Duksin Mordukh Davidovich	1908	Byten	Brest	Ponomarenko	Sovetskaya Belarus
Dukshitskaya Anya Adamovna	1919	Smolevichi	Baranovichi	Chkalov	? 4 "Za Sovetskuyu Belarus"

Name	Year	Origin	Region	Detachment	Brigade
Dukshtein Avner Meyerovich	1904	Bobruisk district, Brozha	Minsk	Parkhomenko	Shchors
Dukshtein Semen Avnerovich	1927	Brozha, Bobruisk district	Minsk	Parkhomenko	Shchors
Dukshtein Sofiya Avnerovna	1929	Bobruisk district	Minsk	Parkhomenko	Shchors
Dukshtulski Zelman Yenaseyevich	1920	getto, Vilno	Vileyka	Voroshilov	Chapayev
Dulets Ilya Yakovlevich	1925	Minsk	Baranovichi	detachment ? 106	
Dulets Nikolai Lvovich	1922	Minsk	Baranovichi		
Dul Roman Zinovevich	1909		Pinsk	Stolin destructive detachment	
Dumskaya Sarra Yefimovna	1912	Minsk	Baranovichi	Chkalov	? 4 "Za Sovetskuyu Belarus"
Dumski Yakov Benyaminovich	1903	Minsk	Baranovichi	Za Sovetskuyu Belarus	Kirov
Dunets Maksim Davidovich	1922	Dyatlovo	Baranovichi	Leninskaya	Borba
Dunets Nikolai Lvovich	1922	Minsk	Baranovichi	detachment ? 106	
Dunets Fanya Davidovna	1920	Dyatlovo	Baranovichi	Kalinin	
Dunn Tsilya Samuilovna (Karaseva Mariya Borisovna)	1914	Minsk	Baranovichi	18th Frunze	Dzerzhinski
Durets Zelik Leibovich	1906	from the encirclement	Minsk	Parkhomenko	Shchors
Durets Mikhail Zelikovich	1924	Osipovichi	Minsk	Parkhomenko	Shchors
Durmashkin Grigori Semenovich	1899	from captivity, Zhitkovichi	Palesye	50st	
Dusovich Samuil Grigorevich	1915	Loev, TsKKP(b)B	Gomel	Za Rodinu (For Motherland)	Molotov
Dukhan Motel Shevelevich	1887	Glussk	Brest	? 99 Gulyaev	Grabko
Dushkin Genya Yosifovna	1919	Novogrudok	Baranovichi	Kalinin	
Dushkin Yakov Rubinovich	1916	Novogrudok	Baranovichi	Kalinin	
Dyman Feliks Khononovich	1927	Minsk	Baranovichi	detachment ? 106	
Dyment Samuil Manulovich	1904	Shklov	Mogilev	8th Zhunin's brigade	? 40
Dyment Samuil Mendelevich	1920	Shklov	Mogilev	Chekist	Kalyushnikov's
Dymshits Yosif Zakharovich	1905	Orsha	Vitebsk	Kirillov	Voroshilov
Dymshits Meyer Moiseyevich	1930		Mogilev		Kazankova
Dymshits Moisei Moiseyevich	1928		Mogilev		Kazankova
Dyshel Abram Zelikovich	1907	Baranovichi	Pinsk	Lenin	Chapayev
Dyshel Aron Zelikovich	1911	Baranovichi	Baranovichi	Grizodubova	Chkalov
Dyatkovski Aron Grigorevich	1925	Minsk	Baranovichi		
Yevelevich Malka Leizerovna	1921	Novogrudok	Baranovichi	Leninskaya	family detachment group
Yevel Grigori Lvovich	1921	from captivity	Vitebsk	Prudnikov's	Luchenok's
Yevnovich Bentsian Nokhimovich	1915	Novogrudok getto	Baranovichi	Kirov	Ordzhonikidze
Yevselevich Rafail Khaimovich	1931	Novogrudok	Baranovichi	Kalinin	
Yevshitski Boris Davidovich	1912	Kosovo	Pinsk	Lenin	Dzerzhinski
Yegudkin Samson Solomonovich	1907	from the encirclement	Gomel	Mstitel (Revenger)	headquarters
Yedelshteen Mosko T.	1917	Domachevo	Brest	Stalin	Voroshilov
Yedinsberg Pinya Yoselevich	1925	Poland	Pinsk	Molotov	Lazo
Yezerski Girsh Yudolevich	1909	Lida	Baranovichi	Pervomaiskaya	Oktyabr
Yezerski Ilya Khaimovich	1922	getto, Vilno	Vileyka	Voroshilov	Kalinin
Yezerski Leizer Khaimovich	1926	Lida	Baranovichi	Kalinin	
Yezerski Meyer Khaimovich	1924	Spadmolkin	Belostok		Boyevoi (Fighting)
Yeinfeld-Zilberman Frida Yefimovna	1901		Baranovichi	Oktyabr	
Yeirush Bentsian Samuilovich	1919	Novogrudok getto	Baranovichi	Kirov	Ordzhonikidze
Yekelchik En Lvovich	1930	Minsk getto	Minsk	3rd Minskaya	brigade headquarters
Yekelchik Shlema Grigorevich	1925	Vidzy	Vileyka	Spartak	? 1
Yelevich Liia Shalymovna	1919	Derechin	Baranovichi	Pobieda	Pobieda
Yelin Isaak Pinkhusovich	1923	Brest	Brest		Kotovski
Yelinski Georgi Gavrilovich	1917		Gomel	Buda-Koshelevskaya	headquarters
Yelinski Naum Khaimovich	1900	iz mestnykh	Baranovichi	Pervomaiskaya	Pervomaiski
Yelovets Mariya Mironovna	1924		Minsk	Suvorov	
Yelkina Elena Grigorevna	1924	Minsk	Baranovichi	Rokossovski	Rokossovski
YYelskaya Raya Alperovna	1913		Baranovichi	Slonim IDC	
Yelchmen Moisei Abramovich	1914	Bryansk getto, Belostok region	Grodno	Vo imya Rodiny (In the name of Motherland)	Zhukov
Yenkin Mikhail Naumovich	1917	from captivity	Vitebsk	Nikitin's	? 1
Erenburg Boris Davidovich	1908	Bobruisk	Palesye	Lelchitskaya	Akhramenko's
Erenburg Grisha Borisovich	1926	Bobruisk	Palesye	Lelchitskaya	Akhramenko's
Erenburg Iser Gimrovich	1891	Shchedrin	Palesye	Lelchitskaya	Akhramenko's
Erenburg Nikolai Naumovich	1928	Shchedrin	Mogilev		? 760 Berezovski
Erenburg Yasha	1929	Belarusian Staff of Partisan Movement	Brest	groups of party leaders	Kachanov's
Yermovski Aizik Simonovich	1911	Novogrudok, getto	Baranovichi	1st Baranovichskaya	Frunze
Yerusalimski Petr Samoilovich	1925	Slutsk	Grodno	Ponomarenko	Ponomarenko
Yeselevich Aron Khaimovich	1922	Slonim district	Brest	Ponomarenko	Sovetskaya Belarus
Yeselevich Kala Aronovna	1925	Stolbtsy	Minsk	Chapayev	Ponomarenko
Yeselevich SOlya Shlemovich	1913	Slonim	Baranovichi	Pobieda	Pobieda

YYeselson David Gdalevich	1910	getto, Dunilovichi	Vileyka	Voroshilov	Suvorov
Yesilevich Abram Gershenovich	1889	Minsk	Baranovichi	Ponomarenko	25 years of the BSSR
Yesilevich Sima Solomonovna	1910	Minsk	Baranovichi	Ponomarenko	25 years of the BSSR
Yesilevskaya GaLya Aronovna	1925	getto N. Sverzhen	Minsk	Chapayev	Ponomarenko
Yesin Zavel Mendelevich	1905		Minsk	Voronyanski	Mstitel (Revenger)
Yesmalski Yuri Aronovich	1916	Poland	Pinsk	Molotov	Kalinin
Yestargovich Sergei Notkovich	1919	Kozyany	Vileyka	Spartak	? 6
Yestarovich Solomon N.	1921	Kozyany	Vileyka	Spartak	? 6
Yetelson David Gdalevich	1910	Volkagato, Vileika region	Minsk	Voroshilov	? 5
Yefman Shaila Leizerovich	1923	local	Baranovichi	Pobieda	Pobieda
Yekhvedov Isaak Gershelevich	1906	from captivity, concentration camp, Mogilev	Mogilev		
Yekhilshchik Izrail Leibovich	1910	Kozyany	Vileyka	Spartak	brigade headquarters
Yeshchin Semen Markovich	1920	from the encirclement	Gomel	Shemyakin's "Vpered (Forward)"	Makagonov's
Zhabinskaya Tamara Moiseyevna	1922	getto	Vileyka	Voroshilov	Istrebitel (Destroyer)
Zhager Tavel Moiseyevich	1922	small town of Zhelubok	Baranovichi	Kirov	Za Sovetskuyu Belarus
Zhelezo Khella	1924	Warsaw	Brest	Lenin	Zhukov
Zhelyubski Nikolai Niselevich	1921	Molchad	Baranovichi	Pervomaiskaya	Zhdanov
Zhelyaskov Matus Yutkovich	1910	Vishnitsy	Brest	Flegontov	Litvinov's
Zhelyakhovskaya Roza Zalmanovna	1928	Glussk	Minsk	Chkalov	Gromov
Zhizhemskaya Khaya Mordukhovna	1923	Lida	Baranovichi	Kalinin	
Zhizhemski Abram Mordukhovich	1926	Lida	Baranovichi	Kalinin	
Zhilin Mikhail Borisovich	1926	Minsk	Minsk	2nd Minskaya	Suvorov
Zhlyakhovski Zakhar Zalmanovich	1925	Glussk	Minsk	Chkalov	Gromov
Zhirmanskaya Khaya Moiseyevna	1919	Zhirmuny	Baranovichi	Kalinin	
Zhirmunski Boris Yakovlevich	1911	Lida	Baranovichi	Kirov	Iskra
Zhitelzeyev Abram Abramovich	1925	Minsk getto	Grodno	Ponomarenko	squadron
Zhito Zdislav Leonovich	1937	Novogrudok	Baranovichi	Kalinin	
Zhito Edit Adamovna	1916	iz mestnykh	Baranovichi	Pervomaiskaya	Pervomaiski
Zhito Yadviga Adamovna	1916	Novogrudok	Baranovichi	Kalinin	
Zhorman Yosif Borisovich	1920	Vileika	Minsk	Kirov	Kirov
Zhornitski Khema Sulevich	1900	Slutsk	Minsk	Suvorov	
Zhuk Abram Solomonovich	1924	Mir	Baranovichi	Chkalov	
Zhuk Fruma Yevelevna	1915	Mir	Baranovichi	Kalinin	
Zhukovitski Isaak Yosifovich	1901	Slavkovichi	Palesye	Lelchitskaya	Tsikunkov's
Zhukovitski Lazar Solomonovich	1922	Gorodishche district	Baranovichi	Pobieda	Pobieda
Zhukovskaya Dora Semenovna	1926	Peski, Mosty	Baranovichi	Pobieda	Budenny
Zhukovski Ilya Semenovich	1905	Radoshkovichi	Minsk	Voronyanski	Kotovski
Zhukovski Itsko Shemelevich	1918	Peski	Baranovichi	Leninskaya	Krasnogvardeiski
Zhuravel Mariya Zalmanovna	1915		Minsk	Voronyanski	Mstitel (Revenger)
Zhukhovetski Grigori Yakovlevich	1907	Kopyl	Belostok		separate detachment Budenny
Zhukhovitskaya Liza Aronovna	1907	detachment Kaganovicha	Pinsk	Kuibyshev	Ordzhonikidze
Zhukhovitskaya Musya Mendeleyevna	1919	Mir	Baranovichi	Kalinin	
Zhukhovitski Aron Abramovich	1907	Ivatsevichi	Brest	Ponomarenko	Sovetskaya Belarus
Zhukhovitski Boris Yosifovich	1904	Baranovichi	Pinsk	Budenny	Kotovski
Zhukhovitski Giles Gershevich	1924	Dyatlovo	Baranovichi	Pobieda	Pobieda
Zhukhovitski Zavel Girshevich	1925	Samoilovichi	Baranovichi	Leninskaya	Borba
Zhukhovitski Izrail Girshevich	1925	Dyatlovo	Baranovichi	Leninskaya	Borba
Zhukhovitski Meisha Aronovich	1923	Novogrudok getto	Baranovichi	Kirov	Ordzhonikidze
Zhukhovitski Nison Abramovich	1924	Novogrudok	Baranovichi	Kalinin	
Zhukhovitski Salomon Lipovich	1909	Molchad	Baranovichi	Kalinin	
ZabYelski Gershon	1910	Slonim	Baranovichi	Pobieda	Pobieda
ZabYelski Yosel Moiseyevich	1923	Ivanovo	Pinsk	Molotov	Shish
Zabets Meyer Leizerovich	1921	Molchad	Baranovichi	Pobieda	Pobieda
Zablotskaya Raya Tevelevna	1923	Lida	Baranovichi	Leninskaya	Borba
Zablotski Bernard Yefimovich	1907	Gorodishche district	Baranovichi	25 years of the BSSR	Grozny
Zablotski Mikhail Shevelevich	1921	Lida	Baranovichi	Leninskaya	Borba
Zabudko Izrail Yefimovich	1918	from the encirclement	Mogilev	208th regiment	
Zavadski Mikhail Volfovich	1915	from the brigade Voroshilova	Vileyka		Za Sovetskuyu Belorussiyu
Zavin Ilya Samuilovich					
Zavin Isaak	1928	Kr. Sloboda, Minsk region	Pinsk	Budenny	Kotovski
Zavin Fedor Ivanovich	1914	concentration camp	Pinsk	Kuibyshev	Shchors
factorynikov Grigori Markovich	1913	Slutsk getto	Minsk	Frunze	Budenny
Zagalski Yosif Abramovich	1890	from captivity	Palesye	? 123	brigade headquarters and administration platoon
Zagel Lyuba Moiseyevna	1919	Slonim	Brest	Sikorski's headquarters	Shchors

Name	Year	Place	Region	Detachment	Brigade/Notes
Zager Mikhail Sakhnovich	1920	Belarusian Staff of Partisan Movement	Vitebsk	2nd Zaslonov	brigade headquarters
Zager Rakhil Isaakovna	1923	Minsk	Baranovichi	detachment ? 106	
Zager Sholom Shneyerovich	1904	Zheludok	Baranovichi	Pervomaiskaya	Oktyabr
Zagovski Rubin Berkovich	1918	Biala PodLyaska	Baranovichi	Lenin's komsomol	Lenin's komsomol
Zadov Yefim Markovich	1926	Shklov	Mogilev	Chekist	? 5
Zaidel Samuil Davidovich	1912	from the encirclement	Vitebsk	Prudnikov's	Tabachnikov's
Zaidel Izrail Abramovich	1909	Slutsk	Baranovichi	Stalin	Budenny
Zaider Isaak Moiseyevich	1926	Braslav district	Vileyka	Zhdanov	
Zaiko EdLya Samuilovna	1921	Raitsy	Baranovichi	Pervomaiskaya	Oktyabr
Zailer Shiya Shmulevich	1922	Oshmiany. Malorita district	Brest	Lenin	Voroshilov
Zainer Fedya Moiseyevich	1912	Kremen	Baranovichi	detachment ? 106	
Zaitsev Mikhail Zakharovich	1922	from captivity	Gomel	Voroshilov	Voroshilov
Zaichik Mordukh Aronovich	1907	Gantsevichi,prison	Minsk	A.Nevski	? 1
Zaichik Mordukh Leibovich	1922	Lenin	Palesye		Ponomarenko
Zaichik Mulya Yosifovich	1917	Mikashevichi	Pinsk	Kirov	Kalinin
Zakgeim Yosif Ilyich	1913	Baranovichi	Baranovichi	Kalinin	
Zakgeim Semen Abramovich	1923	Baranovichi	Baranovichi	Chkalov	
Zakroiski Mordukh Abramovich	1911	Dyatlovo	Baranovichi	Leninskaya	Borba
Zakroiski Samuil Nokhimovich	1919	Postavy	Vitebsk	Lepelskaya Stalin	? 3
Zaks Zinaida Mikhailovna	1910	Grokhovo	Gomel	Za Rodinu (For Motherland)	Stalin
Zalan Basya Abramovna	1901	Minsk	Baranovichi	detachment ? 106	
Zalevyanski Samuil Girshevich	1912	Novogrudok	Baranovichi	Kalinin	
Zalkin Yudel Yankelevich	1913	getto, Vilno	Vileyka	Voroshilov	Suvorov
Zalmanovich Nevakh Bunyaevich	1911		Pinsk	Molotov	Kalinin
Zalovich Khil Efraimovich	1927	Koshalev, Klichev district	Mogilev		? 278
Zalburg Ruva Semenovich	1923	Krasnoye, getto	Baranovichi	Za Sovetskuyu Belarus	Shturm
Zaltsberg Yesel Yankelevich	1921	Lida	Baranovichi	Lenin's komsomol	Lenin's komsomol
Zaltsberg Nina Alterovna	1925	Minsk	Baranovichi	detachment ? 106	
Zaltsman Genrikh Gertskovich	1906	Tseluiki, Bragin district	Palesye		Kotovski
Zaltsman David Yakovlevich	1924	Nichoveshchi, Rovno region.	Pinsk	Shubetidze	brigade headquarters
Zalyukovski Khaim Meyerovich	1921	family detachment camp	Belostok	A.Nevski	
Zamkovaya Polya Abramovna	1927	Novogrudok	Baranovichi	Kalinin	
Zamkovaya Raya Abramovna	1921	Novogrudok	Baranovichi	Leninskaya	Borba
Zamkovaya Khaya Abramovna	1922	Novogrudok	Baranovichi	Leninskaya	family detachment group
Zamkovoi Mikhail Shlemovich	1921	Novogrudok getto	Baranovichi	Kirov	Ordzhonikidze
Zamkovy Leizer Shlemovich	1921	Dyatlovo	Baranovichi	Leninskaya	Borba
Zamkovy Shaya Abramovich	1920	Novogrudok	Baranovichi	Kalinin	
Zamkovy Shlema Yakovlevich	1921	Novogrudok	Baranovichi	Leninskaya	Leninski
Zamoshchik Zalman Movshovich	1922	Korelichi	Baranovichi	Kalinin	
Zamoshchik Moisei Faivelevich	1897	Dvorets	Baranovichi	Kalinin	
Zamoshchik Naum Shimonovich	1909	Dyatlovo getto	Baranovichi	Kirov	Ordzhonikidze
Zamoshchik Rakhelya Elevna	1925	Novogrudok	Baranovichi	Kalinin	
Zamoshchik Sara Nokhimovna	1924	Dvorets	Baranovichi	Kalinin	
Zamoshchik Sara Shinoshovna	1913	Novogrudok getto	Baranovichi	Kirov	Ordzhonikidze
Zamoshchik Sima Elevna	1921	Novogrudok	Baranovichi	Kalinin	
Zamoshchik Khaya Nokhimovna	1902	Dvorets	Baranovichi	Kalinin	
Zamoshchik Elya Meyerovich	1925	Novogrudok	Baranovichi	Oktyabr	
Zamoshchik Yankel Lipovich	1922	Kurenets	Minsk	Voronyanski	Kotovski
Zamushchanski Meyer Samoilovich	1915	getto, Vilno	Vileyka	Voroshilov	Kalinin
Zanbershtein Izrail Yudalevich	1917	Minsk getto	Baranovichi	Stalin	Parkhomenko
Zapesotskaya Tsilya Borisovna	1906	Minsk getto	Minsk	Kirov	? 4
Zapisotskaya Raya Abramovna	1925	Minsk	Baranovichi	detachment ? 106	
Zapnitski Samuil Volfovich	1910	Avgusitov	Brest	Za Sovetskuyu Belarus	Suvorov
Zapolski Isaak Grigorevich	1896	Verkhove, Drissaiski district	Vitebsk	Frunze	brigade headquarters
Zapolski Sholom Mendelevich	1925	getto	Baranovichi	Kirov	Orel
Zaraiskaya Lyusya Aizikovna	1922	Minsk	Minsk		Kalinin
Zarankin Lev Moiseyevich	1921	from captivity	Gomel	1st Gomelskaya	Kalinin
Zaretskaya Raya Solomonovna	1897	Rudensk	Minsk	Belarus	Belarus
Zaretskaya Sonya Davidovna	1925	Novaia Dubrova	Palesye	? 123	Baranova
Zaretski Leonid Naumovich	1910	Bobruisk	Brest	Sikorski's headquarters	Shchors
Zaretski Yakov Moiseyevich	1895		Mogilev	208th regiment	left the detachment from the moment organization
Zarechanskaya Ida Moiseyevna	1916	Lida	Baranovichi	Kalinin	
Zarechanskaya Sara Abramovna	1931	Lida	Baranovichi	Kalinin	
Zarechanski Isaak Abramovich	1919	Lida	Baranovichi	Kalinin	

Zaritskevich Ilya Ilyich	1920	detachment Kotovskogo soedinenie Komarova	Grodno		B.Khmelnitski
Zarutski Boris Rubinovich	1921	Ivanovo	Pinsk	Molotov	Lazo
Zarutski Nikolai Movshevich	1926	Odrizhin, Ivanovo district	Pinsk	Sovetskaya Belarus	Kutuzov
Zarkh Dina Borisovna	1916	Gomel	Gomel	Shchors	Beriya
Zarkhin Kopil Abramovich	1921	Kopatkevichi	Palesye	? 125	Mikhailovski's
Zasetski Khonon Yonovich	1925	Baranovichi	Baranovichi	Kalinin	
Zaslavskaya Liliya	1924	Postavy	Minsk	Zheleznyak	? 5
Zaturanski Leib	1903	Sverzhno	Baranovichi	Kalinin	
Zaturinski Samuil Aizikovich	1908	Shatsk	Mogilev	208th regiment	
Zakharovich Mordukh Isaakovich	1902	Novogrudok	Baranovichi	Shchors	Chapayev
Zashetski Khonon Yosifovich	1922	Baranovichi	Baranovichi	Kalinin	
Zashkov Girsh Movshovich	1929	Ivye	Baranovichi	Kalinin	
Zashchik Rysya Robinovna	1914	Gorodeia	Minsk	Voroshilov	Kutuzov
Zayants Sofiya Lvovna	1919	Minsk	Belostok	Chapayev	Zhukov
Zayats Masha Naumovna	1921	Minsk	Baranovichi	detachment ? 106	
Zbar Grigori Shmerlevich	1915	concentration camp Gantsevichi	Minsk	258th Kuibyshev	Budenny
Zbar Sara Khaimovna	1924	local	Baranovichi	Pobieda	Pobieda
Zvenich Vladimir Noyevich	1923	Gorodishche district	Baranovichi	25 years of the BSSR	Grozny
Zveryankin Izrail Berkovich	1908	Glubokoye	Minsk	Voronyanski	Mstitel (Revenger)
Zvyagilski Aleksandr Abramovich	1906	from captivity	Brest	Za Sovetskuyu Belarus	Suvorov
Zegelman Boris Simonovich	1923	Baranovichi	Baranovichi	Chkalov	? 4 "Za Sovetskuyu Belarus"
Zegerman Vanya Yefimovich	1925	Molchad	Baranovichi	Kalinin	
Zegerman Yakub Efroimovich	1925		Baranovichi	Oktyabr	
Zelevianskaya Khaya Rubinovna	1915	Korelichi	Baranovichi	Kalinin	
Zelikman Nela Davidovna	1936	Minsk	Baranovichi	detachment ? 106	
Zelikman Riva Aronovna	1915	Minsk	Baranovichi	detachment ? 106	
Zelikman Roza Vladimirovna	1925	Minsk	Baranovichi	detachment ? 106	
Zelikovich Gita Leizerovna	1929	Lida	Baranovichi	Kalinin	
Zelikovich Leizer Abramovich	1901	Lida	Baranovichi	Kalinin	
Zelikovich Liza Yosifovna	1902	Lida	Baranovichi	Kalinin	
Zelikovich Meyer Germanovich	1917	from the working Magyar batallion	Pinsk	Sovetskaya Belarus	Chkalov
Zelikovich Simkha Leizerovich	1938	Lida	Baranovichi	Kalinin	
Zelichenok Yakov Zelikovich					
Zelkin Grigori Mordukhovich	1908	Karpilovichi, Oktyabr district	Palesye	Lelchitskaya	Khrapko's
Zelkina Mariya Abramovna	1922	Shklov	Mogilev	Chekist	? 5
Zelberg Shem Borukhovich	1915	Vatsevichi, Kosovski district	Brest	Ponomarenko	Sovetskaya Belarus
Zelvianski Samuil Girshevich	1912		Baranovichi	Oktyabr	
Zeldena Sofiya Yefimovna	1920	from the encirclement	Gomel	1st Gomelskaya	? 1 Chapayev
Zeldon Samuil Gutmanovich	1905	getto, Glubokoye	Vileyka	Gastello	brigade headquarters
Zelkin Grigori Mordukhovich	1908	Glussk district, Podluzhe	Minsk	Parkhomenko	Kirov
Zelkovich Itsko Yakovlevich	1926	Jewish camp, Ivanovo	Pinsk	Molotov	Lazo
Zelkovich Yakov Pinkhusovich	1899	Pinsk	Pinsk	Shubetidze	Ordzhonikidze
Zelmanovich Berko Faivelevich	1926	Novogrudok	Baranovichi	Kalinin	
Zelmanovich Mikhail Matusovich	1922	Baranovichi	Brest	Za Sovetskuyu Belarus	Suvorov
Zemnovich Leonid Ilyich	1915	Sirotinski district	Vitebsk	Korotkin	Voroshilov
Zendel Abram Leibovich	1903	Minsk getto	Baranovichi	18th Frunze	brigade headquarters
Zendel Mikhail Abramovich	1930	Minsk getto	Baranovichi	18th Frunze	brigade headquarters
ZentYelski Itsek					
Zeremski Nokhim Gershovich	1912	Derechin	Baranovichi	Leninskaya	hospital
Zernitskaya Tsilya Alterovna	1923	Dyatlovo	Baranovichi	Leninskaya	Krasnogvardeiski
Zernitski Mikhail Alperovich	1925	Dyatlovo	Baranovichi	Leninskaya	Borba
Zibitsker David Khaimovich	1902	Minsk	Baranovichi	Stalin	Budenny
Zivin Volf Monusovich	1912	Lenin	Pinsk	Komarov-Korzh's	1 group
Zigelvans Khelya Girshevna	1910	br. Rodionova	Minsk	1st Antifashistskaya	
Ziger Leizer Zalmanovich	1903	Minsk	Baranovichi	detachment ? 106	
Zigzon Peisakh Girshevich	1910	Dolginovo	Minsk	Voronyanski	Suvorov
Zilbelgreid Mikhail Abramovich	1919	Minsk	Vitebsk	Nikitin's	? 1
Zilber Khil Gavrilovich	1916	Warsaw	Baranovichi	Kalinin	
Zilberbarg Anna Mironovna	1923	Berezka, Rovno region.	Pinsk		Chukhlai
Zilberberg Shlema Itskovich	1912	N. Sverzhen	Baranovichi	18th Frunze	provisional base of the brigade
Zilberberg Shmul Borisovich	1915	Ivatsevichi	Brest	Ponomarenko	Sovetskaya Belarus
Zilberbord Zhenya Danilovna	1918	Krasnoye district	Mogilev	? 117	? 124
Zilbergaft Yakov Abramovich	1916	Slonim	Pinsk	Lenin	Kutuzov

Zilbergleid Salik Davidovich	1911	Koldychevo, getto	Baranovichi	Pervomaiskaya	Ya.Kolas
Zilbergleit Moisei Solomonovich	1914	Minsk	Baranovichi	detachment ? 106	
Zilbergleit Ruin Berkovich	1902	Minsk getto	Baranovichi	Chkalov	
Zilbergleit Esfir Markovna	1926	Minsk	Baranovichi	detachment ? 106	
Zilbergleit-Gordon Ida Isaakovna	1919	Minsk	Baranovichi	detachment ? 106	
Zilberman Abram Moiseyevich (Gadasyan Suleiman Melekhovich)	1904	Kakoisk, from captivity	Mogilev		? 45 "Za Rodinu (For Motherland)"
Zilberman Girsh Davidovich	1910	Novogrudok	Baranovichi	Leninskaya	family detachment group
Zilberman Yosif Davidovich	1914	Novogrudok getto	Baranovichi	Kirov	Ordzhonikidze
Zilberman Malka Davidovna	1923	Novogrudok	Baranovichi	Leninskaya	family detachment group
Zilberman Mariya Leibovna	1923	Yody	Vileyka	Za Rodinu (For Motherland)	Kirov
Zilberman Peisakh Alterovich	1925	Yody	Vileyka	Spartak	? 3
Zilberman Rafail Davidovich	1902	Yody	Vileyka	Spartak	? 5
Zilberman Tatyana Alterovna	1923	Yody	Vileyka	Spartak	brigade headquarters
Zilberman Frida Yankelevna	1916	Novogrudok	Baranovichi	Leninskaya	family detachment group
Zilberman Yakov Davidovich	1914	Novogrudok	Baranovichi	Leninskaya	family detachment group
Zilberfarb Izrail Shamovich	1923	Omit	Pinsk	Shubetidze	Stalin
Zilberferb Vladimir Khaimovich	1925	Gorodno, Stolin district	Pinsk	Shubetidze	Ordzhonikidze
Zilbershtein Maks Volfovich	1912	Lida	Baranovichi	Kalinin	
Zilbershtein Sara Isaakovna	1901	Lida	Baranovichi	Kalinin	
Zilbershtein Abram Itskovich	1913	getto, Ivatsevichi	Brest	Za Sovetskuyu Belarus	Pozharski
Zilbershtein Izrail Yudelevich	1917	Minsk	Baranovichi	detachment ? 106	
Zilbershtein Irina Davidovna	1924	Warsaw	Pinsk	Molotov	Lazo
Zilbershtein Leib Davidovich	1923	Poland	Brest	Lenin	Zhukov
Zilbershtein Leon Itskovich	1906	Domachevo	Pinsk	Molotov	Potalakh
Zilbershtein Motol Zusmanovich	1905	Vlodava (Poland)	Pinsk	Molotov	Lazo
Zilbershtein Khanka	1927	Warsaw	Brest	Lenin	Zhukov
Zilbershtein Khaya Maksovna	1940	Lida	Baranovichi		
Zilburg Benyamin Isaakovich	1917	Radoshkovichi	Minsk	Voronyanski	Kotovski
Zilburg Ruva Semenovich	1923		Baranovichi	Chkalov	? 4 "Za Sovetskuyu Belarus"
Zilkovich Shlema Yankelevich	1919	Drogichin district	Pinsk	Molotov	Lazo
Zilmanovich Berko Faivelevich	1926	Novogrudok	Baranovichi	Kalinin	
Zimak Aleksandra Gendrikhovna	1922	Alba	Pinsk	Lenin	Kutuzov
Zimak Zyama Osherovich	1920	Alba	Pinsk	Lenin	Kutuzov
Ziman Mikhail Yankelevich	1920	Derechin	Baranovichi	Pobieda	Pobieda
Zimberberg Shevel Abramovich	1896	Pruzhany	Brest	Ponomarenko	Kirov
Zimbergleid Grigori Moiseyevich	1923	Minsk getto	Minsk	Zheleznyak	? 5
Zinger Maks Iserovich	1920	Minsk getto	Baranovichi	Chapayev	Parkhomenko
Zindilovich Sarra Mikhailovna	1907	Ivatsevichi	Brest	Dzerzhinski	Chertkov
Zinchevski Arkadi Naumovich	1925	Starye Dorogi	Minsk	Kirov ? 100	Kutuzov ? 2
Zinyakov Leonid Sergeyevich	1912	from captivity	Mogilev	Chekist	? 60
Zisin Leonid Shevelevich	1918	Dokshitsy	Baranovichi	Ivienets DC CP(b)B company	
Ziskind Tamara Moiseyevna	1911		Baranovichi	Oktyabr	
Zlishkovich Sonya Itskovna	1916	Ivienets	Baranovichi	Kalinin	
Zlotin Leiba Mendelevich	1896	Khotimsk	Mogilev		Za Sovetskuyu Belorussiyu
Zlotin Mikhail Romanovich	1927	Klimovichi	Mogilev		? 45 "Za Rodinu (For Motherland)"
Zlotina Yelizaveta Aronovna	1925	Bratkovichi	Gomel	Shemyakin's "Vpered (Forward)"	Makagonov's
Zlotkin Aleksei Yevelevich	1924	from the encirclement	Palesye	Lelchitskaya	Stalin
Zlotnik Yevsei Yankelevich	1913	Molchad	Baranovichi	Pervomaiskaya	Zhdanov
Zlotnik Isaak Leibovich	1909	Minsk getto	Baranovichi	Za Sovetskuyu Belarus	Shturm
Zlotnik Semen Leibovich	1902	Minsk	Baranovichi	Chkalov	
Zlotnik Fraifel Yevnovich	1914	Novogrudok	Baranovichi	Kalinin	
Zlotova Olga Penkisovna	1917	Ivatsevichi	Brest	Dzerzhinski	Chertkov
Zlotogura Girsh Yosifovich	1906	Derechin	Baranovichi	Pobieda	Suvorov
Zlotsevski Yankel Izrailevich	1924	Belitsa	Baranovichi	Pervomaiskaya	Oktyabr
Zmudyak Abram Danilovich	1923	Kopyl getto	Minsk	Frunze	Budenny
Znesin Saveli Vitalyevich	1913	from captivity	Mogilev	? 121	
Zovin Vladimir Ilyich	1920	Kr. Sloboda, Minsk region	Pinsk	Budenny	Kotovski
Zolan Yevsei Abramovich	1925	Minsk getto	Baranovichi	Chapayev	Parkhomenko
Zolin Lev Abramovich	1924	Minsk	Baranovichi	detachment ? 106	
Zolina Fanya Samuilovna	1912	Smolevichi	Baranovichi	detachment ? 106	
Zolotkovski Abram Yoselevich	1896	Golynka	Baranovichi	Pobieda	Pobieda
Zolotnitskaya Anna	1918	Byten	Brest	Ponomarenko	Sovetskaya Belarus
Zolotovski Abram	1906	Derechin	Baranovichi	Pobieda	Pobieda
Zolotukhina Bronya		Rechitsa	Gomel	Voroshilov	Voroshilov
Zolshtein Lev Shmelevich	1925	Dyatlovo	Baranovichi	Voroshilov	Kalinin

Zomin Naum Samuilovich	1910	Radoshkovichi	Minsk	Voronyanski	Suvorov
Zonenberg Yosif Sigizmundovich	1897	Baranovichi	Baranovichi	Kalinin	
Zorashein Lev Moiseyevich	1921		Gomel	1st Gomelskaya	Kalinin
Zorin Semen Natanovich	1898	Minsk	Baranovichi	detachment ? 106	
Zorina Yelizaveta Zakharovna	1929	Tarkovo	Minsk	Shchors	Voroshilov
Zorina Tamara Zakharovna	1928	Tarkovo	Minsk	Shchors	Voroshilov
Zubarev Lev	1911	Minsk	Baranovichi	Chkalov	
Zubarev Faval Naumovich	1913	Kopyl	Minsk		Chapayev
Zuberman Imre Adolfovich	1914	from the Hungarian army	Brest	Stalin	Chernyak
Zubkovski Aleksandr Izrailevich	1924	Novogrudok	Baranovichi	Kirov	Za Sovetskuyu Belarus
Zubkovski Izrail Berkovich	1898	Novogrudok	Baranovichi	Kirov	Za Sovetskuyu Belarus
Zumer Aron Abramovich	1914	small town of Lenino, Polesskaya obl.	Minsk	Chkalov	Dovator
Zundelevich Sara Mikhailovna	1907	Ivatsevichi	Brest		Budenny
Zuperman Debora Solomonovna	1916	Minsk	Baranovichi	detachment ? 106	
Zuperman Mara Samuilovna	1936	Minsk	Baranovichi	detachment ? 106	
Zusman Roman Yefimovich	1913	Belarusian Staff of Partisan Movement	Vileyka	detachments i gruppy, vyshedshie iz tyla vraga v 1942 godu	Ganeev's group
Zusmanovich Samuil Leizerovich	1896	Novogrudok	Baranovichi	Vpered (Forward)	Roshcha
Zusmanovich Semen Lvovich	1921	Minsk, podpolnyi GK KP(b)B	Minsk	Bragin	Gastello
Zukhovitskaya GaLya Ilinichna	1919	N. Borisov	Vitebsk	Chapayev	detachments
Zyger Leonid Mordukhovich	1914	Zhadun	Baranovichi	Pervomaiskaya	Ya.Kolas
Zyzovski Borukh Shulimovich	1920	Derechin	Baranovichi	Pobieda	Pobieda
Zysk Samuel Abramovich	1918	N. Sverzhen	Minsk	Chapayev	Shchors
Zyskand Tamara Mikhailovna	1915	Novogrudok	Baranovichi	Vpered (Forward)	Chkalov
Zyskind Semen Yuryevich	1912	Baranovichi	Pinsk	Budenny	Ponomarenko
Zysman Ida Aronovga	1924	Minsk	Baranovichi	detachment ? 106	
Zysman Samuil Nokhimovich	1920		Baranovichi	Oktyabr	
Zytsman Yakov Yosifovich	1920	Protskevichi, Slutsk district	Pinsk	Komarov-Korzh's	1 group
Ivanov Semen Ivanovich	1910	from captivity	Palesye	? 123	Kalakin
Ivienetskaya Raya Mikhailovna	1923	Dyatlovo	Baranovichi	Leninskaya	Leninski
Ivienetski Boris Abramovich	1921	Dyatlovo	Baranovichi	Shchuchin IDC	
Ivyenitskaya Riva YeKhilevna	1921	Rozhanka	Baranovichi	Leninskaya	Borba
Ivyenitski Ikhiil Shlemovich	1888	Rozhanka	Baranovichi	Leninskaya	Borba
Ivinitskaya Kellya Moiseyevna	1931	from the civil camp	Vileyka	4th Belorusskaya	? 6
Ivinitskaya Nina Moiseyevna	1925	Disna	Vileyka	4th Belorusskaya	? 2
Ivinskaya BroniSlava (Glory) Yakovlevna	1914	Warsaw	Minsk	Shturmovaya	Grozny
Ivnieva Elena Abramovna	1903	Kopyl	Baranovichi	detachment ? 106	
Ivovich Aron Borukhovich	1924	Urechye, Slutsk district	Minsk	Suvorov	
Igelnik Yosif Notkovich	1914	Stolbtsy	Baranovichi	Kalinin	
Igelnik Roza Leizerovna	1923	Mir	Baranovichi	Kalinin	
Igolnikova Emma Yakovlevna	1927	Zatishe	Palesye	? 123	Krasny Oktyabr
Idelman Yakov Idelevich	1924	Gorodok	Baranovichi	Chkalov	
Idelchik Esfir Yefimovna	1923	Minsk	Baranovichi	detachment ? 106	
Izbutski Motel Abramovich	1913	from captivity	Brest	Za Sovetskuyu Belarus	Suvorov
Izidberg Ilya Leizakhovich	1924	detachment "Mest"	Vileyka	Voroshilov	headquarters' production group
Izikson Abram Samuilovich	1923	Minsk	Baranovichi	Chkalov	
Izikson Peisakh Girshevich	1910	Dolginovo	Minsk	Voronyanski	Kotovski
Izkov Semen Benyaminovich	1928	Samotevichi	Gomel	Shemyakin's "Vpered (Forward)"	Makagonov's
Izraelevich Sima Yankelevna	1906	Novogrudok	Baranovichi	Kalinin	
Izraelevich Khaim Benyaminovich	1901	Novogrudok	Baranovichi	Kalinin	
Izraeli Mariya Yankelevna	1924	Sunchitsy	Baranovichi	Kalinin	
Izraeli Riva Yankelevna	1937	Sunchitsy	Baranovichi	Kalinin	
Izraeli Roza Yankelevna	1927	Sunchitsy	Baranovichi	Kalinin	
Izraeli Yudel Abramovich	1908	Sunchitsy	Baranovichi	Kalinin	
Izrailit Boris Mordukhovich	1902	from the Jewish group, Pruzhany	Brest	Ponomarenko	Gastello
Izrailit Vulf Izrailevich					
Izrailitina Roza Grigorevna	1925	Zhitkovichi	Pinsk	Komarov-Korzh's	1 group
Izrail Girsh Khatskelevich	1913	Glubokoye	Vileyka	Budenny	Lesnoi, special group
Izrail Srulik Abramovich	1908	Derechin	Baranovichi	Leninskaya	hospital
Izrailski Isaak Berkovich	1925	camp Kurenets	Minsk	Voronyanski	Kotovski
Izraelit Leon Mordukhovich	1912	getto, Pruzhany	Brest	Ponomarenko	Kirov
Ikshenshnaider Khaskl Isaakovich	1909	Domanov	Brest	Lenin	Zelenin
Ilevitski Grigori Khaimovich	1922	Slonim	Brest	Sikorski's headquarters	Shchors
Ilvitskaya ULyana Shimovna	1924	Kosovo	Pinsk	Lenin	Kutuzov

Ilvovich Leva Semenovich	1916	Derechin	Baranovichi	Pobieda	Pobieda
Ilinski Naum Khaimovich	1910	Slonim	Baranovichi	Pervomaiskaya	1st May
Ilitovich Izrail Zakharovich	1923	getto	Baranovichi	Kirov	Orel
Ilitovich Sima Elevna	1924	getto	Baranovichi	Kirov	Orel
Ilitskaya Yuliya Semenovna	1924	Kosovo	Brest	Sikorski's headquarters	Shchors
Imberg Alvyezen Izakovich	1917	Slonim	Brest	Sikorski's headquarters	Shchors
Imevich Khaim Semenovich	1914	Derechin	Baranovichi	Pobieda	Pobieda
Inberg Polya Matusovna	1917	malaia group from the forest (KovYelski district)	Pinsk	Sovetskaya Belarus	Kutuzov
Ingberg Zusel Borukhovich	1915	from the forest	Pinsk	Molotov	Kalinin
Indershtein Girsh Movshevich	1902	Dyatlovo	Baranovichi	Leninskaya	family detachment group
Indykh Anna Yosifovna	1924	Minsk	Minsk	2nd Minskaya	Kutuzov
Inzelbukh Moisei Shayevich	1903	Stolbtsy	Minsk	Chapayev	Ponomarenko
Inzelbukh Samuil Shayevich	1903	getto N. Sverzhen	Minsk	Chapayev	Ponomarenko
Yodykman Raisa Matveyevna	1922	Vitebsk	Baranovichi	Lenin's komsomol	Lenin's komsomol
Yokton Sara Moiseyevna	1900	Disna	Vileyka	4th Belorusskaya	? 1
Yonish Musya Salomonovna	1928	Lida	Baranovichi	Kalinin	
Yoselevich Ikhel Aronovich	1914	Dyatlovo	Baranovichi	Leninskaya	Borba
Yoselevich Lyuba Girshevna	1913	Dyatlovo	Baranovichi	Leninskaya	Borba
Yoselevich Roman Pinkhosovich	1918	Dyatlovo	Baranovichi	Leninskaya	Borba
Yoselevich Yudel Zakharovich	1895	Dvorets	Baranovichi	Kalinin	
Yoselevich Yakov Samuilovich	1900	Novogrudok	Baranovichi	Kalinin	
Yoselevskaya Tsilya Girshevna	1907	Minsk	Baranovichi	detachment ? 106	
Yoselevski Bentsiian Shepshelevich	1920	Negnevichi	Baranovichi	Kalinin	
Yoselevski Rubin Pinkhusovich	1918	Dyatlovo	Baranovichi	Kalinin	
Yoselevski Shlema Berkovich	1914	Malkovichi	Pinsk	Komarov-Korzh's	4 group
Yosilevich Afroim Aronovich	1921	Dyatlovo	Baranovichi	Leninskaya	Borba
Yosilevski Abram	1911	Gantsevichi	Pinsk	Budenny	Kotovski
Yofa Kuzma Solomonovich	1906	Jewish camp	Vileyka	Spartak	? 2
Yofe Zalman Mordukhovich	1907	detachment "Mest"	Vileyka	Voroshilov	headquarters' production group
Yofe Klara Fedorovna	1908	Kursk	Baranovichi	detachment ? 106	
Yofe Ninel Naumovna	1936	Minsk	Baranovichi	detachment ? 106	
Yofe Roza Solomonovna	1913	detachment "Mest"	Vileyka	Voroshilov	headquarters' production group
Yofik Anna Semenovna	1921	Orsha	Vitebsk	Sennenskaya brigade	? 150
Yofik Yakov Semenovich	1924	Oboltsy	Vitebsk	1st Zaslonov	Kutuzov
Yoffe Anatoli Yakovlevich	1903	from captivity	Gomel	1st Gomelskaya	Kalinin
Yoffe Boba Itskovna	1923	small town of Belitsa, getto	Baranovichi	Kirov	Ordzhonikidze
Yoffe Boris Shepshelevich	1912	Central Committee of the CP (b) B	Minsk	Dyadi Koli	Burya (Storm)
Yoffe Grigori Samuilovich	1909	Dolginovo	Minsk	Underground RC and DC CP(b)B	Logoisk DC of the CP(b)B
Yoffe Zelik Moiseyevich	1927	Molodechno, getto	Baranovichi	Chkalov	
Yoffe Leonid Mikhailovich	1912	Bobruisk	Gomel	8th Rogachevskaya	? 255
Yoffe Meyer Mentsionovich	1922	Biten, Barnovichi region	Pinsk	Budenny	Ponomarenko
Yoffe Mikhail Grigorevich	1923	Iachnoe, Kalinkovichi district	Palesye	99th Kalinkovichskaya	brigade headquarters and administration platoon
Yoffe Ovsei Abramovich	1914	Novogrudok	Baranovichi	Kalinin	
Yoffe Saveli Yakovlevich	1920	from captivity	Minsk	Ponomarenko	Kalinovski
Yoffe Khaim Abramovich	1922	Novogrudok getto	Baranovichi	Kirov	Ordzhonikidze
Yokhvedovich Golda Davidovna	1922	getto, Pruzhany	Brest	Ponomarenko	Kirov
Yokhelman Abram Isaakovich	1921		Minsk	Voronyanski	Mstitel (Revenger)
Irlikht Aron Isaakovich	1912	N. Sverzhen	Minsk	Chapayev	Ponomarenko
Irman Moisei Shmerkovich	1925	Jewish camp	Vileyka	4th Belorusskaya	? 6
Isakova Tatyana Mikhailovna	1914	Kurnosovo	Minsk	Voroshilov	Kutuzov
Isers Grigori Izrailevich	1923	work camp, Gantsevichi	Pinsk	Molotov	Kalinin
Isers Ivan Izrailevich	1927	work camp, Gantsevichi	Pinsk	Molotov	Kalinin
Isler Riva Moiseyevna	1916	Novogrudok getto	Baranovichi	Kirov	Ordzhonikidze
Issler Genrik Izrailevich	1908		Baranovichi	Oktyabr	
Itkina Nina Yosifovna	1923	st. Slavnoe, Tolochin district	Mogilev	? 61	? 1
Itman Anna Rafailovna	1926	Ziabki	Vileyka	CC of the CP(b)B	brigade sanitary service
Itman Mikhail Rafailovich	1923	Ziabki	Vileyka	CC of the CP(b)B	Denisov
Itman Moisei	1923	Ziabki, Vileika region	Minsk	Voroshilov	? 4
Itman Roza Rafailovna	1928	Ziabki	Vileyka	CC of the CP(b)B	brigade sanitary service
Itman Fanya Borisovna	1901	Ziabki	Vileyka	CC of the CP(b)B	brigade sanitary service
Ikhelchik Shlema Davidovich	1921		Vileyka		Ponomarenko
Ikhilshchik Motka Iserovich	1920	Kozyany	Vileyka	Spartak	brigade headquarters

Ikhteinen Vladimir Leonidovich	1908	Mogilev	Mogilev	? 113	Mogilevski podpolnyi RK KP(b)B
Itskov Semen Benyaminovich	1927	Kostiukovichski district	Gomel	Shemyakin's "Vpered (Forward)"	headquarters
Itskovich Aizik Leibovich	1904	N. Sverzhen	Minsk	Chapayev	Ponomarenko
Itskovich Aleksandr Markovich	1918	working column of the Magyar army	Brest	Dzerzhinski	Molotov
Itskovich Yosif Noselevich	1917	DYevelishki	Baranovichi	Kirov	Baltiets
Itskovich Isaak Davidovich	1923	Mir	Baranovichi	Za Sovetskuyu Belarus	Shturm
Itskovich Meyer Nosonovich	1917		Baranovichi	Oktyabr	
Itskovich Mikhail Zelikovich	1922	st. Sabibor (concentration camp), Poland	Brest	Stalin	Frunze
Itskovich Semen Davidovich	1926	Mir	Baranovichi	Chkalov	
Itskovich Khaim Davidovich	1929	Mir, getto	Baranovichi	Za Sovetskuyu Belarus	Kirov
Itskovich Tsedik Davidovich	1922	Mir	Baranovichi	Chkalov	
Itskovich Shmuil Leibovich	1911	Slonim	Pinsk	Lenin	Frunze
Kabak Guta Davidovna	1922	Novogrudok	Baranovichi	Kalinin	
Kabak Matus Yoselevich	1911	Novogrudok	Baranovichi	Kalinin	
Kabak Mikhail Yosifovich	1917	Novogrudok getto	Baranovichi	Kirov	Ordzhonikidze
Kabak Khana Girshevna	1910	Novogrudok	Baranovichi	Kalinin	
Kabachnik Mikhail Faivelevich	1922	Vasilishki, camp	Belostok	A.Nevski	
Kavalerchik Asya Grigorevna	1924	Glussk	Minsk	Ponomarenko	Selnitski
Kavylin Vladimir Ivanovich	1924		Vitebsk	VLKSM	? 3
Kave Yakov Gershonovich	1919	from the Litovskaya brigade	Baranovichi	detachment ? 106	
Kagan Abram Isaakovich	1909	Pukhovichi	Minsk	Razgrom (Crushing defeat)	
Kagan Berko Moiseyevich	1922	Novogrudok	Baranovichi	Kalinin	
Kagan GaLya Abramovna	1916	Minsk	Baranovichi	detachment ? 106	
Kagan Grigori Venyaminovich	1925	Shchitin	Pinsk	Molotov	Suvorov
Kagan Eva Isaakovna	1924	Minsk	Baranovichi	detachment ? 106	
Kagan Yefim Rafailovich	1913	s/factory Oktyabr	Mogilev	Osipovichskaya VOG	? 215
Kagan Izrail Girshevich	1912	Lyubcha	Baranovichi		
Kagan Yosif Abramovich	1909	Novogrudok	Baranovichi	Kalinin	
Kagan Isaak Kalmanovich	1898	Minsk, getto	Mogilev	208th partisan regiment	? 3
Kagan Isaak Mikhelevich	1914	Vselyub	Baranovichi	Kalinin	
Kagan Isaak Yakovlevich	1898	Minsk	Baranovichi	detachment ? 106	
Kagan Kopel Benyaminovich	1914	Volozhin	Baranovichi	Chkalov	? 4 "Za Sovetskuyu Belarus"
Kagan Kunya Moiseyevna	1917	Mir	Baranovichi	Kalinin	
Kagan Leiba Abramovich	1902	Smolyany	Vitebsk	VLKSM	? 5
Kagan Marusya Yosifovna	1923	Volozhin	Baranovichi	Kalinin	
Kagan Mikhail Abramovich	1893	Novogrudok	Baranovichi	Kalinin	
Kagan Mikhail Grigorevich	1928	Bobruisk	Mogilev	1st Bobruiskaya	? 252
Kagan Mikhail Moiseyevich	1903	Shklov	Mogilev	Chekist	? 20
Kagan Mikhail Samuilovich	1916	from the encirclement	Minsk	Dyadi Koli	Dzerzhinski
Kagan Moisei Yosifovich		Belarusian Staff of Partisan Movement	Vitebsk		
Kagan Polina Yevseyevna	1910	Minsk	Minsk	Underground RC and DC CP(b)B	Minsk underground RC and DC CP(b)B
Kagan Samuil Aizikovich	1912	Novogrudok	Baranovichi		
Kagan Semen Abramovich	1919	Vlodava (Poland)	Pinsk	Molotov	Shish
Kagan Semen Moiseyevich	1926	Mir	Baranovichi	Zhukov	
Kagan Falvyel Gertsevich	1903	Kopyl	Grodno	Kapusta's brigade	
Kagan Fanya Girshevna	1912	Minsk	Baranovichi	detachment ? 106	
Kagan Khaim Faivelevich	1922		Minsk	Voronyanski	Mstitel (Revenger)
Kagan Khana Khaimovna	1916	Ivye	Baranovichi	Kalinin	
Kagan Khaya Yosifovna	1920	Ivye	Baranovichi	Kalinin	
Kagan Yudel Yankelevich	1929	Novogrudok	Baranovichi	Kalinin	
Kagan Yakov Yosifovich	1918	TsK KP(b)B			
Kagan Yankel Benyaminovich	1919	Volozhin	Baranovichi	Chkalov	? 4 "Za Sovetskuyu Belarus"
Kaganovich Abram Khatskelevich	1921	Gorodok	Baranovichi	Chkalov	? 4 "Za Sovetskuyu Belarus"
Kaganovich Vladimir Yosifovich	1922	Mir	Baranovichi	Chkalov	
Kaganovich Yosif Grigorevich	1911	from captivity	Mogilev	? 113	brigade ? 113
Kaganovich Mendel Meyerovich	1921	getto, Pruzhany	Brest	Ponomarenko	Kirov
Kaganovich Moisei Khaimovich	1906	Lida, concentration camp	Belostok	A.Nevski	
Kaganovich Naum Ilyich	1908	Gorodok	Baranovichi	Chkalov	? 4 "Za Sovetskuyu Belarus"
Kaganovich Riva Aronovna	1927	Novogrudok	Baranovichi	detachment ? 106	
Kagonova Anna Aleksandrovna	1916	Slutsk district, Urechye	Minsk	Chkalov	Zheleznyak
Kazhdan Asena Gdalevna	1912	Krasnoye	Vitebsk	1st Belorusskaya	

Kazhdan Berta Abramovna	1915	Minsk	Baranovichi	Kalinin	
Kazhdan Vanya Faivelevich	1925	Derevno	Baranovichi	Kalinin	
Kazhdan Grigori Yefimovich	1905	Minsk	Vitebsk	2nd Belorusskaya	
Kazhdan David Yankelevich	1912	Pleshchenitsy	Vileyka	Kutuzov	
Kazhdan Daniel Davidovna	1909	Minsk getto	Baranovichi	18th Frunze	Frunze
Kazhdan Yosif Izrailevich	1926	Minsk getto	Minsk	Voronyanski	Pobieda
Kazhdan Taiba Peisakhovna	1893	Minsk	Baranovichi	detachment ? 106	
Kazhdan Yakov Markovich	1918	BShPO Moskva	Baranovichi	Stalin	Bolshevik
Kazadaev Yevsei Averkovich	1910	brigade Kalinovskogo	Grodno		Kalinin
Kazimirovskaya Ekaterina Vulfovna	1913	Minsk	Minsk	2nd Minskaya	Kutuzov
Kazinets Abram Beniyaminovich	1891	Minsk	Minsk	Kirov	Kirov
Kazinets Menush Mendelevich	1919	Dokshitsy	Minsk	Voronyanski	Kotovski
Kain Musya Leibovna	1926		Vitebsk	Chapayev	detachments
Kaikov Zalman Samuilovich					
Kaitorovich Shlema Rubinovich	1923		Baranovichi	Pobieda	Pobieda
Kalachik Abram Osherovich	1902	getto	Vitebsk	Nikitin's	? 5
Kalachik Izrail Samuilovich	1928	Novogrudok	Baranovichi	Ivienets DC CP(b)B company	
Kalachik Mikhail Yosifovich	1927	Ivienets	Vileyka	Suvorov	Kutuzov
Kalachik Raisa Aronovna	1919	Rechen, Lyuban district	Minsk	Ponomarenko	Komsomolets
Kalachik Samuil Abramovich	1896	Novogrudok	Baranovichi	Ivienets DC CP(b)B company	
Kaletskaya Sofiya Rafailovna	1923	Pruzhany	Brest	Chapayev	Malenkov
Kalibotski Samuil Solomonovich	1930	Minsk	Baranovichi	detachment ? 106	
Kalivach Abram Borukhovich	1921	concentration camp	Pinsk	Kuibyshev	Shchors
Kalinskaya Sima Abramovna	1915	Novogrudok	Baranovichi	Kalinin	
Kaliskaya Edya Moiseyevna	1909	Lodz	Baranovichi	Kalinin	
Kaliski Abram Aranovich	1909	Lodz	Baranovichi	Kalinin	
Kalman Khana Peisakhovna	1915	Derechin	Baranovichi	Leninskaya	hospital
Kalmanovich Doba Solomonovna	1913	Novogrudok getto	Baranovichi	Kirov	Ordzhonikidze
Kalmanovich Ilya Moiseyevich	1896	from the civil camp	Vileyka	4th Belorusskaya	? 6
Kalmanovich Yosif Aronovich	1925	getto, Vilno	Vileyka	Voroshilov	Pobieda
Kalmanovich Khaim Khononovich	1922	Lida	Belostok	A.Nevski	
Kalmanovich Khena Samuilovich	1914	Novogrudok	Baranovichi	Kalinin	
Kalmykov Abram Isaakovich	1885	Zalese, Polotsk district	Vitebsk	Korotkin	Voroshilov
Kalmykov Yefim Isaakovich	1888	brigade Korotkina	Vitebsk	Stalin (Okhotin's)	artillery division
Kalmykov Izrail Isaakovich	1893	Morsh, Polotsk district	Vitebsk	Korotkin	Voroshilov
Kalmykov Samuil Isaakovich	1880	Zalese, Polotsk district	Vitebsk	Korotkin	Voroshilov
Kalmykov Khaim Isaakovich	1888	Zalese, Polotsk district	Vitebsk	Korotkin	Voroshilov
Kalmykova Leya Samuilovna	1928	Zalese, Polotsk district	Vitebsk	Stalin (Okhotin's)	brigade headquarters
Kalovitski Itsko Moiseyevich	1895	Otiaty, Malorita district	Brest	Lenin	Voroshilov
Kalopnyi Abram Yosifovich	1914	Lida	Baranovichi	Stalin	Suvorov
Kalnitski Miron Borisovich	1905	from captivity	Vileyka	Voroshilov	Chapayev
Kalshtein Movsha Aizikovich	1908	Minsk	Baranovichi	Chkalov	? 4 "Za Sovetskuyu Belarus"
Kam Abram Borisovich	1928	Minsk	Baranovichi	detachment ? 106	
Kamenetskaya Tsilya Sholomovna	1934	Krasnoye	Baranovichi	Za Sovetskuyu Belarus	family detachment
Kamenkovich Berta Zakharovna	1917	Minsk	Baranovichi	Vpered (Forward)	family detachment group
Kamenski Naftaliya Meyerovna	1927	Lida	Baranovichi	Kalinin	
Kamenski Frants Izrailevich	1922	Lida, getto	Baranovichi	Kirov	Ordzhonikidze
Kametski Girsh Shayevich	1925	Kletsk	Minsk	Chapayev	Ponomarenko
Kametski Yakov Shayevich	1926	Kletsk	Minsk	Chapayev	Ponomarenko
Kaminer Mikhail Rakhmilevich	1909	getto, Vilno	Vileyka	Voroshilov	brigade headquarters
Kaminskaya Nina Yakovlevna	1926	Dukora, Minsk	Baranovichi	Leninskaya	hospital
Kaminski Volf Gershonovich	1923	Lida	Baranovichi	Leninskaya	Krasnogvardeiski
Kaminski Lazar Izrailevich	1922	Grodno	Baranovichi	Leninskaya	Niepobedimy (Unde-feated)
Kandelshtein Izrail Itskovich	1909	Pinsk region, Lenino	Minsk	Chkalov	Gromov
Kandelshtein Moisei Vnuk.	1920	Lenino	Brest	Sikorski's headquarters	Shchors
Kandybo Yakov Yefimovich	1913	from captivity	Minsk	Belarus	Belarus
Kantanovich Lyubov Yefimovna	1912	Minsk getto	Minsk	Za Sovetskuyu Belorus-siyu	Uragan
Kantarovich Gersh Leizerovich	1923	Minsk	Baranovichi	detachment ? 106	
Kantarovich Kiva Khaimovich	1911	Minsk	Baranovichi	detachment ? 106	
Kantor Ilya Isaakovich	1915	Belostok	Grodno	Samutin's group	Kirshner's group
Kantor Sara Lazarovna	1906	Derevno	Baranovichi	Kalinin	
Kantor Sonya Rubanovna	1922	Vilno	Minsk	Kalinin	Kalinin
Kantorovich Gesel Yosifovich	1891	Uzda	Baranovichi	Kalinin	
Kantorovich Grigori Rubinovich	1909		Minsk	Voronyanski	Mstitel (Revenger)
Kantorovich David Yakovlevich	1918	Ponarov	Vileyka	Voroshilov	A.Nevski
Kantorovich Enya Lipovich	1920	Vilno	Baranovichi	detachment ? 106	
Kantorovich Yosif Srulevich	1907	iz gruppy Gilchika	Minsk	Chapayev	Chapayev

Kantorovich Nota Mendelevich	1922	family detachment camp	Belostok	A.Nevski	
Kantorovich Riva Markovna	1914	Stolbtsy	Baranovichi	Kalinin	
Kantorovich Susanna Grigorevna	1923	Minsk	Belostok	Ponomarenko	Ponomarenko
Kantorovich Shlema Rubinovich	1923	Novogrudok getto	Baranovichi	Kirov	Ordzhonikidze
Kantorovich Shlema Yankelevich	1921	getto	Vileyka	Voroshilov	Istrebitel (Destroyer)
Kantorovich Yakov Khaimovich	1910	Slutsk	Pinsk	Molotov	Kalinin
Kantorovski Yakov Aronovich	1911	Khrakovichi, Bragin district	Palesye		Kotovski
Kantser Ilya Abramovich	1912	from the encirclement	Minsk	Parkhomenko	Kirov
Kantsiper Boris Aronovich	1918	Kobrin	Pinsk	Molotov	Potalakh
Kantsipolski Novel Davidovich	1923	Baranovichi, from home	Baranovichi	Grizodubova	Matrosov
Kantsler Naum Khononovich	1923	Minsk	Vitebsk	Nikitin's	? 2
Kantsler Sarra Isaakovna	1910	Minsk	Baranovichi	detachment ? 106	
KapaLyan Rakhil Grigorevna	1917	Minsk	Baranovichi	18th Frunze	Kutuzov
Kapelyushnik Mendel Yankelevich	1920	Ivanovo	Pinsk	Shubetidze	Chapayev
Kapelyushnik Shaya Movshevich	1914	Drogichin	Brest	Ponomarenko	Kirov
Kapelyushnikov Yakov Afanasyevich	1888	Bubevo, Surazhski district	Vitebsk	1st Belorusskaya	
Kapilevich Arkadi Natolievich	1928	Pleshchenitsy	Minsk	Voronyanski	Kotovski
Kapilevich David Lazarevich	1922	Belarusian Staff of Partisan Movement	Minsk	Special groups	Dubovik's group
Kapilevich Leizer Zalmanovich	1895	Vileika, getto	Minsk	Shturmovaya	Frunze
Kapilevich Manya Zalmanovna	1908	Minsk	Baranovichi	detachment ? 106	
Kapilevich Mikhail Davidovich	1902	Samokhvalovichi	Minsk	3rd Minskaya	25years of the A-ULCYL
Kapilevich Petr Borisovich	1904	Minsk	Baranovichi	detachment ? 106	
Kapilevich Raisa Borisovna	1924	Ushachi district	Vitebsk	Chapayev	detachments
Kapilevich Ruvim Khaimovich	1912	Khotenchitsy	Minsk	Voronyanski	Kotovski
Kapilevich Yuda Khaimovich	1916	Khotenchitsy	Vileyka	Gastello	Za Sovetskuyu Rodinu
Kapilov Elya Aronovich	1927	Minsk	Baranovichi	detachment ? 106	
Kapilovich Liliya Yefimovna	1921	Novogrudok	Baranovichi	detachment ? 106	
Kaplan Abram Isaakovich	1923	Lida	Baranovichi	Kalinin	
Kaplan Aizik Leizerovich	1925		Baranovichi	Oktyabr	
Kaplan Anna Isaakovna	1915	Derechin	Baranovichi	Leninskaya	hospital
Kaplan Anya Yudelevna	1924	Minsk	Baranovichi	detachment ? 106	
Kaplan Afroim Girsh Leibovich	1915	left by theRK KP(b)B	Palesye	detachment at the headquarters	
Kaplan Boris Samoilovich	1924	Dvinsk	Vileyka	Za Rodinu (For Motherland)	Kirov
Kaplan Vitka Moiseyevna	1920	Minsk	Baranovichi	Chkalov	? 4 "Za Sovetskuyu Belarus"
Kaplan Vladimir Solomonovich	1923	Gorodok	Baranovichi	Chkalov	? 4 "Za Sovetskuyu Belarus"
Kaplan Volf Benyaminovich	1924	Voronovo	Baranovichi	Kalinin	
Kaplan Genya Abramovna	1916	Minsk getto	Minsk	Ponomarenko	Gvardeyets (Guardsman)
Kaplan Grigori Izrailevich	1918	small town of B. Solechniki	Baranovichi	Vpered (Forward)	A.Nevski
Kaplan Grigori Mikhailovich	1925	Minsk getto	Minsk	Zheleznyak	? 5
Kaplan Grisha Davidovich	1925	Minsk	Baranovichi	detachment ? 106	
Kaplan Grisha Isaakovich	1927	Minsk	Baranovichi	detachment ? 106	
Kaplan David Leibovich	1912	Minsk getto	Minsk	Shturmovaya	Grozny
Kaplan Danil Solomonovich	1925	Rakov	Baranovichi	Chkalov	? 4 "Za Sovetskuyu Belarus"
Kaplan Yevgeniya Khaimovna	1923	Vileika	Minsk	Kirov	Kirov
Kaplan Yesel Faivelevich	1922	Radun	Baranovichi	Lenin's komsomol	Lenin's komsomol
Kaplan Ida Nosinovich	1914	Lida	Baranovichi	Kirov	Iskra
Kaplan Ida Yakovlevna	1923	getto N. Sverzhen	Minsk	Chapayev	Ponomarenko
Kaplan Izrail Aronovich	1903	Starobin	Pinsk	Budenny	
Kaplan Yosif Ezorovich	1911	Lida	Baranovichi	Kirov	Iskra
Kaplan Ira Abramovna	1918	Stolbtsy	Baranovichi	Kalinin	
Kaplan Isaak Aleksandrovich	1895	Minsk	Baranovichi	detachment ? 106	
Kaplan Itsko Khaimovich	1915	Viazan	Vileyka	Budenny	
Kaplan Leiba Izrailevich	1920	small town of B. Solechniki	Baranovichi	Vpered (Forward)	A.Nevski
Kaplan Leiba Kastrievich	1907	Yody	Vileyka	Zhdanov	
Kaplan Leiba Noselevich	1922		Baranovichi	Oktyabr	
Kaplan Lina Levikovna	1909	Korelichi	Baranovichi	Kalinin	
Kaplan Matus Abramovich	1927	Molchad	Baranovichi	Kalinin	
Kaplan Meyer Isaakovich	1915	Lida	Baranovichi	Kalinin	
Kaplan Mikhail Shayevich	1925	camp, Lakhva	Palesye	? 125	Bolotnikov's
Kaplan Movsha Ezrovich	1912	Korelichi	Minsk	Chapayev	Ponomarenko
Kaplan Moisei Abramovich	1912	Minsk	Minsk	2nd Minskaya	Kutuzov
Kaplan Natan Yoselevich	1886	Lida	Baranovichi	Kalinin	
Kaplan Nokhim Itskovich	1917	Radun	Baranovichi	Lenin's komsomol	Ivanov's

Kaplan Nokhim Khaimovich	1909	Vileika district, Viazan	Minsk	Dima	
Kaplan Rakhil Isaakovna	1923	Minsk	Baranovichi	detachment ? 106	
Kaplan Raya Yudelevna	1925	Minsk	Baranovichi	detachment ? 106	
Kaplan Roza Meyerovna	1940	Lida	Baranovichi	Kalinin	
Kaplan Roman Moiseyevich	1915	lag. v/pl., Slutsk	Minsk	Suvorov	
Kaplan Samuil Mordukhovich	1923	Minsk	Baranovichi	Ponomarenko	25 years of the BSSR
Kaplan Sara Yankelevna	1913	Lida	Baranovichi	Kalinin	
Kaplan Slava (Glory) Davidovna	1898	Minsk	Baranovichi	detachment ? 106	
Kaplan Srol Aronovich	1903	Starobin	Pinsk	Komarov-Korzh's	Komarov's 3rd group
Kaplan Ura Yakovlevich	1925	N. Sverzhen	Minsk	Chapayev	Shchors
Kaplan Falvyel Elevich	1907	Ivanovo	Pinsk	Molotov	brigade headquarters
Kaplan Fanya Moiseyevna	1924	Minsk getto	Baranovichi	Za Sovetskuyu Belarus	Za Sovetskuyu Belarus
Kaplan Fruma Benyaminovna	1915	Viazan	Vileyka	Budenny	
Kaplan Khaya AntsElevna	1916	Voronovo	Baranovichi	Kalinin	
Kaplan Tsira Aizikovna	1909	Molchad	Baranovichi	Kalinin	
Kaplan Sholim Moiseyevich	Uzda	Baranovichi	detachment ? 106		
Kaplan Elga Isaakovna	1923	Minsk	Baranovichi	detachment ? 106	
Kaplan Yudel Faivelevich	1922	Radun	Baranovichi	Leninskaya	Niepobedimy (Undefeated)
Kaplikskaya Raya Grigorevna	1921	Novogrudok	Baranovichi	Kalinin	
Kaplinskaya Sima Solomonovna	1917	Baranovichi region, Bakhshty	Baranovichi	Vpered (Forward)	Roshcha
Kaplinski Izrail Movshevich	1894	Dyatlovo	Baranovichi	Leninskaya	Borba
Kaplinski Isaak Rafailovich	1909	Baranovichi region, Bakhshty	Baranovichi	Vpered (Forward)	Roshcha
Kaplinski Matvei Barkhovich	1908	getto	Baranovichi	Kirov	Oktyabrski
Kaplinski Mikhail Lvovich	1924	Gorodishche district	Baranovichi	25 years of the BSSR	Grozny
Kaplinski SaLya Isaakovich	1928	Minsk	Baranovichi	detachment ? 106	
Kaplun Grigori Tsalilovich	1911	Minsk	Minsk	Shturmovaya	Grozny
KaPolyan Sonya Abramovna	1908	Shchedrin	Palesye		Kirov
Kapulski Volf Gershenovich	1923	Lida	Baranovichi	Leninskaya	Niepobedimy (Undefeated)
Kapulski Gersh Abramovich	1927	Grodno	Baranovichi	Leninskaya	Niepobedimy (Undefeated)
Kapustyan Moisei Bentsionovich	1922	from the encirclement	Mogilev		? 760 Berezovski
Kaputkin Yakov Nisanovich	1898	Parichi district, Shchedrin	Minsk	Parkhomenko	Shchors
Karagina Zoya Aleksandrovna	1919	Minsk	Baranovichi	Stalin	Kirov
Karantayer Manya Davidovna	1911	Minsk	Baranovichi	detachment ? 106	
Karasik Yosif Mendelevich	1910	Svirski district	Vileyka		Suslov
Karasik Khaim Izrailevich	1912	Osipovichi	Mogilev	1st Bobruiskaya	? 252
Karas Sarra Yosifovna	1926	Minsk	Minsk	Chapayev	Ponomarenko
Karash Abram Pertsevich	1907	Shklyary	Belostok		separate detachment Zhukov
Karber Zlata Volfovna	1926	iz mestnykh	Baranovichi	Lenin's komsomol	Lenin's komsomol
Karelets Samuil Girshevich	1908	Kosovo	Brest	Ponomarenko	Dmitrov
Karelich Gita Samuilovna	1920	Baranovichi	Minsk	Chapayev	Shchors
Karmach Konstantin Aronovich	1927	Minsk	Vitebsk	Nikitin's	? 4
Karnovski Izrail Davidovich	1925	Slonim	Baranovichi	Pobieda	
Karobeinik Boris Zakharevich	1907	Minsk	Baranovichi	detachment ? 106	
Karobeinik Rakhil Abramovna	1909	Minsk	Baranovichi	detachment ? 106	
Karolinski Aron Zelmanovich	1915	Ivanovo	Pinsk	Molotov	Lazo
Karpanos Margis Khaimovich	1918	Minsk	Minsk	3rd Minskaya	Niepobedimy (Undefeated)
Karpel Abram Berkovich	1924	Oshmiany	Baranovichi	18th Frunze	Kotovski
Karpel Leizer Yankelevich	1917	from captivity	Vitebsk	16st Smolenskaya	
Karpik Rakhmel Davidovich	1912	Slonim	Baranovichi	Pobieda	Pobieda
Karpilova Anna KhatskYevna	1917	Minsk getto	Minsk	Rokossovski	Chkalov
Karpinskaya Khelya	1925	Poland	Brest	Lenin	Zhukov
Karpovski Izrail Davidovich	1925	Derechin	Baranovichi	Pobieda	Suvorov
Kartovski Yakub Petrovich	1920	Kopyl	Minsk	Suvorov	
Kartovski Yan Petrovich	1920	Nesvizh	Grodno		Izyumski's
Karcheva Polina Solomonovna	1920	Iurovichi	Palesye		Voroshilov
Karcheva Tamara Solomonovna	1928	Iurovichi	Palesye		Voroshilov
Karchmar Sapel Zelikovich	1897	Volozhin	Baranovichi	Ivienets DC CP(b)B company	
Karsh Bentsion Shulimovich	1898	Lyubashovski district, Volyn region	Pinsk	Sovetskaya Belarus	Kutuzov
Kasimov Abram Leibovich	1916	Kozianski les	Vileyka	Zhdanov	
Kasler Abram Moiseyevich	1911	getto, Pruzhany	Brest	Ponomarenko	Kirov
Kasovskaya Yelena Moiseyevna	1905	Chashniki	Vitebsk	Dubov's	? 3
Kasovskaya Sofiya Moiseyevna	1928	Chashniki	Vitebsk	Dubov's	? 3
Kasovski Naeri Mergovich	1914	Minsk getto	Baranovichi	Stalin	Parkhomenko

Name	Year	Place	Region	Detachment	Unit
Kasperskaya Sara Yakovlevna	1914	Lipen	Mogilev	Osipovichskaya VOG	? 210
Kassinskaya Rakhil Davidovna	1909	Minsk	Baranovichi	Dzerzhinski	Dzerzhinski
Katina Raya Abramovna	1929	Minsk	Baranovichi	detachment ? 106	
Katko Benyamin Leizerovich	1930	Kovel, Ukraine	Brest	Lenin	Voroshilov
Katon Abram Davidovich	1923	from captivity	Minsk	Ponomarenko	Gorbachev
Kaupshtein Mikhail small town of	1903	Dyatlovo	Baranovichi	Pobieda	Pobieda
Kaufman Abram Mendelevich	1905	Belarusian Staff of Partisan Movement	Gomel	Kozhar's	Drozdov's group
Kaufman Volf Isrulevich	1914	Derechin	Baranovichi	Pobieda	Suvorov
Kaufman David Zakharovich	1927	Minsk	Baranovichi	detachment ? 106	
Kaufman Leiba Khemevich	1912	Jewish camp, Rovno region.	Pinsk	Shubetidze	Ordzhonikidze
Kaufman Mikhail Albertovich	1912	Pinsk	Pinsk	Shubetidze	Stalin
Kaufman Movsha Peisakhovich	1920	concentration camp	Pinsk	Kuibyshev	Shchors
Kaufman Sara-Khaya Mendeleyevna	1914	Derechin	Baranovichi	Leninskaya	hospital
Kaufman Fedor Samuilovich	1922	getto, Minsk	Vileyka	Suvorov	
Kats Aizik Yankelevich	1915	getto, Vilno	Vileyka	Voroshilov	Lazo
Kats Aleksandr Khilevich	1919	from behind the Bug, a group from Poland	Pinsk	Molotov	Lazo
Kats Berta Nakhimovna	1876	Smolevichi	Minsk	Voronyanski	Kotovski
Kats Boris Yudelevich	1899	Lakhva	Pinsk	Kirov	Stalin
Kats Ganda (a woman)	1914	Belostok	Grodno	Samutin's group	Kirshner's group
Kats Genya Solomonovna	1921	Smilovichi	Baranovichi	detachment ? 106	
Kats Girsh Abramovich	1926	getto	Vileyka	Voroshilov	Lazo
Kats Grigori Bentsionovich	1907	Jewish camp Dolginovo	Minsk	Voronyanski	Pobieda
Kats Grigori Yakovlevich	1915		Minsk	Voronyanski	Pobieda
Kats Grisha Zolevich	1920	Ivye	Baranovichi	Stalin	Suvorov
Kats David Pavlovich	1919	from the encirclement	Palesye	? 123	Kalakin
Kats Zhenka Lvovich	1925	getto, Disna	Vileyka	1st Suvorov	Bolshevik
Kats Zalman Davidovich	1921	getto, Glubokoye	Vitebsk	Korotkin	Voroshilov
Kats Izrail Mikhailovich	1908	from captivity	Vitebsk	Chapayev	brigade headquarters
Kats Ilya Shayevich	1910	from captivity, Mogilev	Mogilev	? 113	brigade ? 113
Kats Ion Davidovich	1915	Prozoroki	Vileyka	Spartak	? 6
Kats Yosif Isaakovich	1930	Uzda	Baranovichi	Kalinin	
Kats Yosif Yankelevich	1907	from the detachment Lutsenko GrizoDubov's's brigade	Grodno		B.Khmelnitski
Kats Isaak Abramovich	1901	Losha, Uzdenski district	Minsk	Belarus	Belarus
Kats Isidor Germanovich	1905	Lida, getto	Baranovichi	Kirov	Orel
Kats Itska Abramovich	1901	Losha, Uzdenski district	Mogilev	208th regiment	
Kats Lev Isaakovich	1922	iz mestnykh	Baranovichi	Lenin's komsomol	Lenin's komsomol
Kats Leizer Borisovich	1916	from the civil camp	Vileyka	4th Belorusskaya	? 6
Kats Leizer Girshevich	1908	Novogrudok	Baranovichi	Kalinin	
Kats Leonid Samuilovich	1910	Berezino	Minsk	Shchors	Shchors
Kats Lyuba Solomonovna	1921	getto, Glubokoye	Vitebsk	Korotkin	Voroshilov
Kats Lyubov Isaakovna	1920	Vilno	Baranovichi	Lenin's komsomol	Vanda Vasilevskaya
Kats Manya Davydovna	1926	Lakhva	Pinsk	Kirov	
Kats Manya Pavlovna	1921		Palesye	? 123	Vezhnovets'
Kats Mariya Grigorevna	1917	Minsk getto	Baranovichi	Stalin	Kirov
Kats Mariya Isaakovna	1923	small town of Krevo	Baranovichi	Vpered (Forward)	Sibiryak
Kats Meilakh Khilevich	1921	Ivanovo	Pinsk	Molotov	Shish
Kats Mordukh Leibovich	1911	Minsk	Baranovichi	detachment ? 106	
Kats Rakhil Borisovna	1922	from the civil camp	Vileyka	4th Belorusskaya	? 6
Kats Raya Yakovlevna	1922	getto	Vileyka	Voroshilov	Lazo
Kats Ruben Mendelevich	1924	detachment "Mest"	Vileyka	Voroshilov	headquarters' production group
Kats Samuil Shlemovich	1922	detachment "Mest"	Vileyka	Voroshilov	headquarters' production group
Kats Semen Abramovich	1922	Vileika	Vileyka		Suslov
Kats Sigizmund Kalmanovich	1937	Lida	Baranovichi	Kalinin	
Kats Sonya Leibovna	1924	Minsk	Baranovichi	detachment ? 106	
Kats Folek Lipmanovich	1927	getto, Vilno	Vileyka	Voroshilov	brigade headquarters
Kats Foma Zalmanovich	1922	Glubokoye	Vileyka	Spartak	? 1
Kats Khaim Abramovich	1922	Peski, Mosty	Baranovichi	Pobieda	Budenny
Kats Khaim Shamuilovich	1928	Dvorets	Baranovichi	Kalinin	
Kats Shmuil Elevich	1926	Ivye	Baranovichi	Vpered (Forward)	A.Nevski
Kats Sholom Isaakovich	1932	Losha, Uzdenski district	Minsk	Belarus	Belarus
Kats Sholom Itskovich	1892		Mogilev	208th regiment	left the detachment from the moment organization
Kats Edya Samuilovna	1926	Bryansk getto, Belostok region	Grodno	Vo imya Rodiny (In the name of Motherland)	Zhukov
Kats Elya Moiseyevich	1926	Jewish camp	Vileyka	4th Belorusskaya	? 6

Kats Estra	1926	from the civil camp	Vileyka	4th Belorusskaya	? 6
Kats Yuzef Yankelevich	1907	from the concentration camp	Baranovichi	Grizodubova	Chkalov
Kats Yankel Vulfovich	1909	Ivye, getto	Baranovichi	Kirov	brigade headquarters
Katsev Shlema Berkovich	1915	Vasilishki	Baranovichi	Kalinin	
Katsevich Yefim Tevelevich	1925	Postavy	Vileyka		Suslov
Katsevich Mikhail Semenovich	1918	detachment Nikolaeva	Vileyka	1st Suvorov	Bolshevik
Katsenbogen Aleksandr Grigorevich	1916	getto	Vileyka	Voroshilov	brigade headquarters
Katsenbogen Girsh Yakovlevich	1896	Minsk	Baranovichi		
Katsenelenbogen Feliks Semenovich	1883	Torfianoi factory	Baranovichi	18th Frunze	provisional base of the brigade
Katsenelson Berta Grigorevna	1929	Minsk	Baranovichi	Chkalov	reserve group
Katsman		Belarusian Staff of Partisan Movement	Gomel	Kozhar's	Shemyakin's group
Katsman Asya Abramovna	1924	Glussk	Palesye	? 125	Roshchina
Katsman Yefim Borisovich	1913	Minsk	Vitebsk	Nikitin's	brigade administration
Katsman Maks Solomonovich	1929	Minsk	Baranovichi	Zhukov	
Katsman Mark Grigorevich	1915	Kalinkovichi	Vitebsk	Voroshilov	Mstitel (Revenger)
Katsman Mikhail Vulfovich	1908	Mogilev	Gomel	Shemyakin's "Vpered (Forward)"	Makagonov's
Katsnbogin Girsh Yankelevich	1896	Minsk	Baranovichi	detachment ? 106	
Katsnelbogin Lenya Mordukhovich	1935	Minsk	Baranovichi	detachment ? 106	
Katsnelbogin Mordukh Yankelevich	1899	Minsk	Baranovichi	detachment ? 106	
Katsnelbogin Shifra Mordukhovna	1905	Minsk	Baranovichi	detachment ? 106	
Katsnelson Boris Yosifovich					
Katsnelson BroniSlava (Glory) Abramovna	1924	Bobruisk	Mogilev		? 538
Katsnelson Girsh Leibovich	1903	Belarusian Staff of Partisan Movement	Minsk	Special groups	gr. Pekun
Katsnelson Yevgeniya Aronovna	1925	Bobruisk	Palesye	? 123	Krasny Oktyabr
Katsnelson Izrail Yevseyevich	1929	s/factory Oktyabr	Mogilev	Osipovichskaya VOG	? 210
Katsnelson Isaak Zymelevich	1906	Glussk	Minsk	Bragin	Gastello
Katsnelson Liza Borisovna	1908	Minsk	Baranovichi	detachment ? 106	
Katsnelson Lyubov Borisovna	1916	Minsk	Baranovichi	Chkalov	
Katsnelson Moisei Aronovich	1907	Belarusian Staff of Partisan Movement	Minsk	Special groups	Istrebitel (Destroyer)
Katsnelson Naum Yudelevich	1922	Bobruisk	Pinsk	Molotov	Kalinin
Katsnelson Tsilya Aleksandrovna	1916	small town of Urechye Slutsk district	Minsk	Chkalov	Zheleznyak
Katsnelson Tsilya Davidovna	1926	Starye Dorogi	Minsk	Chkalov	Gromov
Katsnelson Yuri V.	1921	Saltanovka	Gomel	1st Gomelskaya	Kalinin
Katsovich Aizik Berkovich	1911		Minsk	Voronyanski	Pobieda
Katsovich Aleksandra Semenovna	1924	Kholopenechski district, Postrozhe	Minsk	Kirov	? 4
Katsovich Boris Samuilovich	1923	Glubokoye	Minsk	Underground RC and DC CP(b)B	Logoisk DC of the CP(b)B
Katsovich Golda Abramovna	1905	Jewish camp	Vileyka	Voroshilov	headquarters' production group
Katsovich Mariya Semenovna	1926	Kholopenechski district, Postrozhe	Minsk	Kirov	? 4
Katsovich Mikhail Shmuilovich	1918	Krivichi	Vitebsk	Chapayev	detachments
Katsovich Semen Movshevich	1893	Dolginovo	Minsk	Kirov	? 4
Katsovich Khasya Yakovlevna	1929	Jewish camp	Vileyka	Voroshilov	headquarters' production group
Katsovich Yankel Mordukhovich	1897	Jewish camp	Vileyka	Voroshilov	headquarters' production group
Kachan Yakov Yosifovich	1918	Belarusian Staff of Partisan Movement	Grodno	Samutin's group	Samutin's group
Kachanovski Sholom Shlemovich	1921	Baranovichi	Baranovichi	18th Frunze	editorial stuff of the newspaper "Za Sovetskuyu Belarus"
Kachevskaya Manya KhatskElevna	1916	Minsk	Baranovichi	detachment ? 106	
Kachevski Peisakh Benyaminovich	1922	Minsk	Baranovichi	detachment ? 106	
Kashetski Shaya Mordukhovich	1902	Kletsk	Minsk	Chapayev	Ponomarenko
Kashitser Isaak Davidovich	1912	Lipovka	Mogilev		? 44
Kashchevskaya Dora Samuilovna	1922	Myadel	Minsk	Zheleznyak	? 2
Kvass Bronya Ilinichna	1916	Baranovichi	Minsk	Chapayev	Shchors
Kvyat Izrail Movshevich	1923		Baranovichi	Pobieda	Pobieda
Kvyat Leizer Khaimovich	1905	detachment "Mest"	Vileyka	Voroshilov	headquarters' production group
Kvyat Moisei Abramovich	1897	Derechin	Baranovichi	Pobieda	Pobieda
Kegeles Matvei Samuilovich	1906	Belarusian Staff of Partisan Movement	Minsk	Special groups	Kunovski's group
Kegrimovski Yuli Yakovlevich	1914	Minsk	Vitebsk	2nd Belorusskaya	

Keizman Abram Mendelevich	1921	concentration camp, Vlodava	Pinsk	Molotov	Kalinin
Keizman Khoma Mendelevich	1924	from the forest, Tomashevka	Pinsk	Molotov	Kalinin
Keiles Mikhail Gidolevich	1915	Grodno	Baranovichi	Leninskaya	Niepobedimy (Undefeated)
Kelman Ira Yefimovna	1924	small town of Vishnevo	Baranovichi	Chapayev	Parkhomenko
Kenigshtein Abram Zavelevich	1926	Nesvizh	Minsk	Chapayev	Ponomarenko
Kerch Isaak Petrovich	1918	Kosovo	Brest	Sikorski's headquarters	Shchors
Kesler Yosif Abramovich	1914	Novogrudok	Baranovichi	Kalinin	
Kesler Katya Isaakovna	1927	Minsk	Baranovichi	detachment ? 106	
Kesler Nina TsezarYevna	1924	getto, Pruzhany	Brest	Za Sovetskuyu Belarus	Chkalov
Kesler Rakhil Moiseyevna	1925	Dvorets	Baranovichi	Kalinin	
Kesler Shlema Leibovich	1915	from the encirclement	Mogilev	Chekist	brigade headquarters
Ketslikh Nevakh Shlemovich	1893	Minsk	Baranovichi	detachment ? 106	
Ketslikh Shlema Nevakhovich	1897	Minsk	Baranovichi	detachment ? 106	
Kibrovski Ilya Khonovich	1926	Martikantsy	Baranovichi	Lenin's komsomol	Kotovski
Kiva Yosif Borisovich	1900	Belostok	Grodno		? 550
Kivelevich Sara Girshevna	1914	Lyubcha	Baranovichi	Kalinin	
Kivilevich Bruno Ilyich	1903	Lida, camp	Belostok	A.Nevski	Kotovski
Kivilevich Sulamif Ilinichna	1917	Lida, camp	Belostok	A.Nevski	Kotovski
Kivovich Abram Khaimovich	1903	Rubezhevichi	Baranovichi	Kalinin	
Kier Boris Lipovich	1901	detachment "Mest"	Vileyka	Voroshilov	headquarters' production group
Kizner Natan Shmeyerovich	1917	Novogrudok, getto	Baranovichi	Lida IDC	
Kizner Nakhman Ilevich	1916		Baranovichi	Oktyabr	
Kizner Roza Abramovna	1911	Novogrudok	Baranovichi	Kalinin	
Kiles Moisei Kidalovich	1915	Grodno	Baranovichi	Lenin's komsomol	Lenin's komsomol
Kil Boris Grigorevich	1914	Ziabki	Vileyka	CC of the CP(b)B	Denisov
Kil Lev Berkovich	1927	Kletsk	Minsk	Chapayev	Ponomarenko
Kil Leiba Grigorevich	1926	Ziabki	Vileyka	CC of the CP(b)B	Denisov
Kimkulkin Faiba Fraimovich	1912	Ivye	Baranovichi	Dzerzhinski	Kotovski
Kinkulkin Moisei Elevich	1922	Ivye	Baranovichi	A.Nevski	brigade headquarters
Kinkulkina Anna Naumovna	1913	Lyakhovichi, Chashniki district	Vitebsk	Dubov's	? 15
Kirzhner Aron Aizikovich	1908	Baranovichi	Baranovichi	Kalinin	
Kirzhner Mikhail Isaakovich	1923	Rakhovichi	Pinsk	Budenny	Voroshilov
Kirzhner Mikhail Semenovich	1932	Lakhva	Pinsk	Kirov	Petrovich's
Kirz Sofiya Khomovna	1924	Ivanovo	Pinsk	Molotov	Lazo
Kirzner Shepsel Novakhovich	1921	Bereznyaki	Pinsk	Molotov	Kalinin
Kirzon Mariya Abramovna	1902	Minsk getto	Baranovichi	Chapayev	Chapayev
Kirman Fishel Leizerovich	1892	Timkovichi, Kopyl district	Minsk	Chapayev	brigade headquarters
Kirshenbaum Yuri Itskovich	1921	Poland	Pinsk	Shubetidze	Kostyushko
Kirshner Zilman Moiseyevich	1919	Belostok	Grodno	Samutin's group	Kirshner's group
Kiselev Yuri Maksimovich	1916	from captivity	Pinsk	Lenin	Frunze
Kiseleva Vera Lvovna	1921	Slutsk	Minsk	Chkalov	Kotovski
Kisel David Romanovich	1908	Minsk	Baranovichi	Dzerzhinski	Dzerzhinski
Kisel Mariya Yuryevna	1916	Minsk	Baranovichi	Dzerzhinski	Dzerzhinski
Kisin Leiba Samuilovich	1923	from the civil camp	Vileyka	4th Belorusskaya	? 6
Kisler Evraim Yoselevich	1925	Belostok	Grodno	Samutin's group	Kirshner's group
Kislovich Girsha Shlemovich	1912	Gurishche, getto	Baranovichi	Stalin	Suvorov
Kisselman Abram Yosifovich	1909	from the encirclement	Minsk	Grishin's 13th regiment	
Kist David Mordukhovich	1922	Krulevshchizna getto	Minsk	1st Antifashistskaya	
Kitaevich Abram Yankelevich	1916	Kosovo	Brest	Dzerzhinski	Chertkov
Kitaevich Solomon Yankelevich	1918	Ivatsevichi	Brest	Dzerzhinski	Molotov
Klaper Grigori Yakovlevich	1924	Minsk	Baranovichi	Ponomarenko	Timoshenko
Klebanova Lyuba Isaakovna	1921	Shepelevichi	Mogilev	Chekist	? 1
Klebanova Tsilya Grigorevna	1907	Minsk	Baranovichi	18th Frunze	Kutuzov
Kleikman Boris Moiseyevich	1905	Slonim	Minsk	Chapayev	Ponomarenko
Klein Sholom Abramovich	1912	Smilovichi	Mogilev	208th regiment	left the detachment from the moment organization
Klein Yakov Leibovich	1917	getto	Vileyka	Voroshilov	Suvorov
Kleinburg Leonid Leonovich	1915	Kobrin	Brest	Za Sovetskuyu Belarus	Chkalov
Kleinst Mulya Osipovich	1920	Bryansk getto, Belostok region	Grodno	Vo imya Rodiny (In the name of Motherland)	Zhukov
Klener Yakov Isaakovich	1915	Krivichi district, Vileika region	Vitebsk	2nd Belorusskaya	
Klerin Misha Yosifovich	1928	Minsk	Baranovichi	detachment ? 106	
Klerin Semen Mendelevich	1921	Budslav, Krivichi district	Vitebsk	Lepelskaya Stalin	? 4
Klet Nosson Shmuilovich	1902	Disna	Vitebsk	Voroshilov	Za Rodinu (For Motherland)
Kletskaya Khana Yosifovna	1927	Viazan, Vileika region	Minsk	Voroshilov	? 6

Kletski Abram Rafalovich	1925	Slutsk	Baranovichi	Zhukov	
Kletski Khona Yosifovich	1925	Ivye	Minsk	Voroshilov	? 6
Kletsman Gllyari Grigorevich	1924		Vitebsk	Nikitin's	? 4
Klechevskaya Mariyasya KhatskElevna	1916	Minsk	Baranovichi	detachment ? 106	
Klechuk Isaak Simkovich	1905	N. Sverzhen	Minsk	Chapayev	Ponomarenko
Kleshchik Mordukh Sholomovich	1912	Timkovichi	Minsk	Chapayev	Ponomarenko
Kligun Shmuel Itskovich	1915	Omit	Pinsk	Shubetidze	Stalin
Klin Yakov Nakhmanovich	1916	Volkovyssk, camp	Belostok	A.Nevski	
Klinski Moisei Davidovich	1913	detachment "Mest"	Vileyka	Voroshilov	headquarters' production group
Klionski David Markovich	1923	from the detachment Parkhomenko	Baranovichi	detachment ? 106	
Klyuch Mikhail Isaakovich		Belarusian Staff of Partisan Movement	Minsk	Special groups	Klyuch's group
KLyaino Yakov Leibovich	1917	getto, Vilno	Vileyka	Voroshilov	Pobieda
KLyamner Yakov Isaakovich	1915	Budslav, Krivichi district	Vitebsk	Stalin (Okhotin's)	Stalin
KLyachkovski Moisei Abramovich	1902	Radoshkovichi	Minsk	Voronyanski	Kotovski
Knel Berka Yoselevich	1915	Braslav district	Vileyka	Zhdanov	
Knel Zinovii Borisovich	1926	Lyuban	Pinsk	Komarov-Korzh's	Komarov's 3rd group
Knel Khana Yeselevna	1915	Sharkovshchina	Vileyka	4th Belorusskaya	? 2
Knikulkin Moisei Elevich	1922	Ivye	Baranovichi	Vpered (Forward)	A.Nevski
Knopmakher Mikhail Yakubovich	1926	Poland	Pinsk	Molotov	Potalakh
Knopmakher Naum Yakubovich	1919	Poland	Pinsk	Molotov	Potalakh
Koberman Elka Yefimovna	1909	Borisov	Baranovichi	detachment ? 106	
Kobzeva Mariya Abramovna	1922	Shklov	Mogilev	Chekist	Kovalev's
Kobrinskaya Tsilya Ilinichna	1914	Lyskovo, Brest region	Grodno	Vo imya Rodiny (In the name of Motherland)	Kutuzov
Kobrovski Samuil Zalmanovich	1906	Baranovichi region	Baranovichi	Pervomaiskaya	Oktyabr
Kovalev's Fanya Aronovna	1915	Bratkovichi	Gomel	Shemyakin's "Vpered (Forward)"	Makagonov's
Kovalevski Monya Yosifovich	1913	Derechin	Baranovichi	Pobieda	Suvorov
Kovalenchik Aleksandr Arkadevich	1916	Luki, Vasilevichski district	Palesye	? 101	brigade headquarters and administration platoon
Kovalenchik Khanan Fedorovich	1912	Kopyl	Minsk	Chapayev	Ponomarenko
Koval Liza Valentinovna	1913	Usakino, Klichev district	Mogilev		? 278
Koval Raya Rafailovna	1911	Mogilev	Mogilev		? 345
Kovalski Venyamin Lyudogovich	1896	Novogrudok	Baranovichi	Vpered (Forward)	Chkalov
Kovalski Matvei Abramovich	1897	Uzda	Minsk	Chapayev	Ponomarenko
Kovalski Yankel Nashevich	1922	Radun	Baranovichi	Lenin's komsomol	Kotovski
Kovarskaya Galina Naumovna	1922	getto, Vilno	Vileyka	Suvorov	
Kovarski Leon Naimovich	1908	Svir	Vileyka	Dovator	Sverdlov
Kovarski Semen Aronovich	1919	Vilno	Vileyka	Voroshilov	brigade headquarters
Kovenskaya Anna Shayevna	1916	Byten	Brest	Sikorski's headquarters	Shchors
Kovenski Zelik Girshevich	1904	Dyatlovo	Baranovichi	Leninskaya	family detachment group
Kovinski Elya Girshevich	1909	Volkovyssk	Baranovichi	Pervomaiskaya	Oktyabr
Kovitskaya Khana Movshevna	1898	Dyatlovo	Baranovichi	Leninskaya	family detachment group
Kovner Emmanuil Borisovich	1903	from captivity, Mogilev	Mogilev	? 113	brigade ? 113
Kogan Aleksandr Yakovlevich	1927	Slizhin, Shklov district	Mogilev	? 115	? 2
Kogan Boris Ivanovich	1923	Ivye	Baranovichi	Stalin	Kirov
Kogan David Zakharovich	1918	from captivity	Grodno		Kalinin
Kogan Dmitri Yosifovich	1909	from captivity	Mogilev	? 14	? 128
Kogan Yosel Abramovich	1912	Vlodava (Poland)	Pinsk	Molotov	Shish
Kogan Maks Samuilovich	1924	Ivye	Baranovichi	Vpered (Forward)	A.Nevski
Kogan Moisei Grigorevich	1923	getto	Vileyka	Voroshilov	Kutuzov
Kogan Tatyana Markovna	1924	Minsk getto	Baranovichi	Stalin	Parkhomenko
Kogan Elya Shmuilovich	1922	Ivye	Baranovichi	Vpered (Forward)	A.Nevski
Kogan Yankel Shmuilovich	1921	Ivye	Baranovichi	Vpered (Forward)	A.Nevski
Kodenchik Grigori Yakovlevich	1911	Molchad	Baranovichi	Pervomaiskaya	Pervomaiski
Kodovets Lev Grigorevich	1921	iz br. Shashury	Minsk	Suvorov	
Kozhukhovich Dina Shlemovna	1924	Novogrudok getto	Baranovichi	Kirov	Ordzhonikidze
Kozhukhovich Movsha Shlemovich	1924	Novogrudok	Baranovichi	Leninskaya	Borba
Kozhushnik Movsha Rakhmielovich	1921	concentration camp	Pinsk	Kuibyshev	Shchors
Kozhushnik Sender Rakhmilevich	1918	concentration camp, Pogost-Zagorodski	Pinsk	Kuibyshev	Shchors
Kozak Movsha Elevich	1904	Dvorets	Baranovichi	Kalinin	
Kozberg Naum Rakhmelevich	1913	Kopyl getto	Minsk	Frunze	Budenny
Kozel Yosif Vulfovich	1926	from captivity, concentration camp, Mogilev	Mogilev	? 121	
Kozel Semen Khaimovich	1920	Baranovichskogo soev. "Bati"	Brest	Flegontov	Litvinov's
Kozinets Beines Mendelevich	1919	Glubokoye	Minsk	Voronyanski	supervision squard of the brigade headquarters

Kozinets Boris Mendelevich	1926	Makovoe, Begomlski district	Vileyka	Frunze	Fighter
Kozliner Abo Abramovich	1910	from the civil camp	Vileyka	4th Belorusskaya	? 6
Kozliner Mikhail Abramovich	1921	small town of Luzhki	Vileyka	Oktyabr	? 3
Kozliner Sara	1905	from the civil camp	Vileyka	4th Belorusskaya	? 6
Kozliner Khaim Abramovich	1917	Vilnius, getto	Baranovichi	Kirov	Ordzhonikidze
Kozlov Mikhail Mikhailovich	1920	from captivity	Mogilev	8th Zhunin's brigade	? 15
Kozlov Mikhail Yakovlevich	1918	Oshmiany, camp, prisoner of war	Baranovichi	Chapayev	Parkhomenko
Kozlova Mariya Mikhailovna	1919	Glinovka, NYevYelski district	Vitebsk	Stalin (Okhotin's)	brigade headquarters
Kozlovskaya Genya Khaimovna	1932	Mishkovichi	Baranovichi	Kalinin	
Kozlovskaya Leya Aronovna	1901	Mishkovichi	Baranovichi	Kalinin	
Kozlovskaya Marusya Khaimovna	1926	Mishkovichi	Baranovichi	Kalinin	
Kozlovskaya Mira Rubinovna	1930	Oshmiany	Baranovichi	Vpered (Forward)	Sibiryak
Kozlovskaya Khaya Khaimovna	1922	Mishkovichi	Baranovichi	Kalinin	
Kozlovski Yosif Khaimovich	1924	Mishkovichi	Baranovichi	Kalinin	
Kozlovski Khaim Yosifovich	1889	Mishkovichi	Baranovichi	Kalinin	
Kozlovski Yakov Mikhailovich	1923	Minsk	Baranovichi	Ponomarenko	25 years of the BSSR
Kozlovski Yakub Moiseyevich	1913	Pruzhany	Brest	Stalin	Chernyak
Koidanovskaya Anna Yakimovna	1915	Slutsk	Minsk	A.Nevski	? 1
Koifman Leizer Aizikovich	1915	from captivity	Vitebsk	Rokossovski	Kotovski
Kokin Lev Yevelevich	1928	Shklov	Baranovichi	Kirov	Ordzhonikidze
Kokin Lev Moiseyevich	1910	Lida	Baranovichi	Kalinin	
Kokina Asya Solomonovna	1918	Shklov district	Mogilev	Chekist	brigade headquarters
Kolachek Samuil Abramovich	1896	Ivienets	Baranovichi	Kalinin	
Kolbasnik Berta Girshevna	1920	Slutsk	Minsk	2nd Minskaya	Kutuzov
Kolbasnik Girsh Moiseyevich	1890	Slutsk	Minsk	2nd Minskaya	Kutuzov
Kolbshtein Izrail Mordukhovich	1908	Dyatlovo	Baranovichi	Leninskaya	family detachment group
Koleditskaya Polya Volfovna	1933	Novogrudok	Baranovichi	Kalinin	
Koleditski Aizik Volfovich	1939	Novogrudok	Baranovichi	Kalinin	
Koleditski Volf Davidovich	1900	Novogrudok	Baranovichi	Kalinin	
Kolmanovich Itska Yankelevich	1926	small town of Trobl, getto	Baranovichi	Kirov	Ordzhonikidze
Kolominski		Belarusian Staff of Partisan Movement	Gomel	Kozhar's	Shemyakin's group
Koltun Khatskel Moiseyevich	1911	getto, Vilno	Vileyka	Voroshilov	brigade headquarters
Koltunova Genya Elikimovna	1922	getto	Vileyka	Voroshilov	Bagration
Kol Samuil Isaakovich	1924	Ivienets	Baranovichi	Kalinin	
Koltrakht Mikhail Mendelevich	1914	from captivity, Bobruisk	Minsk	Parkhomenko	Kirov
Komarnitskaya VatSlava (Glory) Yulyanovna	1912	Warsaw	Baranovichi		
Komarnitski Lekh Genrikhovich	1934	Warsaw	Baranovichi	Kalinin	
Komarov Moris Aronovich	1927	Glussk	Palesye	detachment at the headquarters	
Komissarov Naum Matveyevich	1916	from captivity	Mogilev		? 45 "Za Rodinu (For Motherland)"
Kompnitski David Samundrovich	1925	from captivity	Baranovichi	Grizodubova	
Kondratovskaya Lidiya Arkadevna	1924	Minsk	Baranovichi	Chkalov	? 4 "Za Sovetskuyu Belarus"
Konik Elena GeorgiYevna	1930	Minsk	Baranovichi	detachment ? 106	
Konik Lazar Danilovich	1913	Ananchitsy, Starobin district	Minsk	Dyadi Koli	Stalin
Konlan G.	1927	Rogachev	Gomel		? 1 Rogachevski
Konne (Shuster) Anna Lvovna	1917	Minsk getto	Baranovichi	18th Frunze	Frunze
Konovich Zelda Lazarovna	1933	Lida	Baranovichi	Kalinin	
Konovich Yosif Motolevich	1916	iz partgruppy	Baranovichi	Lenin's komsomol	Matrosov
Konovich Yudel Peisakhovich	1910	Lida	Baranovichi	Kalinin	
Konovich Yankel Motylevich	1912	Sobatintsy	Baranovichi	Lenin's komsomol	Ivanov's
Konokovski Grigori Davidovich	1912	Byten, Baranovichi region	Pinsk	Kuibyshev	Ordzhonikidze
Kononik David Yefimovich	1929	Minsk getto	Minsk	Kirov	Kirov
Kononik Yelizaveta Davidovna	1910	Minsk getto	Minsk	Kirov	Kirov
Konopka Moisei Solomonovich	1922	Lida	Baranovichi	Voroshilov	Kalinin
Konopka Solomon Moiseyevich	1896	Lida	Baranovichi	Voroshilov	Kalinin
Konopko Genya Yefimovna	1931	Lida	Baranovichi	Kalinin	
Konopko Genya Yudelevna	1920	Voronovo	Baranovichi	Kalinin	
Konopko Girsh Yefimovich	1922	Lida	Baranovichi	Kalinin	
Konopko Lyuba Girshevna	1920	Lida	Baranovichi	Kalinin	
Konopko Minya Yudelevna	1929	Voronovo	Baranovichi	Kalinin	
Konopko Rakhil Yankelevich	1881	Voronovo	Baranovichi	Kalinin	
Konopko Riva Yudelevna	1918	Voronovo	Baranovichi	Kalinin	
Konopko Sonya Yudelevna	1924	Voronovo	Baranovichi	Kalinin	
Konopko Elya Yoselevich	1919	Novogrudok	Baranovichi	Kalinin	

Konopko Yudel Leibovich	1879	Voronovo	Baranovichi	Kalinin	
Konopny Abram Yosifovich	1914	Mir	Baranovichi	Kalinin	
Konskavalskaya Masha Yakubovna	1941	Warsaw	Baranovichi	Kalinin	
Konskavalskaya Khana Nokhimovna	1918	Warsaw	Baranovichi	Kalinin	
Kontorovich Ena Lipovich	1918	Minsk	Baranovichi	18th Frunze	Kutuzov
Kontorovich Ida SrolYevna	1915		Baranovichi	18th Frunze	provisional base of the brigade
Kontorovich Shlema Rubinovich	1923	Lida	Baranovichi	Kirov	Ordzhonikidze
Kontorovich Sholom Srolevich	1903	Minsk	Baranovichi	18th Frunze	provisional base of the brigade
Koniukh Maks Khaimovich	1926	Minsk	Baranovichi	detachment ? 106	
Koniukhovski Yakov Gotlibovich	1906	Voronovo	Baranovichi	Lenin's komsomol	Kotovski
Kopanska Roza Rubinovna	1919	getto, Vilno	Vileyka	Voroshilov	Kalinin
Kopach Mikhail Borisovich	1923	Braslav district	Vileyka	Zhdanov	
Kopelevich Abel Semenovich	1906	Minsk	Baranovichi	Chkalov	
Kopelevich Vladimir Semenovich	1907	Minsk	Baranovichi	Chkalov	
Kopelevich Yelizaveta Izrailevna	1909	Minsk	Baranovichi	Vpered (Forward)	family detachment group
Kopelevich Nikolai	1921	Postavy	Minsk	Voroshilov	? 1
Kopelevich Rakhil Girshevna	1914	Minsk	Baranovichi	Za Sovetskuyu Belarus	family detachment
Kopelevich Samuil Zalmanovich	1913	Voronovo	Baranovichi	Oktyabr	
Kopelevich Tsylya Khonovna	1928	Mir	Baranovichi	Kalinin	
Kopelevich Shevel Yankelevich	1896	Novogrudok	Baranovichi	Kalinin	
Kopelevich Shmusl Volfovich	1925	Mir	Baranovichi	Kalinin	
KopElyan Rakhil Grigorevna	1917	Minsk	Baranovichi	Kalinin	
KopElyanskaya Sara Leonidovna	1925	Ivatsevichi	Brest	Sikorski's headquarters	Shchors
Koper Semen Zalmanovich	1918	Miory	Minsk	Voroshilov	? 6
Kopernik Zelda Movshovna	1913	Korelichi	Baranovichi	Kalinin	
Kopershtein Leizer Elevich	1927	Mir	Baranovichi		
Kopershtein Elyash Kushelevich	1900	Mir	Baranovichi		
Kopershtein Ester Elevna	1929	Mir	Baranovichi		
Kopilevich Khatskel Khenokhovich	1922	Lida, camp	Belostok	A.Nevski	
Kopilovich Yuda Khaimovich	1916	Khotenchitsy	Minsk	Voronyanski	Kotovski
Kopil Genrikh Grigorevich	1910	from captivity	Baranovichi	18th Frunze	Frunze
Kopold Boris Moiseyevich	1923	Ivye	Baranovichi	Kalinin	
KoPolyan Sonya Abramovna	1908	Shchedrin	Palesye		Kirov
Kopotnikov Moisei Abramovich	1909	Boyanichi, Lyuban district	Minsk	Ponomarenko	Selnitski
Kopf Lev Yuinovich	1923	getto, Belostokskaya region	Brest		Kutuzov
Kopylevich ElLya Semenovich	1912	Krasnoye, getto	Baranovichi	Chkalov	
Kopytenko Vladimir Petrovich	1909	v. Stankovo	Minsk	Rokossovski	Chkalov
Kopytkina Sima Meyerovna	1905	Shchedrin, Parichi district	Minsk	Parkhomenko	Kirov
Kopytkina Sonya Yakovlevna	1925	Shchedrin, Parichi district	Minsk	Parkhomenko	Kirov
Kopyto Regina Berkovna	1926	getto Warsaw	Grodno	Vo imya Rodiny (In the name of Motherland)	Zhukov
Korenets Mikhail Ilyich	1916	Minsk getto	Baranovichi	Stalin	Parkhomenko
Koren Mikhail Abramovich	1921	Gorodishche district	Baranovichi	25 years of the BSSR	Grozny
Koren Mordukh Ovseyevich	1909		Baranovichi	Oktyabr	
Koren Samuil Yakovlevich	1915	Derechin	Belostok	A.Nevski	
Korestovski Mikhail Borisovich	1905	Gorodishche district	Baranovichi	25 years of the BSSR	Kotovski
Korzh Yakov Shlemovich	1912	Vein, Volyn region	Pinsk	Molotov	Kalinin
Korin Boris Davidovich	1897	Lida	Baranovichi	Kalinin	
Korin Samuil Yankelevich	1915	Derechin	Baranovichi	Pobieda	Pobieda
Korishch Mikhail Ilyich	1916	Minsk getto	Baranovichi	Chapayev	Chapayev
Kormolovski Rakhmel Isaakovich	1913	local	Baranovichi	Pobieda	Pobieda
Korn Abram Khaimovich	1900	Rubezhevichi	Baranovichi	Kalinin	
Korn Boris Solomonovich	1916	work camp, Poland	Pinsk	Molotov	Kalinin
Kornblyum Semen Borukhovich	1921	concentration camp	Pinsk	Kuibyshev	Shchors
Kornfeld Mikhail Volfovich	1909	Poland	Brest	Lenin	Zhukov
Koro Elya Viktorovich	1923	Minsk getto	Baranovichi	Stalin	Parkhomenko
Korob Eliya Zalmanovich	1910	Mery	Vileyka	4th Belorusskaya	? 6
Korobok Rakhil Vulfovna	1922	Minsk getto	Minsk		Mstitel (Revenger)
Korolitski Meyer Peisakovich	1894	Baranovichi	Baranovichi	Kalinin	
Korolitski Movsha Meyerovich	1921	Baranovichi	Baranovichi	Kalinin	
Korol Petr Semenovich	1922	v. Karpilovka	Minsk	Rokossovski	Chkalov
Koron David Elevich	1920	from the encirclement	Vitebsk	Donukalov	brigade headquarters
Korostovski small town ofB.	1905	Molchad	Baranovichi	Pervomaiskaya	Pervomaiski
Korotkov Yevsei Naumovich	1914	from captivity	Gomel	Za Rodinu (For Motherland)	Molotov

Korchminskaya Rozaliya Abramovna	1910	from the encirclement	Baranovichi	Dzerzhinski	Dzerzhinski
Kosei Zelik Ishmonovich	1907	Dyatlovo	Baranovichi	Kirov	Ordzhonikidze
Kosinskaya Lyuba Davidovna	1907	Minsk	Baranovichi	Kalinin	
Kosmaevich Sonya Abramovna	1915		Baranovichi	Oktyabr	
Kosover Leiba Shimonovich	1904	Rubezhevichi	Baranovichi	Kalinin	
Kosover Tsiko Nosovich	1920	Rubezhevichi	Baranovichi	Kalinin	
Kosovskaya Basya	1920	Bastarino, Kosovski district	Brest	Ponomarenko	Sovetskaya Belarus
Kosovski Vladimir Moiseyevich	1926	Viazan, Vileika region	Vitebsk	Dubov's	? 13
Kosovski Leizer Abramovich	1927	Shchuchin	Baranovichi	Kalinin	
Kosovski Mikhail Isaakovich	1915	Slonim	Brest	Sikorski's headquarters	Shchors
Kosovski Naum Meyerovich	1914	Minsk getto	Baranovichi	Chapayev	Parkhomenko
Kosovski Yakov Meyerovich	1924	Minsk getto	Baranovichi	Chapayev	Parkhomenko
Kospershtein Leizer Elevich	1927	Mir	Baranovichi	Kalinin	
Kospershtein Elyash Kushelevich	1900	Mir	Baranovichi	Kalinin	
Kospershtein Ester Elevna	1929	Mir	Baranovichi	Kalinin	
Kost Zelik Semenovich	1907	Ivienets, getto	Baranovichi	Kirov	Ordzhonikidze
Kostanenko Dora Isaakovna	1917	Cherven district, v. Voloduta	Minsk	Kirov	
Kostevich Maksim Venkelevich	1924	Rubezhevichi	Baranovichi	Stalin	Chapayev
KostElyanets Galina Abramovna	1923		Baranovichi	Chkalov	
KostElyanets Ilya Yoselevich	1901	Kosovo	Brest	Ponomarenko	Dmitrov
Kostrol Yakov Girshevich	1906	Dokshitski district, Selishche	Minsk	Zheleznyak	? 5
KostyLyanets Mikhail Yoselevich	1909	Kosovo	Brest	Ponomarenko	Dmitrov
Kostsevich Yankel Mordukovich	1889	Rubezhevichi	Baranovichi	Kalinin	
Kosyver Yosif Mordukhovich	1927	Minsk	Baranovichi	detachment ? 106	
Kot Zalman Shlemovich	1924	Jewish camp	Vileyka	Voroshilov	headquarters' production group
Kot Izrail Moiseyevich	1916	Belostok	Grodno	Samutin's group	Kirshner's group
Kotin Sema Abramovich	1929	Minsk	Baranovichi	detachment ? 106	
Kotin Fima Abramovich	1927	Minsk	Baranovichi	detachment ? 106	
Kotina Rakhil Girshevna	1900	Minsk	Baranovichi	detachment ? 106	
Kotina Sonya Ilinichna	1923	TsK LKSMB, Belarusian Staff of Partisan Movement	Vitebsk	1st Drissenskaya	KIM
Kotler Abram Alterovich	1920		Baranovichi	Oktyabr	
Kotler Izrail Moiseyevich	1920	Ivienets	Baranovichi	Kalinin	
Kotler Khaikem Abramovich	1922	small town of Trobl, getto	Baranovichi	Kirov	Ordzhonikidze
KotLyanik Nina AnufriYevna	1923	Minsk	Minsk	Rokossovski	Chkalov
KotLyar Yosif Gertovich	1902		Vitebsk	1st Drissenskaya	Besstrashny (Fearless)
KotLyar Leonid Abramovich		Dolginovo	Minsk	Voronyanski	Borba
KotLyar Falvyel Nisonovich	1926	Minsk	Baranovichi	Chkalov	? 4 "Za Sovetskuyu Belarus"
KotLyar Sholom Nisonovich	1920	Minsk	Baranovichi	Chkalov	? 4 "Za Sovetskuyu Belarus"
Kotova Breiza Gershevna	1896	Minsk	Baranovichi	detachment ? 106	
Koton Lev Lazarevich	1923	Dolginovo	Minsk	Voronyanski	Kotovski
Kofman Aizik Zoltanovich	1902	from the encirclement	Palesye	2nd Kalinkovichskaya	
Kofman Arkadi Zakharovich	1912	from the encirclement	Palesye	99th Kalinkovichskaya	Voroshilov
Kofman Khaim Yosifovich	1903	Zatishe, Oktyabr district	Palesye	detachment at the headquarters	
Kokh Aron Yakovlevich	1919	Minsk	Baranovichi	Za Sovetskuyu Belarus	Shturm
Kochanovich Vladimir Yosifovich	1922	Mir	Baranovichi	Za Sovetskuyu Belarus	Shturm
Kochenbogin Shlema Girshovich	1927	Minsk getto	Baranovichi	Stalin	Parkhomenko
Kocher Kalman Mordukhovich	1919	from the civil camp	Vileyka	4th Belorusskaya	? 6
Kocher Semen Zalmanovich	1918	getto	Vileyka	Voroshilov	Chapayev
Kocherginski Shmeler Vulfovich	1908		Vileyka	Voroshilov	brigade headquarters
Kocherovski Mikhail Aronovich	1915	Kharkovichi, Bragin district	Palesye		Kotovski
Koshits Moisei Markovich	1900	Minsk	Vitebsk	Nikitin's	? 2
Koshmanovich Itsko Isaakovich	1926	Voronovo	Baranovichi	Kirov	Ordzhonikidze
Koshchanskaya Yudes Mordukhovna	1925	Lida	Baranovichi	Kalinin	
Kravets Boris Yosifovich	1907	Novogrudok	Baranovichi	Kalinin	
Kravets Volf Abramovich	1909	Dyatlovo	Baranovichi	Leninskaya	Borba
Kravets Getsel Mordukhovich	1926	Lenin	Pinsk	Komarov-Korzh's	2 group
Kravets Girsh Borukhovich	1923	from captivity	Palesye	? 225	Chapayev
Kravets Yosif Abramovich	1908	Yelsk, left by RK KP(b)B	Palesye	37th Yelskaya	Bolshevik
Kravets Isaak Mendelevich	1916		Baranovichi	Oktyabr	
Kravets Leva Abramovich	1930	Minsk	Baranovichi	detachment ? 106	
Kravets Lilya Aronovna	1921	Novogrudok	Baranovichi	Kalinin	

Kravets Lyuba Khonovna	1923	Lida	Baranovichi	Leninskaya	Krasnogvardeiski
Kravets Mariya Yosifovna	1911	Lida	Baranovichi	Leninskaya	Borba
Kravets Maya Abramovna	1932	Minsk	Baranovichi	detachment ? 106	
Kravets Mordukh Naftalevich	1904	Lenin	Pinsk	Komarov-Korzh's	2 group
Kravets Roza Mordukhovna	1918	Novogrudok	Baranovichi	Kalinin	
Kravets Solomon Borisovich	1925	Slavkovichi, Glussk district	Brest	? 99 Gulyaev	Voronov's
Kravets Khaim Yosifovich	1911	Novogrudok	Baranovichi	Kalinin	
Kravetskaya Sonya Nokhimovna	1908	Dvorets	Baranovichi	Kalinin	
Kravchenko Boris Yosifovich	1923	Radichevo, Slutsk district	Belostok		separate detachment Budenny
Kravchik Berka Yevseyevich	1913	Lakhva	Palesye	? 130	? 132
Kravchik Girsh Zelikovich	1911	Dvorets	Baranovichi	Kalinin	
Kravchik Kazimir Leizerovich	1917	Poland	Pinsk	Molotov	Kalinin
Kravchik Meyer Yevseyevich	1920	Lakhva	Palesye	? 130	? 132
Kravchik Mordukh Moiseyevich	1916	Kosovo	Brest	Ponomarenko	Sovetskaya Belarus
Kravchik Simon Yevseyevich	1928	Lakhva	Palesye	? 130	? 132
Kravchik Sonya Yosifovna	1925		Palesye	? 130	? 132
Kravchik Sholom Moiseyevich	1924	Kosovo	Brest	Ponomarenko	Sovetskaya Belarus
Kravchik Esfir Solomonovna	1925	Pruzhany	Brest	Ponomarenko	Sovetskaya Belarus
Kravchinskaya Dora Tevelevna	1910	Minsk	Baranovichi	Stalin	Budenny
Kravchinski Vladimir Yosifovich	1908	Minsk	Baranovichi	Stalin	Budenny
Kravchinski Dima Isaakovich	1918	camp, prisoner of war Viazma	Minsk	2nd Minskaya	Sokol
Kraer Zelik Khaimovich	1914	Dyatlovo	Baranovichi	Leninskaya	Borba
Kraer Shifra Khaimovna	1914	Dyatlovo	Baranovichi	Leninskaya	Borba
Kraizelman Raisa Izrailevna	1916	Minsk	Baranovichi	Ponomarenko	Voronov's
Krainovich Bronya Mordukhovna	1914	Dzerzhinsk	Baranovichi	18th Frunze	Frunze
Krais David Solomonovich	1920	Poland, a small partisan group	Pinsk	Molotov	Lazo
Krakov Solomon Khaimovich	1916	Minsk	Baranovichi	Vpered (Forward)	family detachment group
Krakova Yelizaveta Aleksandrovna	1915	Minsk	Baranovichi	Chkalov	reserve group
Krakovski Ruvim Yakovlevich	1920	Sverzhen	Minsk	Chapayev	Ponomarenko
Krakovski Tevel Moiseyevich		Chernikhovo	Baranovichi	Kalinin	
Kramarov Naum Moiseyevich	1905	from the encirclement	Mogilev	Mogilev undergroud of the RC CP(b)B	
Kramarski Yakov Moiseyevich	1902	Nesvizh	Baranovichi	Kalinin	
Kramash Litman Leikovich	1908	Poland	Brest	Stalin	Chernyak
Kramolovski Rakhmil Eskovich	1913	Warsaw	Baranovichi	Pobieda	Pobieda
Krants Movsha Abramovich	1923	Stolbtsy	Baranovichi	Kalinin	
Krants Semen Abramovich	1914	Koldychevo, getto	Baranovichi	Pervomaiskaya	Ya.Kolas
Krasik Mikhail Abramovich	1923	Klimovichi	Vitebsk	Lenin	2nd
Krasilov Etya Yoselevich	1907	Derevno	Baranovichi	Kalinin	
Krasilshchik Isaak Gertsevich	1913	Baranovichi	Pinsk		Chukhlai
Krasilshchik Yakov Vulfovich	1912	from the encirclement	Palesye	? 123	Kalakin
Krasinski Abram Borisovich	1924	Minsk	Baranovichi	detachment ? 106	
Krasinski Berl Nakhmanovich	1890	Minsk	Baranovichi		
Kraskin Khaim Aronovich	1905	Mogilev, concentration camp	Pinsk		? 200
Krasnik Naum Genadevich	1911	Chernevo, Borisov district	Minsk	Shchors	Chapayev
Krasnovski Semen Yankelevich	1890	Derechin	Baranovichi	Pobieda	Pobieda
Krasnovski Yankel Simkhovich	1925	Derechin	Baranovichi	Leninskaya	Leninski
Krasnoperko Anna Davidovna	1925	Minsk	Minsk	Stalin	
Krasnoperko Rakhil Aronovna	1902	Minsk	Minsk	Stalin	
Krasnostavskaya Yevgeniya Lazarevna	1923	Kosovo	Brest	Sikorski's headquarters	Shchors
Kraut Mariya Simonovna	1917	Glubokoye	Vileyka	CC of the CP(b)B	brigade sanitary service
Kraut Mordukh Simonovich	1917	Glubokoye	Vileyka	CC of the CP(b)B	brigade sanitary service
Krein Gita Abramovna	1907				
Kreinin Isaak	1908	Belarusian Staff of Partisan Movement	Palesye		Chapayev
Kreinin Lev Senderovich	1908				
Kremen Zorakh Abramovich	1921	Slonim	Brest		Kotovski
Kremen Khaya Khaimovna	1920	family detachment camp	Belostok	A.Nevski	
Kremen Yankel Izrailevich	1921	Belitsa	Baranovichi	Leninskaya	family detachment group
Kremer Abram Yosifovich	1900	Dokshitsy	Minsk	Zheleznyak	? 1
Kremer Genya Berkovna	1909	Jewish camp Dolginovo	Minsk	Voronyanski	Pobieda
Kremer Zalman Yosifovich	1912	Dokshitsy	Minsk	Zheleznyak	? 1
Kremer Zinaida Maksimovna	1927	Minsk	Vileyka	Frunze	Voroshilov
Kremer Yosif Natanovich	1903	Jewish camp Dolginovo	Minsk	Voronyanski	Pobieda
Kremer Isaak Naumovich	1902	Jewish camp Dolginovo	Minsk	Voronyanski	Pobieda

Name	Year	Origin	Region	Brigade/Unit	Detachment/Group
Kremer Moisei Mendelevich	1926	Kurenets	Vileyka	Voroshilov	brigade headquarters
Kremer Nina Petrovna	1931	Ilya	Minsk	Shturmovaya	Grozny
Kremer Ruvim Zalmanovich	1913	from behind the front line	Vitebsk	Frunze	Petrenko's group
Kremer Khema Yosifovich	1907	from captivity	Mogilev	8th Zhunin's brigade	? 12
Kremer Yankel Yosifovich	1914	Dokshitsy	Minsk	Zheleznyak	? 1
Krechmer Lyuba Pavlovna	1924	Batsevichi, Klichev district	Mogilev		? 115 Dolgov-Rudov's
Krivitskaya Sarra Lazarevna	1917	Starobin	Pinsk	Komarov-Korzh's	4 group
Krivitski Abram Yakovlevich	1915	getto	Vileyka	4th Belorusskaya	? 6
Krivitski Zalman Rubinovich	1926	Krulevshchizna	Minsk	1st Antifashistskaya	? 5
Krivitski Meyer Yankelevich	1912	Leompol	Vileyka	4th Belorusskaya	? 5
Krivoi Khonon Leibovich	1898	Belarusian Staff of Partisan Movement	Brest	groups of party leaders	Za Rodinu (For Motherland)
Krivolapov Yuri Samuilovich	1923	Belarusian Staff of Partisan Movement	Minsk	Special groups	Kaputski's group
Krivosheev Vladimir Abramovich	1902	from the encirclement	Minsk	Parkhomenko	Ordzhonikidze
Krivoshein Grigori Isaakovich	1925	Ukhvala, Krupki district	Mogilev	Ilyin's	? 5
Krivosheina Sima Solomonovna	1929	Minsk	Baranovichi	detachment ? 106	
Krivosheina Esfir Mendeleyevna	1906	Bobr	Baranovichi	detachment ? 106	
Krigel Basya Markovna	1915	Minsk	Baranovichi	detachment ? 106	
Kriger Mariya Borisovna	1907	Minsk	Minsk	2nd Minskaya	Kutuzov
Krimalovski Rakhmil Yoselevich	1913	Derechin	Belostok	A.Nevski	
Krimgolts German Abramovich	1905	br. Rodionova	Minsk	1st Antifashistskaya	
Krimgolts Mikhail Abramovich	1918	br. Rodionova	Minsk	1st Antifashistskaya	
Krimgolts Mulya Samuilovich	1912	br. Rodionova	Minsk	1st Antifashistskaya	? 6
Kriok Galina Semenovna	1927	Galynka, Berezino district	Mogilev		? 278
Krislav Bellya Mikhailovna	1910	Vilno	Baranovichi	Pervomaiskaya	Oktyabr
Kristal Anna Lazarevna	1924	Minsk	Minsk	Rokossovski	Chkalov
Kristal Leonid Aizikovich	1929	Minsk	Baranovichi	detachment ? 106	
Krits German Davidovich	1912	Novogrudok	Baranovichi	Kalinin	
Krichevski Gennadi Petrovich	1936	Minsk	Mogilev	208th partisan regiment	? 4
Kroz Moisei Isaakovich		Belarusian Staff of Partisan Movement	Vitebsk		
Kroik Sonya Yakovlevna	1915	malaia group from the forest (Pinsk)	Pinsk	Sovetskaya Belarus	Kutuzov
Krol Gedali Shmulevich	1922	Poland	Brest	Lenin	Zhukov
Krol Sofiya Lvovna	1916	Minsk	Baranovichi	detachment ? 106	
Kroman David Movshevich	1920	getto, Pruzhany	Brest	Ponomarenko	Kirov
Kron Abram Khaimovich	1900	Rubezhevichi	Baranovichi		
Krotina Manya Lazarevna	1924	Minsk	Baranovichi	detachment ? 106	
Krotina Tanya Lvovna	1923	Minsk	Baranovichi	detachment ? 106	
Krotina Ester Meyerovna	1901	Minsk	Baranovichi	detachment ? 106	
Kroshinskaya Dora Solomonovna	1914	Minsk getto	Baranovichi	18th Frunze	brigade headquarters
Kroshinski Solomon N.	1904	Baranovichi	Pinsk	Budenny	Kotovski
Kroshnits Khaim Yakovlevich	1909	Baranovichi	Pinsk	Budenny	Kotovski
Kru Izidor Germanovich	1905	Belostok	Baranovichi	1st Baranovichskaya	sabotage detachment "Orel"
Kruglikov Gerasim Litmanovich	1910	Slutsk district, Lenino	Minsk	Frunze	Dzerzhinski
Krugly Kalman Shlemovich	1918	concentration camp	Pinsk	Kuibyshev	Shchors
KrugLyanskaya Nina Semenovna	1916	Girivo, Gressk district	Minsk	Voroshilov	B.Khmelnitski
Krugman Isaak Yudelevich	1926	Dyatlovo	Baranovichi	Leninskaya	Borba
Krulevetski Samuil Peisakhovich	1895	concentration camp	Pinsk	Kuibyshev	Shchors
Krulenin Kalman Abramovich	1897	Belarusian Staff of Partisan Movement	Minsk	Special groups	gr. Gerasimovich
Krum Tsemakh Movshovich	1917	Solechniki	Baranovichi	Kalinin	
Krupnik Meyer Yosifovich	1925	Rakitnoe, Rovno region.	Palesye	37th Yelskaya	Za Rodinu (For Motherland)
Krupskaya Leya Pinkhusovna	1903	Lida	Baranovichi	Pervomaiskaya	Oktyabr
Krupski Abram Simkhovich	1922	Lida	Baranovichi	Voroshilov	Kalinin
Krupchik Movsha Itskovich	1911	concentration camp	Pinsk	Kuibyshev	Shchors
Kruspodin Rubin Mendelevich	1907	Zabolote	Baranovichi	Chkalov	? 4 "Za Sovetskuyu Belarus"
Krushgant Sarra Peisakhovna	1913	Minsk	Baranovichi	detachment ? 106	
Krynitski Berko Faivelevich	1893	Mir	Baranovichi	Kalinin	
Krynitski Leizer Abramovich	1907	Mir	Baranovichi	Kalinin	
Kuvelevich Sulamita Ilinichna	1916	Lida	Baranovichi	Kirov	Za Sovetskuyu Belarus
Kugel Berta Lvovna	1921	Minsk	Baranovichi	detachment ? 106	
Kugel Lyubov Naumovna	1925	Minsk	Minsk	3rd Minskaya	25years of the A-ULCYL
Kugel Sofiya Danilovna	1912	Minsk	Baranovichi	Vpered (Forward)	family detachment group
Kugel Elya Isaakovich	1927	Minsk	Baranovichi	detachment ? 106	
Kudevitski Borukh Pinkhusovich	1910	detachment "Mest"	Vileyka	Voroshilov	headquarters' production group

Kudevitski Leiba Pinkhusovich	1913	detachment "Mest"	Vileyka	Voroshilov	headquarters' production group
Kudenchik Grigori Yakovlevich	1911	Gorodishche district	Baranovichi	25 years of the BSSR	Grozny
Kuzevets Anna FoleyYevna	1918	Jewish camp Dolginovo	Minsk	Voronyanski	Pobieda
Kuzevets Yosif Folevich	1920	Jewish camp Dolginovo	Minsk	Voronyanski	Pobieda
Kuzenets Venyamin	1913		Minsk	Voronyanski	Pobieda
Kuzenets Zelik Motovich	1915	Milcha	Minsk	Voronyanski	Pobieda
Kuznets Golda Yakovlevna	1909	Byten	Brest	Ponomarenko	Sovetskaya Belarus
Kuznets Leiba Yoselevich	1893	Byten	Brest	Ponomarenko	Sovetskaya Belarus
Kuznetsov Yosif Zalmanovich	1906	Minsk	Baranovichi	detachment ? 106	
Kuznetsov Leon Davidovich	1908	Tolpino, Chashniki district	Vitebsk	Sennenskaya brigade (Leonov's)	Za Rodinu (For Motherland)
Kuznetsov Mikhail Isakovich	1930	Lida	Baranovichi	Kirov	Za Sovetskuyu Belarus
Kuznetsov Timofei Romanovich	1909	from the encirclement	Mogilev	? 14	? 127
Kuznetsova Vera Semenovna	1924	Rogachev	Gomel	8th Rogachevskaya	? 257
Kuznetsova Fruza Isaakovna	1924	Chubakovo	Mogilev	? 117	? 124
Kukelko Anton Mendelevich	1902	Lomzha	Baranovichi	Kalinin	
Kukerman Roza Yefimovna	1926	Minsk getto	Baranovichi	Ponomarenko	Voronov's
Kulaker Abram Leibovich	1916	Lyakhovichi	Pinsk	Lenin	Kutuzov
Kulaker Sergei Leibovich	1928	from the brigade ismall town of Lenina Pinskogo soedineniia	Belostok		separate detachment Dzerzhinski
Kulakovski A.N.	1914	Derechin	Baranovichi	Pobieda	Pobieda
Kulakovski Yefim Moiseyevich	1923	Kopyl district, Tekhovets	Minsk	Kotovski	Shashury
Kulakovski Semen Moiseyevich	1921	Tekhovka, Kopyl district	Minsk	Voroshilov	Kotovski
Kulevitski David Leibovich	1928	from the civil camp	Baranovichi	Grizodubova	Chkalov
Kulevitski Leiba Itskovich	1898	from the civil camp	Baranovichi	Grizodubova	Chkalov
Kulesh Mikhail Aktonovich	1921	small town of Zhuravichi	Baranovichi	Kirov	Ordzhonikidze
Kumbarg Konstantin Solomonovich		Vitebsk	Smolenski partisan regiment	battallion ? 1	
Kumok Esfir Semenovna	1913	Stolbtsy	Baranovichi	detachment ? 106	
Kunikovski Grigori Davidovich	1912		Pinsk	Lenin	Kutuzov
Kunin-Lakushenko Mikhail Petrovich	1916	from captivity	Minsk	Kirov	Frunze
Kunitsa Moisei Meyerovich	1921	Slonim	Baranovichi	Pobieda	Pobieda
Kuper Samuil Vigdorovich	1913	Jewish camp	Vileyka	Voroshilov	headquarters' production group
Kuper Yasha Moiseyevich	1926	Minsk	Baranovichi	Za Sovetskuyu Belarus	family detachment
Kuperberg Isaak Berkovich	1920	Minsk	Baranovichi	detachment ? 106	
Kuperberg Leib Kopelevich	1921	getto, Vilno	Vileyka	Voroshilov	brigade headquarters
Kuperberg Rakhil Leibovna	1921	getto, Vilno	Vileyka	Voroshilov	brigade headquarters
Kuperman Borukh Yankelevich	1914		Minsk	Voronyanski	Pobieda
Kuperman Zina Semenovna	1927	Belynichi	Mogilev	Chekist	Mon. group
Kuperman Yakov Alekseyevich	1925	Shatski district	Minsk	Voroshilov	Kotovski
Kuperman Yakov Borisovich	1918	from captivity	Vileyka	CC of the CP(b)B	brigade headquarters
Kupershmit Raisa Solomonovna	1905		Palesye	? 130	? 132
Kupershtok FaLya Zelikovich	1919	Minsk	Minsk	2nd Minskaya	Suvorov
Kupchenko-Gerbert Boris Lvovich	1919	from the encirclement	Mogilev	? 13	? 46
Kur Bronya Mordukhovna	1920	Gorodok	Baranovichi	Za Sovetskuyu Belarus	family detachment
Kuranets Rubin Moiseyevich	1926	Disna	Vitebsk	Chapayev	detachments
Kuretski Kopel Davidovich	1907	Nivki, Vileika region	Vitebsk	Chapayev	detachments
Kuretski Nikolai Davidovich	1918	Plino, Vitebsk region	Vitebsk	Ponomarenko	Golovchenko
KurLyand Foma Aronovich	1915	Ukraine	Pinsk	Kirov	Za Rodinu (For Motherland)
Kurman Tsiallov Yefimovich	1923	Minsk	Baranovichi	18th Frunze	Kutuzov
Kurchevski Abram Davidovich	1909	Krynki	Grodno	Samutin's group	Kirshner's group
Kurchik Alik Moiseyevich	1925	Bobruisk	Mogilev	? 537	
Kurshn Yankel Benyaminovich	1897	Rubezhevichi	Baranovichi	Kalinin	
Kusik Freida Donovna	1918	a small group from the forest (Pinsk)	Pinsk	Sovetskaya Belarus	Kutuzov
Kusin Solomon Ilyich		Vileyka	4th Belorusskaya	? 6	
Kusko David Izrailevich	1913	detachment "Mest"	Vileyka	Voroshilov	headquarters' production group
Kustanovich Alter Abramovich	1911	v. Pogost	Minsk	Bragin	Gastello
Kustanovich Dora Borisovna	1899	Lyuban	Minsk	Kirov ? 100	brigade headquarters
Kustanovich Zhenya Osherovich	1927	Lyuban district, Zhivun	Minsk	Bragin	Zaslonov
Kustanovich Yosif Elkonovich	1914	Starye Dorogi	Minsk	Ponomarenko	Gorbachev
Kustanovich Khaim Solomonovich	1927	Lyuban	Minsk	Chkalov	Gromov
Kukharzh Emil Emanovich	1926	camp, prisoner of war	Baranovichi	Komsomolets	Kalinin
Kutsevitskaya Mira Mikhailovna	1913	getto, Vilno	Vileyka	Voroshilov	brigade headquarters
Kutsevitski Samuil Moiseyevich	1911	Vilno, getto	Vileyka	Voroshilov	brigade headquarters

Kutsman Yakov Davidovich	1914	from captivity	Vitebsk	Voroshilov	Bolshevik
Kucher Aizik Moshkovich	1924	Vlodava (Poland)	Pinsk	Molotov	Shish
Kuchinerovski Shaya Peisakhovich	1930	Molchad	Baranovichi	Kutuzov	
Kushelevich Abram Leizerovich	1930	Lida	Baranovichi	Kalinin	
Kushelevich Bellya Berkovna	1898	Lida	Baranovichi	Kalinin	
Kushelevich Yosel Leizerovich	1926	Lida	Baranovichi	Kalinin	
Kushelevich Leizer Khaimovich	1898	Lida	Baranovichi	Kalinin	
Kushelevich Sinai Leizerovich	1930	Lida	Baranovichi	Kalinin	
Kushinskaya Eshka Abramovna	1930	Novogrudok	Baranovichi	Kalinin	
Kushnarev Ilya Davidovich	1923		Vitebsk	Nikitin's	? 3
Kushner Zeidel Khonovich	1892	Novogrudok	Baranovichi	Kalinin	
Kushner Isaak Grigorevich	1924	Lyuban	Minsk	Chkalov	Gromov
Kushner Leya ZeldElevna	1926	Novogrudok	Baranovichi	Kalinin	
Kushner Raisa Borisovna	1918	Peredopy, Klichev district	Mogilev	? 537	
Kushner Raya ZeldElevna	1923	Novogrudok	Baranovichi	Kalinin	
Kushner Khaim Khonovich	1895	Novogrudok	Baranovichi	Kalinin	
Kushner Khana Grigorevna	1909	Minsk	Baranovichi		
Kushner Shevel Khaimovich	1910	small town of Vasilishki	Baranovichi	Vpered (Forward)	A.Nevski
Kushner Shlema Leibovich	1922	Baranovichi	Baranovichi	Kalinin	
Kushner Yankel Tankhelevich	1924	Vasilishki	Baranovichi	Kalinin	
Kushnerovski Shmaya Peisakovich	1929	Molchad	Baranovichi	Kalinin	
Kushnir Grigori Abramovich	1926	concentration camp	Minsk	Chkalov	Zheleznyak
Kushchinskaya Lyuba Girshevna	1894	Novogrudok	Baranovichi	Kalinin	
Kushchinskaya Khaya Zalmanovna	1925	Novogrudok	Baranovichi	Kalinin	
Kushchinskaya Eshka Abramovna	1930	Novogrudok	Baranovichi		
Kushchinski Daniel Mordukhovich	1904	Novogrudok	Baranovichi	Kalinin	
Kushchinski Samuil Mordukhovich	1910	Novogrudok getto	Baranovichi	Kirov	Ordzhonikidze
Laanes Yosif Samuilovich	1916	Belarusian Staff of Partisan Movement	Vitebsk	Belyaev's filmgroups	Mokhnorylov's group
Labeznik Greinom Yakovlevich	1915	Lenino, Pinsk region	Minsk	Ponomarenko	A.Nevski
Labeznik Movsha Yakovlevich	1912	Gantsevichi	Minsk	Bragin	Gastello
Labeznik Faina Yakovlevna	1919	Minsk region	Pinsk	Molotov	brigade headquarters
Labzovski Mikhail Berkovich	1921	Derechin	Baranovichi	Pobieda	Pobieda
Lava Siman		Belostok	Grodno	Samutin's group	Kirshner's group
Lavit Abram Moiseyevich	1920	Lida getto	Baranovichi	Kirov	brigade headquarters
Lavit Isaak Sepselevich	1923	Molodechno, getto	Baranovichi	Za Sovetskuyu Belarus	Shturm
Lavit Leonid Sanovich	1910	Volozhin	Baranovichi	Chkalov	
Lavit Shaya Shlomovich	1916	Volozhin	Baranovichi	Za Sovetskuyu Belarus	Kirov
Lagman Yosif Ilyich	1914	Nesvizh	Grodno	Vo imya Rodiny (In the name of Motherland)	Kutuzov
Lagotker Aizik Benyaminovich	1922	Novogrudok	Baranovichi	Kirov	Ordzhonikidze
Lagun Yakov Yefimovich	1909	Slutsk	Mogilev	partisan regiment ? 277	? 277
Lazarevich Yosif Yustinovich	1921	Zatishe	Brest	Yazykovicha	Bozhenko
Lazovski Isaak Faivelevich	1911	Novogrudok	Baranovichi	Kalinin	
Lazovski Meyer Ovseyevich	1912	Molchad	Baranovichi	Kalinin	
Lazovski Nevakh Yosifovich	1908	Dvorets	Baranovichi	Kalinin	
Laiselfish Irena LeontYevna	1924	Warsaw	Brest	Dzerzhinski	Kalinin
Laitanzen Semen Isaakovich	1918	Minsk	Minsk	3rd Minskaya	Niepobedimy (Unde-feated)
Laksina Sofiya Aronovna	1923	Baranovichi	Brest	Dzerzhinski	Chertkov
Langbord Izrail Khaimovich	1906	Minsk	Baranovichi	detachment ? 106	
Langbort Ovsei Abramovich	1915	Dyatlovo	Baranovichi	Leninskaya	Borba
Langer Mikhail Davidovich	1910	from captivity	Mogilev	Mogilev undergroud of the RC CP(b)B	
Landbord Bella Solomonovna	1910	Minsk	Baranovichi	detachment ? 106	
Landbord Lazar Aizikovich	1930	Minsk	Baranovichi	detachment ? 106	
Landen Aleksei Izakovich	1917	work camp	Pinsk	Molotov	
Lando Natan Borisovich	1912				
Lantsevitskaya Dudis Khaimovna	1920	Derechin	Baranovichi	Pobieda	Pobieda
Lantsevitski Lazar Yankelevich	1922	Volkovysk	Baranovichi	Pobieda	Pobieda
Lantsevitski Movsha Leizerovich	1912	Derechin	Baranovichi	Pobieda	Suvorov
Lantsevitski Tevel Khaimovich	1913	Derechin	Baranovichi	Leninskaya	Leninski
Lantsevitski Yakov Yosifovich	1916	Baranovichi	Baranovichi	detachment ? 106	
Lantsevskaya Yudel Khaimovna	1920	Derechin	Baranovichi	Pobieda	Pobieda
Lapatitski Nona Leibovich	1914	Nesvizh	Minsk	Chapayev	Ponomarenko
Lapido Tsilya Zelikovna	1925	Minsk	Baranovichi	detachment ? 106	
Lapidus Beba Romanovna	1924	Minsk getto	Minsk		Mstitel (Revenger)
Lapidus Vadim Samuilovich	1909	Minsk	Vitebsk	Nikitin's	? 4
Lapidus Genya Girshevna	1904	Minsk	Minsk	2nd Minskaya	Kutuzov
Lapidus Genya Solomonovna	1926	Minsk	Baranovichi	detachment ? 106	
Lapidus Yevsei Girshovich	1918	Minsk getto	Minsk	Ponomarenko	Za Rodinu (For Mother-land)

Lapidus Yefim Izrailevich		Minsk	Baranovichi	Vpered (Forward)	
Lapidus Izrail Abramovich	1909	Minsk	Minsk	2nd Minskaya	Suvorov
Lapidus Maks Samuilovich	1906	Minsk	Vitebsk	Nikitin's	? 4
Lapidus Masha Abramovna	1918	Minsk	Minsk	2nd Minskaya	Kutuzov
Lapidus Mikhail Venyaminovich	1912	from captivity	Minsk	Bragin	Gastello
Lapidus Mikhail Rafailovich	1924	Minsk getto	Minsk	2nd Minskaya	Kutuzov
Lapidus Nikolai Ivanovich	1920	from captivity	Mogilev	? 14	? 128
Lapidus Pavel Abramovich	1921	from captivity	Minsk	Kirov	Budenny
Lapidus Samuil Davidovich	1886	Radoshkovichi	Minsk	Voronyanski	Kotovski
Lapidus Semen Abramovich	1900	Minsk	Minsk	2nd Minskaya	Kutuzov
Lapidus Semen Lvovich	1931	Minsk getto	Baranovichi	Ponomarenko	Voronov's
Lapidus Semen Semenovich	1921	Minsk	Baranovichi	Vpered (Forward)	Chkalov
Lapin Matvei Leontevich	1917	Chigirin, Gomel region	Baranovichi	Rokossovski	Ponomarenko
Lapkovskaya Lyubov Zakharovna	1925	Antonovo, Rossony district	Vitebsk	Stalin (Okhotin's)	brigade headquarters
Lapkovski Leonid Zakharovich	1929	Antonovo, Rossony district	Vitebsk	Stalin (Okhotin's)	Stalin
Lapukh Lyudvik Shayevich	1913	Poland	Brest	Stalin	Chernyak
Lati Malka Davidovna	1923	Novogrudok getto	Baranovichi	Kirov	Ordzhonikidze
Lakhuto David Borisovich	1923	concentration camp Gantsevichi	Minsk	Chkalov	Zheleznyak
Lashitser Genrikh Aronovich	1923	Gorodok	Baranovichi	Chkalov	? 4 "Za Sovetskuyu Belarus"
Lashchinski Leiba Khaimovich	1925	Derechin	Baranovichi	Kirov	Baltiets
Lebski Lev Mironovich	1924	Omsk	Vitebsk	VLKSM	Sibiryak
Lev Bella Shlemovna	1924	Kletsk	Minsk	Suvorov	
Lev Boris Leizerovich	1910	Jewish camp, Drogichin	Pinsk	Shubetidze	Ordzhonikidze
Lev Izrail Isaakovich	1920	getto	Baranovichi	Lenin's komsomol	Kotovski
Lev Yosif Abramovich	1926	Baranovichi	Baranovichi	Kalinin	
Lev Isaak	1910	Derechin	Baranovichi	Pobieda	Pobieda
Lev Mikhail Andreevich	1915	from captivity	Mogilev	? 537	
Levdanskaya Irina Naumovna	1913	Izabelovo, Pukhovichi district	Minsk	Plamya	Slava (Glory)
Levenbuk Gilel Girshevich	1920	Dyatlovo	Baranovichi	Leninskaya	Borba
Levenbuk Ilya Grigorevich	1923	Dyatlovo	Baranovichi	Leninskaya	Krasnogvardeiski
Levenbuk Mira Girshevna	1918	Dyatlovo	Baranovichi	Leninskaya	Borba
Levenchik Grigori Tevelevich	1926	Minsk	Baranovichi	Chkalov	
Levertov Boris Venyaminovich	1899	Central Committee of the CP (b) B	Gomel	Shemyakin's "Vpered (Forward)"	Makagonov's
Levi Sima Shlemovna	1908	local	Baranovichi	Pobieda	Pobieda
Leviev Mikhail Khiiaevich	1920	from captivity	Minsk	Dyadi Koli	Dzerzhinski
Levik Samuil A.	1920	Derechin	Baranovichi	Pobieda	Pobieda
Levin Aizik Ziselevich	1916	Radoshkovichi	Minsk	Voronyanski	Suvorov
Levin Boris Abramovich	1920	from the encirclement	Mogilev	208th regiment	left the detachment from the moment organization
Levin Boris Borisovich	1920		Minsk	Voronyanski	Mstitel (Revenger)
Levin Borukh Samuilovich	1910	Lida	Baranovichi	Leninskaya	family detachment group
Levin Gennadi Yuryevich	1928	Minsk	Baranovichi	Baranovchi underground RC of the CP(b) B and IDC	
Levin Girsh Getselevich	1908	Rubezhevichi	Baranovichi	Kalinin	
Levin Girsh Mordukovich	1911	Rubezhevichi	Baranovichi	Kalinin	
Levin David Yosifovich	1916	Minsk getto	Minsk	Ponomarenko	Za Rodinu (For Motherland)
Levin David Lazarevich	1918	Minski camp, prisoner of war	Minsk		Mstitel (Revenger)
Levin David Moiseyevich	1909	Minsk	Baranovichi	Dzerzhinski	Voroshilov
Levin David Yakovlevich	1929	Stolbtsy	Baranovichi	detachment ? 106	
Levin Yefim Isaakovich	1910	Vilno	Minsk	Voronyanski	Kotovski
Levin Zalman	1909	from the civil camp	Vileyka	4th Belorusskaya	? 6
Levin Zalman Sholomovich	1926	small town of Vishnevo	Baranovichi	Chapayev	Chapayev
Levin Ilya Semenovich	1915	Krevo	Baranovichi	Chkalov	? 4 "Za Sovetskuyu Belarus"
Levin Yosif Samuilovich	1925	small town of B. Solechniki	Baranovichi	Vpered (Forward)	A.Nevski
Levin Itska Yankelevich	1919	Novogrudok getto	Baranovichi	Kirov	Ordzhonikidze
Levin Kopel Tsemakhovich	1901	Ivye	Baranovichi	Kalinin	
Levin Lev Isaakovich	1898	Buda	Mogilev	Osipovichskaya VOG	? 214
Levin Leva Isaakovich	1922	Minsk	Baranovichi	detachment ? 106	
Levin Leiba Leizerovich	1925	Kovali	Palesye	? 123	Krasny Oktyabr
Levin Leonid Markovich	1921	getto	Vileyka	Voroshilov	Istrebitel (Destroyer)
Levin Malka Berkovna	1914	Novogrudok	Baranovichi	Kalinin	
Levin Mikhail Leibovich	1898	small town of Sharkovshchina	Minsk	1st Antifashistskaya	4th

Levin Mikhail Moiseyevich	1928	Jewish camp	Minsk	Voroshilov	Kutuzov
Levin Moisei Mordukhovich	1911	Belarusian Staff of Partisan Movement	Minsk	Special groups	Istrebitel (Destroyer)
Levin Moisei Samuilovich	1914	Belarusian Staff of Partisan Movement			
Levin Naum Davidovich	1915	getto, Glubokoye	Vileyka	Gastello	Zaslonov
Levin Naum Moiseyevich	1917	Minsk	Baranovichi	detachment ? 106	
Levin Rakhmiil Nisonovich	1903	Bobruisk	Palesye	? 225	Chapayev
Levin Rubin Yakubovich	1918	Slonim	Grodno	Samutin's group	Kirshner's group
Levin Samuil Yosifovich	1906	Belarusian Staff of Partisan Movement	Brest	groups of party leaders	Sergeichik's group
Levin Samuil Yudovich	1909	from captivity	Mogilev	? 537	
Levin Samuil Shmuilovich	1898	Novogrudok	Baranovichi	Kalinin	
Levin Semen Yakovlevich	1912	Minsk	Baranovichi	detachment ? 106	
Levin Faiva Mendelevich	1910	Kurenets	Minsk	Voronyanski	Borba
Levin Folya Yudelevich	1926	Batsevichi, Klichev district	Mogilev		25 years Oktyabr
Levin Khaim Leizerovich	1922	from captivity	Palesye	? 123	Krasny Oktyabr
Levin Shendr Samuilovich	1922	small town of Vasilishki	Baranovichi	Vpered (Forward)	A.Nevski
Levin Shmuil Yankelevich	1921	Derechin	Baranovichi	Pobieda	Pobieda
Levin Eshka Samuilovna	1925		Baranovichi	Oktyabr	
Levin Yudel Yudelevich	1912	Novogrudok	Baranovichi	Kalinin	
Levin Iuno Leibovich	1920		Baranovichi	Oktyabr	
Levin Yakov Davidovich	1907	Stolbtsy	Baranovichi	detachment ? 106	
Levin Yakov Leizerovich			Baranovichi	Oktyabr	
Levin Yakov Yudelevich	1925	Batsevichi, Klichev district	Mogilev		25 years Oktyabr
Levin Yankel Benyaminovich	1897	Biniakoni	Baranovichi	Lenin's komsomol	Lenin's komsomol
Levina Anna Lvovna	1924	Pukhovichi	Baranovichi	Pobieda	Pobieda
Levina Anna Lvovna	1916	Minsk	Baranovichi	detachment ? 106	
Levina Basya Venyaminovna	1907	Minsk	Baranovichi	Baranovchi underground RC of the CP(b) B and IDC	
Levina Genya Yakovlevna	1919	Bobruisk district, glass factory	Palesye	? 123	Krasny Oktyabr
Levina Yelena AskarYevna	1924	Minsk	Minsk	Bolshevik	
Levina Ekha Moiseyevna	1917		Minsk	Belarus	Belarus
Levina Luiza Moiseyevna	1936	Minsk	Baranovichi	detachment ? 106	
Levina Mariya Izrailevna	1914	Minsk	Baranovichi	detachment ? 106	
Levina Mira Samuilovna	1907	Minsk	Baranovichi	Kalinin	
Levina Raisa Abramovna	1918	Ivye	Baranovichi	Vpered (Forward)	A.Nevski
Levina Raisa Moiseyevna	1923	Ivye	Baranovichi	Dzerzhinski	Dzerzhinski
Levina Raya Vulfovna	1914	Minsk	Baranovichi	detachment ? 106	
Levina Sara KhatskElevna	1913	Minsk	Baranovichi	Ponomarenko	25 years of the BSSR
Levina Sarra Mironovna	1922	Minsk	Belostok		Boyevoi (Fighting)
Levina Sonya	1925	Zaslavl	Baranovichi	detachment ? 106	
Levina Sonya Osherovna	1906	Stolbtsy	Baranovichi	detachment ? 106	
Levina Fanya Moiseyevna	1926	soviet farm Komintern, Bobruisk district	Palesye	? 100	Za Sovetskuyu Rodinu
Levina Freida Abramovna	1918	Minsk	Baranovichi	detachment ? 106	
Levina Frida Leibovna	1920	Rudensk	Baranovichi	detachment ? 106	
Levina Khana Girshevna	1885	Batsevichi, Klichev district	Mogilev		25 years Oktyabr
Levina Tsilya Faivovna	1924	Ivye	Baranovichi	Chapayev	Parkhomenko
Levina Elya Samuilovna	1925	Novogrudok	Baranovichi	Kalinin	
Levinbuk Zelik Nisanovich	1909	Baranovichi	Baranovichi	Komsomolets	brigade headquarters
Levinbuk Mariya Bentsianovna	1914	Baranovichi	Baranovichi	Komsomolets	brigade headquarters
Levinzon Dina Yakubovna	1907	Alitus	Baranovichi	Lenin's komsomol	Lenin's komsomol
Levinov Semen Ilyich	1900	Shklov district	Mogilev	Chekist	? 1
Levinov Solomon Zusevich	1900	Staro-Sokolniki	Brest	? 8	
Levinskaya Raisa Saulovna	1918	Minsk getto	Baranovichi	18th Frunze	Frunze
Levinson	1905	Mery	Vitebsk	4th Belorusskaya	
Levinson Anatoli Mikhailovich	1913	Vitebsk	Minsk		Chapayev
Levinson Genya Yosifovna	1919	Minsk	Baranovichi	detachment ? 106	
Levinson Lazar Lvovich	1909	from captivity, Zhitkovichi	Palesye	50st	
Levit Adam Kh.	1916	Dyatlovo	Baranovichi	Pobieda	Pobieda
Levit Lev Grigorevich	1916	Vitebsk	Vitebsk	Kirillov	Kirillov's
Levit Mikhail Lvovich	1903	getto, Glubokoye	Vitebsk	Rokossovski	brigade headquarters
Levit Nokhim Kh.	1922	Dyatlovo	Baranovichi	Pobieda	Pobieda
Levit Riva Alperovna	1923	Dyatlovo	Baranovichi	Leninskaya	Borba
Levitan Abram Aronovich	1923	getto, Glubokoye	Vileyka	Voroshilov	Kalinin
Levitan Aron Girshevich	1893	getto, Glubokoye	Vileyka	Voroshilov	Kalinin
Levitan David Samoilovich	1926	Budslav, Krivichi district	Vileyka	Kutuzov	

JEWISH PARTISANS IN BYELORUSSIA 1941-1944 255

Levitan Yefim Borisovich	1910		Baranovichi	Shchuchin IDC	
Levitan Naum Khaimovich	1924	Glussk	Palesye	? 100	Za Sovetskuyu Rodinu
Levitan Rubin Lindovich	1909	getto, Glubokoye	Vileyka	Gastello	Za Sovetskuyu Rodinu
Levitin David Samoilovich	1924	concentration camp	Pinsk	Kuibyshev	Shchors
Levitin Leonid Abramovich	1916	Berlezh, Pukhovichi district	Minsk	Plamya	Slava (Glory)
Levitina Esfir Yakovlevna	1904	Starye Dorogi district, Krinki	Minsk	Kirov ? 100	brigade headquarters
Levitski Naum Yudkovich	1922	Belarusian Staff of Partisan Movement	Gomel	Kozhar's	Shibinski's group
Levitski Osher Levikovich	1907	from captivity	Palesye		Suvorov
Levkov Matvei Yevelevich	1918	getto, Vilno	Vileyka	Voroshilov	Kalinin
Levkovich Mikhail Meyerovich	1923	Belarusian Staff of Partisan Movement	Brest	Ponomarenko	Gastello
Levkovich Nina FadeyYevna	1929	Novogrudok	Baranovichi	Kalinin	
Levkovich Khana Girshevna	1927	Ivye, getto	Baranovichi	Stalin	Suvorov
Levkovich Yakov Kusevich	1924	from the Jewish group, Pruzhany	Brest	Ponomarenko	Gastello
Levus Genya Gutelevna	1930	Minsk	Baranovichi	detachment ? 106	
Levchenko Yevgeniya Ivanovna	1898	Sedcha, Rudnya district	Minsk	2nd Minskaya	Ponomarenko
Levsh Yosif Moiseyevich	1926	Kozyany	Vileyka	Spartak	? 1
Ledvich Elena Borisovna	1892	Bobruisk	Mogilev	partisan regiment ? 277	? 277
Ledvich Nikolai Yakovlevich	1918	Bobruisk	Mogilev	partisan regiment ? 277	? 277
Ledvich Fanya Venyaminovna	1912	Glussk	Minsk	Parkhomenko	Shchors
Leder Girsh Beirakhovich	1926	Ivienets	Baranovichi	Kalinin	
Leib Genakh Shmuilovich	1910	Belostok	Baranovichi	Kalinin	
Leibanovich Nakhama Yevelevna	1922	Rubezhevichi	Baranovichi	Kalinin	
Leibman Zelik Davidovich	1909	Lakhva	Pinsk	Kirov	Za Rodinu (For Motherland)
Leibman MaLya Zalmanovna	1922	Martikantsy	Baranovichi	Lenin's komsomol	Ivanov's
Leibovich Abram Sholomovich	1924	Novogrudok, getto	Baranovichi	Stalin	Suvorov
Leibovich Boris Khaimovich	1912	Dyatlovo	Baranovichi	Leninskaya	Borba
Leibovich Galina Yosifovna	1917	Dyatlovo	Baranovichi	Leninskaya	family detachment group
Leibovich Zalman Notkovich	1923	Novogrudok	Baranovichi	Kalinin	
Leibovich Leizer Khaikelevich	1925	Dyatlovo getto	Baranovichi	Kirov	Ordzhonikidze
Leibovich Mavrikii Oskarovich	1902		Baranovichi	Chkalov	
Leibovich Mikhail Notkovich	1917	Novogrudok	Baranovichi	Kalinin	
Leibovich Nekhama Yevelevna	1922	Rubezhevichi	Baranovichi		
Leibovich Sonya Sholomovna	1921	Novogrudok, getto	Baranovichi	Stalin	Suvorov
Leibovich Tomash Khonovich	1923	Novogrudok	Baranovichi	Pobieda	Pobieda
Leibovich Sholom Movshevich	1882	Novogrudok, getto	Baranovichi	Stalin	Suvorov
Leibovich Elga Abramovna	1903	Minsk	Baranovichi	detachment ? 106	
Leibu Tobis Leibovich	1924	Romania, from the Romanian armyF	Palesye	? 125	Bolotnikov's
Leiderer Bela Nikolayevich	1910	madiary work camp	Palesye	99th Kalinkovichskaya	Kuksa's
Leiderman Viktor Motolevich	1898	Vlodava (Poland)	Pinsk	Molotov	Lazo
Leizerovich Aron Moiseyevich	1913	Dyatlovo	Baranovichi	Leninskaya	family detachment group
Leizerovich Basya Grigorevna	1918	Kishitsy	Mogilev	? 117	? 125
Leizerovich G.B.	1929	Starobin	Pinsk	Budenny	Kotovski
Leizerovich Lyuba Aronovna	1912	Chernevka	Mogilev	? 117	? 125
Leizerovich Matvei Moiseyevich	1897	Chausy	Mogilev	? 117	? 125
Leizerovich Moisei Lazarevich	1899	Dyatlovo	Baranovichi	Leninskaya	Borba
Leizerovich Raisa Moiseyevna	1921	Dyatlovo	Baranovichi	Leninskaya	Krasnogvardeiski
Leizerovich Semen Pavlovich	1906	Chernevka	Mogilev	? 117	? 125
Leizerovich Khaya Movshevna	1921	Dyatlovo	Baranovichi	Leninskaya	Borba
Leizerovski Yosif Shmuilovich	1889	Baranovichi	Baranovichi	Kalinin	
Leikin Semen Savelevich	1922	Minsk	Minsk	Shturmovaya	Grozny
Leikind Semen Grigorevich	1925	Minsk getto	Baranovichi	Chapayev	Parkhomenko
Leinenman Gelya Zelikovna	1919	Khomsk, Drogichin district	Brest	Dzerzhinski	Kalinin
Leitman Khaya Abramovna	1892	Krugloye	Mogilev	? 9	? 539
Lekakh Naum Semenovich	1908		Vileyka	Oktyabr	? 3
Lekakh Khava Leizerovna	1925	Drisa district	Vitebsk	Prudnikov's	Myshko's
Lemberger Leon Itskovich	1922	from behind the Bug, a group from Poland	Pinsk	Molotov	Lazo
Lemesh Girsh Abramovich	1904	getto N. Sverzhen	Minsk	Chapayev	Ponomarenko
Lemper Roza Semenovna	1912	Argelovshchina, Kopyl district	Minsk	Chapayev	Ponomarenko
Lemper Edla Semenovna	1920	Argelovshchina, Kopyl district	Minsk	Chapayev	Ponomarenko
Lenkin Yegor Srulevich	1912	Vitebsk	Vileyka	Gastello	Za Sovetskuyu Rodinu
Lentsevich Vladimir Mikhailovich	1923	v. Sennitsa Minsk district	Minsk	3rd Minskaya	Lazo
Lenchner Aizik Yakovlevich	1923	Minsk	Baranovichi	detachment ? 106	

Name	Year	Origin	Region	Detachment	Brigade
Leokumovich Bela KhatskElevna	1925	Gorodok, Glussk district	Pinsk	Molotov	Kalinin
Leokumovich Yevsei Khatskelevich	1923	Gorodok, Glussk district	Palesye	? 100	Igumnov and Babich's
Leondov Roman Vladimioovich	1921	Golshany, Oshmiany district	Minsk		Chapayev
Lepek Isaak Abramovich	1906	Krivoshin, Lyakhovichi district	Brest	Sikorski's headquarters	Shchors
Lepesheva Emma Semenovna	1917	v. Zaborye	Minsk	Krasnoye znamya (Red Banner)	Voroshilov
Lepshovich Ovsei Nokhimovich	1910	Derechin	Baranovichi	Pobieda	Pobieda
Lerman Godal Vulfovich	1914	Zaostrovichi	Pinsk	Lenin	Kutuzov
Lerman David Alterovich	1912	K. Kashirski	Pinsk	Molotov	Suvorov
Lerman Pesya Itskovna	1919	K. Kashirski	Pinsk	Molotov	Suvorov
Lerner Yosif Berkovich	1921	from captivity	Baranovichi	Kirov	Ordzhonikidze
Les Arkadi Davidovich	1920	from captivity	Brest	Za Sovetskuyu Belarus	Suvorov
Lesnik Abram Elevich	1927	Minsk	Baranovichi	detachment ? 106	
Letilovich Ovsei Naikhamovich	1910	Derechin	Baranovichi	Pobieda	Pobieda
Leus Khatskel Lazarevich	1905	Borisov	Minsk	Dyadi Koli	Gastello
Lekhovitski Dmitri Gershevich	1922	Baranovichi	Baranovichi	Grizodubova	Chkalov
Libentov Mikhail Lvovich	1914	Minsk	Vitebsk	Nikitin's	? 1
Liberman Ada Berkovna	1921	Jewish camp Dolginovo	Minsk	Voronyanski	Pobieda
Liberman Basya Berkovna	1924	Jewish camp Dolginovo	Minsk	Voronyanski	Pobieda
Liberman Isaak Grigorevich	1923	from B. Khmelnitski's detachment	Pinsk	Shubetidze	Stalin
Liberman Leon Angimovich	1922	Volozhin	Baranovichi	Chkalov	? 4 "Za Sovetskuyu Belarus"
Liberman Mariya Grigorevna	1922	Minsk getto	Minsk	2nd Minskaya	Kutuzov
Liberman Mikhail Abramovich	1931	Kurenets	Vileyka		Za Sovetskuyu Belorussiyu
Liberman Sonya Isaakovna	1920	Kopyl	Minsk	Chapayev	Ponomarenko
Liberman Tamara Samoilovna	1918	Warsaw	Grodno	Samutin's group	Kirshner's group
Liberman Khana Pinkhusovna	1916	N. Sverzhen	Minsk	Chapayev	Shchors
Liberman Yankel Itskovich	1903	Gorodnoe	Pinsk	Shubetidze	brigade headquarters
Libershtein Lyuba Rubinovna	1908	Svisloch, Osipovichi district	Baranovichi	detachment ? 106	
Libershtein Fima Nosinovich	1938	Minsk	Baranovichi	detachment ? 106	
Libkovich Nokhim Davidovich	1920	small town ofTraby, Yuratishki district	Baranovichi	Vpered (Forward)	A.Nevski
Libo Renya ZisElevna	1923	Minsk getto	Minsk	2nd Minskaya	Kutuzov
Libo Roza Yakovlevna	1925	Minsk	Baranovichi	detachment ? 106	
Libo Sonya Leibovna	1915	Minsk	Baranovichi	detachment ? 106	
Libova Tatyana Moiseyevna	1910	Minsk	Baranovichi	Kalinin	
Libovich Mikhail Yefimovich	1907	Gorodishche district	Baranovichi	25 years of the BSSR	Kotovski
Livsha Boris Yankelevich	1921	Kozyany	Vileyka	Spartak	? 6
Livshin Grigori Ivanovich	1913	Sharkovshchina	Vileyka	Spartak	? 4
Livshin Yosif Yankelevich	1924	Kozyany	Vileyka	Spartak	? 6
Livshits Abram Moiseyevich	1909	from Dzerzhinski brigade	Baranovichi	detachment ? 106	
Livshits Abrasha Lvovich	1935	Mogilev	Baranovichi	detachment ? 106	
Livshits Avner Yosifovich	1923	getto Tsekhanovets	Grodno	Vo imya Rodiny (In the name of Motherland)	Zhukov
Livshits Aleksandr Yudelevich	1924	Slutsk	Minsk	Ponomarenko	Selnitski
Livshits Anatoli Girshevich	1926	Ozarichi	Palesye	? 123	Kovalenko's
Livshits Aron Moshevich	1928	Minsk	Minsk		Moskva
Livshits Boris Yakovlevich	1921	Kozyany	Vileyka	Spartak	? 1
Livshits Bela Moiseyevna	1913	Osipovichi district	Baranovichi	? 620	
Livshits Vulf Aizikovich	1925	Boyanichi, Lyuban district	Minsk	Ponomarenko	Selnitski
Livshits Galina Aleksandrovna	1925	Volkovshchina, Chashniki district	Vitebsk	Lepelskaya Stalin	? 1
Livshits Girsh Abramovich	1894	Seliba, Berezino district	Mogilev		? 760 Berezovski
Livshits Grigori Samuilovich	1915	prisoners of war camp	Vileyka	Voroshilov	Kalinin
Livshits David Osherovich					
Livshits Dora Borisovna	1914	Dokshitsy	Minsk	Voronyanski	supervision squad of the brigade headquarters
Livshits Dora Yosifovna	1929	Minsk	Baranovichi	detachment ? 106	
Livshits Dora FaivushYevna	1916	Minsk	Baranovichi	Chkalov	? 4 "Za Sovetskuyu Belarus"
Livshits Ignat Danilovich	1905	Minsk	Baranovichi	Chapayev	Parkhomenko
Livshits Izrail Moiseyevich	1922	Budslav, Vileika region	Minsk	Zheleznyak	? 5
Livshits Ilya Abramovich	1898	Seliba, Berezino district	Mogilev		? 760 Berezovski
Livshits Isaak Leibovich	1893	Vitebsk	Vitebsk	Kirillov	Kirillov's
Livshits Klara Abramovna	1937	Minsk	Baranovichi	detachment ? 106	

Livshits Leiba Yevseyevich	1910	Minsk	Vitebsk	Nikitin's	? 4
Livshits Liza Abramovna	1915	Mogilev	Baranovichi	detachment ? 106	
Livshits Liza Kalmanovna	1909	Minsk	Baranovichi	detachment ? 106	
Livshits Meyer Isaakovich	1913	getto, Pruzhany	Brest	Ponomarenko	Kirov
Livshits Mikhail Leibovich	1921		Vitebsk	Chapayev	detachments
Livshits Mikhail Samoilovich	1920	Svisloch	Brest	Za Sovetskuyu Belarus	Suvorov
Livshits Moisei Lvovich	1905	Minsk	Baranovichi	Stalin	Bolshevik
Livshits Raisa Abramovna	1919	Minsk getto	Baranovichi	Stalin	Kirov
Livshits Rozaliya Yosifovna	1904	Minsk	Baranovichi	detachment ? 106	
Livshits Sara Markovna	1914	Shchedrin	Pinsk	Molotov	Kalinin
Livshits Semen Naumovich	1913	Jewish camp	Minsk	Voronyanski	Pobieda
Livshits Simon Shlemovich	1932	Vileika region, Budslav	Minsk	Ponomarenko	Za Rodinu (For Motherland)
Livshits Solomon Leibovich	1920	Lakhva	Palesye	? 130	? 132
Livshits Fruma Alterovna	1912	Volozhin	Baranovichi	Chkalov	
Livshits Tsilya Benyaminovna	1922	getto, Slonim	Brest	Za Sovetskuyu Belarus	Pozharski
Livshits Elka Izrailevna	1897	Dukora	Mogilev	208th regiment	left the detachment from the moment organization
Livshits Elya Gershevna	1924	getto Dolginovo	Minsk	Voronyanski	Pobieda
Livshits Yakov Matveyevich	1905	Nesvizh	Minsk	Voroshilov	Patriots of Motherland
Livshits Yankel Davidovich	1924	Starobin	Pinsk	Komarov-Korzh's	Komarov's 3rd group
Lider Gendel Yosifovich	1910	Mir	Baranovichi	Kalinin	
Lider Miriam GindElevna	1939	Mir	Baranovichi	Kalinin	
Lider Yakha Abramovna	1913	Mir	Baranovichi	Kalinin	
Liderman Mikhail Grigorevich	1925	Glubokoye	Vileyka	4th Belorusskaya	? 1
Lidirman Yankel Gershovich	1929	Vlodava (Poland)	Pinsk	Molotov	Shish
Lidskaya Raya Mikhailovna	1925		Baranovichi	Oktyabr	
Lidskaya Sonya Yosifovna	1923	Volozhin	Baranovichi	Chkalov	
Lidskaya Sonya Isaakovna	1919	Krasnoye, getto	Baranovichi	Za Sovetskuyu Belarus	Shturm
Lidski Aleksei Yosifovich	1915	Gorodok	Baranovichi	Chkalov	
Lidski Boris Fedorovich	1903	from captivity, concentration camp, Mogilev	Mogilev	? 121	
Lidski Mikhail Yosifovich	1916	Krasnoye, getto	Baranovichi	Za Sovetskuyu Belarus	Shturm
Lidski Elya Meilakhovich	1922		Baranovichi	Oktyabr	
Lizenshtat Leiba Moiseyevich	1911	local	Baranovichi	Pobieda	Pobieda
Liker Natan Yosifovich	1912	Slonim	Brest	Sikorski's headquarters	Shchors
Likshtein Boris Shlomovich	1925	camp, Lakhva	Palesye	? 125	Kudravtsa
Limanovich Mulya Aronovich	1930	Alekhnovichi	Baranovichi	Chkalov	? 4 "Za Sovetskuyu Belarus"
Limon Zenon Yudelevich	1908	Novogrudok getto	Baranovichi	Kirov	Oktyabrski
Linik Gersh Yankelevich	1922	Derevno	Baranovichi	Kalinin	
Linkovich Yakub Yeselevich	1913	Vidzy	Vileyka	4th Belorusskaya	? 6
Linkovskaya Dora Samuilovna	1925	getto, Pruzhany	Brest	Ponomarenko	Kirov
Linkovski Aron Shmuilovich	1926	getto, Pruzhany	Brest	Ponomarenko	Gastello
Linkovski Don Yosifovich	1919	from Melnikov's brigade	Vileyka	Kalinin	? 2
Lip Eva Vulfovna	1923		Baranovichi	18th Frunze	provisional base of the brigade
Lip Izrail Yankelevich	1913	Kletsk	Minsk	Chapayev	Ponomarenko
Lipa Grigori Lazarevich	1924	Bryansk getto, Belostok region	Grodno	Vo imya Rodiny (In the name of Motherland)	Zhukov
Lipak Boris Yevseyevich	1906	Minsk	Baranovichi	Vpered (Forward)	Chkalov
Lipelovich Ovsei Nakhmanovich	1910	Derechin	Baranovichi	Leninskaya	
Lipets Roman Lazarevich	1923	Minsk getto	Baranovichi	Chapayev	Parkhomenko
Lipker Grigori Mordukhovich	1926	Minsk	Vitebsk	Nikitin's	? 1
Lipkin David Yevseyevich	1919	from captivity	Minsk	Dyadi Koli	Dzerzhinski
Lipkin Yefim Izrailevich	1904	Borisov	Minsk	Burevestnik	Burevestnik
Lipkind Semen Poulovich	1915		Brest	Lenin	Zelenin
Lipkovich Zelik Yosifovich	1915	Minsk	Baranovichi	Stalin	Budenny
Lipkovich Nokhim Davidovich	1920	Traby	Baranovichi	Kutuzov	
Lipkovich Semen Moiseyevich		small town of Krevo	Baranovichi	Vpered (Forward)	Sibiryak
Lipkovski Abram Yeselevich	1927		Vitebsk	Chapayev	detachments
Lipkovski Don Yeselevich	1919		Vitebsk	Chapayev	detachments
Lipkunski Abram Mikeyevich	1925	Dovgelishki	Baranovichi	Lenin's komsomol	Kotovski
Lipkunski Pinkhus Nokhimovich	1930	small town of Devenovichi	Baranovichi	Vpered (Forward)	Roshcha
Lipnichevski Boris Samuilovich	1918	from the encirclement	Mogilev	? 810	
Lipovetski Dmitri Solomonovich	1912	Puchin, Bragin district	Palesye		Kotovski
Lipovetski Lev Yosifovich	1919	from captivity	Vitebsk	Za Sovetskuyu Belarus	Sibiryak
Lipovski Yosif Yakovlevich	1899	Ivienets, getto	Baranovichi	Stalin	Suvorov
Lipskaya Roza Afroimovna	1907	Svisloch, Osipovichi district	Baranovichi	detachment ? 106	
Lipski Boris Abramovich	1915	getto	Baranovichi	Lenin's komsomol	Kotovski
Lipski Boris Aronovich	1921		Palesye	? 123	komandant platoon

Lipski Feliks Yakovlevich	1938	Minsk	Baranovichi	detachment ? 106	
Lipski Shepsel Yankelevich	1921	Dyatlovo	Baranovichi	Leninskaya	family detachment group
Lipshinskaya Lyuba Moiseyevna	1921		Vitebsk	Chapayev	detachments
Lipshovich Girsh Nokhimovich	1913	Derechin	Baranovichi	Pobieda	Suvorov
Lipshovich Taiba Nokhimovich	1922	Derechin	Baranovichi	Leninskaya	Pobieda
Lipshovich Elik Nokhimovich	1913	Derechin	Baranovichi	Pobieda	Suvorov
Lis Khana KhatskElevna	1913	Mir	Baranovichi	Kalinin	
Lis Yankel Leibovich	1905	Baranovichi, from home	Baranovichi	Grizodubova	Matrosov
Lisgarten Isaak Girshovich	1910	Baranovichi	Baranovichi	Kalinin	
Lisichkin Mikhail	1922	Mogilev	Minsk	Voroshilov	? 4
Lisogurskaya KotLya Meilakovna	1912	Lida	Baranovichi	Kalinin	
Lisogurski Shalom Yankelevich	1911	Lida	Baranovichi	Kalinin	
Lisogurski Yankel Shalomovich	1940	Lida	Baranovichi	Kalinin	
Litavorskaya Grunya Alterovna	1917	v. Zverovshchina	Baranovichi	Kalinin	
Litavorskaya Shifra Alterovna	1921	v. Zverovshchina	Baranovichi	Kalinin	
Litavorski Lipman Alterovich	1925	v. Zverovshchina	Baranovichi	Kalinin	
Litavorski Pinkhos Alterovich	1922	v. Zverovshchina	Baranovichi	Kalinin	
Litvak Moisei Izrailevich	1905	from captivity	Mogilev	? 425	? 425
Litvin Solomon Leibovich	1904	Mogilev	Mogilev	? 121	
Litlovich Elik Nokhimovich	1913	Derechin	Baranovichi	Pobieda	Pobieda
Lifman Shlema Leizerovich	1923	Derechin	Baranovichi	Pobieda	Suvorov
Lifshits Boris Leibovich	1906	Olkeniki	Baranovichi	Kalinin	
Lifshits Elena Izrailevna	1897	Dukora, Minsk region	Minsk	Belarus	Belarus
Lifshits Leiba Girshevna	1871	Olkeniki	Baranovichi	Kalinin	
Lifshits Meyer Isaakovich	1913	Pruzhany	Brest	Ponomarenko	
Lifshits Mordukh Leibovich	1921	from Melnikov's brigade	Vileyka	Kalinin	? 2
Lifshits Khaim Kalmanovich	1896	Uzda	Minsk	Chapayev	Ponomarenko
Lifshits Yankel Moiseyevich	1928	Voronovo	Baranovichi	Kalinin	
Likhtenberg Izak Yevseyevich	1911	Lakhva	Pinsk	Kirov	Petrovich's
Likhtenshtein Gustava Grigorevna	1895	Luninets	Pinsk	Kirov	
Likhtenshtein Ovsei Shlemovich	1923	from the camp	Palesye	? 225	Suvorov
Likhter David Mordukhovich	1913	Dyatlovo	Baranovichi	Leninskaya	Borba
Likhter Yakov Aronovich	1920	from the encirclement	Minsk	Parkhomenko	Shchors
Likhterman Isaak Abromovich	1904	Minsk	Baranovichi	detachment ? 106	
Likhterman Srol Fishelevich	1888	Minsk	Baranovichi	detachment ? 106	
Likhtman Itsek G.	1912	Poland	Brest	Lenin	Zhukov
Likhtman Eda M.	1915	Poland	Brest	Lenin	Zhukov
Litskaya Raya Yosifovna		Gorodok	Baranovichi	Chkalov	? 4 "Za Sovetskuyu Belarus"
Litski Aizik Shelomovich	1907	Gorodishche district	Baranovichi	25 years of the BSSR	Kotovski
Lobanova Fenya Lvovna	1894	Minsk	Minsk	Belarus	Za Rodinu (For Motherland)
Lobzovski Alter Berkovich	1891	Derechin	Baranovichi	Pobieda	Budenny
Lobzovski Girsh Berkovich	1898	Derechin	Baranovichi	Leninskaya	Leninski
Lobzovski Yudel Alterovich	1925	Derechin	Baranovichi	Leninskaya	Leninski
Lovit Isaak Shemshelevich	1923	Gorodok	Baranovichi	Chkalov	? 4 "Za Sovetskuyu Belarus"
Logatker Aizik Bentsionovich	1922	Novogrudok getto	Baranovichi	Kirov	Ordzhonikidze
Logatskaya Lyubov AntonYevna	1914	Slutsk district, Nekrashchi	Minsk	Suvorov	
Lozovski Yefim Volfovich	1922		Minsk	Voronyanski	Mstitel (Revenger)
Loiman David Yankelevich	1904	getto, Glubokoye	Vileyka	1st Suvorov	Voroshilov
Lom Izrail Aizikovich	1914	Skidel	Brest	detachment 346	345
Lopatin Berko Leibovich	1913	Berezhenitsa, Rovno region.	Pinsk	Shubetidze	brigade headquarters
Lopatin Boris Yakovlevich	1900	Lakhva	Pinsk	Kirov	
Lopatukhin Leonid Izrailevich	1912	from the encirclement	Gomel	1st Gomelskaya	Kalinin
Loseva-Yudevich Tatyana Abramovna	1900	Minsk getto	Minsk	Dimy	
Losik Vulf Sholomovich	1902	Minsk	Minsk		Suvorov
Losik Lazar Vladimirovich	1923	Minsk	Minsk	2nd Minskaya	Kutuzov
Los Lev Moiseyevich	1914	Rafalovka	Pinsk	Shubetidze	Chapayev
Lot Yelizaveta Zalmanovna	1907	Minsk	Baranovichi	Vpered (Forward)	family detachment group
Lotvin Leizer Berkovich	1897	Kopyl	Minsk	Chapayev	Ponomarenko
Lotvina Etka SrolYevna	1890	Kopyl	Minsk	Chapayev	Ponomarenko
Lotvina Leya Leizerovna	1921	Kopyl	Minsk	Chapayev	Ponomarenko
Lotvina Yadya Grigorevna	1924	Kopyl	Minsk	Chapayev	Ponomarenko
Lokhozvianski Nema Grigorevich	1921	Baranovichi	Baranovichi	Rokossovski	Rokossovski
Loshitser Genrikh Aronovich	1923	Krasnoye, getto	Baranovichi	Za Sovetskuyu Belarus	Za Sovetskuyu Belarus
Loshitser Zelik Aronovich	1921	Gorodok	Baranovichi	Chkalov	
Loshovich Kasriel Faivelevich	1920	Volkovyssk	Brest	Za Sovetskuyu Belarus	brigade headquarters
Loshchinski Leiba Khaimovich	1925	getto	Baranovichi	Kirov	Baltiets
Luka Ivan Vasilevich	1908	from captivity	Gomel	Voroshilov	headquarters

Lulova GaLya Lazarevna	1914	Krasnoye	Baranovichi	Chkalov	reserve group
Lulova Polya Lazarevna	1914	Krasnoye	Baranovichi	Za Sovetskuyu Belarus	family detachment
Lungin Berka Osherovich	1928	Rubezhevichi	Baranovichi	detachment ? 106	
Lungin Mikhail Leibovich	1930	Minsk	Baranovichi	Kalinin	
Lungin Oser Berkovich	1894	Rubezhevichi	Baranovichi	detachment ? 106	
Luner Abram Yosifovich	1923	getto, Vilno	Vileyka	Voroshilov	Kalinin
Lunin Yudal Movshovich	1890	Minsk	Baranovichi	Vpered (Forward)	Chkalov
Lunina NataLya AvElevna	1892	Minsk	Baranovichi	Vpered (Forward)	Chkalov
Lunskaya Sonya Lazarevna	1914	getto	Vileyka	Suvorov	
Lunyanski Meyer Girshevich	1924	Derechin	Baranovichi	Leninskaya	hospital
Lurye Dmitri Yefimovich	1921	Moskva	Vitebsk	Lenin	2-oi
Lurye Yakov Lvovich	1925	Jewish camp	Vileyka	Spartak	? 2
Luskaya Khana Moiseyevna	1924	Dyatlovo	Baranovichi	Leninskaya	family detachment group
Luskaya Khaya Berkovna	1895	Novogrudok	Baranovichi	Kalinin	
Luski Shimon Solomonovich	1927	Novogrudok	Baranovichi	Kalinin	
Lusski Shimon Moiseyevich	1893	Golynka, Zelva	Baranovichi	Pobieda	Pobieda
Lutskaya Fanya Medovna	1922	Pogost-Zagorodski	Pinsk	Molotov	Kalinin
Lutski David Yankelevich	1920	Vulka	Pinsk	Kirov	Kalinin
Lutski Itsko Yankelevich	1925	Vulka	Pinsk	Kirov	Kalinin
Lutski Mul Lazarevich	1921	detachment Kaganovich	Pinsk	Kuibyshev	Ordzhonikidze
Lutski Pinkhus Yankelevich	1922	Vulka	Pinsk	Kirov	Kalinin
Lutski Semen Itskovich	1922	Vulka	Pinsk	Kirov	
Lysogurski Isaak Girshevich	1910	Baranovichi	Baranovichi	Kalinin	
Lysoyeva Yudif Samuilovna	1916	Belarusian Staff of Partisan Movement	Brest		Selnitski
Lvov Aleksandr Vasilevich	1915	Central Committee of the CP (b) B	Mogilev		? 721
Lvovich Aron Borukhovich		Slutsk district	Minsk	Suvorov	
Lvovich Badaniia Yosifovna	1915				
Lvovich Nekhama Aronovna	1902	Urechye	Baranovichi	detachment ? 106	
Lvovich Sonya Davidovna	1926	Minsk	Baranovichi	detachment ? 106	
Lyubetkina Sima Osherovna	1919	Kozlovshchina, Baranovichi region	Vileyka	Suvorov	brigade headquarters
Lyubetskaya Rakhelya Rubinovna	1944	Naliboki dense forest	Baranovichi	Kalinin	
Lyubetskaya Sonya KushElevna	1906	Mir	Baranovichi	Kalinin	
Lyubetski Abram Rubinovich	1930	Mir	Baranovichi	Kalinin	
Lyubetski Yesel Ivshovich	1917	getto	Baranovichi	Lenin's komsomol	Kotovski
Lyubetski Rubin Aronovich	1901	Mir	Baranovichi	Kalinin	
Lyubetski Samuil Aronovich	1935	Mir	Baranovichi	Kalinin	
Lyubetski Yankel Yudelevich	1921	Radun	Baranovichi	Lenin's komsomol	Lenin's komsomol
Lyubich Yuri Pinkhusovich	1919	from captivity	Pinsk	Budenny	Voroshilov
Lyubichev Ruvim Abramovich	1921		Vileyka	Gastello	brigade headquarters
Lyubner Betya Mikhailovna	1923	Minsk	Baranovichi	Za Sovetskuyu Belarus	family detachment
Lyubovski Zinovii Abramovich	1908	Rechitsa, from captivity	Gomel	Zheleznyak	? 117
Lyubranetskaya Rita Solomonovna	1919	Lodz	Vileyka	Suvorov	brigade headquarters
Lyubranetski Volf			Vileyka	Suvorov	Mstitel (Revenger)
Lyubchanskaya Bellya Rublenovna	1921	Novogrudok	Baranovichi	Kalinin	
Lyubchanskaya Liza AvElevna	1919	Minsk	Baranovichi	detachment ? 106	
Lyubchanskaya Fanya Borukhovna	1922	Novogrudok	Baranovichi		
Lyubchanski Aron Yankelevich	1914	Novogrudok	Baranovichi	Kalinin	
Lyubchanski Mordukh Yankelevich	1912	Novogrudok	Baranovichi	Kalinin	
Lyuminski Yosif Zavelevich	1887	Jewish camp	Vileyka	4th Belorusskaya	? 6
Lyustikman Sara Davidovna	1924	Poland	Pinsk	Molotov	Shish
Lyaderman Idel Gershkovich	1926	Poland	Pinsk	Molotov	Shish
Lyanden Aleksei Izakovich	1917	work camp	Pinsk	Molotov	Shish
Lyanden Elesh Itskovich	1924	Vlodava (Poland)	Pinsk	Molotov	Shish
Lyandman Leiba Borukhovich	1908	concentration camp	Pinsk	Kuibyshev	Shchors
Lyasman Stepan Borisovich	1915	from the detachment Frunze	Pinsk	Kuibyshev	Barutski
Lyatto Samuil Ilyich	1925	from the camp	Baranovichi	Grizodubova	
Lyaufvaner Abram Shmulevich	1907		Brest	Lenin	Zhukov
Lyaufer Rafail Abramovich	1900	N. Sverzhen	Baranovichi	18th Frunze	Dzerzhinski
Lyakh Aron Dubinovich	1922	Belostok	Grodno	Samutin's group	Kirshner's group
Lyakhman Leiba Leizerovich	1896	Disna	Vitebsk	Lenin	3-ii
Lyakhovitskaya Frida Moiseyevna	1919	Nesvizh	Baranovichi	Chkalov	
Lyakhovitski Aleksandr Abramovich	1912	Baranovichi	Pinsk	Budenny	Kotovski
Lyakhovitski Dmitri Gershenovich	1920	detachment named afterChkalov, GrizoDubov's brigade	Grodno		B.Khmelnitski
Lyakhovitski Movsha Zalmanovich	1883	Nesvizh	Baranovichi	Chkalov	
Lyakhovitski Shaya Yeselevich	1924	getto N. Sverzhen	Minsk	Chapayev	Ponomarenko
Lyashitser Genrikh Aronovich	1923	Gorodok	Baranovichi	Chkalov	

Mavzer Albert Naumovich	1930	Minsk	Baranovichi	Ponomarenko	25 years of the BSSR
Magat Aron Notkovich	1913	Lida	Baranovichi	Kalinin	
Magat Lyuba Yankelevna	1921	Lida	Baranovichi	Kalinin	
Magiz Anna Semenovna	1910	Minsk	Baranovichi	detachment ? 106	
Maevskaya Pesya Yudelevna	1918	Dyatlovo	Baranovichi	Leninskaya	family detachment group
Maevskaya Khana Izrailevna	1919	Dyatlovo	Baranovichi	Leninskaya	Borba
Maerovich Isaak Shmuilovich	1918		Baranovichi	Leninskaya	Pobieda
Mazanik Lazar Abramovich	1901	Minsk getto	Minsk	2nd Minskaya	Voroshilov
Mazel Izrail Maksimovich	1916	Minsk	Baranovichi	detachment ? 106	
Mazin Mikhail I.	1924	Mogilev region	Gomel	1st Gomelskaya	Kalinin
Mazo Bella Isaakovna	1905	Borisov	Baranovichi	detachment ? 106	
Mazo Daniil Semenovich		Minsk getto	Minsk		Mstitel (Revenger)
Mazo Meyer Sholomovich	1910	Smolevichi	Baranovichi	detachment ? 106	
Mazo Riva Mikhailovna	1910	Minsk	Minsk	Rokossovski	25 years of Oktyabr
Mazur Shlema Borisovich	1925	Jewish camp, Nevir, Volyn region	Pinsk	Shubetidze	Ordzhonikidze
Mazurek Adam Emmanuilovich	1907	Baranovichi	Baranovichi	Zhukov	
Mazurkevich Esa Yosifovich	1918	N. Sverzhen	Baranovichi	18th Frunze	editorial stuff of the newspaper "Za Sovetskuyu Belarus"
Mazurkevich Semen Yakovlevich	1911	st. Sabibor (concentration camp), Poland	Brest	Stalin	Frunze
Mazurkevich Etya Samuilovna	1913	Ivienets	Baranovichi	Kalinin	
Mazurskaya Lida Isaakovna	1925	from the forest Zvonets, Antopol	Brest		Kotovski
Mazurski Abram Benyaminovich	1907	B. Bolota	Brest		Kotovski
Mazurski Zelman Berkovich	1924	from Poslavy forest	Pinsk	Molotov	Lazo
Mazyn Girsh Pinkhusovich	1920	Nesvizh	Baranovichi	Kalinin	
Mai Moisei Urovich	1925	Minsk	Minsk	Belarus	Belarus
Mai Samuil Borukhovich	1912	detachment Kaganovicha	Pinsk	Kuibyshev	Ordzhonikidze
Maidan Moisei Yankelevich	1913	Stolbtsy	Baranovichi	Kalinin	
Maidel Naum Lvovich	1919	Glussk district, Zastenok	Minsk	Parkhomenko	Kirov
Maiden-Baum Aizik Yankelevich	1907	Jewish camp	Vileyka	Voroshilov	headquarters' production group
Maiden-Baum Mera Khaibovna	1922	Jewish camp	Vileyka	Voroshilov	headquarters' production group
Maizel Alik Naumovich	1930	Minsk	Baranovichi	18th Frunze	Kutuzov
Maizel Boris Isaakovich	1925	Minsk	Brest	detachment 346	345
Maizel Mota Lazarevich	1923	Minsk getto	Minsk	2nd Minskaya	Kutuzov
Maizel Elya Sholomovich	1913		Minsk	Voronyanski	Pobieda
Maizenshtein Ilya Elevich	1922	from captivity	Gomel	Bolshevik	Bolshevik
Maizlis Enta Peisakhovna	1899	Minsk, underground, regional committee of the CP(b)B	Minsk	Voronyanski	Mstitel (Revenger)
Maikon Lipa Moiseyevich	1924	concentration camp Gantsevichi	Minsk	Chkalov	Zheleznyak
Maikon Shaya Motelevich	1906	concentration camp Gantsevichi	Minsk	Chkalov	Zheleznyak
Maimin Vladimir Samuilovich	1926	Polotsk	Vitebsk	3rd Belorusskaya	? 2
Maiski David Lipovich	1906	Vileika	Baranovichi	Baranovchi underground RC of the CP(b)B and IDC	
Maister Leon Solomonovich	1912	Pruzhany	Brest	Brest antifascist committee	
Makarevich Raisa Valentinovna		Plissa	Vitebsk	Sennenskaya brigade (Leonov's)	a contact
Makashevski Mikhail Volfovich	1924		Vileyka	Voroshilov	Bagration
Makover Samuil Davidovich	1922	Minsk, camp, prisoner of war	Baranovichi	Vpered (Forward)	Chkalov
Makovski Yakov Gershovich	1921	Belostok	Grodno	Samutin's group	Kirshner's group
Maksimova Sofiya Antonovna	1920	Zembin	Minsk	Dyadi Koli	Burya (Storm)
Makutonin Isaak Rafailovich	1916	Disna	Vileyka	4th Belorusskaya	? 6
Makutonina Mera Rafalovna	1920	Mery	Vileyka	4th Belorusskaya	? 2
Malakh Genrikh Shemelevich	1918	Slonim	Brest	Sikorski's headquarters	Shchors
Malakhovskaya Gita Yosifovna	1916	detachment Kaganovich	Pinsk	Kuibyshev	Ordzhonikidze
Malakhovski Yakov Grigorevich	1911	Baranovichi	Brest	Dzerzhinski	Molotov
Malik Bentse Mendelevich	1915	K. Kashirski	Pinsk	Molotov	Suvorov
Malikovski Zelik Grigorevich	1912	Slonim	Brest	Sikorski's headquarters	commandant platoon
Malin Isaak Zalmanovich	1912	Glussk	Palesye	? 225	Gastello
Malin Tsukho Natanovich	1924	Novogrudok	Baranovichi	Kalinin	
Malis Itska Natanovich	1924	Mir	Baranovichi	Komsomolets	Kalinin

Malishanskaya Dvoira Khaimovna	1909	Yatra	Baranovichi	Kalinin	
Malishanskaya Mariya Bentsianovna	1921	Mir	Baranovichi	Kalinin	
Malishanskaya Estera Ovseyevna	1923	Molchad	Baranovichi	Kalinin	
Malishanski Abram Volfovich	1918	Mir	Baranovichi	Kalinin	
Malishanski Meyer Ovseyevich	1928	Yatra	Baranovichi	Kalinin	
Malkin Yakov Moiseyevich	1925	Monastyrski district	Vitebsk	Frunze	Petrenko's group
Malovitski Grigori Moiseyevich	1923	Baranovichi	Pinsk	Budenny	Ponomarenko
Malomed Aron Zavalevich	1924	Minsk getto	Minsk	2nd Minskaya	Voroshilov
Malokhovski Benyamin Khonovich	1933	Ivye	Baranovichi	Kalinin	
Malykin Moisei small town of	1900	from the encirclement	Palesye	? 123	Papruga's
Malyn Giler Nakhovich	1926	Glussk	Minsk	Chkalov	Gromov
Malyn Grigori Aronovich	1928	Glussk	Minsk	Chkalov	Gromov
Malyna Etya Zalmanovna	1925	Glussk district, Berezovka	Minsk	Parkhomenko	Kirov
Malbin Lazar Abramovich	1903	Novogrudok	Baranovichi	Kalinin	
Malbina Galina DmitriYevna	1914	Molodechno district	Baranovichi	Beriya	
Maltser Lazar Semenovich	1923		Vileyka	Voroshilov	Bagration
Malyukovski Boris Borisovich	1924	Krasnoye, getto	Baranovichi	Za Sovetskuyu Belarus	Za Sovetskuyu Belarus
Malyatskaya Yelizaveta Yakovlevna	1926	getto	Vileyka	Voroshilov	Slava (Glory)
Man Boris Shlemovich	1919	Minsk getto	Grodno	Ponomarenko	squadron
Mandel Leonid Mendelevich	1928	Slutsk	Minsk	Ponomarenko	A.Nevski
Mandel Mendel Ruvimovich	1896	Slutsk	Minsk	Ponomarenko	A.Nevski
Mandel Raisa Mendeleyevna	1923	Slutsk	Minsk	Ponomarenko	A.Nevski
Mandelbaum Isaak Mordukhovich	1923	Kurenets	Vileyka	Dovator	Suvorov
Manevich Izrail Khaimovich	1904	Belarusian Staff of Partisan Movement	Grodno		Bezlyudov's
Mankovich Yosif Yankelevich	1927	Dyatlovo	Baranovichi	Leninskaya	Borba
Mankovich Isaak Meyerovich	1925	Dyatlovo getto	Baranovichi	Kirov	Ordzhonikidze
Mankovich Isaak Yankelevich	1925	Dyatlovo	Baranovichi	Leninskaya	Borba
Mankovich Movsha Yankelevich	1922	Dyatlovo	Baranovichi	Leninskaya	Borba
Mankovich Rakhil Yefremovna	1924	Grodno, getto	Baranovichi	Kirov	Ordzhonikidze
Mankovich Yankel Isaakovich	1895	Dyatlovo	Baranovichi	Leninskaya	Borba
Mankul Yankel Yosifovich	1910	Dunilovichi	Vitebsk	Rokossovski	Zhukov
Manov Abram Benyaminovich	1919	getto	Vileyka	Voroshilov	Istrebitel (Destroyer)
Manpol Yankel Yosifovich	1910		Vileyka	CC of the CP(b)B	brigade sanitary service
Manskaya Rakhil Shlemovna	1912	Lida, getto	Baranovichi	Kirov	Ordzhonikidze
Manski Aizik Yevelevich	1909	Lida, getto	Baranovichi	Kirov	Ordzhonikidze
Manski Isaak Kalmanovich	1921	getto	Baranovichi	Lenin's komsomol	Kotovski
Manski Misha Kalmanovich	1923	Lida	Baranovichi	Kirov	Ordzhonikidze
MantelmanAnatoli Abramovich	1917	from captivity	Mogilev	Chekist	? 31
Manusevich Moisei Aronovich	1910	Novogrudok	Baranovichi	Kirov	Ordzhonikidze
Manusevich Khaya Abramovna	1912		Baranovichi	Oktyabr	
Mankovski Roman Leibovich	1916	Poland, camp, prisoner of war	Pinsk	Molotov	Kalinin
Mane Mikhail Yankelevich	1921	Radoshkovichi	Baranovichi	Chkalov	
Maniukova Sonya Moiseyevna	1917		Baranovichi	Leninskaya	hospital
Margolin Boris Vulfovich	1927	Moshny	Palesye	? 123	Krasny Oktyabr
Margolin Zelik Berkovich	1909	Gantsevichi	Pinsk	Komarov-Korzh's	4 group
Margolin Ilya Irmeevich	1922	Vasilishki	Baranovichi	Lenin's komsomol	brigade headquarters
Margolin Yosif Vulfovich	1908	Glussk	Palesye	? 123	Krasny Oktyabr
Margolin Matvei Borisovich	1905	from captivity	Vitebsk	Sadchikov's	batalon ? 4
Margolin Meyer Perkhusovich	1906	Belarusian Staff of Partisan Movement			
Margolin Semen Ilyich	1903	Dvinsk	Vitebsk	Stalin (Okhotin's)	Lapenko
Margolin Fima Vladimirovich	1913	Rudobelka	Palesye	? 123	komandant platoon
Margolina Bronya Lazarevna	1912	Glussk	Palesye	? 123	Krasny Oktyabr
Margolina Sonya Yudovna	1917	Minsk	Baranovichi	detachment ? 106	
Margolina Freida Nokhimovna	1904	Checherk	Gomel	1st Gomelskaya	Kalinin
Margolina Yakov Samuilovich	1916	Minsk	Baranovichi	detachment ? 106	
Marich Raisa Borisovna (Chunova Zinaida VasilYevna)	1920	Pogost, Starobin district	Brest	Flegontov	Litvinov's
Markevich Nikolai Nikolayevich	1918	Potreby	Baranovichi	Kalinin	
Markman Yefim Gavrilovich	1895	Urechye	Brest	? 99 Gulyaev	Grabko
Markman Matvei Abramovich	1923	Belarusian Staff of Partisan Movement	Vileyka	Dovator	Sverdlov
Markman Khaim Simkhovich	1918	getto, Glubokoye	Vitebsk	Korotkin	Voroshilov
Markovich Mikhail Naumovich	1916	Omsk	Vitebsk	VLKSM	Sibiryak
Markus Minya Isaakovna	1905	Volkovyssk	Baranovichi	Leninskaya	family detachment group
Markus Sarra			Baranovichi	Leninskaya	Krasnogvardeiski
Maroshek Izrail Davidovich	1918	Minsk	Baranovichi	detachment ? 106	
Maroshek MIlya Leibovna	1915	Khoiniki	Baranovichi	detachment ? 106	
Martkovich Nina Vladimirovna	1917	Timkovichi	Minsk		Chapayev

Martkovski Zavel Aronovich	1914	Novogrudok, getto	Belostok	A.Nevski	
Markhasin Abram Berkovich	1917	Mogilev, concentration camp	Pinsk		? 200
Markhvinskaya Esfir Yefimovna	1923	Mir	Baranovichi	Kalinin	
Markhvinski Yuzef Frantsevich	1910	Nesvizh	Baranovichi	Kalinin	
Marshak Rema Lvovna	1930	Minsk	Baranovichi	detachment ? 106	
Marshak Sonya Naumovna	1913	Minsk	Baranovichi	detachment ? 106	
Marshak Kharin Romanovich	1919	Minsk getto	Baranovichi	Chkalov	
Masarski Aba Abramovich	1889	Sirotino	Vitebsk	Korotkin	? 1
Masarski Roman Lazarevich	1890	Sirotino	Vitebsk	3rd Belorusskaya	? 4
Maslovataia Enta MekhElevna	1911	Novogrudok	Baranovichi	Kalinin	
Maslovaty Gdalya Shlemovich	1922	Novogrudok	Baranovichi	Kalinin	
Matienko Mikhail Abramovich	1912	from captivity	Palesye	? 130	? 133
Matlina Lidiya Solomonovna	1919	Minsk	Baranovichi	detachment ? 106	
Matlovski Yosif Rubinovich	1924	Lida	Baranovichi	Leninskaya	Niepobedimy (Undefeated)
Makhlina Anna Lvovna	1914	Minsk	Baranovichi	detachment ? 106	
Makhlina RivaYefimovna(KupriyanenkoNinaYefimovna)	1918	Minsk	Mogilev	? 537	
Makhlis Mikhail Movshevich	1908	Naliboki	Baranovichi	Kalinin	
Makhover Lev Moiseyevich	1925	Shklov	Mogilev	Chekist	? 20
Makhten Miron Mikhailovich	1922	N. Sverzhen	Minsk	Chapayev	Ponomarenko
Makhtin Abba Khaimovich	1905	Shchedrin	Palesye	? 123	Artyushka's
Mats Zyama Ruvimovich	1913	Bobruisk	Minsk	Chkalov	Dovator
Mats Ilya Abramovich	1929	Svisloch, Osipovichi district	Minsk	Zheleznyak	Olkhovtsa
Matskevich Tatyana Arkadevna	1923	Minsk	Baranovichi	Stalin	Budenny
Matsiukovski Boris Yefimovich	1924	Martikantsy	Baranovichi	Lenin's komsomol	Ivanov's
Machiz Anna Semenovna	1910	Minsk getto	Baranovichi	Zhukov	
Mashkovskaya Yudita TsalYevna	1924	Dyatlovo	Baranovichi	Leninskaya	family detachment group
Mashkovski Ilya Khatskelevich	1921	Slonim	Brest	Sikorski's headquarters	Shchors
Mashkovski Shepsel Isaakovich	1915	Slonim	Brest	Sikorski's headquarters	Shchors
Mashos Petr Ilyich	1920	getto, Vilno	Vileyka	Voroshilov	Chapayev
Mayants Vladimir Ilevich	1922	Gomel	Gomel	formation headquarters of Gomel partisans	
Medvedovski David Izrailevich	1915	Slutsk	Baranovichi	Grizodubova	Chkalov
Medvedski Izrail Isaakovich	1922	Tukhovichi	Brest		Kotovski
Medvetskaya Masha Isaakovna	1924	Dyatlovo	Baranovichi	Leninskaya	Borba
Medvetski Abram Davidovich	1908	Derechin	Baranovichi	Leninskaya	Pobieda
Medvetski Iona Isaakovich	1921	Dyatlovo	Baranovichi	Leninskaya	family detachment group
Medvetski Isaak Abramovich	1892	Dyatlovo	Baranovichi	Leninskaya	Borba
Medlitski Abram Mortkhinovich	1923	Gorodishche district	Baranovichi	Pobieda	Pobieda
Mednik Izrail Gedalevich	1909	Domanovichi, Starobin district	Pinsk	Komarov-Korzh's	Komarov's 3rd group
Mednik Meyer Volkovich	1916	N. Lese, Domachevo district	Brest	Lenin	Zhukov
Mednik Ruvim Moiseyevich	1895	Radoshkovichi	Minsk	Voronyanski	Kotovski
Mednitski David Shmuilovich	1905	Zheludok	Baranovichi	Pervomaiskaya	Oktyabr
Mednitski Zelman Yudelevich	1922	Vasilishki	Baranovichi	Leninskaya	Borba
Medovik Yefim Genokhovich	1911	getto, Pruzhany	Brest	Ponomarenko	Kirov
Medrizh Yelizaveta Aronovna	1920	Baranovichi	Brest	Sverdlov	Chkalov
Medrizh Isaak Novakhovich	1914	Baranovichi	Brest	Sverdlov	Chkalov
Medris Simkha Borisovich	1917	Belostok	Brest	Za Sovetskuyu Belarus	Suvorov
Meyerovich Abram Rubinovich	1913	Voronovo	Baranovichi	Kirov	Ordzhonikidze
Meyerovich Alter Shmoilovich	1912	Kletsk	Minsk	Chapayev	Ponomarenko
Meyerovich Berta Meyerovna	1904	Minsk	Baranovichi	detachment ? 106	
Meyerovich Yevel Bentsionovich	1907	Korelichi getto	Baranovichi	Kirov	Ordzhonikidze
Meyerovich Yevel Rubinovich	1913	Voronovo, getto	Baranovichi	Kirov	Ordzhonikidze
Meyerovich Yosif Shmoilovich	1914	Kletsk	Baranovichi	18th Frunze	provisional base of the brigade
Meyerovich Isaak Shmuilovich	1918	Kalits	Baranovichi	Pobieda	Suvorov
Meyerovich Mordukh Kopelevich	1893	Baranovichi region, Rozhenki	Baranovichi	Vpered (Forward)	Roshcha
Meyerovich Olga Semenovna	1927	Minsk	Baranovichi	detachment ? 106	
Meyerson Antsel Meyerovich	1918		Minsk	Voronyanski	Pobieda
Meyerson Lyubov Yefimovna	1911	Novogrudok	Baranovichi	Vpered (Forward)	Chkalov
Meyerson Moisei Abramovich	1896	Krasnoye, getto	Baranovichi	Za Sovetskuyu Belarus	Shturm
Mezhevetskaya Sofiya Solomonovna	1924	Slonim	Pinsk	Molotov	Shish
Mezheritskaya Yevgeniya Gershevna	1924	Volkovyssk	Brest	Ponomarenko	Kirov
Mekler Lida NakhtolYevna	1925	Dubrovenski district	Mogilev	? 117	? 124
Melamed Gersh Yevelevich	1898	Minsk	Baranovichi	detachment ? 106	
Melamed Leizer Moshkovich	1920	Tomashevka	Brest	Stalin	Frunze

Name	Year	Place	Region	Detachment	Brigade
Melamed Leonid Grigorevich	1928	Minsk	Baranovichi	detachment ? 106	
Melamed Riva Borisovna	1919	Glubokoye	Vileyka	Kutuzov	
Melamed Sarra Savelevna	1902	Minsk	Baranovichi	detachment ? 106	
Melamed Simkha Lakhmanovich	1900	Khomsk, Pinsk region	Brest	Sverdlov	Makarevich
Melamed Estra Borisovna	1917	Dokshitsy	Vileyka	Kutuzov	
Melamedov Mikhail Yefimovich	1917	from captivity, Mozyr	Palesye	? 27 Kirov	Kirov
Melomed Aleksandr Yefimovich	1892	Ivye	Baranovichi	Zhukov	
Melomed Yefim Aleksandrovich	1923	Ivye	Baranovichi	Zhukov	
Melomed Mikhail Aleksandrovich	1926	Ivye	Baranovichi	Zhukov	
Melkovski Zelik Gershelevich	1911	Slonim	Brest	Sikorski's headquarters	Shchors
Melnikov Aleksandr Sergeyevich	1919	Rechitsa	Pinsk	Lenin	Kutuzov
Melnikova Vera Mikhailovna	1907	Minsk district, Kolodishchi	Minsk		Suvorov
Melnikova Marusya Yakovlevna	1928	Minsk district, Kolodishchi	Minsk		Suvorov
Meltser Aizik Rafailovich	1916	Minsk	Baranovichi	detachment ? 106	
Meltser Basya Shayevna	1923	Minsk	Baranovichi	detachment ? 106	
Meltser Isaak Lazarevich	1920	from captivity	Palesye	? 123	Krasny Oktyabr
Meltser Mariya Pavlovna	1920	Karpilovka	Palesye	? 123	Krasny Oktyabr
Meltser Fedosiia Moiseyevna	1919	Minsk getto	Baranovichi	Stalin	Parkhomenko
Meltser Khaya Yankelevna	1909	Glussk	Minsk	258th Kuibyshev	Chapayev
Memkhes Rubin Isaakovich	1924	Disna	Vitebsk	Chapayev	detachments
Menaker Abram Isaakovich	1907	from the concentration camp	Baranovichi	Grizodubova	Chkalov
Menaker Lev Aronovich	1914	Kopyl getto	Minsk	Frunze	Budenny
Menaker Leon Abramovich	1904	Minsk	Minsk	Burevestnik	Burevestnik
Menaker Samuil Yuzefovich	1922	from captivity	Baranovichi	Grizodubova	
Mendalevich Girsh Khmelevich	1914	from the Lyskovski forest	Brest	Ponomarenko	Kirov
Mendelevich Girsh Yosifovich	1903	Baranovichi	Baranovichi	Kalinin	
Mendelevich Lena small town of	1922	Byten	Brest	Ponomarenko	Sovetskaya Belarus
Mendelevich Pinkhos Izrailevich	1902	Veronovo	Baranovichi	Kalinin	
Mendelevich S.M.	1922	Byten	Brest	Ponomarenko	Sovetskaya Belarus
Mendelevich Sholom Tsalkovich	1922	Nachi	Baranovichi	Leninskaya	Niepobedimy (Undefeated)
Mendelevskaya Tsyra Shmuilovna	1899	Turets	Baranovichi	Kalinin	
Mendelevski Benyamin Yoselevich	1897	Turets	Baranovichi	Kalinin	
Mendelevski Yosif Benyaminovich	1943	Turets	Baranovichi	Kalinin	
Mendelevski Simon Davidovich	1924	Vasilishki	Baranovichi	Kalinin	
Mendelevski Shaya Berkovich	1910	Lyubcha, Baranovichi region	Minsk	Chapayev	Shchors
Mendel		Belarusian Staff of Partisan Movement	Gomel	Kozhar's	Shemyakin's group
Mendel Mariya YekhElevna	1925	Dunilovichi, Vileika region	Minsk	Voroshilov	? 5
Menkin Shender Leizerovich	1924	Starobin	Pinsk	Komarov-Korzh's	Komarov's 3rd group
Menkin Yasha Abramovich	1920	Starobin	Pinsk	Komarov-Korzh's	Komarov's 3rd group
Merzon Genya Isaakovna	1922	Slonim	Brest	Sikorski's headquarters	Shchors
Merin Misha Aronovich	1928	Minsk	Baranovichi	detachment ? 106	
Merkina Sarra Leibovna	1897	Shklov	Mogilev	Chekist	Kalyushnikov's
Merlis Abram Mordukhovich	1897	Minsk getto	Baranovichi	Za Sovetskuyu Belarus	Shturm
Merlis Lazar Izrailevich	1924	Minsk getto	Baranovichi	Chapayev	Parkhomenko
Merson Afanasii Moiseyevich	1910	from captivity	Vileyka		Ponomarenko
Merson Grigori	1922	Dolginovo	Vileyka	Dovator	Sverdlov
Merson Samson	1919	Dolginovo	Vileyka	Dovator	Sverdlov
Mesel Genya Yefimovna	1914	Borisov	Baranovichi	Vpered (Forward)	Chkalov
Metlitski Yasha Avseyevich	1933	Ostroshitski gorodok	Baranovichi	detachment ? 106	
Metrik Meyer Afroimovich		Baranovichi			
Metrik Petr Naumovich	1911	Yezerishche	Vitebsk	2nd Belorusskaya	
Mekhenzon Yakov Leibovich	1906	from captivity	Palesye	detachment at the headquarters	
Meshalov Abram Samoilovich	1894	Pogost, Starobin district	Pinsk	Komarov-Korzh's	1 group
Meshalov Yevsei Abramovich	1930	Pogost, Starobin district	Pinsk	Komarov-Korzh's	1 group
Meshelevich Isaak Movshevich	1912	Slonim	Brest	Sikorski's headquarters	Shchors
Meshelevich Mariya SheyYevna	1917	Slonim	Brest	Sikorski's headquarters	Shchors
Migdalovich Grigori Izrailevich	1928	small town of Lenino, Polesskaya obl.	Minsk	Chkalov	Dovator
Migdalovich Meyer Mendelevich	1920	Lenin	Pinsk	Molotov	Kalinin
Migdalovich Moisei Isaakovich	1914	Western Byelorussia, Lenino	Minsk	Chkalov	Dovator
Migdalovich Mordukh Abramovich	1909	concentration camp Gantsevichi	Minsk	258th Kuibyshev	Budenny
Migdalovich Shmuel Khaimovich	1893	Lenino, Pinsk region	Minsk	Ponomarenko	A.Nevski
MidLyanski Abram Moiseyevich	1924		Baranovichi	Oktyabr	

Name	Year	Origin	Region	Unit	Detachment
Mizurek Adam Emmanuilovich	1907	Baranovichi	Baranovichi	Zhukov	
Mikanovskaya Mariya AndreYevna	1920	Warsaw	Palesye	? 130	? 133
Mikkovich Mordukh Meyerovich	1882	Baranovichi	Baranovichi	Kalinin	
Mikulitskaya Ira Mendeleyevna	1922	Lida	Baranovichi	Kirov	brigade headquarters
Mikulitski Samuil Girshevich	1903	Novogrudok	Baranovichi	Kalinin	
Mikulovich Sofiya	1918	Kuzmichi	Vileyka	Dovator	a contact
Mileikovskaya Mira Samuilovna	1921	Krevo	Baranovichi	Chkalov	? 4 "Za Sovetskuyu Belarus"
Mileikovski Yakov Girshevich	1921		Vileyka	Voroshilov	Istrebitel (Destroyer)
Milenkii Zalman Leibovich	1902	Minsk getto	Minsk	3rd Minskaya	Lazo
Milikovski Boris Borisovich	1924	Vishnevo	Baranovichi	Chkalov	? 4 "Za Sovetskuyu Belarus"
Milikovski Semen Yevnovich	1921	Slonim	Brest	Sikorski's headquarters	Shchors
Miller Boris Khatskelevich	1915	small town of Vasilishki	Baranovichi	Kirov	Ordzhonikidze
Miller Isaak Movshovich	1924	Traby	Baranovichi	Kalinin	
Miller Klara Aronovna	1911	Mir	Baranovichi	Zhukov	
Miller Leiba Faivelevich	1924	Sluvshin	Pinsk	Komarov-Korzh's	4 group
Miller Nisel Konelevich	1921		Baranovichi	Pobieda	Pobieda
Miller Yakha Pinkhusovna	1923	Lida	Baranovichi	Kalinin	
Milonaets Dora Yakovlevna	1924	Khorovichi, Rudnya district	Minsk	Pravda (Truth)	Pobieda
Milman Shaya Naumovich	1920	Lakhva	Pinsk	Kirov	Kalinin
Milner Tevel Rafailovich	1906	Sharkovshchina	Vileyka	Spartak	? 4
Milkhman Solomon Vulfovich	1923	Glubokoye	Minsk	Voronyanski	Kotovski
Milchin Meyer Oserovich	1927	Minsk	Baranovichi	detachment ? 106	
Milshtein Abram Davidovich	1908	Rakov, getto	Baranovichi	Stalin	Suvorov
Milshtein Isaak Yefimovich	1918	from the encirclement	Vitebsk	Nikitin's	? 4
Milshtein Semen Borisovich	1910	Nesvizh	Minsk	Voroshilov	Patriots of Motherland
Milyutin Dmitri Abramovich	1910	Braslav district	Vileyka	Zhdanov	
Milyutin Mikhail Berkovich	1923	Braslav	Vileyka	Spartak	? 2
Milyutin Khatskel Samuilovich	1920	getto, Braslav	Vileyka	Voroshilov	Chapayev
Milyutina Emma Yakovlevna	1921	Braslav	Vileyka	Zhdanov	
Mllyavski Vladimir Naumovich	1908	Central Committee of the CP (b) B	Vileyka	Frunze	Fighter
Minaker Ovsei Meyerovich	1923	Novogrudok	Baranovichi	Leninskaya	Borba
Mindalevich Khaim Tsalikovich	1913	Zabolote	Baranovichi	A.Nevski	brigade headquarters
Mindal Lev Ilyich	1924	Vileika district, Sharkova	Minsk	Zheleznyak	? 3
Mindel Dora Yefimovna	1930	Minsk	Baranovichi	detachment ? 106	
Mindel Isaak Shepshelevich	1917	Minsk	Baranovichi	detachment ? 106	
Mindel Lev Abramovich	1904		Minsk	Voronyanski	Mstitel (Revenger)
Mindel Mariya Ekhovna	1924	Dunilovichi	Vileyka	CC of the CP(b)B	Parkhomenko
Mindel Rakhil Solomonovna	1918	Minsk	Baranovichi	detachment ? 106	
Mindel Rubin Mindelevich	1910	Jewish camp	Vileyka	Spartak	? 2
Mindel Sonya Solomonovna	1915	Minsk	Baranovichi	detachment ? 106	
Mindel Shepshel Vulfovich	1874	Minsk	Baranovichi	detachment ? 106	
Mindlin Abram Yakovlevich	1903				
Mindlin Boris Grigorevich	1923	TsK VLKSM	Minsk	Bragin	Gastello
Mindlin David Yakovlevich	1903				
Mindlina Mariya Grigorevna	1927	Turbinka, Petrikov district	Palesye	37th Yelskaya	Bolshevik
Minevich Izrail Khaimovich	1904	Central Committee of the CP (b) B	Baranovichi	Kirov	Orel
Minkin Yosif Mordukhovich	1902	Minsk getto	Minsk	Rokossovski	25 years of Oktyabr
Minkovich Asya Yosifovna	1923	Minsk	Baranovichi	detachment ? 106	
Minkovich Mikhlya Yosifovna	1900	Minsk	Baranovichi	detachment ? 106	
Minkovich Mordukh Meyerovich	1882	Baranovichi	Baranovichi	Kalinin	
Minkovich Riva Yosifovna	1921	Minsk	Baranovichi	detachment ? 106	
Mins Izyuk Rabinovich	1922		Baranovichi	A.Nevski	Kalinovski
Minski David Yefremovich	1930	Slonim	Baranovichi	Pobieda	Pobieda
Mints Zigmunt Genekhovich	1914	Vlotslavsk	Baranovichi	Kalinin	
Mints Mariya Yakovlevna	1926	Bobruisk	Minsk	Bragin	Gastello
Mints Moisei Isarovich	1904	Mashitsy	Brest		Kotovski
Minkov Zalman Abramovich	1897	Khotenchitsy	Minsk	Voronyanski	Kotovski
Minkova Zelda Zalmanovna	1925	Khotenchitsy	Minsk	Voronyanski	Kotovski
Minkova Khaya Zalmanovna	1923	Khotenchitsy	Minsk	Voronyanski	Kotovski
Minkovich Mikhail Shayevich	1903	Byten	Brest	Sikorski's headquarters	commandant platoon
Miranker Girsh Yevelevich	1921	Mir	Baranovichi	Kalinin	
Miranski Aleksei Isarovich	1922	Mir, getto	Baranovichi	Za Sovetskuyu Belarus	Kirov
Miranski Ivan Issarovich	1920	Mir	Baranovichi	Za Sovetskuyu Belarus	Shturm
Miranski Izrail Isarovich	1920	Mir	Baranovichi	Chkalov	
Miranski Eli Isarovich	1922	Mir	Baranovichi	Za Sovetskuyu Belarus	Shturm
Mirzon Yevgeniya Isaakovna	1922	Slonim	Brest		Budenny

Mironchik Abram Moiseyevich	1901	from captivity	Minsk	Death to Fascism	Kutuzov
Mironchik Grigori Mesonovich	1915	Stolbtsy	Baranovichi	Stalin	Bolshevik
Mirskaya Ginda Izrailevna	1910	Dyatlovo	Baranovichi	Leninskaya	Borba
Mirskaya Sofiya Yosifovna	1914	Baranovichi	Baranovichi	Chkalov	? 4 "Za Sovetskuyu Belarus"
Mirski Isaak Izrailevich	1923	getto, Vilno	Vileyka	Voroshilov	Kalinin
Mirski Movsha Borukhovich	1897	Dyatlovo	Baranovichi	Leninskaya	Borba
Mirski Fedor Solomonovich	1916	Minsk	Baranovichi	Vpered (Forward)	Chkalov
Mirson Movsha Abramovich	1904	Gorodok	Baranovichi	Chkalov	? 4 "Za Sovetskuyu Belarus"
Miskin Shlema Girshevich	1887	Baranovichi	Baranovichi	Chkalov	
Misushchina Zelfira Izrailevna	1925	Vilno	Vileyka	Za Rodinu (For Motherland)	Voroshilov
Mitelman Meyer Mortkovich	1919	Poland	Brest	Lenin	Zhukov
Mitelman Sidor Motkovich	1909	a small partisan group	Pinsk	Molotov	Lazo
Mitkovskaya Mina Samuilovna	1924	Vishnevo	Baranovichi	Za Sovetskuyu Belarus	Za Sovetskuyu Belarus
Mitlyanskaya Mera Naumovna	1896	Lida	Baranovichi	Kalinin	
Mitlyanskaya Nakhama Leibovna	1910	Novogrudok	Baranovichi	Kalinin	
Mitlyanskaya Taiba Moiseyevna	1931	Lida	Baranovichi	Kalinin	
Mitlyanski Abram Moiseyevich	1924	Lida	Baranovichi	Kalinin	
Mitlyanski David Moiseyevich	1926	Lida	Baranovichi	Kalinin	
Mitlyanski Samuil Moiseyevich	1922	Lida, getto	Baranovichi	Kirov	Ordzhonikidze
Mityaeva Anna Yosifovna	1919	Vishnevo	Baranovichi	Chapayev	Lazo
Mifsezon Venyamin	1901	Kozianski les	Vileyka	Zhdanov	
Mikhalovskaya Mariya Izrailevna	1922	Lida	Baranovichi	Kalinin	
Mikhalovski Alter Shimanovich	1912	Lida	Baranovichi	Kalinin	
Mikhalson Aleksandr Yakovlevich	1923	getto	Vileyka	Voroshilov	Chapayev
Mikhelson Mikhail Davidovich	1912	from the encirclement	Vitebsk	Kirillov	? 4
Mikhlin Grigori Solomonovich	1913	Khoiniki	Palesye		Chapayev
Mikhnovich Boris Abramovich	1907	Jewish camp	Vileyka	Voroshilov	headquarters' production group
Mitsmakher Abram Osipovich	1916	Domachevo	Brest	Stalin	
Mitsmakher Yakov Yosifovich	1920	Domachevo	Pinsk	Molotov	Lazo
Mishalov Aleksandr Shevelevich	1926	from captivity	Palesye	? 123	Artyushka's
Mishalov Samuil	1914	Lenin	Pinsk	Komarov-Korzh's	4 group
Mishelevich Yosif Yefimovich	1917	Minsk	Minsk	2nd Minskaya	Kutuzov
Mishkin Mikhail Sokhorovich	1925	Slonim	Pinsk	Lenin	Kutuzov
Mishler Fedor Mashkovich	1926	Poland	Brest	Sikorski's headquarters	Shchors
Mishchenko Lyubov Yakovlevna	1914	Kobrin	Pinsk	Kirov	Za Rodinu (For Motherland)
Mlot Maks Abramovich	1909	Volozhin	Baranovichi	Chkalov	? 4 "Za Sovetskuyu Belarus"
Mlynski Boris Markovich	1926	Minsk getto	Minsk	Dyadi Koli	Burya (Storm)
Mnuskin Nevakh Kalmanovich	1905	Dyatlovo	Baranovichi	Leninskaya	Borba
Movshovich David Yoselevich	1910	Develishki	Baranovichi	Kalinin	
Movshovich Iliya Samuilovich	1911	Lida	Baranovichi	Kalinin	
Movshovich Leiba Khaimovich	1923	Novogrudok	Baranovichi	Kalinin	
Movshovich Lyusya Moiseyevna	1925	Baranovichi	Baranovichi	Kalinin	
Movshovich Mikhail Moiseyevich	1926	Minsk getto	Baranovichi	Stalin	Parkhomenko
Movshovich Movsha Girshevich	1897	Baranovichi	Baranovichi	Kalinin	
Movshovich Ovsei Samuilovich	1908	Lida	Baranovichi	Vpered (Forward)	Roshcha
Movshovich Rivka Samuilovna	1878	Lida	Baranovichi	Kalinin	
Movshovich Sara Moiseyevna	1938	DYevelishki	Baranovichi	Kalinin	
Movshovich Khana Samuilovna	1919	Lida	Baranovichi	Kalinin	
Mogid Abram Shmuilovich	1910	Dyatlovo	Baranovichi	Leninskaya	Borba
Mogilevchik Aleksandr Zakharovich	1920	from captivity	Vileyka	Suvorov	
Mogilner Dodel Zavikhovich	1910		Minsk	Ponomarenko	Gorbachev
Modelevich Moisei Lazarevich	1903	Slonim	Brest	Sikorski's headquarters	Shchors
Modlin Boris Yankovich	1920	Jewish camp	Vileyka	Spartak	? 2
Molofei Serafim Romanovich	1920	Kurenetski district	Vileyka	Dovator	Sverdlov
Molochnikov Ignat Danilovich	1905	Minsk	Baranovichi	Stalin	Chapayev
Molchadski Volf Meyerovich	1932	Lida	Baranovichi	Kalinin	
Molchadski Yankel Mordukhovich	1912	small town of Belitsa, getto	Baranovichi	Kirov	Ordzhonikidze
Molchatskaya Raisa Simkhovna	1923		Baranovichi	Slonim IDC	
Molchatski Elya Malakhovich	1893	Baranovichi	Baranovichi	Grizodubova	Chkalov
Molchitski Motel Yakovlevich	1912	Baranovichi, from home	Baranovichi	Grizodubova	Matrosov
Moldan Nevakh Moiseyevich	1911	detachment Kaganovich	Pinsk	Kuibyshev	Ordzhonikidze
Mond Maya Berkovna	1924	Usha district	Vitebsk	Chapayev	detachments
Mond Khaya Berkovna	1922		Vitebsk	Chapayev	detachments
Mondal Leya Khalamovna	1915	detachment Kaganovich	Pinsk	Kuibyshev	Ordzhonikidze

Monski Danel Kalmonovich	1923		Baranovichi	Oktyabr	
Montvilinski Maksim Grigorevich	1895	Minsk getto	Baranovichi	Chapayev	Parkhomenko
Moncher Boris Milovich	1925	getto Tsekhanovets	Grodno	Vo imya Rodiny (In the name of Motherland)	Zhukov
Morgulis Matvei Samuilovich	1909	Porozov district	Brest	Brest antifascist committee	
Mordes Sim Fedorovich	1917	Jewish camp, Belostok	Grodno		Kalinin
Mordetski Khaim Yosifovich	1913	Belostok	Grodno	Samutin's group	Kirshner's group
Mordkovski Zelik Aronovich	1914	Dyatlovo	Baranovichi	Leninskaya	Borba
Mordkovski Noakh Shmuilovich	1911	Molchad	Baranovichi	Kalinin	
Mordkovski Nokhim Mordukhovich	1913		Baranovichi	Oktyabr	
Mordkovski Petr Simonovich	1893	Koldychevo, getto	Baranovichi	Pervomaiskaya	Ya.Kolas
Mordukovich Yankel Itskovich	1927	Ivienets	Baranovichi	Kalinin	
Mordukhovich Rokhmen Izrailevich	1911	Baranovichi	Baranovichi	Vpered (Forward)	Roshcha
Mordukhovich Khaya Davidovna	1920	Baranovichi	Baranovichi	Vpered (Forward)	Roshcha
Mordkhilevich Vova	1930	Minsk	Baranovichi	detachment ? 106	
Mordkhilevich Leonid Lvovich	1930	Moskva	Baranovichi	detachment ? 106	
Morozov Vasili Prokofyevich	1903	from captivity	Vitebsk	Sadchikov's	batalon ? 2
Morozova Mariya Maksimovna	1906	Mozyr	Palesye	99th Kalinkovichskaya	Voroshilov
Mortman Leizer Berkovich	1906	Peredopy	Vileyka	CC of the CP(b)B	brigade sanitary service
Mosarski Boris Meyerovich	1931		Vitebsk	Chapayev	detachments
Mosarski Viktor Aronovich	1930	Shumilino	Vitebsk	Sadchikov's	batalon ? 2
Mosin Grigori Osipovich	1907	Perevoloka	Gomel	Voroshilov	Voroshilov
Moslyanski I.S.	1901	Gressk district	Minsk	Voroshilov	? 1
Motvilinski Maksim Grigorevich	1895	Minsk getto	Baranovichi	Stalin	Parkhomenko
Motienko Mikhail Anatolevich	1913	Brinev	Palesye	? 125	Semko
Motlovskaya Mikhlya Rubinovna	1922	Lida	Baranovichi	Lenin's komsomol	Lenin's komsomol
Motskevich Lev Mikhailovich	1905	Slutsk	Minsk	Suvorov	
Motsnet Ersh Usherovich	1904	N. Sverzhen	Minsk	Chapayev	Ponomarenko
Mochkovskaya Glissa Yefimovna	1918	Novoyelnya	Baranovichi	Kalinin	
Moshkevich Ivan Frantsevich	1919	working column of the Magyar army	Brest	Dzerzhinski	Molotov
Mugerman Miron Naumovich		Palesye		? 135	
Mudrik Nokhim Leibovich	1913	Lida	Baranovichi	Kalinin	
Mudrik Rakhelya Leibovna	1923	Lida	Baranovichi	Kalinin	
Mudrik Khana Leibovna	1922	Lida	Baranovichi	Kalinin	
Muzhatskaya Sofiya Samsonovna	1917	Volkovysk	Belostok	A.Nevski	Kotovski
Mukasei Girsh Yakovlevich	1920	Baranovichi	Baranovichi	Kalinin	
Mukasei Mariya Khanovna	1923	Slonim	Brest	Dzerzhinski	Molotov
Mukasei Mikhail Vladimirovich	1909	Baranovichi	Brest	Dzerzhinski	Kalinin
Mukatser Zakhar Yevseyevich	1919	from captivity	Palesye	? 125	Kudravtsa
Mukashei Rita Khonovna	1920	Slonim	Brest	Sikorski's headquarters	Shchors
Mukosei Ginda	1911	from the civil camp	Baranovichi	Grizodubova	Chkalov
Munets Avsei Abramovich	1914	Yody	Vileyka		Ponomarenko
Munets Moisei Solomonovich	1926	Braslav district	Vileyka	Zhdanov	
Munets Rakhmel Abramovich	1925	Yody	Vileyka		Ponomarenko
Munets Riva Abramovna	1924	Yody	Vileyka		Ponomarenko
Munets Khaim Abramovich	1908	Yody	Vileyka		Ponomarenko
Muravets Boris Samsonovich	1920	Kobrin	Brest		Kotovski
Muravnik Aron Movshevich	1904	Lakhva	Pinsk	Kirov	
Muravnik Lyuba Lvovna	1920	Minsk	Baranovichi	detachment ? 106	
Muravnik Mikhail	1929	Rubel, David-Gorodok district	Pinsk	Sovetskaya Belarus	Kutuzov
Muravchik Zelman Leibovich	1925	Lakhva	Pinsk	Kirov	Za Rodinu (For Motherland)
Muravchik Litman Yudelevich	1917	getto, Vilno	Vileyka	Voroshilov	Pobieda
Muravchik Naum Solomonovich	1918	Lakhva	Pinsk	Kirov	
Muravchik Yakov Grigorevich	1903	family detachment camp	Pinsk	Kirov	
Muravchik Yakov Leibovich	1922	Lakhva	Pinsk	Kirov	Za Rodinu (For Motherland)
Muravchik Yankel Shlemovich	1910	Vulka	Pinsk	Kirov	
Murokh Yevgeniya Yakovlevna	1923	Minsk getto	Baranovichi	18th Frunze	Dzerzhinski
Murokh Sima Izrailevna	1926	Minsk	Baranovichi	detachment ? 106	
Musin Lenya Aronovich	1936	Minsk	Baranovichi	detachment ? 106	
Musina Mariya Grigorevna	1914	v. Motorovo, Pukhovichi district	Minsk	Pravda (Truth)	contacts of the br. "Pravda (Truth)"
Musina Riva YudalYevna	1912	Minsk	Baranovichi	Vpered (Forward)	family detachment group
Musina Tsilya Davidovna	1911	Minsk	Baranovichi	detachment ? 106	
Mutarperl Khaya Shmerkovna	1927		Vitebsk	Chapayev	detachments
Muterpert Dora Aronovna	1906	Dokshitsy	Vileyka	CC of the CP(b)B	Parkhomenko
Muterpert Raisa Davidovna	1929	Dokshitsy	Vileyka	CC of the CP(b)B	Parkhomenko
Mukhina Faina Fedorovna	1922	Vilno	Baranovichi	Stalin	Budenny

Mukhover Bronya Ilkovna		Shklov	Mogilev	Chekist	? 10
Muchnik Ioina Pamfinovich	1927	Mir	Baranovichi	Chkalov	? 4 "Za Sovetskuyu Belarus"
Mushkat Abram Peisakhovich	1922	from Melnikov's brigade	Vileyka	Kalinin	? 2
Mushkat Basya Zalmanovna	1924	Jewish camp	Vileyka	Spartak	? 2
Mushkat Isaak Peisakhovich	1908	from Melnikov's brigade	Vileyka	Kalinin	? 3
Mushkat Leiba Zalmanovich	1914	from captivity	Vileyka	Spartak	? 3
Mushkat Raisa Peisakhovna	1918	from Melnikov's brigade	Vileyka	Kalinin	? 3
Mushkatel Shlema Mendelevich	1920	Stolbtsy	Minsk	Chapayev	Ponomarenko
Myzgaeva Lyubov Yefimovna	1915	Minsk	Minsk	2nd Minskaya	Kutuzov
Myslivchik Mariya Leonovna	1910	Starye Dorogi district, Verkhutino	Minsk	Chkalov	Gromov
Myshelov Aleksandr Mordukhovich	1919	concentration camp Gantsevichi	Minsk	258th Kuibyshev	Chapayev
Myshelov Lipa Mordukhovich	1912	concentration camp Gantsevichi	Minsk	258th Kuibyshev	Chapayev
Myshko'svskaya Dora Girshevna	1897	Kopyl	Minsk	Chapayev	Ponomarenko
Myshko'svski Yankel Srolevich	1895	Kopyl	Minsk	Chapayev	Ponomarenko
Myasnik Bronya Abramovna	1909	Lida	Baranovichi	Leninskaya	hospital
Myasnik Miriam Khaimovna	1935	Lida	Baranovichi	Leninskaya	hospital
Myasnik Khaim Genokhovich	1903	Lida	Baranovichi	Leninskaya	hospital
Nadelson Shlema Abramovich	1918	Slutsk	Pinsk	Komarov-Korzh's	2 group
Nadkovich Yankel	1922	Kozyany	Vileyka	Spartak	? 6
Naerman Tanya MotElevna	1932	Martikantsy	Baranovichi	Lenin's komsomol	Lenin's komsomol
Naigenbauer Abram Itskovich	1917		Baranovichi	Oktyabr	
Naigus Meyer Naumovich	1913	Jewish camp Dolginovo	Minsk	Voronyanski	Pobieda
Naiman Avrum Movshevich	1920	Jewish camp	Pinsk	Shubetidze	Ordzhonikidze
Naiman Simkha Nakhmanovich	1908	Kletsk	Minsk	Chapayev	Ponomarenko
Naimark Aron Girshevich	1916	Dosovichi	Mogilev	polk ? 277	
Naimark Misha Zakharovich	1923	Kopyl	Minsk	Chapayev	Ponomarenko
Naimark Naum Girshevich	1916	Dosovichi	Mogilev	partisan regiment ? 277	? 277
Naifeld Boris Moiseyevich	1912	Baranovichi	Baranovichi	Kalinin	
Naifeld Lyuba Moiseyevna	1912	Baranovichi	Baranovichi	Kalinin	
Naifeld Nadezhda Borisovna	1922	Khorobcha, Gressk district	Minsk	2nd Minskaya	Ponomarenko
Naikhovich Kalman Lazarovich	1913	Gorodishche	Baranovichi	Kalinin	
Namet Isaak Naumovich	1904	Minsk	Mogilev	208th regiment	
Napoleon Rita Maksimovna	1924	Vilno	Vileyka	Suvorov	
Narkunskaya Bunia Abramovna	1921	Lida, getto	Baranovichi	Kirov	Ordzhonikidze
Narkunskaya Minya Yankelevna	1922	Lida	Baranovichi	Kalinin	
Narkunski Abram Idelevich	1915	Ivye	Baranovichi	Kirov	Za Sovetskuyu Belarus
Narkunski Abram Yudelevich	1940	Lida	Baranovichi	Kalinin	
Narkunski Lev Abramovich	1917	Lida, getto	Baranovichi	Kirov	Ordzhonikidze
Narkunski Yudel Abramovich	1910	Zhirmuny	Baranovichi	Kalinin	
Narotski Izrail Sholomovich	1926	Dunilovichi	Minsk	Voronyanski	Kotovski
Narotski Fedor Yosifovich	1926	Vilno, getto	Vileyka	Voroshilov	
Narotski Elyash Yesilevich	1926	getto, Myadel	Vileyka	Voroshilov	Kalinin
Natanblit Dveira Davidovna	1920	Lida	Baranovichi	Kalinin	
Nakhamchik Yefim Zalmanovich	1923	Dzerzhinsk district	Minsk	A.Nevski	? 1
Nakhimovski Yosif Zelikovich	1896	Novogrudok	Baranovichi	Kalinin	
Nakhmanchik Yefim Zalmanovich	1923	Dzerzhinsk district	Brest	? 99 Gulyaev	Grabko
Nevakhovich Shlema Khaimovich	1905	from the encirclement	Baranovichi	25 years of the BSSR	Kotovski
Negnevitskaya Roza Isaakovna	1909	Chernevyachi	Baranovichi	Kalinin	
Negnevitskaya Khaya Isaakovna	1921	Korelichi	Baranovichi	Kalinin	
Negnevitskaya Sheina Yosifovna	1923	Novogrudok	Baranovichi	Kalinin	
Negnevitski Alter Samuilovich	1896	Novogrudok	Baranovichi	Kalinin	
Negnevitski Movsha Samuilovich	1916	Novogrudok	Baranovichi	Kalinin	
Negnevitski Khaim Moiseyevich	1897	Chernevyachi	Baranovichi	Kalinin	
Negnevitski Yakov Isaakovich	1925	Minsk	Baranovichi	detachment ? 106	
Nedlin Nota Zalmanovich	1914	from captivity	Baranovichi	18th Frunze	Frunze
Neiman Abram Yevelevich	1923	Minsk getto	Minsk	1st Minskaya	
Neiman Yefim Yosifovich	1921	from the brigade "Death to Fascism"	Minsk	Ponomarenko	Gvardeyets (Guardsman)
Neiman Mikhail Yosifovich	1898	Borisov district, Brodnya	Minsk	Death to Fascism	Budenny
Neiman Mordukh Yevelevich	1918	Minsk getto	Minsk	1st Minskaya	
Neiman Raisa Yemelyanovna	1926	Peski, Minsk district	Minsk	1st Minskaya	
Neishtat Mikhail Izrailevich	1910		Minsk	2nd Minskaya	Suvorov
Nekrich Isaak Ilyich	1910	Slutsk	Minsk	3rd Minskaya	Niepobedimy (Undefeated)
Nemzer Leon Davidovich	1912	German camp	Pinsk	Molotov	Shish
Nemoi Yankel Shepselevich	1916	Berezovo, Rovno region	Pinsk	Komarov-Korzh's	4 group

Name	Year	Origin	Region	Unit	Sub-unit
Nemchin Elya Mironovich	1919	Mogilev	Mogilev	? 113	brigade ? 113
Nesnevich Isaak Mironovich	1911	Central Committee of the CP (b) B	Minsk	Shturmovaya	Grozny
Nesnevich Mllya Markovna	1912	Minsk	Baranovichi	Chkalov	
Nessel Mikhail Grigorevich	1905	Timonovo	Mogilev		? 45 "Za Rodinu (For Motherland)"
Nestempover Yosif	1920	from behind the front line	Vitebsk	Frunze	Frunze ? 1
Nekhamchik Shevel Khaimovich	1913	from the Jewish camp	Vileyka	Oktyabr	? 2
Nekhenzon Yakov Libovich	1913	Vasilyevichi	Palesye	99th Kalinkovichskaya	Voroshilov
Nekhina Khaya Lvovna	1910	Shchedrin	Palesye	? 123	Kovalenko's
Nikitin Nikolai Mikhailovich	1907	from the encirclement	Vitebsk	Nikitin's	brigade headquarters and reconnaissance platoon
Nikolaev Aleksandr Ivanovich	1910	Koporonka, Komarin district	Palesye		Voroshilov
Nikolaevskaya Galya IsYevna	1919	Novogrudok	Baranovichi	Stalin	Suvorov
Nikolaevskaya Minya Yoselevna	1918	Novogrudok	Baranovichi	Kalinin	
Nikolaevskaya Polya Yudelevna	1918	Dyatlovo	Baranovichi	Leninskaya	Leninski
Nikolaevski Berka Rubinovich	1915	Dyatlovo	Baranovichi	Leninskaya	family detachment group
Nikolaevski Moisei Geselevich	1923	Ivye	Baranovichi	Kalinin	
Ninberg Mariya Matveyevna	1922	Baranovichi	Baranovichi	Chkalov	reserve group
Niselevich Samuil Abramovich	1909	Dyatlovo	Baranovichi	Leninskaya	Borba
Niselbaum Leon Borukhovich	1918	Zburazh, Malorita district	Brest	Lenin	Voroshilov
Nisenbaum Abram Borisovich	1923	Byten	Brest	Ponomarenko	Sovetskaya Belarus
Nisenbaum Lev Solomonovich	1926		Minsk	2nd Minskaya	Kutuzov
Nisenbaum Mikhail Bentsionovich	1916	Nesvizh	Minsk	Chapayev	Ponomarenko
Nisenbaum Khaim Benyaminovich	1908	Radoshkovichi	Minsk	Voronyanski	Kotovski
Niskevich Lilya Mironovna	1915	Minsk	Baranovichi	Chkalov	
Nisnevich Boris Lvovich	1924	Minsk	Baranovichi	detachment ? 106	
Nisnevich Yefim Aronovich	1907	Rudensk	Mogilev	208th partisan regiment	khoziaistvennaia rota
Nisnevich Ida Borisovna	1905	Minsk	Baranovichi	detachment ? 106	
Nisnevich Samuil Volfovich	1911	Shklov district	Mogilev	Chekist	? 1
Nitershul Yosif Kh.	1913	Pruzhany	Brest	Za Sovetskuyu Belarus	Chkalov
Nitlyuk Eidlya Leibovna	1905	Lida	Baranovichi		
Nikhamchik Ginda Elevna	1929	Minsk	Baranovichi	detachment ? 106	
Nitsberg Mikhail Srolevich	1910	Pruzhany	Brest	Ponomarenko	brigade headquarters
Nisht Samuil Shlemovich	1912	Krynki	Grodno	Samutin's group	Kirshner's group
Novik Boris Yudelevich	1922	getto	Baranovichi	Lenin's komsomol	Kotovski
Novik Golda	1923	from the civil camp	Baranovichi	Grizodubova	Chkalov
Novik Zelik Yudelevich	1924	Martikantsy	Baranovichi	Lenin's komsomol	Lenin's komsomol
Novik Zina Yudelevna	1921	getto	Baranovichi	Lenin's komsomol	Kotovski
Novik Roza Aronovna	1903	Minsk	Baranovichi	detachment ? 106	
Novikov David Moiseyevich	1925	Boyanichi, Lyuban district	Minsk	Ponomarenko	Korneyev's
Novitski Leizer Girshevich	1917	Dvorets	Baranovichi	Kalinin	
Novitski Yakov Aronovich	1895	Dvorets	Baranovichi	Kalinin	
Novichenok Isaak Samuilovich	1914	Central Committee of the CP (b) B	Minsk	Shturmovaya	Frunze
Novogrudok Yosif Abramovich	1923	Dyatlovo	Baranovichi	Leninskaya	Borba
Novogrudok Isaak Lazarovich	1912	Dvorets	Baranovichi	Kalinin	
Novogrudok Mikhel Abramovich	1912	Dyatlovo	Baranovichi	Kalinin	
Novogrudok Nikolai Yankelevich	1927	Gorodishche	Baranovichi	25 years of the BSSR	Kotovski
Novodvorets Ilya Egidovich	1925	Shatsk, Rudnya district	Minsk	Belarus	Za Rodinu (For Motherland)
Novodvorski Khaim Samuilovich	1928	Timkovichi getto	Minsk	Frunze	Budenny
NovopLyanski Girsh Leibovich	1923		Baranovichi	Oktyabr	
Novosadskaya Genya Semenovna	1924	Stolbtsy	Baranovichi	Dzerzhinski	Dzerzhinski
Nodelis Khaim Yakovlevich	1919	Minsk, from captivity	Minsk	Shturmovaya	Frunze
Nodel Manboris Grigorevich	1916	Minsk	Belostok	Chapayev	Chapayev
Nodelson Abram Semenovich	1918	Slutsk	Minsk	Dyadi Koli	Stalin
Nozhnitskaya small town ofKh.	1920	Derechin	Baranovichi	Pobieda	Pobieda
Nozik Benya Mordukhovich	1898	Glussk	Minsk	258th Kuibyshev	Chapayev
Nozik Girsh Mikhelevich	1888	Glussk	Palesye	? 123	Pavlovski's
Noiman Shimsha Izrailevich	1914	Lida	Baranovichi	Kalinin	
Nol Abram Lazarevich	1921	Krasnoye, getto	Baranovichi	Chkalov	
Nol Leizer Abramovich	1890	Krasnoye, getto	Baranovichi	Za Sovetskuyu Belarus	Za Sovetskuyu Belarus
Nomkin Grigori Afanasyevich	1905	Jewish camp	Vileyka	Spartak	? 2
Nomkin Yosif Afanasyevich	1903	farm-stead Brudino	Vileyka	Spartak	? 2
Nomkin Matus Avseyevich	1908	getto, Sharkovshchina	Vileyka	Spartak	? 6
Nomkina Belya Yakovlevna	1919	getto, Sharkovshchina	Vileyka	Spartak	? 6
Norman Samuil Davidovich	1924	Vileika	Minsk	Voronyanski	Kotovski
Norotskaya Yelizaveta Yosifovna	1926	Ushachi district	Vitebsk	Chapayev	detachments

Norotski Samuil Abramovich	1907	Myadel	Vileyka	Voroshilov	Suvorov
Norotski Khaim Yosifovich	1928		Vitebsk	Chapayev	detachments
Nosanchuk Mikhail Mordkovich	1911	Rubel, David-Gorodok district	Pinsk	Sovetskaya Belarus	Rokossovski
Notkina Asya Solomonovna	1919	Batsevichi, Klichev district	Mogilev		? 278
Notkovich Kalman Leizerovich	1913	Korelichi	Baranovichi	Kalinin	
Notfeld Boris Moiseyevich	1912	Baranovichi	Baranovichi	Kalinin	
Nokhamkina Fanya Lvovna	1923	Gorodets	Gomel	10st Zhuravichskaya	? 265 Voroshilov
Nokhimovskaya Guta Zelikovna	1920	Korelichi	Baranovichi	Kalinin	
Nokhimovski Gerts Kushelevich	1920	Novogrudok	Baranovichi	Kalinin	
Nudelman Moisei Borisovich		from captivity	Brest	? 8	
Niusbaum Liza GeorgiYevna	1925	getto, Vilno	Vileyka	Voroshilov	Kalinin
Niankovskaya Raya Moiseyevna			Baranovichi	Kalinin	
Niankovski Moisei Salomonovich	1892	Novogrudok	Baranovichi	Kalinin	
Niankovski Teva Moiseyevich	1928	Novogrudok	Baranovichi	Kalinin	
Ovseyevich Sara Ovseyevna	1923	Dyatlovo	Baranovichi	Leninskaya	family detachment group
Ovsievich Tsalya Yosifovich	1924	Lyubcha	Baranovichi	Kalinin	
Oginski Yefim Samuilovich	1922	Minsk	Minsk	2nd Minskaya	Kutuzov
Ogulnik Sofiya Isaakovna	1925	Derechin	Baranovichi	Pobieda	Budenny
Ogulnik Shalom Shmerkovich	1909	Dyatlovo getto	Baranovichi	Kirov	Ordzhonikidze
Ogushevich Ovsei		Slonim	Brest	Sikorski's headquarters	Shchors
Oder Lev Naumovich	1915	Minsk	Minsk	Ponomarenko	Voroshilov
Odes Yevsei Yakovlevich	1923	Minsk	Minsk	2nd Minskaya	Ponomarenko
Odinets Vera Yosifovna	1922	Belarusian Staff of Partisan Movement	Baranovichi	Gruppy partrabotnikov	Shemetovets' group
Odrizhinski Yosif Samuilovich	1912	Odrizhin	Pinsk	Molotov	Potalakh
Odryzhenskaya Genya Moiseyevna	1919	Ivanovo	Pinsk	Molotov	Lazo
Odryzhenski Itsko Itskelevich	1920	Belinsk forest, Pinsk region	Pinsk	Molotov	Lazo
Ozhekhovskaya Galina Abramovna	1921	Lida	Baranovichi	Kalinin	
Ozhekhovskaya Liza Khaimovna	1919	Dyatlovo	Baranovichi	Leninskaya	Borba
Ozhekhovskaya Shifra Yosifovich	1879	Lida	Baranovichi	Kalinin	
Ozhekhovski Zelik Yosifovich	1941	Lida	Baranovichi	Kalinin	
Ozhekhovski Yosif Zelikovich	1917	Lida, getto	Baranovichi	Kirov	Ordzhonikidze
Ozhekhovski Lev Nevakhovich	1918		Baranovichi	Oktyabr	
Ozhekhovski Leiba Motelevich	1921	Korelichi	Baranovichi	Kalinin	
Ozhekhovski Matvei Mendelevich	1921	Derechin	Baranovichi	Pobieda	Pobieda
Ozhekhovski Khonon Zelikovich	1920	getto	Baranovichi	Kirov	Orel
Ozhekhovski Yakov Elyanovich	1920	family detachment camp	Belostok	A.Nevski	
Ozhinski Pin Mikhailovich	1924	Glubokoye	Vileyka	4th Belorusskaya	? 1
Ozhukhovskaya Ester Ovseyevna	1917	Lida, getto	Baranovichi	Kirov	Ordzhonikidze
Ozhukhovski Yosif Ilyich	1926	family detachment camp	Belostok	A.Nevski	
Ozhukhovski Leib Tsalkovich	1916	Lida, getto	Baranovichi	Kirov	Ordzhonikidze
Ozhukhovski Mordukh Itskovich	1897	Novogrudok, getto	Baranovichi	1st Baranovichskaya	Frunze
Ozhukhovski Nokhim Mendelevich	1925	Novogrudok	Baranovichi	Leninskaya	Borba
Ozder Leon Yudelevich	1908	Belostok	Grodno	Samutin's group	Kirshner's group
Ozder Olya Aronovna	1922	Minsk	Baranovichi	detachment ? 106	
Ozerskaya Rakhil Yefimovna	1909	Minsk	Baranovichi	detachment ? 106	
Ozerski Leizer Davidovich	1916	concentration camp	Pinsk	Kuibyshev	Shchors
Ozerianski Boma Yankelevich	1923	Gorodishche district	Baranovichi	25 years of the BSSR	Grozny
Okmenkrug Yefim Isaakovich	1910	Minsk	Vitebsk	Za Sovetskuyu Belarus	? 3
Okonski Shlema Yoselevich	1925	Novogrudok	Baranovichi	Kalinin	
Okonski Efroim Yoselevich	1928	Novogrudok	Baranovichi	Kalinin	
Oksekgrug Klara Isaakovna	1927	Minsk	Baranovichi	detachment ? 106	
Oksenkrug Khaim Isaakovich	1910	Belarusian Staff of Partisan Movement	Brest	groups of party leaders	Mech (Sword)
Okun Boris Borukhovich	1924	from home	Baranovichi	Grizodubova	
Okun Vulf Rubinovich	1898	Minsk getto	Baranovichi	Chapayev	Parkhomenko
Okun Dora Efroimovna	1913	Molodechno	Baranovichi	Chkalov	
Okun Zalman Borukhovich	1915	from home	Baranovichi	Grizodubova	v. Zaluzhe
Okun Iekhiel Khlavnovich	1914	Gorodok	Baranovichi	Chkalov	
Okun Ilya Borisovich	1905	Minsk	Baranovichi	detachment ? 106	
Okun Lenya Isaakovich	1926	Minsk	Baranovichi	detachment ? 106	
Okun Leonid Mikhailovich	1911	Minsk	Mogilev	208th partisan regiment	? 4
Okun Liza Mironovna	1898	Ostroshitski gorodok	Baranovichi	detachment ? 106	
Okun Khana Abramovna	1923	from the civil camp	Baranovichi	Grizodubova	Chkalov
Okun Tsilya Vulfovna	1924	Minsk getto	Baranovichi	Chapayev	Parkhomenko
Olevski Semen Nikolayevich	1919	from captivity	Mogilev	Chekist	Mon. group
Oleinik Zelik Peisakhovich	1913	concentration camp, Logishin	Pinsk	Kuibyshev	Shchors

Olenskaya Regina Yosifovna	1921	Bryansk getto, Belostok region	Grodno	Vo imya Rodiny (In the name of Motherland)	Zhukov
Olenski Abram Yankelevich	1918	Bryansk getto, Belostok region	Grodno	Vo imya Rodiny (In the name of Motherland)	Zhukov
Olenski David Yankelevich	1917	Bryansk getto, Belostok region	Grodno	Vo imya Rodiny (In the name of Motherland)	Zhukov
Olenski Solomon Yankelevich	1925	Bryansk getto, Belostok region	Grodno	Vo imya Rodiny (In the name of Motherland)	Zhukov
Olekh Aron Mendelevich	1913	Volkovyssk, camp	Belostok	A.Nevski	
Ollvyenshtein Shaya Moiseyevich	1912	Nesvizh	Minsk	Chapayev	Ponomarenko
Olomutski Aizik Davidovich	1921	Lyaskovichi	Brest	? 99 Gulyaev	Grabko
Olomutski Volf Davidovich	1908	Lakhva, Pinsk region	Minsk	Ponomarenko	Selnitski
Oldan Yakov Naftolevich	1928	factory Khimik	Baranovichi	Grizodubova	Chkalov
Olkinitskaya Lyubov Movshevna	1916	Orany	Baranovichi	Lenin's komsomol	Lenin's komsomol
Olkhenitski Meyer Khaimovich	1923	Voronovo	Baranovichi	Kalinin	
Olkhenitski Yankel Khaimovich	1925	Voronovo	Baranovichi	Kalinin	
Olkhovoi Lemel Srulevich	1903	Petritskoe, from captivity	Gomel	Za Rodinu (For Motherland)	Za Rodinu (For Motherland)
Olkhovski Mikhail Arkadevichi	1912	from captivity	Vitebsk	1st Drissenskaya	Kirov
Olshan Mirian Isaakovna	1918	Kornashi	Baranovichi	Kalinin	
Olshan Rubin Gertsevich	1920	Vilno	Baranovichi	Kalinin	
Olshanskaya Nadezhda Zakharovna	1914	Minsk	Minsk	2nd Minskaya	Ponomarenko
Olshanski Grigori Naumovich	1928	Shchedrin	Palesye	? 123	25-letiia VLKSM
Olshanski Yosif Zimelevich	1900	Shchedrin	Palesye	? 123	brigade headquarters and administration platoon
Omelinski Moisei Yosifovich	1916	Brest	Pinsk	Molotov	Shish
Omelinski Noakh Yoselevich	1917	Brest	Brest		Kotovski
Omelyanski Moisei B.	1916	Kuzavka, Malorita district	Brest	Lenin	Voroshilov
Ongeiberg Semen Motovich	1927	Slutsk getto	Minsk	32nd Kalinin	Parkhomenko
Opengeim Mariya Samuilovna	1939	Novogrudok	Baranovichi	Kalinin	
Opengeim Ovsei Samuilovich	1925	Novogrudok	Baranovichi	Kalinin	
Opengeim Rubin Samuilovich	1926	Novogrudok	Baranovichi	Kalinin	
Opengeim Samuil Ovseyevich	1905	Novogrudok	Baranovichi	Kalinin	
Opengeim Elka Khaimovna	1905	Novogrudok	Baranovichi		
Oreshovich Lilya Shayevna	1932	Rubezhevichi	Baranovichi	Kalinin	
Orkovich Abram Leibovich	1889	Baranovichi	Baranovichi	Kalinin	
Orkovich Osher Abramovich	1914	Baranovichi	Baranovichi	Kalinin	
Orlik Yefim Berkovich	1927	Bildyuchi	Vileyka	Spartak	? 4
Orlinskaya CheSlava (Glory) Yakovlevna	1905	Slonim	Brest	Sikorski's headquarters	Shchors
Orlinski Abram Meyerovich	1895	Dyatlovo	Baranovichi	Leninskaya	Borba
Orlinski Abram Semenovich	1903	Slonim	Brest	Sikorski's headquarters	Shchors
Orlov Yakov Aleksandrovich	1923	Mogilev	Mogilev	Chekist	? 10
Orlovski Boris Movshevich	1913	Goloburdy, Svisloch district	Brest	Za Sovetskuyu Belarus	Chkalov
Orlyanskaya Khana Isaakovna	1913	Belitsa	Baranovichi	Kalinin	
Orlyanski Zelman Yudovich	1925	Vechishche	Brest	Yazykovicha	Bozhenko
Osadchuk Roman Zakharovich	1918	Lida	Minsk	Shturmovaya	Grozny
Oserovich Khaim Mordukhovich	1926	Warsaw	Baranovichi	Pobieda	Pobieda
Osipova Sima Grigorevna	1919	Minsk getto	Baranovichi	18th Frunze	Dzerzhinski
Oskard Moisei Zakharovich	1923	Bryansk getto, Belostok region	Grodno	Vo imya Rodiny (In the name of Motherland)	Zhukov
Osovskaya Nina Aronovna	1922	Slutsk	Minsk	Dyadi Koli	Stalin
Osovski Isaak Gershevich	1905	Slonim district	Baranovichi	Rokossovski	Dzerzhinski
Osok Ilya Srolevich	1909	Slonim	Pinsk	Lenin	Frunze
Osok Sara Rubinovna	1917	Slonim	Pinsk	Lenin	Frunze
Ostashinskaya AdAsya Abramovna	1912	Novogrudok	Baranovichi	Leninskaya	Borba
Ostashinskaya Lyuba Abramovna	1914	Lida	Baranovichi	Kalinin	
Ostashinskaya Perlya Khaimovna	1924	Novogrudok	Baranovichi	Kalinin	
Ostashinskaya Rakhelya Rubinovna	1918	Novogrudok	Baranovichi	Kalinin	
Ostashinski Abram Isaakovich	1928	Minsk	Baranovichi	Za Sovetskuyu Belarus	family detachment
Ostashinski Grigori Girshevich	1907	Novogrudok, getto	Baranovichi	1st Baranovichskaya	Frunze
Ostashinski Danel Yefimovich	1921	Novogrudok	Baranovichi	Kalinin	
Ostashinski Naum Izraelevich	1904	Lida	Baranovichi	Kalinin	
Ostashinski Khaim Peisakhovich	1891	Novogrudok	Baranovichi	Kalinin	
Ostrov Mikhail Lazarevich	1927	Olkhovichi, Vileika region	Vitebsk	Korotkin	Levkovich's
Ostrovko Zhama Yefremovich	1894	Slonim	Brest	Ponomarenko	Sovetskaya Belarus
Ostrovski German Lipovich	1906	from captivity	Minsk	Zheleznyak	? 2
Ostrometski Samuil Yudelevich	1924	Biten, Barnovichi region	Pinsk	Budenny	Ponomarenko
Ofman Moisei Shlemovich	1925	from the civil camp	Vileyka	4th Belorusskaya	? 6
Offman Vladimir Evgenevich	1912	Desant	Palesye	99th Kalinkovichskaya	Voroshilov

Ocherova Raya Yakovlevna	1924	local	Baranovichi	Pobieda	Pobieda
Osherov Solomon Abramovich	1905	Martynovka	Mogilev		Za Sovetskuyu Belorussiyu
Osherovich Bellya Matusovna	1903	Rubezhevichi	Baranovichi	Kalinin	
Osherovich Lilya Shayevna	1932	Rubezhevichi	Baranovichi		
Osherovich Sofiya Mordukhovna	1924	Derechin	Baranovichi	Pobieda	Budenny
Osherovich Khaim Mordukhovich	1925	Derechin	Baranovichi	Leninskaya	Leninski
Osherovich Khana Mordukhovna	1924	Derechin	Baranovichi	Pobieda	Suvorov
Osherovich Shae Movshovich	1893	Rubezhevichi	Baranovichi	Kalinin	
Osherovskaya Faya Shayevna	1927	Rubezhevichi	Baranovichi	Kalinin	
Osherovski Aron Shmuilovich	1926	Ivye, getto	Baranovichi	Kirov	Ordzhonikidze
Oshman Aron Matusevich	1913	Novogrudok	Baranovichi	Kalinin	
Oshman Isaak Movshevich	1900	Naliboki	Baranovichi	Pervomaiskaya	Oktyabr
Oshman Foma Benyaminovich	1914	Baranovichi, getto	Pinsk		Chukhlai
Oshman Yakov Pinkhusovich	1927	Ivienets	Baranovichi	Kalinin	
Oshman Yankel Matusevich	1915	Ivienets	Baranovichi	Kalinin	
Pabershuk Lyuba Isaakovna	1908	Minsk	Baranovichi	detachment ? 106	
Pabkin Abram Moiseyevich	1908	Sharkovshchina			
Pavlovich Engels Vulfovich	1925	Moskva Central Committee of the CP (b) B	Minsk	Bragin	Gastello
Pave Volf Aizikovich	1925	Grodno	Baranovichi	Lenin's komsomol	Lenin's komsomol
Paglanson Semen Ivanovich	1921	from captivity	Palesye	37th Yelskaya	Za Rodinu (For Motherland)
Pagost Lyuba Yosifovna	1922	Minsk	Baranovichi	detachment ? 106	
Pak Abram Samuilovich	1918	from captivity, Slutsk	Pinsk	Lenin	Frunze
Pak Maksim Abramovich	1924	getto, Vilno	Vileyka		Za Sovetskuyu Belorussiyu
Paktor Abram Yoselevich	1923	Kosovo, Brest region	Belostok	A.Nevski	Kotovski
Paktor Yosif Khaimovich	1915	Kosovo	Brest	Ponomarenko	Dmitrov
Palachankin Aron Davidovich	1924	Minsk	Baranovichi	detachment ? 106	
Palees Gisya Leizerovna	1897	Rubezhevichi	Baranovichi	Kalinin	
Palees Roza Yakovlevna	1928	Rubezhevichi	Baranovichi		
Palei Rakhil Kivovna	1908	Minsk	Baranovichi	detachment ? 106	
Pales Genya AvseYevna	1903	Minsk	Baranovichi	detachment ? 106	
Pales Moisei Shayevich	1903	Minsk	Baranovichi	detachment ? 106	
Pales Sema Moiseyevich	1935	Minsk	Baranovichi	detachment ? 106	
Paller Izya Samuilovich	1914	Taglovshchina	Mogilev	? 117	headquarters
Paloiko Moisei Khaimovich	1913	Osipovichi	Mogilev	Osipovichskaya VOG	? 210
Pam BroniSlava (Glory) Gershevna	1917	Bryansk getto, Belostok region	Grodno	Vo imya Rodiny (In the name of Motherland)	Zhukov
Pam Simon Berkovich	1915	Bryansk getto, Belostok region	Grodno	Vo imya Rodiny (In the name of Motherland)	Zhukov
Paperno Beniiamin Yakovlevich	1909	getto	Baranovichi	Oktyabr	
Papir Zelik Yankelevich	1915	Lyublin	Baranovichi	Vpered (Forward)	Sibiryak
Parent Emma Vladimirovna	1922	Minsk	Baranovichi	detachment ? 106	
Paretskaya Viktoriia Yulyanovna	1918	Warsaw	Baranovichi	Kalinin	
Parkhovnik Venyamin Lvovich	1916	from captivity	Mogilev	Chekist	? 20
Pasalski Mortka Movshevich	1902	Ozeritsa, Slonim	Baranovichi	Pobieda	Budenny
Pasmanik Raisa Borisovna	1924	Kosovo	Brest	Sikorski's headquarters	Shchors
Pasov Shlema Khatskelevich	1901	Molodusha	Mogilev	? 537	
Pasternak Yosif Leizerovich	1910	Baranovichi, from home	Baranovichi	Grizodubova	Matrosov
Pasternak Moshko Abramovich	1917	Poland	Brest	Stalin	Chernyak
Pasternak Shlema Abramovich	1912	Poland	Brest	Lenin	Zelenin
Pasterniak Yankel Aronovich	1923	Gantsevichi, getto	Pinsk	Kuibyshev	
Patashnik Pesya Berkovna	1921	Volozhin	Baranovichi	Za Sovetskuyu Belarus	Kirov
Patent Vladimir Aronovich	1906	Minsk	Vitebsk	Nikitin's	? 1
Patent Izrail Lvovich	1927	Minsk	Baranovichi	detachment ? 106	
Patent Sarra Lvovna	1930	Minsk	Baranovichi	detachment ? 106	
Patent Emma Vladimirovna	1922		Baranovichi		
Patershchuk Lyuba Isaakovna	1907	Minsk	Baranovichi	detachment ? 106	
Patlazhan Semen Elkovich	1919	Yelsk	Palesye	37th Yelskaya	Death to Fascism
Patsovskaya Pesya Izrailevna	1922	Dyatlovo	Baranovichi	Kalinin	
Pashkovski Yudel Izrailevich	1911	Belarusian Staff of Partisan Movement	Mogilev	? 117	gr. Ivleva
Pevzner Manya Grigorevna	1916	Borisov	Baranovichi	detachment ? 106	
Pevzner Samuil Yakovlevich	1902	Krugloye	Mogilev	Chekist	Suvorov
Pevzner-Goland Sarra Grigorevna	1911	Borisov	Baranovichi	detachment ? 106	
Peisakhovich Lev Isaakovich	1914	Vilno	Vitebsk	Rokossovski	Kotovski
Peisakhovich Mariya Solomonovna	1916	Minsk	Baranovichi	detachment ? 106	
Peisakhovich Sergei Grigorevich	1912	Minsk	Minsk	Rokossovski	Chkalov
Peisakhovich Yakov Abramovich	1925	Kopyl getto	Minsk	Frunze	Budenny
Pekarski Isaak Vulfovich	1913	Slonim	Baranovichi	Shchuchin IDC	
Peker Gdalya Mordukhovich	1907	Novogrudok, getto	Baranovichi	Stalin	Ryzhaka

Peker Yosif Gdalevich	1915	Lyakhovichi, Kletsk district	Minsk	Chapayev	Ponomarenko
Peker Yosif Moiseyevich	1913	Kamen	Baranovichi	Kalinin	
Peker Naum Mikhailovich	1923	Slutsk	Minsk	Chkalov	Dovator
Peker Nison Moiseyevich	1912	Mir	Baranovichi	Kalinin	
Peker Yudel Moiseyevich	1915	Mir	Baranovichi	Kalinin	
Pekler Moisei Shmulevich	1906	getto	Vileyka	Voroshilov	Chapayev
Penek Moisei Izrailovich	1917	Lida	Baranovichi	Kalinin	
Perevozkin Leiba Movshevich	1905	Dolginovo	Minsk	Kirov	? 4
Perevozkin Mairon Shayevich	1909	Gorodok	Baranovichi	Chkalov	
Perevozkin Meyer Shmoilevich	1922	Gorodok	Baranovichi	Chkalov	? 4 "Za Sovetskuyu Belarus"
Perevozkin Fedor Leibovich	1913	Gorodok	Baranovichi	Chkalov	? 4 "Za Sovetskuyu Belarus"
Perel David	1913	Slonim	Brest	Sikorski's headquarters	Shchors
Perelgut Mikhail Motolevich	1921	detachment Kirov	Brest	Ponomarenko	Dmitrov
Perelman Anatoli Kadyshevich	1921	Belarusian Staff of Partisan Movement	Minsk	Ponomarenko	brigade headquarters
Perelman Boris Yakovlevich	1908	Central Committee of the CP (b) B	Baranovichi	Baranovchi underground RC of the CP(b) B and IDC	
Perelman Boris Yakovlevich	1924	Minsk	Minsk	Rokossovski	Chkalov
Perelman Bronya Yakovlevna	1920	Minsk	Belostok	A.Nevski	
Perelman Yevgeniya Mikhailovna	1912	Lepel	Vitebsk	VLKSM	? 3
Perelman Ignat Abramovich	1924	Minsk	Baranovichi	detachment ? 106	
Perelman Samuil Aronovich	1924	Novogrudok	Baranovichi	Pobieda	Pobieda
Perelman Semen	1925		Minsk	Voronyanski	Pobieda
Perelman Semen Grigorevich	1920	Gomel, Vitebsk region	Vitebsk	Ponomarenko	Golovchenko
Perendski Abram Yudolevich	1912	Novogrudok getto	Baranovichi	Kirov	Ordzhonikidze
Perepletchik Nokhim Yankelevich	1925	concentration camp Gantsevichi	Brest	? 99 Gulyaev	Grabko
Perets Abram Khaimovich	1925	Novogrudok	Baranovichi	Kirov	Ordzhonikidze
Perlov Yefim Davidovich	1908	Yelsk,left by RK KP(b)B	Palesye	37th Yelskaya	Death to Fascism
Perman Bentsion Shimovich	getto,	Minsk	Chapayev	Ponomarenko	
Pernikov Girsh Abramovich	1914	Mir	Baranovichi	Kalinin	
Pernikov Izrail Aronovich	1926	Mir	Baranovichi	Kalinin	
Pernikov Sara Shlemovna	1913	Mir	Baranovichi	Kalinin	
Perninova Polya Benyaminovna	1925	Minsk	Baranovichi	detachment ? 106	
Pernshtein A.L.	1920	Baranovichi	Baranovichi	Pervomaiskaya	Pervomaiski
Perski Gennadi Shmuilovich	1919	Krasnoye, getto	Baranovichi	Chkalov	
Pertsev Mikhail Yakovlevich	1919	Pinsk	Pinsk	Lenin	Kutuzov
Pertsovskaya Sofiya YevgenyYevna	1922	Tuchki	Gomel	Za Rodinu (For Motherland)	Kalinin
Perchikova Krined (woman)	1919	Belostok	Grodno	Samutin's group	Kirshner's group
Pesetsker Zalka Leibovich	1925	N. Sverzhen	Minsk	Chapayev	Shchors
Pesin German Afanasyevich	1898	Minsk	Mogilev	208th partisan regiment	headquarters
Pesin Gilik Leibovich	1922	Gorodok, Glussk district	Palesye	? 123	Krasny Oktyabr
Pesina Mariya	1926	Parichi	Palesye	? 123	Krasny Oktyabr
Peskin Yuzef Tevelevich	1912	Baranovichi	Baranovichi	Chkalov	
Pestrikov Boris Mikhailovich	1907	Minsk	Minsk	Rokossovski	Chkalov
Pestunovich Sonya Albertovna	1912	Vileika	Minsk	Voronyanski	Kotovski
Petrova Yevgeniya Rafailovna	1918		Brest	Chapayev	Chapayev
Petrovskaya Asya Naumovna	1923	Sirotino	Vitebsk	1st Belorusskaya	
Petrukhovich Lazar Davidovich	1925	Derechin	Baranovichi	Pobieda	Pobieda
Petrukhovich Semen Davidovich	1924	Derechin	Baranovichi	Pobieda	Pobieda
Pecherski Aleksandr Aronovich	1909	from captivity	Brest	Sikorski's headquarters	Shchors
Pivnenko Larisa Yosifovna	1919	Minsk	Mogilev		Za Sovetskuyu Belorussiyu
Pik Movsha Nakhmovich	1911	Kletsk	Brest	Sikorski's headquarters	Shchors
Pikus Fedor Moiseyevich	1900	Belarusian Staff of Partisan Movement	Vitebsk	Belyaev's filmgroups	Tsyganov's group
Piletskaya Dora IshiyYevna	1921	Slonim	Pinsk	Lenin	Kutuzov
Pilovich Semen Zenukovich	1915	Vilno	Vileyka	Suvorov	
Pilovski Izrail Davidovich	1921	getto, Vilno	Vileyka	Voroshilov	Kalinin
Pilts Samuil Yakovlevich	1927	Krasnoye	Baranovichi	Za Sovetskuyu Belarus	family detachment
Pilshchik Khonon Sholomovich	1922	Molchad	Baranovichi	Kalinin	
Pindrik Abram Moiseyevich	1909	Minsk	Minsk	Pravda (Truth)	Kalinin
Pinik Nesha Davidovich	1908	small town of Urechye Slutsk district	Minsk	Chkalov	Zheleznyak
Pinkenberg Gdalya Beneshevich	1929	Minsk getto	Baranovichi	Chapayev	Parkhomenko
Pinsburg David Benesovich	1927	Jewish camp Dolginovo	Minsk	Voronyanski	Pobieda
Pinsker Roza Borisovna	1910	Chebotovichi	Gomel	Shchors	Gastello
Pinski Itsko Leibovich	1905	Byten	Pinsk	Lenin	Frunze

Pinski Lazar Khaimovich	1906	Minsk	Baranovichi	detachment ? 106	
Pinski Leiba Semenovich	1924	Novoselki	Palesye	? 225	Suvorov
Pinkhasik Khana Faitelevna	1927	Minsk	Baranovichi	detachment ? 106	
Pintsev David Solomonovich	1924	Bildyuchi	Vileyka	Spartak	? 6
Pintsova Genya	1926	from the civil camp	Vileyka	4th Belorusskaya	? 6
Pinchanskaya Basya Isaakovna	1911	Stolbtsy	Baranovichi	Kalinin	
Pinchanski Abram Meyerovich	1911	Stolbtsy	Baranovichi	Kalinin	
Pinchevski Yefim Genrikhovich	1925		Pinsk	Molotov	Kalinin
Pinchuk Leiba Notkovich	1896	Novogrudok	Baranovichi	Kalinin	
Piolun Sheina Aronovna	1924	Dyatlovo	Baranovichi	Leninskaya	Borba
Pisetskaya Tsilya Samuilovna	1929	Urechye	Pinsk	Komarov-Korzh's	Komarov's 3rd group
Pisetski Gavriil Abramovich	1912	Western Byelorussia, Morochi	Minsk	Chkalov	Gromov
Pisetski Samuil Shlemovich	1922	from the work camp	Palesye	? 123	Papruga's
Pisetski Shmerka Shlemovich	1926	from the work camp	Palesye	? 123	Papruga's
Pitel Moisei Borisovich	1920	Ivanovo	Pinsk	Shubetidze	Stalin
Pitkovski Abram Aizikovich	1914	Byten	Brest	Sikorski's headquarters	Shchors
PitLyugo EndLya Leibovna	1905	Lida	Baranovichi	Kalinin	
PitLyuk Isaak Khonovich	1927	Lida	Baranovichi	Kalinin	
PitLyuk Khona Aronovich	1896	Lida	Baranovichi	Kalinin	
PitLyuk Tsilya Khonovna	1930	Lida	Baranovichi	Kalinin	
Plavnik Isaak Nokhimovich	1919	Dokshitsy	Minsk	Voronyanski	Kotovski
Plaks L.M.	1911	Bobruisk	Minsk	Rokossovski	25 years of Oktyabr
Platovskaya Raya Mikhailovna	1925	Vitebsk	Baranovichi	Kalinin	
Platovski Elya Salomonovich	1914	Lida	Baranovichi	Kalinin	
Platovski Yankel Lipovich	1915	Lida	Baranovichi	Kalinin	
Pletman Meyer Yankelevich	1913	from captivity, Minsk	Minsk	Shturmovaya	Za Otechestvo (For Fatherland)
Pliner Markiian Abramovich	1914	Vitebsk	Vitebsk	1st Belorusskaya	
Pliskina Ida Yakubovna	1917	Leompol	Vileyka	4th Belorusskaya	? 6
Pliskina Sonya Yakubovna	1926	Leompol	Vileyka	4th Belorusskaya	? 6
Plotkin Aron Samuilovich	1923	Turets	Belostok	A.Nevski	
Plotkin Moisei Khaimovich	1893		Mogilev	Osipovichskaya VOG	? 210
Plotkin Samuil Berkovich	1907	Cherven, Central Committee of the CP (b) B	Minsk	Krasnoye znamya (Red Banner)	Voroshilov
Plotkina Asya Abramovna	1919	Minsk getto	Baranovichi	Chapayev	Lazo
Plotnik Girsh Alterevich	1908	Novogrudok getto	Baranovichi	Kirov	Ordzhonikidze
Plotnik David Aronovich	1913	Belarusian Staff of Partisan Movement	Baranovichi	Gruppy partrabotnikov	Shemetovets' group
Plotnik Leya Isaakovna	1916	Rubezhevichi	Baranovichi	Kalinin	
Plotnik Rakhmil Girshevich	1927	Novogrudok	Baranovichi	Kirov	
Plotnitski Naum Yankelevich	1913	from captivity	Brest	Sikorski's headquarters	Shchors
Plotov Moisei Isaakovich	1917	K. Kashirski	Pinsk	Molotov	brigade headquarters
Plokhotskaya Lyubov Naumovna	1913	Shmaki, Kirovo district	Mogilev	? 537	
Plotskaya Zhenya Mikhailovna	1926	a small group from the forest (Nevel)	Pinsk	Sovetskaya Belarus	Kutuzov
Plotskaya Fanya Mikhelevna	1922	Nevel, Pinsk region	Pinsk	Sovetskaya Belarus	Kutuzov
Plotski Yankel Mikhelevich	1919	Nevel, Pinsk region	Pinsk	Sovetskaya Belarus	Kutuzov
Pluzhitser Meyer Pinkhusovich	1899	Krasnoye district, Smolensk region	Vitebsk	1st Smolenskaya	? 4
Plumian Isaak Abramovich	1908	Sharkovshchina	Vitebsk	Lepelskaya Stalin	cavalry squadron
Plshenitsa Aleksandr Semenovich	1922	Novogrudok	Baranovichi	Kalinin	
Plyut Leonid Gavrilovich	1931	Chashniki	Vitebsk	Dubov's	commandant platoon
Plyut Mariya Semenovna	1909	Chashniki	Vitebsk	Dubov's	commandant platoon
Podberezkin Khaim Leibovich	1905	Gorodok	Baranovichi	Chkalov	
Podberezskaya Zhenya Shmuilovna	1921	Gorodok	Baranovichi	Chkalov	? 4 "Za Sovetskuyu Belarus"
Podberezski Naum Yakovlevich	1905	small town of Vishnevo, Volozhin district, getto	Baranovichi	Chapayev	Chapayev
Podberetski Zinovii Davidovich	1906	small town of Vishnevo	Baranovichi	Chapayev	Chapayev
Poderski Yosif Volfovich	1912	Mir	Baranovichi	Kalinin	
Podolnyi Mikhail Pavlovich	1906	from captivity	Vileyka	Voroshilov	Istrebitel (Destroyer)
Podolskaya Lilya SheyYevna	1919	Slonim	Brest	Sikorski's headquarters	Shchors
Podolski Bension Yosifovich	1911	Minsk getto	Baranovichi	18th Frunze	brigade headquarters
Podolski Yefim Borisovich	1922	from captivity	Brest	Sikorski's headquarters	Shchors
Pozner Anna Mordukhovna	1925	getto	Vileyka	Voroshilov	Propaganda detachment
Pozner Mordukh Tobiyashevich	1901	getto	Vileyka	Voroshilov	Propaganda detachment
Pozniak Abram Lvovich	1908	Mir	Baranovichi	Zhukov	
Pozniak Gita Moiseyevna	1898	Mir	Baranovichi	Kalinin	
Pozniak Zoya Mironovna	1914	Mir	Baranovichi	Zhukov	
Pozniak Maksim Shmoilovich	1921	Rubezhevichi, getto	Baranovichi	Chapayev	Chapayev
Pozniak Khatskel Kivelevich	1905	Ivienets	Baranovichi	Kalinin	
Pozniak Yudel Shlemovich	1927	Mir	Baranovichi	Kalinin	

Pokulov Boris Yefimovich	1922	Bobruisk	Mogilev	partisan regiment ? 277	? 277
Poleshchuk Vladimir Davidovich	1918	Volkovysk, from the German army	Grodno	Chapayev	
Polityko Ekaterina Antonovna	1913	Mogilev	Gomel	1st Gomelskaya	Kalinin
Poloike Yankel Grigorevich	1910	Uzda	Minsk	Chapayev	Ponomarenko
Poloiko Raya Solomonovna	1924	Minsk	Baranovichi	detachment ? 106	
Polonetskaya Esfir Zalmanovna	1907	Miratichi	Baranovichi	Kalinin	
Polonetski Zalman Faivelevich	1944	Miratichi	Baranovichi	Kalinin	
Polonetski Nokhim Gershovich	1911	Byten	Brest	Ponomarenko	Sovetskaya Belarus
Polonetski Falvyel Abramovich	1905	Miratichi	Baranovichi	Kalinin	
Polonski Nota Meyerovich	1921	Kosovo	Brest	Ponomarenko	Sovetskaya Belarus
PolnYakov Boris Elevich	1904	Anapole, Cherven district	Minsk	Pravda (Truth)	Pravda (Truth)
Polyak David Moiseyevich	1918	Krasnopolye district	Mogilev		? 41
Polyak Ekaterina Isaakovna	1913	Minsk	Baranovichi	Ponomarenko	25 years of the BSSR
Polyak Zalman Isaakovich	1912	Minsk	Baranovichi	Ponomarenko	25 years of the BSSR
Polyak Liza Vladimirovna	1913	Slutsk	Baranovichi	detachment ? 106	
Polyanski Miron A.	1912	Dyatlovo	Baranovichi	Leninskaya	Krasnogvardeiski
Polyatskin Anatoli Gdalevich	1925	Minsk getto	Minsk	Voronyanski	Pobieda
Polyatskina Zina Gdalevna	1923	Minsk getto	Minsk	Voronyanski	Pobieda
Polyachek Solomon Rudolfovich	1927	Lida	Belostok	A.Nevski	
Pomeranets Avodia Senerovich	1923	Belostok	Grodno	Samutin's group	Kirshner's group
Pomeranets Aron Khaimovich	1903	Odrizhin	Pinsk	Molotov	Potalakh
Pomeranets Shaya Kubovich	1920	getto, Pruzhany	Brest	Ponomarenko	Kirov
Pomerchik Leizer Rubinovich	1895	Turets	Baranovichi	Kalinin	
Pomerchik Malkim Rubinovna	1891	Turets	Baranovichi	Kalinin	
Pomiranets Semen Abramovich	1926	from the family detachment	Brest	Ponomarenko	Kirov
Ponchak Yanek Khaskelevich	1924	German work camp, Poland	Pinsk	Molotov	Kalinin
Ponyatik Samuil Elevich	1918	Baranovichi, from home	Baranovichi	Grizodubova	Matrosov
Popichka Movsha Motolevich	1920	Drizhin	Brest	Yazykovicha	Bozhenko
Pordes Mauvritsi Samuilovich	1914	Lida	Minsk	Chapayev	Ponomarenko
Port Leizer Abramovich	1903	Vileika district, Oshmiany	Minsk	Kirov	Frunze
Port Roman Meilovich	1916	Mir	Baranovichi	Chkalov	
Portnaia Sarra Elevna	1930	Minsk	Baranovichi	detachment ? 106	
Portnik Zyama Samuilovich	1925	Berezino	Minsk	Razgrom (Crushing defeat)	
Portnik Leonid Samsonovich	1929	Berezino	Minsk	Krasnoye znamya (Red Banner)	Krasnoye znamya (Red Banner)
Portnik Petr Samuilovich	1932	Berezino	Minsk	Razgrom (Crushing defeat)	
Portnoi Mikhail Solomonovich	1926	Minsk	Baranovichi	detachment ? 106	
Portnoi Peisakh Lazarovich	1910	Novogrudok	Baranovichi	Kalinin	
Portnoi Rakhmel Yankelevich	1913		Baranovichi	Oktyabr	
Portnoi Sima Lazarovna	1916	Novogrudok	Baranovichi	Kalinin	
Porus Isaak Elyashevich	1922	getto	Vileyka	Suvorov	
Postirniak Yankel Aronovich	1923	Lenin	Pinsk	Molotov	Kalinin
Postolov Dmitri Yosifovich	1910	Borisov	Minsk	Belarus	Belarus
Potashinskaya Raya Yefimovna	1906	Minsk	Baranovichi	detachment ? 106	
Potashkina Anna Izrailevna	1922	Suvalki	Baranovichi	Kalinin	
Potashnik Abram Yefimovich	1913		Minsk	Voronyanski	Mstitel (Revenger)
Potashnik Leiba Beisovich	1910	detachment "Mest"	Vileyka	Voroshilov	headquarters' production group
Potashnik Maks Osherovich	1915	Golshany	Baranovichi	Kalinin	
Potashnik Pesya Berkovna	1922	Volozhin	Baranovichi	Chkalov	reserve group
Potashnik Yudel Berkovich	1897	Volozhin	Baranovichi	Za Sovetskuyu Belarus	family detachment
Potashova Khaya Khaimovna	1891	Ulla	Vitebsk	Chapayev	detachments
Pochakovski Kushel Zalmanovich (Isaakovich)	1902	Gorodishche	Baranovichi	Kalinin	
Pochta Ida Pavlovna	1926	Minsk	Baranovichi	detachment ? 106	
Pochtar Moisei Samoilovich	1923	Vasilishki	Baranovichi	Lenin's komsomol	Lenin's komsomol
Pravda (Truth) Iakop Mordkovich	1917	Gnevchitsy, Ivanovo district	Pinsk	Molotov	Potalakh
Praver Filip Mendelevich	1910	Stanislav, Ukraine	Brest	Sikorski's headquarters	Shchors
Prazdnik Aizik Borisovich	1924	Belarusian Staff of Partisan Movement	Gomel	Kozhar's	gr. Tikhomirova
Prais Itska Berkovich	1906	Kletsk district	Baranovichi	Zhdanov	
Pres Sofiya Aizikovna	1924	Baranovichi, from home	Baranovichi	Grizodubova	Matrosov
Presman Yefim Moiseyevich	1923	Minsk	Baranovichi	Stalin	Budenny
Presman Lets Alterovna	1924	Dvorets	Baranovichi	Kalinin	
Presman Yakov Grigorevich	1898	Minsk	Baranovichi	detachment ? 106	
Press Boris Moiseyevich	1926	Minsk	Baranovichi	detachment ? 106	

JEWISH PARTISANS IN BYELORUSSIA 1941-1944 275

Pressman Khona Gertsovich	1920	Naliboki	Baranovichi	Kalinin	
Pribulski Boris Isaakovich	1928	Kosovo	Brest	Ponomarenko	Sovetskaya Belarus
Pribulski Yakov Isaakovich	1927	Kosovo	Brest	Ponomarenko	Sovetskaya Belarus
Prigozhina Basya Samuilovna	1922		Gomel	1st Gomelskaya	Chapayev
Primet Aron Isaakovich	1914	from the encirclement	Mogilev	partisan regiment ? 277	? 277
Pritykina Zinaida Semenovna	1912		Baranovichi	Leninskaya	Leninski
Prokopets David Yakovlevich	1920	from the encirclement	Mogilev	Chekist	? 5
Pronyagina Ira LeontYevna	1924	Tukhovichi (Slonim)	Brest	Sikorski's headquarters	
Protas David Nevakhovich	1930	Mir	Baranovichi	Kalinin	
Protas Mariyasha Davidovna	1906	Mir	Baranovichi	Kalinin	
Protas Sofiya Borisovna	1923	Mir	Baranovichi	Chkalov	
Protasevich Aleksandr Markovich	1923	from captivity	Minsk	Kirov	Kirov
Proshchitski Leizer Abovich	1897	concentration camp	Pinsk	Kuibyshev	Shchors
Pruzhanski Genikh Zelmanovich	1923	Jewish camp, Ivanovo	Pinsk	Shubetidze	Stalin
Pruzhanski Nakhman Zavelevich	1920	Ivanovo	Pinsk	Shubetidze	Chapayev
Prupes Leonid Izrailevich	1915	Pavlovichi, Mogilev region	Minsk	Belarus	Belarus
Prupes Movsha Girshevich	1925	concentration camp, Logishin	Pinsk	Kuibyshev	Shchors
Prus Leonid Vulfovich	1911	from captivity	Minsk	Shchors	Shchors
Prusak Moisei Peisakhovich	1910	Borisov	Minsk	Shchors	brigade headquarters
Pruslina Bella Mendeleyevna	1912	Minsk (a contact)	Minsk	Kalinin	Kalinin
Pruslina Khasya Mendeleyevna	Minsk	Minsk	Suvorov		
Pruss Sonya Zelikovna	1921	Minsk	Baranovichi	detachment ? 106	
Puzyritski Yokhel Yudelevich	1904	Voronovo	Baranovichi	Kirov	Za Sovetskuyu Belarus
Pulik Aron-Leib Srolevich	1920	Ivanovo	Pinsk	Molotov	Lazo
Pupkin David Elevich	1902	Krivoselki, Baranovichi region	Minsk	Chapayev	Shchors
Pupkin Ilya Khaimovich	1915	Dyatlovo	Baranovichi	Kalinin	
Pupko Gita Yankelevna	1916	getto	Baranovichi	Kirov	Orel
Pupko Yosif Movshovich	1939	Lida	Baranovichi	Kalinin	
Pupko Isaak Grenimovich	1903	Lida	Baranovichi	Vpered (Forward)	A.Nevski
Pupko Itska Rafailovich	1905	getto	Baranovichi	Kirov	Orel
Pupko Kalman Rafailovich	1914	Lida, getto	Baranovichi	Kirov	Orel
Pupko Kellya Moiseyevna	1886	Lida	Baranovichi	Kalinin	
Pupko Lazar Semenovich	1908	Baranovichi	Baranovichi	Pervomaiskaya	
Pupko MariyaGoncharov's detachment	1913	Baranovichi	Baranovichi	Pervomaiskaya	
Pupko Masha Semenovna	1936	Lida	Baranovichi	Kalinin	
Pupko Mikhail Pinsovich	1910	Voronovo, getto	Baranovichi	Kirov	Ordzhonikidze
Pupko Rakhil Aizikovna	1902	getto	Baranovichi	1st Baranovichskaya	Stalin
Pupko Samuil Rakhmilevich	1878	Lida	Baranovichi	Kalinin	
Pupko Semen Meilakhovich	1909	Lida	Baranovichi	Kalinin	
Pupko Khaim Zakharovich	1907	Lida	Baranovichi	Kalinin	
Pupko Khinkha Samuilovna	1915	Lida	Baranovichi	Kalinin	
Pupko Shura Samuilovna	1914	Lida	Baranovichi	Kalinin	
Pupkho Rakhmiel Shmuilovich	1914	Lida	Baranovichi	Kalinin	
Purin Semen Yankelevich	1915	Serniki, Rovno region.	Pinsk	Molotov	Kalinin
Pukhovitski Abram Rakhmilevich	1922	Chashniki	Vitebsk	VLKSM	Raitsev's
Pukhovitski Arkadi Isaakovich	1923	Chashniki	Vitebsk	Kirillov	Kirillov's
Puchinski Arkadi Lazarevich	1916	Minsk getto	Minsk	2nd Minskaya	Molotov
Puchinski Yakov Senderovich	1926	Minsk	Baranovichi	detachment ? 106	
Pshenitsa Aleksandr Semenovich	1925		Baranovichi	Oktyabr	
Pshenitsa Sonya Berkovna	1922	Korelichi	Baranovichi	Kalinin	
Pshepyurko Yosif Davidovich		Minsk	Chapayev	Ponomarenko	
Pshipiurko Yosif Borisovich	1923	Kletsk	Grodno	Vo imya Rodiny (In the name of Motherland)	Kutuzov
Pianin Abram Yakovlevich	1907	Slutsk	Minsk	Chkalov	Gromov
Pianina Genya Solomonovna	1924	Glussk	Minsk	A.Nevski	? 1
Pen Aleksandr Grigorevich	1919	from captivity	Minsk	Voronyanski	Kotovski
Rabets Abram Isaakovich	1900	Novogrudok	Baranovichi	Kalinin	
Rabets Khatskel Yudelevich	1889	Gorodishche district	Baranovichi	25 years of the BSSR	Kotovski
Rabinovich Aron Motelevich	1908	Novogrudok	Baranovichi	Kalinin	
Rabinovich Basya Mordukhovna	1917	Dyatlovo	Baranovichi	Kalinin	
Rabinovich Boris Naumovich	1922	Belarusian Staff of Partisan Movement	Minsk	Special groups	Kunovski's group
Rabinovich Vita Yosifovna	1927	Minsk	Baranovichi	detachment ? 106	
Rabinovich Ginda Rubinovna	1917	Mir	Baranovichi	Kalinin	
Rabinovich Yefim Zelikovich	1917	Poland, Vinnitsa	Brest	Lenin	Zhukov
Rabinovich Izrail Davidovich	1921	Slonim	Brest	Sikorski's headquarters	Shchors
Rabinovich Izrail Maikhrovich	1918	from captivity	Vitebsk	Frunze	Frunze ? 1
Rabinovich Izrail Yakovlevich	1915	Minsk	Baranovichi	detachment ? 106	
Rabinovich Yosif Kivelevich	1910	Vishnevo	Baranovichi	Za Sovetskuyu Belarus	family detachment

Rabinovich Yosif Yudelevich	1924	Gorodok	Baranovichi	Chkalov	? 4 "Za Sovetskuyu Belarus"
Rabinovich Isaak Semenovich	1912	Slonim	Brest	Sikorski's headquarters	
Rabinovich Kalman Moiseyevich	1910	from the civil camp	Vileyka	4th Belorusskaya	? 6
Rabinovich Lazar Ekhelevich	1911	Baranovichi, getto	Baranovichi	Za Sovetskuyu Belarus	Kirov
Rabinovich Lyubov Lazarevna	1919	Lenin	Pinsk	Lenin	Kutuzov
Rabinovich Mikhail Abramovich	1911	Lenin	Pinsk	Budenny	Kotovski
Rabinovich Mikhail Solomonovich	1927	Braslav district	Vileyka	Zhdanov	
Rabinovich Motel Volfovich	1915	work camp	Pinsk	Molotov	Shish
Rabinovich Noakh Davidovich	1914	Korelichi	Baranovichi	Kalinin	
Rabinovich Roza Rubinovna	1913	Mir	Baranovichi	Kalinin	
Rabinovich Samuil Rubinovich	1906	Mir	Baranovichi	Kalinin	
Rabinovich Fanya Mordukhovna	1915	Gorodok	Baranovichi	Chkalov	? 4 "Za Sovetskuyu Belarus"
Rabinovich Khaim Alterovich	1922	Mir, getto	Baranovichi	Za Sovetskuyu Belarus	Shturm
Rabinovich Khana Yosifovna	1919	small town of Vishnevo	Baranovichi	Chapayev	Parkhomenko
Rabinovich Sholom Isaakovich	1900	Gorodok	Baranovichi	Chkalov	? 4 "Za Sovetskuyu Belarus"
Rabinski Mech (Sword)islav Germanovich	1914	Lodz	Baranovichi	Kalinin	
Rabkin Abram Moiseyevich	1908	Sharkovshchina			
Rabunski Mendel Isaakovich	1927	Kurenets	Vileyka	Gastello	Bochkova
Rabunski Mulya Isaakovich	1921	Maly Kurenets	Vileyka	Gastello	Shchors
Ravets Girsh Simkhovich	1919	Dyatlovo	Baranovichi	Leninskaya	Borba
Ravets Isaak Abramovich	1908	Dyatlovo	Baranovichi	Leninskaya	
Ragovina Khana Borisovna	1907	Minsk	Baranovichi	detachment ? 106	
Radashkevich Nekhama Leizerovna	1929	Dolginovo	Minsk	Voronyanski	Kotovski
Radashkovich Izrail Yakovlevich	1914		Minsk	Voronyanski	Mstitel (Revenger)
Radashkovich Isaak Yankelevich	1922	Dolginovo	Minsk	Voronyanski	Borba
Radashkovich Leib Yankelevich	1910		Minsk	Voronyanski	Mstitel (Revenger)
Radkevich Raisa Yefimovna	1918	Minsk	Palesye	? 100	Za Sovetskuyu Rodinu
Radkevich Ruta Borisovna	1912	Pruzhany	Brest	Brest antifascist committee	
Radunski Izrail Isaakovich	1930	Minsk	Baranovichi	detachment ? 106	
Razvaski Aron Peisakhovich	1922	Dyatlovo	Baranovichi	Leninskaya	family detachment group
Razvaski Volf Movshevich	1904	Ruda Yavorskaya	Baranovichi	Leninskaya	Borba
Razin Abram Yekhimovich	1921	Novogrudok	Baranovichi	Kirov	Ordzhonikidze
Razinovski Aron Borisovich	1922	Belarusian Staff of Partisan Movement	Minsk	Special groups	Baranovski's group
Razmarin Benyamin Nokhimovich	1908	Poland	Brest	Sikorski's headquarters	Shchors
Razmarina Rakhil Mikhailovna	1915	Poland	Brest	Sikorski's headquarters	Shchors
Raznova Mira Khaimovna	1922	Novogrudok getto	Baranovichi	Kirov	Ordzhonikidze
Raznova Sara Khaimovna	1925	Dyatlovo	Baranovichi	Leninskaya	family detachment group
Razovskaya Fanya Lvovna	1927	Pristroma, Smolevichi district	Minsk	Shturmovaya	Za Otechestvo (For Fatherland)
Razron Genya Solomonovna	1918		Palesye	? 123	Zhulega's
Raiman Yevgeniya Lazarevna	1919	Borisov	Minsk	Kirov	Za Pobiedu (For the Victory)
Raines Genya Yudelevna	1924	Minsk	Baranovichi	detachment ? 106	
Raines Leya Yudelevna	1931	Minsk	Baranovichi	detachment ? 106	
Raines Semen Faitelevich	1926	Minsk	Baranovichi	detachment ? 106	
Raines Faitel Nevakhovich	1904	Minsk	Baranovichi	detachment ? 106	
Raitman Itsko Fishelevich (Voloshanov Grigori Filippovich)	1918	Kakoisk, from captivity	Mogilev		? 45 "Za Rodinu (For Motherland)"
Raif Frida Yakovlevna	1920	Lida	Baranovichi	Kalinin	
Raifer Nakhman Nakhmanovich	1911	Novogrudok	Baranovichi	Kalinin	
Raikh Khaim Leibovich	1896	from captivity	Baranovichi	Grizodubova	
Raikhel Yevel Shmerkovich	1911	Postavy	Vileyka	Voroshilov	Suvorov
Raikhel Leiba Vulfovich	1918	Bildyuchi	Vileyka	Spartak	? 4
Raikhelson Benyamin Leibovich	1921	Rubezhevichi	Baranovichi	Kalinin	
Raikhelson Kira Aleksandrovna	1916	Minsk getto	Minsk	Underground RC and DC CP(b)B	Minsk underground CC of the CP(b)B
Raikhelson Khaya Borisovna	1922	Rubezhevichi	Baranovichi	Kalinin	
Raikhes Galina Yakovlevna	1922	Vilno	Vileyka	Suvorov	
Raikhlin Tevel Gitelevich	1903	Minsk	Minsk	Rokossovski	Chkalov
Raikhlin Yulf Leibovich	1912	Minsk getto	Grodno	Ponomarenko	squadron
Raikhlina Mariya Mikhailovna	1922		Gomel	Voroshilov	Frunze
Raikhlina Ester Televna	1925	Minsk	Baranovichi	detachment ? 106	
Raikhman Girsh Shimanovich	1918	Yaskovichi	Pinsk	Budenny	Voroshilov
Raikhman Khaim Teevich	1924	Minsk	Minsk	Rokossovski	Chkalov
Rak Leya Zalmanovna	1918	Novogrudok	Baranovichi	Kalinin	
Rak Khaya Zalmanovna	1920	Novogrudok	Baranovichi	Kalinin	
Rakover Yosif Rakhilovich	1905	Novogrudok	Baranovichi	Leninskaya	hospital

Rakovin Yosif Gershevich	1925	Volozhin	Baranovichi	Chapayev	Parkhomenko
Rakovich Mikhail Mordukhovich	1922	Novogrudok	Baranovichi	Leninskaya	Niepobedimy (Undefeated)
Rakovich Khonon Geselevich	1904	Mir	Baranovichi	Kalinin	
Rakov-Livshits Aleksandr Yudolevich	1924	Slutsk	Minsk	Ponomarenko	Gorbachev
Rakovski Abram Rubinovich	1914	local	Baranovichi	Pobieda	Pobieda
Rakovski Abram Yakovlevich	1911	Novogrudok, getto	Baranovichi	1st Baranovichskaya	Frunze
Ralkina Fanya Yevnovna	1915	Minsk	Baranovichi	detachment ? 106	
Ralkovski Isaak Makeevich	1923	Novogrudok	Baranovichi	Pobieda	Pobieda
Ram Elyakh Gotlevich	1916	Minsk	Minsk	Ponomarenko	Voroshilov
Ramendik Tatyana Naumovna	1918	Shklov	Mogilev	Chekist	? 10
Ramkova Yevdokiya Lvovna	1923	st. Slavnoe, Tolochin district	Mogilev	? 61	? 2
Ranenson Tatyana Zakharovna	1924	Belgres, Orsha district	Vitebsk	16st Smolenskaya	? 4
Rapoport Abram-Yakov Yosifovich	1902	Lenin	Brest	Sikorski's headquarters	Shchors
Rapoport Galina AvseYevna	1917	Minsk	Minsk	Shturmovaya	Grozny
Rapoport Leiba Davidovich	1909	Glubokoye	Vileyka	CC of the CP(b)B	Parkhomenko
Rapoport Mikhail Shenderovich	1924	Petrikov district	Palesye	? 125	Bolotnikov's
Rapoport Raisa Davidovna	1915	Glubokoye	Vileyka	CC of the CP(b)B	Parkhomenko
Rapoport Raisa Samuilovna	1924	Ivienets	Baranovichi	Dzerzhinski	Dzerzhinski
Rapoport Rakhil Samuilovna	1911	Minsk	Baranovichi	detachment ? 106	
Rapoport Sasha Khaimovna	1929	escaped the shooting	Vitebsk	Chapayev	detachments
Rapoport Fanya Yankelevna		Minsk	Voronyanski	Borba	
Rapoport Tsilya Rubinovna	1921	from captivity	Baranovichi	Chkalov	
Rappoport Zalman Samuilovich	1906	Glubokoye	Vitebsk	Rokossovski	Zhukov
Rasin Boris Moiseyevich	1914	Bobovka	Gomel	10st Zhuravichskaya	? 265 Voroshilov
Rasin Moisei Naumovich	1888	Bobruisk district, Telusha	Minsk	Bragin	Gastello
Rasina Lyubov Moiseyevna	1930	Bobruisk district, Telusha	Minsk	Bragin	Gastello
Rasina Roza Shlemovna	1888	Bobruisk district, Telusha	Minsk	Bragin	Gastello
Raskina Yevgeniya Yosifovna	1913	Minsk	Baranovichi	Kalinin	
Raskina Esfir Solomonovna	1902	Ostrov, Rudensk district	Minsk	Kirov	Kirov
Ratevski Shmuil Vasilfovich	1920	Derechin	Baranovichi	Pobieda	Pobieda
Ratner Boris Abramovich	1924	Minsk	Baranovichi	detachment ? 106	
Ratner BronyaGoncharov's detachment	1915	Shepelevichi	Mogilev	Ilyin's	? 24
Ratner Khena Yakovlevna	1922	Novogrudok getto	Baranovichi	Kirov	Ordzhonikidze
Rafimovich Marilya	1919	Belostok	Grodno	Samutin's group	Kirshner's group
Rakhelzon Shmul Isaakovich	1922	Bryansk getto, Belostok region	Grodno	Vo imya Rodiny (In the name of Motherland)	Zhukov
Rakhliel Roman Yefimovich	1909	Klichev district	Mogilev	? 61	? 2
Rakhlin Sergei Ivanovich	1910	Rechitsa	Minsk	Parkhomenko	Kirov
Rakhlis Mariya Movshevna	1919	Gorodok	Baranovichi	Za Sovetskuyu Belarus	family detachment
Rakhman Abram Moiseyevich	1914	Lida	Baranovichi	Kalinin	
Rakhmanov Abram Samuilovich	1925	Glussk	Palesye	? 123	Krasny Oktyabr
Rakhmanchik Khana Semenovna	1922	Minsk	Baranovichi	detachment ? 106	
Rakhmanchik Raya Leonidovna	1922	Uzlyany	Baranovichi	Chkalov	reserve group
Rakhmilevich Yosif	1887		Baranovichi	Slonim IDC	
Rachenert Rakhil Samuilovna	1911	Minsk	Baranovichi	detachment ? 106	
Rachkovskaya Golda Pershovna	1915	Rubezhevichi	Baranovichi	Kalinin	
Rachkovski Isaak Maksovich	1923	Novogrudok, getto	Baranovichi	Kirov	Ordzhonikidze
Rev Boris Yeselevich	1904	Dyatlovo	Baranovichi	Pobieda	Pobieda
Redkin Abram Yefimovich	1924	Molodechno, getto	Baranovichi	Chkalov	
Reer Khaim Leibovich	1911	Ilya	Minsk	Voronyanski	Kotovski
Reznik Abram Davidovich	1886	Baranovichi	Baranovichi	Kalinin	
Reznik Boris Abramovich	1917	Mir	Baranovichi	Za Sovetskuyu Belarus	family detachment
Reznik Boris Shlemovich	1909		Vileyka	Voroshilov	Istrebitel (Destroyer)
Reznik Isaak Khaimovich	1925	Novogrudok	Baranovichi	Kalinin	
Reznik Mendel Borukhovich	1906	Lida	Baranovichi	Leninskaya	Niepobedimy (Undefeated)
Reznik Mikhail Isaakovich	1916	Novogrudok getto	Baranovichi	Kirov	Ordzhonikidze
Reznik Movsha Berkovich	1880	Mir	Baranovichi	Kalinin	
Reznik Moisei Davidovich	1908	Minsk, from captivity	Minsk	Shturmovaya	Frunze
Reznik Naum Borisovich	1904	Slutsk	Minsk	2nd Minskaya	Kutuzov
Reznik Petr Yevseyevich	1920	from captivity	Minsk	Shturmovaya	Shturm
Reznik Polya Vulfovna	1923	Mir	Baranovichi	Za Sovetskuyu Belarus	family detachment
Reznik Rakhil Mordukhovna	1918	Ivanovo	Pinsk	Shubetidze	Nemytov
Reznik Semen Borisovich		Western Byelorussia	Minsk	Chkalov	Zheleznyak
Reznik Khana Ilyichna	1898	Novoyelnya	Baranovichi	Kalinin	
Reznik Yuden Markovich	1905	Jewish camp	Pinsk	Molotov	Lazo

Reznik Yael Yosifovna	1934	Novoyelnya	Baranovichi	Kalinin	
Reznik Yankel Todorovich	1908	from captivity	Pinsk	Molotov	Kalinin
Reznikov Aleksandr Georgievich	1914	from captivity	Minsk	Bragin	Dovator
Reznikov Matvei Yakovlevich	1907	Minsk	Minsk	3rd Minskaya	Voroshilov
Reznikov Fedor Davidovich	1914	Slepen	Mogilev	? 17	headquarters
Reznikova Basya Khaimovna	1921	Samotevichi	Gomel	Shemyakin's "Vpered (Forward)"	Makagonov's
Reznitskaya Dora IlYevna	1919	Krasnoye	Baranovichi	Za Sovetskuyu Belarus	family detachment
Reznitski Aron Kiselmanovich	1910	from the encirclement	Palesye	? 225	Suvorov
Reznitski David Semenovich	1912		Baranovichi	Oktyabr	
Reznitski Lev Isaakovich	1915	Krasnoye	Baranovichi	Za Sovetskuyu Belarus	family detachment
Reznitski Sholom Girshevich	1908	Lida	Baranovichi	Leninskaya	Borba
Reznov Movsha Yefimovich	1927	Dyatlovo	Baranovichi	Kalinin	
Reznov Khaim Leibovich	1893	Dyatlovo	Baranovichi	Kalinin	
Reznova Mira Khaimovna	1922	Novogrudok	Baranovichi	Kirov	Ordzhonikidze
Reznova Sara Yefimovna	1923	Dyatlovo	Baranovichi	Kalinin	
Reider Yosif Borisovich	1909	Minsk	Baranovichi	Chkalov	? 4 "Za Sovetskuyu Belarus"
Reider Mikhail Yosifovich	1935	Minsk	Baranovichi	Chkalov	? 4 "Za Sovetskuyu Belarus"
Reider Pinya Meyerovich	1901	Selivanovka	Gomel	8th Rogachevskaya	? 255
Reidman Aleksandr Yudelevich	1914	Gomel, from captivity	Gomel	Voroshilov	headquarters
Reiza Grigori Yosifovich	1911	getto	Baranovichi	Kirov	Oktyabrski
Reizel Aizik Kleinovich	1926	Glussk	Palesye		Slavkovicha
Reizel Boris Kleinovich	1929	Glussk	Palesye		Slavkovicha
Reizer Osher Borisovich	1909	Minsk	Baranovichi	Za Sovetskuyu Belarus	Za Sovetskuyu Belarus
Reiman Viktor Leontevich	1918	from the encirclement	Baranovichi	Voroshilov	Voroshilov
Rein Abram Isaakovich	1910	getto, Sventiany	Vileyka	Voroshilov	Bagration
Reingold Abram Geselevich	1905	Slutsk	Pinsk	Komarov-Korzh's	2 group
Reingold Abram Yoselevich	1885	Pogost, Starobin district	Pinsk	Budenny	Voroshilov
Reingold Benya Itskovich	1921	Rakhovichi	Pinsk	Budenny	Voroshilov
Reingold Isaak Abramovich	1923	Slutsk	Pinsk	Komarov-Korzh's	2 group
Reingold Khaim Abramovich	1925	Slutsk	Pinsk	Komarov-Korzh's	2 group
Reines Yefim Neverovich	1897	Minsk	Baranovichi	Ponomarenko	Budenny
Reiser Izrail Lazarevich	1923	Stolbtsy	Baranovichi	detachment ? 106	
Reiser Lazar Meyerovich	1888	Stolbtsy	Baranovichi	detachment ? 106	
Reitkop Mikhail Mordukhovich	1912	getto, Pruzhany	Brest	Ponomarenko	Kirov
Reitkop Frida Yakovlevna	1915	getto, Pruzhany	Brest	Ponomarenko	Kirov
Relkin Abram Yosifovich	1914	Minsk	Mogilev	208th partisan regiment	? 3
Relkina Fanya Enovna	1916	Minsk	Minsk	Burevestnik	Burevestnik
Rengold Sholom Yevseyevich	1908	Kr. Sloboda, Minsk region	Pinsk	Lenin	Kutuzov
Rendel Shneer Rakhmovich	1924	getto, Myadel	Vileyka	Voroshilov	Kalinin
Resel Dvoira Moiseyevna	1915	Mir	Baranovichi	Kalinin	
Resel Mordukh Moiseyevich	1924	Mir	Baranovichi	Kalinin	
Ref Boris Yosifovich	1906	Dyatlovo	Baranovichi	Pobieda	Suvorov
Ref Solomon Yosifovich	1910	from captivity	Pinsk		Chukhlai
Ref Khava Davidovna	1923	Baranovichi, getto	Pinsk		Chukhlai
Rekhelson Yosif Semenovich	1911	Sitno, Polotsk district	Vitebsk	3rd Belorusskaya	? 1
Rekhtman Meyer Shlemovich	1916	Minsk	Baranovichi	18th Frunze	Kutuzov
Rivin Aizik Moiseyevich	1912	Minsk getto	Baranovichi	Chapayev	Parkhomenko
Rivin Grigori Maksimovich	1903	Minsk	Baranovichi	Dzerzhinski	Kotovski
Rivkin Grigori Antonovich	1921	from captivity	Mogilev	polk ? 600	
Rivkin Solomon Markovich	1914	from captivity	Vitebsk	Prudnikov's	Tabachnikov's
Rivkina Berta Yefimovna	1928	Minsk	Baranovichi	detachment ? 106	
Rivosh Isaak Solomonovich	1923	Braslav	Vileyka	Voroshilov	brigade headquarters
Rier Yevna Neukhovich	1914	Ilya	Minsk	Voronyanski	Borba
Riza Nekhemya Yosifovna	1913	Stolbtsy	Baranovichi	Kalinin	
Rizova Liliya Yefimovna	1919	Minsk getto	Minsk	3rd Minskaya	Niepobedimy (Undefeated)
Riklin Leiba Yankelevich	1889	Gantsevichi	Pinsk		Chukhlai
Rinetski Tevel Shimonovich	1919	Sokolovo	Baranovichi	Kalinin	
Rir Berka Vasilevich	1904	Dyatlovo	Baranovichi	Pobieda	Pobieda
Risina Dina Grigorevna	1917	Korma	Gomel	10st Zhuravichskaya	? 260 Kalinin
Riskina Basya Abramovna		Shklov	Mogilev	Chekist	? 10
Ritkon Semen Mordukhovich	1910	Pruzhany	Brest	Za Sovetskuyu Belarus	Chkalov
Ritman Viktor Elevich	1925	Dokshitsy	Baranovichi	Baranovchi underground RC of the CP(b) B and IDC	
Ritts Solomon Izrailevich	1922	from the encirclement	Vitebsk	Prudnikov's	Grinenko's's
Roberman Khotia Kalmanovich	1922	Rovenskaya Sloboda	Gomel	Voroshilov	Voroshilov
Robok Genekh Yoselevich	1918	Nesvizh	Minsk	Chapayev	Ponomarenko
Rovin Aizik Moiseyevich	1912	Minsk getto	Baranovichi	Stalin	Parkhomenko

JEWISH PARTISANS IN BYELORUSSIA 1941-1944   279

Name	Year	Origin	Region	Brigade	Unit
Rogalin Isaak Khonovich	1919	getto	Vileyka	Voroshilov	Istrebitel (Destroyer)
Rogal Zelik Leibovich	1921	Lida, concentration camp	Belostok	A.Nevski	
Rogatinskaya Yelizaveta Albertovna	1914	Lenino	Grodno	Kapusta's brigade	hospital
Rogatinski Mordukh Rubinovich	1911	Lyubcha	Baranovichi	Kalinin	
Rogov Izrail Vulfovich	1922	Vilno, getto	Baranovichi	Stalin	Budenny
Rogov Samuil Girshevich	1924	Volozhin	Baranovichi	Chkalov	? 4 "Za Sovetskuyu Belarus"
Rogova Fruma Ershovna	1929	Gorodok	Baranovichi	Chkalov	? 4 "Za Sovetskuyu Belarus"
Rogovin Aron Moiseyevich	1914	Gorodok, getto	Baranovichi	Chkalov	
Rogovin Zelik Moiseyevich	1923	Gorodok	Baranovichi	Chkalov	
Rogovin Yosif Girshevich	1925	Volozhin	Baranovichi	Dzerzhinski	Dzerzhinski
Rogovin Isaak Yakovlevich	1923	Gorodok	Minsk	Voronyanski	Kotovski
Rogovin Sima Khonovich	1925	Volozhin	Baranovichi	Chkalov	? 4 "Za Sovetskuyu Belarus"
Rogovina Fanya Yosifovna	1920	Gorodok, getto	Baranovichi	Chkalov	
Rogovskaya Khaya Itskovna	1924	Radun	Baranovichi	Lenin's komsomol	Lenin's komsomol
Rogovski Nema Itskovich	1921	Orany	Baranovichi	Lenin's komsomol	Lenin's komsomol
Rogozhin Lazar Grigorevich	1923	Volozhin	Baranovichi	Za Sovetskuyu Belarus	Kirov
Rodenshtein Yankel Leibovich	1923		Baranovichi	Pobieda	
Rodshtein Lev Semenovich	1913		Minsk	Voronyanski	Mstitel (Revenger)
Rozhanko Leon Leontevich	1909	Vlodava (Poland)	Pinsk	Molotov	Lazo
Rozhanskaya Mariya Markovna	1922	Karpilovka, Oktyabr district	Minsk	Ponomarenko	Kalinovski
Rozhanskaya Sima Semenovna	1922	Glussk	Minsk	Chkalov	Dovator
Rozhanski David Danilovich	1924	otr. ismall town of Chkalova	Brest	Dzerzhinski	Selnitski
Rozhanski Yosif Mairilovich	1901	Byten, Baranovichi region	Brest	Za Sovetskuyu Belarus	Suvorov
Rozhanski Meyer Abramovich	1924	Molchad	Baranovichi	Kalinin	
Rozhanski Moisei Abramovich	1906	Baranovichi, from home	Baranovichi	Grizodubova	Matrosov
Rozhanski Nekhama Ovseyevich	1917	Baranovichi	Baranovichi	Chkalov	? 4 "Za Sovetskuyu Belarus"
Rozhkovski Isaak Maksimovich	1923	Novogrudok	Baranovichi	Pobieda	Pobieda
Rozblat Bronislav Selmanovich	1914	Ilya	Minsk	Voronyanski	Kotovski
Rozvazhski Arkadi P.	1922	Dyatlovo	Baranovichi	Leninskaya	
Rozeiman Lilya Semenovna	1927	Kozel, KrugLyanski district	Mogilev	Chekist	? 31
Rozeiman Roza Semenovna	1924	Shklov district	Mogilev	Chekist	Suvorov
Rozeiman Sara Leibovna	1900	Mogilev	Mogilev	Chekist	Suvorov
Rozemberg Roza Abramovna	1900	Minsk getto	Minsk		Mstitel (Revenger)
Rozemberg Sema Vulfovich	1929	Minsk getto	Minsk		Mstitel (Revenger)
Rozen Yulyan Itskovich	1917	Gorodishche district	Baranovichi	25 years of the BSSR	Grozny
Rozenbaum Aron Girshevich	1924	getto, Pruzhany	Brest	Ponomarenko	Kirov
Rozenbaum Makar Yankelevich	1920	Poland	Pinsk	Molotov	Lazo
Rozenbaum Raisa SrulYevna	1904		Brest	Ponomarenko	Kirov
Rozenbaum Khaim Girshevich	1922	getto, Pruzhany	Brest	Ponomarenko	Kirov
Rozenbaum Khaim Yakovlevich	1901	Pruzhany	Brest	Ponomarenko	Kirov
Rozenberg Aleksandra Lazarevna	1925	Derechin	Baranovichi	Pobieda	Budenny
Rozenberg Vladislav Abramovich	1916	Drogichin district	Pinsk	Molotov	Lazo
Rozenberg Leizer Berkovich	1899	Derechin	Baranovichi	Pobieda	Budenny
Rozenberg Leya Moiseyevna	1904	Derechin	Baranovichi	Pobieda	Budenny
Rozenberg Mariya Lazarevna	1928	Derechin	Baranovichi	Pobieda	Budenny
Rozenberg Pesya Volfovna	1920	getto	Vileyka	Voroshilov	Istrebitel (Destroyer)
Rozenberg Semen Grigorevich	1914	from the Kletnianskaya brigade	Mogilev		Bolshevik
Rozenberg Shifra Lazarevna	1921	Derechin	Baranovichi	Pobieda	Pobieda
RozenBlyum Lazar Moiseyevich	1909	Novogrudok	Baranovichi	Dzerzhinski	Kotovski
Rozenvasser Moisei Motelevich	1906	Slonim	Brest	Sikorski's headquarters	Shchors
Rozenvaian Lev Ikhimovich	1922	Belostok	Grodno	Samutin's group	Kirshner's group
Rozengarten Monik Shmoilovich	1914	Poland, a small partisan group	Pinsk	Molotov	Lazo
Rozengauz Genya Moiseyevna	1913	Grodno	Baranovichi	Kalinin	
Rozengauz Isaak Moiseyevich	1909	Novogrudok	Baranovichi	Kalinin	
Rozenkind Yudel Khaimovich	1907	Dolginovo	Minsk	Kirov	? 4
Rozenovich Girsh Yosifovich	1916		Baranovichi	Lenin's komsomol	Lenin's komsomol
Rozental Isaak Moiseyevich	1924		Baranovichi	Pobieda	Pobieda
Rozenfeld Boris Moiseyevich	1870		Palesye	? 125	brigade headquarters and administration platoon
Rozenfeld Genya Yudelevna	1915		Baranovichi	Leninskaya	hospital
Rozenfeld David Lazarevich	1912	Dyatlovo	Baranovichi	Leninskaya	Leninski
Rozentsveig Sarra Nokhimovna	1919	Novogrudok	Baranovichi	Voroshilov	Voroshilov
Rozentsveig Yulii Berkovich	1911	small town of Derechin	Baranovichi	Voroshilov	Voroshilov

Rozensher Monek Isaakovich	1912	German work camp	Pinsk	Molotov	Kalinin
Rozenshtein David Yosifovich	1903	Belarusian Staff of Partisan Movement	Grodno	Samutin's group	Samutin's group
Rozenshtein Kiva Davidovich	1912	getto N. Sverzhen	Minsk	Chapayev	Ponomarenko
Rozenshtein Yankel Leibovich	1923	Derechin	Baranovichi	Pobieda	Molotov
Rozes Mikhail Srulevich	1918	from the forest, Domachevo	Brest	Stalin	Voroshilov
Rozzhavski Girsh Yudelevich	1916	Dyatlovo	Baranovichi	Leninskaya	Borba
Rozin Abram Yekhimovich	1921	Novogrudok getto	Baranovichi	Kirov	Ordzhonikidze
Rozin Abram Khaimovich	1917	Minsk getto	Grodno	Chapayev	
Rozin Girsh Gilelovich	1932		Mogilev	208th regiment	left the detachment from the moment organization
Rozin Zisel Meyerovich	1912	Novogrudok	Baranovichi	Kalinin	
Rozin Ilya Isaakovich	1903	Timkovichi, Kopyl district	Minsk	Voroshilov	Kotovski
Rozin Yosif Lvovich	1922	from the Litovskaya brigade	Baranovichi	detachment ? 106	
Rozin Karl Borisovich	1910	Ozarichi	Minsk	Bragin	Gastello
Rozin Mikhail Yefimovich	1923	Minsk	Minsk	Rokossovski	25 years of Oktyabr
Rozin Simkha Mikhailovich	1915	Nesvizh	Minsk	Chapayev	Ponomarenko
Rozin Solomon Grigorevich	1905	concentration camp, Mogilev	Gomel	Shemyakin's "Vpered (Forward)"	Makagonov's
Rozina Genya Ruvinovna	1923	Urechye	Palesye	? 225	Chapayev
Rozina Katya Elevna	1908	Minsk	Baranovichi	detachment ? 106	
Rozman Grigori Abramovich	1922	concentration camp, Mogilev	Gomel	8th Rogachevskaya	? 255
Rozmarina Genya Fominichna	1917	Uzda	Minsk	Chapayev	Ponomarenko
Rozov Gelya Abramovich	1913	getto Pleshchenitsy	Minsk	Voronyanski	Pobieda
Rozov Isaak Khaimovich	1914	getto	Vileyka	Voroshilov	Suvorov
Rozov Semen Yudovich	1929	Ushachi	Vitebsk	Dubov's	? 3
Rozova Khana Girshevna	1909	Minsk	Baranovichi	detachment ? 106	
Rozovskaya Khaya Matusovna	1913	Minsk	Baranovichi	detachment ? 106	
Rozovski Abram Ilyich	1924	Minsk	Minsk	3rd Minskaya	25years of the A-ULCYL
Rozovski Tevel Abramovich	1905	Rubezhevichi	Baranovichi	Kalinin	
Roizman Leonid Markovich	1915	Mikhnovichi	Vitebsk	Nikitin's	? 1
Roitman Itsko Fishelevich	1918	from captivity, Kokoisk	Mogilev		? 45 "Za Rodinu (For Motherland)"
Roitman Nevel Yakutovich	1923	Baranovichi, from home	Baranovichi	Grizodubova	Matrosov
Roitman Rakhil Bernardovna	1923	Baranovichi, from home	Baranovichi	Grizodubova	Matrosov
Rok Leon Semenovich	1919	getto	Vileyka	Voroshilov	Istrebitel (Destroyer)
Rolbina Lena Yevelevna	1927	Minsk	Baranovichi	detachment ? 106	
Rolnik Anna Markovna	1900	Minsk	Baranovichi	detachment ? 106	
Rolnik Arkadi Sidorovich	1915	Poland	Pinsk	Molotov	Shish
Rolnik Mateum Moiseyevich	1927		Baranovichi	Kalinin	
Rolnik Mikhel Shmerkovich	1910	Mir	Baranovichi	Kalinin	
Rolnik Pesya Abramovna	1921	Mir	Baranovichi	Kalinin	
Rolnik Fanya Yakovlevna	1912	Minsk	Baranovichi	detachment ? 106	
Romanov Aleksandr Pavlovich	1922		Vitebsk	1st Zaslonov	Kutuzov
Romanova Esfir Solomonovna	1916	Chereya, Chashniki district	Vitebsk	Sadchikov's	battallion ? 3
Romanovskaya Lidiya Borisovna	1923	Lakhva	Pinsk	Kirov	
Romanovski Vladimir Irmovich	1919	Minsk	Mogilev	Osipovichskaya VOG	? 210
Romanovski Lazar Shevelevich	1925	Byaloloza	Baranovichi	Kalinin	
Romanovski Shaya Berkovich	1910	Gorodishche district	Baranovichi	25 years of the BSSR	Grozny
Rosen Adalo Korolevich	1916		Brest	Lenin	Zhukov
Rosin Nikolai Yakovlevich	1918	from the encirclement	Minsk	Ponomarenko	brigade headquarters
Rosinovskaya Yonakh-Kuno Tevelevna (Romanovskaya Ekaterina Anatolevna)	1908	Orsha	Vitebsk	1st Zaslonov	brigade headquarters
Rossa Isaak Mordukhovich	1918	Slonim	Brest		Kotovski
Rosianskaya Sara	1911	Kosovo	Brest	Ponomarenko	Sovetskaya Belarus
Rosianski Ya.	1919	Kosovo	Brest	Ponomarenko	Sovetskaya Belarus
Rotanel Sofiya Moiseyevna	1922		Baranovichi	Pobieda	Pobieda
Rotenberg Semen Yonovich	1917	Tomashevka	Pinsk	Molotov	Shish
Rotenberg Ella Godinovna	1924	getto, Pruzhany	Brest	Ponomarenko	Kirov
Rotkovich Aleksei Mordukhovich	1920	Baranovichi, getto	Pinsk		Chukhlai
Rotkop Shlema Niskovich	1918	concentration camp	Pinsk	Kuibyshev	Shchors
Rotman Khaim Bentsianovich	1910	Lida	Baranovichi	Vpered (Forward)	Bolshevik
Rotmanski Yudel Am.	1916	Kobrin	Brest		Kotovski
Rotopel Sofiya Khaimovna	1921	Derechin	Baranovichi	Pobieda	Pobieda
Rotshild Yakov Leopoldovich	1923	Minsk getto	Minsk	Belarus	Belarus
Rotshtein Samuil Vigdorovich	1929	Ivye	Baranovichi	Kalinin	
Rokhkin Meyer Aronovich	1915	Peski	Baranovichi	Leninskaya	Krasnogvardeiski
Rokhlin Aizik Shlemovich					

Name	Year	Place	Region	Detachment	Brigade
Rokhlin Mikhail Moiseyevich	1919	from the encirclement	Mogilev	? 810	
Rokhman Abram Moiseyevich	1914	Lomzha	Baranovichi	Kalinin	
Rokhman Zalman Mikhailovich	1915	Kaunas	Vileyka		Suslov
Rochkei Savek Girshevich	1906	Baranovichi	Brest	Za Sovetskuyu Belarus	Suvorov
Roshkin Genya Yudelevna	1913	Dyatlovo	Baranovichi	Leninskaya	family detachment group
Rubanovich Yefim Demianovich	1922	getto, Vilno	Vileyka	Voroshilov	Kalinin
Rubanovich Sofiya Bentsianovna	1924	Vilno	Vileyka		Suslov
Rubakha Nikita Grigorevich	1910	Yaskovichi	Brest	Dzerzhinski	Chertkov
Rubakha Osher Niselevich	1906	Gantsevichi	Pinsk	Molotov	Shish
Rubezhevski Boris Salomonovich	1921	Naliboki	Baranovichi	Kalinin	
Rubezhevski Isaak Salomonovich	1907	Naliboki	Baranovichi	Kalinin	
Rubezhin Vilik Semenovich	1928	Minsk getto	Baranovichi	18th Frunze	Dzerzhinski
Rubel Gdal Mordukhovich	1912	Gorodok	Baranovichi	Chkalov	? 4 "Za Sovetskuyu Belarus"
Rubenchik Abram Izrailevich	1927	Minsk	Baranovichi	Za Sovetskuyu Belarus	family detachment
Rubenchik Asya Naumovna	1922	Minsk	Baranovichi	Chkalov	
Rubenchik Benyamin Markovich	1910	Uzlyany, Rudnya district	Minsk	2nd Minskaya	Shchors
Rubenchik Benyamin Mordukhovich	1904	from the forest	Minsk	3rd Minskaya	Lazo
Rubenchik Genrikh	1906	Minsk	Baranovichi	18th Frunze	Kutuzov
Rubenchik Genya Elevna	1929	Minsk	Baranovichi	detachment ? 106	
Rubenchik Grisha Yosifovich	1929	Minsk	Baranovichi	detachment ? 106	
Rubenchik Eva Izrailevna	1925	Minsk	Baranovichi	Chkalov	? 4 "Za Sovetskuyu Belarus"
Rubenchik Izrail Iselevich	1901	Minsk	Baranovichi	detachment ? 106	
Rubenchik Nekhama Abramovna	1904	Minsk	Baranovichi	detachment ? 106	
Rubenchik Samuil F.	1911	Minsk	Vitebsk	Nikitin's	? 1
Rubin Berka Mendelevich	1895	small town of Vishnevo	Baranovichi	Chapayev	Parkhomenko
Rubin Berka Yankelevich	1887	Parichi district, Kovchitsy	Minsk	Parkhomenko	Kirov
Rubin Grigori Mendelevich	1919	Knyaginino	Minsk	Voronyanski	Mstitel (Revenger)
Rubin Grigori Samuilovich	1925	Minsk	Baranovichi	Kalinin	
Rubin David Isaakovich	1914	Minsk	Mogilev	208th regiment	
Rubin Kopyl Moiseyevich	1900	from the civil camp	Vileyka	4th Belorusskaya	? 6
Rubin Lev Borisovich	1924	Minsk	Baranovichi	Ponomarenko	25 years of the BSSR
Rubin Lev Mendelevich	1926	Dolginovo	Minsk	Voronyanski	Kotovski
Rubin Mendel Khaimovich	1919	Lyakhovichi	Pinsk	Lenin	Dzerzhinski
Rubin Pavel Markovich	1927	Minsk	Baranovichi	detachment ? 106	
Rubin Shlema Aronovich	1911	Kartuz-Bereza district	Brest	Ponomarenko	Kirov
Rubin Yankel Srulevich	1920	Jewish camp Dolginovo	Minsk	Voronyanski	Pobieda
Rubina Zlata Samoilovna	1923	Volkovyssk, camp	Belostok	A.Nevski	
Rubina Raya Moiseyevna	1923	Minsk	Baranovichi	detachment ? 106	
Rubina Roza Semenovna	1924	Mogilev	Baranovichi	detachment ? 106	
Rubina Sofiya Solomonovna	1920	Minsk	Baranovichi	Vpered (Forward)	Chkalov
Rubina Emma Mikhailovna	1924	small town of Vishnevo, Volozhin district, getto	Baranovichi	Chapayev	Parkhomenko
Rubinich Khaim Izrailevich	1893	Lenin	Pinsk	Budenny	Kotovski
Rubinov Mikhail Alkhonovich	1921	from the encirclement	Grodno		Izyumski's
Rubinovich Yerukhim Yankelevich	1922	Lida	Baranovichi	Vpered (Forward)	A.Nevski
Rubinovich Samuil Volfovich	1925	Lida	Baranovichi	Kalinin	
Rubinovich Sara Volfovna	1888	Lida	Baranovichi	Kalinin	
Rubinovich Khana Yosifovna	1920	Vishnevo	Baranovichi	Stalin	Chapayev
Rubinson Benyamin Nevakhovich	1888	Minsk	Baranovichi	detachment ? 106	
Rubinson Kalman Yankelevich	1901	Minsk	Minsk	2nd Minskaya	Kutuzov
Rubinson Shlema Yosifovich	1890	Glussk	Palesye	? 123	brigade headquarters and administration platoon
Rubinchik Ana Aronovna	1923	Bobruisk	Mogilev		? 760 Berezovski
Rubinchik Anna Izrailevna	1914	Minsk	Mogilev	208th regiment	
Rubinchik Sofiya Aronovna	1925	Bobruisk	Mogilev		? 760 Berezovski
Rubinchik Khana Izrailevna	1914	Minsk	Minsk	Belarus	Belarus
Rubinshtein Benyamin Mendelevich	1914	Domachevo	Pinsk	Molotov	Lazo
Rubinshtein Boris Semenovich	1923	Minsk	Vitebsk	Nikitin's	? 2
Rubinshtein Genya Nevakhovna	1917	Minsk	Baranovichi	detachment ? 106	
Rubinshtein Gita	1887	Bryansk getto, Belostok region	Grodno	Vo imya Rodiny (In the name of Motherland)	Zhukov
Rubinshtein Zelik Failovich	1914	Zheludok	Baranovichi	Pervomaiskaya	Oktyabr
Rubinshtein Zina Isaakovna	1911	Minsk	Baranovichi	Chkalov	reserve group
Rubinshtein Izik Abramovich	1913	Minsk getto	Minsk	Shchors	Voroshilov
Rubinshtein Isaak Rafailovich	1927	Minsk	Baranovichi	detachment ? 106	
Rubinshtein Isaak Samuilovich	1919	Korelichi	Baranovichi	Kalinin	
Rubinshtein Lidiya Maksimovna	1916	Rovno region.	Baranovichi	Leninskaya	Niepobedimy (Undefeated)
Rubinshtein Mariya Isaakovna	1914	Minsk	Baranovichi	Chkalov	reserve group

Rubinshtein Osher Abramovich	1913	Rovno region.	Baranovichi	Leninskaya	Niepobedimy (Undefeated)
Rubinshtein Pinus Meyerovich	1910	Derechin	Baranovichi	Leninskaya	hospital
Rubinshtein Roza Lipovna	1924	Grodzyanka	Mogilev		? 760 Berezovski
Rubinshtein Rubin Solomonovich	1920	Lida	Baranovichi	Kirov	Iskra
Rubinshtein Sonya Shayevna	1917	Minsk	Baranovichi	detachment ? 106	
Rubinshtein Sofiya Gershevna	1930	Bryansk getto, Belostok region	Grodno	Vo imya Rodiny (In the name of Motherland)	Zhukov
Rubinshtein Fanya Solomonovna	1914	Minsk	Baranovichi	detachment ? 106	
Rubinshtein Khana Gershevna	1922	Bryansk getto, Belostok region	Grodno	Vo imya Rodiny (In the name of Motherland)	Zhukov
Rubinshtein Khenrik Shimonovich	1902	getto, Brest	Pinsk	Molotov	Suvorov
Rubinshtein Edya Samuilovna	1913	Ivienets	Baranovichi	detachment ? 106	
Rubinshtein Ester Semenovna	1913	Minsk	Baranovichi	detachment ? 106	
Rubinshtein Yankel Leibovich	1923	Derechin	Baranovichi	Leninskaya	Pobieda
Rubnich Aron Shevelevich	1924	Lenino	Palesye	? 100	Budenny
Rubnich Izrail Shevelevich	1926	Lenino	Mogilev	208th partisan regiment	? 1
Rudashevskaya Sofiya Borisovna	1914	Minsk	Baranovichi	detachment ? 106	
Rudenko Iadviga Mair	1912	Slonim district	Baranovichi	Rokossovski	Rokossovski
Ruder Yerukhim Ziskovich	1899	Budnishki, Beshenkovichi district	Vitebsk	Sennenskaya brigade (Leonov's)	B.Khmelnitski
Ruderman Aizik Faibishevich	1913	Minsk getto	Baranovichi	Chapayev	Chapayev
Ruderman Isaak Meyerovich	1906	Vileika	Minsk	Voronyanski	Suvorov
Ruderman Maks Naumovich	1899	Samokhvalovichi	Baranovichi	Stalin	Budenny
Ruderman Marik Maksovich	1930	Minsk	Baranovichi	Ponomarenko	Timoshenko
Ruderman Mira Matveyevna	1926	Minsk getto	Baranovichi	Stalin	Parkhomenko
Ruderman Mikhail Grigorevich	1925	Minsk	Baranovichi	Za Sovetskuyu Belarus	family detachment
Ruderman Sonya Abramovna	1908	Minsk	Baranovichi	detachment ? 106	
Ruderman Yakov Davidovich	1923	Glubokoye	Minsk	Voronyanski	Suvorov
Rudetski Boris Ilyashevich	1916	Poland, camp, prisoner of war	Pinsk	Molotov	Kalinin
Rudin Afroim Zalmanovich	1902	Smolyany	Vitebsk	VLKSM	? 5
Rudinitski Mikhail Vin.	1921	Vilno	Vileyka	Voroshilov	Suvorov
Ruditser Abram Isaakovich	1924	Minsk getto	Baranovichi	18th Frunze	Frunze
Ruditser Bela Nisinovna	1906	Rudobelka	Palesye	? 123	brigade headquarters and administration platoon
Ruditser Yosif Leibovich	1914	Minsk	Mogilev	208th regiment	
Ruditser Mikhail Mordukhovich	1924	Minsk	Mogilev	208th regiment	
Ruditser Nadia Mordukhovna	1916	Medvezhino, Minsk region	Mogilev	polk ? 15	
Ruditser Naum Lvovich	1905	Minsk	Mogilev	208th partisan regiment	? 1
Ruditser Neiakh-Abram Mikhailovich	1907	Minsk	Baranovichi		
Ruditser Khaya Mordukhovna	1916	Minsk	Mogilev	208th regiment	
Ruditski Lev Abramovich	1911	Garnitsa, Smolevichi district	Minsk	Razgrom (Crushing defeat)	
Rudkovskaya Lyubov Igorevna	1921	Minsk getto	Minsk	2nd Minskaya	Kutuzov
Rudnik Rakhilya Yosifovna	1920	Vishnevo	Baranovichi	Chkalov	
Rudnik Fedor Aizikovich	1916	camp Kurenets	Minsk	Voronyanski	Kotovski
Rudnitser Neiiakh-Abram Mikhelevich	1907	Minsk	Baranovichi	detachment ? 106	
Rudnitskaya Elena Lvovna	1918	Kurenets, Vileika region	Vitebsk	Chapayev	detachments
Rudnitskaya Lyuba Yudelevna	1918		Baranovichi	Oktyabr	
Rudnitskaya Fanya Semenovna	1911	Minsk	Baranovichi	detachment ? 106	
Rudnitski Beshamil Germinovich	1924	Volkovyssk	Baranovichi	Pobieda	Pobieda
Rudnitski Semen Grigorevich	1925	Veiskishki	Vileyka	Voroshilov	Slava (Glory)
Rudnitski Semen Mikhailovich	1914	from captivity	Mogilev	? 425	battallion ? 3
Rudnitski Falvyel Germinovich	1920	Volkovyssk	Baranovichi	Pobieda	Pobieda
Rudnitski Khaim Yudelevich	1922	Slutsk	Minsk	Dyadi Koli	Stalin
Rudnitski Sholim Rafailovich	1908	Stolbtsy	Baranovichi	detachment ? 106	
Rudnitski Yakov Khaimovich	1910	Novogrudok getto	Baranovichi	Kirov	Ordzhonikidze
Rudnitski Yankel Abramovich	1907	Novogrudok	Baranovichi	Kirov	Ordzhonikidze
Rudski Mordko Yankelevich	1911	Odrizhin	Pinsk	Molotov	Potalakh
Rudshtein Galina Aizikovna	1913	Slonim	Brest	Sikorski's headquarters	Shchors
Ruzha Vulf Shmulevich	1916	getto N. Sverzhen	Minsk	Chapayev	Ponomarenko
Ruzha Movsha Itskovich	1911	Koldychevo, getto	Baranovichi	Pervomaiskaya	Zhdanov
Ruzhanskaya (Malskaya) Khana Yudelevna	1921	Dyatlovo	Baranovichi	Leninskaya	Borba
Ruzhanski Nakhamia Ovseyevich	1917	from the detachment Chapayev	Baranovichi	Za Sovetskuyu Belarus	Za Sovetskuyu Belarus
Ruza Gersh Yosifovich	1911		Baranovichi	Oktyabr	
Ruzova Rita Samuilovna	1922	Minsk	Baranovichi	Vpered (Forward)	family detachment group
Rukshin Izrail Abramovich	1919	Yody	Vileyka		Ponomarenko
Rukshin Meyer Khonovich	1902	Zamoshe, Braslav district	Vileyka	Zhdanov	

JEWISH PARTISANS IN BYELORUSSIA 1941-1944 283

Rukshin Srol Abovich	1919	Yody	Vileyka		Ponomarenko
Rukshin Srol Meyerovich	1909	Zamoshe, Braslav district	Vileyka	Zhdanov	
Rumanov Grisha Samuilovich	1934	Minsk	Baranovichi	detachment ? 106	
Rumanova Yevgeniya Grigorevna	1909	Minsk	Baranovichi	detachment ? 106	
Rumshitski Khaim Mordulevich	1912	Lida	Baranovichi	Vpered (Forward)	Bolshevik
Rusak Solomon Izrailevich	1917	Minsk getto	Baranovichi	18th Frunze	brigade headquarters
Rusakov I.Sh.	1912	Osipovichi	Mogilev	1st Bobruiskaya	destroying platoon
Rutbart Grisha Sulimovich	1916	Belostok	Grodno	Samutin's group	Kirshner's group
Rutman Ilya Borisovich	1906	Minsk underground	Mogilev	152-oi partisan regiment	? 152
Rutshtein Abram Izrailevich	1926	Glubokoye	Vileyka	4th Belorusskaya	? 1
Rutshtein Aleksandr Abramovich	1905	family detachment camp	Belostok	A.Nevski	
Rufaizen Osfald Ilyich	1922	Mir	Baranovichi	Stalin	Budenny
Rutski Vladimir Isaakovich	1927	Borovki, Lepel district	Vitebsk	Dubov's	? 1
Rybak Abram Shlemovich	1902	from the civil camp	Vileyka	4th Belorusskaya	? 6
Rybak Nookh Isaakovich	1917	getto	Baranovichi	1st Baranovichskaya	Besstrashny (Fearless)
Rybak Khana Meyerovna	1913	Novogrudok	Baranovichi	Kalinin	
Rybak Shlema Yefremovich	1914	Novogrudok	Baranovichi	Kalinin	
Rybak Ester Abramovna	1920	getto	Baranovichi	1st Baranovichskaya	Besstrashny (Fearless)
Rybakova Ida Ruvimovna	1902	Minsk getto	Baranovichi	Shchuchin IDC headquarters' company	Ivienets underground DC of the CP(b)B
Rybnik Adam Leibovich	1919	getto, Pruzhany	Brest	Ponomarenko	Kirov
Rybnikov Anton Antonovich	1919		Brest	Ponomarenko	Kirov
Ryvkin Zisel Srulevich	1900	Minsk	Vitebsk	Nikitin's	? 2
Ryvkin Yosif Srolevich	1914		Vitebsk	Nikitin's	
Ryvkin Isaak Emanuilovich	1910	Veselovo, Borisov district	Minsk		Suvorov
Ryzhii Lev Borisovich	1913	Minsk, camp, prisoner of war	Vileyka	Frunze	Voroshilov
Ryza Khema Yosifovich	1913	Koldychevo, getto	Baranovichi	Pervomaiskaya	Ya.Kolas
Ryklin Moisei Leibovich	1920	Pinsk region, Lenino	Minsk	Chkalov	Dovator
Rymar Khaim Velvelevich	1918	Lakhva	Pinsk	Kirov	Kalinin
Rymburg Yosif Shayevich	1904	Bobruisk	Palesye	Lelchitskaya	Khrapko's
Rynkovskaya Sofiya Grigorevna	1894	Velizh	Vitebsk	Korotkin	Levkovich's
Ryskina Zinaida Grigorevna	1915	Minsk	Baranovichi	Vpered (Forward)	Chkalov
Rys Liza Yefimovna	1905	Minsk	Baranovichi	detachment ? 106	
Rys Roza Davidovna	1935	Minsk	Baranovichi	detachment ? 106	
Rytkov Leiba Zinglevich	1923	Pruzhany	Brest	Za Sovetskuyu Belarus	Chkalov
Riabets Movsha Abelevich	1886	Molchad	Baranovichi	Pervomaiskaya	
Riabets Freida Leibovna	1918	Gorodishche district	Baranovichi	25 years of the BSSR	Grozny
Riabikov Yefim Borisovich	1911	Borisov	Minsk	3rd Minskaya	Niepobedimy (Undefeated)
Riaznitski David Semenovich	1912	Novogrudok getto	Baranovichi	Kirov	Ordzhonikidze
Savelson David Izrailevich	1914	Zareche	Minsk	Voronyanski	Suvorov
Savenko Zhenya Khaimovna	1924	Nesvizh	Baranovichi	Chapayev	Parkhomenko
Savikovski Lenya Aronovich	1928	Minsk	Baranovichi	detachment ? 106	
Savin Naum Yoselevich	1924	Mir	Baranovichi	Zhukov	
Savitskaya Dusha Yankelevna	1921	Dyatlovo	Baranovichi	Leninskaya	family detachment group
Savitskaya Leya Mordukhovna	1920	Dyatlovo	Baranovichi	Kalinin	
Savitskaya Khaya Greinomovna	1923	Dyatlovo	Baranovichi	Leninskaya	Borba
Savitskaya Tsylya Yankelevna	1922	Lida	Baranovichi	Kalinin	
Savitski Gerts Yudelevich	1922	Dyatlovo	Baranovichi	Leninskaya	Krasnogvardeiski
Savitski Isaak Mordukhovich	1912	Dyatlovo	Baranovichi	Leninskaya	Borba
Savitski Leizer Greinomovich	1920	Dyatlovo	Baranovichi	Leninskaya	Borba
Savitski Leizer Yudelevich	1924		Baranovichi	Oktyabr	
Savitski Meyer Mikhailovich	1923	Dyatlovo	Baranovichi	Leninskaya	Krasnogvardeiski
Savitski Mitia Semenovich	1916	Lida	Baranovichi	Kalinin	
Savitski Khaim Mordukhovich	1904	Dyatlovo	Baranovichi	Leninskaya	Borba
Savchits Fima Yakovlevich	1909	from the prisoners of war camp	Baranovichi	Grizodubova	
Savchits Tsita Leibovna	1922	from captivity	Baranovichi	Grizodubova	
Savchuk Revveka Grigorevna	1907	Minsk	Baranovichi	detachment ? 106	
Sagalovich Avram Itskovich	1929	Lenino	Palesye	? 100	Budenny
Sagalovich Grigori Itskovich	1922	getto	Brest	? 99 Gulyaev	Grabko
Sagalovich David Moiseyevich	1927	Minsk	Baranovichi	detachment ? 106	
Sagalovich Dora Ilinichna	1934	Minsk	Baranovichi	detachment ? 106	
Sagalovich Isaak Davidovich	1923	Timkovichi, Kopyl district	Minsk	Chapayev	Shchors
Sagalovich Modes Davidovich	1918	Minsk getto	Baranovichi	Stalin	Parkhomenko
Sagalovich NataLya Elevna	1923	Lida	Baranovichi	18th Frunze	Frunze
Sagalovich Rubin Leibovich	1920	Ivienets	Baranovichi	Zhukov	

Sagalovich Tsalko Itskovich	1924	Glussk	Palesye	? 100	Budenny
Sagalovich Elya Itskovich	1920	getto	Brest	? 99 Gulyaev	Grabko
Sagalovich Yakov Yudelevich	1908	camp Kurenets	Minsk	Voronyanski	Kotovski
Sagalchik Anna Markovna	1916	Minsk	Baranovichi	detachment ? 106	
Sagalchik Aron Solomonovich	1927	Minsk	Baranovichi	Chkalov	? 4 "Za Sovetskuyu Belarus"
Sagalchik Bellya Gershevna	1903	Minsk	Baranovichi	detachment ? 106	
Sagalchik Moisei Khaimovich	1927	Minsk	Baranovichi	detachment ? 106	
Sagalchik Faiva Abramovich	1900	Samokhvalovichi	Baranovichi	detachment ? 106	
Sagalchik Fruma Gershevna	1906	Samokhvalovichi	Baranovichi	detachment ? 106	
Sagalchik Khana Abramovna	1902	Minsk	Baranovichi	detachment ? 106	
Sagutin-Iazmir Ruvim Tsadikovich	1904	Minsk	Minsk	2nd Minskaya	Kutuzov
Sadovskaya Sofiya Semenovna	1912	Minsk	Baranovichi	Chkalov	
Sadovski Boris Yeselevich	1906	Starobin	Pinsk	Komarov-Korzh's	1 group
Sadovski Igor Yefimovich	1933	Minsk	Baranovichi	Chkalov	
Sadovski Isaak Khaimovich	1914	Timkovichi	Vileyka	Zhdanov	
Sadovski Mitsik Khamelevich	1924	Soly	Baranovichi	Leninskaya	Niepobedimy (Undefeated)
Sadovski Khaim Shimelevich	1925	Radun	Baranovichi	Lenin's komsomol	Lenin's komsomol
Sadovski Shlema Elevich	1925	camp, Gantsevichi	Palesye	? 100	Za Sovetskuyu Rodinu
Sadovski Elya Abramovich	1887	Gantsevichi	Palesye	? 100	Za Sovetskuyu Rodinu
Saet Yefim Samoilovich	1911	Rakhovets district	Brest	Sikorski's headquarters	Shchors
Said Abram Khatskelevich	1921	Slonim district	Brest	Sikorski's headquarters	Shchors
Saimer Zalman Motkovich	1923	Myadel	Vitebsk	2nd Belorusskaya	
Sak Moisei Girshevich	1896	Glussk	Palesye	Lelchitskaya	Shantar's
Sakovich Berta Grigorevna	1910	Minsk	Minsk	Stalin	
Sakomski Semen Grigorevich	1902	Minsk	Minsk	Zheleznyak	? 5
Salamon Leiba Fiselevich	1926	getto	Vileyka	Voroshilov	Bagration
Salutskaya Gutia Izrailevna	1922	Derechin	Baranovichi	Pobieda	Molotov
Salutski Karsel Mordukhovich	1910	Zelva	Baranovichi	Pobieda	Pobieda
Salutski Movsha Mordukhovich	1909	Zelva	Baranovichi	Pobieda	Pobieda
Salutski Moisei Izrailevich	1924	Derechin	Baranovichi	Pobieda	Pobieda
Salutski Natan Khonovich	1922	Zelva	Baranovichi	Pobieda	Pobieda
Salmon Isaak Shimelevich	1923	local	Baranovichi	Pobieda	Pobieda
Samershtein Leya Yosifovna	1907	Poland	Pinsk	Molotov	Kalinin
Samovar Isaak Nokhimovich	1909	Ikiziya	Vileyka	Za Rodinu (For Motherland)	Kirov
Samoilovski Mikhail Moiseyevich	1916	detachment Shchors	Minsk	Shchors	Bolshevik
Samsonovich Girsh Mendelevich	1910	Novogrudok	Baranovichi	Kalinin	
Samsonovich Yosif Ikhilevich	1895	Turets	Baranovichi	Kalinin	
Samsonovich Sheina Nokhimovna	1917	Baranovichi	Baranovichi	Kalinin	
Samsonovich Yudel Mendelevich	1912	Gorodishche	Baranovichi	Kalinin	
Sandler Isaak Naumovich	1923	Bobruisk	Palesye	? 123	Vezhnovets'
Sandler Mikhail Yosifovich	1915	Krivik	Gomel	Shchors	Beriya
Sandler Roza Izrailevna	1913	Minsk	Baranovichi	detachment ? 106	
Saplitski Gennadi Itskovich	1911	Traiki	Baranovichi	Pervomaiskaya	Ya.Kolas
Sapozhnikov Daniil Markovich	1907	Bobruisk	Mogilev	11st Bykhovskaya	? 325
Sapozhnikov Ida Zelikovna	1910	Lida	Baranovichi	Kalinin	
Sapozhnikov Moisei Abramovich	1913	Starye Dorogi	Minsk	Chkalov	Dovator
Sapozhnikov Osher Mordukhovich	1900		Baranovichi	Oktyabr	
Saposhnik Leib Davidovich	1925	Lida	Baranovichi	Kalinin	
Saragovich Shlema Leibovich	1909	Yody	Vileyka	Spartak	? 6
Saulski David Berkovich	1915	camp, Volkovyssk	Brest	Ponomarenko	brigade headquarters
Safrov Urka Solomonovich	1926	Druya	Vileyka	Kalinin	? 3
Sakhrai Motya Girshevich	1915	Mogilev	Mogilev	partisan regiment ? 277	? 277
Sveranovski Leib Isaakovich	1893	Turets	Baranovichi	Kalinin	
Sverdel Boris Markovich	1915	escapee	Vileyka	Suvorov	
Sverdel Genya Solomonovna	1912	escapee	Vileyka	Suvorov	
Sverdlina Roza Zyndelevna	1919	Glubokoye	Vileyka	4th Belorusskaya	brigade headquarters
Sverdlov Mikhail Osherovich	1925	getto	Vileyka	Voroshilov	Bagration
Sverdlov Samuil Monusovich	1903	Rogachev	Gomel		? 1 Rogachevski
Sverdlova Asya Naumovna	1922	Polotsk	Vitebsk	Chapayev	detachments
Sverdlova Sonya Naumovna	1923	Polotsk	Vitebsk	Chapayev	detachments
Sverzhenskaya Esfir Yefimovna	1923	Mir	Baranovichi	Chkalov	
Sverzhinskaya Bellya Mikhelevna	1896	Minsk	Baranovichi	detachment ? 106	
Svetitskaya Tiviia Yankelevna	1908	Nachi, Lida district	Baranovichi	Leninskaya	Niepobedimy (Undefeated)
Svetitski Abram Yankelevich	1905	Nachi, Lida district	Baranovichi	Leninskaya	Niepobedimy (Undefeated)
Svinik Dvoira Yosifovna	1905	Ivienets	Baranovichi	Kalinin	
Svinik Sholom Abramovich	1923	Ivienets	Baranovichi	Kalinin	
Svinkina Olga Zakharovna	1910	Minsk	Baranovichi	Kalinin	
Svirnovskaya Mira Vulfovna	1912	Glussk	Minsk	Bragin	Gastello

Svirskaya Yelizaveta Abovna	1925	getto	Vileyka	Voroshilov	Chapayev
Svirski Boris Yakovlevich	1921	Sventiany	Vileyka	CC of the CP(b)B	Parkhomenko
Svirski Viktor Elekimovich	1920	getto, Vilno	Vileyka	Voroshilov	Kalinin
Svirski David Elkimovich	1923	Myadel	Vileyka	Voroshilov	Kalinin
Svirski Ilya Solomonovich	1925	Kozyany	Vileyka	Spartak	? 1
Svirski Naum Abovich	1922	getto	Vileyka	Voroshilov	Chapayev
Svirski Yakov Natanovich	1908	Sutin	Minsk	2nd Minskaya	Kutuzov
Svistun Anna Abramovna	1925	Oboltsy, Senno district	Vitebsk	Sennenskaya brigade (Leonov's)	Filippova
Svistunov Efrem Yefremovich	1905	from the encirclement	Gomel	1st Gomelskaya	? 1 Chapayev
Svistunov Leon Yefremovich	1912	Kamenka	Gomel	1st Gomelskaya	? 1 Chapayev
Svoiski Salei Mendelevich	1908	from captivity	Vitebsk	Nikitin's	? 1
Svyatov Abram Rakhmilevich	1899	Zholudok	Baranovichi	Kalinin	
Svyatoi Girsh Abramovich	1922		Baranovichi	Oktyabr	
Svyatoi Mordukh Rakhmilevich	1902	Zheludok	Baranovichi	Pervomaiskaya	Oktyabr
Sgotski Leiba Khaimovich	1924		Baranovichi	Pobieda	Pobieda
Sevilson Moisei Khaimovich	1904		Minsk	Voronyanski	Borba
Sevrin Khaim Nisonovich	1895	Lenin	Pinsk	Kirov	Petrovich's
Segal Ilyash Khononvich	1906	getto, Pruzhany	Brest	Ponomarenko	Kirov
Segal Samuil Khononvich	1903	getto, Pruzhany	Brest	Ponomarenko	Kirov
Segalovich Yekhil Letovich	1919	Rubezhevichi	Baranovichi	Kalinin	
Segalovich Rakhmil Elevich	1925	Rubezhevichi	Baranovichi	Kalinin	
Segalovich Rubin Isaakovich	1924	Ivienets	Baranovichi	Kalinin	
Segalovich Sonya Isaakovna	1914	Rubezhevichi	Baranovichi	Kalinin	
Segalovich Feiga Elevna	1918	Rubezhevichi	Baranovichi	Kalinin	
Segalovich Elya Khilevich	1888	Rubezhevichi	Baranovichi	Kalinin	
Segalovich Estera Abramovna	1888	Rubezhevichi	Baranovichi	Kalinin	
Segal Girsh Aronovich	1924	Slonim	Baranovichi	Kalinin	
Segal Izrail Yakovlevich	1894	Sukhovchitsy	Brest		Kotovski
Segal Isaak Aleksandrovich	1921	Divinishki	Baranovichi	Leninskaya	Borba
Segal Leiba Yakovlevich	1908	Sukhovchitsy	Brest		Kotovski
Segal NataLya Mordukhovna	1919	Nevir, Volyn region	Pinsk	Shubetidze	Ordzhonikidze
Segal Khaim Yakovlevich	1897	Sukhovchitsy	Brest		Kotovski
Segal Sholom Khaimovich	1920	Indura, Grodno district	Brest	detachment 346	345
Segel Aron Vladimirovich	1919	from captivity	Palesye	? 123	Death to Fascism
Segel Grigori Tsalkovich	1909	from the Jewish group, Pruzhany	Brest	Ponomarenko	Gastello
Segel Izrail Lvovich	1923	Western Belarus	Minsk	Kalinin	Kalinin
Segen Mariko Khononovich	1908	getto, Pruzhany	Brest	Ponomarenko	Kirov
Seifor Moisei Isaakovich	1925	Slonim	Brest	Sikorski's headquarters	Shchors
Sematnitskaya Serafima Abramovna	1923	Sedlets district	Baranovichi	25 years of the BSSR	Kotovski
SemeNenya Mariya Yakovlevna	1913	Lyuban	Minsk	258th Kuibyshev	Budenny
Semernitskaya Faina Lvovna	1913	Stolbtsy	Mogilev	? 61	? 61
Senderovskaya Mirra Menakhimovna	1926	Dyatlovo	Baranovichi	Leninskaya	family detachment group
Senderovskaya Tsilya Menakhimovna	1927	Dyatlovo	Baranovichi	Leninskaya	family detachment group
Senderovski Grigori Mekhanovich	1932	Dyatlovo	Baranovichi	Leninskaya	Borba
Serafimovich Lev Ivanovich	1925	Minsk	Minsk	Parkhomenko	Kirov
Serbryannik Leiba Samsonovich	1915	Svalovichi, Volyn region	Pinsk	Molotov	Lazo
Servianski Noakh Notovich	1908	Slonim	Brest	Za Sovetskuyu Belarus	Chkalov
Serebrevskaya Mariya Leizerovna	1914	Skiporovichi	Baranovichi	Pobieda	Suvorov
Serebrevskaya Matlya Shayevna	1935	Velikaya Svorzhva	Baranovichi	Kalinin	
Serebrevskaya Slava (Glory) Shayevna		Velikaya Svorzhva	Baranovichi	Kalinin	
Serebrevski Genn Shmuilovich	1907		Baranovichi	Pobieda	Suvorov
Serebrevski Shaya Geselevich	1896	Velikaya Svorzhva	Baranovichi	Kalinin	
Serchuk Daniil Yakovlevich	1920	Ivanovo	Pinsk	Shubetidze	Chapayev
Setler Gershun Motelevich	1924	Slonim	Minsk	Rokossovski	25 years of Oktyabr
Sigalov Yakov Petrovich	1921	from captivity, Smorgon	Minsk	Dimy	
Siderovich Elya Arkadevna	1936	Lida	Baranovichi	Kalinin	
Siderovich Esia Davidovna	1908	Lida	Baranovichi	Kalinin	
Sidorevski Khaim Abramovich	1911	Mogilev	Mogilev	? 121	
Sidorianski Abram Borukhovich	1909	concentration camp	Pinsk	Kuibyshev	Shchors
Silchinskaya Raisa Mikhailovna	1927	Mogilev	Mogilev		? 41
Simanovich Nina Davidovna	1913	Sviridonovka, Mozyr district	Palesye	37th Yelskaya	Bolshevik
Simakhovich Solomon Abramovich	1910	Subotniki	Baranovichi	Kalinin	
Simkhovich Mariya Markovna	1905	Starye Dorogi	Minsk	Kirov ? 100	brigade economical service
Simkhovich Ruva Nevelevich	1923	Minsk	Baranovichi	detachment ? 106	
Simkhovich Khaya Berkovna	1914	Gorodok	Minsk	Voronyanski	Mstitel (Revenger)

Simkhovich Tsilya Ilinichna	1912	Ukhvala, Krupki district	Mogilev	8th Zhunin's brigade	? 30
Sinalevich Falvyel Isaakovich	1923	Sobatintsy	Belostok	A.Nevski	
Sinder Boris Faivelevich	1910	Mir	Brest		Kotovski
Sinder David Mendelevich	1926	Mir	Baranovichi	Chkalov	
Sinder Yefim Izrailevich	1923	getto	Baranovichi	Za Sovetskuyu Belarus	Kirov
Sinder Yosif Mendelevich	1912	Mir, getto	Baranovichi	Za Sovetskuyu Belarus	Kirov
Sinder Masha Faivelevna	1921	Mir	Baranovichi	detachment ? 106	
Sinder Fima Faivelevich	1923	Mir	Baranovichi	Komsomolets	? 1 komsomolski
Sinderman Sonya Benyaminovna	1923	Minsk	Baranovichi	Kalinin	
Sinderovskaya Riva Menakhenovna	1920	Dyatlovo	Baranovichi	Kalinin	
Sinderovskaya Iakhna Elevna	1887	Dyatlovo	Baranovichi	Kalinin	
Sinderuk Volf Davidovich	1922	Pogost	Mogilev	208th partisan regiment	? 3
Sindor Mariya Faivelevna	1921	Mir	Baranovichi	Kalinin	
Sinelnikova Sofiya Pavlovna	1909	Rudnya, Smolensk region	Baranovichi	Leninskaya	Leninski
Sinuk Vita Lvovna	1932	Ivye	Baranovichi	Kalinin	
Sinuk Lev Moiseyevich	1900	Ivye	Baranovichi	Kalinin	
Sinuk Sima Moiseyevna	1905	Ivye	Baranovichi	Kalinin	
Siper Semen Abramovich	1922	Belarusian Staff of Partisan Movement	Vileyka	Dovator	Furmanov
Sirotkin Mikhail	1922	Minsk	Baranovichi	detachment ? 106	
Sisauri Mariya Girshevna	1920	Vyazan, Vileika region	Minsk	Voroshilov	? 6
Siterman Grisha Abramovich	1910	Minsk	Baranovichi	detachment ? 106	
Siterman Ida Yevseyevna	1917	Minsk	Minsk	Shturmovaya	Grozny
Sitorman Sarra Abramovna	1916	Minsk	Baranovichi	Ivienets DC CP(b)B company	
Situn Valentin Averkovich	1925	v. Stankovo	Minsk	Rokossovski	Chkalov
Skarbun Lazar Shevelevich	1922	Kosovo	Brest	Ponomarenko	Sovetskaya Belarus
Skvortsova Ida Markovna	1902	Chashniki	Vitebsk	Dubov's	? 2
Skiba David Izrailevich	1913	Mir	Baranovichi	Kalinin	
Sklyut Grigori Abramovich	1916	Volozhin	Baranovichi	Za Sovetskuyu Belarus	destroying battallion
Sklyut Mikhail Abramovich	1923	Volozhin	Baranovichi	Chkalov	
Skorokhod Yakub Izrailevich	1922	Baranovichi	Pinsk	Budenny	Ponomarenko
Skrabun Yankel Elevich	1925	Dyatlovo	Baranovichi	Pobieda	Pobieda
Skuza Viktor Faivelevich	1928	Derechin	Baranovichi	Leninskaya	Leninski
Slabodkin Grigori Isaakovich	1915	Braslav district	Vileyka	Zhdanov	
Sladovnik Leya Moiseyevna	1925	Radun	Baranovichi	Lenin's komsomol	Lenin's komsomol
Slepyan Grigori Grigorevich	1925	Minsk	Baranovichi	detachment ? 106	
Slepyan Sofiya Abramovna	1928	Minsk getto	Minsk	Za Sovetskuyu Belorussiyu	Uragan
Slivkin Pinkhus Isaakovich	1925	Mokhra, Ivanovo district	Pinsk	Shubetidze	brigade headquarters
Slivkina Roza Yosifovna	1922	Gressk	Minsk	Chapayev	Ponomarenko
Slobodkin Leiba Grigorevich	1906	Rubezhevichi	Baranovichi	Chapayev	Parkhomenko
Slobodski Shelsel Yakovlevich	1922	Lida	Baranovichi	Kalinin	
Slodovik Zyama Moiseyevich	1923	Radun	Baranovichi	Lenin's komsomol	Lenin's komsomol
Slonim Fanya Aronovna	1904	Novogrudok, getto	Baranovichi	Stalin	Ryzhaka
Slonimskaya Guta Shmuilovna	1927	Byten	Pinsk	Lenin	Kutuzov
Slonimskaya Nakhama Movshevna	1900	Baranovichi region	Baranovichi	Vpered (Forward)	Chkalov
Slonimski Izrail Faibovich	1898	Baranovichi region	Baranovichi	Vpered (Forward)	Chkalov
Slonimski Leon Abramovich	1898	Mogilev	Mogilev	Chekist	? 5
Slonimski Srol Shmulevich	1923	Byten	Pinsk	Lenin	Frunze
Slonimchik Miriam Yefimovna	1924	Lida	Baranovichi	Kalinin	
Sloush Naum Samoilovich	1923	Minsk	Baranovichi	Ponomarenko	Budenny
Sludski Ilya Borisovich	1916	camp, prisoner of war, Belostok	Vileyka	Gastello	brigade headquarters
Slukhovski Abram Motelevich	1907	Minsk	Baranovichi	Ponomarenko	25 years of the BSSR
Slukhovski Aron Natanovich	1904	Minsk	Baranovichi	Stalin	Budenny
Slutskaya Genya Izrailevna	1918	Minsk getto	Minsk	3rd Minskaya	Niepobedimy (Undefeated)
Slutskaya Dora Borisovna	1920	Maryina Gorka	Minsk		Stalin
Slutskaya Sonya Borukhovna	1924	Lenin	Pinsk	Kirov	
Slutskaya Yakha Davidovna	1918	Novogrudok	Baranovichi	Kalinin	
Slutski Borukh Leibovich	1902	Western Byelorussia, Lenino	Minsk	Chkalov	Dovator
Slutski Girsh Yankelevich	1927	Lenin	Palesye	? 225	Pakushi
Slutski Lev Berkovich	1922	Bereznyaki	Pinsk	Molotov	Kalinin
Slutski Naum Moiseyevich	1924	Minsk getto	Minsk	3rd Minskaya	Niepobedimy (Undefeated)
Slutski Samuil Abramovich	1924	Sverzhen	Minsk	Chapayev	Ponomarenko
Slutski Srol Nokhimovich	1882	Bereznyaki	Pinsk	Molotov	Kalinin
Slutski Khaim Gershenovich	1920	from captivity	Baranovichi	Grizodubova	
Slutski Yudel Davidovich	1924	Novogrudok	Baranovichi	Kalinin	
Sluchak David Volfovich	1907	Stolbtsy	Baranovichi	detachment ? 106	

JEWISH PARTISANS IN BYELORUSSIA 1941-1944   287

Name	Year	Place	Region	Unit	Sub-unit
Sluchak Shevel Isaakovich	1922	Lyuban district, Zagale	Minsk	Chkalov	Gromov
Smirnova Liza Aronovna	1921	small town of Kurenets, Vileika region	Baranovichi	Vpered (Forward)	A.Nevski
Smirnovski Fedor Girshevich	1916	Belarusian Staff of Partisan Movement	Brest	Flegontov	Litvinov's
Smoler Grigori Davidovich	1905	Belostok	Baranovichi	18th Frunze	Kutuzov
Smolinski Lev Gavrilovich	1902	Slonim	Brest	Ponomarenko	brigade headquarters
Smolinski Meyer Samuilovich	1917	Slonim	Pinsk	Lenin	Kutuzov
Smolkin Abram Solomonovich	1922	Belarusian Staff of Partisan Movement	Gomel	Kozhar's	gr. Krishneva
Smolyanskaya Frida Solomonovna	1927	Minsk	Baranovichi	detachment ? 106	
Smolyanski Mikhail Abramovich	1922	Novogrudok	Baranovichi	Chkalov	reserve group
Smolyanski Solomon Solomonovich	1883	Minsk	Baranovichi	detachment ? 106	
Smolyar Grigori Davidovich	1905	Minsk	Baranovichi	Stolbtsy zone	
Smuza Viktor Faivelevich	1930	local	Baranovichi	Pobieda	Pobieda
Smushkevich Genya Abramovna	1922	Yody	Vileyka	Spartak	? 5
Smushkevich David Abramovich	1925	Yody	Vileyka	Spartak	? 5
Smushkevich Peisakh Abramovich	1921	Sharkovshchina	Vileyka		Ponomarenko
Snadover Grigori Simonovich	1916	Lyubashov, Volyn region	Pinsk	Sovetskaya Belarus	Kutuzov
Sniadovich Faya Volfovna	1924	Baranovichi	Baranovichi	Kalinin	
Sniadovski Solomon Abramovich	1912	Molchad	Baranovichi	Kalinin	
Sobelman Natan Mikhailovich	1921	N. Sverzhen	Baranovichi	Zhdanov	
Soberman Berko Leibovich	1929	Malorita	Brest	Lenin	Voroshilov
Sobol Ilya Kunovich	1925	Poland	Brest	Lenin	Zhukov
Sobol Mariya	1927	Korona, Brest region	Brest	Lenin	Zhukov
Sobol Pelageya Zilmanovna	1923	Rovenski district	Pinsk	Sovetskaya Belarus	Chkalov
Soguitski Khaim Gershenovich	1920	getto	Brest	? 99 Gulyaev	Grabko
Sokobenzon Yankel Movshevich	1912	Jewish camp	Vileyka	Voroshilov	headquarters' production group
Sokol Pinya Kuselevna	1923	K. Kashirski	Pinsk	Shubetidze	Ordzhonikidze
Sokolik Srol Yosifovich	1912	Slonim	Pinsk	Lenin	Frunze
Sokolov Mikhail Abramovich	1931	Kurenets	Vileyka		Za Sovetskuyu Belorussiyu
Sokolova Nelya Zakharovna	1924	Bobruisk	Pinsk	Molotov	Kalinin
Sokolovskaya Zlata Khaikelevna	1922	Lida	Baranovichi	Kalinin	
Sokolovski Adam Abramovich	1916	Belostok	Grodno	Samutin's group	Kirshner's group
Sokolovski Eina Moiseyevich	1920	Lida	Baranovichi	Kalinin	
Sokolovski Sholom Abovich	1904	concentration camp	Pinsk	Kuibyshev	Shchors
Sokolskaya Rita Romanovna	1923	getto	Baranovichi	Kirov	brigade headquarters
Sokolski Abram Davidovich	1903	Loev, RKKP(b)B	Gomel	Za Rodinu (For Motherland)	Za Rodinu (For Motherland)
Sokolski Yakov Natanovich	1899	Radoshkovichi	Minsk	Voronyanski	Kotovski
Solin Vulf Khaimovich	1922	from the Litovskaya brigade	Baranovichi	detachment ? 106	
Solovei Leiba Gilevich	1898	from captivity	Mogilev	Chekist	? 31
Soloveichik Leizer Abramovich	1912		Vileyka	Gastello	Bochkova
Soloveichik Manya Vladimirovna	1928	Minsk	Baranovichi	detachment ? 106	
Soloveichik Tsilya Samuilovna	1918	Glubokoye	Minsk	Voronyanski	supervision squard of the brigade headquarters
Solovskaya Sara SrulYevna	1923	concentration camp	Pinsk	Kuibyshev	Shchors
Soloveva Genya Moiseyevna	1918	Orsha	Mogilev	? 35	
Soloveva Sofiya Moiseyevna	1920	Orsha	Mogilev	? 35	
Solodovnik Yelizaveta Moiseyevna	1925	getto	Baranovichi	Lenin's komsomol	Kotovski
Solomon Eduard Borisovich	1923	from the encirclement	Vitebsk	Prudnikov's	Grinenko's
Solomonnik Grigori Lvovich	1912	Minsk	Baranovichi	Kutuzov	
Solomonov Genrikh Geshevich	1913	Gorelets	Minsk	2nd Minskaya	Suvorov
Solomian Faina Moiseyevna	1915	Pinsk	Pinsk	Shubetidze	Kostyushko
Solomianski Volf Mendelevich	1917	Lyubcha	Baranovichi	Leninskaya	Borba
Solomianski Falvyel Elevich	1908		Minsk	Voronyanski	Mstitel (Revenger)
Solutski Natan Khonovich	1922	Zelva	Baranovichi	Leninskaya	Pobieda
Solfrin Mikhail Moiseyevich	1926	Kopys	Mogilev	? 425	
Solts Betya Yankelevna	1918	Lida	Baranovichi	Kalinin	
Solts Leiba Volfovich	1916	Lipnishki	Baranovichi	Kalinin	
Sonkin Meyer Mordukhovich	1906	Minsk	Baranovichi	detachment ? 106	
Sonkin Motya Meyerovich	1931	Minsk	Baranovichi	detachment ? 106	
Sorkina Olga Borisovna	1925	Drogino	Gomel	Bolshevik	Bolshevik
Soroka Mikhail Pavlovich	1905	v. Sorokovshchina	Minsk	Rokossovski	Chkalov
Sorokin Boris Yefimovich	1919	Minsk	Baranovichi	detachment ? 106	
Sorokin Moisei Ionovich	1910	Otruba	Gomel	Voroshilov	Voroshilov
Sorokin Moisei Khaimovich	1923	Minsk	Baranovichi	detachment ? 106	
Sorotskin Semen Ilyich	1916	from captivity	Mogilev	Chekist	? 5
Sosekski Anatoli Shimonovich	1904	Jewish camp, Vileika	Minsk	Bolshevik	

Name	Year	Origin	Region	Unit	Brigade/Detachment
Sosinskaya Basya Folevna	1924	Jewish camp, Dolginovo	Minsk	Voronyanski	Pobieda
Sosinski Yosif Rafailovich	1922	Dolginovo	Minsk	Voronyanski	Mstitel (Revenger)
Soskovski Khonya Yosifovich	1914	Derechin	Baranovichi	Pobieda	Pobieda
Sosland Revekka Davidovna	1922	Minsk	Minsk	Belarus	Belarus
Sosman Ida Simonovna	1922	Moskva	Vitebsk	Korotkin	Voroshilov
Sosman Sofiya Davidovna	1919	Glubokoye	Vileyka	CC of the CP(b)B	Parkhomenko
Sosnovik Genya Yakovlevna	1923	Yody	Vileyka	Spartak	? 6
Sosnovik Yosif Semenovich	1918	Glubokoye	Vileyka	4th Belorusskaya	? 4
Sosnovik Peisakh Zalmanovich	1914	Glubokoye	Vileyka	Za Rodinu (For Motherland)	Zhdanov
Sosnovich Yevgeniya Yakovlevna	1923	Sharkovshchina district	Vitebsk	Rokossovski	Zhukov
Sosnovski Khendrik Yosifovich	1914	Dyatlovo	Baranovichi	Pobieda	Pobieda
Sokhrai Motya Girshevich	1913	Mogilev	Mogilev		? 278
Sokhrin Mikhail Moiseyevich	1926	Belarusian Staff of Partisan Movement	Brest	groups of party leaders	Sokolovski's group
Soshin Roman Borisovich	1917	Kopyl	Minsk	Underground RC and DC CP(b)B	Minsk underground CC of the CP(b)B
Spevak Isaak Zalmanovich	1928	Minsk	Baranovichi	detachment ? 106	
Spivak Boris Ionovich	1903	Parkhomovichi	Mogilev	152-oi partisan regiment	? 152
Spivak Mira Aronovna	1924	Belarusian Staff of Partisan Movement	Vileyka		Manakhova
Spira Nikolai Ignaitovich	1916	from the Hungarian army	Brest	Stalin	Chernyak
Sragovich Movsha Shevelevich	1898	Stolbtsy	Baranovichi	Kalinin	
Srebnyi Yesel Leizerovich	1928	Mir	Baranovichi	Kalinin	
Stavitski Maksim Rafailovich	1923	Warsaw	Belostok	A.Nevski	
Staklitski Abram Zakharovich	1927	N. Sverzhen	Baranovichi	18th Frunze	Lenin
Stalper Mulya Girshevich	1925	Novy Pogost	Vileyka	Kalinin	? 3
Stambler Zalman Elevich	1910	brigade "Zvezda"	Vitebsk	2nd Zaslonov	Oktyabr
Stanislavski Mikhail Yakovlevich	1915	Senno	Vitebsk	Sennenskaya brigade (Leonov's)	A.Nevski
Stanitski Yosif Khaimovich	1923	getto	Baranovichi	Lenin's komsomol	Kotovski
Stankevich Roman Vladimirovich	1930	Bobruisk	Palesye	? 225	Suvorov
Starobin Leizer Peisakhovich	1922	Radoshkovichi district, Serodudovshchina	Minsk	Zheleznyak	? 3
Starobin Ruvim Elevich	1926	Mordosy	Minsk	Voronyanski	Borba
Starobin Semen Samuilovich	1922	Radoshkovichi	Minsk	Shturmovaya	Shturm
Starobin Tanik Samuilovich	1924	Radoshkovichi	Minsk	Shturmovaya	Shturm
Starobin Elya Peisakhovich	1924	Radoshkovichi	Minsk	Shturmovaya	Shturm
Starobinets Ilya Samuilovich	1922	Belarusian Staff of Partisan Movement	Mogilev	Chekist	brigade headquarters
Starobinets Moisei Davidovich	1910	Minsk, prisoners of war camp	Baranovichi	Za Sovetskuyu Belarus	Shturm
Starodvorskaya Bela Khonovna	1926	Lida	Baranovichi	Kirov	Ordzhonikidze
Starodvorskaya Roza Beinesovna	1895	Lida	Baranovichi	Kalinin	
Starodvorskaya Sheina Khononovna	1935	Lida	Baranovichi	Kalinin	
Starodvorski Zendel Leibovich	1910	Lida	Baranovichi	Kalinin	
Starodvorski Khonon Kopelevich	1895	Lida	Baranovichi	Kalinin	
Starodvorski Yankel Khonovich	1921		Baranovichi	Oktyabr	
Stepak Yosif Itskovich	1916	K. Kashirski	Pinsk	Shubetidze	Kostyushko
Sterenzad Genrikh Moseevich	1930	Minsk	Baranovichi	detachment ? 106	
Sterin Moisei Borisovich	1897	Glussk	Minsk	Parkhomenko	Shchors
Stoler Semen Yakovlevich		Gomel	? 225 A.Suvorov	Chkalov	
Stoler Shlema Zelikovich	1925	Korelichi	Baranovichi	Kalinin	
Stolovitskaya Sara Volfovna	1898	Lida	Baranovichi	Kalinin	
Stolovitskaya Khana Lvovna	1930	Lida	Baranovichi	Kalinin	
Stolovitski Lev Yakovlevich	1897	Lida	Baranovichi	Kalinin	
Stolovitski Mikhail Levovich	1926	Lida	Baranovichi	Kalinin	
Stolovitski Khaim Gedaimovich	1916	Baranovichi	Brest	Dzerzhinski	brigade headquarters
Stolyar Boris Natanovich	1921	Vishnevo, getto	Baranovichi	Za Sovetskuyu Belarus	Za Sovetskuyu Belarus
Stolyar Vilik Shlemovich	1931	Minsk	Baranovichi	detachment ? 106	
Stolyar Geles Meyerovich	1913	Yody	Vileyka		Ponomarenko
Stolyar Zalman Shlomovich	1925	Gorodok	Baranovichi	Za Sovetskuyu Belarus	family detachment
Stolyar Itsko Movshevich	1906	Berezniki	Pinsk	Budenny	Ponomarenko
Stolyar Meyer Khaimovich	1912	getto	Baranovichi	Lenin's komsomol	Kotovski
Stolyar Khaim Mordukhovich	1916	Minsk getto	Baranovichi	Shchors	Chapayev
Stolyar Edya Zelikovna	1920	Yody	Vileyka		Ponomarenko
Stolyar Yudel Yosifovich	1903	Korelichi getto	Baranovichi	Kirov	Ordzhonikidze
Stolyarov Isaak Safronovich	1900	Rubashino	Vitebsk	1st Zaslonov	Kutuzov

Name	Year	Place	Region	Detachment	Brigade
Stotskaya Vasilisa Moiseyevna	1918	v. Selets, Starye Dorogi district	Minsk	Frunze	Kirov
Stotskaya Eva Moiseyevna	1924	Ivye	Baranovichi	Kalinin	
Stotski Mendel Bentsionovich	1914	family detachment camp	Belostok	A.Nevski	
Stravchinski Natan Yakovlevich	1913	getto, Pruzhany	Brest	Za Sovetskuyu Belarus	Pozharski
Strasenbegr Aron Izrailevich	1925	Mir	Baranovichi	Kalinin	
Strasenbegr Khaya Aronovna	1932	Mir	Baranovichi	Kalinin	
Strasenbegr Sheina Shmuilovna	1905	Mir	Baranovichi	Kalinin	
Strelets Itska Abramovich	1883	Lyuban	Minsk	Ponomarenko	Gorbachev
Strizhen Boris Yakovlevich	1915	Chashniki	Vitebsk	Kirillov	Kirillov's
Strikhovski Khaim Lipmanovich	1918	from the detachment Kotovski, Grodno	Brest	Flegontov	brigade headquarters
Strogovich Khaim Ruvimovich	1922	Glubokoye	Minsk	1st Antifashistskaya	brigade hospital
Strongina Mira Shayevna	1923	Minsk getto	Baranovichi	Chapayev	brigade headquarters
Strugach Leiba Mordukhovich	1887	Minsk, Uzlyany	Minsk	2nd Minskaya	Kutuzov
Strugach Meyer Mordukhovich	1885	Minsk getto	Minsk	2nd Minskaya	Kutuzov
Strut Falvyel Shmulevich	1905	Domachevo	Brest	Lenin	Voroshilov
Stul Boris Yankelevich	1911	Biniakoni	Baranovichi	Lenin's komsomol	Lenin's komsomol
Stul Semen Gershkovich	1921	Poland	Pinsk	Molotov	Shish
Subbotnik Yosif Leonidovich	1896	small town of Vishnevo	Baranovichi	Chapayev	Parkhomenko
Sudakov Andrei Antonovich	1918	from captivity	Vileyka	Zhdanov	
Suller Efroim Aronovich	1923	Mir	Baranovichi	Kalinin	
Sulkin Matus Mendelevich	1907	Sharkovshchina	Vileyka	1st Suvorov	Chkalov
Sulman Blyuma Grigorevna	1908	Zabote, Shklov district	Mogilev	Chekist	? 5
Sulskaya Yelizaveta Vulfovna	1926	Minsk getto	Minsk	Rokossovski	Chkalov
Sutin Isaak Yudelevich	1923	Stolbtsy	Baranovichi	detachment ? 106	
Sutin Yudel Isaakovich	1886	Mir	Baranovichi	detachment ? 106	
Sutina Eva Polisovna	1925	Minsk	Baranovichi	Chkalov	? 4 "Za Sovetskuyu Belarus"
Sutina Rakhil Lazarevna	1924	Stolbtsy	Baranovichi	detachment ? 106	
Sutina Roza Leizerovna	1908	Minsk	Baranovichi	detachment ? 106	
Sutkevich Zelik Borisovich	1920	Disna	Vileyka	4th Belorusskaya	? 1
Sukhavitskaya Klara Isaakovna	1929	Minsk	Baranovichi	detachment ? 106	
Sukhareva Serafima Goncharov's detachment	1893		Minsk	Grishin's 13th regiment	
Sukharski Nota Izrailevich	1897	Novogrudok	Baranovichi	Kalinin	
Sukhman Moisei Zalmanovich	1904	Pukhovichi district	Minsk	Stalin	
Sutskever Abram Gertsovich	1913	getto	Vileyka	Voroshilov	brigade headquarters
Sutskever Polya Samuilovna	1920	Minsk	Baranovichi	detachment ? 106	
Sutskever Fanya Solomonovna	1921	Minsk	Baranovichi	Za Sovetskuyu Belarus	family detachment
Sutskever Frida Yakovlevna	1917	getto	Vileyka	Voroshilov	brigade headquarters
Sushkevich Zinaida Borisovna	1920	from the civil camp	Vileyka	4th Belorusskaya	? 2
Sushkevich Peisakh Abramovich	1921	Yody			
Schenskovich Aleksandra NikolaYevna	1898	Minsk	Baranovichi	Kalinin	
Schenskovich Nikolai Ignatovich	1894	Minsk	Baranovichi	Kalinin	
Schenskovich Tamara Petrovna	1932	Minsk	Baranovichi	Kalinin	
Sytko Pavel Zalmanovich	1893	Bereznyaki	Pinsk	Molotov	Kalinin
Tabak Taiba Peisakhovna	1928	Bryansk getto, Belostok region	Grodno	Vo imya Rodiny (In the name of Motherland)	Zhukov
Tabakman Nisun Yosifovich	1905	Baranovichi, getto	Baranovichi	Grizodubova	Matrosov
Tabarisski Moisei Rafailovich		Minsk	Voronyanski	Borba	
Tabakhovich Grigori Nosevich	1911	getto, Sharkovshchina	Vileyka	Voroshilov	Chapayev
Tabius Leiba Leibovich	1922	from captivity	Palesye	detachment at the headquarters	
Taborinski Boris Izrailevich	1917	st. Sabibor (concentration camp), Poland	Brest	Stalin	Frunze
Tavbin Semen Markovich	1891	Kurino	Vitebsk	Groza	
Tavger Bodana Gershenovna	1913	small town of Krivichi Vileika region	Minsk	Starik (Old man)	
Tavger Klara Grigorevna	1916	Vileika region, Krivichi.	Minsk	Kirov	Za Pobiedu (For the Victory)
Tavritskaya Grunya Abramovna	1915	Novogrudok	Baranovichi	Kalinin	
Tavritski Yosif Danilovich	1910	Novogrudok getto	Baranovichi	Kirov	brigade headquarters
Tavritski Isaak Davidovich	1904	Novogrudok	Baranovichi	Kalinin	
Tavshtein Lev Davidovich	1920	from captivity	Gomel	Voroshilov	headquarters
Tavshunski Shlema Abramovich	1925	Ivye	Vitebsk	Nikitin's	? 4
Tainovskaya Berta Afroimovna	1915	Minsk	Baranovichi	detachment ? 106	
Tainovski ??? Avseyevich	1932	Minsk	Baranovichi	detachment ? 106	
Tainovski Mikhail Aronovich	1916	Minsk	Baranovichi	Vpered (Forward)	Bolshevik
Taikhman Orsmall	1910	Magyar army	Brest	Lenin	Zhukov
Taits Anna Markovna	1905	Minsk	Baranovichi	Vpered (Forward)	Chkalov
Taits Yevsei Kalmanovich	1908	Druya	Vileyka	4th Belorusskaya	? 1

Taits Izrail Samuilovich	1926	Svintyany	Vitebsk	Lenin	? 1
Taits Isaak Samuilovich	1923	getto	Vileyka	Voroshilov	Chapayev
Taits Mark Yuryevich	1927	Minsk	Baranovichi	Vpered (Forward)	Chkalov
Taits Mosia Borisovich	1931	Minsk	Baranovichi	detachment ? 106	
Taits Yuri Ilyich	1902	Minsk	Baranovichi	Vpered (Forward)	Chkalov
Tamarina Dora Aronovna	1912	Minsk	Baranovichi	detachment ? 106	
Tamarkin Mikhail Yosifovich	1912	from the detachment Budenny	Baranovichi	detachment ? 106	
Tamarkin Stanislav Lvovich	1930		Minsk	Grishin's 13th regiment	
Tanenbaum Boris Shayevich	1908	from the forest	Pinsk	Molotov	Kalinin
Tanenbaum Volf Genrikhovich	1912	Lida	Baranovichi	1st Baranovichskaya	sabotage detachment "Orel"
Tanenbaum Yosif Zelikovich	1915	concentration camp, Vlodava	Pinsk	Molotov	Kalinin
Tanenbaum Liza Yosifovna	1912	Lida	Baranovichi	1st Baranovichskaya	sabotage detachment "Orel"
Taptunov Rafail Leibovich	1893	Ermilovski	Mogilev	? 115	? 2
Taras Raya Girshevna	1927	Minsk	Baranovichi	detachment ? 106	
Taras Sarra Girshevna	1922	Minsk	Baranovichi	detachment ? 106	
Taras Fanya Girshevna	1924	Minsk	Baranovichi	detachment ? 106	
Tarashinski Moisei Sh.	1923	Lida	Baranovichi	Pobieda	Pobieda
Tartakovski Dmitri Yosifovich	1923	Logoisk	Minsk	Voronyanski	Kotovski
Tartatski Morfen Leibovich	1925	Belostok	Grodno	Samutin's group	Kirshner's group
Taruch Rita Moiseyevna	1925	Zareche, Shklov district	Mogilev	Chekist	Kalyushnikov's
Tatarkina Mariya Pinkhusovna	1906	Stolbtsy	Baranovichi	Kalinin	
Tatarskaya Mina	1920	Minsk	Baranovichi	detachment ? 106	
Tatarkhina Elena Abramovna	1925	Lodz	Baranovichi	Kalinin	
Taub Nina Salomonovna	1906	Lida	Baranovichi	Kalinin	
Taub Salomon Ovseyevich	1893	Lida	Baranovichi	Kalinin	
Tauger Khaim Grigorevich	1910	Krivichi, Vileika region	Minsk	Belarus	Belarus
Tvoretski Isaak Mdeevich	1917	Kena	Vitebsk	Lepelskaya Stalin	? 8
Teif Abrasha Sholomovich	1927	Smilovichi	Baranovichi	detachment ? 106	
Teif Basya Yosifovna	1907	Samokhvalovichi	Baranovichi	detachment ? 106	
Teif Mikhail Romanovich	1927	Samokhvalovichi	Baranovichi	detachment ? 106	
Teif Motka Isaakovich	1902	Minsk getto	Minsk	3rd Minskaya	brigade headquarters
Teisheva Tamara Maksimovna	1929	v. Korobchi	Minsk	3rd Minskaya	brigade headquarters
Temchin Boris Pavlovich	1924	Minsk	Minsk	2nd Minskaya	Ponomarenko
Tender Yosif Sigmuntovich	1915	from the Hungarian army	Brest	Stalin	Chernyak
Tenenbaum Yosif Leibovich	1923	Domachevo	Pinsk	Molotov	Lazo
Tenenbaum Leiba Abramovich	1899	Radoshkovichi	Minsk	Voronyanski	Kotovski
Tenenbaum Mikhail Viktorovich	1908	getto	Baranovichi	Kirov	brigade headquarters
Tenenbaum Falvyel Abramovich	1911	Ivatsevichi	Brest	Ponomarenko	Sovetskaya Belarus
Tenenbaum Frida Shmuilovna	1914	Slutsk	Baranovichi	Zhdanov	
Teper Sofiya Leibovna	1925	getto	Vileyka	1st Suvorov	Voroshilov
Teplitski Abram Borisovich	1900	Krasnoye	Baranovichi	Za Sovetskuyu Belarus	destroying battallion
Teplitski Shlema Abramovich	1926	Krasnoye, getto	Baranovichi	Za Sovetskuyu Belarus	Za Sovetskuyu Belarus
Teplovich Maksim Solomonovich	1921	Postavy	Minsk	Voroshilov	? 1
Teplovich Neima Solomonovna	1926	Postavy	Vileyka	Dovator	Sverdlov
Teplovich Fanya Mendeleyevna	1898	Postavy	Vileyka	Dovator	Sverdlov
Terebilo Boris Zakharovich	1926	Serniki, Rovno region.	Pinsk	Shubetidze	Chapayev
Terushkin Monus Elevich	1904	Starye Dorogi	Minsk	Ponomarenko	Gorbachev
Tiktin Lilya Isayevna	1923	Lida	Baranovichi	Kalinin	
Tiles Zelik Gilevich	1918	Dokshitsy	Vileyka	Kutuzov	
Tiles Yakha Izrailevna	1924	Novogrudok	Baranovichi	Kalinin	
Tiliman Maks Gershkovich	1914	Poland	Brest	Stalin	Chernyak
Tilshchik Khonon Sholomovich	1922	Molchad	Baranovichi	Kalinin	
Timerman Grigori I.	1923	Goncharov's detachment	Vileyka	1st Suvorov	Bolshevik
Timkind Moisei Mirovich	1922		Vileyka	CC of the CP(b)B	Furmanov
Tipershtein Peisakh Isaakovich	1925	Baranovichi, from home	Baranovichi	Grizodubova	Matrosov
Tipershtein Sonya Isaakovna	1921	Baranovichi, from home	Baranovichi	Grizodubova	Matrosov
Tishkova Galina Isaakovna	1926	Gorodok	Baranovichi	Chkalov	
Tkach Yevsei Borukhovich	1896	Khvorostovo, Lenino district	Pinsk	Komarov-Korzh's	2 group
Tkach Mikhail Aizikovich	1920	from the encirclement	Vitebsk	Lepelskaya Stalin	? 4
Tkach Mordukh Ovseyevich	1924	Khvorostovo, Lenino district	Pinsk	Komarov-Korzh's	2 group
Tkach Shlema Ovseyevich	1926	Khvorostovo, Lenino district	Pinsk	Komarov-Korzh's	2 group
Tobchik Lipa Shlemovich	1910	Lenin	Pinsk	Komarov-Korzh's	4 group
Tokarski Zalya Shmerkovich	1909	Minsk	Minsk	2nd Minskaya	Kutuzov
Toker Gdalya Naftalevich	1925	Zheludok	Baranovichi	Leninskaya	Borba

JEWISH PARTISANS IN BYELORUSSIA 1941-1944

Topelson Mira Yakovlevna	1916	Minsk	Baranovichi	detachment ? 106	
Topor Mendel Kalmanovich	1909	Stolbtsy	Baranovichi	detachment ? 106	
Topormandon Don Gershovich	1914	from the ROA	Vitebsk	Prudnikov's	
Topchik Boris Shlemovich	1920	concentration camp Gantsevichi	Minsk	Chkalov	Zheleznyak
Topchik Yankel Shlemovich	1906	Lenin	Palesye	50st	
Torikis Nina Borisovna	1926	Porechye, Pukhovichi district	Minsk	2nd Minskaya	Molotov
Torfshtein Aron Pinkhusovich	1920	Warsaw	Baranovichi	Kalinin	
Traevitski Berko Shayevich	1921	Baranovichi	Baranovichi	Kalinin	
Trainer Isaak Yakovlevich	1928	Shklov	Gomel	1st Gomelskaya	? 1 Chapayev
Trakinski Volf Moiseyevich	1922	Smorgon	Vileyka		Suslov
Trakinski Semen Moiseyevich	1925	Smorgon	Vileyka		Suslov
Trakhtenberg Boris Isaakovich	1924	from the Jewish camp, Minsk	Minsk	2nd Minskaya	Suvorov
Trakhtenberg Lev Davidovich	1938	Mogilev	Baranovichi	detachment ? 106	
Trakhtenberg Liza Borisovna	1917	Mogilev	Baranovichi	detachment ? 106	
Trakhtenberg Yulyan Mironovich	1927	getto, Vilno	Vileyka	Voroshilov	Kalinin
Tratsevitski Izrail Abramovich	1911	Gorodishche	Baranovichi	Kalinin	
Trebukhovskaya Larisa Samuilovna	1924	Zaostrovichi	Pinsk	Lenin	Kutuzov
Trebukhovskaya Lidiya Samuilovna	1922	Zaostrovichi	Pinsk	Lenin	Dzerzhinski
Trebukhovski Boris Gilmovich	1920	Kletsk district, Zaostrovelo	Minsk	32nd Kalinin	Parkhomenko
Trebukhovski Grigori Shlemovich	1916	Zaostrovichi	Pinsk	Lenin	Dzerzhinski
Treiger Naum Yefimovich	1924	Belarusian Staff of Partisan Movement	Minsk	Special groups	Zagorodnev's group
Treister Anna Abramovna	1925	Minsk	Baranovichi	detachment ? 106	
Treister Mikhail Abramovich	1927	Minsk	Baranovichi	detachment ? 106	
Treister Rakhil Khononovna	1894	Druya	Baranovichi	detachment ? 106	
Trestman Yakov Grigorevich	1898		Baranovichi		
Tribut Stefanida Davidovna	1929	Bryansk getto, Belostok region	Grodno	Vo imya Rodiny (In the name of Motherland)	Zhukov
Tribut Khaim Aratovich	1925	Bryansk getto, Belostok region	Grodno	Vo imya Rodiny (In the name of Motherland)	Zhukov
Tribukh Ilya Mendelevich	1907	from captivity	Baranovichi	Grizodubova	
Tribukh Sara IlyashYevna	1915	from captivity	Baranovichi	Grizodubova	
Trifsik Isaak Grigorevich	1910	Polotsk	Vitebsk	Voroshilov	Death to Fascism
Trovba Feliks Khaimovich	1914	from the camp	Baranovichi	Grizodubova	
Troyetski Berka Moiseyevich	1897	Novogrudok getto	Baranovichi	Kirov	Ordzhonikidze
Troyetski Gerts Solomonovich	1928	Novogrudok getto	Baranovichi	Kirov	Ordzhonikidze
Troyetski Solomon Moiseyevich	1902	Novogrudok getto	Baranovichi	Kirov	Ordzhonikidze
Trokhman Mikhail Anatolevich	1918	Belarusian Staff of Partisan Movement	Grodno	groups sent to part. det. and brigades in 1942-1943	
Trotskaya Nina Isaakovna	1922	Dunilovichi	Minsk	Voronyanski	Mstitel (Revenger)
Trubovich Bela Yosifovna	1924	Baranovichi	Grodno	Chapayev	
Truch Rita Moiseyevna	1925	Zarechye	Mogilev	Chekist	
Tubashevich Yudel Isaakovich	1894	Jewish camp	Vileyka	Voroshilov	headquarters' production group
Tukalovskaya Genya Moiseyevna	1902	Lida	Baranovichi	Kalinin	
Tukalovski Mones Yekhilevich	1902	Lida	Baranovichi	Kalinin	
Tulchinski Moisei Sulimovich	1909	from captivity	Baranovichi	Leninskaya	family detachment group
Tumin Gariya Mikhailovna	1934	Minsk	Baranovichi	detachment ? 106	
Tumin Mikhail Yakovlevich	1907	Minsk	Baranovichi	detachment ? 106	
Tunet Boris Girshevich	1896	Minsk	Baranovichi	detachment ? 106	
Tunik Abram Pinkhusovich	1914	Minsk	Minsk	Voronyanski	Kotovski
Tunik Boris Girshevich	1895	Minsk	Baranovichi	detachment ? 106	
Tunik Boris Shayevich	1907	Minsk	Baranovichi	detachment ? 106	
Tunik Girsh Abramovich	1891	Baranovichi, getto	Baranovichi	18th Frunze	Frunze
Tunik Izya Lvovich	1933	Minsk	Baranovichi	detachment ? 106	
Tunik Lev Grigorevich	1900	Minsk	Baranovichi	detachment ? 106	
Tunik Manya Borisovna	1928	Minsk	Baranovichi	detachment ? 106	
Tunik Roza Borisovna	1925	Minsk	Baranovichi	detachment ? 106	
Tunik Fima Lvovich	1928	Minsk	Baranovichi	detachment ? 106	
Tunik Tsilya Yosifovna	1926	Minsk	Baranovichi	detachment ? 106	
Tunik Shifra Grigorevna	1899	Minsk	Baranovichi	detachment ? 106	
Tunik Esfir Borisovna	1919	Minsk	Baranovichi	detachment ? 106	
Tunkelshvarts Dmitri Yosifovich	1924	Ivanovo	Pinsk	Shubetidze	Stalin
Turetskaya Mila Bentsianovna	1928	Minsk	Baranovichi	detachment ? 106	
Turetskaya Tsilya Bentsianovna	1932	Minsk	Baranovichi	detachment ? 106	
Turetski Aron Yekhilevich	1901	Sverzhno	Baranovichi	Kalinin	
Turetski Vladimir Moiseyevich	1917	Minsk	Mogilev	208th regiment	
Turetski Isaak Nokhimovich	1923	Stolbtsy	Minsk	Chapayev	Shchors

Turetski Meyer Abramovich	1910	Minsk getto	Baranovichi	18th Frunze	Frunze
Turetski Yuri Markovich	1922	from captivity	Vitebsk	VLKSM	? 3
Turkenich Abram Yankelevich	1922	Serniki, Rovno region.	Pinsk	Molotov	Shish
Turkenich Genakh Einovich	1922	Serniki, Rovno region.	Pinsk	Shubetidze	Chapayev
Turkenich Leiba Mordukhovich	1910	Lakhva	Pinsk	Kirov	Kalinin
Turkenich Movsha Gershovich	1905	Jewish camp, Stolin district	Pinsk	Shubetidze	Ordzhonikidze
Turkenich Movsha Einovich	1920	Serniki, Rovno region.	Pinsk	Shubetidze	Chapayev
Turkenich Naum Gershovich	1908	Jewish camp, Pinsk district	Pinsk	Shubetidze	Ordzhonikidze
Turts Ida Simonovna	1902	Sl. Kuchenka, Kopyl district	Minsk	Chapayev	Ponomarenko
Turchel Semen Mikhailovich	1909	Mir	Baranovichi	Stalin	Kirov
Turshneider Grisha Shlemovich	1927	Minsk	Baranovichi	detachment ? 106	
Tufman Pinya Lazarevich	1921	Derechin	Baranovichi	Pobieda	Pobieda
Tukh Raisa Moiseyevna	1922	Slonim	Brest	Sikorski's headquarters	Shchors
Tukhman Mikhail Yudelevich	1917	Kartuz-Bereza	Brest	Ponomarenko	Dmitrov
Tyles Gdali Grigorevich	1929	Minsk	Baranovichi	detachment ? 106	
Tymas Yosif Yefimovich	1912	Kurenets	Vileyka	Budenny	Budenny
Tynkovitskaya Dora Leibovna	1914	Dyatlovo	Baranovichi	Leninskaya	Borba
Teklin Grigori Mikhailovich	1923	Slutsk	Pinsk	Komarov-Korzh's	2 group
Teper Sara Leibovna	1924	Dunilovichi, Vileika region	Minsk	Voroshilov	? 5
Uvekhina Khaya Yosifovna	1911	Minsk	Baranovichi	detachment ? 106	
UzLyan Gedali Abramovich	1906	Minsk	Mogilev	208th regiment	
Ulert Isaak Khaimovich	1918	Korelichi	Baranovichi	Kalinin	
Ulman Boris Zalmanovich	1924	Kozyanski forest	Vileyka	Voroshilov	A.Nevski
Ulyanski Yevsei Aizikovich	1910	Byten	Brest	Sikorski's headquarters	
Uman Raya Yankelevna	1911	Doboska	Mogilev	partisan regiment ? 277	? 277
Umbras Isaak Tsalevich	1914	Sventyany	Vileyka	Gastello	Zaslonov
Unikovski Genrikh Abramovich	1913	Stolbtsy	Baranovichi	Grizodubova	Chkalov
Urvich F.Kh.		Moskva	Minsk		Braeva
Urvich Iakob Gdalevich	1919	Zelva	Baranovichi	Pobieda	Pobieda
Urechskaya Larisa Naumovna	1900	Rechitsa	Gomel	Voroshilov	Budenny
Uritski Moisei Meyerovich	1908	from the encirclement	Minsk	Ponomarenko	brigade headquarters
Faberson Ruva Shepselevich	1929	Minsk	Baranovichi	detachment ? 106	
Fabritski Yankel Nakhmanovich	1910	getto Belostok	Grodno	Vo imya Rodiny (In the name of Motherland)	Zhukov
Faiber Nota Khaimovich	1922	Kopyl	Minsk	Chapayev	Ponomarenko
Faibyshev David Benyaminovich	1906	from captivity Minsk	Minsk	Burevestnik	Burevestnik
Faivelevich Benyamin Girshevich	1921	Korelichi	Baranovichi	Kalinin	
Faivelevich Movsha Leizerovich	1895	Novogrudok	Baranovichi	Kalinin	
Faivuzhinski Mordukh Shmeyerovich	1925	Dyatlovo	Baranovichi	Leninskaya	Borba
Faigelson Zalman Esenovich	1923	Glubokoye	Minsk	Voroshilov	? 5
Faigenbaum Aron Movshevich	1923	Sverzhen	Minsk	Chapayev	Ponomarenko
Faigenbaum Flanka Germanovna	1913	Belostok	Baranovichi	Pobieda	Pobieda
Fain Vasili Sergeyevich	1923	Minsk getto	Minsk	3rd Minskaya	Lazo
Fain Grisha Borisovich	1904	Logoisk	Baranovichi	detachment ? 106	
Fain Zilman Leibovich	1913	Belostok	Grodno	Samutin's group	Kirshner's group
Fain Isaak Davidovich	1908	Minsk, prison	Minsk	Za Sovetskuyu Belorussiyu	Kutuzov
Fain Faiva Meyerovich	1923	Minsk	Minsk	3rd Minskaya	Niepobedimy (Undefeated)
Fain Yakov Yudelevich	1902		Minsk	2nd Minskaya	Stalin
Fainberg Abram Movshevich	1922	Lakhva	Pinsk	Kirov	
Fainberg Anna Grigorevna	1918	v. Motorovo, Pukhovichi district	Minsk	Pravda (Truth)	contacts of the br. "Pravda (Truth)"
Fainberg Yosif Yakovlevich	1923	Orsha	Vitebsk	1st Belorusskaya	
Fainberg Mota Khaimovich	1926	Kopyl, getto	Baranovichi	18th Frunze	Kotovski
Fainberg Slava (Glory) Movshovich	1898	Kopyl	Minsk	Chapayev	Ponomarenko
Fainberg Khaim Abramovich	1892	Kopyl	Minsk	Chapayev	Ponomarenko
Fainberg Shender Leibovich	1915	from the Litovskaya brigade	Baranovichi	detachment ? 106	
Fainberg Yudel Khaimovich	1924	Kopyl	Minsk	Chapayev	Ponomarenko
Fainblyum David Zalmanovich	1909	Krivichi	Vileyka	Gastello	Zaslonov
Fainbron Emmanuil Isaakovich	1922	from the encirclement	Mogilev	? 61	? 1
Faingilerint David Mendelevich	1913	from the encirclement	Vitebsk	Prudnikov's	Grinenko's
Faingold Samuil Grigorevich	1907	Ugly	Vitebsk	Chapayev	Ushachi of the CP(b)B
Fainer Moisei Leibovich	1917	Pogost, Starobin district	Minsk	Dyadi Koli	Stalin
Fainer-Gershun Alfred Langenovich	1909		Palesye	Lelchitskaya	Gorodiatichi Yefremov's detachmnt
Fainshtein Leva Zyselevich	1909	Minsk	Baranovichi	detachment ? 106	
Fainshtein Naum Lvovich	1923	Minsk	Vitebsk	2nd Zaslonov	Komlev's

Fainshtein Roza Fruimovna	1910	Brest	Brest		Kotovski
Faiser Gesel Meyerovich	1898	Stolbtsy	Baranovichi		
Faitelevich Motel Movshevich	1908	Baranovichi	Baranovichi	Za Sovetskuyu Belarus	family detachment
Faitelson Yefim Pavlovich	1906	from captivity	Mogilev		? 721
Faikh Genrikh Natanovich	1911	Derechin	Baranovichi	Leninskaya	Borba
Faikhel Aron Berkovich	1925	Kozyany	Vileyka	Spartak	? 1
Falda Khaim Movshovich	1910	Molchad	Baranovichi	Kalinin	
Falevich Vladimir Zelikovich	1907	Gansovichi, Pinsk region	Palesye		Volkov's
Falevich Yulya Gerasovna	1906	Slutsk	Minsk	Chapayev	Ponomarenko
Falikson Yefim Mironovich (Bednitski Bronislav Adamovich)	1909	from the encirclement	Vitebsk	1st Zaslonov	Kutuzov
Falk Abram Isaakovich	1910	Stolin	Baranovichi	Kalinin	
Falkovich Mikhail	1928	Stolbtsy district	Baranovichi	Zhukov	
Faltsaid Sara Ilyamovna (Leonova Mariya Grigorevna)	1905	Mogilev	Mogilev	? 113	brigade ? 120
Falshtein Naum Lvovich	1923	Minsk	Vitebsk	Nikitin's	
Farber Mariya Semenovna	1922	Orsha	Mogilev	Chekist	? 20
Farber Mikhail Davidovich	1925	Kopyl	Minsk	Chapayev	Ponomarenko
Farber Moisei Markovich	1898	Botki	Belostok	Vo imya Rodiny (In the name of Motherland)	
Farber Raisa Semenovna	1924	Orsha	Mogilev	Chekist	Kalyushnikov's
Farberov David Lvovich		from the encirclement	Mogilev	Chekist	brigade headquarters
Faronovski Tsylya Yosifovich	1924	Baranovichi	Baranovichi	Kalinin	
Farfel Gershan Samuilovich	1895	Mir	Baranovichi	Kalinin	
Farfel David Grigorevich	1920	Minsk	Baranovichi	detachment ? 106	
Farfel Elka Girshevna	1920	Minsk	Baranovichi	detachment ? 106	
Faterson Serafima Lazarevna	1929	Minsk getto	Baranovichi	Stalin	Parkhomenko
Faya Shlema Zalmanovich	1901	Novogrudok getto	Baranovichi	Kirov	Oktyabrski
Fegel Yankel Naukhovich	1901	Postavy, getto	Vileyka	Dovator	Sverdlov
Fegelman Abram Leibovich	1912	Glubokoye	Minsk	Voroshilov	? 6
Fegelman Abram Samuilovich	1917	Sharkovshchina	Vitebsk	Lepelskaya Stalin	sabotage detachment
Fegelman Semen Berkovich	1913		Minsk	Voronyanski	Mstitel (Revenger)
Fedorov David Ilyich		Mogilev	polk ? 113		
Fedorovich Pavel Grigorevich	1904	Lenin	Pinsk	Komarov-Korzh's	4 group
Fediuk Matvei Mikhailovich	1905	Lyakhovichi, Kletsk district	Minsk	Chapayev	Shchors
Feigel Gutman Khonovich	1920	Kozyany	Vileyka		Ponomarenko
Feigel Motel Yosifovich	1923	Vilno	Vileyka	Spartak	? 6
Feigel Oskar Lazarevich	1925	Vidzy, getto	Vileyka	Spartak	? 1
Feigel Shimon Abramovich	1912	Baranovichi	Baranovichi	Kalinin	
Feigel Shlema Lazarevich	1927	Kozyany	Vileyka	Spartak	? 1
Feigelman Avner Leibovich	1913	Glubokoye	Vileyka	Voroshilov	brigade headquarters
Feigelman Masha Lvovna	1930	Smilovichi	Baranovichi	detachment ? 106	
Feigelman Khaim Srolevich	1910		Baranovichi	detachment ? 106	
Feigelson Don Yosifovich	1925	Glubokoye	Vileyka		Ponomarenko
Feigelson Zalman Yosifovich	1915	Glubokoye	Vileyka		Ponomarenko
Feigelshtein Yakov Aronovich	1912		Pinsk	Shubetidze	Stalin
Feigin Moisei Markovich	1924	Minsk getto	Minsk	Ponomarenko	Za Rodinu (For Motherland)
Feigin Solomon Shlemovich	1919	Minsk getto	Baranovichi	Chapayev	Parkhomenko
Feigin Tsodek Grigorevich	1911	Slutsk	Pinsk	Lenin	Dzerzhinski
Feigina Gesia Lvovna	1917	Gorodok, Glussk district	Palesye	Lelchitskaya	Shantar's
Feiman Basya Bentsionovna	1915	Gorodok	Baranovichi	Chkalov	? 4 "Za Sovetskuyu Belarus"
Feiman Revekka Abramovna	1905	Minsk	Baranovichi	detachment ? 106	
Feiser Gesel Meyerovich	1898	Stolbtsy	Baranovichi	Kalinin	
Fel Zalman Srulevich	1921	local	Baranovichi	Pobieda	Pobieda
Felgman Rafail N.	1921	Sharkovshchina district	Vileyka	Spartak	? 6
Feldgman Semen N.	1910	Sharkovshchina district	Vileyka	Spartak	? 6
Feldman Anatoli Mordukhovich	1912	left by theRK KP(b)B	Palesye	? 125	brigade headquarters and administration platoon
Feldman Anna Markovna	1912	Orsha	Mogilev	? 113	brigade ? 120
Feldman Anna Mikhailovna	1916	Kostyukovichi	Mogilev		? 44
Feldman Aron Abramovich	1921	Lakhva	Brest	Sikorski's headquarters	Shchors
Feldman Grigori Moiseyevich	1913	Minsk getto	Minsk	2nd Minskaya	Kutuzov
Feldman Ida Isaakovna	1910	Lida	Baranovichi	Kalinin	
Feldman Ilya Naumovich	1920	Belarusian Staff of Partisan Movement	Pinsk	Komarov-Korzh's	Komarov's 3rd group
Feldman Isaak Moiseyevich	1903	Minsk getto	Minsk	2nd Minskaya	Suvorov
Feldman Itsko Izrailevich	1914	concentration camp, Pogost-Zagorodski	Pinsk	Kuibyshev	Shchors

Feldman Itsko Yosifovich	1904	Negovishchi, Rovno region.	Pinsk	Shubetidze	Chapayev
Feldman Mariya Isaakovna	1912	Shpilki	Baranovichi	Stalin	Kirov
Feldman Motel Movshevich	1923	Glinka, Stolin district	Pinsk	Shubetidze	Chapayev
Feldman Naum Lvovich	1900	Minsk	Baranovichi	Stalin	Kirov
Feldman Pinya Berkovich	1898	Lagoisk	Baranovichi	Kalinin	
Feldman Pinya Gershkovich	1907	Poland, a small partisan group	Pinsk	Molotov	Lazo
Feldman Riva Faitelevna	1920	Bogushevsk	Mogilev	Ilyin's	? 24
Feldon Abram Gertsovich	1921	Lida	Baranovichi	Kirov	Iskra
Feldon Ignatii Gertsovich	1918	Lida	Baranovichi	Kirov	Iskra
Feldon Mariya Berkovna	1924	Lida	Baranovichi	Kirov	Za Sovetskuyu Belarus
Feldshtein Rafail Lazarevich	1907	Minsk getto	Baranovichi	Chapayev	Parkhomenko
Ferdman Leib Zalmanovich	1907	Lida	Baranovichi	Kalinin	
Ferstenberg Lyudvig Izrailevich	1914	Derechin	Baranovichi	Pobieda	Pobieda
Fertman Nina	1926	Repin, Oktyabr district	Minsk	Bragin	Panfilov
Fetershtein Roza Davydovna	1918	Minsk getto	Minsk	Pravda (Truth)	Ponomarenko
Figa Leon Simkhovich	1913	Slonim	Baranovichi	Leninskaya	family detachment group
Figo Leib Yankelevich	1913	Stobtsy	Baranovichi	Stalin	
Figotski David Leizerovich	1913	Bryansk getto, Belostok region	Grodno	Vo imya Rodiny (In the name of Motherland)	Zhukov
Fidelgolts Lev Bentianovich	1912	Gorodok	Baranovichi	Chkalov	? 4 "Za Sovetskuyu Belarus"
Fidelgolts Ester Movshevna	1911	Gorodok	Baranovichi	Chkalov	? 4 "Za Sovetskuyu Belarus"
Fidelman Ilya Grigorevich	1916	from captivity	Mogilev	? 13	? 719
Fik Khaim Yankelevich	1908	from captivity	Mogilev	Chekist	? 20
Fiksman Gdalya Shlemovich	1897	concentration camp Gantsevichi	Minsk	258th Kuibyshev	Chapayev
Filer Rakhil Isaakovna	1907	Timkovichi	Minsk	Chapayev	Ponomarenko
Filnar Boris Semenovich	1908	getto	Vileyka	Spartak	? 6
Fimer Mikhail Gilevich	1917	Mery, Braslav district	Vileyka	Zhdanov	
Finkel Anton	1919	Slonim	Brest	Sikorski's headquarters	Shchors
Finkel Volf Shakhanovich	1921	Slonim	Brest	Sikorski's headquarters	Shchors
Finkel Lazar Shakhnovich	1921	Slonim	Brest	Sikorski's headquarters	Shchors
Finkel Natan Khaimovich	1919	Slonim	Brest	Ponomarenko	Sovetskaya Belarus
Finkelberg Yosif Khaimovich	1918	Berezino district, Pruzhanka	Minsk	3rd Minskaya	Niepobedimy (Undefeated)
Finkelberg Elya Yosifovich	1900	Loev, TsKKP(b)B	Gomel	Za Rodinu (For Motherland)	Za Rodinu (For Motherland)
Finkelshtein Abram Khaimovich	1930	Bryansk getto, Belostok region	Grodno	Vo imya Rodiny (In the name of Motherland)	Zhukov
Finkelshtein Anna Khaimovna	1932	Bryansk getto, Belostok region	Grodno	Vo imya Rodiny (In the name of Motherland)	Zhukov
Finkelshtein Borukh Froimovich	1903	Bazhen	Pinsk	Budenny	Kotovski
Finkelshtein Yosif Aronovich	1924	Jewish camp,	Pinsk	Shubetidze	Ordzhonikidze
Finkelshtein Yosif Lazarevich	1914	Dyatlovo	Baranovichi	Leninskaya	Borba
Finkelshtein Leiba Shlemovich	1911		Baranovichi	Oktyabr	
Finkelshtein Leon Froimovich	1907	Byten	Brest	Sikorski's headquarters	Shchors
Finkelshtein Lyubov Mordukhovna	1913	Dyatlovo	Baranovichi	Leninskaya	Borba
Finkelshtein M.L.	1906	Bryansk getto, Belostok region	Grodno	Vo imya Rodiny (In the name of Motherland)	Zhukov
Finkelshtein Sofiya Khaimovna	1928	Bryansk getto, Belostok region	Grodno	Vo imya Rodiny (In the name of Motherland)	Zhukov
Finkelshtein Khaim Berkovich	1894	Bryansk getto, Belostok region	Grodno	Vo imya Rodiny (In the name of Motherland)	Zhukov
Firer Berko Movshevich	1914	Lakhva	Pinsk	Kirov	
Firshtenberg Lyudovil Izrailevich	1911	Zelva	Baranovichi	Pobieda	Suvorov
Fiterson Aron Gertsevich	1897	Minsk	Baranovichi	detachment ? 106	
Fiterson Grisha Nisinovich	1927	Minsk	Baranovichi	detachment ? 106	
Fiterson Izrail Yudelevich	1901	Minsk	Baranovichi	detachment ? 106	
Fiterson Nenya Izrailevich	1926	Minsk	Baranovichi	detachment ? 106	
Fiterson Revekka Mikhelevna	1902	Minsk	Baranovichi	detachment ? 106	
Fiterson Sarra Lazarevna	1929	Minsk getto	Baranovichi	Chapayev	Parkhomenko
Fiterson Fanya Semenovna	1928	Minsk	Baranovichi	detachment ? 106	
Fiterson Fima Bentsionovich	1940	Minsk	Baranovichi	detachment ? 106	
Fish Liza Leibovna	1922	Kletsk	Minsk	Chapayev	Ponomarenko
Fish Mikhail Eremovich	1910	Stolbtsy	Minsk	Chapayev	Ponomarenko
Fisher Lazar Khaivisovich	1906	Braslav	Vileyka	Za Rodinu (For Motherland)	Kirov
Fisher Samuil Andreevich	1918		Mogilev	208th regiment	left the detachment from the moment organization
Fisher Fanya Moiseyevna	1904	Ignalina	Vileyka	Voroshilov	headquarters' production group

Fisher Shevel Nosonovich	Slonim	Pinsk	Lenin	Kutuzov	
Fishkin Aleksandr Yefimovich	1907	from captivity	Mogilev	1st Bobruiskaya	? 252
Fishkin Aleksei Mordukhovich	1924	detachment "Mstitel (Revenger)"	Vileyka	Voroshilov	Suvorov
Fishkin Eina Gershovich	1913	Rubezhevichi	Baranovichi	18th Frunze	Kutuzov
Fishkin Yosif Shepselevich	1920	Rubezhevichi	Baranovichi	Chapayev	brigade headquarters
Fishkin Shepsel Yeselevich	1888	Rubezhevichi	Baranovichi	Chapayev	Chapayev
Fishkin Yuzef Shepshelevich	1920	Rubezhevichi	Baranovichi	Stalin	Chapayev
Fishkina Elena ShepsElevna	1927	small town of Dvorets, getto	Baranovichi	Chapayev	Chapayev
Fishkina Roza Solomonovna	1915	Shklov district	Mogilev	Chekist	? 1
Fishman Abram Davydovich	1919	N. Sverzhen	Minsk	Chapayev	Ponomarenko
Fishman Abram Zelikovich	1924	Glussk	Minsk	Ponomarenko	Gorbachev
Fishman Brokha Shlemovna	1919	Lakhva	Pinsk	Kirov	Stalin
Fishman Yelizaveta Simonovna	1915	Glussk	Minsk	Chkalov	
Fishman Zelik Abramovich	1891	from the encirclement	Minsk	Ponomarenko	Gorbachev
Fishman Ivan Davydovich	1919	getto N. Sverzhen	Minsk	Chapayev	Ponomarenko
Fishman Isaak Ilyich	1925	from the camp, Lokhva	Palesye	? 123	Artyushka's
Fishman Kalman Abramovich	1896	Glussk	Palesye	Lelchitskaya	Tsikunkov's
Fishman Keson Kolmovich	1920	Glubokoye	Vileyka	Budenny	Lesnoi, special group
Fishman Lyubov Elevna	1921	Glubokoye	Vileyka	Budenny	Lesnoi, special group
Fishman Sonya Isaakovna	1909	Glussk	Minsk	Chkalov	Dovator
Fishman Foma Shmuilovich	1926	Poland	Pinsk	Molotov	Shish
Fishtenberg Mordukh	1918	Lashchi	Baranovichi	Pobieda	Pobieda
Flaks Mikhail Yefimovich	1927	Minsk	Baranovichi	detachment ? 106	
Fleisher Yosif Grigorevich	1907	Slutsk	Minsk	Chkalov	Dovator
Fleisher Yosif Itskovich	1907	Belitsa	Baranovichi	Leninskaya	family detachment group
Fleisher Semen Davidovich	1919	German work camp	Pinsk	Molotov	Kalinin
Fleishter Mera Shmulevna	1917	Lida	Baranovichi	Leninskaya	Niepobedimy (Undefeated)
Flerans Izak Yakovlevich	1916	Novogrudok	Baranovichi	Vpered (Forward)	Chkalov
Flekhtman Grigori Berkovich	1906	Krasnoye	Baranovichi	Chkalov	? 4 "Za Sovetskuyu Belarus"
Fligelman Samuil Abramovich	1908	from captivity, Minsk	Minsk	Shturmovaya	Frunze
Flyaks Sarra Abramovna	1904	Minsk	Baranovichi	detachment ? 106	
Flyaks Yakov Vladimirovich	1920	Duntsy, Lyuban district	Belostok	A.Nevski	
Flyaster Tsodok Mendelevich	1913	Mlava	Baranovichi	Kalinin	
Fogel Ziskind Mendelevich	1904	Warsaw	Baranovichi	Za Sovetskuyu Belarus	family detachment
Fogel Yosif Lazarevich		Minsk	Shturmovaya	Grozny	
Foerman Aleksandr Aronovich	1908	working column of the Magyar army	Brest	Dzerzhinski	Molotov
Foldmak Aron Abramovich	1901		Brest	Ponomarenko	Sovetskaya Belarus
Forleiter Saul Abramovich	1907	Tomashevka	Brest	Stalin	Frunze
Forfman Vulf Izrailevich	1911	Kurenets	Vileyka	Voroshilov	Istrebitel (Destroyer)
Fradin Isaak Davidovich	1917	Loev, TsKKP(b)B	Gomel	Za Rodinu (For Motherland)	Stalin
Fradkin Moisei Gilerovich	1923	Gorodok	Baranovichi	Chkalov	
Fradkin Yakov Gilkovich	1922	Polochany	Baranovichi	Chkalov	? 4 "Za Sovetskuyu Belarus"
Fraint Sonya Lvovna	1913	Minsk	Baranovichi	Kalinin	
Fraiberg Motol Berkovich	1905	Tolmachevka	Pinsk	Molotov	Lazo
Fraigenbaum Aron Moiseyevich	1923	Novy Sverzhen	Minsk	Chapayev	Shchors
Fraiman Genya Abramovna	1922	N. Sverzhen	Minsk	Chapayev	Shchors
Fraiman Grisha	1930	Minsk	Baranovichi	detachment ? 106	
Fraiman Leonid Isaakovich	1915	Minsk	Baranovichi	detachment ? 106	
Fraiman Khana Abramovna	1917	Ruzhana	Baranovichi	Kalinin	
Fraint Boris Fishelevich	1941	Lida	Baranovichi	Kalinin	
Fraint Guta Abramovna	1910	Lida	Baranovichi	Kalinin	
Fraint Fishel Berkovich	1910	Lida	Baranovichi	Kalinin	
Fran Lyubov Danilovna	1930	getto Belostok	Grodno	Vo imya Rodiny (In the name of Motherland)	Zhukov
Fratkin Girsh Gilnovich	1921	Krasnoye, getto	Baranovichi	Za Sovetskuyu Belarus	Za Sovetskuyu Belarus
Freidbort Falvyel Solomonovich	1922	getto, Pruzhany	Brest	Ponomarenko	Kirov
Freidenshtein Yefim Ilyich	1919	getto, Vilno	Vileyka	Voroshilov	Chapayev
Freidkin Mikhail Vulfovich	1924	Jewish camp	Vileyka	4th Belorusskaya	? 6
Freidland Ema AlekseYevna	1922	Minsk	Minsk	Starik (Old man)	
Freiman Mosha Yakovlevich	1913	Krugloye	Mogilev	Chekist	Suvorov
Freintman Voldo Shayevich	1926	Rubezhevichi	Baranovichi	Kalinin	
Freintman Feiga Shayevna	1925	Rubezhevichi	Baranovichi	Kalinin	
Freintman Shaya Mendeleyevna	1895	Rubezhevichi	Baranovichi	Kalinin	
Freitok Yuzef Khelevich	1923	Vlodava (Poland)	Pinsk	Molotov	Lazo

Name	Year	Place	Region	Unit	Detachment
Frenkel Abram Simkhovich	1914	Radoshkovichi	Minsk	Voronyanski	Kotovski
Frenkel Alter Shmulevich	1913	N. Sverzhen, camp	Baranovichi	Zhdanov	
Frenkel Zyama Moiseyevich	1913	Bobruisk	Minsk	Chkalov	Dovator
Frenkel Matvei Borisovich	1912	from the encirclement	Palesye	? 123	Death to Fascism
Frenkel Pinkhas Khatskelevich	1922		Baranovichi	Oktyabr	
Frenkel Yakov Isaakovich	1921	Lida, getto	Baranovichi	Kirov	Orel
Frenkin Grigori Bentsionovich	1913	from captivity	Mogilev	208th partisan regiment	khoziaistvennaia rota
Frid Aleksei Zalmanovich	1926	Lapichi	Mogilev	Osipovichskaya VOG	? 210
Frid Boris Lvovich	1925	Minsk	Minsk	2nd Minskaya	Suvorov
Frid Ida Abramovna	1902	Minsk	Baranovichi	detachment ? 106	
Frid Ilya Abramovich	1922	Smilovichi	Minsk	Plamya	Slava (Glory)
Frid Polya Yefimovna	1923	Minsk	Baranovichi	detachment ? 106	
Fridberg Isaak Orelovich	1918	getto, Pruzhany	Brest	Ponomarenko	Kirov
Fridberg Leon Orelovich	1916	getto, Pruzhany	Brest	Ponomarenko	Kirov
Fridberg Peisakh Ilyich	1918	Novogrudok	Baranovichi	Kalinin	
Fridberg Sholom Elevich	1916	getto N. Sverzhen	Minsk	Chapayev	Ponomarenko
Fridburg Isaak Markovich	1909	from captivity	Pinsk	Komarov-Korzh's	2 group
Fride Yakub Yanokhovich	1922	from captivity	Baranovichi	Grizodubova	
Fridzon Rozaliya Zakharovna	1903	Minsk	Baranovichi	Ponomarenko	Timoshenko
Fridlyan Zalman Srolevich	1907	Minsk	Mogilev	208th regiment	
Fridlyand Anatoli Vladimirovich	1940	Minsk	Baranovichi	detachment ? 106	
Fridlyand Asya Davidovna	1926	Minsk	Baranovichi	Ponomarenko	Budenny
Fridlyand Berta Davidovna	1927	Minsk	Baranovichi	detachment ? 106	
Fridlyand Yosif Abramovich	1913	Minsk	Baranovichi	detachment ? 106	
Fridlyand Lyubov Grigorevna	1918	Slavnoye, Tolchin district	Mogilev		Chapai
Fridlyand Moisei Semenovich	1903	Minsk getto	Baranovichi	Ponomarenko	Vasilevski
Fridlyand Solomon Izrailevich	1907	Minsk getto	Minsk	Belarus	Za Rodinu (For Motherland)
Fridlyand Sofiia Yuryevna	1910	Minsk	Baranovichi	detachment ? 106	
Fridlyand Sofiya Yosifovna	1903	Minsk getto	Baranovichi	Ponomarenko	Vasilevski
Fridlyand Khasya Davidovna	1901	Minsk	Baranovichi	detachment ? 106	
Fridlyand Ema AlekseYevna	1922	Minsk getto	Minsk	Ponomarenko	Za Rodinu (For Motherland)
Fridman Abram Meyerovich	1918	Dolginovo	Minsk	1st Antifashistskaya	
Fridman Abram Moiseyevich	1905	Kopyl	Minsk	Chapayev	Shchors
Fridman Ada Borisovna	1926		Vitebsk	Chapayev	detachments
Fridman Aleksei Meyerovich	1923	Glubokoye, getto	Minsk	1st Antifashistskaya	
Fridman Anton Lazarevich	1886	Senno	Vitebsk	Sadchikov's	battallion ? 3
Fridman Anton Moiseyevich	1921	Ruzhany	Brest	Ponomarenko	Kirov
Fridman Aron Abramovich	1906	Koldychevo, getto	Baranovichi	Pervomaiskaya	Ya.Kolas
Fridman Aron Zelikovich	1912	Poland	Brest	Lenin	Zhukov
Fridman Basya Izrailevna	1922	Dokshitsy	Vileyka	Kutuzov	
Fridman Boris Isaakovich	1915	Ziabki	Vileyka	CC of the CP(b)B	Parkhomenko
Fridman Vera Samuilovna	1919	Lyuban	Minsk	Underground RC and DC CP(b)B	Logoisk DC of the CP(b)B
Fridman Grigori Abramovich	1931	Minsk	Baranovichi	detachment ? 106	
Fridman Grigori Izrailevich	1900	Minsk	Minsk	Chapayev	Chapayev
Fridman Dasha Natanovna	1919	Minsk	Baranovichi	detachment ? 106	
Fridman Dora Moiseyevna	1923	Jewish camp	Vileyka	Voroshilov	headquarters' production group
Fridman Yevgeniya Aronovna	1922	Tulgovichi, Khoiniki district	Palesye		Kotovski
Fridman Yefim Isaakovich	1914	from captivity	Vitebsk	Ponomarenko	
Fridman Yosif Davidovich	1922	Bronnaya Gora	Brest	Ponomarenko	Kirov
Fridman Yosif Solomonovich	1912	Minsk	Minsk	2nd Minskaya	Suvorov
Fridman Isaak Yoselevich	1926	Vlodava (Poland)	Pinsk	Molotov	Lazo
Fridman Isaak Moiseyevich	1903	Minsk	Minsk	2nd Minskaya	Suvorov
Fridman Larisa Ilnichna	1927	Minsk	Baranovichi	detachment ? 106	
Fridman Mikhail Abramovich	1923	N. Sverzhen	Minsk	Chapayev	Shchors
Fridman Mikhail Leibovich	1926	Pleshchenetski district	Vileyka	Kutuzov	
Fridman Mikhail Meyerovich	1926	Dolginovo	Vitebsk	Stalin (Okhotin's)	Kutuzov
Fridman Mikhail Meyerovich	1915	Dolginovo	Minsk	1st Antifashistskaya	
Fridman Mikhail Rubinovich	1925	Smolevichi	Baranovichi	Vpered (Forward)	Chkalov
Fridman Movsha Khatskelevich	1920	Baranovichi	Baranovichi	Za Sovetskuyu Belarus	family detachment
Fridman Moisei Abramovich	1925	Kopyl	Minsk	Chapayev	Ponomarenko
Fridman Moshka Abramovich	1912	l/vpl. Malyshevichi	Brest	Flegontov	Litvinov's
Fridman Nokhim Izrailevich	1902	Slutsk	Palesye	? 100	Igumnov and Babich's
Fridman Rakhelya Gershevna	1920	Lida	Baranovichi	Kalinin	
Fridman Rita Abramovna	1928	Minsk	Baranovichi	detachment ? 106	
Fridman Sarra Shayevna	1901	Kopyl	Minsk	Chapayev	Ponomarenko
Fridman Sofiya Moisevna	1916	getto, Pruzhany	Brest	Ponomarenko	Kirov
Fridman Teodor Adolfovich	1913	Magyar work camp	Palesye	99th Kalinkovichskaya	Kuksa's

Fridman Khaim Davidovich	1904	Vileika, getto	Minsk	Kirov	? 4
Fridman Yankel Faigusevich	1919		Minsk	Voronyanski	Mstitel (Revenger)
Fritsalis Leizer Movsovich	1912	Vileika region	Belostok	A.Nevski	
Frisher Gerts Shimonovich	1921	Mir	Baranovichi	Kalinin	
Frudkin Zisia Shayevich	1926	Minsk	Baranovichi	detachment ? 106	
Fruktebaum Anna Borisovna	1918	getto	Vileyka	Suvorov	
Fruman Rafail Mikhailovich	1908	Zaostrovichi	Pinsk	Lenin	Kutuzov
Frundyler Roman Solomonovich	1909	Borisov	Minsk	Shchors	Bolshevik
Fuks Boris Yosifovich	1923	Braslav district	Vileyka	Zhdanov	
Fuks Kastrol Zalmanovich	1910	from the civil camp	Vileyka	4th Belorusskaya	? 6
Fuks Leiba Shlemovich	1874	Bobruisk district, Bogushevka	Minsk	Bragin	Gastello
Fuks Meita Lvovna	1926	Bobruisk district, Bogushevka	Minsk	Bragin	Gastello
Fuks MotLyu Moshkovich	1913	from captivity	Mogilev	Chekist	? 10
Fuks Sima Lvovna	1920	Bobruisk district, Bogushevka	Minsk	Bragin	Gastello
Fuks Fanya Davidovna	1917	from the civil camp	Vileyka	4th Belorusskaya	? 6
Fuksik Vladimir Moiseyevich	1921	from captivity	Mogilev	? 537	
Fukson Moisei Grigorevich	1906	Glussk	Minsk	Parkhomenko	Kirov
Fukson Falvyel Nokhimovich	1905	from the encirclement	Palesye		Kirov
Funt Movsha Aronovich	1901	N. Sverzhen	Minsk	Chapayev	Ponomarenko
Funt Natan Samuilovich	1919	Lida	Baranovichi	Leninskaya	Borba
Furleiter Kalman Khaimovich	1927	Stolbtsy	Baranovichi	Kalinin	
Furleitor Sholko Abramovich	1907	Domachevo	Brest	Lenin	Zhukov
Furman Girsha Rubinovich	1926	Pozovshchina, Vitebsk region	Vitebsk	Ponomarenko	Kirov
Furman David Abramovich	1912	detachment Zhukov	Pinsk	Kuibyshev	Ordzhonikidze
Furman David Yefimovich	1888	detachment Kaganovich	Pinsk	Kuibyshev	Ordzhonikidze
Furman Yevel Berkovich	1903	Myadel	Minsk	Voronyanski	Mstitel (Revenger)
Furman Zarakh Davidovich	1925	detachment Kaganovich	Pinsk	Kuibyshev	Ordzhonikidze
Furman Leiba Davidovich	1923	concentration camp, Pogost-Zagorodski	Pinsk	Kuibyshev	Shchors
Furman Liza Mikhailovna	1907	br. Lenin	Pinsk	Kuibyshev	Ordzhonikidze
Furman Misha Movshevich	1924	concentration camp, Luninets	Pinsk	Kuibyshev	Shchors
Furman Movsha Yankelevich	1898	concentration camp	Pinsk	Kuibyshev	Shchors
Furman Moisei Meyerovich	1913	Dolginovo	Minsk	Underground RC and DC CP(b)B	Logoisk DC of the CP(b)B
Furman Rafail Mikhailovich	1908	Zaostrovichi	Pinsk	Lenin	
Furman Sara Izrailevna	1898	detachment Kaganovich	Pinsk	Kuibyshev	Ordzhonikidze
Furman Faikin Isaakovich	1909	Belarusian Staff of Partisan Movement	Pinsk	groups in the region	gr. Ignetenko
Furman Khaim Davidovich	1920	concentration camp, Logishin	Pinsk	Kuibyshev	Shchors
Furmanov Yefim Isaakovich	1909	Belarusian Staff of Partisan Movement	Pinsk	Budenny	Ponomarenko
Khavkin Mikhail Erofeevich	1907	Pinsk	Pinsk	Shubetidze	Ordzhonikidze
Khavkin Mordukh Mendelevich	1907		Vitebsk	1st Drissenskaya	Besstrashny (Fearless)
Khadan Etya Yoselevich	1907	Lida	Baranovichi	Kalinin	
Khaet Yosif Yumanovich	1923	Kopyl getto	Minsk	Frunze	Budenny
Khaet Isaak Meyerovich	1913	Minsk	Baranovichi	Stalin	Budenny
Khaet Liza Yefimovna	1923	Minsk	Baranovichi	detachment ? 106	
Khazan Vova Yakovlevich	1927	Minsk	Baranovichi	detachment ? 106	
Khazan Yosif Aronovich	1910	Pruzhany	Brest	Brest antifascist committee	
Khazan Samson Mendelevich	1906	Dzerzhinsk district, from captivity	Baranovichi	Stalin	Ryzhaka
Khazan Khana Moiseyevna	1915	Sharkovshchina	Vitebsk	Rokossovski	Dzerzhinski
Khazanovski Lazar Naumovich	1914	Vileika	Minsk	Voronyanski	Mstitel (Revenger)
Khaimovich Abram Khaimovich	1900	Mir	Baranovichi	Kalinin	
Khaimovich Rakhmiel Yevelevich	1926	Novogrudok	Baranovichi	Kalinin	
Khaimovich Tevel Khaimovich	1906	Mir	Baranovichi	Kalinin	
Khain Semen Solomonovich	1914	from the soviet rear	Vitebsk	Donukalov	Rodina
Khait Lev Yakovlevich	1920	Kartuz-Bereza	Pinsk	Budenny	Ponomarenko
Khaikin Yevgeni Markovich	1913	Moskva	Vitebsk	Dubov's	? 8
Khaikin Ilya Khatskelevich	1893	from the forest	Minsk	Belarus	Belarus
Khaikina Yelizaveta Leonovna	1920	Beshenkovichi	Vitebsk	Sennenskaya brigade (Leonov's)	Karantova
Khaimovich Anna Savelevna	1897	Mir	Baranovichi	Zhukov	

Name	Year	Place	Region	Detachment	Brigade
Khaimovich Boris Markovich	1920	small town of Vselyub, Novogrudok district	Baranovichi	Chapayev	Parkhomenko
Khaimovich Boris Faivelevich	1910	Khotimsk	Mogilev	208th partisan regiment	? 1
Khaimovich Sara Bentsianovna	1930	Mir	Baranovichi	Zhukov	
Khaitman Yakov Semenovich	1931	Azarichi	Minsk	Bragin	Gastello
Khaitovich David Grigorevich	1925	from the camp	Baranovichi	Grizodubova	
Khaitovich Mikhail Yudelevich	1910	Mir	Baranovichi	Zhukov	
Khaitovich Sima Shlemovich	1909	Novogrudok	Baranovichi	Kalinin	
Khaifets Sonya Naumovna	1914	Minsk	Baranovichi	detachment ? 106	
Khalipskaya Anna Moiseyevna	1931	Minsk	Baranovichi	detachment ? 106	
Khalipskaya Dora Isaakovna	1906	Minsk	Baranovichi	detachment ? 106	
Khalipski Izya Moiseyevich	1934	Minsk	Baranovichi	detachment ? 106	
Khalfina Mariya Isaakovna	1925	Minsk	Baranovichi	detachment ? 106	
Khamarski Yesel Yankelevich	1923	Eishishki	Baranovichi	Lenin's komsomol	Lenin's komsomol
Khamelyanski Semen Markovich	1915	Minsk	Mogilev		Slavny
Khanales Pavel Yakovlevich	1925	Gorodishche, getto	Baranovichi	Pervomaiskaya	Zhdanov
Khaneles Grigori Borisovich	1925	Molchad	Baranovichi	Pervomaiskaya	Pervomaiski
Khanin Ivan Leonovich	1925	Minsk getto	Baranovichi	Stalin	Parkhomenko
Khanin Yosif Mikhailovich	1920	Molodechno	Baranovichi	Za Sovetskuyu Belarus	Za Sovetskuyu Belarus
Khanin Mikhail Lvovich	1924	Minsk getto	Baranovichi	Chapayev	Furmanov
Khanin Nikolai Lvovich	1925	Minsk getto	Baranovichi	Chapayev	Furmanov
Khanovich Lidiya Sholokhovna	1915	Vilno	Vileyka	Suvorov	
Khantsevitski Tevel Khaimovich	1913	Derechin	Baranovichi	Pobieda	Pobieda
Kharlip Mariya Abramovna	1922	Mir	Baranovichi	Za Sovetskuyu Belarus	Shturm
Kharlip Moisei Vulfovich		Minsk	Baranovichi	detachment ? 106	
Khartova Liliya Yefimovna	1923	Minsk	Minsk	Rokossovski	Furmanov
Khartova Polina Antonovna	1902	Minsk	Minsk	Rokossovski	Dzerzhinski
Kharkhas Shlema Meyerovich	1918	Mir, getto	Baranovichi	Za Sovetskuyu Belarus	Za Sovetskuyu Belarus
Kharkhurin Yefim Abramovich	1923	Glussk district, Gorodok	Minsk	Parkhomenko	Kirov
Kharkhurin Khonya Aronovich	1895	Gorodok, Glussk district	Palesye	? 123	Death to Fascism
Kharkhurin Shaya Abramovich	1927		Palesye	? 123	Vezhnovets'
Khasin Aleksandr Isaakovich	1922	Belarusian Staff of Partisan Movement	Brest	groups of party leaders	Sokolovski's
Khasin Aron Borisovich	1906	Minsk	Baranovichi	18th Frunze	Frunze
Khasin Zundul Gilerovich	1913	from captivity	Minsk	Dyadi Koli	Stalin
Khasin Semen Solomonovich	1914	Belarusian Staff of Partisan Movement	Brest	groups of party leaders	Za Rodinu (For Motherland)
Khasman Mikhail Yosifovich	1905	collective farm Krasny Bereg	Mogilev	Chekist	? 31
Khasman Khaya Khaimovna	1921	Lida	Baranovichi	Kalinin	
Khatskilevich Yankel Nivakhovich	1925	Slonim	Brest		Budenny
Khatskin Izrail Abramovich	1933		Baranovichi	Kalinin	
Khachkovski Mikhail Naumovich	1914	Belarusian Staff of Partisan Movement	Belostok	Chapayev	Zhukov
Khvediuk Mota Mikhelevich	1905	Lyakhovichi, Kletsk district	Minsk	Chapayev	Ponomarenko
Khedekel Fruma Berkovna	1917	from the detachment "Spartak"	Vileyka	4th Belorusskaya	? 6
Kheiman Klara Moiseyevna	1920	Glussk	Brest	? 99 Gulyaev	brigade headquarters
Kheiman Matvei Moiseyevich	1924	Glussk	Brest	? 99 Gulyaev	brigade headquarters
Kheiman Khana Moiseyevna	1920	Germanova Sloboda, Minsk region	Minsk	Chkalov	Dovator
Kheifets Asher Samoilovich	1920	Lakhva	Pinsk	Kirov	
Kheifets Berko Shayevich	1919	Voronovo	Baranovichi	Kalinin	
Kheifets Yevel Shayevich	1911	Lida	Baranovichi	Kalinin	
Kheifets Zelik Leibovich	1910	concentration camp, Lakhva	Pinsk	Kuibyshev	Shchors
Kheifets Manya Solomonovna	1927	Minsk	Baranovichi	detachment ? 106	
Kheifets Movsha Zelmonovich	1913	Lakhva	Pinsk	Kirov	
Kheifets Roza Ovseyevna	1922	from the brigade Suvorov	Vileyka		Za Sovetskuyu Belorussiyu
Kheifets Roman Abramovich	1927	Western Byelorussia, Lokhva	Minsk	Chkalov	Dovator
Kheifets Roman Zelikovich	1924	Lakhva	Palesye	? 100	Za Sovetskuyu Rodinu
Kheifets Semen Shmoilovich	1923	Lokhva	Palesye	? 225	Suvorov
Kheifets Sonya Naumovna	1914	Minsk	Baranovichi		
Kheifets Khaim Ruvimovich	1925	Lyuban district, Sosny	Minsk	Frunze	Budenny
Kheifets Shlema Gershevich	1896	Borisov	Baranovichi	detachment ? 106	
Kheifets Shlema Isaakovich	1924	Lakhva	Palesye	? 125	Bolotnikov's
Kheifets Yankel Davidovich	1921	Puchiny, Logishin district	Pinsk	Kuibyshev	Shchors

Kheifits Marusya Ovseyevna	1922		Vileyka	Dovator	Sverdlov
Kheifits Khaya Zalmanovna	1924	Lakhva	Pinsk	Kirov	
Khenchinski Maks Shlemovich	1898	Lyntupy	Vileyka	Voroshilov	Suvorov
Khernas Esfil Leibovich	1913	Jewish camp	Vileyka	Voroshilov	headquarters' production group
Khetskel Aleksei Moiseyevich	1931	Nevery	Vitebsk	Rokossovski	Lenin
Khidekil Rakhmil Davidovich	1894	Mery, Braslav district	Vileyka	Zhdanov	
Khiker Zus Markovich	1926	Boyanichi, Lyuban district	Minsk	Ponomarenko	Korneyev's
Khilkevich Vera AnanYevna	1920		Pinsk	Molotov	Kalinin
Khinevich Sofiya Moiseyevna	1921	Mir	Baranovichi	Zhukov	
Khinich Aron Izrailevich	1912	Starobin	Minsk	Dyadi Koli	Stalin
Khinich Zelik Shimanovich	1913	Lenin	Pinsk	Molotov	Kalinin
Khinich Lipa Srolevich	1921	Lenino district, Pinsk region, v. Bereznyaki	Minsk	Stalin	
Khinich Srol Gertsevich	1887	Lenino district, Pinsk region	Minsk	Stalin	
Khinich Khaim Srolevich	1916	Lenino district, Pinsk region, v. Bereznyaki	Minsk	Stalin	
Khishel Zyama Abramovich	1924	Minsk	Baranovichi	Stalin	Budenny
Khishin Girsh Mordukhovich	1926	Minsk	Baranovichi	detachment ? 106	
Khlasnovich Meyer Alterovich	1911	Molchad	Baranovichi	Kalinin	
Khlebnik Rubin Leibovich	1915	Dyatlovo getto	Baranovichi	Kirov	Ordzhonikidze
Khmelnitski Kusim Leizerovich	1911	Derechin	Baranovichi	Pobieda	Suvorov
Khmelnitski Shimon Khaimovich	1906	Belostok	Baranovichi	Kalinin	
Khodak Falvyel Aronovich	1927	Derevno	Baranovichi	Kalinin	
Khodak Elya Aronovich	1927	Derevno	Baranovichi	Kalinin	
Khodas Vera Moiseyevna	1927	Madilo	Minsk	Voronyanski	Borba
Khodas Isaak Neukhovich	1880	detachment "Mest"	Vileyka	Voroshilov	headquarters' production group
Khodas Itska Shnerovich	1928	Balashi	Vileyka	Gastello	Bochkova
Khodas Leon Mendelevich	1915	Danilovichi	Vileyka	Voroshilov	Kalinin
Khodas Meyer Izrailevich	1922	Kobylnik	Vileyka	Voroshilov	Istrebitel (Destroyer)
Khodas Nikolai Motovich	1929	Krivechi district	Minsk	Voronyanski	Borba
Khodas Sofiya Motovna	1927	Krivechi district	Minsk	Voronyanski	Borba
Khodas Shiker Isaakovich	1928	Jewish camp	Vileyka	Voroshilov	headquarters' production group
Khodash Petr Yakovlevich	1917	Smolevichi	Baranovichi	Dzerzhinski	Dzerzhinski
Khodos Boris Matveyevich	1924	Myadel	Minsk	Voronyanski	Mstitel (Revenger)
Khodos Grigori Davidovich	1924	Myadel	Vileyka	Voroshilov	Kalinin
Khodos Grigori Yevelevich	1907	from the civil camp	Vileyka	4th Belorusskaya	? 6
Khodos Grigori Tanovich	1928	Kurenets	Vileyka	Dovator	Dzhioyev
Khodos David Khaimovich	1897	Myadel	Minsk	Kirov	? 4
Khodos Zelik Tanovich	1921	Kurenets	Vileyka	Dovator	Dzhioyev
Khodos Mariya Abramovna	1923		Minsk	Voronyanski	Pobieda
Khodos Rakhmal Markovich	1926	getto, Myadel	Vileyka	Voroshilov	Kalinin
Khodos Tana Mikhelevich	1890	Kurenets	Vileyka	Dovator	Dzhioyev
Khodos Fima Zalmanovich	1928	Jewish camp	Vileyka	Voroshilov	headquarters' production group
Khodos Khevus Yudelevich	1905		Minsk	Voronyanski	Pobieda
Khodosh Aleksandra Lipovna	1917	Novogrudok	Baranovichi	Kalinin	
Khodosh Berta Bentsianovna	1924	Minsk	Baranovichi	Kalinin	
Khodosh Fruma Yoselevich	1924	Novogrudok	Baranovichi	Kalinin	
Khodykin Vasili Ilyich	1912	Radzinski forest	Brest	Sikorski's headquarters	Shchors
Khodyrker Isrol Froimovich	1885	Stolbtsy	Baranovichi	detachment ? 106	
Khozanovich Yefim Filipovich	1926	Minsk	Vileyka	Frunze	Fighter
Khozoi Ruvim Yakovlevich	1903	Bobr	Mogilev	Ilyin's	? 30
Khoina Abram Itskovich	1919	German work camp, Poland	Pinsk	Molotov	Kalinin
Kholmentskaya Eva Semenovna	1924	Orsha	Vitebsk	Kirillov	Voroshilov
Kholmianskaya Mariya Semenovna	1928	Orsha	Vitebsk	1st Zaslonov	Kutuzov
KhOlyavski Abram Borisovich	1920	Minsk	Minsk	2nd Minskaya	Kutuzov
KhOlyavski Samuil Borisovich	1928	Minsk	Minsk	2nd Minskaya	Kutuzov
KhOlyavski Sholom Isaakovich	1914	Nesvizh	Minsk	Chapayev	Ponomarenko
Khomeli Mirosha Borisovich	1925	Gorodishche district	Baranovichi	Pobieda	Pobieda
KhomElyanski Semen Moiseyevich	1915	Mogilev	Gomel	8th Rogachevskaya	? 255
Khomik Solomon Yefimovich	1928	Minsk	Minsk	Dyadi Koli	Dzerzhinski
Khoneli Abram Yankelevich	1922	Gorodishche district	Baranovichi	Pobieda	Pobieda
Khonyak Estera Khilevna	1927	Derechin	Baranovichi	Pobieda	Suvorov
Khopman Isaak Aberovich	1894	Ozarichi	Palesye	Lelchitskaya	Akhramenko's
Khorlap Lev Yefimovich	1912	Minsk	Minsk	2nd Minskaya	Kutuzov
Khoroneko Tsilya Bentsianovna	1912	Shchedrin	Palesye		Kirov
Khoroshukha Lazar Semenovich	1916	Belostok	Grodno	Samutin's group	Kirshner's group

Name	Year	Place	Region	Unit	Detachment
Khoroshchanski David Girshevich	1924	Kosovo	Brest	Ponomarenko	Sovetskaya Belarus
Khosid Girsh Niselevich	1924	Grodno	Baranovichi	Kalinin	
Khurgin Benyamin Yankelevich	1931	Rubezhevichi	Baranovichi	Kalinin	
Khurgin Izrail Vulfovich	1906	Minsk, prison	Minsk	2nd Minskaya	Suvorov
Khurgin Lazar Borisovich	1925	Minsk	Baranovichi	Ponomarenko	25 years of the BSSR
Khurgin Leiba Yankelevich	1929	Rubezhevichi	Baranovichi	Kalinin	
Khurgin Naum Davidovich	1910	Parichi	Mogilev	1st Bobruiskaya	? 252
Khurgin Khatskel Borisovich	1928	Minsk	Baranovichi	Ponomarenko	25 years of the BSSR
Khurgin Yankel Benyaminolvich	1897	Rubezhevichi	Baranovichi		
Khurgina Amaliia Moiseyevna	1926	Minsk	Baranovichi	detachment ? 106	
Khurgina Rakhelya Yankelevna	1904	Rubezhevichi	Baranovichi	Kalinin	
Tsalikhin Mark Naumovich	1914	Buda-Koshelevo	Gomel		Kotovski
Tsalkind Mendel Abramovich	1900	Glubokoye	Vitebsk	Rokossovski	Zhukov
Tsalkovich Izrail Ilyich	1902	N. Sverzhen	Minsk	Chapayev	Shchors
TsaLyuk Esfir Leibovna	1916	Minsk	Baranovichi	Stalin	Budenny
Tsarinski Izrail Girshevich	1907	Lyakhovichi, getto	Baranovichi	Kirov	brigade headquarters
Tsvaiberg Efroim Khiletsevich	1900	Minsk getto	Baranovichi	Ivienets DC CP(b)B company	
Tsvasman Daria Borisovna	1924	Filipovichi	Palesye	? 125	brigade headquarters and administration platoon
Tsvei David Mikhailovich	1916	getto, Vilno	Vileyka	Voroshilov	Kalinin
Tsveigorin Mikhail Lvovich	1910	Minsk getto	Baranovichi	Ponomarenko	Vasilevski
Tsveronovski Leiba Aronovich	1893	Mir	Baranovichi	Kalinin	
Tsvibak Oskar Gershkovich	1917	Poland	Brest	Stalin	Chernyak
Tsvik Izrail Mendelevich	1907	Mir	Baranovichi	Za Sovetskuyu Belarus	Za Sovetskuyu Belarus
Tseitlin Naum Alterovich	1917	concentration camp, Mogilev	Gomel	8th Rogachevskaya	? 258
Tseitlina Aleksandra Borisovna	1922	Shklov	Mogilev	Chekist	? 20
Tseitlina Sofiya Alferovna	1903		Baranovichi	Slonim IDC	
Tselniker Pinkhas Khaimovich	1905	Belostok	Grodno	Samutin's group	Kirshner's group
Tsemakhov Grigori Yakovlevich	1919	Vitebsk	Vitebsk	1st Drissenskaya	brigade headquarters
Tsemokh Semen Zavelevich	1920	getto	Vileyka	Voroshilov	Grozny
Tsenisevich Foma Isaakovich	1922	Vileika region	Vileyka	4th Belorusskaya	? 6
Tsentsiper Leonid Abramovich	1923	Minsk	Minsk	Belarus	Belarus
Tsepelevich Enta Aronovna	1905	Lida	Baranovichi	Kalinin	
Tsepelevich Zalman Yudelevich	1910	Lida	Baranovichi	Kirov	Iskra
Tsepelevich Lazar Leibovich	1914	getto, Sharkovshchina	Vileyka	Voroshilov	Chapayev
Tsepelevich Khana Isaakovna	1922	from the civil camp	Vileyka	4th Belorusskaya	? 6
Tseplovich Boris Yosifovich	1913	Postavy	Vileyka	Spartak	? 1
Tsekhanovich Khaim Grigorevich	1897	v. Urechye	Minsk	Bragin	Gastello
Tsekhnovich Grigori Khaimovich	1925	v. Urechye	Minsk	Bragin	Gastello
Tsekhnovich Ida Khaimovna	1927	v. Urechye	Minsk	Bragin	Gastello
Tsekhnovich Fanya Abramovna	1898	v. Urechye	Minsk	Bragin	Gastello
Tsibulski Nikolai Savelevich	1930	Bagrinova, Tolochin district	Mogilev	Chekist	? 1
Tslvyes Gitia Shenderovna	1891	Minsk	Baranovichi	detachment ? 106	
Tsivin Gilel Aronovich	1905	from the encirclement	Mogilev	? 61	? 61
Tsigelnitskaya Tsylya Genakhovna	1921	Lida	Baranovichi	Kalinin	
Tsiimer Boris Semenovich	1921	Kozyany	Vileyka	Spartak	? 6
Tsiimer Rafail Zalmanovich	1915	Zazvorinets	Vileyka	Spartak	? 6
Tsikelevich Yankel Nevakhovich	1925	Slonim	Brest	Sikorski's headquarters	Shchors
Tsiklik Boris Yankelevich	1917	concentration camp Gantsevichi	Brest	? 99 Gulyaev	Grabko
Tsiklik Gdaliia Yankelevich	1906	concentration camp Gantsevichi	Brest	? 99 Gulyaev	Grabko
Tsiklik David Yankelevich	1920	concentration camp Gantsevichi	Brest	? 99 Gulyaev	Grabko
Tsiklik Yudel Leibovich	1909	Lenin	Pinsk	Komarov-Korzh's	1 group
Tsiklin David Zelikovich	1891	Lenino, Pinsk region	Minsk	Ponomarenko	A.Nevski
Tsiklin N.E.	1928	Lenin	Pinsk	Budenny	Kotovski
Tsiklin Shlema Davidovich	1927	Lenino, Pinsk region	Minsk	Ponomarenko	A.Nevski
Tsikman Abram Berkovich	1902	Minsk	Baranovichi	Chkalov	
Tsiler Shlema Zalmanovich	1921	Sharkovshchina	Vitebsk	4th Belorusskaya	
Tsimbal Sonya Meyerovna	1918	Minsk	Baranovichi	detachment ? 106	
Tsimbal Tsadik Yosifovich	1913	from captivity	Brest	Sikorski's headquarters	commandant platoon
Tsimberknop Pelageya Moiseyevna	1920	st. Krynki, Western railway	Vitebsk	Donukalov	Rodina
Tsimer Gllya Solomonovna	1926	Sharkovshchina	Vitebsk	Rokossovski	Kotovski
Tsimer Slava (Glory) Samuilovich	1929	Braslav district	Vileyka	Zhdanov	
Tsimer Solomon Khaimovich	1890	Sharkovshchina	Vitebsk	Rokossovski	Kotovski
Tsimer Tsilya Samuilovna	1925	Lapushino, Sharkovshchina district	Vitebsk	Rokossovski	Shchors
Tsimerblat Ziskin					

Tsimerman Aizik Solomonovich	1916	Logoisk	Minsk	Kirov	Kirov
Tsimerman Vladimir Isaakovich	1922	Vileika	Vitebsk	Ponomarenko	Golovchenko
Tsimerman Grigori Isaakovich	1923	from Utkin's brigade	Vileyka	Kalinin	? 1
Tsimerman Daniil Yosifovich	1915	Kurenets	Vileyka		Suslov
Tsimerman Rozaliya Simkhovna	1913	from the forest	Pinsk	Molotov	Kalinin
Tsimerman Shimon Ilyich	1924	getto	Vileyka	Voroshilov	brigade headquarters
Tsimkovski Zyama Mendelevich	Palesye	Glusskaya ? 100	Za Sovetskuyu Rodinu		
Tsimmer Zalman Samuilovich	1921		Vileyka	1st Suvorov	Voroshilov
Tsimmer Ida Lipovna	1925	Germanovichi	Vileyka	1st Suvorov	Chkalov
Tsimmer Leiba Zalmanovich	1911	Sharkovshchina	Vileyka	Spartak	? 6
Tsimmer Lipa Mordukhovich	1905	Krulevshchizna	Minsk	1st Antifashistskaya	? 5
Tsimmer Lyuba Zalmanovna	1921	Sharkovshchina	Vileyka	1st Suvorov	Voroshilov
Tsimmer Mira	1880	from the civil camp	Vileyka	4th Belorusskaya	? 6
Tsimmer Solomon Solomonovich	1921	Jewish camp	Vileyka	4th Belorusskaya	? 6
Tsimmer Shlema Zalmanovich	1921	from the civil camp	Vileyka	4th Belorusskaya	? 6
Tsimmerman Grigori Itskovich	1923	Kurenets, Vileika region	Vitebsk	Chapayev	detachments
Tsimmerman Khatskel Isaakovich	1922	Kurenets, Vileika region	Vitebsk	Chapayev	detachments
Tsimmershok Riva Sheisovna	1922	getto, Vileika	Vileyka	Voroshilov	Suvorov
Tsimsher Isaak Semenovich	1923	Kozyany	Vileyka	Spartak	? 4
Tsin David Yosifovich	1918	Vlodava (Poland)	Pinsk	Molotov	brigade headquarters
Tsinkina Yadia Elevna	1922	Baranovichi	Baranovichi	Chkalov	reserve group
Tsipelevich Polina Borisovna	1919	Glubokoye	Minsk	1st Antifashistskaya	
Tsipershtein Sender Movshevich	1925	concentration camp	Pinsk	Kuibyshev	Shchors
Tsipershtein Yulya Erokhimovna	1923	Pogost-Zagorodski, getto	Pinsk	Molotov	Shish
Tsipilevich Asya Borisovna	1925	Jewish camp, Luzhki	Vileyka	Spartak	? 2
Tsipilevich Leon Isaakovich	1929	Lida, getto	Baranovichi	Kirov	Ordzhonikidze
Tsipin Isaak Davidovich	1913	Peski	Baranovichi	Leninskaya	Borba
Tsipin Mikhail Konstantinovich	1916	Belarusian Staff of Partisan Movement	Pinsk	groups in the region	Bobrov's group
Tsipin Nisel Abramovich	1916		Baranovichi	Leninskaya	Pobieda
Tsipina Beila Leibovna	1922	Kletsk	Minsk	Chapayev	Ponomarenko
Tsipkina Genya Yoselevna	1917	Minsk	Baranovichi	detachment ? 106	
Tsipkina Nella Grigorevna	1936	Minsk	Baranovichi	detachment ? 106	
Tsiplin Yudel Leibovich	1909	concentration camp	Pinsk	Kuibyshev	Shchors
Tsipukova Yokha Isaakovna	1924	Glubokoye	Vitebsk	Rokossovski	Kotovski
Tsirinski Izrail Gershonovich	1907	Lyakhovichi	Baranovichi	Kirov	brigade headquarters
Tsirinski Meyer Grigorevich	1895	getto, Ushachi	Vitebsk	Ponomarenko	hospital
Tsirinski Nenya	1922	Slonim	Brest	Sikorski's headquarters	Shchors
Tsirkin Motel Mendelevich	1889	Osipovichi	Palesye	? 100	Za Sovetskuyu Rodinu
Tsirlin Anatoli Abramovich	1924	Minsk	Baranovichi	Ponomarenko	25 years of the BSSR
Tsirlin Samuil Yankelevich	1892	Minsk getto	Minsk	3rd Minskaya	Lazo
Tsirlina ... Grigorevna	1928	Minsk	Baranovichi		
Tsirlina Katya Izrailevna	1922	Minsk	Baranovichi	detachment ? 106	
Tsirlina Rakhil Davidovna	1904	Minsk	Baranovichi	detachment ? 106	
Tsirlina Faina Romanovna	1918	Minsk getto	Minsk	2nd Minskaya	Kutuzov
Tsirulnik Gennadi Khaimovich	1930	getto	Vileyka	Voroshilov	Istrebitel (Destroyer)
Tsirulnik Khaya Itskovna	1917	Lida	Baranovichi	A.Nevski	Kalinovski
Tsirulskaya Elena Yosifovna	1921	Viazan, Vileika region	Minsk	Voroshilov	? 6
Tsitver Yakov Grigorevich	1905	Minsk, underground, regional committee of the CP(b)B	Minsk	Voronyanski	Mstitel (Revenger)
Tsitron Boris Mendelevich	1918	getto, Vileika	Vileyka	Suvorov	
Tsitron-Rubina Sonya Naumovna	1920	getto, Vileika	Vileyka	Suvorov	
Tsishkovski Zakhar Mendelevich	1908	Bogushevka, Bobruisk district	Palesye	? 100	Igumnov and Babich's
TsiYurin Abram Naumovich	1918	Minsk	Baranovichi	18th Frunze	Kutuzov
Tslaf Ilya Zakharovich	1912	Rechitsa			
Tsodenkman Raisa Matveyevna	1923	from the forest	Baranovichi	Kirov	Ordzhonikidze
Tsofin Grigori Moiseyevich	1917	Gorodok	Baranovichi	Chkalov	? 4 "Za Sovetskuyu Belarus"
Tsofina Yevgeniya Gershevna	1916	Gorodok	Baranovichi	Za Sovetskuyu Belarus	family detachment
Tsofina Khana Gershevna	1916	Gorodok	Baranovichi	Chkalov	? 4 "Za Sovetskuyu Belarus"
Tsubrevich Anton Aleksandrovich	1880	Vileika region	Vileyka	4th Belorusskaya	? 6
Tsudkevich Mikhail Godelevich	1909	Gorodishche district	Baranovichi	25 years of the BSSR	Grozny
Tsuker Anna Davidovna	1914	Minsk getto	Baranovichi	18th Frunze	Frunze
Tsuker Girsha Abramovich	1931	Radun	Baranovichi	Leninskaya	Niepobedimy (Undefeated)
Tsuker Enta Isaakovna	1897	Minsk	Baranovichi	detachment ? 106	
Tsuker Yefim Arkadevichi	1902	Jewish camp Dvorets	Baranovichi	Ivienets DC CP(b)B company	

Tsuker Yefim Lazarevich	1912	Minsk getto	Baranovichi	18th Frunze	Frunze
Tsuker Lyubov Yankelevna	1914	Jewish camp Dvorets	Baranovichi	Ivienets DC CP(b)B company	
Tsukerkop Meilakh Pinkhusovich	1918	Kotsenets	Baranovichi	Kalinin	
Tsukerkorn Samson	1920	Baranovichi	Pinsk	Budenny	Kotovski
Tsukerman Abram Borisovich	1907	Gorodok	Baranovichi	Chkalov	? 4 "Za Sovetskuyu Belarus"
Tsukerman Aizik Aronovich	1906	Minsk getto	Baranovichi	Chapayev	Parkhomenko
Tsukerman Andrei Grigorevich	1921	Volkovyssk, camp	Belostok	A.Nevski	
Tsukerman G.Ts.	1924	Derechin	Baranovichi	Pobieda	Pobieda
Tsukerman Gerts Davidovich	1892	Krivichi district	Minsk	Zheleznyak	? 5
Tsukerman Girsh Itskovich	1922	Derechin	Belostok	A.Nevski	
Tsukerman Ida Yakovlevna	1924	Minsk	Baranovichi	detachment ? 106	
Tsukerman Yosif Isaakovich	1918	Staroselye	Mogilev	Chekist	? 31
Tsukerman Leonid Aleksandrovich	1927	Minsk getto	Baranovichi	Ponomarenko	Voronov's
Tsukerman Lyubov Yefimovna	1923	Minsk, getto	Minsk	Belarus	Bolshevik
Tsukerman Mariya Isaakovna	1920	Staroselye	Mogilev	Chekist	? 31
Tsukerman Meilokh Pinkhusovich	1918	Dvorets	Baranovichi	Leninskaya	Borba
Tsukerman Raya Borisovna	1919	Gorodok	Baranovichi	Kalinin	
Tsukerman Roza Borisovna	1920	Molodechno	Baranovichi	Kalinin	
Tsukerman Roza Yefimovna	1926	Minsk	Baranovichi	Stalin	Budenny
Tsukerman Semen Izrailevich	1926	Minsk	Minsk	3rd Minskaya	Lazo
Tsukerman Felya Movshevna	1923	concentration camp	Pinsk	Kuibyshev	Shchors
Tsukerman Khaim Gutelevich	1921	Lebedevo	Baranovichi	Chkalov	? 4 "Za Sovetskuyu Belarus"
Tsukurman Rakhil Solomonovna	1898	Minsk	Baranovichi		
Tsurkova Gerna Abramovna	1897	Baranovichi, from home	Baranovichi	Grizodubova	Matrosov
Tsurkovich David Berkovich	1898	Lenin	Pinsk	Kirov	Kalinin
Tsutkevich Mikhail Godelevich	1909	Baranovichi	Baranovichi	Pervomaiskaya	Zhdanov
Tsfasman Zinaida Zakharovna	1922	village of Kozlovichi Slutsk district	Minsk	Chkalov	Gromov
Tsybulnik Ida Moiseyevna	1898	Minsk	Baranovichi	Kalinin	
Tsygelnitskaya Tsylya Enukhovna	1921	Lida	Baranovichi	Vpered (Forward)	Roshcha
Tsylman Abram Berkovich	1902	Minsk	Baranovichi	Vpered (Forward)	Chkalov
Tsypin Nisel Abramovich	1916	Peski, Mosty	Baranovichi	Pobieda	Suvorov
Tsyrinski Girsh Davidovich	1910	Novogrudok	Baranovichi	Kalinin	
Tsyrkin Grigori Elkonovich	1912				
Tsyrkin Gutman Mendelevich	1902	Parichi district, Kovchitsy	Minsk	Parkhomenko	Kirov
Tsyrkin Leonid Zakharovich	1929	Antonovo, Rossony district	Vitebsk	Stalin (Okhotin's)	Stalin
Tsyrkin Motel Mendelevich	1889	Osipovichi	Pinsk	Molotov	Kalinin
Chaikovski Yakov Abramovich	1914	from captivity	Gomel	1st Gomelskaya	Suvorov
Chan Yosif Abramovich	1907	Dvorets	Baranovichi	Kalinin	
Chan Malka Peisakovna	1916	Dvorets	Baranovichi	Kalinin	
Chankevich Genya Salomonovna	1924	Lida	Baranovichi	Kalinin	
Charlin Yakov Yakovlevich	1911	left by the RK KP(b)B	Palesye	? 125	Kudravtsa
Charnaia Esfir Isaakovna	1923	Minsk	Minsk	2nd Minskaya	Kutuzov
Charno Samuil Ivanovich	1911	Vilno	Minsk	Voronyanski	Mstitel (Revenger)
Charny Abram Barukhovich	1917	Rubezhevichi, getto	Baranovichi	Zhukov	
Charny Bemus Borkhovich	1913	Uzlyany	Mogilev	208th regiment	
Charny Boris Grigorevich	1912	Rudensk	Minsk	Belarus	Stalin
Charny Izrail Yakovlevich	1897	Mir	Baranovichi	Za Sovetskuyu Belarus	Za Sovetskuyu Belarus
Chauski Isaak Grigorevich	1906				
Chauchinski Yosif Davidovich	1915	Minsk getto	Vileyka	Frunze	Voroshilov
Chatski Yosif Marovich	1884	Baranovichi	Brest	Sverdlov	Bozhenko
Chemerinski Abram Bentsionovich	1894	Dyatlovo	Baranovichi	Leninskaya	family detachment group
Cheremashnyi Maton Rubinovich	1915	Belostok	Grodno	Samutin's group	Kirshner's group
Cherepakha Yevel Khaimovich	1891	Minsk	Baranovichi	Vpered (Forward)	Chkalov
Cherepakha Ilya Shmuilovich	1912	Minsk	Baranovichi	Vpered (Forward)	Chkalov
Cherne David Samuilovich	1914	from captivity	Minsk	Voroshilov	Patriots of Motherland
Chernevin Foma Mironovich	1908	Baranovichi	Baranovichi	Vpered (Forward)	Sibiryak
Chernevich Abram Shmuilovich	1908	Novogrudok	Baranovichi	Kalinin	
Chernevich Notek Abramovich	1930	Novogrudok	Baranovichi	Kalinin	
Chernik Yevgeniya Abramovna	1912	Antopol	Brest		Kirov
Chernin Grigori Ilyich	1905	Minsk getto	Baranovichi	Chapayev	Parkhomenko
Chernin Izrail Yakovlevich	1924	Starye Dorogi	Minsk	Ponomarenko	Gorbachev
Chernina Raisa Isaakovna	1909	Minsk	Baranovichi	Za Sovetskuyu Belarus	family detachment
Cherno Khana Yakovlevna	1919	Minsk getto	Baranovichi	Stalin	Parkhomenko
Chernoglaz Zus Yakovlevich	1903	Yelsk	Palesye	37th Yelskaya	brigade headquarters and administration platoon
Chernozubovski Aizik L.	1918	from the civil camp	Baranovichi	Grizodubova	Chkalov
Chernyi Izrail Yakovlevich	1897	Mir	Baranovichi	Chkalov	

Name	Year	Place	Region	Detachment	Brigade
Chernyi Ilya Aronovich	1915	Poland, camp, prisoner of war	Pinsk	Molotov	Kalinin
Chernyi Kusel Lvovich					
Chernyi Khaim Isaakovich	1904	Novogrudok	Baranovichi	Kalinin	
Chernyavski Aron Elkovich	1912	from captivity	Vileyka	Budenny	Budenny
Chernyak Aleksandr Mordukhovich	1922	Shchuchin	Baranovichi	Leninskaya	Borba
Chernyak Girsh Mordukhovich	1919	Shchuchin	Baranovichi	Leninskaya	Borba
Chernyak David Mikhailovich	1921	Central Committee of the CP (b) B	Vileyka	Kutuzov	
Chernyak Lazar Yefimovich	1901	from the encirclement	Minsk	A.Nevski	Bondarovets
Chernyak Lazar Mordukhovich	1918	Shchuchin	Baranovichi	Leninskaya	Borba
Chernyak Lev Grigorevich	1919	Minsk	Baranovichi	detachment ? 106	
Chernyak Mikhail Yefimovich	1909	Gorki	Gomel	Shemyakin's "Vpered (Forward)"	rota ? 1
Chernyak Moisei Nisanovich	1909	Bobruisk, from the encirclement	Minsk	Parkhomenko	Shchors
Chernyak Petr Aronovich	1909	Antopol	Brest		Kirov
Chernyak Shas Mordukhovich	1922	Shchuchin	Baranovichi	Leninskaya	Krasnogvardeiski
Chernyak Yakov Lvovich	1904	Central Committee of the CP (b) B	Vileyka	Kutuzov	
Chernyakov Yakov Moiseyevich	1909	Central Committee of the CP (b) B	Minsk	Special groups	Chervyakov's group
Chernyakhovskaya Iakhna Manusovna	1916	Slonim district	Baranovichi	Rokossovski	Dzerzhinski
Chernyakhovski Izrail Esaulovich	1885	Slonim district	Baranovichi	Rokossovski	Dzerzhinski
Chertov Viktor Yakovlevich	1913	from the encirclement	Vitebsk	Nikitin's	? 1
Chertova Raya Abramovna	1913	Minsk	Baranovichi	Stalin	Budenny
Chertova Tamara Sholomovna	1905	Minsk	Baranovichi	detachment ? 106	
Chertok Abram Ovseyevich	1921	Novogrudok, getto	Baranovichi	1st Baranovichskaya	Frunze
Chertok Izak Gershevich	1917	K. Kashirski	Pinsk	Molotov	Suvorov
Chertok Nokhim Movshevich	1914	Slonim	Pinsk	Lenin	Dzerzhinski
Chertok Saul Shmulovich	1903	Minsk	Baranovichi	Chkalov	
Chertok CheSlava (Glory) Ivanovna	1923		Minsk	Voronyanski	Mstitel (Revenger)
Cherchevski Tsoden Yosifovich	1914	getto, Pruzhany	Brest	Ponomarenko	Kirov
Cherches Yefim Mikhailovich	1925	Minsk getto	Minsk	Pravda (Truth)	Pobieda
Chesler Samuil Abramovich	1920	Mir	Baranovichi	Za Sovetskuyu Belarus	Shturm
Chekhanovskaya Roza Davidovna	1925	Minsk	Baranovichi	detachment ? 106	
Chechik Boris Alekseyevich	1908	Viten, Vileika region	Vitebsk	Sadchikov's	battallion ? 1
Chechik David Aronovich	1926	farm-stead Tupik, Rovno region	Palesye	37th Yelskaya	Bolshevik
Chizhikova Dora Karlovna	1907	from the detachment Budenny	Baranovichi	detachment ? 106	
Chikatovskaya Dora Vladimirovna	1915	Minsk	Minsk	Bolshevik	
Chirlin Edit Yankelevich	1911	left by the OK KP(b)B	Brest	Yazykovicha	Lenin's komsomol
Chornyi Boris Grigorevich	1912	Gorelets, Pukhovichi district	Minsk	2nd Minskaya	Stalin
Chuevskaya Genya Lvovna	1913	Uzda	Minsk	Rokossovski	Chkalov
Chunts Mikhail Grigorevich	1915	Central Committee of the CP (b) B	Pinsk	Budenny	Ponomarenko
ChYakubovich Aron Pinkhusovich	1911	Novogrudok	Baranovichi		
Shabakovskaya Matlya Meyerovna	1917	Novogrudok	Baranovichi	Kalinin	
Shabakovski David Kalmanovich	1915	Novogrudok	Baranovichi	Kalinin	
Shabakovski Samuil Khaimovich	1914	Dyatlovo	Baranovichi	Leninskaya	Borba
Shabsai Ovsei Zemelevich	1924	Slonim	Brest	Sikorski's headquarters	Shchors
Shadovski Dmitri Semenovich	1925	Radun	Baranovichi	Voroshilov	Kalinin
Shain Yakov Markovich	1916	contact	Minsk		Moskva
Shaikevich Galina Lazarevna	1909	Minsk	Minsk	Stalin	
Shaikevich Nina Yosifovna	1925		Minsk	2nd Minskaya	Kutuzov
Shaikova Nina Danilovna	1919	Krasino district	Mogilev	? 117	? 124
Shalamson David Markovich	1925	Beshenkovichi	Vitebsk	Bogushevskaya	Lazo
Shalin Volf Khaimovich	1922	Vilno	Baranovichi	Kalinin	
Shalman Rafail Venyaminovich	1897	Minsk	Minsk	2nd Minskaya	Kutuzov
Shalobinskaya Sima Isaakovna	1920	Derechin	Baranovichi	Pobieda	Pobieda
Shaloumova Sofiya Yakovlevna	1904	Tikhany, Orsha district	Vitebsk	1st Belorusskaya	
Shames Yakov Abramovich	1919	from captivity, Minsk	Minsk	Shturmovaya	Grozny
Shamis Raisa Abramovna	1916		Vitebsk	2nd Belorusskaya	
Shamis Simkhai Levich	1910	K. Kashirski	Pinsk	Sovetskaya Belarus	Kutuzov
Shandorovich Yakov Samoilovich	1894	from the encirclement	Palesye	? 123	Death to Fascism
Shanovich Elena Davidovna	1926	Vetka	Gomel	1st Gomelskaya	Kalinin
Shapiro Anna Yevseyevna	1922	Minsk getto	Minsk	3rd Minskaya	25years of the A-ULCYL
Shapiro Boris Markovich	1926	small town of Urechye Slutsk district	Minsk	Chkalov	Dovator
Shapiro Vera Abramovna	1913	Zamoshe, Braslav district	Vileyka	Zhdanov	

Shapiro Grigori Semenovich	1917	Bykhov	Mogilev	152-oi partisan regiment	battallion ? 1
Shapiro Gutel Gutelevich	1922	Novogrudok	Baranovichi	Kalinin	
Shapiro David Vulfovich	1914	Smorgon	Vileyka		Suslov
Shapiro Dina Ashelevna	1914	Smorgon	Vileyka		Suslov
Shapiro Dora Irmovna	1925	Postavy	Minsk	Underground RC and DC CP(b)B	Logoisk DC of the CP(b)B
Shapiro Elion Izrailevich	1904		Palesye	? 27 Kirov	Kirov
Shapiro Izrail Venyaminovich	1923	Lyuban district, Iushkovichi	Minsk	Chkalov	Gromov
Shapiro Isaak Davidovich	1907	Bereza, Volynskaya region	Brest	Flegontov	Boyevoi (Fighting)
Shapiro Isaak Yefimovich	1911	Gomel	Gomel	Bolshevik	Chapayev
Shapiro Isaak Irshevich	1927	Jewish camp	Vileyka	Voroshilov	headquarters' production group
Shapiro Lazar Khaimovich	1912	detachment "Komsomol"	Vileyka	Voroshilov	Suvorov
Shapiro Larisa Borisovna	1925	Selishche, Klichev district	Mogilev		? 278
Shapiro Leon Yosifovich	1906	getto, Glubokoye	Vileyka	1st Suvorov	Komsomolets
Shapiro Mariya Yosifovna	1924	Zaslavl	Baranovichi	Chkalov	
Shapiro Meyer Isarovich	1925	detachment Kaganovich	Pinsk	Kuibyshev	Ordzhonikidze
Shapiro Mikhail Shamshevich	1914	Pruzhany	Brest	Za Sovetskuyu Belarus	Chkalov
Shapiro Moisei Davidovich					
Shapiro Moisei Zalmanovich	1921	Svisloch, Osipovichi district	Mogilev		? 760 Berezovski
Shapiro Moisei Ovseyevich	1904		Baranovichi	Shchuchin IDC	
Shapiro Moisei Shmoilovich	1899	small town of Vishnevo	Baranovichi	Chapayev	Chapayev
Shapiro Pelageya Leibovna	1909	Bereza, Volynskaya region	Brest	Flegontov	Boyevoi (Fighting)
Shapiro Pina Khaimovna	1915	Kurenets	Vileyka	Dovator	Furmanov
Shapiro Rakhmel Vulfovich	1910	Jewish camp	Vileyka	Voroshilov	headquarters' production group
Shapiro Ruva Yankelevich	1909	Minsk	Baranovichi	detachment ? 106	
Shapiro Samuil Yefimovich	1902	Dzerzhinsk	Baranovichi	Stalin	
Shapiro Samuil Khonovich	1923	from the brigade Suvorov	Vileyka	Voroshilov	Lazo
Shapiro Semen Irmovich	1912	Dolginovo	Minsk	Underground RC and DC CP(b)B	Logoisk DC of the CP(b)B
Shapiro Sonya Benyaminovna	1919	Slutsk	Pinsk	Komarov-Korzh's	1 group
Shapiro Sofiya Yefimovna	1902	Dzerzhinsk district	Baranovichi	Stalin	Bolshevik
Shapiro Fima Grigorevich	1927	Minsk	Baranovichi	detachment ? 106	
Shapiro Khana Gdalevna	1912	Minsk	Baranovichi	detachment ? 106	
Shapiro Yakov (Khaim) Aronovich	1923	camp Kurenets	Minsk	Voronyanski	Kotovski
Shapochnik Ilya Srulevich	1921	Molodechno	Baranovichi	Chkalov	? 4 "Za Sovetskuyu Belarus"
Shapsai Avsei Zimelevich	1924	Slonim	Brest	Sikorski's headquarters	commandant platoon
Sharstinskaya Polina	1900	Dobrush	Gomel	Stalin	Budenny
Shatov Nikolai Ivanovich	1911		Mogilev		Slavny
Shafer Zhorzh Abramovich	1912	Minsk, camp, prisoner of war	Vileyka	Frunze	Voroshilov
Shafran Shmul Yankelevich	1911	Poland	Brest	Stalin	25-letiia Sovetskoi Belarusi
Shafran Yakov Semenovich	1918	Vileika	Vileyka	Voroshilov	Lazo
Shafranski Khaim Gershonovich	1925	Zheludok	Baranovichi	Leninskaya	Krasnogvardeiski
Shaft Zelda Yankelevna	1914		Baranovichi	Oktyabr	
Shaft Zina Aizikovna	1915	Baranovichi	Baranovichi	Vpered (Forward)	A.Nevski
Shakhnovich M.	1910	Jewish camp	Vitebsk	4th Belorusskaya	
Shakhnovich Sheval Leibovich	1915	Zheludok	Baranovichi	Lenin's komsomol	Lenin's komsomol
Shats Vilgelm Germanovich	1904	Kurenets	Minsk	Voronyanski	Kotovski
Shats Mira Mikhailovna	1914	Slutsk	Minsk	Dyadi Koli	Stalin
Shatski Abram Khaimovich	1901	from the concentration camp	Baranovichi	Grizodubova	Chkalov
Shatsman Vladimir Yoselevich	1918	from captivity	Pinsk	Molotov	Kalinin
Shvaiko Abram Girshevich	1914	Lakhva	Pinsk	Kirov	Stalin
Shvarts Abram Semenovich	1925	getto	Vitebsk	Nikitin's	? 5
Shvarts Iser Nokhimovich	1906	Ivye	Baranovichi	Kalinin	
Shvarts Lyudmila Aronovna	1920	getto, Vilno	Vileyka	Voroshilov	Pobieda
Shvarts Meyer Semenovich	1928	getto	Vitebsk	Nikitin's	? 5
Shvarts Rakhil Moiseyevna	1910	Ivye	Baranovichi	Kalinin	
Shvarts Semen Mirovich	1895	getto	Vitebsk	Nikitin's	? 5
Shvarts Semen Naumovich	1925	Minsk	Baranovichi	Dzerzhinski	Dzerzhinski
Shvarts Fanya Iserovna	1932	Ivye	Baranovichi	Kalinin	

Name	Year	Place	Region	Unit	Sub-unit
Shvarts Yudel Isaakovich	1915	Lida	Baranovichi	Kalinin	
Shvartsbart Khaim Davidovich	1911	Dibki, Belostokskaya obl.	Minsk	Ponomarenko	A.Nevski
Shvartsbord Mordukh Matusovich	1902	Rakov	Baranovichi	detachment ? 106	
Shvartsman Leiba Yeselevich	1921	Lenino, Pinsk region	Minsk	Ponomarenko	A.Nevski
Shvartsman Samuil Yakovlevich	1910	Belarusian Staff of Partisan Movement	Grodno	Samutin's group	gr. Kazakova
Shvartsshtein Genik Yakovlevich	1926	getto	Baranovichi	Lenin's komsomol	Kotovski
Shvedski Isar Yankelevich	1910	Dvorchany	Baranovichi	Lenin's komsomol	Kotovski
Shveidel Aron Izrailevich	1923	Slutsk	Pinsk	Komarov-Korzh's	2 group
Shverdinovski Girsh Yankelevich	1905	Starobin	Pinsk	Komarov-Korzh's	Komarov's 3rd group
Shvets Aleksandr Markovich	1905	Glussk	Minsk	Ponomarenko	Selnitski
Shvets Anna Moiseyevna	1898	Kopyl	Minsk	Chapayev	Shchors
Shvets Snaia Mironovich	1905	from the encirclement	Minsk	Underground RC and DC CP(b)B	Minsk underground CC of the CP(b)B
Shvindler Mira Samuilovna	1921	Belarusian Staff of Partisan Movement	Brest	groups of party leaders	Krotov's group
Shvoren Aron Girshevich	1923	Lakhva	Belostok	A.Nevski	
Shvorets Lilya Aronovna	1921		Baranovichi	Oktyabr	
Shebes Froim Srolevich	1888	Starye Dorogi	Minsk	Ponomarenko	A.Nevski
Shevakh Lev Bentsianovich	1924	Volozhin	Baranovichi	Chkalov	? 4 "Za Sovetskuyu Belarus"
Shevakhovich Aizik Nokhimovich	1922	Grodno	Baranovichi	Kirov	Za Sovetskuyu Belarus
Shevakhovich Berko Movshovich	1897	Lida	Baranovichi	Kalinin	
Shevakhovich Sonya Borisovna	1922	Lida	Baranovichi	Kirov	Iskra
Shevakhovich Khaya Moiseyevna	1901	Lida	Baranovichi	Kalinin	
Shevakhovich Yankel Berkovich	1927	Lida	Baranovichi	Kalinin	
Shevelevich Gita Elevna	1922	Minsk	Minsk	Shturmovaya	Frunze
Shevel Yakov Leibovich	1902	Belarusian Staff of Partisan Movement	Baranovichi	Gruppy partrabotnikov	Krastin's group
Shevrin Khaim Nisonovich	1895	Gantsevichi	Pinsk	Kirov	
Shevrina Fanya Khaimovna	1927	Lenin	Pinsk	Kirov	
Shevtsova Sonya Yakovlevna	1902	Bobruisk	Palesye	? 100	Igumnov and Babich's
Shedletski Yevsei Lvovich	1922	Minsk	Mogilev	208th regiment	
Sheikman Savik Yosifovich	1910	Jewish camp	Vitebsk	4th Belorusskaya	
Sheiler Mendel Khaimovich	1894	Mery	Vileyka	4th Belorusskaya	? 6
Shein I.A.					
Shein Lev Aleksandrovich	1915		Minsk	Razgrom (Crushing defeat)	
Sheinberg Lyuba Lvovna	1927	Minsk	Baranovichi	detachment ? 106	
Sheinberg Tevel	1923	Minsk	Baranovichi	18th Frunze	Kutuzov
Sheiner Zhenya Shmuilovich	1911	from the civil camp	Vileyka	4th Belorusskaya	? 6
Sheiner Yosif Khatskelevich	1909	Druya	Vileyka	4th Belorusskaya	? 2
Sheiner Menfel Khonovich	1894	Mery	Vileyka	4th Belorusskaya	? 2
Sheiner Khaim Yankelevich	1926	from the civil camp	Vileyka	4th Belorusskaya	? 6
Sheinin Marik Grigorevich	1932	Minsk	Baranovichi	detachment ? 106	
Sheinin Semen Leibovich	1911		Mogilev		Kazankova
Sheinker Asya Yakovlevna	1916	Minsk	Baranovichi	detachment ? 106	
Sheinman Mikhail Yakovlevich	1923	Mozyr district	Palesye	Lelchitskaya	Gorodiatichi Yefremov's detachmnt
Sheikhatovich Leva Mordukhovich	1902	Minsk	Baranovichi	Vpered (Forward)	Chkalov
Sheleman Yankel Mendelevich	1925	Novogrudok	Baranovichi		
Shelk Irma	1917		Brest	Za Sovetskuyu Belarus	Chkalov
Shelkovich Kalman Shevelevich	1910	Novogrudok	Baranovichi	Komsomolets	Kalinin
Shelkovich Sofiya Leibovna	1923	Derechin	Baranovichi	Pobieda	Pobieda
Shelomson David Mendelevich	1924	Bashenkovichi	Vitebsk	Sennenskaya brigade (Leonov's)	Vanteyev's
Shelkhatovich Leva Mordukhovich	1902	Minsk	Baranovichi	Chkalov	
Shelkevich Khaya E.	1926	Derechin	Baranovichi	Pobieda	Pobieda
Shelkovich Kalman Shevelevich	1910	Novogrudok	Baranovichi	Kalinin	
Shelyubinskaya Fanya Isaakovna	1923	Derechin	Baranovichi	Pobieda	Pobieda
Shelyubskaya Yudif Abramovna	1925	Slonim	Minsk	Burevestnik	Burevestnik
Shelyubski Viktor Isaakovich	1901	Derechin	Baranovichi	Leninskaya	hospital
Shelyubski Yosif Davidovich	1930	small town of Vishnevo	Baranovichi	Chapayev	Furmanov
Shelyubski Naum Isaakovich	1920	Novogrudok	Baranovichi	Kirov	Ordzhonikidze
Shelyubski Efroim Shlemovich	1903	Novogrudok	Baranovichi	Kalinin	
Shemshelevich Tema Moiseyevich	1906	Jewish camp	Vileyka	Voroshilov	headquarters' production group
Shemyatovets Ivan Vasilevich	1905	Minsk	Baranovichi	Kalinin	
Shenvald Pavel Lyudvikovich	1920	Lida	Baranovichi	Kalinin	
Shendlin Grigori Solomonovich	1915	Glubokoye	Minsk	1st Antifashistskaya	
Shenitski A.S.	1902	Baranovichi	Baranovichi	Pervomaiskaya	Pervomaiski
Shenitski Mikhail Yakovlevich	1924	Mozyr	Baranovichi	Grizodubova	Chkalov

Shenker Leontii Izrailevich	1912	Domanovo	Brest	Dzerzhinski	Molotov
Shenkman Abram-Movsha Yankelevich	1902	Glussk	Minsk	Ponomarenko	Gorbachev
Shenkman Vladimir Grigorevich	1895	getto, Glubokoye	Vileyka	CC of the CP(b)B	brigade sanitary service
Shenkman Mikhail	1913	from captivity	Vitebsk	Prudnikov's	Tabachnikov's
Shenkman Pavel Abramovich	1928	Glussk	Minsk	Ponomarenko	Gorbachev
Shenkman Samuil Abramovich		Minsk	Ponomarenko	Selnitski	
Shenkman Tatyana Grigorevna	1923	Glubokoye	Vileyka	CC of the CP(b)B	Denisov
Sheper ??? Izrailovich	1909	Belostok	Grodno	Samutin's group	Kirshner's group
Shepetinskaya Raya Isaakovna	1926	Slonim	Pinsk	Lenin	Kutuzov
Shepetnitski Izrail Leizerovich	1911	Ozernitsy	Baranovichi	Lenin's komsomol	Ponomarenko
Shepetnitski Movsha Lezerovich	1909	Slonim district	Baranovichi	Rokossovski	Ponomarenko
Shepetnitski Srol Leizerovich	1911	Ozeritsy	Baranovichi	Pobieda	Pobieda
Shepilenko Sofiya Timofeyevna	1913		Minsk	Voronyanski	Mstitel (Revenger)
Shepitinski Grigori Shlemovich	1925	Slonim	Pinsk	Lenin	Dzerzhinski
Shepitinski Yakov Isaakovich	1920	Slonim	Pinsk	Lenin	Dzerzhinski
Shepper Yosif Aronovich	1920	Galyk	Pinsk	Molotov	Shish
Shepsenvol Emma Naumovna	1926	Minsk	Baranovichi	detachment ? 106	
Shepsman Yasha Mendelevich	1925	Minsk	Baranovichi	Za Sovetskuyu Belarus	family detachment
Shepsonval Borukh Bentsiyanovich	1906	Radoshkovichi	Minsk	Voronyanski	Kotovski
Shepsonval Semen Yakovlevich	1927	Minsk getto	Baranovichi	Stalin	Bolshevik
Shepsonval Yakov Yefimovich	1926	Minsk getto	Baranovichi	Stalin	Bolshevik
Shepsonval Yakov Shayevich	1905	Minsk getto	Baranovichi	Stalin	Bolshevik
Sheptinskaya Eva Moiseyevna	1900	Lida, getto	Baranovichi	Pervomaiskaya	Zhdanov
Sheptinskaya Mariya Solomonovna	1925	Lida, getto	Baranovichi	Pervomaiskaya	Zhdanov
Sheptinski Solomon Ekhelevich	1888	Lida, getto	Baranovichi	Pervomaiskaya	Zhdanov
Shepshelevich Yakha Abramovna	1924	Dyatlovo	Baranovichi	Leninskaya	family detachment group
Sher Aron Lazarevich	1921	from captivity, Slutsk	Pinsk	Lenin	Frunze
Sher Ester Davidovna	1895	Minsk	Baranovichi	detachment ? 106	
Sheranski Fedor Yankelevich	1927	local	Baranovichi	Pobieda	Pobieda
Sherer Adam Borukhovich	1914	Slonim	Baranovichi	Vpered (Forward)	Sibiryak
Sheres Tuvia Efroimovich	1920	getto, Vilno	Vileyka	Voroshilov	Chapayev
Shereshovski Leizer Gershkovich	1909	Motol	Brest	Sverdlov	Makarevich
Sherman Yona	1897		Brest	Ponomarenko	Kirov
Sherman Leon OBoyatizovich	1896	Braslav	Vileyka	4th Belorusskaya	? 5
Sherman Mikhail Leonovich	1921	Braslav	Vileyka	4th Belorusskaya	? 5
Sherman Raisa Grigorevna	1914	Minsk	Minsk	Voronyanski	Kotovski
Sherman Roman Konstantinovich	1919	from captivity	Mogilev	? 537	
Sherman Semen Markovich	1918	Simferopol	Vitebsk	Nikitin's	? 1
Sherman Khaim Naftolovich	1916	Kletsk	Minsk	Chapayev	Ponomarenko
Sherman Tsalya Ilyich	1929	Minsk	Baranovichi	detachment ? 106	
Sherman Yudelis Benusovich	1915	from the Litovskaya brigade	Baranovichi	detachment ? 106	
Sherman Yakov Elevich	1903		Brest	Ponomarenko	Kirov
Sheftel Mariya I.	1919	small town of Khimry, Baranovichi region	Baranovichi	Vpered (Forward)	A.Nevski
Sheftel Sima Elevna	1921	Ivye	Baranovichi	Vpered (Forward)	A.Nevski
Sheshunski Lazar Gertsovich	1908	Minsk	Vitebsk	Nikitin's	? 1
Shidletski Fedor Davidovich	1924	Minsk	Minsk	Belarus	Belarus
Shikman Mikhail Khatenovich	1913	from captivity	Vitebsk	Prudnikov's	Myshko's
Shllyin's Genya Borisovna	1925	Bustki	Vileyka	Voroshilov	A.Nevski
Shiling Motik Abramovich	1919	from home	Baranovichi	Grizodubova	
Shilov David Moiseyevich	1899	Orsha	Mogilev	Chekist	? 1
Shilovitski Izrail Khaimovich	1915	Dyatlovo getto	Baranovichi	Kirov	Ordzhonikidze
Shimanovich Boris Isaakovich	1924	Naliboki	Baranovichi	Dzerzhinski	Dzerzhinski
Shimanovich Gita Yevelevna	1930	Rubezhevichi	Baranovichi	Kalinin	
Shimanovich Ilya Vulfovich	1916	Stolbtsy	Baranovichi	detachment ? 106	
Shimanovich Isaak Faibovich	1892	Naliboki	Baranovichi	Dzerzhinski	Dzerzhinski
Shimanovich Kiva Yevelevich	1901	Naliboki	Baranovichi	Kalinin	
Shimanovich Leya Elevna	1933	Rubezhevichi	Baranovichi		
Shimanovich Manya Borisovna	1918	Rubezhevichi	Baranovichi	Kalinin	
Shimanovich Movsha Borisovich	1930	Rubezhevichi	Baranovichi	Kalinin	
Shimanovich Fats Leibovich	1903	Rubezhevichi	Baranovichi	Kalinin	
Shimanovich Khasya Borisovna	1926	Rubezhevichi	Baranovichi	Kalinin	
Shimanovich Yakov Viktorovich	1919	from behind the front line	Minsk	Voronyanski	Mstitel (Revenger)
Shimanskaya Vera Mikhailovna	1912	Minsk	Pinsk		Chukhlai
Shimanskaya Zoya Yosifovna	1919	?	Baranovichi	Zhukov	
Shimanskaya Sonya Leizerovna	1917	Dvorets	Baranovichi	Kalinin	
Shimberg Mota Lvovna	1927	Minsk, getto	Baranovichi	Stalin	
Shimberg Khaim L.	1922	from the village	Vileyka	Budenny	Molotov
Shimonovich Shaya Khaimovich	1924	Mir	Baranovichi	Kalinin	
Shimshelevich Aron Ruvimovich	1878	Vileika	Minsk	Voronyanski	Kotovski

Shinder Rina Khaimovna	1904	Belostok	Grodno	Samutin's group	Kirshner's group
Shinitski Ovsei Solomonovich	1912	Gorodishche district	Baranovichi	25 years of the BSSR	Grozny
Shinker Lev Izrailevich	1912	Byten district	Brest	Sverdlov	Bozhenko
Shirokova Galina Ilinichna	1910	v. Kolodezhi	Minsk	Krasnoye znamya (Red Banner)	Krasnoye znamya (Red Banner)
Shitman Viktor Yakovlevich	1920	reccon. adm, RKKA, sent by the front staff	Gomel	formation headquarters of Gomel partisans	
Shif Yakov Maksimovich	1923	Minsk	Minsk	2nd Minskaya	Suvorov
Shifin Maksim Yosifovich	1918	Volkovyssk, camp	Belostok	A.Nevski	
Shifman Aron Izrailevich	1907	concentration camp	Pinsk	Kuibyshev	Shchors
Shifman Yosif Mikhailovich	1915	Poland	Pinsk	Molotov	Kalinin
Shifmanovich Nokhim Gertsevich	1922	Zheludok	Baranovichi	Leninskaya	Borba
Shifmanovich Yankel Yankelevich	1909	Zheludok	Baranovichi	Kalinin	
Shifrina Asya Vladimirovna	1915	Minsk	Baranovichi	detachment ? 106	
Shifris Aron Yakovlevich	1925	Baranovichi	Baranovichi	Grizodubova	Chkalov
Shikhman Ushar Borisovich	1922	Vinnitsa region	Brest	Ponomarenko	Kirov
Shishkevich Semen Mironovich	1913	N. Borisov	Minsk	Shchors	Chapayev
Shishko Falvyel Davidovich	1912	family detachment camp	Belostok	A.Nevski	
Shkirber Khenik Shmuilovich	1916		Minsk	Voronyanski	Pobieda
Shklovin Moisei Zalmanovich	1904	Molodechno district	Baranovichi	Chkalov	
Shklyut Aron Girshevich	1906		Vitebsk	Nikitin's	? 2
Shklyanevich Mendel Moiseyevich	1928	Mir	Baranovichi	Chkalov	
Shklyar Girsh Yakovlevich	1908	Grozovo, Minsk region	Minsk	Chapayev	Ponomarenko
Shklyar Zisia Srulevich	1921	from the encirclement	Mogilev	Mogilev undergroud of the RC CP(b)B	
Shklyar Isaak Mordukhovich	1916	Lida	Baranovichi	Kalinin	
Shklyar L.Kh.	1913		Minsk	Voroshilov	? 1
Shklyar Leizer Elevich	1922		Baranovichi	Oktyabr	
Shklyar Leon Elevich	1915	Tikhovka, Kopyl district	Minsk	Voroshilov	Patriots of Motherland
Shklyar Lyuba Zalmanovna	1912	Grozovo, Minsk region	Minsk	Chapayev	Ponomarenko
Shklyar Mora Meyerovna	1888	Grozovo, Minsk region	Minsk	Chapayev	Ponomarenko
Shklyar Pesya Volfovna	1922	Mir	Baranovichi	Chkalov	
Shklyar Frida Davidovna	1922	Lida	Baranovichi	Kalinin	
Shklyar Khaim Grigorevich	1890	Belarusian Staff of Partisan Movement	Palesye		Volkov's
Shklyar Khaim Mordukhovich					
Shklyar Khaya Samuilovna	1916	Grozovo	Baranovichi	18th Frunze	editorial stuff of the newspaper "Za Sovetskuyu Belarus"
Shklyar Shender Girshevich	1902	Lyuban district, Starosek	Minsk	Bragin	Davyvoda
Shkolnik Anna Abramovna	1914	Batsevichi, Klichev district	Mogilev	152-oi partisan regiment	battallion ? 3
Shkolnik Girsh Leizerovich	1879	Korelichi	Baranovichi	Kalinin	
Shkolnik Dunia Abramovna	1918	Batsevichi, Klichev district	Mogilev	partisan regiment ? 277	? 277
Shkolnik Zalman Izrailevich	1916	Yody	Vileyka	Spartak	? 3
Shkolnik Nina Faivelevna	1925	Kosov, Baranovichi region	Brest	Za Sovetskuyu Belarus	Suvorov
Shkolnik Perets	1912	Yody	Vileyka		Ponomarenko
Shkolnik Sofiya Abramovna	1924	Batsevichi, Klichev district	Mogilev	152-oi partisan regiment	battallion ? 3
Shkolnikovich Yakov Alterovich	1925	Dvorets	Baranovichi	Kalinin	
Shlapakova Lidiya Yakovlevna	1925	Sloboda	Minsk	Voronyanski	Kotovski
Shlapovit Armin AksemElyanovich	1919	from the working Magyar batallion	Pinsk	Sovetskaya Belarus	Chkalov
Shleimovich Abram Moiseyevich	1898	Kopyl	Minsk	Chapayev	Ponomarenko
Shleimovich Naum Abramovich	1907	Novogrudok	Baranovichi	Kirov	Za Sovetskuyu Belarus
Shleimovich Ruvim Abramovich	1924	Kopyl	Minsk	Chapayev	Ponomarenko
Shleimovich Sonya Rubinovna	1898	Kopyl	Minsk	Chapayev	Ponomarenko
Shleimovich Khaim Leizerovich	1914	Kopyl	Minsk	Chapayev	Ponomarenko
Shlemovich Khaim Zelikovich	1922	Turets	Baranovichi	Kalinin	
Shlesberg Izrail Isaakovich	1916	Naliboki	Baranovichi	Kalinin	
Shlesberg Perla Shlemovna	1915	Naliboki	Baranovichi	Kalinin	
Shlesberg Khaim Isaakovich	1914		Baranovichi	Rokossovski	
Shlekhter David Izrailevich	1924	Belostok	Baranovichi	Vpered (Forward)	A.Nevski
Shlekhter Moisei Nokhimovich	1912		Baranovichi	Oktyabr	
Shlipok Sara Leibovna	1917	Bereznyaki	Pinsk	Molotov	Kalinin
ShLyapin Yakov Grigorevich	1924	Lyuban district, Zhivun	Minsk	Bragin	Zaslonov
ShLyakhtovich Abram Isaakovich	1897	Lukov	Baranovichi	Kalinin	
Shmaragd Anna Sheyevna	1920	Warsaw	Baranovichi	detachment ? 106	
Shmeberg Khaim Isaakovich	1914	Naliboki	Baranovichi	Kalinin	

Shmeyerovich Girsh Khaimovich	1924	small town of Zheludok, getto	Baranovichi	Kirov	Ordzhonikidze
Shmerkin Aleksei Anatolevich	1927	Kopys, Orsha district	Vitebsk	1st Zaslonov	Kutuzov
Shmerkovich Abram Zalmanovich	1896	from the encirclement	Minsk	Bragin	Gastello
Shmerkovich Genya Meyerovna	1941	Voronovo	Baranovichi	Kalinin	
Shmerkovich Kellya Yankelevna	1921	Lida	Baranovichi	Kalinin	
Shmerkovich Meyer Yosifovich	1911	Voronovo	Baranovichi	Kalinin	
Shmerkovich Tevel Girshevich	1911	Novogrudok	Baranovichi	Kalinin	
Shmerkovich Yankel Girshevich	1905	Nesvizh	Baranovichi	Kalinin	
Shmerlis Zoya Yakovlevna	1929	Minsk	Baranovichi	detachment ? 106	
Shmetsler Mundak		from captivity	Gomel	Voroshilov	Voroshilov
Shmidt Grigori Bunimovich	1909	Serniki, Rovno region.	Pinsk	Shubetidze	Nemytov
Shmirkovich Yakub Gershevich	1905	Stolbtsy	Baranovichi	Kutuzov	
Shmit Yosif Grigorevich	1927	Lida	Baranovichi	Kalinin	
Shmuilovich Yosif Berkovich	1907	Momad	Baranovichi	Kalinin	
Shmuilovich Abram Tsalkovich	1927	Ivye, getto	Baranovichi	Stalin	Kirov
Shmuilovich Kiva Girshevich	1909	Novogrudok	Baranovichi	Kalinin	
Shmuilovich Lets Elevna	1902	Naliboki	Baranovichi	Kalinin	
Shmuilovich Maksim Abramovich	1910	Vselyub	Baranovichi	Kalinin	
Shmuilovich Matvei Aronovich	1917	Novogrudok getto	Baranovichi	Kirov	Ordzhonikidze
Shmuilovich Mikhail Mikhailovich	1924	Zhadun	Baranovichi	Pervomaiskaya	Ya.Kolas
Shmuilovich Moisei Mendelevich	1913	iz mestnykh	Baranovichi	Lenin's komsomol	Lenin's komsomol
Shmuilovich Mordukhai Shlemovich	1921	Gorodishche district	Baranovichi	25 years of the BSSR	Grozny
Shmuilovich Nikolai Mikhailovich	1921	Molchad	Baranovichi	Pervomaiskaya	Zhdanov
Shmukler Basya Isaakovna	1925	Ivye	Baranovichi	Kalinin	
Shmukler Yosif Abramovich	1893	v. Osipovichi	Vileyka		Za Sovetskuyu Belorus- siyu
Shmukler Isaak Movshovich	1890	Ivye	Baranovichi	Kalinin	
Shmukler Mordukh Mikhailovich	1924	Ivye	Baranovichi	Pervomaiskaya	Oktyabr
Shmukler Taiba Yankelevna	1902	Ivye	Baranovichi	Kalinin	
Shmukler Frida Isaakovna	1900	Ivye	Baranovichi	Kalinin	
Shmukler Khaya Isaakovna	1924	Ivye	Baranovichi	Kalinin	
Shmukler Tsilya Khenrikovna	1918	Stolbtsy	Minsk	Chapayev	Ponomarenko
Shmukler Shlema Beinusovich	1914	Kletsk	Minsk	Chapayev	Ponomarenko
Shmulevich Aleksandr Ilyich	1889	Minsk	Baranovichi	detachment ? 106	
Shmulevich Lazar Aleksandrovich	1923	Minsk getto	Baranovichi	Chapayev	Parkhomenko
Shmulevich Malka Bentsionovna	1925	Dyatlovo	Baranovichi	Leninskaya	Leninski
Shmulevich Matus Abramovich	1903		Baranovichi	Oktyabr	
Shmushkevich Fanya Gerasimovna	1923	Mir	Baranovichi	Za Sovetskuyu Belarus	Shturm
Shmushkovich Zusman Yankelevich	1886	concentration camp	Pinsk	Kuibyshev	Shchors
Shmushkovich Yakov Ostapovich	1926	Mir	Baranovichi	Zhukov	
Shnaider Mariya Berkovna	1937	Lida	Baranovichi	Kalinin	
Shnaider Nakhama Peisakovna	1905	Lida	Baranovichi	Kalinin	
Shnaiderler Kusel Girshovich	1919	Baranovichi	Brest	Za Sovetskuyu Belarus	brigade headquarters
Shneer David Moiseyevich	1904	Osveia	Vitebsk	Frunze	Frunze ? 1
Shneider Yefim Semenovich	1920	Minsk, Uzlyany	Minsk	2nd Minskaya	Kutuzov
Shneider Zhenya Samuilovich	1911	Jewish camp	Vileyka	4th Belorusskaya	? 6
Shneider Zusman Shmuilovich	1911	Mery	Vileyka	4th Belorusskaya	? 6
Shneider Mikhail Semenovich	1929	Minsk	Minsk	2nd Minskaya	Kutuzov
Shneider Mikhail Yankelevich	1911	Shchuchin	Baranovichi	Leninskaya	Borba
Shneider Nikhama Girshevna	1910	concentration camp, Krasnopolye	Gomel	Bolshevik	Bolshevik
Shneider Samuil Yosifovich	1915	Lida	Baranovichi	Kirov	Iskra
Shneider Semen Davidovich	1885		Minsk	2nd Minskaya	Kutuzov
Shneider Yankel Kalmanovich	1908	Ikiziya	Vileyka	Za Rodinu (For Motherland)	Kirov
Shneiderman Khelya Shulymovna	1924	from the forest	Pinsk	Molotov	Kalinin
Shneiderovich Mikhail Peisakhovich	1910	Minsk	Baranovichi	Chkalov	reserve group
Shneidman Meyer Shpatovich	1915		Vileyka	Gastello	brigade headquarters
Shneidman Sholom Shlemovich	1918	Smorgon	Baranovichi	Chkalov	
Shniper Moisei Aronovich	1911	Minsk	Minsk	Rokossovski	25 years of Oktyabr
Shnitman Asya Ilinichna	1923	Minsk getto	Baranovichi	Ivienets DC CP(b)B company	
Shnitman Yevsei Lvovich	1911	Minsk	Mogilev	208th regiment	
Shnitman Mariya Yefimovna (Mina Khaimovna)	1912	Minsk	Baranovichi	18th Frunze	Kutuzov
Shnitman Naum Shayevich	1907	Rakov	Baranovichi	Chkalov	
Shnitman Raya Khaimovna	1921	Dobraya	Mogilev	? 117	? 125
Shnitser Abram Borisovich	1924	Shklov	Mogilev	Chekist	? 20
Shnitser Zalman Geselevich	1895		Gomel	1st Gomelskaya	Kalinin
Shnitser Mariya Borisovna	1926	Shklov	Mogilev	Chekist	
Shnur Ilya Berkovich	1921	Slonim	Brest	Sikorski's headquarters	Shchors
Shnur Edvard Berkovich	1921	Slonim	Brest	Sikorski's headquarters	Shchors

Sholyukovski Semen Isaakovich	1912	Derechin	Baranovichi	Pobieda	Pobieda
Shor Ilya Mikhailovich	1917	from the prisoners of war camp Minsk	Minsk	Burevestnik	Gromov
Shossarski Viktor Abramovich	1930	Shumilino	Vitebsk	Ponomarenko	Chapayev
Shostak Polya Mordukhovna	1923	Minsk	Baranovichi	detachment ? 106	
Shostak Sonya Mordukhovna	1927	Minsk	Baranovichi	detachment ? 106	
Shostskis Mikhail Isaakovich	1911	Minsk	Vitebsk	Nikitin's	? 1
Shofer Izrail Abramovich	1921	Vilno	Vileyka		Suslov
Shofer Rafal Zalmanovich	1891	Novogrudok	Baranovichi	Kalinin	
Shokhman Boris Moiseyevich	1910	Bobruisk	Minsk	Kotovski	Shashury
Shpadel Abram Yankelevich	1908	Ivienets	Baranovichi	Kalinin	
Shpadel Eva Movshovna	1912	Ivienets	Baranovichi	Kalinin	
Shpaer Feliks Moiseyevich	1908	st. Lesnaya, Baranovichi region	Brest	Ponomarenko	Sovetskaya Belarus
Shpaizer Izrail Abramovich	1896	Kastekovtsy	Vileyka	Kutuzov	
Shpak Vladimir Petrovich	1918	from captivity	Pinsk	Lenin	Kutuzov
Shpak Gersha Berkovich	1887	Bryansk getto, Belostok region	Grodno	Vo imya Rodiny (In the name of Motherland)	Zhukov
Shparber Ruben Aronovich	1926	getto Dolginovo	Minsk	Voronyanski	Pobieda
Shparber Khaim Zelmanovich	1908	Krichev, from captivity	Mogilev	? 17	? 1
Shparberg Genya Izrailevna	1925	Kurenets	Baranovichi	Komsomolets	Kalinin
Shparberg Gita Khaimovna	1916	Minsk getto	Baranovichi	Stalin	Parkhomenko
Shparberg Izrail Zalmanovich	1924		Minsk	Voronyanski	Mstitel (Revenger)
Shparberg Isaak Yakovlevich	1923	Minsk getto	Baranovichi	Stalin	Parkhomenko
Shparkman Yosif Solomonovich	1918	Novogrudok, getto	Baranovichi	Stalin	Suvorov
Shparkman Sonya Leibovna	1917	Novogrudok, getto	Baranovichi	Stalin	Suvorov
Shper Yosif Aronovich	1920	Domachevo	Brest	Stalin	Voroshilov
Shpetorko Yosif Borisovich	1923	Kletsk	Minsk	Chapayev	Ponomarenko
Shpigel Aleksandr Lazarevich	1910	from ikhomirov's detachment	Brest	Flegontov	Litvinov's
Shpiz Raikhel Mendelevich	1919	getto	Vileyka	Voroshilov	Suvorov
Shpiler Irina Viktorovna	1922	Minsk getto	Grodno	Ponomarenko	Sokol
Shpilman Isaak Aizikovich	1918	from captivity	Minsk	Zheleznyak	? 5
Shpilman Tadzik Moiseyevich	1929	small town of Turets	Baranovichi	Chapayev	Chapayev
Shpilman Fedor Moiseyevich	1928	Turets	Baranovichi	Stalin	Chapayev
Shpirer Iadviga Moiseyevna	1917	Volkovyssk	Baranovichi	Chkalov	
Shpitalnik Yefim Moiseyevich	1910	from the encirclement	Minsk	Parkhomenko	Shchors
Shpitalnyi Boris Yakovlevich	1920	from captivity	Minsk	Voronyanski	Kotovski
Shpitalnyi Yefim Zalmanovich	1923	Western Byelorussia	Minsk	Chkalov	Gromov
Shpits Dmitri Moiseyevich	1913	Yukhnovichi	Pinsk	Shubetidze	Stalin
Shpitser Abram Borisovich	1924	Shklov	Mogilev		Yakimov's
Shporer Viktor Gershovich	1915	Poland	Pinsk	Molotov	Shish
Shporer Leon Gershkovich	1917	Vlodava (Poland)	Pinsk	Molotov	Shish
Shpreiregin Boris Samuilovich	1923	camp Kremenets	Minsk	Voronyanski	Suvorov
Shpreregent Leonid Samuilovich	1926	Pleshchenitsy	Minsk	Kalinin	Kalinin
Shpreregent Samuil Khaimovich	1884	Pleshchenitsy	Minsk	Kalinin	Kalinin
Shpringer Grigori Isaakovich	1929	Gorodok	Baranovichi	Chkalov	? 4 "Za Sovetskuyu Belarus"
Shpringer Yevgenii Itskovich	1922	Krasnoye, getto	Baranovichi	Chkalov	
Shpringer Sergei Itskovich	1924	Krasnoye, getto	Baranovichi	Chkalov	
Shpunt Shlema Shmuilovich	1880	Denisovichi, Krupki district	Mogilev	Ilyin's	? 30
Shraibaum Basya Pinusovna	1915	Dyatlovo	Baranovichi	Leninskaya	Leninski
Shraiber Vladimir Itskovich	1925	Mir	Baranovichi	Chkalov	
Shraiber Yosif Vilgelmovich	1915	Yugoslavian army	Palesye		Chapayev
Shraiber Yuzef	1915	detachment Suvorov	Palesye		Kotovski
Shraibman Leiba Lazarevich	1925		Minsk	Voronyanski	Mstitel (Revenger)
Shriro Shlema Yudelevich	1909	Glubokskoe getto	Minsk	1st Antifashistskaya	
Shtaiman Ilya Maksimovich	1904	Minsk	Minsk	Zheleznyak	? 1
Shtain Mariya Mairamovna	1914	Slonim	Brest	Sikorski's headquarters	Shchors
Shtal Lyait Khaimovich	1902	from captivity	Minsk	Zheleznyak	? 5
Shtambaum Semen Mikhailovich	1915	Savchenki	Vitebsk	Korotkin	? 1
Shtarkman Yosif Solomonovich	1917	Ivienets	Baranovichi	Stalin	Suvorov
Shtarkman Sonya Leibovna	1917	Ivienets, getto	Baranovichi	Stalin	Suvorov
Shteiman Feiga Yoselevna	1917	Minsk	Baranovichi	detachment ? 106	
Shteiman Yakov Isaakovich	1925	Minsk getto	Minsk	3rd Minskaya	Lazo
Shteim-Gard Faiva Yoselevich	1922	Jewish camp	Vileyka	Voroshilov	headquarters' production group
Shtein Boris Lvovich	1920	Kopyl getto	Minsk	Frunze	Budenny
Shtein Isaak	1916	Slonim	Brest	Sikorski's headquarters	Shchors
Shtein Nina Yosifovna	1926	Minsk	Minsk	Stalin	
Shtein Sara Yakovlevna	1924	Yody	Vileyka	Spartak	? 1
Shtein Semen	1921	Yody	Vileyka	Spartak	? 6

Shtein Tatyana	1924	Molodechno	Baranovichi	Chkalov	? 4 "Za Sovetskuyu Belarus"
Shteinbakh Grigori Abramovich	1903	Gomel	Gomel	formation headquarters of Gomel partisans	
Shteinbakh Grigori Zakharovich	1903	Grodno	Gomel		Kirov
Shteinberg Vladimir Lvovich	1913	Slonim	Pinsk	Budenny	Kotovski
Shteinblat Boris Solomonovich	1913	N. Sverzhen	Minsk	32nd Kalinin	Parkhomenko
Shteingart Yuri Matveyevich	1921		Vitebsk	Nikitin's	
Shteingrat Yefim Yosifovich	1920	Kobylniki, Myadel district	Vitebsk	Chapayev	detachments
Shtenberg Aleksandr	1918	Hungary, from the Magyar army	Palesye	? 125	Lukianchika
Shtengert Zalman Lvovich	1923	Dunilovichi	Vitebsk	Dubov's	? 4
Shtengort Solomon Isaakovich	1909	Bereznyaki	Vitebsk	Za Sovetskuyu Belarus	
Shterinfeld Shapsai Meyerovich	1907	Baranovichi	Brest	Sverdlov	Bozhenko
Shterkman David Timofeevich	1927	Ostrov, Lyakhovichi district	Pinsk	Molotov	Shish
Shterkman Kisel Timofeevich	1930	Ostrov, Lyakhovichi district	Pinsk	Molotov	Shish
Shtern Semen Abramovich	1924	Belostok	Grodno	Samutin's group	Kirshner's group
Shternbaum Monya Itskovich	1915	Lyubashov, Volyn region	Pinsk	Sovetskaya Belarus	Kutuzov
Shtiz Raikhel Mendelevich	1919	getto, Vilno	Vileyka	Voroshilov	Pobieda
Shtilman Aleksandr Isaakovich	1923	from captivity	Minsk	Shchors	Shchors
Shtok Sara	1922	Poland	Brest	Lenin	Zhukov
Shtokk Fana Ivanovna	1926	Kopyl getto	Minsk	Frunze	Budenny
Shtoltsman Rakhil Yosifovna	1914	Krasnaya Sloboda	Baranovichi	Kirov	
Shtravkhler Ionas Germanovich	1913	from captivity	Pinsk	Shubetidze	Kostyushko
Shtukmaister Mikhail Konstantinovich	1911	Chereya	Gomel	8th Rogachevskaya	? 255
Shtukmaister Mikhail Moiseyevich	1893	small town of Bobr	Minsk	Ponomarenko	Gvardeyets (Guardsman)
Shub Abram Isaakovich	1913	from the civil camp	Vileyka	4th Belorusskaya	? 6
Shub Mariya Isaakovna	1917	Chernevichi, Borisov district	Minsk	Shchors	Bolshevik
Shubaev Aleksandr Mikhailovich	1917	st. Sabibor (concentration camp), Poland	Brest	Stalin	Frunze
Shugol Gavriil Borisovich	1907	Belarusian Staff of Partisan Movement	Vileyka	Suvorov	
Shugol Zalman Borisovich	1892	from the civil camp	Vileyka	4th Belorusskaya	? 6
Shud Ivan Moiseyevich	1925	Krivichi	Vitebsk	Chapayev	detachments
Shud Ida Moiseyevna	1921		Vitebsk	Chapayev	detachments
Shud Sara Moiseyevna	1927		Vitebsk	Chapayev	detachments
Shulevich Mariya Yosifovna	1924	Ivanovo	Pinsk	Molotov	Lazo
Shulelisskaya Yevgeniya	1924	detachment Kalinin	Vileyka	Voroshilov	Suvorov
Shulelisski Yakov Lazarevich	1922	detachment Kalinin	Vileyka	Voroshilov	Suvorov
Shulin Yakov Mendelevich	1913	Shklov	Mogilev	Chekist	? 5
Shulgin Monya Abramovich	1913	Belarusian Staff of Partisan Movement	Gomel	Kozhar's	Shemyakin's group
Shuldkrot Basya LeontYevna	1910	Kuzmichi, Lyuban district	Minsk	Ponomarenko	A.Nevski
Shulken Raya Kheinovna	1920	Malinovka	Minsk	Voronyanski	Pobieda
Shulkin Khaim Sholomovich	1900	Minsk getto	Minsk	3rd Minskaya	Lazo
Shulman Abram Tankhelevich	1908	Baranovichi, getto	Baranovichi	Lida IDC	
Shulman Anna Lazarevna	1917	Radoshkovichi	Minsk	Shturmovaya	Shturm
Shulman Aron Semenovich	1905	Krivichi getto	Minsk	Kirov	? 4
Shulman Boris Nisonovich	1921	Maiski	Gomel		Kotovski
Shulman Venyamin Aronovich		Belarusian Staff of Partisan Movement	Vitebsk		
Shulman Grigori Zalmanovich	1907	Radoshkovichi	Minsk	Voronyanski	Kotovski
Shulman Dora Yevseyevna	1925	Chernevka, Borisov district	Minsk	Shchors	brigade headquarters
Shulman Yevsei Semenovich	1907	small town of Krivichi, Vileika region	Minsk	Starik (Old man)	
Shulman Yevsei Yakovlevich	1912	Zamoste	Palesye		Voroshilov
Shulman Ida Vladimirovna	1902	getto Knyaginino	Minsk	Voronyanski	Pobieda
Shulman Izrail Abramovich	1920	Nivki, Vileika region	Vitebsk	Chapayev	detachments
Shulman Ilya Srulevich	1911	Nivki	Minsk	Voronyanski	Kotovski
Shulman Mikhail Vulfovich	1921	Nivki, Vileika region	Vitebsk	Ponomarenko	Kirov
Shulman Moisei Semenovich	1912	Kurenets	Minsk	Voronyanski	Kotovski
Shulman Moisei Shabseevich	1910	small town of Lenino, Polesskaya region	Minsk	Parkhomenko	Shchors
Shulman Natan Pinkhusovich	1909	Vileika	Baranovichi	Leninskaya	Borba
Shulman Nekhama Abramovna	1912	Radoshkovichi	Minsk	Voronyanski	Kotovski
Shulman Olga Gdalevna	1906	Nivki, Vileika region	Vitebsk	Ponomarenko	Dovator

JEWISH PARTISANS IN BYELORUSSIA 1941-1944   311

Shulman Riva Abramovna	1917	Molodechno	Vitebsk	Ponomarenko	Kirov
Shulman Rubin Itselevich	1911	Krivichi	Minsk	Voronyanski	Kotovski
Shulman Samuil Volfovich	1921	Plinki, Vitebsk region	Vitebsk	Ponomarenko	Kirov
Shulman Samuil Moiseyevich	1914	from the German prison in Mozyr	Palesye	99th Kalinkovichskaya	Voroshilov
Shulman Faiba Yankovich	1897	Smilovichi	Mogilev	208th regiment	
Shulman Khaya GElevna	1908	Nivki, Vileika region	Vitebsk	Ponomarenko	Dovator
Shulman Etka Abramovna	1928	Ugrimovichi	Vitebsk	Chapayev	detachments
Shuman Fira Grigorevna	1922	getto, Vilno	Vileyka	Voroshilov	brigade headquarters
Shumakher Izrail Borisovich	1920	from the encirclement	Vitebsk	2nd Zaslonov	detachment razvedki
Shumakher Mikhail Isaakovich	1919	getto	Vileyka	Voroshilov	Istrebitel (Destroyer)
Shupakevich Raya Mordukhovna	1924	Minsk	Baranovichi	detachment ? 106	
Shur Chernya Yudovna	1903	Staroselye	Mogilev	Chekist	brigade headquarters
Shusland Shepsel Yakovlevich	1908	Minsk	Baranovichi	18th Frunze	Kutuzov
Shusman Leonid Meyerovich	1923	Mir	Baranovichi	Za Sovetskuyu Belarus	Shturm
Shusman Raisa Grigorevna	1914	Minsk	Minsk	Voronyanski	Borba
Shusser Nadezhda Grigorevna	1898	Lepel	Baranovichi	detachment ? 106	
Shuster Aron Girshevich	1912	Pruzhany	Brest	Ponomarenko	brigade headquarters
Shuster Boris Davidovich	1926	Ivanovo	Pinsk	Molotov	Lazo
Shuster Boria Naumovich	1932	Minsk	Baranovichi	detachment ? 106	
Shuster Galina Semenovna	1923	Mir, getto	Baranovichi	Za Sovetskuyu Belarus	Kirov
Shuster Girsh Berkovich	1922		Minsk	Ponomarenko	Selnitski
Shuster Girsh Semenovich	1923	Mir	Baranovichi	Za Sovetskuyu Belarus	Shturm
Shuster Golda Yudelevna	1922	Lenin	Pinsk	Kirov	Petrovich's
Shuster David Khononovich	1916	Dolginovo, Vileika region	Vitebsk	Frunze	brigade headquarters
Shuster Yelizaveta Mordukhovna	1910	Pruzhany	Brest	Ponomarenko	Dmitrov
Shuster Zelik Yudelevich	1924	Glussk	Palesye	? 100	Budenny
Shuster Zinaida Lvovna	1928	Minsk getto	Baranovichi	18th Frunze	Frunze
Shuster Yosif Ovseyevich	1909	Novogrudok getto	Baranovichi	Kirov	Ordzhonikidze
Shuster Isaak Pinkhusovich	1914	Novogrudok	Baranovichi	Kalinin	
Shuster Itsko Alterovich	1912	Jewish camp, Ivanovo	Pinsk	Shubetidze	Ordzhonikidze
Shuster Masha Zelikovna	1893	Lenin	Pinsk	Kirov	
Shuster Mina Elevna	1910	Minsk	Baranovichi	detachment ? 106	
Shuster Movsha Vsevolodovich	1917	from the forest	Pinsk	Molotov	Lazo
Shuster Rakhil Naumovna	1925	Minsk	Baranovichi	detachment ? 106	
Shuster Run Gershevich	1910	Pruzhany	Brest	Ponomarenko	Dmitrov
Shuster Semen Volfovich	1924	Rubezhevichi	Baranovichi	18th Frunze	Kutuzov
Shuster Faigel Alterovich	1898	Jewish camp, Ivanovo	Pinsk	Shubetidze	Ordzhonikidze
Shuster Khaim Fishelevich	1921	Belostok	Grodno	Samutin's group	Kirshner's group
Shuster Khonya Yudelevich	1928	Lenin	Pinsk	Kirov	
Shuster Shamshon Movshevich	1916	Belarusian Staff of Partisan Movement	Baranovichi	Pervomaiskaya	Zhdanov
Shuster Elyusya Yakovlevich	1931	Minsk	Baranovichi	detachment ? 106	
Shuster Elya Yosifovich	1922	Timkovichi	Minsk		Chapayev
Shuster Yudel Khaimovich	1893	Lenin	Pinsk	Kirov	
Shuster Iukel Aronovich	1927	K. Kashirski	Pinsk	Shubetidze	Kostyushko
Shusterman Abram Girshevich	1928	Lenino, Pinsk region	Minsk	Ponomarenko	A.Nevski
Shusterman Abram Isaakovich	1923	concentration camp Gantsevichi	Minsk	Chkalov	Zheleznyak
Shusterman Girsh Isaakovich	1891	Lakhva, Pinsk region	Minsk	Ponomarenko	A.Nevski
Shusterman Mikhail Semenovich	1906	Dvina district	Brest	Sikorski's headquarters	
Shusterman Yakov Girshevich	1927	Lakhva, Pinsk region	Minsk	Ponomarenko	A.Nevski
Shusterovich Venyamin Yegorovich	1902	Slonim	Brest	Sikorski's headquarters	Shchors
Shusterovich Khaya Yosifovna	1908	Novoselki, Borisov district	Minsk	Shchors	Bolshevik
Shut Lazar Izrailevich	1916	from Melnikov's brigade	Vileyka	Kalinin	? 2
Shut Rakhil Izrailevna	1912	from Melnikov's brigade	Vileyka	Kalinin	? 2
Shutan Mikhail Grigorevich	1924	Vileika region, Svent-sani	Minsk	Kalinin	Kalinin
Shukh Zalman Zalmanovich	1922	Baranovichi, from home	Baranovichi	Grizodubova	Matrosov
Shukh Monakh Germanovich	1916	from the Hungarian army	Brest	Stalin	Chernyak
Shukhman Leonid Meyerovich	1923	Gorodok	Baranovichi	Chkalov	
Shukhman Fanya Semenovna	1919	Sloboda	Gomel	Shemyakin's "Vpered (Forward)"	Makagonov's
Shushan Dora Aronovna	1924	Baranovichi	Baranovichi	Kalinin	
Shushan Zelik Naumovich	1912	village of Khukhrovo	Baranovichi	Kalinin	
Shushan Moisei Aronovich	1925	Baranovichi	Baranovichi	Kalinin	
Shushan Osher Naumovich	1913	Baranovichi	Baranovichi	Kalinin	
Shushan Shepsel Naumovich	1912	village of Lurovo	Baranovichi	Kalinin	
Shchekin Fedor Zalmanovich	1924	Orsha	Vitebsk	1st Zaslonov	Dyadia Kostya
Shcherbakov Izrail Mordovich	1913	getto	Vitebsk	Nikitin's	? 6

Shcherbakov Semen Mordovich	1919	getto	Vitebsk	Nikitin's	? 6
Shcherbakovskaya Raisa Borisovna	1923	Kabnia	Vitebsk	Lenin	Frunze
Shchukin Ilya Ilyich	1902	from captivity	Brest	Dzerzhinski	Chertkov
Shchupak David Moiseyevich	1906	Bobruisk	Minsk	Chkalov	Gromov
Evenchik Yakov Moiseyevich	1916	Minsk	Baranovichi	Dzerzhinski	Dzerzhinski
Evilevich Malka Leizerovna	1926	Novogrudok	Baranovichi	Leninskaya	Leninski
Edelbaum Genrikh Mikhailovich	1918	Belarusian Staff of Partisan Movement	Mogilev	Chekist	? 1
Edelberg Anna Moiseyevna	1925	Vlodava (Poland)	Pinsk	Molotov	Kalinin
Edelman Asya Zalmanovna	1914	getto, Vileika	Vileyka		Za Sovetskuyu Belorussiyu
Edelman Boris Lazarevich	1924	Vileika	Vileyka	Kalinin	? 2
Edelman German Yefimovich	1913	getto, Vileika	Vileyka		Za Sovetskuyu Belorussiyu
Edelman Gulli Lipmanovich	1897	Rakov	Baranovichi	Chkalov	
Edelshtein Abram Gershevich	1911	Domachevo	Brest	Lenin	Zelenin
Edelshtein Izrail Leizerovich	1922	Eishishki	Baranovichi	Lenin's komsomol	Lenin's komsomol
Edelshtein Yosif Arkadevichi	1912	from captivity	Minsk	Belarus	Za Rodinu (For Motherland)
Edelshtein Moisei Lipovich	1926	Epshishki	Baranovichi	Kalinin	
Edelshtein Rafail Lvovich	1922	iz politsii	Mogilev	? 13	? 719
Ezrakh Samuil Yevelevich	1920	Minsk	Baranovichi	detachment ? 106	
Eig Naum Yudelevich	1905	Minsk	Minsk	2nd Minskaya	Suvorov
Eig Fanya Lvovna	1925	Smilovichi	Baranovichi	detachment ? 106	
Eig Khasya Berkovna	1906	Minsk getto	Minsk	2nd Minskaya	Suvorov
Eig Esfir Yakovlevna	1898	Minsk	Baranovichi	detachment ? 106	
Eiges David Peisakhovich	1928		Vileyka		Ponomarenko
Eidel D.S.	1921	Ostrov	Baranovichi	Pervomaiskaya	Pervomaiski
Eidelzon Kalman Abramovich	1913	getto, Glubokoye	Vitebsk	Korotkin	Voroshilov
Eidelman Ilya Lipmanovich	1898		Baranovichi	Chkalov	
Eidelman Yosif Shlemovich	1924	Zaskovichi, Molodechno district	Minsk	Voroshilov	? 6
Eidelman Petr Yudelevich	1924	Radoshkovichi	Minsk	Bolshevik	
Eidelman Faiba Gdalevich	1909	Gorodok	Baranovichi	Chkalov	
Eidelman Khonya Yudelmovich	1922		Minsk	Voronyanski	brigade hospital
Eidelman Shepsha Borisovich	1905	from the civil camp	Vileyka	4th Belorusskaya	? 6
Eidelman Yulyan Yosifovich	1913	Gorodok	Baranovichi	Stalin	Suvorov
Eidelman Yakov Gdalevich	1924	Krasnoye	Baranovichi	Za Sovetskuyu Belarus	destroying battallion
Eidelman Yakov Faibovich	1913	Lida getto	Baranovichi	Vpered (Forward)	
Eidin Yosif Venyaminovich	1915	Minsk camp, prisoner of war	Minsk	3rd Minskaya	Lazo
Eidym Yosif Senderovich	1923	Dirosslo	Baranovichi	Kalinin	
Eingel Samuil Aizikovich	1927	from the civil camp	Vileyka	4th Belorusskaya	? 6
Einoig Lazar Motelevich	1916	Slutsk	Minsk	2nd Minskaya	Kutuzov
Eife Khatskel Abramovich	1907	getto, Vilno	Vileyka	Voroshilov	headquarters' production group
Eitser Mikhail Mikhailovich	1917	Uzda	Minsk	Chapayev	Ponomarenko
Ekkman Yankel Leibovich	1906	Dolginovo	Vileyka	Kutuzov	
Elevich David Elevich	1898	Novogrudok getto	Baranovichi	Kirov	Ordzhonikidze
Elevich Leya Sholomovna	1919	Derechin	Baranovichi	Leninskaya	Leninski
Elenberg Genya Zelikovna	1922	Mir	Baranovichi	Kalinin	
Elenberg Elena Khaimovna	1943	Mir	Baranovichi	Kalinin	
Elenberg Khaim Mendelevich	1913	Mir	Baranovichi	Kalinin	
Elenbukh Izrail Mordukhovich	1913	Minsk	Baranovichi	detachment ? 106	
Elentukh Boris Abramovich	1913	Minsk	Mogilev	Osipovichskaya VOG	? 210
Elentukh Boris Yakovlevich	1928	Minsk getto	Baranovichi	Za Sovetskuyu Belarus	Shturm
Elentukh Symon Izrailevich	1926	Minsk	Baranovichi	Za Sovetskuyu Belarus	family detachment
Elishkovich Sonya Itskovna	1916	Ivienets	Baranovichi		
Elomnitski Vulf Davidovich	1908	Lakhva	Baranovichi	Kirov	
Elbert Simon Menashevich					
Elvin Yefim Markovich	1925	Smolensk	Mogilev		Chapai
Elkanovich Mina Efroimovna	1918	Minsk	Baranovichi	detachment ? 106	
Elkina BroniSlava (Glory) Yosifovna	1924	Starye Dorogi district	Minsk	Kirov ? 100	Kutuzov ? 2
Elkina Elena Grigorevna	1924	Minsk	Baranovichi	Vpered (Forward)	Bolshevik
Elkina Zhenya Davidovna	1901	Starye Dorogi	Minsk	Kirov ? 100	brigade headquarters
Elkina Roza Yosifovna	1925	Starye Dorogi district	Minsk	Kirov ? 100	Kutuzov ? 2
Elkina Sofiya Pavlovna	1925	Minsk	Minsk	Shturmovaya	Grozny
Elkind Zyama Izrailevich	1908	Borisov	Baranovichi	detachment ? 106	
Elkind Ida Lazarovna	1910	Borisov	Baranovichi	detachment ? 106	
Elkind Moisei Grigorevich	1924	Minsk getto	Baranovichi	Chapayev	Parkhomenko
Elkind Roza Zalmanovna	1936	Minsk	Baranovichi	detachment ? 106	

JEWISH PARTISANS IN BYELORUSSIA 1941-1944   313

Elman Aleksandr Benyaminovich	1919	detachment n/a Kirov, brigade n/a Ponomarenko	Grodno		Kalinin
Elman Yosif Venyaminovich	1922	Pruzhany	Brest	Ponomarenko	Kirov
Elman Isaak Faivelevich	1890	Radoshkovichi	Minsk	Voronyanski	Kotovski
Elman Fanya Isaakovna	1923	Radoshkovichi	Minsk	Voronyanski	Kotovski
Elman Shmul Benyaminovich	1919	Ruzhany	Brest	Ponomarenko	Kirov
Elperina BroniSlava (Glory) Genrikhovna	1909	Minsk	Baranovichi	Chkalov	
Elterman Genya Aronovna	1918	Minsk	Minsk	2nd Minskaya	Kutuzov
Elterman Roza Notovna	1915	Gorodok	Baranovichi	Chkalov	
Elterman Foma Natovich	1922	Gorodok	Baranovichi	Chkalov	
Engel Dora Movshevna	1919	getto, Slutsk	Pinsk	Budenny	Voroshilov
Engel Meyer Davidovich	1915	Ivanovo	Pinsk	Shubetidze	Stalin
Engel Nosel Davidovich	1920	K. Kashirski	Pinsk	Shubetidze	Chapayev
Engel Roza	1923	from the civil camp	Vileyka	4th Belorusskaya	? 6
Engel Tevel Shmuilovich	1914	Ivye	Baranovichi	Kalinin	
Engelshtern Leizer Abramovich	1900	Vilno	Baranovichi	Kalinin	
Engorn Grisha Isaakovich	1914	Yody	Vileyka	Spartak	? 5
Enzemski Sholom Borukhovich	1918		Baranovichi	Oktyabr	
Entin Lev Grigorevich	1919	RKKA	Minsk	Special groups	Chervyakov's group
Entin Semen Mikhailovich	1910	from the prisoners of war camp Bobruisk	Minsk	Parkhomenko	Ordzhonikidze
Epelbaum Abram Zundolevich	1924	Iasevichi	Brest	Ponomarenko	Dmitrov
Epelbaum Isaak Mordukhovich	1907	Ivanovo	Pinsk	Molotov	Potalakh
Epelman Mikhail Yosifovich	1924	getto	Minsk	Razgrom (Crushing defeat)	
Epelman Tsilya Yosifovna	1921	getto	Minsk	Razgrom (Crushing defeat)	
Epelshtein Stepan Yakubovich	1923	concentration camp, Vlodava	Pinsk	Molotov	Kalinin
Epengeim Raya Izrailevna	1924	Minsk	Baranovichi	detachment ? 106	
Epshtein Aizik Yevseyevich	1924	Glussk	Brest	? 99 Gulyaev	Grabko
Epshtein Aizik Meyerovich	1895	Klichev	Mogilev	partisan regiment ? 277	? 277
Epshtein Aleksandr Lvovich	1917	from captivity	Mogilev		? 345
Epshtein Aleksandr Mikhailovich	1898	Glussk	Palesye	Lelchitskaya	Tsikunkov's
Epshtein Aleksandr Samuilovich	1925	Shchedrin	Palesye	? 123	Artyushka's
Epshtein Aleksei Petrovich	1920	from captivity	Vileyka	Frunze	special group Bogatyreva
Epshtein Anatoli Ilyich	1917	Minsk getto	Baranovichi	Chapayev	Parkhomenko
Epshtein Anna Mikhailovna	1915	Polotsk	Minsk	Chapayev	Ponomarenko
Epshtein Basya Mikhailovna	1901	Minsk	Baranovichi	detachment ? 106	
Epshtein Boris Fomich	1926	concentration camp Gantsevichi	Minsk	Chkalov	Zheleznyak
Epshtein Vladimir Abramovich	1910	Slutsk	Baranovichi	Zhdanov	
Epshtein David Motolevich	1924	Lyakhovichi	Pinsk	Lenin	Kutuzov
Epshtein Elena Vladimirovna	1921	Glussk	Palesye	? 123	Krasny Oktyabr
Epshtein Yelizaveta Moiseyevna	1907	Usakino, Klichev district	Mogilev		? 760 Berezovski
Epshtein Izrail Samuilovich	1924	Shchedrin	Palesye		Kirov
Epshtein Ilya Mikhailovich	1917	Minsk getto	Baranovichi	Ponomarenko	Vasilevski
Epshtein Leiba Yankelevna	1904	Novy Sverzhen	Baranovichi	Kalinin	
Epshtein Leya Borisovna	1922	Novogrudok	Baranovichi	Kalinin	
Epshtein Leon Nakhmanovich	1901	Vilno	Baranovichi	Kalinin	
Epshtein Liba Aronovna	1918	Lida	Baranovichi	Kalinin	
Epshtein Mariya Venyaminovna	1923	Minsk	Minsk	2nd Minskaya	Kutuzov
Epshtein Mikhail Yevseyevich	1926	Glussk	Palesye	? 100	Budenny
Epshtein Misha Solomonovich	1932	Minsk	Baranovichi	detachment ? 106	
Epshtein Monya Isaakovich	1923	Molchad	Baranovichi	Pobieda	Pobieda
Epshtein Mofisa Samoilovich	1910	Gorodishche district	Baranovichi	Pobieda	Pobieda
Epshtein Nokhim Borukhovich	1909	Lenin	Pinsk	Komarov-Korzh's	4 group
Epshtein Peisakh Yankelevich	1911	Novy Sverzhen	Baranovichi	Kalinin	
Epshtein Raisa Mironovna	1925	Minsk getto	Grodno	Ponomarenko	Sokol
Epshtein Regina Leonovna	1939	Vilno	Baranovichi	Kalinin	
Epshtein Samuil Abramrvich	1891	Shchedrin	Palesye		Kirov
Epshtein Samuil Girshevich	1910	from captivity	Grodno	Vo imya Rodiny (In the name of Motherland)	Kutuzov
Epshtein Sonya Aizikovna	1918	Glussk	Minsk	Ponomarenko	Selnitski
Epshtein Sofiya Yefimovna	1927	Klichev	Mogilev		? 760 Berezovski
Epshtein Sofiya Markovna	1909	Rudnya, Smolensk region	Baranovichi	Leninskaya	Leninski
Epshtein Khaim Vulfovich	1916	Klichev	Mogilev	partisan regiment ? 277	Klichev DC of CP(b)B
Epshtein Khaim Leibovich	1922	Dyatlovo	Baranovichi	Leninskaya	Leninski
Epshtein Khana Shevelevna	1898	Rubezhevichi	Baranovichi	Kalinin	
Epshtein Khaya Aronovna	1924	Derechin	Baranovichi	Pobieda	Pobieda

Epshtein Khonya Borisovich	1928	Shepelevichi	Mogilev	Chekist	? 31
Epshtein Tsilya Izrailevna	1915	otr. n/a Shchors, br. n/a Chapaev	Minsk	A.Nevski	Stalin
Epshtein Tsypa Markovna	1906	Vilno	Baranovichi	Kalinin	
Epshtein Yakov Khononovich	1922	concentration camp Gantsevichi	Brest	? 99 Gulyaev	Grabko
Erdman Naum Borisovich	1904	Minsk	Baranovichi	detachment ? 106	
Erenburg Boris Davidovich	1903	Kitin, Parichi district	Palesye	? 123	Kovalenko's
Erenburg Boris Leibovich	1898	Parichi, from captivity	Palesye		Volkov's
Erenburg Grigori Borisovich	1927	Kitin, Parichi district	Palesye	? 123	Kovalenko's
Erenburg Nikolai Naumovich	1928	Shchedrin	Mogilev	208th regiment	left the detachment from the moment organization
Erkin Girsha Nasonovich	1903	N. Belitsa	Gomel	Bolshevik	Bolshevik
Erlakh Yankel Shevelevich		Palesye	otdelnyi Lelchitski		
Erlikh Aleksandra Khilevna	1925	N. Sverzhen	Minsk	Chapayev	Ponomarenko
Erlikh Isaak Abramovich	1935	Dokudovo	Baranovichi	Kalinin	
Erlikh Semen Moshkovich	1925	Vlodava (Poland)	Pinsk	Molotov	Lazo
Erlikhman Movsha Barukhovich	1915	Baranovichi	Baranovichi	Kalinin	
Erman Semen Moiseyevich	1916	Makarovo	Grodno		Za Rodinu (For Motherland)
Eskin Semen Naumovich	1919	Belarusian Staff of Partisan Movement	Baranovichi	Pervomaiskaya	Oktyabr
Esterkin Idel Shmerkovich	1917	Stolbtsy, getto	Baranovichi	Chapayev	Parkhomenko
Esterovich Solomon Natanovich	1920	Kozyany	Vileyka	Spartak	? 1
Estrein Isaak Samuilovich	1916	Baranovichi	Baranovichi	Kalinin	
Estrin Abram Leizerovich	1908	from captivity	Mogilev	? 537	
Estrin Venia Shlemovich	1917	Jewish camp	Vileyka	Spartak	? 2
Estrin Izrail Shlemovich	1923	from the civil camp	Vileyka	4th Belorusskaya	? 6
Estrin Meyer Shlemovich	1912	Jewish camp	Vileyka	Spartak	? 2
Estrin Noson Shlemovich	1914	from the detachment "Spartak"	Vileyka	4th Belorusskaya	? 6
Estrin Semen Zalmanovich	1919	Sharkovshchina	Vileyka	1st Suvorov	Chkalov
Estrina Mllya Movshevna	1924	Kurenets	Vileyka	Dovator	Furmanov
Estrina Sarra Moiseyevna	1918	Minsk	Baranovichi	detachment ? 106	
Estrov Yosif Vulfovich	1913	from the civil camp	Vileyka	4th Belorusskaya	? 6
Estrov Shepsha Vulfovich	1900	from the civil camp	Vileyka	4th Belorusskaya	? 6
Eskin Semen Naumovich	1919	Belarusian Staff of Partisan Movement	Baranovichi	Gruppy partrabotnikov	Chertkov's group
Etkin Mikhail Mendelevich	1925	Krulevshchizna	Vitebsk	Rokossovski	Kotovski
Etman Leiba Abramovich	1907	from the civil camp	Vileyka	4th Belorusskaya	? 6
Yudevich Dmitri Meyerovich	1911	Pruzhany	Brest	Chapayev	Malenkov
Yudevich Regina Yefimovna	1915	Pruzhany	Brest	Chapayev	Malenkov
Yudina Lyuba	1922	from the civil camp	Vileyka	4th Belorusskaya	? 6
Yudkevich Naum Vladimirovich	1914	from captivity	Minsk	A.Nevski	Lomatko
Yudkevich Sima Abramovna	1907	st. Lesnaya, Baranovichi region	Brest	Ponomarenko	Sovetskaya Belarus
Yudkovski Aleksandr Yefimovich	1912	Byten	Brest	Ponomarenko	Sovetskaya Belarus
Yudkovski Boris Yefimovich	1906	Byten	Brest	Ponomarenko	Sovetskaya Belarus
Yudovich Yakov Movshevich	1920	Yachnoye, Kalinkovichi district	Brest	? 99 Gulyaev	Grabko
Yuzhuk Itsko Gershevich	1925	detachment Kaganovich	Pinsk	Kuibyshev	Ordzhonikidze
Yukshtein Genya Gelevichuvna	1925	Poland	Brest	Stalin	Chernyak
Yukshtein Mikhail Gelevich	1922	Poland	Brest	Stalin	Chernyak
Yulevich Rozaliya Abramovna	1924	Lenin	Pinsk	Molotov	Kalinin
Yulevich Khaim Mordukhovich	1924	concentration camp. Gantsevichi	Minsk	A.Nevski	Bondarovets
Yungelson Rufim Maksimovich	1923	from the civil camp	Vileyka	4th Belorusskaya	? 6
Yuryevich Yankel Nosovich	1904	Rakhovichi	Pinsk	Lenin	Chapayev
Yurkanski Shlema Khaimovich	1925	Lida	Baranovichi	Kalinin	
Yutilevskaya Lyubov Girshevna	1916	Byten	Brest	Ponomarenko	Sovetskaya Belarus
Yushkevich P. M.		Minsk	Minsk	Shturmovaya	Grozny
Yablonka Leizer Shlemovich	1918	Poland	Brest	Stalin	Chernyak
Yablonka Semen Aronovich	1918	Poland	Pinsk	Molotov	Shish
Yablonski Boris Zelmanovich	1921	Kobrin	Pinsk	Molotov	Suvorov
Yabloshevskaya Anna Markovna	1915	Minsk	Minsk	Bolshevik	
Yablynko Khenek Khonovich	1920	getto N. Sverzhen	Minsk	Chapayev	Ponomarenko
Yazvin Itska Izrailevich	1920	Berezovo, Gressk district	Minsk		Chapayev
Yakimovskaya Zhenya	1923	Slonim	Brest	Ponomarenko	Sovetskaya Belarus
Yakimovski Abram Berkovich	1920	detachment Kaganovich	Pinsk	Kuibyshev	Ordzhonikidze
Yakobi Semen Yosifovich	1920	from captivity	Vitebsk	Nikitin's	? 6

Yakobson Lazar Leonidovich	1912	Minsk	Vileyka	Frunze	brigade headquarters
Yakovchuk Mariya Moiseyevna	1910	Orsha	Mogilev	? 35	
Yakubov Semen Isaakovich	1904	from the encirclement	Gomel	1st Gomelskaya	? 1 Chapayev
Yakubovich Aleksandr Grigorevich	1916	Minsk getto	Baranovichi	Shchors	Shchors
Yakubovich Yelizaveta Yevseyevna	1916	Minsk getto	Baranovichi	Shchors	Chapayev
Yakubovich Ivan Yakovlevich	1915	working column of the Magyar army	Brest	Dzerzhinski	Molotov
Yakubovich Meyer Berkovich	1911	Novoyelnya	Baranovichi	Kalinin	
Yakubovich Natan Abramovich	1905	getto	Vileyka	Voroshilov	Chapayev
Yakubovich Serafima Davydovna	1920	Gorodishche district	Baranovichi	25 years of the BSSR	Budenny
Yakubovich Yulyan Yankelevich	1918	Belostok	Grodno	Samutin's group	Kirshner's group
Yakubovich Yakov Abramovich	1912	N. Sverzhen	Minsk	Chapayev	Ponomarenko
Yakubovski Aron Pinkhusovich	1911	Novogrudok	Baranovichi	detachment ? 106	
Yakshinko Ianina Ivanovna	1909	s/k Rusinovo	Vitebsk	Nikitin's	brigade headquarters and reconnaissance platoon
Yaloveser Vera MozElevna	1925	Minsk	Baranovichi	Chkalov	reserve group
Yalovitser Bentsian Modelevich	1927	Minsk	Baranovichi	detachment ? 106	
Yalovitser Yosif Modelevich	1923	Minsk	Baranovichi	Ponomarenko	
Yalovski Yudel Yoselevich	1915	Turets	Baranovichi	Kalinin	
Yamnik Mendel Aizikovich	1923	Minsk	Baranovichi		
Yaninski Yakov Avelevich	1921	Novogrudok	Baranovichi	Pobieda	Pobieda
Yaniska Sheina Rubinovna	1914	detachment "Mest"	Vileyka	Voroshilov	headquarters' production group
Yankelevich Arkadi Markovich	1909	from behind the Bug	Brest		Kotovski
Yankelevich Boris Mordukhovich	1913	Novogrudok	Baranovichi	Kalinin	
Yankelevich Volf Elyashevich	1910	Lida	Baranovichi	Lenin's komsomol	Lenin's komsomol
Yankelevich Izrail Yudelevich	1910	Novogrudok	Baranovichi	Oktyabr	
Yankelevich Yosif Kopelevich	1902	Minsk	Minsk	2nd Minskaya	Kutuzov
Yankelevich Yosif Simkhovich	1915	Kopyl	Minsk	Chapayev	Ponomarenko
Yankelevich Lev Abramovich	1924	Radun	Baranovichi	Lenin's komsomol	Lenin's komsomol
Yankelevich Lev Moiseyevich	1913	Kopyl getto	Minsk	Frunze	Budenny
Yankelevich Mariya Abramovna	1902	Minsk	Minsk	2nd Minskaya	Kutuzov
Yankelevich Movsha Yudelevich	1920	Slonim	Brest	Sikorski's headquarters	Shchors
Yankelevich Nota Davidovich	1898	Lyubcha	Baranovichi	Kalinin	
Yankelevich Ruvim Benyaminovich	1909	Baranovichi	Minsk	Voroshilov	Kotovski
Yankelevich Khaya Moiseyevna	1922	Novogrudok	Baranovichi	Kirov	Ordzhonikidze
Yankelevich Yakov Yudelevich	1904	Novogrudok	Baranovichi	Oktyabr	
Yankelevski Shepshel Abramovich	1900	Turets, Grodno region	Minsk	Chapayev	brigade headquarters
Yankel Shlema Movshovich	1904	Kopyl	Minsk	Chapayev	Ponomarenko
Yankilevich Rubin Yakovlevich	1904	Ivye	Baranovichi	Kirov	Iskra
Yanovitski Moisei Mendelevich	1911	from captivity	Mogilev	1st Bobruiskaya	? 751
Yanovich Ivan Yosifovich	1929	Mery	Vileyka	4th Belorusskaya	? 6
Yanovich Konstantin Osipovich	1905	Vileika region	Vileyka	4th Belorusskaya	? 6
Yanovskaya Khaya Girshevna	1923	Myadel district	Vitebsk	2nd Belorusskaya	
Yanson Volf Davidovich	1918	Novogrudok	Baranovichi	Kalinin	
Yanus Kopelman Sh.	1927	Poland	Brest	Lenin	Zhukov
Yanushevich Boris Abramovich	1916	Derechin	Baranovichi	Pobieda	Pobieda
Yanushevich Lev Abramovich	1913	Derechin	Baranovichi	Pobieda	Pobieda
Yanushkevich Khana NusElevna	1919	Derechin	Baranovichi	Leninskaya	hospital
Yanushkevich Tsilya Zelmanovna	1915	Derechin	Baranovichi	Leninskaya	hospital
Yarmovski Shlema Shimonovich	1907	Novogrudok	Baranovichi	Kalinin	
Yaskulski Shlema Itskovich	1925	Khomsk	Pinsk	Molotov	Shish
Yastshomb Mark Moiseyevich	1901	v. Osipovichi	Vileyka		Za Sovetskuyu Belorussiyu
Yastshomb Roza Samuilovna	1909	v. Osipovichi	Vileyka		Za Sovetskuyu Belorussiyu
Yasyuchenya Sofiya Davidovna	1919	B. Raevka, Kopyl district	Minsk	Chapayev	Shchors
Yatvitski Khaim B.	1925	Dyatlovo	Baranovichi	Pobieda	Pobieda
Yakhliel Roman Yefimovich	1909	Klimovichi district	Mogilev	? 61	
Yakhnes Isaak Berkovich	1916	Gorodok	Baranovichi	Za Sovetskuyu Belarus	family detachment
Yakhnich Naum Isaakovich	1922	Starobin	Pinsk	Komarov-Korzh's	Komarov's 3rd group
Yakhnich Yankel Isaakovich	1923	Starobin	Pinsk	Komarov-Korzh's	1 group

List of 1023 Fallen Jewish Partisans

#	Name	Year	Place	Date	Region	Unit
1	Abelshtain Azriel Leizerovich	1923	Eishinki	03/03/1944	Baranovichi	Lenin Comsomol
2	Abramov Mikhail Yosifovich	1917		04/08/1942	Minsk	Stalin
3	Abramov Mikhail Isaakovich			04/02/1942	Baranovichi	Ponamorenko
4	Abramovich Itska Aizikovich	1923	Zheludok	22/03/1944	Baranovichi	
5	Abramovich Leiba Leizerovich	1916	Dvorets	01/05/1943	Baranovichi	Kirov
6	Abramovich Mikhail	1915	Ostra	29/12/1942	Baranovichi	25 years of the BSSR
7	Abramovich Sarra Salomonovna	1923	Mir	01/08/1943	Baranovichi	Za Sovetskuyu Belarus
8	Abramski Yona Yefimovich	1912	Suvalki	01/06/1943	Baranovichi	Za Sovetskuyu Belarus
9	Aginski Fedor Borisovich	1904	Grodno	24/07/1943	Baranovichi	Chapayev
10	Agulnik Mikhail Rubovich	1921	Derechin	10/06/1944	Baranovichi	Pobieda
11	Aizenberg David Aizikovich	1904	Logoisk	24/06/1944	Minsk	Dyadya Koya's
12	Ainbinder Viktor Borisovich	1925		01/10/1943	Minsk	Narodnye mstiteli
13	Ainshtein Mikhail	1913	Deri	01/07/1943	Brest	Ponamorenko
14	Akselrod Boris-Yuda Leibovich	1914	Minsk	05/06/1944	Baranovichi	Ponamorenko
15	Akselrod Zyama Izrailevich	1916	Minsk	18/11/1943	Baranovichi	
16	Akselrod Mikhail Berkovich	1922	Borki	03/09/1943	Baranovichi	Za Sovetskuyu Belarus
17	Aksenkrug Khaim Isaakovich	1910			Mogilev	
18	Albertshtein Meyer Leibovich	1910	Ive	22/03/1943	Baranovichi	Kirov
19	Algerovich N.			02/07/1943	Minsk	Stalin
20	Alperovich Afroim	1925	Minsk	01/08/1943	Baranovichi	Chapayev
21	Alperovich Genya Shlemovich	1927		18/11/1943	Vileika	Voroshilov
22	Alperovich Yosif Mendelevich	1904		25/12/1942	Vitebsk	Chapayev
23	Alperovich Motak Rubinovich	1924		20/02/1944	Vitebsk	Ponamorenko (Utkina)
24	Antlyas Shaya Itskovich	1919	Luninets district, Lakhva	24/08/1943	Minsk	Kotovski
25	Arisman Yosif Yefimovich	1922	Minsk	24/01/1944	Baranovichi	
26	Aronov Abram Isaakovich	1923	Mogilev	13/08/1942	Mogilev	? 47 "Pobieda"
27	Atlas Eugeni	1913		01/12/1943	Baranovichi	Lenin's
28	Baran Isaak Faivovich	1924	Voronovo	21/12/1943	Baranovichi	Kirov
29	Barats Yonas Zelikovich	1903	Minsk	05/08/1943	Baranovichi	Chapayev
30	Barch Lev Movshevich	1924	Alitus	14/06/1944	Baranovichi	Lenin Comsomol
31	Barshai Yakov Grigorevich	1914		19/06/1944	Minsk	Dyadya Koya's
32	Basikhis Lev Borisovich	1902	Minsk	01/03/1943	Minsk	Narodnye mstiteli
33	Baskina			02/07/1943	Minsk	Stalin
34	Bass S.			02/07/1943	Minsk	Stalin
35	Begelman Anatoli Borisovich	1915	Nikopol	18/05/1944	Minsk	Burevestnik
36	Bekenshtein Ilya Mordukhovich	1924	Derechin	01/03/1944	Baranovichi	Pobieda
37	Beker Ivan Yemelyanovich	1909		01/05/1943		Neulovimye
38	Bekker Isaak Zelikovich	1916		14/04/1943	Vitebsk	Prudnikov's
39	Bekker Sofia Isaakovna	1924	Sinaiskie Kolonny, Bar. obl, Zelv r-n	17/06/1944	Baranovichi	Pobieda
40	Belenki Aizik Grigorevich	1915		19/05/1943	Brest	party leadres' groups sent to the region
41	Beloboroda Yosif Izrailevich	1907	Warsaw	30/03/1944	Baranovichi	
42	BiYelsk Ida Khonovna		Novogrudok	01/10/1943	Baranovichi	Kirov
43	Belyavski Leonid Abramovich	1922		17/05/1943	Vitebsk	Za Sovetskuyu Belarus
44	Bendtsman Isaak Mordukhovich	1905			Minsk	Chkalov
45	Benenski Yosif			01/12/1942	Baranovichi	Lenin's
46	Benuman Khaya Moiseyevna	1918			Minsk	Chkalov
47	Berger Yakov Ruvinovich	1914	Kopyl	16/02/1944	Belostok	
48	Bergfart Nikolai Yevseyevich	1920		15/08/1944	Vitebsk	1st Zaslonov
49	Berezin Aron Matveyevich	1911		02/09/1943	Brest	
50	Berezovski Shade Yakovlevich	1919		25/02/1944	Pinsk	Pinsk
51	Berzon Aron Mendelevich	1915		06/06/1944	Vileika	4th Byelorussian
52	Berkovich Aron Sholomovich	1921	Radun	24/01/1944	Baranovichi	Lenin Comsomol
53	Berkovich Mikhail Berkovich	1925	Stolbtsy	01/06/1943	Baranovichi	Za Sovetskuyu Belarus
54	Berman Yosif Yankelevich	1912		04/05/1944	Vileika	CC of the CP(b)B
55	Berman Yudik Yankelevich	1912			Minsk	Frunze
56	Bernak Izrail Leizerovich	1928		25/03/1943	Minsk	
57	Bernak Sholom Leizerovich	1893	Mir	07/01/1944	Baranovichi	
58	Bernshtein Shavel Aizikovich	1898		07/03/1942	Mogilev	? 208 Stalin
59	Binun Pavel Yefimovich	1910		12/07/1942	Minsk	Narodnye mstiteli
60	Birman Boris Abramovich	1918	Olsa	12/07/1944	Vileika	1st Suvorov
61	Blat Isaak Leibovich	1919		19/01/1944	Vileika	Voroshilov
62	Blyakhman Abram Moiseyevich	1898	Dyatlovo	30/05/1943	Baranovichi	Lenin's
63	Blyakhman Leonid Yosifovich	1925		12/09/1942		Frunze
64	Blyakhman Samuil Abramovich	1921	Dyatlovo	25/04/1944	Baranovichi	Kirov
65	Bobrov David Samuilovich	1914		03/05/1944	Pinsk	Kuibyshev
66	Bobrovitski Abram Leizerovich	1913	Mir	01/08/1943	Baranovichi	Za Sovetskuyu Belarus
67	Bozina Anna Mikhailovna	1923		18/02/1943		1st Smolenskaya
68	Boretski Boris Lazarevich	1921	Molchad	20/07/1943	Baranovichi	25 years of the BSSR

JEWISH PARTISANS IN BYELORUSSIA 1941-1944

69	Borzon Aron Mendelevich	1915		06/06/1944	Vitebsk	4th Byelorussian
70	Borzon Olga	1909		02/09/1942	Minsk	2nd Minsk
71	Borski Tlya Mordukhovich	1920	Leningrad	22/07/1942	Baranovichi	Stalin
72	Borsuk Moisei Yakovlevich	1923		13/03/1942	Minsk	37th Parkhomenko
73	Borusiak Pinkhus Mikhailovich	1910	Derechin	17/06/1944	Baranovichi	Pobieda
74	Borushanski Meyer Tankhelevich	1918	Minsk	29/07/1943	Baranovichi	Stalin
75	Botvinnik Benyamin	1903		29/01/1943	Baranovichi	? 2 Zhukov
76	Botvinnik Isaak Mordukhovich	1922	Minsk	06/09/1943	Baranovichi	? 18 Frunze
77	Boyarskaya Tsipa Yoselevna	1916	Vasilishki	09/02/1944	Baranovichi	Lenin's
78	Boyarski Arkadi Markovich	1922	Dnepropetrovsk	18/11/1943	Vileika	Voroshilov
79	Boyarski Ilya Mordukhovich	1920		22/07/1942	Minsk	
80	Boyarski Samuil Libovich	1915	Dyatlovo		Baranovichi	Lenin's
81	Branovitski Adam Zakharovich	1911		07/09/1943	Baranovichi	Grizodubova
82	Breido Isak Markovich	1917			Baranovichi	1st Baranovichi
83	Breslin Kiva			01/12/1942	Baranovichi	Lenin's
84	Briner Anna Zalmanovna	1908	Minsk		Baranovichi	18th Frunze
85	Briner David Khaimovich	1904	Minsk		Baranovichi	18th Frunze
86	Briner Klara Davidovna	1934	Minsk		Baranovichi	18th Frunze
87	Bronitski L.			02/07/1943	Minsk	Stalin
88	Brum Isaak Nokhimovich	1916	Belostok	27/12/1943	Brest	Ponamorenko
89	Buzin Adam Semenovich			30/03/1943	Brest	
90	Burgin Rafail Mikhailovich	1920		14/04/1943	Mogilev	1st Bobruisk
91	Busel Izrail Tsalevich	1915	Dyatlovo	16/07/1943	Baranovichi	Lenin's
92	Butynski Boris Grigorevich	1904	Minsk		Minsk	Pravda
93	Bukhtan Faiko Samuilovich	1917		25/05/1943	Mogilev	? 17 Kataev's
94	Bushlin Yosif Zelikovich	1922	Dyatlovo	25/04/1944	Baranovichi	Kirov
95	Byk Leiba Solomonovich	1927	Vileika region	04/05/1944	Minsk	? 100 Kirov
96	Vaiman Martyn Moiseyevich	1890			Vileika	
97	Vainshtein Yefim Yakovlevich	1895		01/06/1942	Baranovichi	Ponamorenko
98	Vaikhanski Abram	1912			Vitebsk	3rd Byelorussian
99	Valks Yevel Ilich	1918	Nachi	05/12/1943	Minsk	Shchors
100	Vantrub Movsha Itskovich	1915		03/07/1944	Pinsk	Lenin
101	Vargavtik Khaim Izrailevich			01/12/1941	Polesye	
102	Varfman Motkha Simkhovich	1921		03/05/1944	Vitebsk	Chapayev
103	Varshavski Shmaya Abramovich	1913	Mosty	17/07/1943	Baranovichi	Kirov
104	Vasemblyum Meyer Gertovich	1914		06/06/1944	Minsk	Shturmovaya
105	Vasilevitski Yosif Kasyanovich	1904		20/09/1941	Polesye	? 130
106	Vasilkova Faina Vasilevna	1924	Vitebsk	1942	Vitebsk	1st Vitebsk
107	Vashkevich A.	1938		02/07/1943	Minsk	Stalin
108	Veif Monas Khaimovich	1907		27/12/1943	Vitebsk	2nd Drissna
109	Veksler Moisei Borisovich	1922		08/07/1944	Pinsk	Kirov
110	Velikovski Ruvim Izrailevich	1909			Brest	party leadres' groups sent to the region
111	Vecherbin Yuri Leibovich	1912	Bobruisk	28/04/1943	Minsk	
112	Vigdorchik Lazar Niselevich	1913	Minsk region	20/07/1942	Minsk	Plamya
113	Vigmaister David Abramovich	1912	Slonim		Baranovichi	Lenin's
114	Viling Isaak Moiseyevich	1912	Borisov	06/08/1943	Mogilev	1st Bobruisk
115	Vilinski			01/11/1941	Vitebsk	2nd Byelorussian
116	Vishnevich Meyer Yankelevich	1922	Vyshinki	09/05/1944	Belostok	Vo imya Rodiny (In the name of Motherland)
117	Vladavski Venyamin	1914		03/10/1943	Pinsk	Sovetskaya Belarus
118	Vovk Vladimir Aleksandrovich	1915	Moskva	06/04/1944	Minsk	Shchors
119	Voikhanski Yefim Semenovich	1906		12/08/1942		1st Byelorussian
120	Voichik Yuri Georgievich			06/06/1944	Minsk	underground organization of Gressk district
121	Volovysski Leonid Abramovich	1929	Zheludok	24/10/1943	Baranovichi	Voroshilov
122	Volodko Leiba Leibovich	1914	Kozyany	23/12/1943	Vileika	Spartak
123	Volchek Boris Mikhailovich	1913	Minsk	15/12/1943	Minsk	
124	Volmark Mendel Shevalevich	1916		01/07/1943	Baranovichi	Lenin's
125	Volfson Izrail Abramovich	1920	Svintyany	21/07/1944	Vileika	Voroshilov
126	Vorobeichik Berta Semenovna	1913			Vitebsk	Chapayev
127	Voronna Mariya	1924	Slonim	01/01/1943	Brest	Ponamorenko
128	Vykhos Leiba Abramovich	1892		01/03/1944	Polesye	? 123
129	Gavbinder Mikhail Abramovich	1921		04/12/1942	Mogilev	? 14
130	Gazevich Samuil Yeselevich	1927	s/kh Zhaly	10/04/1944	Minsk	? 121 Bragin
131	Gazenpud David Lazarevich	1903	Minsk	22/03/1944	Baranovichi	Vpered
132	Gaitler Aron Girshevich	1924	Warsaw	28/03/1943	Minsk	Shturmovaya
133	Galik Srol Yeselevich	1903		01/12/1943	Polesye	? 125
134	Galinder Galina Zakharovna	1922	Terdovo, Mogil.region	22/07/1943	Baranovichi	
135	Galbershtein Ida Samuilovna	1921	Kurenets	13/01/1944	Minsk	Narodnye mstiteli Voronianski
136	Galdshtin Natan Solomonovich	1924		11/06/1944	Minsk	

#	Name	Year	Place	Date	Region	Unit
137	Gammer			02/07/1943	Minsk	Stalin
138	Garber Samuil			01/12/1942	Baranovichi	Lenin's
139	Garde Aron Berkovich	1924	Ostralenko	01/06/1943	Baranovichi	Za Sovetskuyu Belarus
140	Garelchik Simon Isaakovich	1905		12/03/1943	Polesye	? 125
141	Gebelev Mikhail Lvovich	1905	Minsk	15/08/1942	Vitebsk	Kutuzov
142	Gelemson Mikhail Isaakovich	1915		07/03/1942	Mogilev	? 208 Stalin
143	Geller Galina Borisovna	1924	Vilno	10/04/1944	Baranovichi	Pobieda
144	Gelmovski Tevel Shevelevich	1914	Rubezhevichi	27/07/1943	Baranovichi	18th Frunze
145	Gelfond Leonid Yefimovich	1924		14/07/1942	Vitebsk	Frunze
146	Genesov Eugeni Semenovich	1929	Orsha	06/05/1944	Vitebsk	Sadchikov's
147	Genina Raisa Yefimovna	1923	Minsk	27/07/1943	Baranovichi	Stalin
148	Gertsman Perets Girshevich	1900		10/05/1944	Vileika	Oktyabr
149	Gershanovskaya Sarra Semenovna	1895	Novogrudok	09/07/1944	Baranovichi	
150	Gershanok B.A.	1897	Rogachev	28/08/1941	Gomel	8th Rogachev
151	Gershman Moisei Mikhailovich	1912		11/11/1942	Polesye	? 123
152	Gershman Nokhim Itskovich	1903		11/09/1942	Polesye	? 123
153	Geskin Yakov Yosifovich	1913	Borisov	02/04/1944	Minsk	Smert fashizmu (Death to fascism)
154	Gibkhina Vera Yefimovna	1927		15/04/1943	Mogilev	
155	Gimborg Moisei Abramovich	1900		25/09/1943		
156	Gindin Mikhail Abramovich	1900	Ulla	06/05/1944	Vitebsk	Chapayev
157	Ginzburg Grigori Ivanovich	1899		01/09/1942	Mogilev	? 208 Stalin
158	Gitlits Semen Abramovich	1879		07/05/1944	Vitebsk	Ponamorenko (Utkina)
159	Glazman Izrail Yosifovich	1921	Mogilev		Brest	Ponamorenko
160	Glezer David Khaimovich	1916	Dokshitsy	31.06.1944	Baranovichi	A.Nevski
161	Gleizer Genakh Simonovich	1907		06/06/1944	Vitebsk	4th Byelorussian
162	Gleizer Girsha Simonovich	1897	Leompol	06/06/1944	Vileika	4th Byelorussian
163	Glinnik Dina Davidovna		Slutsk	01/03/1944	Minsk	Dyadya Koya's
164	Gnesin Faiba Mironovich	1921		01/04/1944	Vitebsk	Kutuzov
165	Godes Mikhail Yefimovich	1928	Minsk	30/07/1943	Baranovichi	18th Frunze
166	Godin Petr Yurevich	1925		02/10/1943	Gomel	Ponamorenko
167	Golub Lazar Moiseyevich	1923		15/01/1943	Minsk	2nd Minsk
168	Golubkin Mikhail Lvovich	1908			Vitebsk	Lenin
169	Golberg Zalman Markovich	1892	Minsk	21/08/1943	Baranovichi	Chapayev
170	Golberg Yosif Zalmanovich	1904	Pogost, Storobin district	25/02/1943	Pinsk	Budenny
171	Golberg Samuil Khaimovich	1907		02/03/1943	Minsk	2nd Minsk
172	Golbershtein Ida	1921	Kurenets	13/01/1944	Minsk	Nikitina
173	Goldin Yosif Mordukhovich	1877		01/08/1942	Mogilev	Chekist
174	Goldina Lyubov Mikhailovna	1917	Minsk	23/07/1943	Baranovichi	Ponamorenko
175	Goldshtein Natan Solomonovich	1924	N. Sverzhen	11/08/1944	Baranovichi	
176	Gomon Girsh Zalmanovich	1913		01/11/1941	Polesye	Yelsk ? 37 (Mishchenko)
177	Gonchar Khona Girshevich	1921	Derechin	16/07/1943	Baranovichi	Lenin's
178	Gordon Isaak Meyerovich	1907		05/05/1944	Vitebsk	Chapayev
179	Gordon Tankhel Yefimovich	1903	Vasilishki	08/07/1944	Baranovichi	
180	Gordun Khaim Ivanovich	1909		18/09/1943	Vileika	Spartak
181	Gorelik Manya	1920		01/05/1944	Polesye	
182	Gorelik Simon Isaakovich	1905		01/04/1943	Polesye	? 125
183	Gorenkrig Shaya Meilekhovich	1921	Stolbtsy	16/03/1943	Baranovichi	Za Sovetskuyu Belarus
184	Gormiza Rubin Getselevich	1923	Zvinets district	22/07/1942	Baranovichi	Stalin
185	Gormiza Sadol Getselevich	1922	Rubezhevichi	22/07/1942	Baranovichi	Stalin
186	Gorfinkel Venyamin Yakovlevich	1924	Minsk	20/12/1943	Minsk	2nd Minsk
187	Gorfinkel Khonek Nutovich			01/03/1943	Baranovichi	Lenin's
188	Gorshtein Yakov Motulevich	1920		20/04/1944	Vitebsk	Chapayev
189	Gofman Arkadi Isaakovich	1923	Bobruisk	23/09/1943	Mogilev	? 152
190	Gofman Bronya Shlemovna	1926	Vidzenski r-n	23/12/1943	Vileika	Spartak
191	Gofman Izrail Leizerovich	1898		06/06/1944	Vileika	Oktyabr
192	Grabovski Aleksandr Yakovlevich		Leningrad	30/10/1942	Minsk	Razgrom
193	Gradonchik Yakov Abramovich	1913	Lida	04/11/1943	Baranovichi	Kirov
194	Grayer Azik Yakovlevich	1924	Ivenets district	22/07/1942	Baranovichi	Stalin
195	Graiver Yakub Aizikovich	1925		05/06/1944	Belostok	Kalinovski
196	Graifer Leiba Mordukhovich	1898	Glussk	05/09/1942	Minsk	? 37 Parkhomenko
197	Grachuk Yakub Lazarevich	1924	Vasilishki	01/02/1943	Baranovichi	Lenin's
198	Gress Yankel Solomonovich	1924		27/05/1944	Baranovichi	Grizodubova
199	Gribets Abram Leibovich	1923	Starobin	28/02/1943	Pinsk	Budenny
200	Grigoreva Mira Andreyevna	1921		03/05/1944	Vitebsk	Danukalov
201	Gridenchik Sara Moiseyevna	1914	Lida	23/07/1943	Baranovichi	Kirov
202	Grimberg Zina Berkovna	1916	Glussk	01/04/1944	Minsk	? 25 Ponamorenko
203	Grin Benyamin Davidovich	1909		01/03/1943	Baranovichi	Lenin's
204	Guberman Estra Solomonovna	1923		01/05/1944	Vitebsk	Dzerzhinski

205	Gulis Anna Maksimovna	1912	Belostok	25/08/1943	Vileika	Frunze
206	Gulkovich Efraim Ganokhovich	1922	Mir	04/04/1944	Baranovichi	Za Sovetskuyu Belarus
207	Gurvich Aleksandr Semenovich	1897	Rakov	01/10/1943	Baranovichi	Chapayev
208	Gurvich Vladimir Lvovich	1919		11/10/1943	Brest	Dzerzhinski
209	Gurvich Leiba Kopelevich	1914		05/11/1943		Voroshilov
210	Gurevich Izrail Yosifovich	1903		12/04/1944	Polesye	? 123
211	Gurevich Moisei Lvovich	1912	Mogilev	24/01/1942	Mogilev	? 277 Izokh's
212	Gurevich Revekka Girshevna	1910	Vetka	05/01/1942	Minsk	Chervenski DC of the CP(b)B
213	Guryan Gita Moiseyevna	1923	Rubezhevichi		Baranovichi	18th Frunze
214	Guryan Leiba Erzerovich	1915		27/01/1944	Vileika	Za Rodinu
215	Gutalevski Girsh Faivelevich	1917	Lida	26/08/1944	Baranovichi	
216	Gutin Lev Abramovich	1909	Kopys	10/11/1943	Mogilev	? 122 "Za Rodinu"
217	Gutkovich Leiba Yankelevich	1899				1st Byelorussian
218	Dagutski Yudel Abramovich	1925	Baranovichi	01/10/1943	Baranovichi	Kirov
219	Dvoretski Mairam Movshevich			01/12/1942	Baranovichi	Lenin's
220	Dvoretski Mota Abramovich	1920	Dvorets	01/05/1943	Baranovichi	Kirov
221	Dvorkin Abram Girshevich	1894		13/02/1944	Polesye	? 123
222	Dvorkin Yosif Niselevich	1906		01/09/1941	Gomel	Voroshilov
223	Deich Meyer Zalmonovich	1910		06/06/1944	Vitebsk	4th Byelorussian
224	Deminson Nikolai Borisovich	1916	Vileika region	04/05/1944	Minsk	1st Antifascist
225	Demski David Usharovich	1916				Bogushevsk
226	Denershtein Semen Markovich	1924		14/06/1943	Minsk	Ponamorenko
227	Diminshtein Berta Leibovna	1920		28/10/1942	Minsk	Narodnye mstiteli
228	Dinershtein Neukh Lvovich	1915	Vileika	29/09/1944	Minsk	Narodnye mstiteli
229	Dlot Yuri Aizikovich	1910	Pudenichi	11/10/1942	Minsk	Narodnye mstiteli Voronianski
230	Dobkin Arkadi Davidovich	1920	Belynichi	07/10/1943	Gomel	8th Rogachev
231	Dobrin Efroim Lazarevich	1923	Mir	03/07/1944	Baranovichi	Za Sovetskuyu Belarus
232	Dogor Yakov Abramovich	1897	Bobruisk	01/08/1943	Mogilev	
233	Dombrovski Leo Ivanovich	1903	Krasnoye	04/05/1944	Minsk	1st Antifascist
234	Domnich Yakov Izrailevich	1910	Starobin	27/07/1943	Minsk	Dyadya Koya's
235	Donda Yosif Moisevich	1921		11/06/1944	Vileika	Suvorov (Khomchenko)
236	Dondo Alter Leibovich	1922		06/06/1944	Vitebsk	4th Byelorussian
237	Dorin Vladimir Moiseyevich	1920		13/08/1942	Polesye	Yelsk ? 37 (Mishchenko)
238	Dorosinskaya Sara Yeselevna	1921		06/05/1943	Baranovichi	
239	Dreer Zakhar Moiseyevich	1925	Berkovo	21/05/1944	Minsk	? 37 Parkhomenko
240	Dubrovski Grigori Isaakovich	1918		17/10/1943	Polesye	Kalinkovichi ? 99
241	Dubrovski Izrail Zusevich	1919		15/10/1943	Polesye	Kalinkovichi ? 99
242	Dubchanski Khaim Yekhenovich	1913		05/05/1943	Baranovichi	A.Nevski
243	Dukhan David Borukhovich	1905		29/01/1943	Polesye	123 Oktyabrskaya
244	Dymant Solomon Danilovich	1921		29/08/1942	Vileika	Kutuzov
245	Yevnovich Ilya Nokhimovich	1908	Novogrudok	01/06/1944	Baranovichi	Kirov
246	Yegudkin Mikhail Mikhailovich	1912	Gomel	06/04/1944	Mogilev	? 61
247	Yekelchik Moisei Lazarevich	1908		05/05/1942	Minsk	Minsk underground
248	Yelshakova Khana Grigorevna	1924	Vishnevo	03/01/1943	Baranovichi	Chapayev
249	Yelkanovich Samuil Isaakovich	1909	Shklov	27/07/1942	Mogilev	Chekist
250	Yeselevski Aron Moiseyevich	1891		08/02/1943	Baranovichi	? 2 Zhukov
251	Yesepkin Yakov Solomonovich	1919	ChElyabinskaya region	05/06/1944	Minsk	Burevestnik
252	Yekhilevski Leonid Semenovich	1917		28/06/1943	Vitebsk	Za Sovetskuyu Belarus
253	Zhelikhovski Abram Grigorevich	1906		01/07/1943	Baranovichi	Vpered
254	Zhelyakhovski Zakhar Zalmanovich	1925		25/03/1944	Minsk	Dyadya Koya's
255	Zhilinskaya Sofia Aleksandrovna	1923	Rakov		Minsk	Shturmovaya
256	Zhilitski Yakov Efremovich	1921	Khoiniki	17/02/1944	Minsk	Frunze
257	Zhikhmanovich Shlema Gertsevich	1925	Zheludok	19/03/1944	Baranovichi	Lenin's
258	Zhuk Abram Gershovich	1893	Mir	09/07/1944	Baranovichi	
259	Zhustkovski Mikhail Rubinovich	1913	Warsaw	08/07/1944	Minsk	Narodnye mstiteli
260	Zhukhovitskaya Pesya Yakovlevna	1888	Derevnoe	24/04/1944	Baranovichi	
261	Zhukhovitski Aleksei Samoilovich	1920		01/03/1943	Baranovichi	Lenin's
262	Zavin Vladimir Isaakovich	1913		15/05/1944	Pinsk	Kuibyshev
263	Zager Izrail Girshenovich	1912	Minsk	18/11/1943	Baranovichi	
264	Zaidenknon Isaak Pavlovich	1904		19/08/1942	Baranovichi	Ponamorenko
265	Zalatorski Mordukh Aizikovich	1924		09/02/1944	Baranovichi	? 2 Zhukov
266	Zaltsman Abram Yakovlevich	1906			Mogilev	? 208 Stalin
267	Zaltsman Lazar Yidolevich	1916	Rovno	26/05/1944	Vileika	Voroshilov
268	Zaltsman Shlema Gertskovich	1922	Minsk	07/06/1944	Minsk	3rd Minsk
269	Zaretski Mikhail			20/02/1942	Polesye	? 123
270	Zverzhinski Aron Abramovich	1903	Sloboda	19/10/1943	Baranovichi	Za Sovetskuyu Belarus
271	Zelikman Abram Markovich	1912		01/05/1944	Minsk	Shturmovaya
272	Zeldovich			02/07/1943	Minsk	Stalin

273	Zilberman Yankel Antonovich	1921	Iody, Sharkovshchinski r-n, Vit. region	08/10/1943	Vitebsk	
274	Zilbershtein Azim Davidovich			08/05/1944	Brest	
275	Zimanski Semen Abramovich	1920	Suvalki	08/02/1943	Baranovichi	25 years of the BSSR
276	Zimnovoda Pinkhus Abramovich	1912	Baranovichi	23/02/1943	Brest	shtab Sikorskogo i regionnoi shtab
277	Zinger Aron Davidovich	1928	Minsk	24/06/1944	Minsk	Dyadya Koya's
278	Zisgolts Aron Leizerovich	1918	Slutsk	13/02/1943	Minsk	2nd Minsk
279	Ziskent Motka Leibovich	1915	Golinovo	18/05/1944	Vileika	Frunze
280	Zifkovich Basya Isaakovna			18/12/1943	Vileika	Voroshilov
281	Zmeyev Moisei Aronovich	1916		06/06/1944	Vitebsk	4th Byelorussian
282	Zolotkovski Elya Abramovich	1924		05/08/1942	Baranovichi	Pobieda
283	Zoolovich Khil Efroimovich	1927	Polsha	12/01/1944	Mogilev	
284	Zubarev	1922	Grozovo	14/12/1942	Minsk	Chapayev
285	Zusman Samuil	1925	Warsaw	20/05/1944	Baranovichi	Kirov
286	Zukhovitskaya Tsilya Ilinichna	1919		03/03/1943	Vitebsk	2nd Byelorussian
287	Zyskant Motka Leibovich	1915		18/05/1944	Vileika	Frunze
288	Idilevich Yakov Moiseyevich	1905	Vilno	21/03/1944	Vileika	Voroshilov
289	Izakov Boris Mendelevich	1925		13/03/1944	Minsk	Dyadya Koya's
290	Izrailit Vulf Izrailevich	1898		01/11/1941	Vitebsk	2nd Byelorussian
291	Izrailitin Girsh Moiseyevich	1901		25/05/1943	Minsk	13 polk Grishina
292	Ilyatovich Elyash Yankelevich	1893		01/10/1943	Baranovichi	Kirov
293	Yosilevich Eduard Yosifovich	1925	Sloboda	08/08/1943	Minsk	Stalin
294	Yoffe Abram Semenovich	1906		05/11/1941	Vitebsk	1st Vitebsk
295	Yokhai David Khaimovich	1924	Kurenets	07/01/1944	Vileika	Voroshilov
296	Itman Khana Rafailovna	1916			Vileika	CC of the CP(b)B
297	Itskov Lev Yosifovich	1899		29/03/1944	Baranovichi	1st Baranovichi
298	Itskovich Leib Davidovich	1920	Mir	01/06/1943	Baranovichi	Za Sovetskuyu Belarus
299	Itskovich Solomon Izrailevich	1926	Baranovichi	17/12/1943	Baranovichi	Lenin's
300	Kabak Yosif Yudelevich	1924		29/03/1943	Baranovichi	A.Nevski
301	Kabanov Semen Nokhimovich	1919		12/02/1942		Smolenskoe partizanskoe pole
302	Kagan Alter Isaakovich	1923	Dyatlovo	25/04/1944	Baranovichi	Kirov
303	Kagan Genrikh Yakovlevich	1913		24/04/1944	Vileika	Spartak
304	Kagan E.A.					Rossonskaya podpolnaya partorganizatsia
305	Kagan Izrail Yurevich	1912	Mestino	06/02/1943	Mogilev	? 277 Izokh's
306	Kagan Lev Matveyevich	1923	Bobruisk	19/06/1944	Brest	Ponamorenko
307	Kagan Mikhail Yosifovich	1919		23/03/1943	Pinsk	Sovetskaya Belarus
308	Kagan Naum Yefimovich	1908		06/12/1943	Baranovichi	? 19 Molotov
309	Kagan Naum Markovich	1925	Minsk	01/08/1943	Baranovichi	Chapayev
310	Kagan Samuil Moiseyevich	1915	Minsk	15/05/1943	Baranovichi	Ponamorenko
311	Kagan Yakov Abromovich	1910		03/03/1942		Zaborskaya podpolnaya partino-komsomllskaya organizatsia
312	Kagan Yakov Moiseyevich	1902		02/07/1943	Vileika	Frunze
313	Kaganovich Natel Khatskelevich	1924	Gorodok	01/11/1943	Baranovichi	Za Sovetskuyu Belarus
314	Kaganovich Nakhum	1923		08/08/1943		LepYelsk Stalin
315	Kazinets Abel Mendelevich	1914		01/05/1944	Vileika	Frunze
316	Kazinets Isai Pavlovich	1910		07/05/1942	Minsk	Minsk underground
317	Kaim Mariya Lvovna	1925		05/06/1944	Vitebsk	Ponamorenko (Utkina)
318	Kaidanov Semen Moiseyevich	1905		08/12/1943	Minsk	Narodnye mstiteli
319	Kaller Teodor Borisovich	1912	Glussk	13/03/1942	Minsk	? 37 Parkhomenko
320	Kalmykova Mariya Samuilovna	1924			Vitebsk	Dzerzhinski
321	Kamenetski Aron Mordukhovich	1908	Shchuchin	01/09/1943	Baranovichi	Lenin's
322	Kamenetski Mikhail Semenovich	1917		23/09/1943	Minsk	37th Parkhomenko
323	Kamenetski Motel Yankelevich	1920	Shchuchin		Baranovichi	Lenin's
324	KaMinsk Eva Savelevna	1915		03/06/1944	Vileika	Oktyabr
325	Kanonik David Yefimovich	1929			Minsk	Kirov
326	Kantsenbogin Shlema Girshevich	1927	Minsk	06/03/1944	Baranovichi	Chapayev
327	Kapilevich Monus Samuilovich	1917	Dokshitsy	03/06/1944	Minsk	Narodnye mstiteli
328	Kaplan Abram Yefimovich	1926		03/07/1943	Baranovichi	Ponamorenko
329	Kaplan YYelizaveta Yakovlevna	1922		01/02/1943	Pinsk	Budenny
330	Kaplan Leiba Khaimovich	1908	Viazyn	15/05/1943	Vileika	Budenny
331	Kaplan Khaim Izrailevich	1904			Minsk	Chkalov
332	Kaplan Khaim Mendelevich	1906		27/03/1942	Minsk	Chkalov
333	Kaplinski Girsh Yakovlevich			01/12/1942	Baranovichi	Lenin's
334	Kaplunov Boris Yosifovich	1917		01/11/1942	Pinsk	Molotov
335	Kapotnikov Moisei Aizikovich	1900	Warsaw	10/04/1944	Minsk	? 25 Ponamorenko
336	Kapulski Abram Alterovich	1902	Grodno	21/04/1944	Baranovichi	Lenin Comsomol
337	Karo Elya Vikentevich	1923	Minsk	09/01/1944	Baranovichi	Chapayev
338	Karpilov Moisei Khatskevich	1911	Minsk	08/02/1942	Baranovichi	Rokossovskogo

339	Kasmai Kushel Izrailevich	1922		09/01/1944	Baranovichi	Lazo
340	Kaufman Boris Naumovich	1921	Pogost	15/07/1942	Mogilev	? 277 Izokh's
341	Kats Gershel Elevich	1901	Lida	22/03/1944	Baranovichi	Vpered
342	Kats Samuil Abramovich	1908		07/11/1943	Vitebsk	4th Byelorussian
343	Kats Sofia Markovna	1921		21/11/1942	Vitebsk	Stalin
344	Kats Shlema Shalmovich	1916	Stolbtsy	22/07/1942	Baranovichi	Stalin
345	Kats Elya Khaimovich	1893	Ive	16/02/1944	Baranovichi	A.Nevski
346	Katsevich Zelik	1912	Minsk	22/07/1942	Baranovichi	Stalin
347	Katsevich Mikhail	1922		01/11/1943		Kalinin
348	Katsman Aron Mendelevich	1898		01/01/1944	Vitebsk	Kutuzov
349	Katsnelson Beus	1881		01/05/1944	Polesye	? 225
350	Katsnelson E.M.	1905	Rogachev		Gomel	8th Rogachev
351	Katsnelson Irma Navtolevich	1903	Minsk	20/02/1943	Vitebsk	Kutuzov
352	Katsnelson Khaim Davidovich	1922	Starye Dorogi	20/06/1943	Minsk	Chkalov
353	Katsnelson Yudol Zalmanovich	1909	Bobruisk	18/04/1944	Minsk	? 37 Parkhomenko
354	Katsovich Yosif Samuilovich	1927			Minsk	Bolshevik
355	Katsovich Lev Ototsevich	1913	Budslav	17/05/1944	Minsk	Narodnye mstiteli
356	Kats-Terenteva Yekaterina Borisovna	1905		25/05/1943	Mogilev	
357	Kachan Yakov Moiseyevich	1902		02/07/1943	Minsk	Frunze
358	Kashevich Maksim Venkelevich	1924	Rubezhevichi	27/07/1943	Baranovichi	Chapayev
359	Kashkan Semen Yakovlevich	1910		22/06/1944	Minsk	Smert fashizmu (Death to fascism)
360	Keimakh David Ilich				Minsk	Dyadya Koya's
361	Kesler Izrail Izrailevich	1905	Naliboki	06/02/1944	Baranovichi	
362	Kivkin Yosif Srulevich	1914			Vitebsk	Nikitina
363	Kivovich Abram Davidovich	1925	DElyatichi	17/01/1944	Baranovichi	Vpered
364	Kivovich Kusha Kushelevich	1920		27/12/1943	Baranovichi	Zhukova
365	Kirman David Semenovich	1922	Zvinets district	22/07/1942	Baranovichi	Stalin
366	Kisetski Samuil Shlemovich	1922		01/04/1944	Polesye	? 123
367	Kitrova Lyuba Fedorovna	1924		03/06/1944	Vitebsk	Voroshilov
368	Kleinbok Lazar Moiseyevich	1923		17/06/1944	Minsk	Spetsgruppy
369	Kleiner Sarra Moiseyevna	1919	Glussk	14/07/1943	Minsk	Chkalov
370	Kleorin			02/07/1943	Minsk	Stalin
371	Kletski Faiva Yosifovich	1923		29/11/1942	Vileika	Voroshilov
372	Kliger Betseler Girshevich	1912		25/11/1943	Polesye	? 225
373	Klikfeld Nina Yakovlevna	1926	Derechin		Baranovichi	Pobieda
374	Klinbok Lazar Moiseyevich	1923	ChElyabinskaya region	15/06/1944	Minsk	Frunze
375	Knuman Yakov Davidovich	1914		04/05/1944	Vitebsk	Voroshilov
376	Kovalev Mikhail Grigorevich	1916		01/04/1943	Gomel	Zhelezniak
377	Koval Mikhail Aronovich	1924	Iasenski	24/01/1944	Mogilev	Chekist
378	Koval Foma Borisovich	1920		17/05/1944	Minsk	? 121 Bragin
379	Kovner Yefim Mordukhovich	1896	Minsk	15/12/1942	Baranovichi	Rokossovskogo
380	Kogan Grigori Grigorevich	1907		05/05/1943	Baranovichi	A.Nevski
381	Kogan Isaak Izrailevich			12/02/1942	Mogilev	? 61
382	Kogan Rita Zalmanovna	1922		29/08/1943	Vileika	CC of the CP(b)B
383	Kozik Isaak Leibovich	1923		28/03/1942	Polesye	? 225
384	Kozinets Abel Mendelevich	1914	Dokshitsy	01/05/1944	Vileika	
385	Kozinets Movsha Mendelevich	1921	Dokshitsy	01/05/1944	Vileika	
386	Kozlovski Yefim Rubinovich	1925	Oshmiany	03/02/1944	Baranovichi	
387	Kolodenich Mikhail Izrailevich	1913		27/10/1943	Brest	Ponamorenko
388	Kolodkin Boris Konstantinovich	1925	Minsk	01/10/1943	Baranovichi	Chapayev
389	Koltuv Genakh Shmerkovich	1897		12/04/1944	Polesye	? 123
390	Kondelshtein Moisei Vitskelevich			22/02/1943	Brest	
391	Koninshtein Abram	1918		27/07/1942	Baranovichi	? 2 Zhukov
392	Kopelevich Kopel Yudolevich	1921	Zhuprany	28/12/1943	Vileika	Dovatora
393	Kopelevich Yakov Vladimirovich	1927			Minsk	Frunze
394	Kopotnikov Moisei Aleks.	1909		10/04/1944	Minsk	25-ia Ponomarenko
395	Kostelyanets Abram Pavlovich	1885		01/07/1943	Minsk	Chkalov
396	Kostelyanets Olga Arkadevna	1903	Minsk	02/08/1943	Baranovichi	Chapayev
397	Kotina Sonya Abramovna	1922	Minsk	01/08/1943	Baranovichi	Chapayev
398	Kotov Mikhail Grigorevich	1892	Minsk	23/07/1942	Baranovichi	Vpered
399	Kotchen Aleksandr Yefimovich	1922	Evpatoria	16/09/1943	Mogilev	Demidova
400	Kokh Isaak Yakovlevich	1923	Mir	16/03/1943	Baranovichi	Za Sovetskuyu Belarus
401	Kocherzhinski Grigori Yankelevich	1912		09/12/1943	Vileika	Voroshilov
402	Kravets Leva Grigorevich	1921	Leningrad	19/12/1943	Minsk	Suvorov
403	Kravitski Zaiman Robinovich	1926	Vileika region	04/05/1944	Minsk	? 100 Kirov
404	Kravchuk Yakov Isaakovich	1921		07/06/1944	Minsk	Zhelezniak
405	Krashevski Mota	1916	Belostok region	01/02/1942	Mogilev	Osipovichskaya
406	Kreinis Boris Nikolayevich	1927		22/05/1944	Minsk	Shturmovaya

407	Kremgolts Mulia Solomonovich	1912	Lyublin	04/05/1944	Minsk	1st Antifascist
408	Kremgolts Yakub Abramovich	1910	Lyublin	04/05/1944	Minsk	1st Antifascist
409	Kremer Aleksandr Moiseyevich	1921		05/06/1944	Vileika	Spartak
410	Krechmar Ilya Naumovich	1924	Seliba	28/10/1943	Mogilev	? 277 Izokh's
411	Kreshkevich Levi Volfovich	1915	Warsaw	04/05/1944	Minsk	1st Antifascist
412	Krivitskaya Raisa Samuilovna	1911		06/06/1944	Vitebsk	4th Byelorussian
413	Krivitski Grigori				Minsk	Chapayev
414	Krivitski Rufka Mendelevich	1932		06/06/1944	Vitebsk	4th Byelorussian
415	Krivoshein Boris Isaakovich	1927	Ukhvala	18/05/1944	Mogilev	? 8 Ilina
416	Krigel Lazar	1905	Minsk	01/08/1943	Baranovichi	Chapayev
417	Kriger Taisia Maksimovna	1926	Minsk	13/11/1943	Minsk	2nd Minsk
418	Krimgolts Yakov Abramovich	1910			Minsk	1st Antifascist
419	Krichevski Venyamin Isaakovich	1907		20/06/1943	Minsk	Kirov
420	Krichevski Petr Grigorevich	1909		01/04/1942	Mogilev	? 208 Stalin
421	Kroz Gleb Petrovich	1899		06/06/1944	Vitebsk	2nd Zaslonov
422	Krol Lev Grigorevich	1908		01/01/1942	Mogilev	
423	Kru Elya Naumovna	1907	Belostok	18/05/1944	Baranovichi	Kirov
424	Krugly Akiva Shlemovich	1918		14/04/1944	Pinsk	Kuibyshev
425	Krugman Yudel Yurkovich			01/12/1942	Baranovichi	Lenin's
426	Krupenya Kalman Abramovich	1900		10/01/1943	Belostok	Vo imya Rodiny (In the name of Motherland)
427	Kugel Yefim Ilich	1924	Minsk	23/12/1943	Baranovichi	18th Frunze
428	Kugel Yasha Abramovich			25/11/1943	Baranovichi	
429	Kuznets Khatskel Shimsovich	1915		13/02/1943	Pinsk	Budenny
430	Kuznetsov Isaak Mikhailovich	1922		21/10/1941	Vitebsk	Kutuzov
431	Kukut Lev			01/08/1941	Mogilev	
432	Kulik Lev Yakovlevich	1908		12/12/1942	Minsk	
433	Kurlyand Tspal Yemelyanovich	1923	Minsk	15/07/1943	Baranovichi	? 18 Frunze
434	Kurlyanski Semen Davidovich	1924	Litva	03/02/1944	Baranovichi	Lenin Comsomol
435	Kusik Aron Mendelevich	1909		21/01/1944	Pinsk	Sovetskaya Belarus
436	Kusik Menta Mendelevna	1915		03/10/1943	Pinsk	Sovetskaya Belarus
437	Kustanovich Vladimir Elkovich	1914	St. Dorogi	01/03/1942	Minsk	? 25 Ponamorenko
438	Kustanovich Ida Yefimovna	1925	Lyuban	03/03/1944	Minsk	? 100 Kirov
439	Kukharchik Mikhail Abramovich	1922		05/08/1943	Vitebsk	Chapayev
440	Kushner Boris Khaimovich	1917	Minsk	10/04/1944	Baranovichi	
441	Kushner Khatskel Abramovich	1914		19/04/1942	Vitebsk	1st Byelorussian
442	Kushnir Leonid Isaakovich	1920	Ukraina	27/04/1944	Vileika	
443	Kushchinski Zalman Abramovich	1894	Novogrudok	28/04/1944	Baranovichi	
444	Lando Zakhar Mikhailovich	1908	Vitebsk	01/08/1943	Baranovichi	Chapayev
445	Lantsevitski Faivel Mordukhovich	1908	Dyatlovo	19/03/1944	Baranovichi	Lenin's
446	Lapidus Mariya Grigorevna	1916	Minsk	13/02/1944	Minsk	Ponamorenko
447	Laskin Solomon Abramovich	1893		01/01/1942	Vitebsk	Kutuzov
448	Laufer				Minsk	Nikitina
449	Lakhter Yosif Mordukhovich	1905		01/06/1943	Baranovichi	Lenin's
450	Lebedkin Nevakh Yankelevich			01/12/1942	Baranovichi	Lenin's
451	Lev Khonon Sholomovia	1923		24/06/1944	Belostok	Kalinovski
452	Levin Abram Isaakovich	1911		05/05/1943	Baranovichi	A.Nevski
453	Levin Aron Lipovich	1927		01/10/1942	Vitebsk	Gudkova
454	Levin Grigori Ziselevich	1925	Radoshkovichi	18/05/1944	Vileika	Frunze
455	Levin Zalman Yanovlevich	1908		01/02/1944	Polesye	? 123
456	Levin Izrail Samuilovich	1907		30.02.1944	Polesye	? 123
457	Levin Isaak Noselevich	1923	Vselyub	03/08/1943	Baranovichi	Chapayev
458	Levin Mendel Zalmanovich	1899		06/09/1943	Baranovichi	1st Baranovichi
459	Levin Moisei Leibovich	1908		03/03/1942	Minsk	Minsk underground
460	Levin Motka Girshevich	1909			Minsk	Frunze
461	Levin Roman Yefimovich	1910		09/09/1942		
462	Levin Ruvim Mendelevich	1898		01/08/1942	Brest	Stalin
463	Levin Fedor Davidovich	1926	Glubokoe	06/06/1944	Vileika	4th Byelorussian
464	Levina Danya Yakovlevna	1924	Minsk	01/08/1943	Baranovichi	Chapayev
465	Levina Ekha Moiseyevna	1917			Minsk	Belarus
466	Levina Fanya Yakovlevna	1922	Minsk	01/08/1943	Baranovichi	Chapayev
467	Levinson Yelizaveta Isaakovna	1910		05/06/1944	Minsk	Shturmovaya
468	Levinson Khaim Yankelevich	1916		04/06/1944	Vitebsk	4th Byelorussian
469	Levit Meyer Zalmanovich	1919			Vitebsk	Kutuzov
470	Levitan Mikhail Semenovich	1912	Minsk	13/03/1942	Minsk	? 37 Parkhomenko
471	Levitski Ivan Vasilevich	1919		01/02/1943	Minsk	Chkalov
472	Levkovich Abram Leibovich	1918	Novoelnia		Baranovichi	Pobieda
473	Levoronchik Yevsei Venyaminovich	1916	Dyatlovo	13/07/1943	Baranovichi	Lenin's
474	Ledvich Shaya Tolevich	1908	Glussk	05/09/1942	Minsk	? 37 Parkhomenko

JEWISH PARTISANS IN BYELORUSSIA 1941-1944   325

475	Leib Motya Yudelevich	1910		01/04/1943	Baranovichi	Lenin's
476	Leibovich Mikhail Askarovich	1903	Mozyr	09/09/1943	Mogilev	? 61
477	Leibovich Yuri Notkovich	1924	Novogrudok	09/07/1944	Baranovichi	
478	Leinus Yakov Izrailevich	1901		01/06/1944	Minsk	Dyadya Koya's
479	Leitos Lev	1918		15/12/1941	Gomel	Bolshevik
480	Leifman Moisei Leibovich	1899		20/11/1941		
481	Lekakh Nadezhda Fedorovna	1917		05/05/1944	Vileika	Oktyabr
482	Lekakh Semen Mankovich	1924		03/09/1943	Vitebsk	Prudnikov's
483	Lelchuk Girsh Osherovich			10/11/1942	Polesye	Lelchitskaya
484	Lemze Khaim Ia.	1906	Ivenets	22/07/1942	Baranovichi	Stalin
485	Lepshevich Teiba Nokhimovna	1921		01/09/1943	Baranovichi	Lenin's
486	Lepshovich Khaim Nokhimovich	1910	Derechin	17/06/1944	Baranovichi	Pobieda
487	Leus Leva Khatskelevich	1923	Shamkino	06/07/1942	Minsk	Dyadya Koya's
488	Libman E.M.	1915		1942	Gomel	8th Rogachev
489	Livshits David Aronovich	1915	Zvinets district	22/07/1942	Baranovichi	Stalin
490	Livshits Eugeni Borisovich	1913	Ushachi	06/03/1943	Vitebsk	1st Byelorussian
491	Livshits Yosif Tsedikovich	1926	Komarovichi	27/02/1944	Minsk	
492	Livshits Tsilya Yakovlevna	1903	Kostyukovichi	05/03/1942	Mogilev	
493	Lidkovski Isaak Abramovich	1919		01/04/1943	Baranovichi	Lenin's
494	Lidskaya Raya Yosifovna	1922	Gorodok	01/08/1943	Baranovichi	Za Sovetskuyu Belarus
495	Lidski Meyer Khaimovich	1923			Baranovichi	Lidski MRTs
496	Lidski Rakhmil Khaimovich	1921			Baranovichi	Lidski MRTs
497	Lin Boris Izrailevich	1915	Vselyub	22/03/1944	Baranovichi	Vpered
498	Lin Lolya Yankelevna	1925		20/11/1943	Baranovichi	? 2 Zhukov
499	Lis Ruvim Khaimovich	1913	Zakhody	14/11/1941	Polesye	
500	Lisnevski Ilya Yevseyevich	1924	Vilno	21/04/1943	Baranovichi	Voroshilov
501	Lisovskaya Dora Berkovna	1915	Derechin		Baranovichi	Lidski MRTs
502	Litmanovich Mikhail Ilich	1908		23/02/1944	Minsk	Dyadya Koya's
503	Likhovitski David Markovich	1908	Vilno	01/11/1943	Baranovichi	Vpered
504	Likhtenshtein Moisei Klementevich	1888	Luninets	10/04/1944	Pinsk	Kirov
505	Likhter Yefim Yakovlevich			22/06/1944	Minsk	Spetsgruppy
506	Likhter Yosif Mordukhovich	1905	Dyatlovo	16/06/1943	Baranovichi	Lenin's
507	Likhter Rakhmel Mordukhovich	1917	Dyatlovo		Baranovichi	Lenin's
508	Lobzovski Mikhail Berkovich	1921	Derechin		Baranovichi	Lenin's
509	Lopatin Boris Yakovlevich	1900		02/11/1943	Pinsk	Kirov
510	Loshitser Aron Aizikovich	1903	Gorodok	12/01/1943	Baranovichi	
511	Luzanski Yosif Mikhailovich	1902	Bobruisk	24/02/1943	Minsk	? 25 Ponamorenko
512	Lunin Grigori Izrailevich	1921	Volozhin	30/04/1943	Baranovichi	Za Sovetskuyu Belarus
513	Lusskaya Sarra Meyerovna	1902	Derechin	01/03/1943	Baranovichi	Lenin's
514	Lusskin Ofer Samoilovich	1906	Karelichi	22/07/1942	Baranovichi	Stalin
515	Lyubranetski Vatsek	1902	Lodz	11/04/1944	Baranovichi	Suvorov
516	Lyustik Roman Semenovich	1918		08/07/1943	Minsk	Razgrom
517	Lianger Yosif Venyaminovich	1920		31/10/1943	Brest	party leadres' groups sent to the region
518	Liakhovitski Foma Yosifovich	1921		24/02/1944	Vileika	Za Rodinu
519	Magadovski Girsh Girshevich	1916	Grodno	27/07/1944	Baranovichi	Lenin Comsomol
520	Mazurkevich Isaak Aronovich	1899	Novogrudok	08/12/1943	Baranovichi	
521	Maze Leizer Yoselevich	1922	Baranovichi	17/03/1944	Minsk	Chapayev
522	Maizel			01/11/1941	Vitebsk	2nd Byelorussian
523	Makutonin Sholom Rafailovich	1913		06/06/1944	Vitebsk	4th Byelorussian
524	Makutonina Mera Rafolovna	1920		06/06/1944	Vitebsk	4th Byelorussian
525	Malikhovski Semen Evnovich	1921		22/02/1943	Vitebsk	Kutuzov
526	Malkin	1919	Gorodok	24/01/1943	Baranovichi	Za Sovetskuyu Belarus
527	Malkin Yankel Leibovich	1907		06/06/1944	Vileika	4th Byelorussian
528	Mandel Taiba Isaakovich	1896		06/04/1944	Minsk	25-ia Ponamorenko
529	Mankovich Mendel Meyerovich	1923	Dyatlovo	18/03/1943	Baranovichi	Lenin's
530	Margolin Vulf Itskovich	1885		01/04/1944	Polesye	? 123
531	Margolin Isaak Yankelevich	1923	Shatsk	31/05/1944	Belostok	Kalinovski
532	Margolin Meyer Perkhusovich	1904		09/03/1943		VLKSM
533	Markman Mira Yakovlevna	1911	Minsk	15/05/1943	Baranovichi	Ponamorenko
534	Markus Shlema Abramovich	1910	Volkovyssk		Baranovichi	Lenin's
535	Marochnik Aleksei Kharitonovich	1921	Shchitno	28/01/1943	Brest	Ponamorenko
536	Martman Leizer Berkovich	1906	Peredolog, Vileika region	12/06/1944	Minsk	Voroshilov
537	Maslyanski Izrail Semenovich	1901		13/05/1944	Minsk	Kalinin
538	Massarski Grigori	1920		05/09/1942	Vitebsk	Za Sovetskuyu Belarus
539	Matusevich Raisa Semenovna	1909	Minsk	02/06/1944	Minsk	Spetsgruppy
540	Mats Grigori Afanasevich	1918	Svisloch	06/05/1943	Mogilev	? 152
541	Meyerson Gershon Abramovich	1922	Dolginovo		Minsk	Voroshilov
542	Meyerson Samson Abramovich	1920	Dolginovo		Minsk	Voroshilov
543	Mekel David Girshevich	1893		01/09/1943	Baranovichi	Lenin's

544	Melamed Fima Aleksandrovich	1922		01/07/1943	Baranovichi	Zhukova
545	Melnik Mikhail Ivanovich	1919		06/06/1943	Minsk	37th Parkhomenko
546	Meltser Ovsei Girshevich	1902	Zabereze	01/09/1943	Baranovichi	Kirov
547	Memokovski Semen Evnovich			22/03/1943	Brest	
548	Merlis Yakov Borisovich	1917		06/07/1943	Vitebsk	Leonova
549	Mertsev Mikhail Antonovich	1920		10/01/1943	Belostok	Vo imya Rodiny (In the name of Motherland)
550	Mesezhnikov Lev Samuilovich	1908		04/04/1943	Vitebsk	Prudnikov's
551	Militsin Aron Nisovich	1910		01/01/1943	Mogilev	
552	Milkin Rakhmeil			01/01/1943	Minsk	Narodnye mstiteli
553	Milman Boris Naumovich	1921		16/08/1942	Vitebsk	Korotkina
554	Mindel Issak			12/10/1943		
555	Mindel Fima Solomonovich	1918	Minsk	06/07/1944	Baranovichi	
556	Minkin Yakov Mendelevich	1922		16/02/1944	Brest	party leadres' groups sent to the region
557	Minkovich Solomon Yosifovich	1925	Minsk	23/12/1943	Baranovichi	? 18 Frunze
558	Mins Khaim Rubinovich	1914		29/03/1943	Baranovichi	A.Nevski
559	Mireiko Miron Aronovich	1924	Ukhvala	08/11/1942	Mogilev	? 8 Ilina
560	Mirkin Zakhar Yefimovich	1911				
561	Mitel Zyama Abramovich	1924	Minsk	26/07/1943	Baranovichi	Ponamorenko
562	Mishels Afroim Mendelevich	1919		26/06/1943	Mogilev	1st Bobruisk
563	Mishler Estra Mashkovna	1923	Polsha	01/04/1944	Brest	shtab Sikorskogo i regionnoi shtab
564	Mlotok Fedor Yosifovich	1923	Lenino	27/09/1942	Minsk	Frunze
565	Movshovich Abram Khaimovich		Novogrudok	19/04/1944	Baranovichi	Kirov
566	Morozovski Izrail Lvovich	1910	Glussk	31/12/1941	Polesye	
567	Mudrik Abram Leibovich	1924	Lida	06/07/1944	Baranovichi	
568	Muzykant Anatoli Aronovich	1915		01/11/1941	Vitebsk	Kutuzov
569	Mukman Leizer Berkovich	1906		12/06/1944	Vileika	
570	Muler Rubin Moiseyevich	1896	Ivenets	22/07/1942	Baranovichi	Stalin
571	Munits Alter Getolovich	1909		06/06/1944	Vitebsk	4th Byelorussian
572	Murog Airin Girshevich	1923	Minsk	25/05/1944	Minsk	3rd Minsk
573	Musin Shlema Ilich	1914		23/03/1944	Vitebsk	4th Byelorussian
574	Mushkin Mikhail Samuilovich	1914	Briansk	30/04/1943	Brest	Chapayev
575	Myshalov Semen	1914		23/05/1944	Pinsk	Budenny
576	Miadlinski Mikhail	1913	Molchad	15/08/1943	Baranovichi	25 years of the BSSR
577	Navrotski Yosif Shlemovich	1882			Vitebsk	Chapayev
578	Nalibotski Vulf Borukhovich	1919		15/01/1943	Minsk	2nd Minsk
579	Naroiki Khaim Yosifovich	1928				Chapayev
580	Natkovich Yankel Nesterovich	1922		20/01/1944	Vitebsk	Spartak
581	Neishtat Mikhail Izrailevich	1910		17/06/1943	Minsk	2nd Minsk
582	Neusikhina Bella Yakovlevna	1914	Minsk	30/07/1943	Baranovichi	18th Frunze
583	Nekhnevitski Kopl Alterovich	1923		21/06/1943	Baranovichi	? 19 Molotov
584	Nikitin-Shleikher Ivan Ivanovich (Sona Yosifovich)	1910		03/07/1943		1st Smolenskaya
585	Nisebaum Yasha Sholomovich	1923		10/07/1943	Minsk	Stalin
586	Nisnevich Isaak Mironovich	1911	Cherven	01/06/1944	Minsk	Shturmovaya
587	Novitski Shimon Girshevich	1915	Dvorets	01/05/1943	Baranovichi	Kirov
588	Novogrodor Khaim Yosifovich	1926	Lenino	25/04/1944	Minsk	
589	Novosadski Naum Semenovich	1928	Molodechno	03/11/1943	Baranovichi	Dzerzhinski
590	Nozik Afroim Pinkhusovich	1915	Glussk	20/06/1944	Minsk	? 37 Parkhomenko
591	Nozik Itskho Leibovich	1923		01/12/1941	Polesye	? 225
592	Nozik Ruva	1914	Glussk	15/02/1942	Minsk	? 37 Parkhomenko
593	Norotski Yosif Shlemovich	1882		15/01/1943	Vitebsk	Chapayev
594	Notkovich Yankel Nesterovich	1922		20/01/1944	Vileika	Spartak
595	Nusenson Yefim Davydovich	1912	Minsk	27/07/1943	Baranovichi	Stalin
596	Nusenson Faivel Aronovich	1914	Minsk	01/10/1943	Baranovichi	Chapayev
597	Nus Fedor Maksimovich	1919	Kharkov	28/07/1943	Belostok	Kalinovski
598	Ogur Nokhim Abrasimovich	1911		01/06/1944	Minsk	Frunze
599	Ogushevich Avsei Kototovich			02/04/1944	Brest	
600	Odrizhinski David Meyerovich	1921		22/08/1943	Gomel	Molotov
601	Ozhekhovski Ena Khaimovich			01/12/1942	Baranovichi	Lenin's
602	Ozerski Arkadi Abramovich	1913	Moskva	10/04/1944	Minsk	? 161 Kotovski
603	Ozerski Zinovi Lvovich	1927	Minsk	18/11/1943	Baranovichi	
604	Okun Zalman Mironovich	1907		01/03/1942	Minsk	Minsk underground
605	Okshenkrug Yefim Isaakovich	1910		14/05/1944	Vitebsk	Za Sovetskuyu Belarus
606	Opengeim Grigori Shavelevich	1897	Minsk	01/06/1944	Minsk	Kirov
607	Opengeim Dora Solomonovna	1896	Minsk		Baranovichi	
608	Opengeim Lenia Yefimovich	1926	Minsk	18/11/1943	Baranovichi	
609	Opengeim Fanya Yefimovna	1915	Minsk		Baranovichi	
610	Ostashinskillya Shlemovich	1911	Novogrudok	09/07/1944	Baranovichi	

611	Otlivankin Yosif Zalmanovich	1913	Bykhov	28/08/1942	Mogilev	? 425
612	Osherovski Yudel Abramovich	1905		15/05/1944	Pinsk	Kuibyshev
613	Oshmianski Aleksandr Moiseyevich	1919	Odessa	18/10/1943	Mogilev	? 208 Stalin
614	Oshnek Alla Robertovna	1924		25/08/1942		Danukalov
615	Pavlovski Benia	1924	Vilno	22/07/1944	Vileika	Voroshilov
616	Pave Shlema Aizikovich	1923	Grodno	20/06/1944	Baranovichi	Lenin Comsomol
617	Paikin Abram Moiseyevich	1908	Sharkovshchina	08/10/1943	Vitebsk	
618	Pales Yakov Nokhimovich	1888	Rubezhevichi	09/07/1944	Baranovichi	
619	Paretski Yosif Arkatovich	1907		01/04/1943	Brest	Ponamorenko
620	Patent Aron Vulfovich	1898		01/05/1942	Minsk	2nd Minsk
621	Pakhutskaya Raisa Semenovna	1894	Ivenets		Baranovichi	
622	Pakhutski Lev BentsYonovich	1880	Warsaw	06/07/1944	Baranovichi	
623	Patsovski Grigori Tsalevich	1915	Dyatlovo	09/07/1944	Baranovichi	
624	Pashkevich			02/07/1943	Minsk	Stalin
625	Pevzner Mark Isaakovich	1922	Moskva	21/07/1944	Mogilev	Osipovichskaya
626	Pekar Sonya Rakhmulovna	1920	Vilno	28/05/1944	Vileika	Voroshilov
627	Peker Avsei Yakovlevich	1927	Stolbtsy		Baranovichi	
628	Peker Yakov Aronovich	1903	Stolbtsy		Baranovichi	
629	Peller Galina Borisovna	1924	Vilno	10/04/1944	Baranovichi	Pobieda
630	Perevozkin Aizik Yankelevich	1913	Malinovka		Minsk	Narodnye mstiteli Voronianski
631	Perevozkin Yosif Abramovich	1911	Malinovka		Minsk	Narodnye mstiteli Voronianski
632	Perelman Samuil Rubinovich	1921		01/04/1943	Baranovichi	Lenin's
633	Perelshtein Anna Lipovna	1920	Baranovichi	07/06/1943	Baranovichi	1st Maya
634	Perlov Itsek Pelkovich	1905		06/06/1944	Vitebsk	4th Byelorussian
635	Perlov Itsik Pelkovich	1905		06/06/1944		4th Byelorussian
636	Perlov Moisei Khaimovich	1912	Beskatovo	30/10/1943	Vitebsk	Kutuzov
637	Perchenok Girsh Aizikovich	1902	Minsk		Baranovichi	
638	Perchenok Sema Girshevich	1923	Minsk		Baranovichi	
639	Pesin Gershon Aronovich	1898	Minsk	17/09/1943	Mogilev	? 208 Stalin
640	Petrovitski Khaim Raivelevich		Minsk	13/03/1944	Minsk	Dyadya Koya's
641	Petrukovich Movsha Yevseyevich	1886			Baranovichi	Pobieda
642	Petrukhovich Movsha Yevseyevich	1888	Derechin		Baranovichi	Pobieda
643	Pildus Rafail Samuilovich	1909		26/10/1943	Vitebsk	4th Byelorussian
644	Pinski Avsei Yosifovich	1913	Baranovichi	18/09/1943	Baranovichi	Za Sovetskuyu Belarus
645	Pisarevich Samuil Yevseyevich	1908	Starobin	04/08/1942	Pinsk	Budenny
646	Pisetski Leiba Shlemovich	1925		22/05/1943	Polesye	? 123
647	Plavchik Mikhail Yakovlevich	1912	Ostrov	18/11/1943	Baranovichi	
648	Pliski Leizer Borisovich	1908		10/01/1944	Vileika	
649	Plisskin Izrail Platsklevich	1904		04/05/1944	Vileika	Oktyabr
650	Ploten Kheta Leizerovich	1907		13/08/1942	Baranovichi	? 2 Zhukov
651	Pludo Leiba Mikhailovich	1920	Derechin	01/09/1943	Baranovichi	Lenin's
652	Pogov Izrail Ulfovich	1922	Vilno	06/07/1944	Baranovichi	Ponamorenko
653	Podberezki Efroim Leibovich	1914	Gorodok	18/04/1944	Baranovichi	Za Sovetskuyu Belarus
654	Podmaza Khatskel	1895	Minsk	02/07/1944	Minsk	Plamya
655	Poznyak Abram Yakovlevich	1922	Mir	01/06/1943	Baranovichi	Za Sovetskuyu Belarus
656	Poznyakov Mikhail Abelevich	1908	Zaskovichi	10/03/1943	Vileika	Voroshilov
657	Poloiko Isaak Moiseyevich	1913	Lapichi, Osipovich. r-n	05/05/1944	Mogilev	Osipovichskaya
658	Poloiko Liza Samuilovna	1919	Minsk	15/10/1943	Mogilev	Demidova
659	Polyatskina Sara Gdalevna	1921	Minsk	02/06/1944	Mogilev	
660	Pomeranets Izrail	1906		18/12/1943	Pinsk	Molotov
661	Poniatchik Anatoli Ilich	1925	Ivatsevichi	17/12/1943	Pinsk	Lenin
662	Popernik Solomon Abramovich	1918	Senno	13/11/1943	Vitebsk	2nd Zaslonov
663	Portnov Abram Samuilovich	1922	Baranovichi	13/04/1944	Pinsk	Budenny
664	Potashev Pavel Khaimovich	1891		04/05/1944	Vitebsk	Chapayev
665	Potekhin Grigori Moiseyevich	1921	Slutski r-n, Ureche	08/06/1943	Minsk	Chkalov
666	Press Yankel Solomonovich	1924		26/05/1944	Minsk	Grizodubova
667	Pruslin Matvei Mendelevich	1905			Minsk	Minsk underground
668	Ptushkina Raisa Izrailevna	1918	Minsk	01/08/1943	Baranovichi	Chapayev
669	Pulis Anna	1912		25/08/1943	Vileika	Frunze
670	Pupkin	1882		29/01/1943	Baranovichi	? 2 Zhukov
671	Pupko Boris	1919		01/07/1942	Minsk	Minsk underground
672	Pupko Monekh Ivanovich	1923	Lida	19/11/1943	Belostok	A.Nevski
673	Pen Aleksandr Grigorevich	1919		28/07/1943	Minsk	Narodnye mstiteli
674	Rabinovich Dora Leizerovna	1923	Gorodok	01/09/1943	Baranovichi	Za Sovetskuyu Belarus
675	Rabinovich Isaak Shlemovich	1925	Dyatlovo	17/02/1943	Baranovichi	Lenin's
676	Rabinovich Leon Borukhovich	1921	Volozhin	30/04/1943	Baranovichi	Za Sovetskuyu Belarus
677	Rabinovich Matvei				Vileika	Spartak
678	Rabinovich Eizer Meyerovich	1921	Gorodok	04/09/1944	Baranovichi	Za Sovetskuyu Belarus
679	Ravinski Abram Yonovich	1921	Lyubcha	22/07/1942	Baranovichi	Stalin

680	Raginski Vladimir	1919	Klimovichi	01/09/1943	Mogilev	
681	Radimonski Yakov Anisimovich	1914	Lida	08/06/1943	Baranovichi	Kirov
682	Raek Boris Khaimovich	1910		20/06/1942	Vitebsk	Za Sovetskuyu Belarus
683	Razvadski Yosif Movshevich	1895	Novogrudok		Baranovichi	Kirov
684	Raiko Anna Fadeyevna	1912		01/06/1944	Minsk	Dyadya Koya's
685	Raikh Rakhil Genokhovna			01/12/1942	Baranovichi	Lenin's
686	Raikhman Aizik Davidovich	1904		20/11/1941	Polesye	Lelchitskaya
687	Raikhman Mikhail Vulfovich	1901		18/09/1941	Pinsk	Kirov
688	Rapoport Galina Yevseevna	1917	Volozhin	01/06/1944	Baranovichi	
689	Rapoport Semen Grigorevich	1922	Minsk	1942	Minsk	Narodnye mstiteli
690	Raskin Yefim Semenovich	1925	Minsk	18/11/1943	Baranovichi	
691	Rasovski Lev	1908		15/10/1941	Polesye	? 125
692	Rakhman Zundol Abramovich	1925	Glussk	22/07/1942	Baranovichi	Stalin
693	Revin Grigori Maksimovich	1903	Minsk	12/05/1943	Baranovichi	
694	Revinski Abram Yontovich	1921		22/07/1942	Minsk	Stalin
695	Regenbogen Eugenya Samuilovna	1918	Minsk	24/06/1944	Minsk	Smert fashizmu (Death to fascism)
696	Reznikov Leonid Isaakovich	1909	d. Berezovka Glusski r-n	20/12/1943	Minsk	Parkhomenko
697	Reingold Sonya Leonidovna	1921	Petrikov	05/05/1943	Mogilev	? 277 Izokh's
698	Reikhtman Zalman Davidovich			01/11/1941	Polesye	Lelchitskaya
699	Rier Khaim Leibovich	1911	Ilia	08/11/1943	Minsk	Narodnye mstiteli
700	Rikhter Vladimir Bronislavovich			01/08/1942	Mogilev	1st Bobruisk
701	Rober Grigori Yakovlevich	1919	Odessa		Baranovichi	Chapayev
702	Rozhkin Abram Yudelevich			01/12/1942	Baranovichi	Lenin's
703	Rozet Galina Moiseyevna	1928		05/05/1944	Vileika	Oktyabr
704	Rozin			03/05/1942	Minsk	Voroshilov
705	Rozin Grisha Gavrilovich	1892	Dukora	07/09/1943	Minsk	Belarus
706	Rozinkind yuzel Khaimovich	1907	Dolginovo	12/05/1944	Minsk	Kirov
707	Rozran Roza Zalmanovna (doctor)	1916	Ozarichi	14/04/1944	Polesye	? 100 Kulikovski
708	Rolnik Roza Mikhailovna	1925	Minsk	22/06/1944	Minsk	Smert fashizmu (Death to fascism)
709	Romanovski Meyer Zalmanovich	1922		05/05/1943	Baranovichi	A.Nevski
710	Romanski Yudel Abramovich	1916		11/09/1943	Brest	
711	Rotgarbe Khaim Shepshelevich	1924	Raigrad	17/12/1943	Baranovichi	? 18 Frunze
712	Rotenberg Mikhail Yakovlevich	1901		05/05/1943	Vileika	
713	Rubakha Shmul Khatskelevich	1912		12/11/1943	Pinsk	gruppy po regioni
714	Rubin David Vladimirovich	1927	Krasnoye	01/06/1944	Minsk	Shturmovaya
715	Rubin Lazar Yakovlevich	1913		27/06/1944	Belostok	Kalinovski
716	Rubin Sasha Aronovich	1911	Pruzhany	29/07/1943	Brest	Ponamorenko
717	Rubinovich Samuil Osherovich	1906	Mir	03/09/1944	Baranovichi	
718	Rubinchik Benyamin Mordukhovich	1904			Minsk	3rd Minsk
719	Rubinshtein Aizik Yeremeyevich	1923	Lenin	09/01/1944	Belostok	A.Nevski
720	Rubinshtein Genya Girshevna	1918	Briansk	18/04/1944	Minsk	Shturmovaya
721	Rubinshtein Leizer Mordukhovich	1924	Lenino	08/04/1944	Minsk	
722	Rubinshtein Moisei Gershovich	1926	Lenino	08/04/1944	Minsk	
723	Rubinshtein Yakov Romanovich	1922	Krugloe	27/04/1943	Mogilev	? 277 Izokh's
724	Ruderman Izrail Khaimovich	1920		26/03/1943	Vitebsk	4th Byelorussian
725	Ruderman Sima Khaimovna	1921		12/09/1942	Minsk	Narodnye mstiteli
726	Ruditser Giler Mordukhovich	1911	Minsk	10/02/1944	Mogilev	? 208 Stalin
727	Rudnik Abram Leibovich	1909	Gorodok	20/10/1943	Baranovichi	Chapayev
728	Rudnik Lazar Ryzhikovich	1914	Radoshkovichi		Vileika	Frunze
729	Rudyka Faiva Aizikovich	1916	Galenovo		Vileika	Frunze
730	Ruzhanski Meyer Velvelevich	1916	Mosty	17/07/1943	Baranovichi	Lenin's
731	Rutman Mikhail Lazarevich	1913		01/04/1944	Brest	Za Sovetskuyu Belarus
732	Rybak David Elevich	1917	Kopyl	06/06/1944	Belostok	
733	Ryvkin Grigori Antonovich	1921	Nikolaev	27/05/1943	Mogilev	? 600 Mednikova
734	Ryskin Mikhail Solomonovich	1923		18/08/1944	Minsk	Dyadya Koya's
735	Ryabkin Isaak			01/04/1942	Pinsk	Budenny
736	Savgiski Yevel Shmuilovich	1911		05/05/1943	Baranovichi	A.Nevski
737	Savinski Meyer Leibovich	1899		06/06/1944	Vitebsk	4th Byelorussian
738	Sagelchik Khaim Abramovich	1902	Pukhovichi	18/11/1943	Baranovichi	
739	Sakin Aron Moiseyevich	1917	Mogilev	01/03/1944	Mogilev	? 121
740	Salitan				Vitebsk	Frunze
741	Sapozhnikov Semen			01/12/1942	Baranovichi	Lenin's
742	Saragovich Khaim Rubinovich	1922	Glubokoe	04/05/1944	Minsk	? 100 Kirov
743	Svirski Movsha Yosifovich	1907	Ivenets	22/07/1942	Baranovichi	Stalin
744	Svistun Leonid Abramovich	1924	Oboltsy, Senninski r-n	03/03/1944	Vitebsk	Leonova
745	Seifer Anna Lvovna	1924	Pukhovichi		Baranovichi	Pobieda
746	Senderovski Movsha Menakhimovich	1917	Dyatlovo	27/05/1943	Baranovichi	Lenin's

747	Serebrin Boris Semenovich	1922		10/05/1943	Baranovichi	Lazo
748	Serebryanich Vladimir Solomonovich	1923	Mir	25/03/1943	Baranovichi	Za Sovetskuyu Belarus
749	Simenovich Yefim Davidovich			12/06/1943	Mogilev	
750	Simkin David Lvovich	1913		08/02/1944	Vitebsk	1st Vitebsk
751	Simonovich Aron Itskovich	1925		10/02/1944	Baranovichi	Lazo
752	Simkhovich Monus Abramovich	1914	Radoshkovichi	08/07/1944	Minsk	Narodnye mstiteli
753	Sinyagov Boris Markovich	1914		22/12/1941	Brest	Stalin
754	Sirotin Solomon Elevich	1914		07/03/1944	Mogilev	? 61
755	Siterman Yakov Moiseyevich	1922	Minsk	11/12/1943	Minsk	Shturmovaya
756	Skvortsov Yefim Isaakovich			05/06/1944	Vitebsk	Dubova
757	Sklyut Maks Abramovich	1910	Smorgon	12/07/1944	Baranovichi	Za Sovetskuyu Belarus
758	Slepoi David Khonovich	1917	Proskurov	10/12/1943	Belostok	Kalinovski
759	Slomka Khaim Matusovich	1917	Snedovo	13/03/1943	Baranovichi	Lenin's
760	Slonim Penya Zaumnovich	1899	Novogrudok	25/07/1942	Baranovichi	Stalin
761	Sloush Yuzik Yuzofovich	1921	Minsk	18/07/1942	Baranovichi	Ponamorenko
762	Slutski Boris Isaakovich	1922	Minsk	1942	Vitebsk	Nikitina
763	Slutski Isaak Yosifovich	1912		01/04/1944	Minsk	? 100 Kirov
764	Slutski Yankel Isaakovich	1915	Karelichi	01/10/1943	Baranovichi	Kirov
765	Smilovitski Yakov Ilich	1929	Gomel	10/07/1944	Baranovichi	
766	Smirin Isaak Markovich	1920		29/08/1942	Vitebsk	Frunze
767	Smolinski Meyer Samoilovich	1917		11/07/1944	Belostok	Kalinovski
768	Smushkevich Aron Rafailovich	1913		11/05/1944	Baranovichi	? 19 Molotov
769	Snitovski Rubin Isaakovich	1919	Karelichi	22/07/1942	Baranovichi	Stalin
770	Snitovski Shaya Isaakovich	1923	Pogost-Zagorski	22/07/1942	Baranovichi	Stalin
771	Snovski Semen Rubinovich	1912		28/09/1943	Brest	
772	Sokol Ronia Kiselevna	1920	K. Kashirski	24/12/1943	Pinsk	Pinsk Shubetidze
773	Sokol Sergei Grigorevich	1920		08/04/1944	Pinsk	Pinsk
774	Sokolova Nina Mikhailovna	1921	Velizh	03/03/1943	Vitebsk	Kutuzov
775	Solomko Khaim Motusovich	1917		01/04/1943	Baranovichi	Lenin's
776	Solomyanskaya Masha Mendelevna	1921	Lyubcha		Baranovichi	Lenin's
777	Sorokina Klava yuzefovna	1912		09/04/1944	Polesye	? 123
778	Sosnovskaya Sofia Yosifovna	1914	Derechin	10/04/1944	Baranovichi	Pobieda
779	Sterin Boris Movshevich	1924		01/04/1942	Polesye	? 225
780	Stolov Matyas Efroimovich	1922		25/04/1942	Minsk	Minsk underground
781	Strelets Aron Itskovich	1919	Lyuban	15/09/1942	Minsk	? 25 Ponamorenko
782	Suler Yefim Naumovich	1924	Minsk	20/04/1944	Baranovichi	Shchors
783	Sulman Isaak Samuilovich			16/02/1943	Baranovichi	Lenin's
784	Sulski Grigori Moiseyevich	1924	Minsk	08/02/1944	Baranovichi	Rokossovskogo
785	Sumkovich Peisakh Abramovich	1921	Iody, Sharkovshchinski r-n, Vit. region	08/03/1943	Vitebsk	
786	Surpin Yefim Germanovich	1924	Glussk	28/06/1944	Polesye	
787	Surpina Danya Gershevna (m/s)	1922		29/05/1943	Polesye	? 123
788	Sukhan Tsalya Isaakovich	1924	St. Dorogi	13/02/1942	Minsk	
789	Sukhman Gdalya Pausovich	1903	Dukora	02/02/1944	Minsk	Belarus
790	Sushkevich Estera Mendelevna	1918	Glubokoe	01/05/1944	Vitebsk	Korotkina
791	Tabak Shaya Mendelevich	1919	Briansk-Belostokski	30/04/1944	Belostok	Vo imya Rodiny (In the name of Motherland)
792	Taninbaum Ivan Yemelyanovich	1916		22/06/1943	Minsk	Narodnye mstiteli
793	Tanfel Fruma Rakhmiyelevna	1922	Ive	25/03/1944	Baranovichi	Stalin
794	Taporovski Grigori Abramovich	1921	Vilno	19/07/1944	Vileika	
795	Tatarski Grigori Yeliseyevich	1920	Boianichi, Lyubanski r-n	15/04/1944	Minsk	Ponamorenko
796	Telekhanovski Movsha Izrailevich	1903			Brest	
797	Tenenbaum Leiba Peisakhovich	1910		06/12/1942	Baranovichi	? 2 Zhukov
798	Tiger Leonid Rafailovich	1901	Grudinets	28/08/1943	Baranovichi	Kirov
799	Timon Yosif Motolevich	1921		31/03/1943	Pinsk	Lenin
800	Tikhok Yefim Sergeevich	1919	Rechki	04/03/1943	Minsk	Shturmovaya
801	TrilesnikIlya Semenovich	1907	Klichev	12/07/1942	Mogilev	? 425
802	Trok Faifa Khonovich	1911	Iody, Sharkovshchinski r-n, Vit. region	07/06/1944	Vitebsk	
803	Tunik Moisei Yudelevich	1908	Stolbtsy	06/07/1944	Baranovichi	
804	Turgel Semen Mikhailovich	1908	Mir	13/12/1942	Baranovichi	Stalin
805	Tukhbinder Simon Lvovich	1908		11/09/1943	Mogilev	? 208 Stalin
806	Uzdenski Khatskel Faivelevich	1904	Grozovo	05/06/1944	Minsk	Suvorov
807	Ulman Naum Shmuilovich	1924	Dunilovichi	18/11/1943	Vileika	Voroshilov
808	Uritski Aizik Lakhmanovich	1927	Myshenki, Kopytkevichski r-n	03/04/1944	Polesye	? 125
809	Fabrikant Roman Leibovich	1919	Dukora	04/03/1943	Minsk	Shturmovaya
810	Faershtan David Germanovich	1912		01/06/1944	Brest	Stalin
811	Fainfeld Leiba	1925		01/04/1944	Polesye	? 123

812	Farber Anton			29/01/1943	Mogilev	
813	Farfel Samuil Faivelevich	1921	Nesvizh	27/07/1942	Baranovichi	? 2 Zhukov
814	Faut Ilya Peisokhovich	1922	Ivenets	22/07/1942	Baranovichi	Stalin
815	Faut Mikhail Moiseyevich	1922	Ivenets	22/07/1942	Baranovichi	Stalin
816	Faut Moisei Peisakhovich	1914	Ivenets	22/07/1942	Baranovichi	Stalin
817	Fegelmakh Abram Shmuilovich	1917		05/05/1944	Vitebsk	Stalin
818	Fedorovich Yefim			13/09/1942	Vitebsk	Kutuzov
819	Feigel Mikhail Khaimovich	1915	Glubokoe	19/02/1944	Minsk	Narodnye mstiteli
820	Feigelman Rubin	1926	Bildyuchi	28/08/1943	Vileika	Za Rodinu
821	Feldman Viktor Naumovich	1925		19/06/1942	Baranovichi	Ponamorenko
822	Feldman Grigori Markovich	1909	Lida	29/12/1943	Baranovichi	Kirov
823	Feldman Yakov Khatskelevich	1925	Klichev	10/01/1942	Mogilev	? 277 Izokh's
824	Fidler Vladimir Abramovich	1920	Kurenets	28/05/1944	Minsk	Narodnye mstiteli
825	Filtser David Abramovich	1913		01/05/1944	Minsk	Shturmovaya
826	Fiterson Zalman Lazarevich	1923	Minsk	21/02/1944	Baranovichi	? 18 Frunze
827	Fish Semen Yosifovich	1917		09/08/1943	Vitebsk	Osveiskaya Frunze
828	Fisher Boris Semenovich	1908		18/09/1943	Vileika	Spartak
829	Fishkin Aleksei Girshevich	1926	Minsk	18/11/1943	Minsk	106-oi detachment
830	Fishkin Mota Shevelevich	1922	Rubezhevichi	22/07/1942	Baranovichi	Stalin
831	Fishkin Yudel Srolevich	1892	Minsk		Baranovichi	
832	Fishman Eva Alekseevna	1924	Glussk	09/04/1944	Minsk	Dyadya Koya's
833	Flatsbaum Izakh Leibovich	1921	Ivenets	22/07/1942	Baranovichi	Stalin
834	Flatsbaum Natan Leibovich	1918	Novogrudok	22/07/1942	Baranovichi	Stalin
835	Fleisher Yosif Mirovich	1913	Lida	08/06/1943	Baranovichi	Kirov
836	Fokin Nikolai Semenovich	1927	Polotsk	03/05/1944	Vitebsk	Za Sovetskuyu Belarus
837	Fradkin Mendel Shlemovich	1899		04/05/1944	Vitebsk	Voroshilov
838	Fratkin Mikhail Ginerovich	1923	Gorodok	01/02/1943	Baranovichi	Chapayev
839	Frid Abram Yankelevich	1895	Minsk region	25/07/1944	Minsk	Plamya
840	Frid Ruvim Yakovlevich	1910		01/10/1941	Vitebsk	Kutuzov
841	Frid Samuil Zalmanovich	1911		06/04/1942	Mogilev	? 208 Stalin
842	Fridliand Boris	1918		29/01/1943	Baranovichi	? 2 Zhukov
843	Fridliand Elya Kalmanovich	1923	Minsk	18/10/1943	Baranovichi	Chapayev
844	Fridman Vladimir Isaakovich	1924		27/02/1943	Mogilev	? 17 Kataev's
845	Fridman Eugeni			01/01/1943	Minsk	Narodnye mstiteli
846	Fridman Mitia Meyerovich	1921	Dolginovo	05/05/1944	Minsk	Bolshevik
847	Fridman Nina Leibovna	1922		15/06/1944	Vileika	Kutuzov
848	Fridman Nokhim Abramovich	1924	Kartuz-Bereza	20/08/1944	Brest	Za Sovetskuyu Belarus
849	Fridman Roman Abramovich	1908	Lodz	16/06/1944	Baranovichi	1st Maya
850	Fridman Samuil Izrailevich	1905		04/05/1944	Vitebsk	Ponamorenko (Utkina)
851	Fridman Sofia Isaakovna	1920		01/06/1944	Vileika	Kutuzov
852	Fridman Sokhor Itskovich	1894		20/02/1944	Vitebsk	Chapayev
853	Frumkin Leva Shayevich	1924	Minsk	01/08/1943	Baranovichi	Chapayev
854	Fuks David Yekhelevich	1901		03/06/1944	Vitebsk	Voroshilov
855	Fuks Solomon Yakovlevich	1919	Dyatlovo		Baranovichi	Lenin's
856	FuntIlya Peisokhovich	1922		22/07/1942	Minsk	Stalin
857	Funt Mikhail M.	1914		22/07/1942	Minsk	Stalin
858	Funt Moisei Peisokhovich	1914		22/07/1942	Minsk	Stalin
859	Furman Yosif Gershevich	1922	Lida		Baranovichi	Zhukova
860	Khabai Naum Grigorevich	1924	Minsk	01/08/1943	Baranovichi	Chapayev
861	Khavkin Yefim Timofeevich	1915		07/04/1943	Brest	? 99 Guliaeva
862	Khavkin Yosif Leibovich				Mogilev	
863	Khazanovich Lev Filippovich	1912	Minsk	04/05/1944	Minsk	Dyadya Koya's
864	Khazanovich Tatiana Filipovna	1924	Minsk	01/08/1943	Baranovichi	Chapayev
865	Khaikin David Naumovich	1921		19/05/1943	Brest	party leadres' groups sent to the region
866	Khaikinzon Leonid Yefimovich	1922		11/05/1944	Vitebsk	Za Sovetskuyu Belarus
867	Khaitin				Minsk	Nikitina
868	Khanin Lekum Yankelevich	1903		15/04/1944	Minsk	
869	Khanchinski Isak Shmuilovich	1920	Peski, Most. r-n, Baranovichi region	10/04/1944	Baranovichi	Pobieda
870	Khapman Itska Abelevich	1894		25/05/1944	Polesye	? 123
871	Kharik Grigori Solomonovich	1898	Smolevichi	24/06/1944	Minsk	Dyadya Koya's
872	Kharkhas Yosif Meyerovich	1923	Mir	01/08/1943	Baranovichi	Za Sovetskuyu Belarus
873	Kharkhurgin Grigori Mikhailovich	1921			Baranovichi	Ponamorenko
874	Kharkhurin Abram Aronovich	1892	Rudobelka	01/02/1943	Polesye	? 123
875	Kharkhurin Aron Khonovich	1922	Glussk	24/06/1942	Minsk	? 37 Parkhomenko
876	Kharkhurin Grigori Isaakovich	1900		01/02/1944	Polesye	? 123
877	Khvayevski Shenufr Avseyevich	1920		28/08/1943	Baranovichi	A.Nevski
878	Khvoevski Movsha Benyaminovich	1883	Lida	04/02/1944	Baranovichi	
879	Khvoshchyanski Mikhail Mikhailovich	1914		25/05/1944	Vitebsk	Groza

880	Khedekal Isaak Berkovich	1915		26/10/1943	Vitebsk	4th Byelorussian
881	Kheifets Mikhail Yevseyevich	1926		03/05/1944	Vileika	
882	Kheifets Movsha Zalmanovich	1913		24/04/1944	Pinsk	Kirov
883	Khenin Boris Markovich	1910	Leningrad	22/07/1942	Baranovichi	Stalin
884	Khentov Lev Aronovich	1923			Minsk	Minsk underground
885	Kheus Leva			08/07/1943	Vitebsk	Kutuzov
886	Khidritskaya Anna Moiseyevna	1917	Minsk	30/07/1943	Baranovichi	18th Frunze
887	Kholodenko Mikhail Izrailevich	1913		19/06/1944	Brest	Ponamorenko
888	Khomelyanski Yakov Osherovich	1918	Mogilev	19/03/1944	Mogilev	? 121
889	Tseitnin Mikhail Solomonovich	1902	Shklov	04/11/1943	Mogilev	Chekist
890	Tsepelevich Abram Zalmanovich	1917		04/08/1943	Vileika	
891	Tsepelevich Leiba Isaakovich	1910		26/10/1943	Vitebsk	4th Byelorussian
892	Tsekhnovich Khaim Grigorevich	1897	Ureche	01/04/1944	Minsk	? 121 Bragin
893	Tsikinski Semen Isaakovich	1913	Zabereze	01/08/1943	Baranovichi	Chapayev
894	Tsimmer Lipa-Peisakh Mordokhovich	1905	Sharkovshchina	04/05/1944	Minsk	? 100 Kirov
895	Tsinkin Yosif Naftanovich	1912	Mir	01/06/1943	Baranovichi	Za Sovetskuyu Belarus
896	Tsiporin Abram Naumovich	1918	Minsk	27/11/1942	Baranovichi	? 18 Frunze
897	Tsipota Zoia Avramovna	1921		06/10/1944	Minsk	Dyadya Koya's
898	Tsirkin Gutman Mendelevich	1902	Kovtichi	19/12/1943	Minsk	? 37 Parkhomenko
899	Tsirulnik Lazar Movshevich	1913		05/05/1943	Baranovichi	A.Nevski
900	Tsuker Ira Shmulevna	1923	Nerchukha		Brest	Ponamorenko
901	Charno Grisha Yankelevich	1925	Sedlets	18/11/1943	Baranovichi	
902	Charno Khana Yakovlevna	1919	Minsk		Baranovichi	
903	Charnyi Boris Berkovich	1903		05/03/1942	Mogilev	? 208 Stalin
904	Chausovski Samuil Davydovich	1916	Ukraina	23/06/1942	Mogilev	Demidova
905	Chernaya Sofia Borisovna	1921	Mir	01/06/1943	Baranovichi	Za Sovetskuyu Belarus
906	Chernin Grigori Maksimovich	1915	Minsk	02/05/1944	Vileika	Frunze
907	Chernovoi Mosha Izrailevich	1917	Novogrudok	22/07/1942	Baranovichi	Stalin
908	Cherny David Yakovlevich	1923		21/08/1942	Gomel	Zhelezniak
909	Cherny Miron Zalmanovich	1918		18/11/1942	Vitebsk	Groza
910	Cherny Mikhail Beirakhovich	1926	Mir	01/08/1943	Baranovichi	Za Sovetskuyu Belarus
911	Cherny Faiva Aronovich	1917	Derevo		Baranovichi	
912	Chernyak Basya	1923		13/06/1944	Minsk	Shturmovaya
913	Chechik Motel Aronovich	1927	khutor Tupik, Rovenskaya region	18/07/1943	Polesye	Yelsk ? 37 (Mishchenko)
914	Chipchin Mikhail Borisovich	1902		07/05/1942	Minsk	Minsk underground
915	Chikhonovetskaya Tselya	1925		01/06/1943	Pinsk	Molotov
916	Shayevich Isaak Abramovich	1920		15/09/1941	Gomel	Bolshevik
917	Shapiro Boris Moiseyevich	1924			Minsk	Chkalov
918	Shapiro Lev Yakovlevich	1924	Minsk	01/06/1944	Minsk	Shturmovaya
919	Shapiro Solomon Yefimovich	1896	Minsk	30/04/1943	Minsk	Shturmovaya
920	Shapiro Sholom	1914	Postavy	18/11/1943	Vileika	Voroshilov
921	Sharman Boris Gilevich	1919	Vilno	12/12/1943	Vileika	Voroshilov
922	Shafer Semen Yakovlevich	1922		04/06/1944	Brest	Za Sovetskuyu Belarus
923	Shvarts Sergei Grigorevich	1919		31/08/1942	Vitebsk	
924	Shvedchikova Raisa Aleksandrovna	1917	Minsk	12/06/1943	Minsk	Za Sovetskuyu Belarus
925	Shevakhovich Mariya Bonisovna	1924	Lida	02/09/1943	Baranovichi	Kirov
926	Shevchik Kirill Leibovich	1912		14/07/1942	Brest	
927	Sheinberg Anatoli Lvovich	1923	Minsk	01/08/1943	Baranovichi	Chapayev
928	Sheinberg Raisa Isaakovna	1923	Minsk	01/08/1943	Baranovichi	Chapayev
929	Sheinberg Sofia Lvovna	1925	Minsk	01/08/1943	Baranovichi	Chapayev
930	Sheinberg T.			06/07/1943	Minsk	Stalin
931	Sheinin Lazar Yakovlevich	1925	Kostyukovichi	05/03/1942	Mogilev	
932	Shelyubskaya Sima Isakovna	1931	Derechin	19/06/1944	Baranovichi	Pobieda
933	Shelyubski David Yitskovich	1909	Vishnevo	05/03/1944	Baranovichi	Chapayev
934	Shelyubski Nikolai Niselevich	1921	Molchad	02/07/1944	Baranovichi	1st Maya
935	Shelyubski Semen	1913		01/12/1943	Baranovichi	Lenin's
936	Shemper Mikhail Borisovich	1917	Odessk. region	17/05/1944	Mogilev	? 208 Stalin
937	Shenderovich Boris Semenovich	1919	Rogachev	24/12/1942	Mogilev	? 14
938	Shenkman Shaya Yosifovich	1910		06/06/1944	Vitebsk	4th Byelorussian
939	Shepitinski Gera Isaakovich	1922		10/03/1943	Pinsk	Lenin
940	Sheps Mariyan Lazarevich	1922	Stolbtsy	22/07/1942	Baranovichi	Stalin
941	Sherman Isaak Lvovich			01/12/1941	Mogilev	
942	Shilavitskaya Sofia Khaimovna			01/12/1942	Baranovichi	Lenin's
943	Shilavitskaya Fruma Khaimovna			01/12/1942	Baranovichi	Lenin's
944	Shilon Viktor Borisovich	1925	Postavy	04/12/1943	Vileika	Dovatora
945	Shimanski Viktor Isaakovich	1914	Derechin	10/04/1944	Baranovichi	Pobieda
946	Shimanski Izrail Menakhelevich	1883	Dvorets	09/07/1944	Baranovichi	
947	Shimanski Moisei Izrailevich	1917	Dvorets	01/05/1943	Baranovichi	Kirov

948	Shikhmanovich Shlema Gertsevich	1925	Zheludok	19/03/1944	Baranovichi	Lenin's
949	Shklyut Girsh Movshevich	1898	Naliboki	01/08/1943	Baranovichi	
950	Shklyut Khonia Solomonovich	1908	Naliboki	16/06/1944	Baranovichi	
951	Shklyarevich Mordukh Khananaevich	1898			Brest	
952	Shkolnikovich Simkha Azreilovich	1918	Karelichi	22/07/1942	Baranovichi	Stalin
953	Shlapakov Yevsei Evdovich	1889		04/05/1944	Vitebsk	Voroshilov
954	Shleikher-Nikitin Sanna Yosifovich	1910		03/07/1943	Vitebsk	1st Smolenskaya
955	Shlidov Boris Yefimovich			07/05/1943	Gomel	Voroshilov
956	Shmeltser Mundan			15/08/1942	Gomel	Voroshilov
957	Shmerkovich Feiga Samuilovna	1894	Novogrudok	02/04/1944	Baranovichi	
958	Shmidt Yudel Novshevich	1912	Maryupol	01/06/1943	Brest	
959	Shmuilovich Abram Matusovich	1923	Naliboki	16/04/1944	Baranovichi	
960	Shmukler Boris Lvovich	1910	Kholopenichi	04/05/1944	Minsk	Dyadya Koya's
961	Shmulevich David Mironovich	1922	Kletsk	30/04/1944	Minsk	Chapayev
962	Shmulevich Sara Bentsionovna			01/12/1942	Baranovichi	Lenin's
963	Shmulov Yefim Davidovich	1922		08/07/1943	Vitebsk	Voroshilov
964	Shmushkevich Mikhail Aleksandrovich	1924		28/08/1943	Minsk	2nd Minsk
965	Shnaer Frida Moiseyevna	1922		24/02/1944	Vitebsk	4th Byelorussian
966	Shneider Lyudvig Amelyanovich	1916	Grodno	22/07/1944	Vileika	Voroshilov
967	Shneiderman Boris	1917		18/12/1943	Pinsk	Molotov
968	Shneiderman Izmail Zelikovich	1915		03/05/1944	Vitebsk	Donukalov
969	Shnit Mikhail Mironovich	1923	Rakov	17/10/1943	Baranovichi	Za Sovetskuyu Belarus
970	Shnitman Eta Khaimovna	1923		03/07/1942	Mogilev	
971	Sholkov Sholom Abramovich	1917	Vilno	18/11/1943	Baranovichi	
972	Shpaitsman Samuil Khaimovich			05/04/1944	Pinsk	Molotov
973	Shpakovskaya Darya Yosifovna	1918	Zgoda	19/12/1943	Minsk	? 37 Parkhomenko
974	Shparberg Raisa Izrailevna	1919	Minsk	01/08/1943	Baranovichi	Chapayev
975	Shpigel Mariyan Yankelevich	1908	Baranovichi	15/10/1942	Baranovichi	Stalin
976	Shpilman Moisei Borisovich	1905	Turets	26/07/1942	Baranovichi	Chapayev
977	Shteingard Semen Isaakovich	1922		20/05/1944	Vitebsk	Za Sovetskuyu Belarus
978	Shtemberg Khaim Solomonovich	1922	Khotianets	21/06/1944	Vileika	Budenny
979	Shternberg Grigori Moiseyevich	1917		01/09/1942	Pinsk	Lenin
980	Shtykin David Leizerovich	1921	Molchad	01/05/1943	Baranovichi	Kirov
981	Shulkov Mikhail Stepanovich	1922	Slutsk	10/05/1944	Mogilev	Chekist
982	Shulken Raya Khaikovna	1920			Minsk	Narodnye mstiteli
983	Shulkina Khaya Yosifovna	1922		27/08/1942	Minsk	Narodnye mstiteli
984	Shulman Zalman Berkovich	1914			Vitebsk	Kutuzov
985	Shulman Kopel Mendelevich	1904		04/05/1944	Vitebsk	2nd Ushachskaya
986	Shulman Moisei Gdalovich	1907	Nivki, Vileika region	04/04/1943	Vitebsk	Chapayev
987	Shulman Sergei Abramovich	1920		04/05/1944	Vitebsk	Ponamorenko (Utkina)
988	Shulman Khena Moiseyevna	1909	Pudenichi	10/10/1942	Minsk	Narodnye mstiteli Voronianski
989	Shulski Nikolai Aleksandrovich	1894	Leningrad	01/06/1944	Vileika	Frunze
990	Shuster Abram Khonovich	1921	Dolginovo	09/03/1943	Vitebsk	Frunze
991	Shuster Lipa Moiseyevich	1924	Timkovichi	01/07/1943	Minsk	Chapayev
992	Shuster Moisei Srulevich	1919		01/12/1943	Minsk	Ponamorenko
993	Shut Ida Moiseyevna	1925	Krivichi	05/05/1944	Vitebsk	Chapayev
994	Shut Raisa Moiseyevna	1923		05/05/1944	Vitebsk	Chapayev
995	Shcheglov Matvei Samuilovich	1900	Minsk	16/06/1944	Minsk	Narodnye mstiteli
996	Shcherbakovski Abram Borisovich	1920		04/05/1944	Vitebsk	Lenin
997	Shchurak Aleksandr Mikhailovich	1910	Stalino	24/06/1944	Minsk	Dyadya Koya's
998	Ezrakh Semen Samuilovich	1897	Minsk	06/07/1944	Baranovichi	
999	Eiks Yefim Yakovlevich	1918	Rudensk	18/04/1943	Minsk	3rd Minsk
1000	Eishishkin Lazar Khaimovich	1922	Vasilishki		Baranovichi	Lenin's
1001	Eishtein Leiba yudkovich	1907		12/04/1944	Minsk	Chkalov
1002	Elevich Leiba Sholomovich	1914	Derechin	17/12/1943	Baranovichi	Lenin's
1003	Elevich Khaim Sholomovich	1912	Derechin	17/12/1943	Baranovichi	Lenin's
1004	Elperina Sara Ilinichna	1921		01/10/1943	Minsk	Narodnye mstiteli
1005	Epshtein Alter Mikhailovich	1898		13/04/1944	Polesye	? 100 Kulikovski
1006	Epshtein Blyuma Samuilovna	1902		13/04/1944	Polesye	? 100 Kulikovski
1007	Epshtein Yevel Vulfovich	1904		10/10/1942	Mogilev	
1008	Epshtein Leiba yulevich	1907		12/04/1944	Minsk	? 100 Kirov
1009	Epshtein Mark Borukhovich	1926	Novogrudok	09/07/1944	Baranovichi	
1010	Epshtein Foma Alekseyevich	1886	Timkovichi	18/02/1944	Minsk	Dyadya Koya's
1011	Erenburg Isaak Gilerovich	1891	Shchedrin	11/02/1944	Polesye	? 123
1012	Estrov Izrail Vulfovich	1913		04/06/1944	Vitebsk	4th Byelorussian
1013	Estrov Nikolai Izrailevich	1923		18/04/1944	Vileika	Oktyabr
1014	Estrova Khaimina Yankelevna	1924		06/06/1944	Vitebsk	4th Byelorussian
1015	Ekhembaum Evgenya Grigorevna	1923	Slonim	02/09/1944	Brest	

1016	Ekhshtein Boris Mikhailovich	1907		01/03/1943	Vitebsk	Lioznenskaya Kirillov
1017	Yudelevich Yosif Isaakovich	1917	Dyatlovo	16/06/1943	Baranovichi	Lenin's
1018	Yuzhuk Girsha Moiseyevich	1921		28/05/1944	Pinsk	Kuibyshev
1019	Yurshan Isaak Faivelevich	1923	Mir	01/08/1943	Baranovichi	Za Sovetskuyu Belarus
1020	Yakubovich Semen Davidovich	1920		14/06/1944	Vitebsk	2nd Zaslonov
1021	Yasilevich Leiba Davidovich	1922	Dyatlovo		Belostok	A.Nevski
1022	Yatvitski Leizer Benyaminovich	1918	Dvorets	01/05/1943	Baranovichi	Kirov
1023	Yakhimovich Stanislav Pavlovich	1920		08/03/1943	Minsk	Stalin

Acknowledgements

Sincere gratitude and acknowledgements to Michail Izrailski for his invaluable assistance in the work with archival materials and their processing carried out in the course of several years.

Thanks to Valentina Moroz, specialist on public relations of the MJCH, for permanent support.

Many thanks to Sergei Vladimirovich and Artem Moroz for their professionalism and regular assistance in making a computer data base, their patience while checking the lists.

Gratitude for the assistance

To the workers of the National Archive of the Republic of Belarus with Vyacheslav Dmitrievich Selemenev at the head, leading researcher Eugeni Ivanovich Baranski, workers of the reading room – Nina Iosifovna Malakhova and Yelena Valeryevna Vasilyeva. Our work would have been impossible without their attention and help.

To the workers of the archive of the Institute of memory of the victims of the Shoa and Heroism of the Jewish people Yad Vashem (Jerusalem): Nadya Cohen, Masha Ionina, Rita Margolina, Bella Nocham, Meri Ginzburg.

To the volunteers of the Museum of History and Culture of the Jews of Belarus Michail Akkerman, Irina Barkan, Yelizaveta Kirilchenko and also to the worker of the Museum Veronika Rusakova.

To the former partisans: Zvi Shefet, Yakov Grinshtein, Aleksandr Bogen, Ben-Zion Dagan, Raisa Gitlina, Sholom Kholyavski, Mark Taiz, Anna and Aleksandr Zakharov, Yakov Shepetinski, Vyacheslav Tamarkin, Abram Rubinchik (Israel); Jack (Yidel) Kagan (Great Britain); Vladimir Rubezhin, Michail Treister, Michail Kantarovich, Grigori Dorski, Uri Kaplan, Yekaterina Klimovich, Anna Gorelik, Yakov Mogilnitski (Minsk).

To the children of the former partisans Orna Shuman, Aleksander Turecki (Israel); Lyubov Kostyuchenko (Vileika, Belarus); Vladimir Sverdlov, Zinaida Nikodimova, Anna Kustanovich, Frida Reizman, Svetlana Ivanchenko, Sofia Savikovskaya, Yelizaveta Kirilchenko (Minsk); Iosif Liberman (Pinsk); Olga Gorokhova (St. Petersburg); Feliks Lipski (Germany).

To those who helped the Museum: Clara and Abram Urevich, Faina Tureckaya, Semen Goldberg, Bella Balabanskaya, Nella Rasovskaya (Israel); Marina Shedikova, Svetlana Papernaya, Tamara Levina, Mila Sokolenko, Vladimir Mekhov, Eugeni Tsirinski (Minsk).

To Tamara Vershitskaya, the director of the Museum of History and Regional Studies in Novogrudok, Olga Kolosova, deputy director of the Museum of History and Regional Studies in Vileika, Andrei Vashkevich, researcher of the Museum of History and Archeology in Grodno, workers of the Museum of Belarusian Polesye in Pinsk.

Special gratitude and acknowledgements are to my husband Mark Pikman for understanding, support and patience through the years of work on this book.

Gratitude for the assistance in publishing the book

Committee on the matters of religions and nationalities at the Soviet of Ministers of the Republic of Belarus

Union of Belarusian Jewish public organizations and communities

Belarusian public union of the Jews – former prisoners of ghettos and Nazi camps

Office of the American Jewish united distribution committee "Joint" in the Republic of Belarus

Agency for Israel "Sokhnut" in the Republic of Belarus

Charity organization "Hesed-Rakhamim"

Jewish cultural society "Emuna"

Minsk charity society "Gilf"

and personally

Iosif Liberman (Pinsk) and Yuri Dorn (Minsk)

Museum of History and Culture of the Jews of Belarus

National Archive of the Republic of Belarus

Republican Foundation "Holocaust"

Reference book

We stood shoulder to shoulder…
The Jews in the partisan movement of Belarus. 1941-1944

Compiled by:

Director of the Museum of History and Culture of the Jews of Belarus
Kandidat of historical sciences
I.P. Gerasimova

Editor:	A.Shulman
Computer model and make-up:	D. Bogorad, A.Frumin
Proof-reader:	Ye. Grin
Publishing house:	"Asobny Dakh", Minsk

www.ingramcontent.com/pod-product-compliance
Lightning Source LLC
Chambersburg PA
CBHW080845230426
43662CB00013B/2027